D1195803

The
Opponents
of Paul
in Second
Corinthians

The Opponents of Paul in Second Corinthians

DIETER GEORGI

Fortress Press   Philadelphia

Translated from the German *Die Gegner des Paulus im 2. Korintherbrief: Studien zur Religiösen Propaganda in der Spätantike* (Neukirchen-Vluyn: Neukirchener Verlag, 1964). Dieter Georgi has supervised the translation and revised the original material slightly.

Library of Congress Cataloging in Publication Data

Georgi, Dieter.
The opponents of Paul in Second Corinthians.

Translation of: Die Gegner des Paulus im 2. Korintherbrief.
Originally presented as the author's thesis (doctoral) —Heidelberg, 1957.
Includes bibliographies and indexes.
1. Bible. N.T. Corinthians, 2nd—Criticism, interpretation, etc. I. Title.
BS2675.2.G4413 1986   227'.3067   84-47917
ISBN 0-8006-0729-5

K106K84   Printed in the United States of America 1–729

Contents

Preface

Habent sua fata libelli, "little books have a fate of their own." This certainly is true for this early work of mine. The discussion of Paul's opponents in Corinth was initially conceived as merely a brief excursus of at most three pages in a dissertation on 2 Cor. 2:14—7:4, particularly on 2 Cor. 3 and 4. Günther Bornkamm had suggested that I explore the relationship between Gnosticism and Apocalypticism. On the advice of Ernst Käsemann and Bornkamm, I chose the text as a crystallizing agent for that exploration. The intended title of that thesis was "Apostolate and Saving Event." When I began working on the project, I did not yet know about the difference between the opponents in 1 Cor. and 2 Cor.; I did not contemplate writing on the θεῖος ἀνήρ, the Jewish mission, or Jewish Apologetics. In fact, my working hypothesis at the time was that of my teachers Bornkamm and Rudolf Bultmann, namely, that Paul's opponents in the entire Corinthian correspondence were the same, that is, Gnostics. The doubt my other teacher, Käsemann, sowed had not yet had an effect on me. I believed that Paul shared some of the opposition's Gnostic presupposition but qualified it critically with the help of apocalyptic motifs.

But then the excursus grew into a study of its own. A comparison of the texts forced me to see the differences between 1 Cor. and 2 Cor.; in 2 Cor., Paul is the Gnostic, not his rivals. Bultmann had already recognized an increase of Gnostic motifs in Paul's language in 2 Cor., but Bultmann had not drawn any consequences for his understanding of the opposition.

As the texts forced me to acknowledge those differences, it was necessary to make some adjustments. The original project had to be postponed. I had not lost interest in Gnosticism or Apocalypticism, or in their convergence in 2 Cor., but in order to understand this phenomenon properly I first had to come to grips with the additional phenomenon which the texts made me see. New vistas in Paul's religious environment opened themselves to me and offered new explanations for old problems. Thus a new work evolved, one which I decided to do first.

As the initial excursus on the opponents grew into a study of its own, it conflicted with my professional training and was delayed. A first version was presented as a thesis for my church exams in 1955. A second, more elaborate version was submitted to the Theological Faculty at Heidelberg as a doctoral thesis in 1957. When the thesis was to be published, I went through it once more, thoroughly. Since Jewish mission had found little attention in scholarship and since its integration into Hellenistic missionary activity was of essential importance for understanding the presuppositions and working conditions of Paul's opponents, I enlarged the middle part of the thesis considerably, that is, the discussion of the religio-historical background. The book finally appeared in 1964. Some of the reviewers tore me to shreds; most of them, however, were very positive and encouraging. The book experienced what Terentius Maurus says further in the Latin passage quoted above: *pro captu lectoris,* "just as the reader grasps it" (*Carmen Heroicum* 258).

In the meantime, I had been invited to the United States, and here I found that I had become very much identified with the book. "Oh, the 'Gegner'!" was a frequent reaction during introductions. Questions about a translation were raised frequently, but my previous experience with revising the work made me fearful that I might be tempted to rewrite the book completely once more.

Finally, dear colleagues and friends of mine in the United States decided to take matters into their own hands and to produce a translation draft which my son Martin was to edit. That would bring the book completely into the country where it had found the warmest welcome and where it has had the greatest impact. My ideas about the "state of the question," particularly the religio- and social-historical aspects, would be reserved for an epilogue.

The reader will see that while I have not been converted on my major positions, they have gained new perspectives and thus, I hope, more depth. The methodological dimensions have become clearer to me, too, and so have the theological and hermeneutical conditions and consequences of my approach, and certainly also the political sides of it.

I hope that at least occasionally the virtues of the English language will benefit the reading of the book. The heavy German style of the original may have occasionally turned into something clearer, less weighty, and less mysterious. What the German really meant finally came out in English.

My thanks go first to the translators: Harold Attridge, Isabel and Thomas Best, Bernadette Brooten, Ron Cameron, Frank Fallon, Stephen Gero, Renate Rose, Herman Waetjen, and Michael Williams, who are to be credited with many improvements over the original manuscript. Helmut Koester and George MacRae initiated and organized the enterprise. I am very grateful to them. This book is a testimony to George's care. It is dedicated to his memory. Martin Georgi gave formal cohesion to the pluralistic effort. His patience deserves as much appreciation as his imagination and stimulation.

Many other friends were of assistance: Bruce Beck, Joseph Bessler, Lukas Bormann, John Daniels, Reiner Dietrich, Sarah Doering, Thomas Neufeld, René Rüttimann, Philip Sellew, Nathan Stoltzfus, Hans Christoph Stoodt. They helped also to minimize the difficulties caused by the physical dimension of the "translation" from one library system into another (and back), increased by my move from Cambridge, Massachusetts, to Frankfurt am Main. The major task of typing the main text was performed brilliantly by Mary Picard. For typing the epilogue I am indebted to Sharon Fortenberry and Renate Rüttimann.

The reader will benefit from the enormous help I have received from all these people. They have made the book more readable and understandable. But this does not burden any one of them with any responsibility for the outcome. That has to rest with me, particularly any blame. The people of Fortress Press, particularly Norman A. Hjelm and John A. Hollar, need to be praised for their friendly patience as well as for their proficiency and competence.

P.S. As regards translations of texts found in LCL the English version of that edition is usually followed unless indicated by [ ] or (my ed.). The spelling has been modernized.

DIETER GEORGI
Frankfurt am Main

Abbreviations

AAWH	Abhandlungen der Akademie der Wissenschaften zu Heidelberg
AGJU	Arbeiten zur Geschichte des antiken Judentums und des Urchristentums
AJP	*American Journal of Philology*
AnBib	Analecta biblica
ANRW	*Aufstieg und Niedergang der Römischen Welt,* edited by Hildegard Temporini and Wolfgang Haase. Berlin: De Gruyter.
APOT	R. H. Charles, ed., *Apocrypha and Pseudepigrapha of the Old Testament*
ARW	*Archiv für Religionswissenschaft*
ATANT	Abhandlungen zur Theologie des Alten und Neuen Testaments
ATR	*Anglican Theological Review*
AusBR	*Australian Biblical Review*
BA	*Biblical Archaeologist*
BAGD	W. Bauer, *A Greek-English Lexicon of the New Testament,* trans. W. F. Arndt and F. W. Gingrich, rev. F. W. Gingrich and F. W. Danker (2d ed.; Chicago: Univ. of Chicago Press, 1979).
BBB	Bonner biblische Beiträge
BEvTh	Beiträge zur evangelischen Theologie
BFCTh	Beiträge zur Förderung christlicher Theologie
BHT	Beiträge zur historischen Theologie
BJRL	*Bulletin of the John Rylands University Library of Manchester*

BTB	*Biblical Theology Bulletin*
BZ	*Biblische Zeitschrift*
BZNW	Beihefte zur *Zeitschrift für die neutestamentliche Wissenschaft*
CBQ	*Catholic Biblical Quarterly*
CIJ	Corpus inscriptionum Judaicarum
Ep. Arist.	*Epistle of Aristeas*
Epictetus	
Diss.	Epictetus, *Dissertations*
EPRO	Études préliminaires aux religions orientales dans l'empire romain
EvTh	*Evangelische Theologie*
Eusebius	
Hist. Eccl.	*Ecclesiastical History [Historia ecclesiastica]*
Praep. Ev.	*Preparation for the Gospel [Praeparatio evangelica]*
FRLANT	Forschungen zur Religion und Literatur des Alten und Neuen Testaments
GCS	Griechische christliche Schriftsteller
HAW	Handbuch der Altertumswissenschaft
HDR	Harvard Dissertations in Religion
HKNT	Handkommentar zum Neuen Testament
HNT	Handbuch zum Neuen Testament
HTR	*Harvard Theological Review*
ICC	International Critical Commentary
IDBSup	Supplementary Volume to G. A. Buttrick, ed., *Interpreter's Dictionary of the Bible* (Nashville: Abingdon Press, 1976)
Ignatius	
Eph.	*Letter to the Ephesians*
Magn.	*Letter to the Magnesians*
Phld.	*Letter to the Philadelphians*
Smyrn.	*Letter to the Smyrnaeans*
Trall.	*Letter to the Trallians*
Int	*Interpretation*
JAC	*Jahrbuch für Antike und Christentum*
JBC	R. E. Brown et al., eds. *The Jerome Biblical Com-*

	mentary (Englewood Cliffs, N.J.: Prentice-Hall, 1968).
JBL	*Journal of Biblical Literature*
JJS	*Journal of Jewish Studies*
Josephus	
Ant.	*Antiquities*
Apion	*Against Apion*
JW	*The Jewish War*
Life	*The Life*
JQR	*Jewish Quarterly Review*
JRS	*Journal of Roman Studies*
JTS	*Journal of Theological Studies*
KNT	Kommentar zum Neuen Testament
LCL	Loeb Classical Library
LSJ	H. G. Liddell, R. Scott, and H. S. Jones, *A Greek-English Lexicon* (Oxford: Clarendon Press, 1940)
MeyerK	H. A. W. Meyer, Kritisch-exegetischer Kommentar über das Neue Testament
MNTC	Moffatt New Testament Commentary
NovT	*Novum Testamentum*
NPNF	Nicene and Post-Nicene Fathers
NTS	*New Testament Studies*
PGM	K. Preisendanz, ed., *Papyri graecae magicae*
Philo	
Abr.	*De Abrahamo* [*On Abraham*]
Cont.	*De vita contemplativa* [*On the Contemplative Life*]
Decal.	*De decalogo* [*On the Decalogue*]
Det.	*Quod deterius potiori insidiari soleat* [*The Worse Attacks the Better*]
Deus	*Quod deus immutabilis sit* [*On the Unchangeableness of God*]
Flacc.	*In Flaccum* [*Flaccus*]
Her.	*Quis rerum divinarum heres sit* [*Who is the Heir*]
Leg. Gai.	*De legatione ad Gaium* [*On the Embassy to Gaius*]
Mig.	*De migratione Abrahami* [*On the Migration of Abraham*]
Moses	*De vita Mosis* [*Moses*]

Mut.	*De mutatione nominum* [*On the Change of Names*]
Post.	*De posteritate Caini* [*On the Posterity and Exile of Cain*]
Praem.	*De praemiis et poenis* [*On Rewards and Punishments*]
Q. Gen.	*Quaestiones in Genesin* [*Questions on Genesis*]
Sacr.	*De sacrificiis Abelis et Caini* [*On the Sacrifice of Abel and Cain*]
Somn.	*De somniis* [*On Dreams*]
Spec.	*De specialibus legibus* [*On the Special Laws*]
Virt.	*De virtutibus* [*On the Virtues*]
Pliny	
Epist.	*Epistles*
PW	Pauly-Wissowa, *Real-Encyclopädie der classischen Altertumswissenschaft*
PWSup	Supplement to PW
RAC	*Reallexikon für Antike und Christentum*
RB	*Revue biblique*
RGG	*Die Religion in Geschichte und Gegenwart*, 3d ed.
RHPR	*Revue d'histoire et de philosophie religieuses*
RVV	Religionsgeschichtliche Versuche und Vorarbeiten
SBL	Society of Biblical Literature
SBLASP	Society of Biblical Literature Abstracts and Seminar Papers
SBLDS	SBL Dissertation Series
SBLMS	SBL Monograph Series
SBS	Stuttgarter Bibelstudien
SBT	Studies in Biblical Theology
SCHNT	Studia ad corpus hellenisticum novi testamenti
SHAW.PH	Sitzungsberichte der Heidelberger Akademie der Wissenschaften. Philosophisch-historische Klasse
Sib. Or	*Sibylline Oracles*
SJLA	Studies in Judaism in Late Antiquity
SNTSMS	Society for New Testament Studies Monograph Series
SO	Symbolae osloenses
SPB	Studia postbiblica

Str-B	H. Strack and P. Billerbeck, *Kommentar zum Neuen Testament*
StTh	*Studia Theologica*
SUNT	Studien zur Umwelt des Neuen Testaments
SyBU	Symbolae biblicae upsalienses
SyBuSup	Supplement to SyBU
TAPA	*Transactions of the American Philological Association*
TDNT	G. Kittel and G. Friedrich, eds., *Theological Dictionary of the New Testament* (Grand Rapids: Wm. B. Eerdmans, 1964–76).
ThF	Theologische Forschung
TU	Texte und Untersuchungen
UNT	Untersuchungen zum Neuen Testament
VD	*Verbum domini*
VF	*Verkündigung und Forschung*
WdF	Wege der Forschung
WMANT	Wissenschaftliche Monographien zum Alten und Neuen Testament
WUNT	Wissenschaftliche Untersuchungen zum Neuen Testament
ZKG	*Zeitschrift für Kirchengeschichte*
ZMR	*Zeitschrift für Missionskunde und Religionswissenschaft*
ZNW	*Zeitschrift für die neutestamentliche Wissenschaft*
ZNWSup	Supplement to ZNW
ZRGG	*Zeitschrift für Religions- und Geistesgeschichte*
ZSTh	*Zeitschrift für systematische Theologie*
ZThK	*Zeitschrift für Theologie und Kirche*
ZWTh	*Zeitschrift für wissenschaftliche Theologie*

Introduction

HISTORY OF MODERN RESEARCH ON
PAUL'S OPPONENTS IN CORINTH

Early biblical interpretation considered Paul's disputes with his opponents in the Second Letter to the Corinthians a last purge with only marginal importance to the letter as a whole. It was a purge, so they thought, of a minority which was somewhat stubborn and slow of mind. John Chrysostom, for example, thought that Paul only had to overcome the last barriers of pride in these opponents of Jewish origin.[1] And John Calvin wrote: "Some wicked persons, despising Paul's authority, persisted in their obstinancy."[2] In the eyes of these commentators, the polemics in 2 Cor. were merely an appendix to those found in 1 Cor. They saw the opposition to Paul, which appears in both letters, in essentially psychological terms. This is clearly the case with John Calvin in the introduction to his commentary on 1 Cor.:[3]

> During Paul's absence false apostles had crept in, not, in my opinion, to disturb the Church openly with wicked doctrines, or designedly to undermine sound doctrine; but priding themselves in the splendour and magnificence of their address, or rather, being puffed up with an empty loftiness of speech, they looked upon Paul's simplicity, and even the Gospel itself, with contempt. They afterwards, by their ambition, gave occasion for the Church being split into various parties; and, last of all, reckless as to everything, provided only they were themselves held in estimation, made it their aim to promote their own honour, rather than Christ's kingdom and the people's welfare.

In support of his opinion, Calvin stated that Paul debated against actual heresy in a very different manner, as, for example, in the Letter

1

to the Galatians. In that letter Paul calls heresy by name—but he does not do so in 2 Cor.

A dramatic change occurred in the nineteenth century: the polemics in 2 Cor. were seen as the climax of the disputes, not as an appendix to them. Indeed, they were thought to reveal the essential characteristics of the anti-Pauline opposition, which came to be understood as a determined theological counterposition in matters of church policy. Therefore, it was believed, the history of early Christianity had to be rewritten in the light of 2 Cor. and the Corinthian correspondence in general. Ferdinand Christian Baur was the first to formulate such far-reaching hypotheses. The title of the work in which he presented these ideas for the first time was trailblazing in itself: "The Christ Party in the Corinthian Community, the Contrast of Pauline and Petrine Christendom, the Apostle Peter in Rome." In this work, Baur first proposed the concept of history which he later expanded on in several other publications and brought to its crowning glory in his brilliant book on Paul, especially in its second edition.[4]

Following a suggestion of Johann S. Semler,[5] Baur distinguished two types of early Christianity: (1) the law-obedient, particularistic Jewish Christians led by Peter (Judaizers) and (2) the law-free, universalist Gentile Christians led by Paul (Paulinists). Biblical scholars prior to Baur had seen Paul's disputes with the false apostles merely as marginal events in the development of early Christianity. For Baur, however, the unity of early Christianity consisted in the persistent, passionate disputes between the two above-mentioned groups and their final reconciliation in Catholicism. This thesis of the great theologian of Tübingen became the subject of theological research for the next one hundred years. In fact, the problem stated by Baur is still with us today despite obituaries and furious rampages to the contrary.[6]

The conflict in Corinth was the starting point for Baur's investigation of early Christianity. Baur was convinced that the controversy arose with a visitation of Judaizers to the Pauline community (as was their custom elsewhere). These intruders rapidly found followers in Corinth. They could not only cite their own Jewish origin but also—unlike Paul—point to their authorization by the first apostles, especially Peter. They could also emphasize the agreement of their own doctrines and teachings with those of the first Christians. Thus they presented themselves to the young church in Corinth as representatives of authentic (in the sense of original) Christianity, as the true followers of Christ (2 Cor. 10:7); they were regarded among the Corinthians as the "Christ party" (1 Cor. 1:12). Paul, the innovator, had nothing to say against their message and claim. He lacked the direct link to the early church and the authorization by the first apostles, a lack which was only aggravated by his frail appearance. According to Baur, "the Judaizing Christ party," which was identical with the group led by Peter, advocated the precedence of Jewish tradition. It also developed a messianic christology in a Jewish sense. The nomistic criticism of Paul's theology was temporarily suppressed in a hypocritical manner. The opponents even gave up, for a while, circumcision and other legal demands, because of their bitter experiences in the Galatian churches and the special character of pagan Corinth.

Baur's thesis led to continued study of the historical forces active in the early church; the many errors connected with his advance into a new field of research were of a constructive nature. The scholarly reaction to his programmatic tract resembled that of a stirred-up hornet's nest. Soon, however, Baur's critics found a point of view which, at least at the surface, permitted them to ignore his critical advances; it became downright fashionable to accuse him of dogmatism and to dismiss him as a Hegelian. But hardly anybody succeeded in shaking off the spell of Baur's historical vision, nor was anybody able to overcome its increasing rigidity by a new attempt to study and interpret the variety in the life of the early church. Such an investigation should have been the natural outgrowth of Baur's work. Despite all the complaints about his one-sidedness, Baur's critics generally simply modified his hypothesis. For example, a connection between Paul's opponents and the first apostles was often denied,[7] since direct references in the text are missing. There was disagreement about the origin of the opponents from the Jewish sphere. Many scholars even portrayed the Judaizers as disciples of Jesus by pointing to 2 Cor. 5:16.[8] Opinions varied on how long the Judaizers stayed in Corinth and on the extent of their influence on the Corinthian Christians.

All past and present advocates of the "Judaizer" hypothesis had difficulty explaining Paul's polemic against libertinistic tendencies, the disputes about *sophia* and *gnosis*, and Paul's criticism of the self-glorification of his opponents, as found in 2 Cor. The "Judaizer" hypothesis also seemed inadequate for dealing with questions such as:

- What role did Christology play in the dispute?
- Do differences exist in this respect between 1 and 2 Cor.?
- Why was there bound to be a dispute about the concept of *pneuma*? (2 Cor. 11:4)

The so-called Apollos party was often used to explain the above-mentioned problems, even though neither this "party" nor any of the "parties" of 1 Cor. are mentioned in 2 Cor. The advocates of the "Judaizer" hypothesis had the greatest trouble explaining Paul's lack of polemic against nomism, since nomism was supposed to be characteristic of the Judaizers. 2 Cor. 3 and 2 Cor. 11:15 cannot be used for drawing any conclusions about the existence of nomism. This becomes evident if one compares these passages with Paul's polemic in Galatians. In particular, there was no insistence on circumcision in Corinth.

After Baur, the nineteenth century saw no further significant advances in this area of research,[9] but the situation began to change at the turn of the century. Richard Reitzenstein and Wilhelm Bousset were among those scholars who used a history-of-religions approach in trying to prove that the Gnostic movement developed at the same time or even prior to the early church.[10] They also tried to argue that the early church itself was not free of Gnostic influences.

The work of these scholars received some unexpected support from the NT scholar Wilhelm Lütgert, who belonged to the Greifswald school.[11] His exegetical studies may have begun as an apologetic attempt to refute Baur's conception of history. The "Paulinism" of the Greifswald school could explain Lütgert's efforts as well as his failure. But whoever reads Lütgert's studies on the problem of enthusiasm in early Christianity in context—especially his investigations into the problems of the Pauline communities—must recognize his large-scale exegetical effort to extract, from the historical material at our disposal, signs of an early Gnostic movement of Jewish origin. So Baur's alternative received its fatal blow from studies which again started from investigations of Paul's opponents in Corinth. Biblical research gained new vigor and became more colorful than it had been for a long time. Lütgert finally took seriously the fact that Paul's attacks on his opponents in 1 and 2 Cor. (his most violent attacks apart from Galatians) do not include anti-Judaizing polemics against nomism. On the basis of 2 Cor. 11:4, Lütgert showed that the teachings of Paul's opponents were based on a different concept of *pneuma* together with a different, pneumatic christology. Previous biblical research had claimed that Paul's opponents were nomistic pneumatics. Lütgert portrayed them as pure pneumatics and termed the attribute of nomism only a scholarly creation. Thus he was able to explain the libertinism and the boasting self-confidence of the Corinthian opposition. Paul's opponents were enthusiasts and Gnostics, and not former Pharisaic scribes; they were people who did not care about tradition and authority, who expected nothing of the future, but who believed that they already possessed everything in the present. According to these liberal Jewish Christians, Paul had only gone halfway; they were more Pauline than Paul, argued Lütgert.

But this thesis of Lütgert did not account for the Jewish (Palestinian) origin of these heretics in 2 Cor. He did not do justice to their propagandistic, even missionary strength or to the spread of the movement they had kindled. Nor was he able to explain the following:

- Why did these people care so much about certain titles common to the early Christian communities?
- What was their relationship to the rest of the organizational structure of the early church?
- Why did they insist on letters of recommendation?

To all these questions posed by Baur, Lütgert had no satisfactory answer. Further problems which remain unresolved and had first been raised by the "Judaizer" hypothesis are:

- Why was the person of the earthly Jesus important for Paul's opponents?
- How can the special role which scripture played for them be explained?

Lütgert had no convincing answers. But above all he did not succeed, even in his later works, in giving a clear-cut profile of the characteristic features of these Gnostics. One reason was probably his attempt to include all opposition to Paul in this one group. Fundamentally a biblicist, Lütgert also shied away from any support which could have come from the study of the history of religions. His work and that of Bousset were not tied to each other at all.

Adolf Schlatter tried to strengthen Lütgert's hypothesis by using religio-historical insights.[12] He rightly looked to Judaism in order to find the conditions which made the Gnostic movement (as postulated by Lütgert) possible, yet his construction of a religio-historical background for Paul's opponents remains strangely artificial. Schlatter was simply not prepared to imagine any other religio-historical trend in the NT than one relating to Jesus, orthodox Judaism, and the OT. Deducing a gnostic movement directly from orthodox Pharisaic theology was to remain a futile attempt.

The interpretation of Kirsopp Lake was more promising.[13] On the basis of the differences in Paul's polemics of 1 and 2 Cor., Lake concluded (a novelty!) that Paul's opponents in the two letters must also have been different. Pointing to Philo and the Jewish-Alexandrian theology (which so far had only been used to describe the Apollos party), Lake characterized Paul's opponents in 2 Cor. as nonlegalistic, allegorizing pneumatics. Lake's exegesis had a notable influence on Alfred Plummer and Robert H. Strachan, yet they also did not completely abandon Baur's "Judaizer" hypothesis and still ascribed Judaizing tendencies to Paul's opponents in 2 Cor. Strachan, however, first formulated the important hypothesis that Exodus 34 forms a basis of the exegesis and theology of Paul's opponents.[14]

In the meantime, biblical scholars had recognized at last that Paul fought on different fronts in the two letters. However, they still divided the opposition to him in the following manner: the opponents in the first letter were considered pneumatics or Gnostics, while those in the second letter were thought to be Judaizers (usually also with Gnostic tendencies). According to Hans Windisch, the opposition at the time 1 Cor. was composed was mainly an inner-Corinthian one (pneumatics and Gnostics);[15] this group was joined before the writing of 2 Cor. by a group of Jewish "wandering preachers" who soon led the opposition.[16] This theory accounts for the fact that the polemics in 2 Cor. have clearly increased, that they are directed at outsiders, and that they concern subject matters largely different from 1 Cor. But Windisch and others who argued in a similar way were unable to explain the difference or why it was possible for the two groups to combine. Even qualifying the agitators as gnostic Judaizers (on the basis of the heresy mentioned in Colossians) did not help to resolve the problems. There was no explanation as to why in 2 Cor. the στοιχεῖα speculations are not mentioned as an element of the heresy, although in the Colossian and Galatian heresies they provide the connection between Torah and the Gnostic myth. Furthermore, in Colossians and Galatians the opponents are described as posing typical legalistic demands missing in 2 Cor. The opponents against whom Paul fights in 2 Cor. also do not seem to demand circumcision, which the Colossian heretics probably considered an initiatory rite.[17]

Among contemporary scholars, Rudolf Bultmann presents the Corinthian opponents as representatives of the Gnostic movement.[18] His various studies follow the research of Reitzenstein, Bousset, and Lütgert. The illustration of Bultmann, supplemented by his student Walter Schmithals,[19] seems to do justice to Paul's opposition in 1 Cor. In 2 Cor., however, the situation is different, as becomes evident from the tone of Paul's arguments. The foreign agitators who had arrived *in the meantime* cannot simply be identified as fellow party-members of the Corinthian Gnostics. After all, it is remarkable that in 2 Cor.—as opposed to 1 Cor.—Paul no longer attacks the Gnostic redeemer-myth. On the contrary, he can now speak about "gnosis" in decidedly positive terms and use Gnostic motifs more directly than before.[20]

It was Ernst Käsemann who first drew attention to the fact that Paul's opponents in 2 Cor. are not Gnostics.[21] He also stressed that Paul no longer polemicizes against libertinism (apart from the stereotypical formulations in 2 Cor. 6:14—7:1 and 12:20). Those objections, which had led Baur to his "Judaizer" hypothesis, were now raised by Käsemann against the gnostic hypothesis (as formulated by Bultmann): the emphasis on the Jewish, even Palestinian, background and the insistence on tradition by Paul's opponents in 2 Cor. Yet the theories developed by Käsemann, Bultmann, and Schmithals disregard a major issue: they do not explain the understanding of scripture that Paul's opponents hold (see 2 Cor. 3). Käsemann's study is unfortunately limited to 2 Cor. 10—13, which leads him to the idea of ascribing to these opponents a purely legal understanding of tradition, very similar to that of the rabbis. It is true that in NT times spirit and law were connected, but how is it possible to associate ecstatic pneumatism and a rabbinic concept of tradition, and enthusiasm and the principle of legitimacy?

With good reason Bultmann and Schmithals also question the strength of Baur's hypothesis as modified by Käsemann (following the example of Reitzenstein), namely, that the opponents were a visitation committee from Jerusalem. Paul's complicated diction in 2 Cor. 10—13 can hardly be explained as a carefully constructed indirect polemic against the first apostles via the "visitors" from Jerusalem. No, Paul's polemic is rather to be explained as an ironic response to the boastful attitudes of his opponents. In this respect Bultmann has clearly refuted the arguments of Käsemann. After all, the first apostles are not mentioned in 2 Cor., and Paul was not afraid, should the need arise, to attack them pointedly over the heads of their partisan followers, as in Galatians. But thanks to Käsemann we have been made aware of the singular *claim* of Paul's opponents, particularly as expressed in their titles. The significance of these titles cannot be explained simply by a "pneumatic self-assurance," and even less by a claimed Gnostic origin of the term "apostle" (contrary to Schmithals), for one can disregard the dubious nature of this religio-historical derivation of the title "apostle" and ask: how about the other titles to which Paul's opponents laid claim?

Käsemann also shows how much the opponents desired "to measure" themselves and tries to present their "canon" as a principle of tradition and legitimacy of the Jerusalem church. Although such a historical categorization is impossible (as Bultmann has shown), the question remains *why* the opponents in their missionary claims and their attacks on Paul are concerned with the right "measure." Käsemann supports his hypothesis by pointing to the opponents' letters of recommendation. While Bultmann succeeds in refuting Käsemann's assertion of a Jerusalem origin for these letters, he is unable (just as Schmithals) to explain why Gnostic pneumatics should have valued letters of recommendation.

Modern research has shown that Paul's opponents in 2 Cor. must have had a different christology. Käsemann's objections to the as-

sumption of a "Gnostic" christology have not been refuted by
Schmithals. Käsemann does not, however, describe the christology
of these opponents clearly. The advocates of the Gnostic hypothesis,
on the other hand, stumble over 2 Cor. 5:16. And finally, against
which Jewish Jesus-believers could Paul be arguing in the erratic
manner of 2 Cor. 3? Why was the understanding of scriptures of
these Jewish Christians no hindrance for the alliance with the Corinthian Gnostics? In the following I will try to answer these questions.[22]

REASONS FOR LIMITING THIS STUDY TO
2 COR. 2:14—7:4 AND 10—13

In the last section I briefly listed some arguments for not extending the study of Paul's opponents to 1 Cor. In the next section
further chronological reasons will justify limiting this study to the
time period of 2 Cor. But first the textual problems have to be clarified, since 2 Cor. is now a single literary unit.[23]

Even casual inspection of 2 Cor. reveals the abrupt transition
from chap. 9 to chap. 10.[24] It is impossible to agree with Chrysostom and say that Paul, at an appropriate moment and after sufficient
preparation of the Corinthians, here finally addresses graver matters (εὐκαίρως λοιπὸν τῶν ἐπιτιμητικωτέρων ἅπτεται λόγων).[25] The
problem is this εὐκαίρως λοιπόν. Are we really dealing here with an
"appropriate moment"? Paul has just urgently asked for active and
existential participation in the collection for Jerusalem. And then a
scathing philippic which gives the Corinthians no quarter! I cannot
see how anyone could attribute strategy to Paul in order to explain
this striking contrast. From a tactical point of view, having a philippic in chaps. 10—13 follow a request for money is not very
shrewd.[26] The appeal for a voluntary contribution to the Jerusalem
collection would have no chance of success if followed by attacks and
reproaches, and not until 12:16–18 does Paul respond to accusations regarding the collection and the way in which he raised the
money. In the two chapters (8—9) concerning the Jerusalem collection there is no mention of these problems.

Placing chaps. 1—7 ahead of 8—13 increases the tactical difficulties and leads to a number of logical inconsistencies.[27] In chaps.
10—13 Paul is attacking the church in Corinth sharply. He doubts

their faith and expects a cold reception at his next visit. He is forced to argue against specific calumnies.[28] Paul is threatening to come to Corinth and to show no mercy in judging those who disobey. On the other hand, in 1:1—2:13 and especially in 1:23—2:11 and 7:5 the dispute between Paul and his community is treated as something belonging to the past. These passages do not contain any tensions which could justify the polemics of chaps. 10—13. The Corinthians have shown Titus that they are prepared to show obedience again. In some passages we even find almost verbatim correspondence: 1:23 with 13:2; 1:24 with 13:5; 2:3 with 13:10; 2:9 with 10:6; 7:16 with 10:1.[29] But if the order of the chapters is not changed, the passages from chaps. 10—13 would retract or ignore what has been said in the earlier chapters.

Thus neither tactical nor logical reasons can be found to justify the present sequence of the chapters of 2 Cor. Therefore some scholars make Paul's psyche responsible for the drastic changes of mood. Hans Lietzmann, for instance, remarked that a sleepless night could adequately explain the abrupt transition from 2 Cor. 9 to 2 Cor. 10.[30] But what a strange explanation! Paul's psyche would then surely be a case for psychopathology.

No wonder scholars look for a different reason. Some point to the arrival of new information in order to explain Paul's sudden and total change of tone.[31] But the letter does not speak of such news, and no reason for the assumption that Paul might have suppressed such news can be found. Bousset's argument (based on the introductory phrase of 2 Cor. 10 with its stress on the "I") that Paul had taken the pen from his secretary in order to write with his own hand instead of dictating yields new difficulties,[32] for in that case Paul would earlier have kept his opinion to himself; chaps. 1—9 would represent an ambiguous document. Even if Paul did pick up the pen, why did he do so, and why did he write in such a tone? This question would still remain unanswered. Günther Bornkamm rightly asks "how our letter could have been sent in its present form, which in the first part does not allow the restored rapport between Paul and his community to be clouded in any way, yet shows the struggle at its height in the last part."[33]

For all these reasons one must look for a larger unit than one single letter, a unit which is able to encompass these tensions. Placing the pieces of the letter in a larger time frame enables the observer to view better the color and life of these events and interchanges. Now it becomes clear that the last four chapters of 2 Cor. form a fragment of a separate letter written before the conciliatory parts of 2 Cor. and presupposed in them. This reconstructed letter can be identified as the "letter of sorrow" (*Schmerzensbrief*) conjectured from 2 Cor. 2:4 and 7:8.[34]

This hypothesis, first developed by Adolf Hausrath, has found much support.[35] It does, however, leave some unanswered questions,[36] for it is very difficult to reconcile the mention of a person who treated Paul unjustly and had since been punished by the congregation (see 2:1–11 and 7:5–12[37]) with the absence of this person and the specific event from chaps. 10—13. The advocates of this "division hypothesis" tried to resolve the problem in various ways.[38] At first, the ἀδικήσας was identified with the incestuous person of 1 Cor. 5 as traditional exegesis also advocated. The lost piece of the letter of sorrow would then have dealt with the personal dispute of this man with Paul. But such a solution has rightly been declared to be off the mark and quite impossible. There is more to be said for the hypothesis that the offender represented a case example of the successful agitation which Paul's opponents had stirred up within his community. In this case there would be no need to mention the incident at great length in the letter of sorrow, but Paul could not have been totally silent about the event and the person in question. Bornkamm explains their absence from the supposed fragment of the letter of sorrow with two assumptions:

> (1) that the chapters known to us are only one fragment of the letter of sorrow, though surely the most important one, and (2) that a later editor, probably a Christian from the Corinthian community who compiled parts of Paul's extensive correspondence with the community in order to make it available to others, did not again include the incident in the last part of the letter since it had been mentioned already in the letter of reconciliation as being settled.[39]

That the editor was not concerned with details is already shown by his omission of the names of the envoys responsible for the collection in chaps. 8 and 12 (except for Titus) and in chap. 9 (here including Titus).

A further and even greater hindrance to the "four-chapter hypothesis" seems to be the suppression of the object of dispute in 1:23—2:11 and in 7:5–16.[40] Bornkamm believes that if the opponents were wandering preachers (which will be shown to be the case below), then they could have already left before Paul wrote the more autobiographical portions of his letter. There would be no need to mention them again.

> Moreover, there can be no doubt that the conflict stirred up by the false apostles had reached its climax in this very incident. It is understandable that Paul now refers only to the conflict in general, since he is fighting to win back the community. The ἀδικήσας is a member of that community. He was not one of the false apostles, but one who had been misled by them; thus he is still living in the community and subjected to its disciplinary measures.[41]

The remaining chapters of 2 Cor. also have numerous awkward breaks and transitions. The segment 6:14—7:1 has been inserted in its present position;[42] the two framing verses 6:13 and 7:2 match each other well, but this cannot be said of their relationship to 6:14 or 7:1.[43] 7:2 immediately follows 6:13 with no noticeable influence of the statements between. In addition, the content of 6:14—7:1 has not been prepared for by the previous verses of chap. 6. This small passage also has several *hapax legomena*. 7:1 is particularly difficult to associate with Paul's usual terminology and point of view. Nowhere else does Paul speak of a "defilement of the flesh," for the flesh is for Paul sinful in itself, whenever this term is not used simply to designate human mortality. It is even more unusual for Paul to speak of a "defilement of the spirit." The concepts of cleansing, sanctification, and perfection, presupposed in this passage, are also non-Pauline. Likewise Paul does not mention elsewhere the notion of ethical development expressed here. The form of the passage is that of a prophetic saying. It strongly resembles the Qumran texts in language and philosophy.[44] Thus this prophetic saying has its likely origin in Jewish circles of Jesus believers in Palestine. It is impossible to say how it came to Corinth.

In 2 Cor. 2:13 Paul suddenly stops narrating the events of his journey from Asia Minor to Macedonia, but in 7:5 he resumes at exactly the same point. The piece between is complex and entangled. Many attempts have been made to explain this sequence,[45] but the text does not give much support to the many psychological speculations.[46] Reordering the verses does not help much either.[47] It could be done only in conjunction with changes in the established text of 2:14—7:4, which would be difficult to justify. It is, however, possible to show that the segment 2:14—7:4 forms a unit, with the exception of the inserted passage 6:14—7:1.[48]

The section 2:14—7:4 (without 6:14—7:1) also differs from the surrounding passages in content. Its character is almost entirely polemical. According to these polemical remarks, the community is still on the side of the opposition, and Paul has to fight vigorously for acknowledgment. According to 1:1—2:13 and 7:5–16, however, Paul has in the meantime regained his authority among the Corinthians. The didactic passages in 2:14—7:4 resemble a theological dispute with a heresy, of which there is nothing in 1:1—2:13 or in 7:5–16.[49] In 2:14—7:4, on the other hand, no reference is made to the peace agreement initiated by Titus. Such a reference would have fit well in 3:1–3, for instance. Even the last verses of this passage, 6:11–13 and 7:2–4, do not fit into the letter of reconciliation.[50] Paul's pleading and urging, especially the bitter tone of 6:11–13, speaks against such an interpretation. Paul has to implore the community to grant him the trust and confidence which he has already reestablished in 2:1–11 and 7:5–12.

There is much closer correlation between section 2:14—7:4 and chaps. 10—13 with respect to form as well as to substance. In both cases Paul is fighting the alliance of the Corinthian community with outside agitators, sometimes using similar ideas and wording.[51] But still, 2:14—7:4 and 10—13 are fragments of different letters, for regardless of the similarity in subject and terminology, there is a clear difference in tone between the two fragments. In 2:14—7:4 Paul is still courting the Corinthians. His attacks are directed more at the opponents who are staying in Corinth than at the Corinthian community itself. In chaps. 10—13, however, the antagonism between Paul and his opponents also divides Paul and his community.[52] Compared with the discussion in 2:14—7:4, the polemics of 10—13 are considerably sharper and, above all, much more personal. Unlike 2:14—7:4, there are no passages of a truly didactic nature here.[53]

The difference is also visible in Paul's use of the καύχησις motif.[54] In 7:4 Paul's understanding of boasting is fairly unambiguous, whereas in chaps. 10—13 it is more dialectical. The words of praise for his community in 7:4 are absent from chaps. 10—13. A notable difference also exists between Paul's statements about self-commendation in 3:1 and 5:12, on the one hand, and those in 10:7 and 11:5, 18, 23 on the other.[55] In the latter passages Paul is forced to commend himself despite his objections to self-commendation in 2:14—7:4. To justify himself he cites the attacks of his opponents and the reaction of the Corinthian community. The fact that Paul rejects any kind of self-commendation in 2:14—7:4 but then is forced to use it after all (although in the form of a fool's speech) makes me believe that a turn for the worse took place between the period when 2:14—7:4 was written and the time when Paul was forced, later on, to write chaps. 10—13.[56]

The development described above leads me to the conclusion that 2:14—7:4 and chaps. 10—13 do not belong together, even though both fragments address the danger that the community might desert Paul for his opponents. The similarity as well as dissimilarity of the two passages is best explained in the following way. When Paul was writing 2:14—7:4 the community seemed in danger of accepting the arguments of the recently arrived opponents. But Paul still had reasons to hope that he might be able to keep the community from succumbing. When Paul was writing chaps. 10—13, however, the situation seemed practically hopeless, for the community appeared to be firmly in the hands of his opponents. But after the arrival of the philippic (2 Cor. 10—13) the tide unexpectedly turned. The majority of the Corinthian church took Paul's side again. Paul's messenger, Titus, who arrived after the letter of sorrow, appeared to have succeeded in turning the situation around. Thus 2:14—7:4 was probably written before chaps. 10—13.[57] If this assumption is correct, then 2:14—7:4 is a fragment, in fact the most important fragment, of one of those letters at which Paul's opponents and the community were scoffing (2 Cor. 10:10).

THE COURSE OF EVENTS

Discussion of the textual limits for this study must be complemented by an investigation of the *time frame* in question. A more precise determination of the chronology encourages Schmithals to work with a wide textual basis, that is, to take into account all fragments of the Corinthian correspondence which have been transmitted to us. He believes that all fragments should be included in the analysis since the intervals between them are relatively short.[58] According to Schmithals, the first and the last fragments are separated by only eight months. This supports his conviction that the entire Corinthian correspondence concerns only a *single* dispute with *one and the same* group of people. He says: "It would be most unusual if two completely different heresies had been able to secure admission in the community at about the same time and then similarly had disappeared again at the same time."[59] Qualifying his statement somewhat, he continues: "Such a remarkable coincidence naturally would be theoretically possible, but it is obvious that it would be a more than rare accident. One could arrive at such an assumption only if Paul's polemic were clearly directed against *two* opposing fronts."[60]

But do not various indications in the texts point to a hectic and eventful development during this time period (accepting the eight-month proposal for now)? First I would like to ask only what exactly must have happened during this period, postponing the problem of the history of the opposition in order not to prejudice the result.[61]

Paul's first letter to the Corinthians (of which we know) already dealt with the tensions and difficulties in the community. This letter is mentioned in 1 Cor. 5:9. Whether parts of this letter are preserved in the canonical 1 Cor. is a question I shall leave aside.[62] The Corinthians sent a delegation from the community to Paul with an answering letter. There can be no doubt that parts (or perhaps all) of 1 Cor. refer to it.[63] According to 1 Cor. 4:17 and 16:5–11, Paul had sent Timothy to Corinth to set matters right before sending his letter, perhaps even before the arrival of the delegation. The statements and allusions of Paul found in 1 Cor. 16 suggest that he did not intend to come to Corinth for several more months. The instructions for the Jerusalem collection, which was being reactivated at the time, are meant to cover a longer time period. Moreover, Paul mentions in 16:5–9 that he will be busy in Ephesus for a while longer because of new missionary possibilities. After finishing this mission successfully, he planned first to visit the communities in Macedonia and only then come to Corinth. He intended to remain in Corinth until the following spring and then possibly to travel with the others to Jerusalem (see 16:3).

Timothy's visit and Paul's letter had some success.[64] One indication we have for this is that Titus, whom Paul had sent to Corinth shortly afterward, was well received and successful in organizing the collection for Jerusalem (2 Cor. 12:18; 8:5, 10; 9:2), for in the meantime Paul had changed his original plan to let the Corinthians themselves organize the collection. In fact, the dispatch of Titus seems to have been a response to the desire of the *Corinthians* to complete the collection rapidly. His journey was not a result of tensions between Paul and the community. Even at the time when Paul wrote the philippic, he could still count on the positive influence from Titus's visit (2 Cor. 12:16–18). Apparently the urging of the Corinthians also caused Paul to change his own travel plans. Since he could not come immediately, he probably sent Titus as his representative. But through Titus he must have made it known to the Corinthians that he would come to them directly from Ephesus as soon as possible. He would then go to Macedonia from Corinth and return to Corinth again before departing for Jerusalem (2 Cor. 1:15–16). How much the Corinthians counted on Paul's visit can be seen from the fact that they still blamed him for not having kept his itinerary even after the reconciliation had taken place.

After Titus had left Corinth new tensions arose, causing Paul to change his travel plans once again. The following events must have taken place:

1. Paul sent a letter (including 2:14—7:4) to Corinth, trying to redress the situation and to persuade those who seemed hesitant and undecided in their loyalty to him.
2. Paul briefly visited Corinth (2 Cor. 2:1; 12:14; 13:1), at which time the conflict reached its climax (2 Cor. 2:1–11 and 7:5–16).[65]
3. Paul wrote the "letter of sorrow" (including 2 Cor. 10—13) from Ephesus.

In 2 Cor. 1:8–11 Paul implies that he had since been imprisoned and nearly killed.[66] It seems that during his imprisonment he wrote the letters to Philippi, fragments of which are preserved in the canonical letter.[67] The information about the imprisonment as well as the help and illness of Epaphroditus (Phil. 2:25–30) points to an imprisonment of several months' duration.

Apparently Paul had sent Titus to Corinth before he was put in prison.[68] After his release, Paul set out to Macedonia (via Troas) in order to meet Titus on the way (2 Cor. 2:12–13). In Macedonia he was evidently confronted with the spreading Philippian heresy (compare 2 Cor. 7:5 with 8:2).[69] Finally Titus arrived and brought good news to Paul about the situation in Corinth (7:5–16), where peace reigned once again. Paul then wrote the letter of reconciliation (including 1:1—2:13 and 7:5–16).

After the problems in Macedonia were settled, Paul urged the Macedonians to complete the collection. According to 2 Cor. 8:1–6, the Macedonians themselves had taken the initiative, perhaps in order to help Paul overcome his disappointment about the dismal situation he had first encountered in their communities. Paul writes and reports about this development to the Corinthians and asks them to bring their own collection to a conclusion too.

There seems to be a break between 2 Cor. 7:16 and 8:1. 2 Cor. 8 presupposes a totally different situation. I am inclined to believe that the fragment of another letter begins here.[70] The appeal for the collection is combined with a recommendation of Titus, who was ready to depart for Corinth again, and of two companions (2 Cor. 8:16–24). They are supposed to prepare for the conclusion of the collection. After writing this letter about the collection (2 Cor. 8), Paul apparently wrote a short second letter addressed to all the churches in the province of Achaia. This letter is preserved in 2 Cor. 9. Shortly afterward, Paul himself went to Corinth where, according to Acts 20:3, he stayed for three months. During this period the collection was completed and the delegation for Jerusalem was chosen. Paul also wrote the Letter to the Romans, thereby preparing a new phase of his missionary work.

These various events would already seem to conflict with any simple and uniform interpretation of the situation in the Corinthian community. It seems that the successive visits—first of Timothy, then of Titus (his first visit to organize the collection)—speak for a clear break between different time periods. During the visits of Timothy and Titus the situation in the Corinthian church seems to have been calm, whereas tensions existed before and after. This break must be placed between the time periods described in 1 and 2 Cor.

Finally, I believe Schmithals's time period of eight months (or a little more) to be too short.[71] According to a brief but reliable remark in Acts 19:8, Paul was active in Ephesus for three months in the synagogue, and then, after breaking with the Jewish synagogue, he worked in this capital of the province of Asia and its surroundings for another two years (Acts 19:10). Acts 20:31 even speaks of an approximate period of three years in Ephesus. The difference between two and a quarter and three years can be explained by Paul's imprisonment (reported in 2 Cor. 1:8–11 and Phil. 1:7–26). Luke keeps silent about this incident.[72] The incidental reference in Acts 19:22 to Paul's staying in Asia "for a while" also seems to hint at the duration of the imprisonment. Since ancient references to specific time periods are always approximate, I assume that the Corinthian correspondence extends over a period of about two and a half years (two and a quarter years of actual work and three months in prison). This assumption is confirmed by other observations, which I discuss elsewhere.[73]

I suggest that the fragment 2:14—7:4 was composed in the summer of 54 C.E. and the letter of sorrow in the fall of that same year. The letter of reconciliation and the letters about the collection would then have been written during the summer and fall of 55 C.E. Unlike Schmithals, I recommend starting with a relatively small textual basis and then deciding how much more can be safely integrated. Because Paul's polemic shows most clearly in 2 Cor. 10—13, this passage should be discussed first. An added advantage is that this fragment contains numerous allusions to the self-designations of Paul's opponents. Therefore, I would now like to ask exactly what these self-designations are meant to express.

NOTES

1. John Chrysostom, *Homilies on the Epistles of Paul to the Corinthians* (NPNF ser. 1, vol. 12; Edinburgh: Clark, 1889), Homily 1 on 2 Cor., 271–72 and Homily 21 on 2 Cor., 375–78.

2. John Calvin, *Commentary on the Epistles of Paul the Apostle to the*

Corinthians (Calvin's Commentaries 20; Grand Rapids: Baker Book House, 1981 repr.) 2:102.

3. Ibid., 1:37–38.

4. Ferdinand Christian Baur, "Die Christuspartei der korinthischen Gemeinde" (1831; repr. in *Ausgewählte Werke in Einzelausgaben* [ed. Klaus Scholder; 5 vols.; Stuttgart: Fromann, 1963] 1:1–164); idem, *Paul the Apostle* (trans. A. Menzies; 2d ed.; 2 vols.; London and Edinburgh: Williams & Norgate, 1875–76).

5. Baur was influenced mainly by Semler, not by Hegel, when he began his historical analysis of early Christianity. Speculative philosophy provided Baur only with the intellectual tools to work out in full the differences he had discovered in the development of early Christianity and to use them as a key for historical understanding.

6. Cf. also Ernst Käsemann's introduction to Baur's *Ausgewählte Werke*, 1:viii–xxv.

7. Critical biblical scholars (cf., e.g., Otto Pfleiderer, *Der Paulinismus: Ein Beitrag zur Geschichte der urchristlichen Theologie* [2d ed.; Leipzig: Reisland, 1890] 315–22) expressed at least occasionally some doubts as to the *justification* of the Judaizing opponents for appealing to the first apostles. Others limited the relationship of the opponents to the first apostles in only conceding that they might have been legitimized by a certain group in the community at Jerusalem, the circle around James. See Karl Holsten, *Das Evangelium des Paulus* (2 vols.; Berlin: Reimer, 1880) 1:215–32.

8. Albert Klöpper, *Kommentar über das zweite Sendschreiben des Apostels Paulus an die Gemeinde zu Korinth* (Berlin: Reimer, 1874) 93; Adolf Hausrath, *Der Apostel Paulus* (Heidelberg: Bassermann, 1872) 381–82; Holsten, *Paulus*, 1:223–24; Paul Wilhelm Schmiedel, *Die Briefe an die Thessalonicher und an die Korinther* (2d ed.; HKNT 2/1; Freiburg: Mohr, 1892) 62.

9. A good summary can be found in Wilhelm Lütgert, *Freiheitspredigt und Schwarmgeister in Korinth: Ein Beitrag zur Charakteristik der Christuspartei* (BFCTh 12/3; Gütersloh: Bertelsmann, 1908) 41–101.

10. Richard Reitzenstein (*The Hellenistic Mystery-Religions: Their Basic Ideas and Significance* [trans. John E. Steely; Pittsburgh Theological Seminary Monographs 15; Pittsburgh: Pickwick, 1978] 59–71.) continues, strangely enough, to believe that Paul's opponents in 2 Cor. were Judaizing visitors. Cf. also Wilhelm Bousset, "Gnosis," PW 7 (1912) 1502–34; idem, *Hauptprobleme der Gnosis* (FRLANT 10; Göttingen: Vandenhoeck & Ruprecht, 1907).

11. Lütgert, *Freiheitspredigt*. See also idem, *Die Irrlehrer der Pastoralbriefe* (BFCTh 13/3: Gütersloh: Bertelsmann, 1909); idem, *Die Vollkommenen im Philipperbrief und die Enthusiasten in Thessalonich* (BFCTh 13/6; Gütersloh: Bertelsmann, 1909); idem, *Amt und Geist im Kampf* (BFCTh 15/4, 5; Gütersloh: Bertelsmann, 1911).

12. Adolf von Schlatter, *Die korinthische Theologie* (BFCTh 18/2;

Gütersloh: Bertelsmann, 1914); idem, *Paulus, der Bote Jesu: Eine Deutung seiner Briefe an die Korinther* (Stuttgart: Calwer, 1934).

13. Kirsopp Lake, *The Earlier Epistles of St. Paul* (London: Rivingtons, 1927) 219–35.

14. R. H. Strachan, *The Second Epistle of Paul to the Corinthians* (MNTC; London: Hodder & Stoughton, 1935) 25.

15. Hans Windisch, *Der zweite Korintherbrief* (MeyerK 6; Göttingen: Vandenhoeck & Ruprecht, 1924) 25–26 and elsewhere.

16. Windisch believes that the Jewish wandering preachers could have arrived in Corinth before 1 Cor. was written but that they did not begin their campaign until after the Corinthians had received Paul's letter.

17. For the heresy of Colossians, cf. Günther Bornkamm, "Die Häresie des Kolosserbriefes" (1948), in *Das Ende des Gesetzes: Gesammelte Aufsätze 1* (2d ed.; BEvTh 16; Munich: Kaiser, 1958) 139–56.

18. Esp. Rudolf Bultmann, *TDNT*, 1:709–11; idem, *Exegetische Probleme des zweiten Korintherbriefes: Zu 2. Kor. 5:1–5; 5:11–16; 10:10–13; 12:21* (SyBUSup 9; Uppsala: Wretmans, 1947).

19. For a detailed discussion of the work on *gnosis* by Walter Schmithals (*Gnosticism in Corinth: An Investigation of the Letters to the Corinthians* [trans. John E. Steely; Nashville: Abingdon, 1971]), esp. of his religio-historical propositions, cf. Dieter Georgi, Review of W. Schmithals, *Die Gnosis in Korinth*, in *VF* (1958–59) 90–96. In the later edition of his book Schmithals has modified his views on *gnosis*, particularly with respect to the redeemer myth.

20. Georgi, ibid.

21. Ernst Käsemann, "Die Legitimität des Apostels: Eine Untersuchung zu II Korinther 10—13," *ZNW* 41 (1942) 33–71.

22. A strange interpretation has been presented by Johannes Munck (*Paul and the Salvation of Mankind* [trans. Frank Clarke; Atlanta: John Knox, 1977]). He believes that the dispute between Paul and the Corinthian church existed already in a highly polemical form before the opponents arrived in Corinth (pp. 170–71). This is correct if one takes into consideration 1 Cor. only, but it becomes wrong if Paul's main opponents in 2 Cor. are also seen as *Corinthian* Christians whom Paul attacks for the same reasons as in 1 Cor. Paul mentioned the visiting Jewish Christians only (so Munck) because they arrived in Corinth at an inappropriate moment, i.e., before Paul had been able to reestablish firmly his authority in the Corinthian church. In view of the violence of Paul's polemic against the intruders, Munck's interpretation seems unacceptable: "The real opponents, here as elsewhere in the letter, are the Corinthians themselves, their false picture of the apostle, which now finds support in the behaviour of the apostles from outside, and their continued difficulty in humbling themselves under the suffering Christ and his suffering apostle and the message of the suffering for the Church in the world. . . . The visiting apos-

tles are only a subordinate theme, which has become important because the Corinthians saw something great in them and their demeanour, and because Paul thought he saw in them a temptation to apostasy" (Munck, *Paul*, 186). Does Munck not refute himself with these arguments? If this "temptation" was only a "subordinate theme," why were the Corinthians so impressed (2 Cor. 3:1; also 2:17; 4:2; 5:12; and esp. chap. 11)? And how do we explain the length and seriousness of Paul's reply? The "temptation for apostasy" describes a truly new situation, a situation far more serious than that at the time of 1 Cor. The case of Munck clearly demonstrates that a mere denial of Baur's questions does not lead very far.

23. For literary criticism of 2 Cor., see also Schmithals, *Gnosticism*, and Günther Bornkamm, *Die Vorgeschichte des sogenannten zweiten Korintherbriefes* (SHAW.PH 2; Heidelberg: Winter, 1961).

24. Cf. the survey of scholarly opinions in Windisch, *2. Korintherbrief*, 12–18, 288–89.

25. Chrysostom, *Homilies*, 375.

26. Alfred Plummer, *A Critical and Exegetical Commentary on the Second Epistle of St. Paul to the Corinthians* (ICC 34; Edinburgh: Clark, 1948). On the argument that the request for the collection is meant to prepare the polemic against the opponents, cf. ibid., xxx. On the assumption that 2 Cor. 1—9 is deliberately preparing the arguments in chaps. 10—13, cf. Windisch, *2. Korintherbrief*, 15.

27. Cf. esp. Plummer, *2 Corinthians*, xxx–xxxi.

28. Cf., e.g., 2 Cor. 10:2, 7, 10, 12–13; 11:6, 7, 16; 12:16–18.

29. Cf. Plummer, *2 Corinthians*, xxxi–xxxii.

30. Hans Lietzmann, *An die Korinther I–II* (4th ed.; HNT 9; Tübingen: Mohr, 1949) 139.

31. Among modern authors, see Adolf Jülicher, *Einleitung in das Neue Testament* (7th rev. ed. with Erich Fascher; Tübingen: Mohr, 1931) 99–100. Against this argument, see Plummer, *2 Corinthians*, xxxv; and Windisch, *2. Korintherbrief*, 15–16.

32. Wilhelm Bousset, "1. und 2. Korinther," in *Die Paulinischen Briefe und die Pastoralbriefe* (ed. Wilhelm Bousset and Wilhelm Heitmüller; 3d ed.; *Die Schriften des Neuen Testaments 2*; Göttingen: Vandenhoeck & Ruprecht, 1917) 171–72, 205–6.

33. Bornkamm, *Vorgeschichte*, 19 (my trans.).

34. Modern scholars have nearly unanimously accepted the idea that Paul had probably written another letter to the Corinthians *before* 1 Cor. They disagree, however, on the question of an "interim letter" which Paul is to have sent between 1 and 2 Cor. (against this last proposal, cf. the detailed contribution of Eduard Golla (*Zwischenreise und Zwischenbrief: Eine Untersuchung* . . . [*BS* 20/4; Freiburg: Herder, 1922]). But cf. the excursus in Lietzmann, *Korinther*, 104–5; and Windisch, *2. Korintherbrief*, 80.

35. Cf. Bornkamm, *Vorgeschichte*, 16–21. On the question of identifying

2 Cor. 10—13 with the letter of sorrow or a fragment of it, see the excellent survey in Plummer, *2 Corinthians*, xxx–xxxvi. Bibliography in Windisch, *2. Korintherbrief*, 12–13. Windisch himself does not think that chaps. 10—13 form the letter of sorrow. Following Max Krenkel (*Beiträge zur Aufhellung der Geschichte und der Briefe des Apostels Paulus* [Braunschweig: Schwetschke, 1890]), he believes that these chapters represent a fragment of a later letter, which was written when the dispute suddenly reemerged after Paul had already sent the letter of reconciliation. This time the polemic between Paul and his opponents became particularly violent, more violent than ever before.

This would mean that the community Paul addresses in 10:10 had in the meantime entirely forgotten that in earlier days it had accepted Paul's authority after being confronted with a single letter. According to Windisch, the opponents would only now have become truly successful in their agitation among the Corinthians. However, the opponents are no longer mentioned in the letter of reconciliation (as if they had left).

All this seems very unlikely. Also, in such a case, the Letter to the Romans, which was written in Corinth, would probably show traces of the dispute (cf. what Windisch himself has to say about the composition of Romans and its significance for the understanding of the situation in Corinth [in *2. Korintherbrief*, 432]). But Romans was written in an atmosphere of tranquility. All these arguments are also valid against Munck (*Paul*, 168–70), who defended the idea that 2 Cor. 10—13 was written after chaps. 1—9.

36. Objections other than the ones discussed here are less important, as, e.g., the one by Jülicher, (*Einleitung*, 97) that the letters mentioned in 10:10 must have included the letter of sorrow in particular because Paul speaks of their "weightiness." This is wrong, for the community reacted to the letter of sorrow with submission and not with protest. Paul's letters were no longer scoffed at, but on the contrary highly appreciated.

Even the second visit Paul planned (2 Cor. 1:15–16) cannot be used as an argument against the division hypothesis. The interim visit, the interim letter, and Paul's travel plan (1:15–16) do not need to be exclusive of each other. Cf. the discussion by Strachan, *2 Corinthians*, 62–69; Windisch, *2. Korintherbrief*, 60–61; and Lietzmann, *Korinther*, 102–3.

The assumption that 2 Cor. forms a unit is untenable, even if it is assumed that Paul addressed two different groups at the same time, a submissive majority (in chaps. 1—9) and a rebellious minority (chaps. 10—13). First, it would be unusual to distinguish between different addressees in one and the same letter. Second, this distinction in address would have to be mentioned in some way in the letter, but we find nothing of the sort. In 2 Cor. Paul addresses in fact only one group, the Corinthian community. The intruding opponents are attacked via that community in both fragments: in 2:14—7:4 and in chaps. 10—13 (cf. Plummer, *2 Corinthians*, xxxv).

37. The same issue is at stake in 2:1–11 and 7:5–16. See Windisch, *2. Korintherbrief*, 224.

38. A summary of the various opinions is found in ibid., 237–39; cf. also the discussion by Lietzmann, *Korinther*, 104–5.

39. Bornkamm, *Vorgeschichte*, 19 (my trans.).

40. Windisch, *2. Korintherbrief*, 14; Bornkamm, *Vorgeschichte*, 19–20.

41. Bornkamm, *Vorgeschichte*, 19–20 (my trans.).

42. There is discussion of this segment in Schmiedel, *Briefe*, 252–54; and Windisch, *2. Korintherbrief*, 211–20, esp. 219–20; also Jülicher, *Einleitung*, 87. Bornkamm (*Vorgeschichte*, 32) also argues for nonauthenticity. Kümmel (in Lietzmann, *Korinther*, 260) and Nils Dahl (*Das Volk Gottes: Eine Untersuchung zum Kirchenbewusstsein des Urchristentums* [Darmstadt: Wissenschaftliche Buchgesellschaft, 1963] 221, 324 n. 43) have tried to prove its authenticity. Schmithals (*Gnosticism*, 94) also believes that the piece is Pauline, although not in its proper place. It is impossible to consider 6:14—7:1 as a continuation of the ethical exhortation of 6:1–2. First, 6:1–2 is not a moral parenesis. Second, 6:1–2 continues smoothly in 6:3–10 (Bultmann, *Probleme*, 20). The debate on the apostolic mission constitutes the central issue of the dispute, not an excursus, for the existence of the church depends on the interpretation of that mission. However, 6:14—7:4 is irrelevant for this problem.

43. Lietzmann, *Korinther*, 129, again assumes a pause in dictation here.

44. Cf. Karl Georg Kuhn, "Die Schriftenrollen vom Toten Meer," *EvTh* 11(1951/52) 74; and "Les rouleaux de cuivre de Qumran," *RB* 61 (1954) 203 nn. 1, 2.

45. The abrupt transition is recognized by nearly all commentators.

46. Refutation of the psychological explanations by Windisch, *2. Korintherbrief*, 96, 224–25.

47. Against ibid.

48. Cf. also Schmithals, *Gnosticism*, esp. 98–101. Schmithals and I came to similar conclusions independently of each other. Cf. also Bornkamm, *Vorgeschichte*, 21–24.

49. Schmithals, *Gnosticism*, 98.

50. So also ibid., 99.

51. Similar personal apologies are found in 1 Cor. 3; 4; and 9. The motivation is also comparable. But there is a difference: in 1 Cor. the attacks come directly from the Corinthian church and not from outside agitators.

52. This would also explain why in 2:14—7:4 Paul rarely uses ἐγώ but mostly ἡμεῖς, even when referring to himself, whereas in chaps. 10—13 ἐγώ is predominant. This different terminology reflects theological disputes. Cf. below, pp. 229–41.

53. All these arguments are also found in Schmithals, *Gnosticism*, 98.

54. Cf. Plummer, *2 Corinthians*, xxxii, based on Lake and Kennedy. But Plummer uses these observations to separate chaps. 1—9 from 10—13. He

also draws attention to the fact that the strong words ἄφρων (11:16, 19; 12:6, 11) and ἀφροσύνη (11:1, 17, 21) are used only in chaps. 10—13, not in 1—9 (which means that they are also not used in 2:14—7:4). Other such aggressive words are also absent from chaps. 1—9.

55. Ibid., xxxiii. But Plummer sees 3:1 and 5:12 as quotations from chaps. 10—13.

56. Plummer assumes the contrary, a development from chaps. 10—13 to 2:14—7:4. This could be possible only if 2:14—7:4 belonged to 1:1—2:13 and 7:5–16.

57. Schmithals (*Gnosticism*, 99) reaches the same conclusions.

58. Ibid., 113–14.

59. Ibid., 113.

60. Ibid., 114.

61. This problem is discussed in more detail and depth in D. Georgi, *Die Geschichte der Kollekte des Paulus für Jerusalem* (ThF 38; Hamburg: Reich, 1965).

62. Cf. Bornkamm, *Vorgeschichte*, 34 n. 131.

63. 1 Cor. 1:11; 7:1, 25; 8:1; 12:1; 16:1, 12, and others.

64. See also Bornkamm, *Vorgeschichte*, 9 n. 13. More details in Georgi, *Kollekte*.

65. Schmithals is correct insofar as Paul did not "flee" Corinth (*Gnosticism*, 104). But Paul must have debated the painful event for the first time in the letter of sorrow. Because he then mentions it (the ἀδικία) explicitly in the letter of reconciliation, it must have happened on the occasion of his short interim visit, for the λύπη of which he speaks in 2:1–11 must have some relation to this visit (cf. also 13:2). Therefore, it is more likely that the letter which included the fragment 2:14—7:4 was written *before* Paul's interim visit (against Schmithals, *Gnosticism*, 104–13), for the tone of this fragment is still so conciliatory that one can hardly imagine that the ἀδικία had already taken place when 2:14—7:4 was written. The interval between the short visit and the letter of sorrow would be too long if one were to follow the assumption of Schmithals. Although chaps. 10—13 cannot be qualified as being purely emotional (Schmithals' hypothesis about what happened during Paul's short visit could imply such a suggestion), these chapters show a strong personal reaction. Paul does not refer to new information or to reports but to a personal experience which is still vivid in his memory. Cf. Bornkamm, *Vorgeschichte*, 23 n. 89.

66. More details in Georgi, *Kollekte*. Cf. also the bibliography there of earlier works, as well as a critique of the different approach taken by Schmithals to the dating of Paul's imprisonment, and Bornkamm, *Vorgeschichte*, 9 n. 13.

67. For convincing criticism of Philippians, cf. the article by Walter Schmithals, "Die Irrlehrer des Philipperbriefes," *ZThK* 54 (1957) 297–341.

68. 2 Cor. 1:8–11 seems to imply that the Corinthians were not too well

informed about Paul's imprisonment. The visit of Titus is mentioned in 2 Cor. 2:12–13 and 7:5–11, 13–15.

69. More details in Georgi, *Kollekte*.

70. For literary criticism of 2 Cor. 8 and 9, see ibid.

71. I discuss the problems of chronology of Paul's missions in ibid.

72. Cf. Ernst Haenchen, *The Acts of the Apostles: A Commentary* (trans. Bernard Noble and Gerald Shinn; ed. Hugh Anderson and R. McL. Wilson; Philadelphia: Westminster, 1971) 568–70.

73. Georgi, *Kollekte*.

1

The Missionary Role of the Opponents

THE OPPONENTS' SELF-DESIGNATIONS FOR THE TASK

The self-designations of the opponents either are cited directly by Paul or may be extracted indirectly from ironical or sarcastic inversions. Of those titles which disclose the opponents' view of their task, only the title διάκονος Χριστοῦ is quoted directly by Paul, in 2 Cor. 11:23.[1] This will be a good starting point for a discussion of their self-understanding.[2]

Διάκονος Χριστοῦ

According to the context of 11:23, the opponents regard διάκονος Χριστοῦ as a designation of respect.[3] Paul does not dispute his opponents' right to this title. He also does not play off his apostolate against their diaconate in the phrase ὑπὲρ ἐγώ.[4] That would not be spoken παραφρονῶν. Judging from 11:13–15, moreover, Paul regards the title "apostle" and the title "deacon" as parallel;[5] surely the opponents do too. Because the opponents, just as Paul, have called themselves διάκονοι Χριστοῦ, their common understanding of the concept διάκονος and of the title διάκονος Χριστοῦ must be investigated, and their use of the term scrutinized for possible differences in meaning.

The usual translation of διάκονος is "servant," but in the texts of antiquity the servant in a sociological or legal sense is generally designated by ὑπηρέτης or παῖς, or—if he is an administrator—by οἰκονόμος.[6] Of course, διάκονος frequently means the "waiter" at a table, and this leads to the description of cult assistants as διάκονοι too.[7] If one can assume that the concept already describes a rela-

27

tionship of trust in these instances, then this becomes even clearer with further examples. Thus orderlies of a field general are called διάκονοι. In Aeschines (*Ctesiphon* 55.33), διακονία is the special mission granted through an election. Correspondingly, Pollux (8.115, 137) speaks of διακονίαι δημόσιαι. In these instances, δια-κονία means less the office of special responsibility than the task connected with the office. Finally, the διάκονος can also be the "messenger." This meaning is found in Aeschylus,[8] Sophocles,[9] and Aristophanes.[10] Only a small step further is the use of this term for "envoy" and of διακονία for "embassy." Evidence for this is found once in Thucydides[11] and Pollux,[12] but especially in Epictetus.[13] Epictetus (*Diss.* 3.22.69) asks

> if the Cynic ought not to be free from distraction, wholly devoted to the διακονία τοῦ θεοῦ, free to go about among men, not tied down by the private duties of men, nor involved in relationships which he cannot violate and still maintain his role as a good and excellent man, whereas, on the other hand, if he observes them, he will destroy the messenger (ἄγγελος), the scout (κατάσκοπος), the herald (κῆρυξ) of the gods, that he is.

The διακονία of the true Cynic therefore consists in being messenger, scout, the herald of the gods.

In *Diss.* 3.24.64–66 the mission of the Cynic to the world is described still more clearly:

> But what was the manner of his [Diogenes's] loving? As became a διά-κονος of Zeus, caring for men indeed, but at the same time subject unto God. That is why for him alone the whole world, and no special place, was his fatherland.

Thus the διακονία of the Cynic is the expression of his world-encompassing missionary consciousness. He sees himself as God's representative in the world; he has a mission in and to the entire world. Accordingly, the διάκονος θεοῦ is the envoy of God in the sense of being his authorized representative. He executes this function as a world missionary. How much the Cynic is defined by his task may be discerned from *Diss.* 3.26.28:

> Does God so neglect his own creatures, his διάκονοι, his witnesses (μάρτυρες), whom alone he uses as examples (παραδείγματα) to the

uninstructed, to prove that he both is, and governs the universe well, and does not neglect the affairs of men, and that no evil befalls a good man either in life or in death?

Then the Cynic's relationship with God is compared to the relationship between soldier and general (3.26.29): "I obey, I follow, lauding my commander, and singing hymns of praise about his deeds." In the next paragraph this is carried over directly to the relationship with God: "For I came into the world when it so pleased him, and I leave it again at his pleasure, and while I live this was my function . . . to praise unto God, to myself and to others be it to one or to many."

There are many other impressive examples for the fateful fusion of the Cynic with his assigned task. I would like to make only one further reference, which shows once again how this self-understanding may be encompassed by the concept of διάκονος (*Diss*. 4.7.20):

> But always I wish rather the thing which takes place. For I regard God's will as better than my will. I shall attach myself to him as a διάκονος and follower (ἀκόλουθος). My choice is one with [him], my desire one with [him], in a word: my will is one with his will.

The intensity of the relation between God and his διάκονος could hardly be expressed any more strongly. Indeed, the thoughts expressed here are characteristically Stoic; yet it is significant that διάκονος can be used to describe this relationship with God as it is externally manifested and proclaimed.

The meaning of "envoy" for διάκονος (in the sense of responsible, fateful representation and manifestation) will do justice to most NT passages in which διάκονος appears, rather than the meaning of "servant," for which the function of the "waiter" at the table stands in the background. The NT term almost never involves an act of charity. Instead, nearly all instances are meant to refer to acts of proclamation. In 1 Thess. 3:2, Timothy is characterized as διάκονος τοῦ θεοῦ ἐν τῷ εὐαγγελίῳ τοῦ Χριστοῦ. In 1 Cor. 3:5, the missionaries Apollos and significantly even Paul are presented as διάκονοι.

In my opinion, Paul is alluding to the proclaimers with the term διάκονοι even in Phil. 1:1.[14] Because of the juxtaposition of ἐπίσκοποι and διάκονοι, exegetes have generally been tempted to find beginnings of the later, ecclesiastical differentiation of "bishops" and "deacons" in this passage. But no further basis exists for the assumption of a developed ecclesiastical organization of a vertical structure in the Pauline community in Philippi. The Philippian correspondence yields almost nothing for a legal and titular classification of specific functions of community life. Only the special and particular activity of Epaphroditus is singled out. He is called a "community delegate" (ὑμῶν ἀπόστολος in 2:25) because of his delivery of the community donation. It is hard to believe that the organization of this collection would have required a special permanent personnel structure, and even harder to believe that the organizers were necessarily given titles. Moreover, Phil. 1:1 was written a long time after the delivery of that collection.[15] The earlier note of thanks in 4:10–20 likewise mentions only Epaphroditus and no other officeholders, particularly no special ones.

In my opinion, the evidence presented by Martin Dibelius for a technical use of διάκονος helps as little as does the evidence given for ἐπίσκοπος. This is true not only for the cultic examples but also for the economic evidence preferred by Dibelius. All the previous observations suggest instead a synonymous use of διάκονοι and ἐπίσκοποι as designations for proclaimers, most of all because ἐπισκοπεῖν can also describe the preaching of popular philosophy. Evidence for this is found in Epictetus,[16] but also in Dio Chrysostom and in Lucian.[17] Paul would then be greeting (missionary) proclaimers present or living in Philippi.[18] This would correspond well with the special role of missionary activity in the aforementioned letter fragment.[19]

Apparently the Philippian community, which after all was entirely self-dependent at a very early date, had energetically taken up missionary proclamation in the vicinity.[20] If individual persons had become especially active because they could invest more time and strength in the effort than others, that is not surprising.

In the deutero-Pauline letters, it seems that διάκονος and its derivatives are also used in a similar meaning. Col. 1:7, 23, and 25 allude to acts of proclamation, the last two passages referring to Paul. In Col. 4:7, Tychicus is probably being presented as a preacher—at least the author of Ephesians understood it in this sense, as Eph.

6:21 shows. And in Eph. 3:7 the missionary function of Paul is circumscribed with the phrase τοῦ εὐαγγελίου διάκονος.

In both the Pastoral Epistles and in Ignatius, διάκονος appears as a separate, official function. But in both cases the elements of church order presented give more of an ideal program than a description of reality. This shows not the least with the office of διάκονος. The reality the authors in question have to work with does not fit the ideal they wish to see.

In 1 Tim. 3:8–13 an office is described, but Timothy is still called a διάκονος (1 Tim. 4:6). Since the mystery of faith is entrusted to the deacons as officeholders (3:9), acts of proclamation seem to be assumed as their essential task still. If they are warned of shameful greed (3:8), then that must not necessarily indicate a charitable or administrative activity of theirs. On the contrary, accusations of personal enrichment are often raised against religious propagandists in antiquity. I shall discuss this topic later.[21]

In Ignatius the integration of the deacons into a hierarchical structure with subordination under the bishops and presbyters appears on the surface as a matter of course.[22] But Ignatius has to deal with a reality different from his wishful thinking and adjuration, for when individual deacons are mentioned, it is not always apparent that they are being subordinated to a hierarchical structure, although Ignatius pushes for it. The deacons mentioned (Ignatius: *Eph*. 2:1; *Magn*. 2; *Phld*. 11:1–2; *Smyrn*. 10:1) can leave their communities for a fairly long time and presumably frequently as well.[23] But if they, apparently unlike the bishops,[24] were able to do this, they could hardly have been administrative assistants of the bishops, and certainly not officers entrusted with charitable work. They can scarcely be considered purely as community employees with a limited sphere of activity.[25] Apparently, in practice they still function as "envoys."

Trall. 2:3 also says more about the "deacons" than that they were merely involved in charity. Analogous to 1 Tim. 3:9, they are said to be in charge of the mysteries of Jesus Christ, which probably means that they are held to be proclaimers.[26]

Only in Acts 6:1–2 is the activity of the διάκονοι interpreted as table service and charitable work and thus associated with common

Greek usage of the term.[27] But this interpretation is not followed as the narration continues. The only precise statements about the seven deacons concern the preaching of Stephen and Philip.[28] And Acts 6:4 calls the office of the apostle a διακονία τοῦ λόγου. The accounts of the missionary accomplishments of Stephen and Philip are certainly the original ones.[29]

In addition, διακονία also frequently designates acts of proclamation. This is certainly the case in 1 Cor. 16:15 (Stephanas and the members of his household); Rom. 11:13; Acts 1:17, 25; 6:4; 20:24; 21:19; Eph. 4:12; 1 Tim. 1:12; and 2 Tim. 4:5 (cf. also Heb. 1:14). It is probably the case in 1 Cor. 12:5; Rom. 12:7; Col. 4:17; and 2 Tim. 4:11.[30]

One may conclude that, like Paul and other early Christian proclaimers, the opponents of Paul thought of themselves as envoys of Christ, as Christ's personal representatives. Accordingly, the adversaries of Paul functioned principally as Jesus-missionaries.[31] They apparently differed from Paul in demonstratively emphasizing the importance of their role, or—to use the words of Paul (11:16–23)—they boasted and bragged about it. The task of the rest of this inquiry will be to show the objective reasons for this difference. Close examination of the terms used makes it appear that different convictions about the proper manner and legitimate basis of representation are involved. This analysis is confirmed by 2 Cor. 5:18–20.

Ἀπόστολος Χριστοῦ

In 2 Cor. 11:13 Paul designates his opponents as ψευδαπόστολοι. He would not have done this had the adversaries not seen themselves as ἀπόστολοι. The expression ὑπερλίαν ἀπόστολοι is probably an ironic restatement of the opponents' claim to be apostles; the notion that with the phrase "superapostles" Paul meant the first apostles is contrived.[32] Therefore the phrase ἀπόστολοι Χριστοῦ in 2 Cor. 11:13 quotes a self-designation of the opponents. Paul cannot and does not want to flaunt a personal "apostolic office" before them. He uses no formal reasons in wresting from them their claim to be apostles of Christ, and he accuses them not simply of unauthorized employment of the title.[33] After all, one should notice that Paul first speaks of the term "apostle" in 11:5, and there reacts as if attacked. Moreover, he cannot just cut the ground from under their feet with a sudden attack, but must instead fight hard to keep some room for himself to stand on. From the beginning of chap. 10 on, the argument is over how to appear in public. Here significant differences exist, and the manner of appearance seems to justify the claim of being an apostle on both sides. This shows that a generally accepted understanding of the image of an apostle did not exist as yet and could not be used as a basis for comparison. This leads to the subject of the "apostolate" in the early church in general.

The "apostolate" in the early church has been researched repeatedly, but many questions have not been sufficiently clarified.[34] The earlier attempt to start from Luke's understanding of the apostle is rejected with good reasons in the majority of the newer works;[35] Luke's concept proves to be fictitious.[36] On the other hand, it seems to be similarly uncritical to start from Paul's image of the apostle as typical for the early church, a procedure followed especially by Schmithals.[37] Schmithals then attempts to differentiate somewhat by drawing parallels only to the apostolic office of the church, and also by identifying two Gnostic apostolates, a Jewish one and a Jewish-Christian one. He regards the Gnostic apostolate as the earliest one in the church.[38] But Walter Bauer's *Orthodoxy and Heresy in Earliest Christianity* should demonstrate in particular that boundaries between church and (Gnostic) heresy in the first two centuries were very fluid. *The* church existed as little in NT times as did *the* Gnosticism or *the* Gnostic heresy.

Paul can be said to have understood himself as belonging with the other apostles,[39] yet it must be recognized that Paul claims to have a peculiar understanding of the "apostle."[40] He says he is sent to the *nations* (Rom. 1:5, and Romans passim; but also Gal. 1:16). Furthermore, Paul's position on the question of financial support must also be recalled, especially his presentation in 1 Cor. 9. One should not say that Paul proceeded apologetically in the passages in which he speaks of the "apostolate."[41] That would look as if he had an image of *the* "apostolate" or an apostolic institution to defend. True, he passionately defends his belonging to the circle of apostles.[42] But nowhere is a general image of the "apostolate" evoked, not even in 1 Cor. 9:1–2; nowhere is a common understanding of the "apostolate" referred to as having been worked out, agreed to, and established. In the bitter discussions it would have been of substantial help if Paul had been able to refer to such an agreed-upon institution. Schmithals could object that Paul possessed as little an original understanding of the "apostolate" as had the other apostles of Jesus, that they had instead adopted that of Gnosticism. Then the church's apostles, as plagiarists, would naturally have had a difficult position vis-à-vis the Gnostic critique of the church's understanding of the apostolate.[43]

Nevertheless, the thesis of the origin of the early Christian "apostolate" in Gnosticism is not convincing. I do not want to embark on a discussion of the religio-historical assessment.[44] Günter Klein has already called attention to a substantial contradiction.[45] If Gnostic self-understanding and apostolic consciousness were identical in Gnosticism, and that means at the same time for every Gnostic, then a special apostolic *claim* of a definite, defined circle of persons could not develop. I would like to observe further that, given this identity of Gnostic self-understanding and Gnostic apostolate, I do not understand why one would have attacked and disputed the Pauline apostolate instead of simply Paul's view of faith's self-understanding as expressed by Paul. And if Paul's understanding of the apostolate was attacked at all, then surely, according to Schmithals's thesis, all forms of exclusiveness would have had to be denied and a democratization supported. Precisely the opposite, however, took place. The opponents of Paul emphasized exclusiveness; Paul certainly did not (so without exception in 2 Cor.).

Schmithals also cannot show sufficient reasons for adoption of a Gnostic apostolate by the early church. To explain that it was adopted because the mission carried on by the Gnostic apostles was copied only shifts the problem.[46] Aside from the fact that the evidence presented for this is insufficient, no reason or necessity is given for this assimilation. The eschatological vantage point, from which Paul sees his missionary work in both the first and the last segment of his preserved correspondence (1 Thessalonians 1—2 and Romans 15), does not derive from Gnosticism, although certain Gnosticizing (actualizing) accents are present.[47] The perception of time in Rom. 11:25–32, in fact, that of the entire chapter, also contradicts the Gnostic perception. I can find here no Gnostic saying.[48] The tradition of Matthew 10 illustrates that even on Palestinian soil there was a completely eschatologically oriented mission of Jesus-believers.[49] The eschatological moments are not secondary here but integral, with no trace of Gnostic background. Schmithals does not seriously probe the possibility of a connection between the early mission of the early church and the non-Gnostic Jewish mission. He concludes that Paul was unaware that his understanding of the "apostolate" originated with Gnosticism, that he adopted the church's understanding of the apostolate as a matter of course.[50] But in that case one would definitely expect Paul to vigorously and confidently resort to such a general understanding on the part of the church.

The various investigations of the Pauline and early Christian "apostolate" do not adequately recognize that Paul never, even when hard pressed, "quoted" a generally held definition of the apostle. It seems to be a justified *argumentum e silentio* to conclude from this absence that at the time of Paul a general and concrete understanding or image of the apostle did not yet exist.

The vehemence of the discussion also speaks for the unclear understanding of "apostle" in Pauline times. An objection that could be raised is that the intensity of the disagreement instead speaks for the existence of an object of controversy, namely, the "apostolate." I do not want to answer this objection directly, but rather to raise the question of how, for example, Paul can mention apostles of the community (2 Cor. 8:23; Phil. 2:25).[51] Schmithals stands the question on its head when he asserts that "Paul can call these fellow workers in the service of the ministry 'apostles' only because it does not even enter his mind that one could give them and their service the description of 'apostolic.'"[52] Similarly,

> Paul can casually call the three brethren from Macedonia apostles only because he has no idea that one could confuse these ἀπόστολοι ἐκκλησιῶν with the ἀπόστολοι Χριστοῦ, or even posit any commonality between them. Thus for Paul the two forms of the apostolate have nothing to do with each other.[53]

What must still be proven is presupposed here.

So long as one is not yet tied to a particular thesis, one will assume that the varying use of one and the same term by the same author is an indication that the term is not yet fixed. Expressed differently, the function designated with the term ἀπόστολος is not yet confined to any office. The opening of Galatians shows the degree to which the functional character of the term is still relevant for Paul. And even though the following passages certainly deal with the understanding of "apostle," in the first sentence the term is used not as a noun but as a verb.[54]

To be sure, there was agreement in the early church that being an envoy applied to the self-understanding and life style of certain people *in a special degree* and, above all, *on a long-term basis*. This shows in the matter-of-factness with which one could continually characterize certain persons as apostles, using the term as a designation of one's calling.

But the "special" circle of persons was stretched widely. This one can see from such passages as 1 Thess. 2:7; 1 Cor. 4:9; 9:5–6; 12:28; Rom. 16:7; Rev. 2:2; and *Didache* 11.3–6; and from the observations in 2 Cor. mentioned above as well. A numerical limit is nowhere given in the early texts.[55] Paul mentions only a temporal limit in 1 Cor. 15:7–8: he sees himself as the last of those called to be apostles. All apostles he knows of, therefore, received their calling between the years 30 and 35.[56] Clearly Paul is only making a judgment based on personal experience, not giving a generally recognized dogmatic definition. However, this Pauline judgment gains theological relevance in the dispute with the Gnostics in 1 Cor. The thesis that the appearances of Christ had come to an end with the last callings of apostles means that faith is not enveloped in a timeless, mystical experience of identity,[57] but that faith also has a past and thereby the dimension of time. This is then extended to the concept of faith having a future. In his judgment expressed in 1 Cor. 15:7–8, Paul was just as mistaken as he was in expecting the early parousia.

This is made obvious in Rev. 2:2 and *Didache* 11.3–6, passages from the last decades of the first century.[58] Persons eighty years old or older are certainly not meant here, but that is what one would have to assume if these apostles were identical with those mentioned by Paul in 1 Cor. 15:7. Schmithals, in his book on the apostolate, has denied anew that these passages supply any conclusive evidence for the general early "Christian" view of the apostle (pp. 167–68, 170–72). In this Schmithals has precursors.[59] But he then interprets these passages according to his thesis of the Gnostic origin and the Gnostic background of the concept of the "apostolate." He claims that in the Apocalypse Gnostic apostles are being fought, while the *Didache*, just as the apostles mentioned there, is said to be on the boundary between the church and Gnosticism, with the apostles more on the heretical side.

The tendency of a collected work like the *Didache* is difficult to determine. Nevertheless, the selection and order of the material seems to show a non-Gnostic imprint and an antipneumatic interest, especially concerning actual church organization.[60] The *Didache* as a whole is a document of early Catholicism. The same branch of the church which is seeking to institutionalize its functions must, at the same time, make allowance for the fact that free charismatics who are called apostles still exist. These persons, like the redactor of the *Didache*, equate religion and spirituality with stability and institutionalized control; they are troublesome for theologians. But the very inability to dispute the right of those migrant preachers to call themselves apostles shows that they had that right. Surely one would also have liked to brand these wandering apostles as heretics. But contrary to the claim of Schmithals, this was just not possible. So one had to come to terms with them. In an excellent discussion of this topic,[61] Klein has brought forth further reasons that show us why we "must retain the *Didache* as an important testimony against an absolute restriction of the apostolate to the generation of Paul."[62]

In the Apocalypse passage referred to, Jewish Gnostics are in fact being fought.[63] Nevertheless, it does not follow that at the time of the Apocalypse only heretical apostles still existed, and no more apostles of the church. On the contrary, the author of the Apocalypse cannot simply dismiss even heretical apostles as obvious usurpers of the office, an office to which they would not be entitled because it had been restricted to a particular time and particular people. If this had been so, John could have said, they are not apostles, for there can no longer be any. The apocalyptist and the congregations to whom he writes reckon, at least on principle, with the *possibility* of apostles appearing in the present. It is even more probable that they also know of several contemporary apostles. Klein has shown that the references to the circle of the twelve in the Apocalypse cannot be used as a counterargument.[64]

It also seems that the Apocalyptic critic still lacks a strong image of the "apostolate" in his arsenal. John's critique has to rest on general theological arguments and moral accusations. Because these persons are heretics, they cannot be considered authentic apostles. The congregation in Ephesus is praised because they have understood this (cf. 2:2 with 2:6).[65]

All these "envoys" of the early church have in common their constant traveling and acts of proclamation; at any rate, these are always included when the activity of the apostles is mentioned.[66] One can thus designate the apostles of the early church as (professional) missionaries, and this corresponds to the functional character of the term ἀπόστολος.[67]

At this point I would like to take up the possible objection mentioned above, that is, that a very broad understanding of the "apostolate" could not have led to disputes. The fact that it did is connected with the widespread missionary interest of the early church. I do not want to cite any texts for this, since this would first demand a long and complicated discussion of authenticity and dating. I think the reference to a sure historical phenomenon will suffice as proof: a community that in just six short years could establish a great number of congregations over a range of 700 kilometers (comparable to the distance from Boston to Washington, D.C.) must have had an enormous interest in missionary activity. It was technically impossible for all members of the early faith communities to engage in missionary work to the same degree. But then the people who were able to dedicate their entire time and strength to the mission must have been held in special esteem, for these persons and their performance embodied, so to speak, the missionary will of the entire community. This is reflected in the very early text Acts 13:1–3. It is only natural that some rivalry came into being. Paul testifies to that in 1 Cor. 15:10 (cf. also Phil. 1:15). It was likewise to be expected that occasionally a missionary's abilities were doubted. Someone who was blamed for being of no use as a missionary and, because of proven incompetence, no longer had the right to be one must have been hurt in a community so strongly centered on mission.

Such criticism provoked defense and countercriticism, and the dispute necessarily included attempts to find makeshift standards for a legitimate "apostolate." On the other hand, attention was also paid to success because of the rivalry, and success became a criterion in the debate. In my opinion, we have now reached the historical basis to understand the conduct of Paul's opponents in 2 Cor. 10—13. Paul ironically refers to their behavior with the designation "superapostles," not only because they apparently rated themselves quite highly, but also because they had gained prestige. This is supported by his twice saying, "I am not in the least inferior to these superapostles" (2 Cor. 11:5; 12:11). It is also significant that "*signs of* the apostolate" play a role in the discussion (12:12). Certainly the congregation can be blamed indirectly and directly for the dispute over the "apostolate." Both Paul and the opponents presented themselves to the judgment of the community, and apparently the community had demanded this.[68]

This is not surprising in a community which was organized around the mission. The difference between Paul and his opponents seems to lie in the fact that Paul presented himself (to judge also from his other letters) only to his own communities, whereas the opponents also presented themselves to other communities they encountered on their missionary journeys. Naturally, it must have been especially painful to have one's ability and right to missionary activity disputed in front of or even by the communities one had personally established.

With this I have already advanced far into the analysis of the opponents' self-understanding. There is not yet enough material to be able to do this more completely. But this much may be stated here: the opponents of Paul were missionaries of the early church who thought they were good at what they were doing, apparently with good reasons. In so doing they had not necessarily acted contrary to the general practice of their contemporaries and the applicable criteria; on the contrary, one may ask whether the zeal of professional missionaries of the early church is not manifested here before a congregation with a missionary interest.

Ἐργάτης

In using the phrase ἐργάται δόλιοι (2 Cor. 11:13), Paul appears to treat a further self-designation of the opponents with irony, as the trend of the entire sentence makes clear.[69] Paul also calls his opponents in Philippians (κακοὶ) ἐργάται (3:2). Surely the false teachers of Philippians, whose "vocation" Paul only refers to with the term mentioned, were wandering proclaimers, that is, missionaries.[70] Although the functional designation is consistent with 2 Cor. 11:13, it is a mistake to assume the same circle of opponents in both cases.[71] Today not all questionable ministers belong to the same movement or group either.

Paul likes to paraphrase missionary activity with such words as "to toil" or "collaboration." To designate the activity of mission as (difficult) work was not, however, an idiom only of Paul. Parallels are also found for this in the rest of the NT.[72] Not only in 1 Cor. 3:13–15 and 9:6–11 but also in the Synoptic sayings (Matt. 9:37–38 and par.; Matt. 10:10 and par.) and in John 4:35–38 there are conceptions and images transferred directly or indirectly from the work sphere to the work of mission.[73] 1 Tim. 5:18 and *Didache* 13.2 pick up the work of God in Matt. 10:10.[74] In 2 Tim. 2:15–16, ἐργάτης also characterizes the proclaimer of God. And elsewhere it seems that ἔργον and ἐργάζεσθαι occasionally allude to proclaiming (so, e.g., Matt. 21:28; ἔργον especially in the Pastorals).[75]

The third self-designation of the opponents of Paul thus also shows them to us as missionaries who want to be and can be compared to other missionaries of the early church.[76] It should be noted that designating the early missionaries of Jesus as "workers" associated apparently as a matter of course the conception of the "paid laborer." That is expressed in Matt. 10:10 and in parallel passages such as 1 Cor. 9:6.

THE OPPONENTS' SELF-DESIGNATIONS OF ORIGIN

In the catalog of the opponents' merits (2 Cor. 11:22–23) and before the designation of function διάκονος Χριστοῦ, Paul mentions three self-designations of a different nature: Ἑβραῖοι, Ἰσραηλῖται,

and σπέρμα 'Αβραάμ. These designations refer not to acquired attributes or functions but rather to origin. In the mouths of the opponents, however, they would not only have contained simple
biographic information but also have pointed to a special authorization. It is no accident that these designations of origin usher in the
designation of function διάκονοι Χριστοῦ. Designations of origin
and function must have complemented one another not only in the
perception of the opponents but also in the perception of the public.
The "whence" must have implied and determined the "what for."[77]

Ἑβραῖος

It is significant that 'Ιουδαῖοι does not appear among the designations of origin. This would merely have been the familiar name of
the people, easily associated with a disdainful undertone for non-
Jewish ears.[78] On the other hand, the expressions "Hebrews," "Israelites," and "seed of Abraham" sounded *eminent*. These terms
belonged to an elegant mode of expression.[79] For a long time a particular group within Judaism had already made it its business to
make the eminence of Judaism understood by the pagans. I refer to
Hellenistic-Jewish Apologetics,[80] a branch of the Jewish wisdom
movement.[81]

It is known that the Apologists frequently concealed those motifs
of the OT Jewish religion which appeared or must have appeared as
strange in the discussion with pagan or Jewish critics. Most of the
difficulties of the tradition were mastered by interpretation. Often-
times ingenious explanations helped to purify or protect traditional
peculiarities against misunderstanding, distortion, or suspicion, especially coming from pagan anti-Semitism. But the interpretation
went beyond mere defense. It did not decide to level all differences. Features peculiar to Judaism were often purposefully retained, even emphasized in some respects. For example, not only
monotheism and the law in general but also certain commandments
(such as the commandments concerning the Sabbath and purity)
were stressed, and the characteristic traits of Jewish history and
people were not concealed. That cannot be explained on the basis of
apologetics alone.[82] A truly positive tendency must have stood behind this. It consisted in having the pagans comprehend the special

characteristic of Judaism as inclusive, not exclusive. The concern of the Apologists was to bring out that which was peculiar to Judaism as that which was valid and essential for humankind, as the original source and final goal of human life and thought. Evidence for this will be offered in the following section.

The designation Ἑβραῖος is already part of this tendency. As an adjective, Ἑβραῖος means the speech and writing peculiar to the Palestinian Jews and then their geographic and cultural characteristics in general.[83] Thus a "Hebrew" would represent the features peculiar to this eastern people as manifested in speech, tradition, culture, and religion. In addition, Ἑβραῖος often appears as an archaic name for the Jewish people and finally attains the character of a designation of honor.[84] It is therefore not surprising that the term attained a mysterious ring.[85] There seems to be no contradiction between these different nuances of the word, but rather an inner relationship.[86] I would like to demonstrate this with the help of some examples from Hellenistic-Jewish Apologetics.

According to the author of the *Epistle of Aristeas*, the Hebrew script of the original of the Jewish laws, preserved in Jerusalem, in and of itself lets the holy document of Judaism tower over other literary works. Thus the Torah cannot be treated the same as other books (*Ep. Arist.* 3, 11, 30; cf. 176). This special treatment is also appropriate because of its content, since it is the law "which is full of wisdom and without error" and whose conceptions are "holy and venerable" (31). The history and law of Judaism are things that are not immediately accessible to everyone but are surrounded by a mysterious veil, as is proper for something extraordinary. Thus the Torah must be translated with great care and under royal protection and at first it was only for royal use. But the placement of the translation in the royal library in Alexandria reveals that despite their mysterious peculiarities the holy scriptures are not reserved for the Hebrews. They can also be entrusted to pagans of good will. The special possession of the people of God can awe these pagans, whose respect leads them to inquire further.

The respectful treatment of the Hebrew documents by Philadelphus is contrasted with earlier attempts at translation, which were entirely inappropriate (*Ep. Arist.* 31). The *Epistle of Aristeas* underlines further through the *argumentum e silentio* that out of respect for the content of the law the truly great pagans avoided any reference to what was only inadequately known before the (correct) translation. Aristobulus, on the contrary, claims that the pagan philosophers had known these imperfect translations of the Hebrew writings.[87] Precisely because they had made use of these poor translations, they were only insufficiently able to recognize and to transmit the actual truth and wisdom. But the "Hebrew" philosopher Aristobulus was able to recognize the roots behind these half-truths, and from this knowledge of the source he was able to bring to its proper goal and fruition that which was understood only inadequately by the Greek philosophers.

Occasionally the designation "Hebrew" is even brought into immediate association with the beginnings of Jewish wisdom and thus with wisdom in general. Thus Artapanus says that the Jews called themselves "Hebrews" from the time of Abraham.[88] In the following sections the Apologist then describes Abraham as the first sage to whom the others owed their wisdom.

Thus the term "Hebrews" is used not only in discussing the present peculiarities of the Palestinian Jews but specifically in discussing the special past of these peculiar people.[89] Indeed, the present characteristics of the Palestinian Jews are grounded in the past and thus are found there in a much purer form. The tragedian Ezekiel, as well as Philo and Josephus, typically uses the designation "Hebrews" in this way.[90] It crops up mainly when "the special" and "essential" become manifest to the outside world, especially when a *particular life style* is envisaged. Thus in Philo's tractate *De Josepho*,[91] which is substantially influenced by Apologetics, Joseph says to the wife of Potiphar (42): "We children of the Hebrews follow laws and customs which are especially our own. Others are. . . ." This destiny is conditioned more by society than by biology. Thus in another Apologetic work, *De Abrahamo*, Philo writes of Hagar (251): "an Egyptian by birth, but a Hebrew by choice."

In 4 Maccabees (closely associated with Apologetics)[92] the Hebrews portrayed also incorporate a definite way of life which is oriented to the ancestral tradition—and thus they become models.[93] It is significant that the author is able to present this behavior which is bound to tradition as an indication of truly philosophic conviction, as an expression of the philosophic virtues.[94] Thus the view is directed not only toward internal phenomena of Judaism but also toward the pagan world.

So it could only please the Apologists if the pagans found Jewish thought and behavior to be something extraordinary, if only they took it not as something strange or even absurd but as something which was surrounded by mystery. In his *apologia*, Josephus, not without reason, finishes the section in which he speaks about the universality and the constance of obedience to the law among the Jews by a comparison with the mysteries.[95] To be sure, the term "Hebrew" does not appear here, but the tendency expressed in its use clearly comes to light.

> Could there be a more saintly government than that exercised in accord with the Torah? Could God be more worthily honored than through the entire community being trained towards religion—the priests are entrusted with the special charge of it, and the whole *constitution of the community is something like a mystery rite*? For that which others can maintain zealously for no longer than only a few days, *although they indeed call it mysteries and mystery rites*, we maintain with delight and unflinching determination all our lives (*Apion* 2.188–89, my ed.).

Surely with these questions and arguments Josephus counts on the agreement of his pagan readers. Therefore, a more familiar type of argumentation must be involved—leaving open the question whether it was a manner of proof that was common only in Judaism and its sphere or whether it was even more widely used.

In any case, the evidence shows that with the designation Ἑβραῖος the pagans already associated the idea of something special in the sense of mysterious. So in a symposium setting, *Quaestiones Convivales* 4.6 (2.671c), Plutarch has one partner in the dialogue ask another: "So, do you thus reckon and allot the native god . . . Dionysus, to the secret rites of the Hebrews?"[96] This question, which examines a previously suggested relationship, is then actually answered by the statement that the Jewish worship resembles the Dionysiac mysteries. The subject had previously been the strange views and practices of the Jews; now it is made clear that behind it a highly impressive mystery cult lies hidden. The question cited above marks the actual transition in the dialogue, and it is significant that the religious community suddenly has a different name in this question. Having spoken previously of the "Jews," the questioner now speaks of "Hebrews" and thus titles the following.[97]

Lucian recounts that Alexander of Abonuteichos announced the epiphany of his divinity by uttering what sounded like Hebrew or Phoenician (13).[98] Alexander, who had prepared well for the proclamation of the new deity by extensively using contemporary religious ideas,[99] surely chose a Semitic language deliberately.[100] Apparently the foreign element was to announce at the same time both the mysterious and thereby also the divine; in this way Alexander must have hoped to comply with contemporary ideas and criteria.[101]

When adversaries of Paul praised themselves before their audience as "Hebrews," they could count on attention, they could build on their listeners' expectation of something special which was grounded in their Hebrew origin, in Hebrew history and culture. Thus the self-designation "Hebrews" would also encompass the context of religious propaganda. Indeed, on the basis of the previous observations I would like to postulate that Paul's antagonists took over the standards and methods already tested and used by the mission of Hellenistic-Jewish Apologetics.

Surely the outside agitators who came to Corinth did not stem from families who had resided in the diaspora for many generations but rather from ones who had dwelled in Palestine until very recently. Perhaps they themselves had been born and raised in Palestine. A knowledge of Hebrew or Aramaic is to be supposed,[102] and of course these wandering preachers had mastered Greek.

Here I must reckon with the fundamental objection that Palestinian origin and tradition would exclude a familiarity with the practices of Hellenistic-Jewish Apologetics and propaganda. However, this objection can be made only under the influence of the rabbinic dogma that Palestine had remained essentially an anti-Hellenistic oasis from the time of the Maccabees. But here one should not just accept later assertions, descriptions, and discussions as accurate reports from an earlier time. One must instead reckon with tendentious distortions and constructions. The events of 70 C.E. played a decisive role after all. Even if later statements or legal rulings on the relationship of Jews and pagans should stem from the time before 70, one must still investigate whether they were really valid and accepted previously. The historical evaluation of Pharisaic rabbinic regulations must differentiate between the ideal and the real more sharply than previous scholarship has done.

As counterexamples I shall not overrate the presence of Jewish Hellenists and Jewish-Hellenistic synagogues (Acts 6:1 and 9:20) in Jerusalem;[103] that would refer only to Greek-speaking Jews in Jerusalem who originally came from the diaspora, from families that had lived for a long time outside the boundaries of Palestine. These Hellenistic Jews, who now lived in Palestine again, were everything but "Hebrews." Thus Acts 6:1 speaks of discord between Hebrews and Hellenists. The Hellenization of the royal court does not provide an immediate argument for some general tolerance in Palestine toward Hellenism either, because the later Hasmoneans and the Idumeans were severely criticized. But then it is curious that although Herod and his successors were indeed clearly influenced by Hellenism and even founded temples to honor men,[104] nevertheless the Jews permitted and frequently praised the sumptuous enlargement of the temple by these politically calculating kings. This does not speak for a widespread and blind puritanical zeal.

The Jewish ossuaries found in Palestine, with their countless pagan motifs, indicate even more strongly a widespread infection of indigenous Judaism by Hellenistic rituals. For these and similar questions newly posed by archaeology, I would like to refer to the monumental work of E. R. Goodenough, *Jewish Symbols in the Greco-Roman Period*.

Thus nothing contradicts the assumption that the adversary wandering preachers who invaded Corinth were of Palestinian origin and nevertheless followed the traditional propaganda methods of Hellenistic-Jewish Apologetics. By referring to their special Jewish characteristics, they advertised for their cause, the Jesus faith, as the outgrowth and climax of the Hebrew tradition—as will be shown more extensively later on. The second designation of origin, Ἰσραηλῖται, will show more clearly that not only the cultural but also the historical-religious characteristics were significant.

Ἰσραηλίτης

In the internal use of Judaism, "Israelite" was the self-designation of the Jews.[105] In Hellenistic Judaism that was no longer a matter of course.[106] Here one still spoke of Israelites, but it was not a common self-designation anymore. In Hellenistic-Jewish Apologetics it appears in Demetrius, Philo, and Josephus. The infrequency can be partially explained from the fragmentary character of the tradition. In addition, a certain reserve toward the term must also be assumed. This reserve cannot be explained by a desire to conceal the name "Israelite" from the pagans. In *Embassy to Gaius* (*Leg. Gai.* 4), Philo explicitly praises the Jews in front of pagans as Israelites. Josephus likewise speaks of the Israelites in his works, which are also destined for pagans.[107]

Josephus's use of Ἰσραηλῖται outlines the basis for the reserve toward the term. Josephus speaks of "Israelites" only in the description of the Jewish past.[108] In contrast, he also applies to contemporary Jews the term "Hebrew," which he uses in the narrative of the past interchangeably with "Israelite." This indicates that the name "Israelite" belongs to the special *history of Jewish faith*.

While the designation "Hebrews" refers mainly to those peculiarities of the Jews which were manifest to the outside world and were determined more by form, the term "Israelite" apparently refers to their special faith. The frequent reference to special origin and significance of the name demonstrates that this was meant. In his otherwise brief presentation, Demetrius gives a fairly detailed description of the Jabbok scene and expressly mentions the words of the angel that Jacob should be called Israel from then on.[109] Demetrius notes the repetition of this onomastic saying in Gen. 35:10, which is rarely observed by other authors.[110]

It is true that no tractate *De Jacobo* of Philo has been preserved. Still, he also states for pagans in the passage from the *Embassy to Gaius*, mentioned above, the basis for the fame of the Israelites. They are the race of those who, like their ancestors, are capable of seeing God, who are thus true philosophers, who are able to fulfill what is truly willed by the philosophers. Here, as also otherwise in his allegories on "Israel,"[111] which are more speculatively and mystically determined, Philo follows the etymology given in Genesis 32 to "Pniel," which, contrary to the text, he transfers to "Israel."

Josephus comments otherwise.[112] He understands the renaming of Jacob (Israel) truly as an honoring of the *theomachus* ("the one who battles with God") who was able to overcome the messenger of

God. Thus, for Josephus "Israel" is the epithet of a quasi-divine figure. Naturally the race of the "Israelites" has a part in that.[113] The first passage in which there is mention of "Israelites" (*Ant.* 2.202) shows that already. The Israelites prove themselves to be fully superior to the Egyptians; and in the midst of the Israelites Moses grows up, all the more something like a demigod (*Ant.* 2.205–7).

When Josephus no longer speaks of Israelites in the narration of the postexilic history, one cannot conclude from this that he considered extinguished the growing power which had been manifested in the history of the Jewish people since Jacob. On the contrary, the *Antiquities* of Josephus seeks to prove that the so-called Jews of the present have their roots in the famous ancient people of the Israelites, indeed, that they are none other than the Israelites of the heroic period.[114] They have the same power and the same promise. Josephus is convinced that the Jewish people settled in the Roman Empire represent only a small percentage of the descendants of the Israelites. Of the descendants of the twelve tribes, only those from two live in the Roman world empire, the others dwell in the east, on the other side of the Euphrates (*Ant.* 11.133). Thus, according to Josephus the Israelites have become a people who surpass all boundaries, the boundaries of time as well as the boundaries of space. A people which is anchored in history in this manner and which has been able thus to spread itself throughout the world, even the unknown world, must be a great people in the truest sense of the word. But this greatness is rooted in religious particularity, in the special concern of God, which he has shown to this people in its past. Concerning that neither Josephus nor the Apologists allow any doubt.[115]

Thus the designation "Israelite" pointed mainly to the past as the root and source of the religious strength of the Jews, a strength which ought to be and should be realized in the present. The reserve in the use of the term thus seems to be explained by a concern to maintain its "heroic" character and not to make it a part of everyday speech.[116] If someone boasted about one's Israelite origin, then one's religious superiority which was conditioned by the predetermined past was meant. But that signified for Hellenistic Judaism not something private or exclusive; and even less so for the

Apologists. To use a verbal image—one pointed to a spring which had been dammed up so that it could overflow all the more abundantly.

Josephus (*Ant*. 4.237)[117] writes similarly as he generalizes OT instructions concerning conduct toward widows, orphans, and strangers:[118]

> God bestows this abundance of good things not for our enjoyment alone, but that we may also share them generously with others, and He is desirous that by these means the special favour that He bears to the people of Israel and the bounty of His gifts may be manifested to others also, when out of all that superabundance of ours they too receive their share from us.[119]

The special characteristics of that which was Israelite pointed beyond the limits of the people, according to Hellenistic-Jewish understanding. This can be shown with the third designation of origin of the opponents of Paul.

Σπέρμα ᾿Αβραάμ

At first glance the height of religious (and ethnic) isolationism seems to have been reached with this self-designation. Passages such as John 8:33 and 37 as well as rabbinic parallels could likewise support this charge.[120] In the Hellenistic-Jewish book 4 Maccabees, the reference to Abraham also seems to be in the service of downright Jewish segregation, even strangeness and perversion in the eyes of the Gentiles. For instance, the sacrifice of Isaac is vividly praised as a shining model,[121] and the example set by the Jewish mother and her seven sons proves true kinship to Abraham. But this appears to be valid only for the Israelites as descendants of Abraham (18:1).[122]

The author of 4 Maccabees argues, however, that this is not particularistic, that on the contrary it is an especially impressive example of true piety as the right philosophic attitude, which arises only from true philosophy. This becomes clear from the contexts of 4 Macc. 18:1, 20, 23, and especially 7:19 and 15:28.[123] The author does not mean to be parochial at all; on the contrary, the examples and their utilization fit well into the framework of Hellenistic rhetoric, and the author's vivid style comes less from Jewish roots than from pagan roots, in particular from the diatribe of popular philosophy.[124] With that we have entered into a broader realm of discourse, including not only moral edification but also propaganda. Propaganda and moral edification appear to be closely related to each other here.

In proper Hellenistic-Jewish Apologetics the life of Abraham was understood even more emphatically as exemplary for one's own situation. The problem of being Jewish in a pagan environment could be presented by the example of the primeval wanderer. To be sure, one saw in him the ancestor of the Jewish people, but at the same time one also knew of his close connection to paganism.[125] The origin of Abraham in the land of the Chaldeans and his later relationship to the Phoenicians and Egyptians were often emphasized. The departure from his father's house was understood not as a route to isolation or to the Palestinian backcountry but rather as a departure for the wide world. Indeed, for the Apologists, Abraham counted as the actual beginning of a great world.

Before Abraham there was the epoch of the Titans and the giants, the time of uncivilized primitiveness according to the anonymous author.[126] Even the tower of Babel was not considered a cultural achievement but the product of Cyclopean simplicity[127] or, to use the words of Josephus, a manifestation of barbarian tyranny.[128] The actual development of nations was not thought to have begun until after this. According to Josephus, after the destruction of the tower divine compulsion forced people to do as punishment what they previously had not wanted to do: colonize the earth.[129] Cleodemus Malchus in particular widens the OT description of Abraham as father of the nations (Gen. 17:4–5) to the claim that the actual civilized nations all stemmed from Abraham,[130] the nations in the east, the south, and the southwest.[131] Abraham first started colonization,[132] a claim whose ambitious nature can be judged only in relationship to the colonialist pride of Greek and Hellenistic provenance. It is significant that Cleodemus places Abraham in time and in order of precedence even before the Greek hero Heracles, who was generally considered the conveyer of divine order and founder of human well-being.[133] In all this Abraham was seen as the precursor.

For Hellenistic-Jewish Apologists, Abraham was the best of the best and thus the predestined ruler according to the criteria of the Hellenistic royal ideology.[134] The puzzling pericope on the battle of the kings (Genesis 14) contributed to this. Abraham was considered a victorious military leader. There even existed a tradition (probably as a development of Gen. 14:15 and 15:2) that Abraham had been king of Damascus for a while. To be sure, this tradition is preserved for us only in pagan sources; nevertheless it is probably of Jewish origin. Josephus offers the following citation from the historical work of Nicolaus of Damascus:

> Abram(es) reigned (in Damascus),[135] [a foreigner] who had come with an army from the country beyond Babylon called the land of the Chaldees. But, not long after, he left this country also with his people for the land then called Canaan but now Judaea, where he settled, he and his numerous descendants, whose history I shall recount in another book. The name of Abram is still celebrated in the region of Damascus, and a village is shown that is called after him "Abram's abode."[136]

To judge from this, Abraham was occasionally even described as a sometime ruler over pagans.[137]

The emphasis on Abraham's erudition also fits within this picture of royal supremacy. For the Hellenistic world the great ruler was also the light of the peoples.[138] The Apologists expressed this especially by emphasizing the astrological knowledge of Abraham. Astrology, the mysterious art of the East, was considered the root and crown of all knowledge in the Hellenistic period, the real manifestation of wisdom and the surest access to the divine.[139] The Apologists asserted no less than that the world owed the gift of astrology, that is, the Chaldean art, to Abraham, the former Chaldean and later ancestor of the Jews.[140] Either he had perfected this art and then spread it,[141] or he had even founded it.[142]

But as one with this the Apologists saw Abraham's experience of God and his piety. These were at the core of the special capabilities and gifts which made Abraham the center of the cultured world. Thus the anonymous author says:

> In the tenth generation in the Babylonian city of Camarinae, which some call Uria (which means city of the Chaldaeans), Abraham was born who surpassed everyone in *nobility* and *wisdom*; he also founded

> astrology, i.e. the Chaldaean (art),[143] and he pleased God by his *dis-position for piety*.[144]

The reciprocal dependence of the observation of cosmic phenomena and of the experience and knowledge of God is expressed by Josephus in a way that is exemplary for developed Apologetics (*Ant.* 1.154–56):

> He (Abraham) left Chaldaea, God having bidden him to remove to Canaan, and there he settled, and left the country to his descendants. *He was a man of ready intelligence on all matters, persuasive with his hearers*,[145] and not mistaken in his inferences. Hence he began to have more lofty conceptions of virtue than the rest of mankind, and *determined to reform and change the ideas universally current concerning God*.[146] He was thus the first boldly to declare that *God*, the creator of the universe, is *one*, and that, if any other being contributed aught to man's welfare, each did so by His command and not in virtue of its own inherent power. This he inferred from the changes to which land and sea are subject, from the course of sun and moon, and from all the celestial phenomena; for, he argued, were these bodies endowed with power, they would have provided for their own regularity, but, since they lacked this last, it was manifest that even those services in which they cooperate for our greater benefit they render not in virtue of their own authority, but through the might of their commanding sovereign, to whom alone it is right to render our homage and thanksgiving.

Here the knowledge of the cosmos, especially of the stars, is clearly seen as a sequence of steps, as a path leading to the knowledge of God.[147] For instance, a tradition incorporated in Wisdom 13 is characteristic of this. The pagans are here reproached (1b):

> And they were unable even from the good things that are seen to infer him who exists, nor did they recognize the craftsman while paying heed to his works. . . . (3) Those in whose beauty they took delight (i.e., the cosmic things) they took for gods, they should know how much better than these the ruler is, for the author of beauty created them. (4) And if people were driven to astonishment about [their] power and working, they should have concluded from them how much more powerful is he who formed them. (5) *For from the greatness and beauty of creatures their originator is perceived by way of analogy*,[148] (9) for if they had the power to infer so much that they could investigate the world, how did they fail to find sooner the Lord of these things?[149]

Natural knowledge of God and natural theology were the main concerns of the Hellenistic-Jewish Apologists.[150] The early "Christian" Apologists took this up later.[151] Thereby the proximity as well as the superiority of the Jewish faith to paganism could be made clear. The same reality was involved, but the Apologists claimed a deeper understanding and thus also a more intensive grasp and a more comprehensive mastery of it.[152]

The remarks of Josephus on Abraham, cited above, imply the thought that Abraham ascribed universal validity and obligation to his views, indeed, that he also advertised for them.[153] How Abraham is presented is already significant: as a man "of ready intelligence on all matters, persuasive with his hearers." But according to the narrative of Josephus, Abraham failed in his missionary effort for monotheism, of which he was the first supporter. The text continues:

> It was in fact owing to these opinions (what had previously been said about Abraham) that the Chaldaeans and the other peoples of Mesopotamia rose against him, and he, thinking fit to emigrate, at the will and with the aid of God, settled in the land of Canaan. Established there he built an altar and offered a sacrifice to God.

This is not meant to express a final withdrawal of Abraham: no resignation after first missionary failures.

Josephus (*Ant.* 1.161–68) has Abraham migrate to Egypt—true to the biblical account (Gen. 12:10). Yet the reasons offered by Josephus for this journey are not only that there was a famine but also that Abraham "was of a mind . . . to hear what their priests said about the gods; intending, if he found [them] more excellent than [himself], to [follow them], or else to convert them to [the] better, should he [appear better disposed]." *Engaging in competition* is spoken of here: not only will the better person win, but he can and may convert the loser to his side (cf. the two concepts καταϰο-λουθεῖν and μεταϰοσμεῖν ἐπὶ τὸ βέλτιον).

In this competition superior religious knowledge is demonstrated by superior ability, which also involves "worldly things." Abraham then also established contact with the most learned Egyptians (1.165): "where his virtue (ἀρετή)[154] and reputation became still more conspicuous." The Egyptians did not show themselves to be a culturally (and also politically) unified people. Abraham was able to show them the hollowness of their arguments (1.167–68):

> Thus gaining their admiration at these meetings as a man of extreme sagacity, gifted not only with high intelligence but with power to convince his hearers on any subject which he undertook to teach,[155] he introduced them to arithmetic and transmitted to them the laws of astronomy. For before the coming of Abraham the Egyptians were ignorant of these sciences, which thus travelled from the Chaldaeans into Egypt, whence they passed to the Greeks.

Just as religious and cultural capabilities are seen here as being more or less identical, so religious and cultural mission are regarded almost as one.[156] The religious power of Abraham is obviously taken for granted even in passages where it is not mentioned explicitly; after all, his superiority must have a reason.[157] The successes of Abraham are clearly demonstrations of an inner strength. In the competition, not only the greater achievement of Abraham but also his extraordinary power become evident.[158]

The strong emphasis on the influence of Abraham is obviously connected to the process of inference (already observed above) from the experienced effects to their real causes. So it is also not surprising that this physico-theological knowledge can easily turn into cosmic mysticism. In the pseudonymous Testament of Orpheus the pagan Orpheus says: "My child, I shall show you,[159] if I catch sight of the traces and the strong hand of the mighty God. However, I do not see him personally; for he has enclosed himself in a cloud which is thin for me but with a tenfold layer for all (other) humans."[160] Despite the inaccessibility of God for all humans, even for the distinguished Orpheus, one person, Abraham, is given a greater possibility:

> For no one saw the ruler of mortals except the single person (μουνογενής), the former branch of the tribe of the Chaldaeans;[161] for he was experienced in the starry street and how the movement of the spheres revolves around the earth in the same circle and around its own axis; (how) the winds travel around the air and around the flood of water; (how) there appears the light of the fire produced by power.[162]

Evidently the knowledge of Abraham was able to go so far on this path until it experienced at least the majesty of God, for after this cited description of the cosmic view the appearance of God is thus paraphrased:

> He himself now stands firm again above the great heaven upon a golden throne; the earth lies under (his) feet. His right hand he has stretched out over the boundary of the ocean. The foundation of the mountains shakes from within through (his) anger, and it cannot endure the ruling power. He himself is fully a heavenly being, and (yet) he brings everything on earth to its goal. To him personally belong the beginning and the middle as well as the end.[163]

But since then this majestic final point of the heavenly vision of Abraham also beckons to others as their goal; the continuation of the Testament of Orpheus clearly presents that which was only hinted at by the introduction.[164] What Abraham first experienced and saw is passed on to other men: "Just as it was a word of the ancients, so the one who was born from the water (Moses) ordered it on the basis of the law given by God, (he) who received (it) in twofold statute."[165] What this twofold statute is becomes clear from the context as well as from the style of the whole;[166] it is the Jewish tradition in twofold form: an unessential, exoteric form and an essential, esoteric form.[167] Naturally, the previously explained vision of Abraham is the content of the esoteric communication; it is an experience which as with Abraham so also later is alloted only to someone *special*.

The final, complete inference from the effects to their causes is this penetration of a cloud, the unveiling of a mystery; this remains wrapped in a mystical fog for the broad mass. With good reason, the Testament of Orpheus immediately presents itself as a mystery speech, and thus the following conclusion is connected to that which is cited above: "In another way (than the asserted twofold way) it is not permitted to speak. And thus I quake in (my) members in the spirit."[168]

Of course, the Apologists must say at the same time that there is a relationship between the cosmic and God (as between both Mosaic traditions). An advancement of knowledge by the process of inference mentioned is only then possible: "From the heights he (God) dominates everything in *one* order."[169] But the knowledge of this unity is not given to all. Thus a typical mysterious ending follows:

"Approach *with your thoughts* (i.e., the spirit), yet restrain your *tongue*; let the statement sink into your breast."[170] Further below the relationship between this cosmic mysticism and the double form of the Jewish tradition must be investigated more precisely, especially to determine whether there is an association between the technique of mystical experience and the method of interpreting the tradition.[171]

The passages cited until now have already shown how much of a missionary effect a reference by Jews to the figure of Abraham could have. A passage in Philo which I have been made aware of by Moriz Friedländer can complete and summarize the result very nicely.[172] The text is from the section "De Nobilitate" of the tractate *De Virtutibus (On the Virtues)*, which Friedländer used to determine the missionary conception of Philo and of the Jewish Apologists.[173] Philo clearly expresses his intent in the introduction to this section. The connection of this tract to the previous one on μετάνοια has to be considered too. Philo writes in this introduction (*Virt.* 187):

> This shows also that those who hymn nobility of birth as the greatest of good gifts and the source too of other great gifts deserve no moderate censure, because in the first place they think that those who have many generations of wealth and distinction behind them are noble, though neither did the ancestors from whom they boast descent find happiness in the superabundance of their possessions. For the true good cannot find its home in anything external, nor yet in things of the body, and further not even in every part of the soul, but only in its sovereign part (the νοῦς is meant).

Thus in the following Philo wants to show that proper nobility (valid before God and perceptive humans), namely, wisdom, is not inborn. It soon becomes clear that this is aimed especially at the security and pride of his own Jewish people, at their confidence in their natural descent.

Abraham offers the principal example that true nobility is not inherited but consists of wisdom. In *Virt.* 212 Philo says of him, *"The most ancient member of the Jewish people was a Chaldaean by birth."*[174] This emphatic statement that a pagan stands at the beginning of Jewish history breaks the principle of a natural determinacy. This principle is replaced by another, which the following will then discuss. There is a break then with the older Apologetic view that Abraham was founder or mediator of astrology. Instead of this the assertion is made here and elsewhere in Philo that astrology as such leads away from authentic knowledge of God. But it will be shown that there is no real contradiction with the older Apologetic conception, namely, that true knowledge of God and genuine knowledge of the world coincide. This is true because the persistent questioning about the proper cause of the many effects observed leads to the true originator, and this in turn teaches one to understand the world correctly.

Philo narrates further on Abraham:

His father was an astronomer (i.e., an astrologer), one of those who study the lore of that (astrological)[175] science, and think that the stars and the whole heaven and universe are gods, the authors, they say, of the events which befall each man for good or for ill, and *hold that there is no originating cause outside the things we perceive by our senses.*[176] What could be more grievous than this or could prove more the ignobility in the soul, which through knowledge of the many, the secondary, the created, moves to ignorance of the One and Primal, the Uncreated and Maker of the universe, who is the very best because of this and myriads of other things which because of their majesty no human reason can grasp? (*Virt.* 212–13, my ed.)[177]

Abraham turns from this corrupting view:

Perception of these truths (i.e., into this pernicious folly) and divine inspiration induced him to leave his native country, his race and paternal home, knowing that if he stayed the delusions of the polytheistic creed would stay within him and render incomplete the discovery of the One, who alone is eternal and the Father of all things, conceptual and sensible, whereas if he (i.e., Abraham) emigrated, the delusion would also emigrate from his mind which would change the false opinion toward the truth. At the same time, also, the yearning with which he yearned to know the Existent was fanned by oracular sayings. With these to guide his steps, he went forth never faltering in his ardour to seek for the One, nor did he pause until he received clearer visions, not of his essence, for that is impossible, but of his existence and (his) providence. And, therefore, *he is the first person spoken of as believing in God, since he was the first to possess a firm and unswerving notion that there is one Cause above all, and that it provides for the world and all that there is therein. And having gained faith, the most*

> *certain of the virtues, he gained with it all the other virtues, so that by*
> *those who had received him he was regarded as a king,*[178] *not because*
> of the armament, layperson that he was, *but because of the majesty of*
> *soul, for he possessed royal thinking. Indeed, they continued to treat*
> *him with a respect which subjects pay to a ruler, being awestruck at*
> *the all-embracing greatness of his nature which was more perfect than*
> *usual among people.* (*Virt.* 214–17, my ed.)[179]

Nature in the previous sense of biological determinacy is clearly no
longer meant here; this nature is gained by higher perception. The
knowledge of God bestows outstanding capabilities, gives a royal
character, and compels the surroundings to respectful recognition.

The Apologetic conception of Abraham as a kingly person has thus
remained and has even been intensified. Abraham as the first believer is designated by Philo very clearly as a *pneumatic*; later he receives a *divine* superiority. But at the same time it remains clear
that Abraham is meant to present a possibility which is also offered
to others, since it is in general the true possibility of human existence. Unlike in other texts of Philo, the beyond is not seen here in
opposition to the worldly; it is understood not as the abolition of the
human but as the exaltation of the human (*Virt.* 217, my ed.).[180]

> For the company also which he sought was not the same (as they
> sought), but oftener under inspiration another more august. *Thus*
> *whenever he was possessed, everything in him changed to something*
> *better, eyes, color, stature, carriage, movements, voice. For the divine*
> *spirit whenever it was breathed upon him from on high made its lodg-*
> *ing in his soul, and invested his body with singular beauty, his words*
> *with persuasiveness, and his hearers with understanding.*[181]

The statement is not about an escape from the world but about a
demonstration to the world, to the point of strengthening the possibilities of communication (through endowment with the power of
persuasion, on the one hand, and understanding, on the other).

Pneumatic and prophetic gifts here clearly coincide with missionary skill, not least of all because Abraham shares the prerequisites of
the others: the general human condition as well as the initial lack of
faith and finally the possibility of conversion. This connection is secured by the further statements of Philo, although at first it appears
as if Abraham is someone entirely different (218).

> Would you not say that this lone wanderer without relatives or friends was of the highest nobility, he who craved for kinship with God and strove by every means to live in familiarity with him, he who while ranked among the prophets, [an order] of such high excellence, put his trust in nothing created rather than in the Uncreated and Father of all, he who as I have said was regarded as a king by those in whose midst he settled, a sovereignty gained not with weapons, nor with mighty armies, as is the way of some, but by the election of God, the friend of virtue, who rewards the lovers of piety with imperial powers to benefit those around them?

Abraham shows to those who want to see it, to those who are ready to follow his path, the enormous possibilities of human existence.

With this constant increase in status and potential revealed as a growing offer, the continuation of the text is also no longer surprising (219):

> He (Abraham) is the standard (κανών!) of nobility for all proselytes, who, abandoning the ignobility of strange laws and monstrous customs which assigned divine honours to stocks and stones and soulless things in general, *have come to settle in a better land, in a commonwealth full of true life and vitality, with truth as its director and president.*[182]

In all the texts treated here, the term σπέρμα ’Αβραάμ does not appear. Instead of this the very involved phrase τῶν Αβραμιαίων σπερμάτων ἀπόγονοι is used in 4 Macc. 18:1 and is immediately complemented by παῖδες ’Ισραηλῖται, which means that the author is not using a *terminus technicus* in referring to the descendants of Abraham. Nevertheless, the examples cited have been able to show how the appeal to the figure of Abraham could be understood among Hellenistically oriented Jews and to what extent a missionary concern could be attached to it. The parallels cited by Herman L. Strack and Paul Billerbeck from rabbinic Judaism do have the Hebrew equivalent (זרעו של אברהם or זרע אברהם) for the Greek term, but except for *Targum* Ps. 22:31 they reveal the exact opposite of a missionary consciousness.[183] *Targum* Ps. 22:31 reads: "The seed of Abraham will serve before God and announce the power of Yahweh's might to the last generation (in the Messianic period)."[184] This statement has a clear eschatological orientation.

On the other hand, I shall show that the opponents of Paul were influenced instead by an eschatological hope, which corresponded to the mentality of Hellenistic Judaism. Their interest was primarily in the past for the sake of the present. In the present, what was original should appear more strongly than previously and should be spread even further—for the sake of the divine in the human. The designations of function and origin of Paul's adversaries already pointed to the intellectual world of Hellenistic Judaism. It will become apparent how this attitude, so confident of itself and its commission, was expressed in the conduct and the preaching of the outside agitators in Corinth. The question of how all this can be combined with the claim of the opponents to be missionaries of Jesus should not be neglected. But first it is advisable to describe the field on which the missionaries fought by Paul moved: religious propaganda in Judaism, in paganism, and in the first generation of the early church. Of course, an exhaustive picture cannot be offered, although it would be timely to complete the investigations of Schürer, Wendland, Harnack, Reitzenstein, and Cumont and to develop a comprehensive portrayal from them.[185]

NOTES

1. It is surprising that Walter Schmithals disputes the quotelike character of this very passage (*Gnosticism*, 207–8), because elsewhere he constantly discovers allusions to and quotations from the opponents' statements. In opposition to Schmithals, other exegetes consider the dispute with the opponents in this section especially concrete. It provides the surest reference points for determining the nature and origin of the opponents.

2. Cf. also the phrase διάκονοι τῆς δικαιοσύνης in 2 Cor. 11:15.

3. Cf. 2 Cor. 11:21b. With τις the same persons are referred to as in the following (Windisch, *2. Korintherbrief*, 350). Cf. also ibid., 352, for this passage.

4. Against Käsemann ("Legitimität," 42) and Schlatter (*Korinthische Theologie*, 110; and *Paulus*, 636–37).

5. Alfred Plummer on 2 Cor. 11:23: "διάκονος is used here as equivalent to 'apostle'" (*A Critical and Exegetical Commentary on the Second Epistle of St. Paul to the 2 Corinthians* [ICC 34; Edinburgh: Clark, 1948] 321). Cf. Lietzmann, *Korinther*, 150.

6. Hans Lietzmann, "Zur altchristlichen Verfassungsgeschichte," *ZWTh* 55 (1913) 106. Lietzmann writes there: "the word διάκονος (as well as διακονία, διακονεῖν) is found in the literature of the most diverse services but is almost never a technical designation of the servant and accordingly is seldom met in inscriptions and papyri" (my trans.).

7. Lietzmann, "Verfassungsgeschichte," 106–7; Martin Dibelius, *An die Thessalonicher 1, 2, an die Philipper* (3d ed.; HNT 11; Tübingen: Mohr, 1937) 61. On the following, cf. LSJ, "διάκονος," "διακονία," "διακονεῖν"; see also James H. Moulton and George Milligan, *The Vocabulary of the Greek Testament Illustrated from the Papyri and Other Non-Literary Sources* (London: Hodder & Stoughton, 1914–29), and BAGD on the same words. But most important is *Thesaurus Stephanus*, from which the following passages have been selected.

8. Aeschylus, *Prometheus* 942.

9. Sophocles, *Philoctetes* 497; frag. 133.

10. Aristophanes, *Ecclesiazusae* 1116d.24, 197.

11. Thucydides 1.133: ὡς οὐδὲν πώποτε αὐτὸν ἐν ταῖς πρὸς βασιλέα διακονίαις παραβάλοιτο, προτιμηθείη δ᾿ ἐν ἴσῳ τοῖς πολλοῖς τῶν διακόνων ἀποθανεῖν.

12. Pollux 8.137 of the πρεσβευτής: ὁ δὲ πρεσβευτής, εἴη ἂν καὶ ἄγγελος καὶ διάκονος, ἑτέρας δὲ χρείας, κῆρυξ καὶ σπονδοφόρος.

13. On the following, cf. above all Eduard Norden, *Beiträge zur Geschichte der griechischen Philosophie* (*Jahrbuch für Klassische Philologie*, Sup. 19 [1893] 365–462); in addition, cf. Kurt Deissner, "Das Sendungsbewusstsein der Urchristenheit," *ZSTh* 7 (1929–30) 782–85; Karl H. Rengstorf, "ἀποστέλλω κτλ," *TDNT*, 1:398, 407–13; and Walter Schmithals, *The Office of the Apostle in the Early Church* (Nashville: Abingdon, 1969) 111–14.

14. It is impossible to give an overview of the secondary literature on this passage and its problems here. Along with the essay of Lietzmann, one should consult esp. Dibelius (*Thessalonicher, Philipper*), the commentary on Philippians by Ernst Lohmeyer (*Die Briefe an die Philipper, an die Kolosser und an Philemon* [10th ed.; MeyerK 9 Göttingen: Vandenhoeck & Ruprecht, 1954]) and F. W. Beare (*A Commentary on the Epistle to the Philippians* [London: Black, 1959]) for this passage.

15. See the literary critical analysis of Schmithals ("Irrlehrer").

16. Epictetus gives parallels to the phrase ἐπιφοιτᾶν ἀνθρώποις = to seek out humanity (in the passage in *Diss.* 3.22.69, cited above) in *Diss.* 3.22.72: τοὺς ἄλλους ἐπισκοπεῖν; in *Diss.* 3.22.77: οἱ ἐπισκοποῦντες πάντας ἀνθρώπους; and in 3.22.97: τὰ ἀνθρώπινα ἐπισκοπῇ.

17. Dio Chrysostom 9.1: ἐπισκοπῶν τοὺς ἀνθρώπους. Lucian, *Dialogues of the Dead* 20.2: ὡς ἐπισκοπῆς ἅπαντας. Hermes describes Menippus, who is descending into Hades, in this way and Diogenes Laertius (6.102) portrays Menedemus as ἐπίσκοπος ἀφῖχθαι ἐξ ᾅδου τῶν ἁμαρτανομένων. Even if the noun is documented first in the third century C.E., the idea clearly stands in the Menippean tradition. Norden's sharp differentiation (*Beiträge*, 378 n. 1) between κατάσκοπος and ἐπισκοπεῖν and then also ἐπίσκοπος (more strongly still by K. H. Rengstorf [*TDNT*, 1:409 n. 19] and H. W. Beyer [*TDNT*, 2:607 n. 5]) seems unwarranted, for in the first place

ἐπισκοπεῖν in Epictetus clearly interprets the older title κατάσκοπος, and in the second place Menedemus is in the tradition of the Cynic-Stoic popular philosophy. The trend from κατάσκοπος by way of ἐπισκοπεῖν to ἐπίσκοπος is unmistakable. Since we are dealing with the essentially nonliterary tradition of Cynic-Stoic popular philosophy, the dating of literary evidence cannot be a decisive factor. It seems that Philo's designation of Moses (Her. 30) and of Eleazar and Ithamar (Somn. 2.186) as ἐπίσκοπος can be explained most easily by some connection of Philo with the Cynic-Stoic tradition.

18. It should be observed that the ἐπίσκοποι and διάκονοι are not set before or above the other members of the community. They belong within the community. Thus the letter actually would not have been addressed to them for subsequent delivery to the community.

19. Phil. 1:5, 7b, 12–18; 2:1, 15; 4:5.

20. 1 Thess. 2:1–2 and Acts 16:11–40 let it appear that Paul's stay in Philippi was only brief and not very successful. When he wrote the Letter to the Thessalonians, Paul regarded his work in Philippi mainly in negative terms. That makes the later impression left by the Philippian correspondence all the more astonishing. The community, left alone by Paul after a few weeks and entirely self-dependent, had progressed splendidly. It had begun proselytizing on its own much earlier and more vigorously than other communities. In their preaching they perhaps imitated the Cynic-Stoic wandering preachers, after receiving their original encouragement from Paul. In any case, it appears that the particular mentioning of the ἐπίσκοποι and διάκονοι in the opening of Philippians is Paul's compliment to the independent proclamation activity which was so effective in the community and its vicinity, and a compliment to its chief representatives. Placing the ἐπίσκοποι before the synonymous expression διάκονοι could signify that only someone who is really concerned with human beings, that is, an ἐπίσκοπος similar to the Cynic-Stoic popular philosophers, can properly carry out his embassy to humanity, his proclamation (be a διάκονος).

21. See below, pp. 98–102, 109, 238–42.

22. Cf. Walter Bauer, Die Briefe des Ignatius von Antiochien und der Polykarpbrief (HNT supp. vol., Die Apostolischen Väter 2; Tübingen: Mohr, 1920) 202.

23. Not sufficiently considered by Bauer (Ignatius).

24. Ignatius, Phld. 10.2; Eph. 2.1; Magn. 2; Trall. 1.1. Cf. Bauer, Ignatius, 203.

25. Bauer (Ignatius, 203) says: "For the accomplishment of such tasks the deacons are apparently rather well qualified, since their office confines them not so narrowly to the home congregation" (my trans.). But Bauer says nothing about the positive significance this has for an understanding of the activity and task of the deacons.

26. See above, p. 31. The prototype for both passages appears to have been 1 Cor. 4:1.

27. On the problems of the first two verses of Acts 6, cf. Ernst Haenchen (*The Acts of the Apostles: A Commentary* [trans. Bernard Noble and Gerald Shinn; ed. Hugh Anderson and R. McL. Wilson; Philadelphia: Westminster, 1971] 259–62). Haenchen follows with a circumspect and illuminating discussion of the whole difficult section. In tracing the history of the term, it is noteworthy that Luke avoids the use of the title διάκονος. This could be a confirmation that the use of the term in the church, even of Luke's time, was still reserved for a function other than that given in Acts 6:1–2.

28. Hans Lietzmann sees them taking missionary work as their main task (*The Beginnings of the Christian Church* [trans. B. L. Woolf; New York: Scribner's, 1937] 89). Even more decisive is Haenchen, *Acts*, 259–62. A compromise solution is considered by F. J. Foakes-Jackson and Kirsopp Lake (*The Acts of the Apostles* [5 vols.; *The Beginnings of Christianity*, part 1; London: Macmillan, 1920–33] 5:149), namely, "that the Seven were themselves apostles before they were appointed as charity commissioners."

29. So most of all Haenchen (*Acts*), who also clarified the tendency of the Lukan report in Acts 6—8.

30. The designation of the collection for the community in Jerusalem presents a special problem. In my work on the collection (Georgi, *Kollekte*, 59–60) I discuss which meaning the term διακονία has there and the extent to which it corresponds with the meaning of the term as previously evaluated and the extent to which it does not.

The passages in the *Didache*, the *Shepherd of Hermas*, and *1 Clement* I need not discuss further. There the deacons are clearly seen as officials of the community and as subordinated to the bishops. The meaning of "assistant" pushes to the fore. Nevertheless, even here the functions still appear to be aligned more strongly to proclamation and similar activities than to acts of charity. Measured by this, Acts 6:1–2 appears to be an exception.

31. This already gives a preliminary answer to the question posed by Käsemann ("Legitimität," 41; my trans.): "Why does Paul here apparently not pierce the spheres of the *scandala intima* of the early church? Both in 1 Cor. and in Galatians he demonstrates his superiority by shifting the largely subjective battles to an objective plane. What compels him then in 2 Cor. to contend in the marshes of personal rivalry, so to speak, and yet to assert in 2 Cor. 11:3–4, 13–22, the existence of serious differences?" Because Paul has encountered on his own turf people who have the same task as he does, who are of the same rank as he is, and who therefore are seen by the community to be in the same category. Cf. also the next note.

32. This thesis of Schlatter and Käsemann is refuted especially by Bultmann (*Probleme*, 25–30). Käsemann ("Legitimität," 47–48) distinguishes between the ὑπερλίαν ἀπόστολοι and the ψευδαπόστολοι. In his opinion, the opponents had appealed to the first apostles without full authorization. Paul, in turn, had not attacked the first apostles but nevertheless had to take into consideration the claim of the opponents that they had been sent by the first apostles. Because of this ambiguous starting point, the discus-

sion may also have been so hermaphroditic, as it were. (The distinction mentioned had already been made by Reitzenstein [*Mystery-Religions*, 466] in a less refined form and refuted by Lietzmann [*Korinther*, 148–49].) On the dialectic observed by Käsemann, cf. Bultmann (*Probleme*, 26–27), Bultmann writes: "His [Paul's] position is determined, after all, by the fact that the community was impressed by competitors who are superior to Paul in their eyes. Paul woos the community by complying with their weakness and doing what he actually should not do" (ibid., 26; my trans.). Paul shows no trace of inhibitions toward the ὑπερλίαν ἀπόστολοι (ibid., 29). He is inhibited only by the situation there. On the ὑπερλίαν ἀπόστολοι (as the opponents themselves), cf. also Windisch (*2. Korintherbrief*) and Lietzmann (*Korinther*) on 11:5 and 12:11.

33. Käsemann ("Legitimität," 37; my trans.) also notes that the opponents saw themselves as apostles of Christ, as ἐργάται, as διάκονοι. He correctly observes that Paul did not acknowledge the opponents this honor. Certainly also "the vehemence with which he . . . reviles them . . . is without parallel even for him." But this very vehemence is best explained when one recognizes that Paul actually could not decisively contest the opponents' right to the title of apostle on formal grounds. So already Schmiedel, *Briefe*. Of course, the whole passage does not reflect merely a general admonition to the community, but rather a real exchange of arguments pro and con (against Schlatter and Munck). The opponents were not obscure people, let alone shadows in the fantasy of individual members of the community or of Paul, but people against whom it paid to defend oneself (Lietzmann, *Korinther*, 149).

34. The following should be noted in particular: Hans von Campenhausen, *Ecclesiastical Authority and Spiritual Power in the Church of the First Three Centuries* (trans. J. A. Baker; Stanford: Stanford University Press, 1969); idem, "Der Urchristliche Apostelbegriff," *StTh* 1 (1947) 96–130; Karl Heinrich Rengstorf, *Apostolate and Ministry: The New Testament Doctrine of the Office of the Ministry* (trans. Paul D. Pahl; St. Louis: Concordia, 1969); Schmithals, *Office of Apostle*.

35. Cf. on this point esp. the work of Günter Klein (*Die zwölf Apostel: Ursprung und Gehalt einer Idee* [FRLANT NF 59; Göttingen: Vandenhoeck & Ruprecht, 1961]).

36. Klein has provided an interesting and generally compelling attempt to classify this concept of the apostle within the theology of Luke and the history of the early church.

37. Schmithals, *Office of Apostle*, 21–44, 58–59.

38. Most of all in the third section of ibid., 96–191.

39. Ibid., 59.

40. This is stressed most of all by Gerhard Sass (*Apostelamt und Kirche: Eine theologisch-exegetische Untersuchung des paulinischen Apostelbegriffs* [Forschungen zur Geschichte und Lehre des Protestantismus 9/2;

Munich: Kaiser, 1939]). The sentence following in the German original above has been changed, now reflecting more fully Paul's understanding of himself as being representative.

41. Schmithals, *Office of Apostle*, 21, esp. n. 7.

42. Most of all in Gal. 1—2 and in 1 Cor. 9, 15.

43. This is what Schmithals is out to prove in his book on the apostolate. Cf. esp. *Office of Apostle*, 198–230.

44. On the Gnostic understanding, cf. my discussion in Review of W. Schmithals, *Die Gnosis in Korinth*.

45. Klein, *Zwölf Apostel*, 63 n. 277.

46. Schmithals, *Office of Apostle*, 201–30.

47. So perhaps the motif of λογικὴ λατρεία in Rom. 15:16, 28–32. Details on this are in Georgi, *Kollekte*.

48. Against Schmithals, *Office of Apostle*, 203–4.

49. Cf. below, pp. 165–67.

50. Schmithals, *Office of Apostle*, 198.

51. Cf. on this Werner Georg Kümmel, *Kirchenbegriff und Geschichts-bewusstsein in der Urgemeinde und bei Jesus* (Göttingen: Vandenhoeck & Ruprecht, 1968) 5; on 2 Cor. 8:23, cf. Georgi, *Kollekte*.

52. Schmithals, *Office of Apostle*, 61.

53. Ibid., 102–3.

54. Campenhausen ("Apostelbegriff," 98 n. 1) calls attention to this, following Zahn and Schlier.

55. On the problem of the circle of the twelve, cf. the discussion by Klein. Beyond this, a *communis opinio* is very slowly developing that—no matter how early the conception of the circle of the twelve arose—the identification of the circle of the twelve and the circle of the apostles is in any case late by comparison and cannot be taken into consideration for determining the original understanding of the apostolate.

56. On the dating of the conversion of Paul, cf. Haenchen, *Acts*, 64–65.

57. As it must be assumed for the Corinthian heretics. They adhered to the tradition of the resurrection of Jesus but denied their own resurrection from the dead. In connection with their repeatedly apostrophized understanding of *gnosis* and their negative attitude vis-à-vis the demands of genuine community, that can only mean that just as the later Gnostics of the Pastorals, they said, "ἀνάστασιν ἤδη γεγονέναι" (2 Tim. 2:18), and gave reasons for this christologically, i.e., from the resurrection of Christ experienced and carried out in Gnosticism. In addition, cf. Kümmel (in Lietzmann, *Korinther*, 192–93, and the literature cited there); against Schmithals (*Gnosticism*, 155–59).

58. For the Apocalypse, the time in question is that of Domitian; for the *Didache*, it is the turn of the century. Whereas this dating of the Apocalypse is widely accepted, it is still disputed for the *Didache*. Cf. Molland, "Apostellehre," *RGG*, 1:508, and the literature cited there.

59. Cf. the particulars on this and the discussion in Klein, *Zwölf Apostel*, 50–52, 75–80. In my opinion, the Ephesians passages adduced by Klein (ibid., 66–75) do not speak for apostles of the second generation.

60. On the problem of the apostles in the *Didache*, I would especially like to refer to the essay of Gerhard Sass ("Die Apostel in der Didache," in Werner Schmauch, ed., *In Memoriam Ernst Lohmeyer* [Stuttgart: Evangelisches Verlagswerk, 1951] 233–39). One should also not forget the comprehensive and fundamental inquiry into the expansion of the circle of the apostles until the second century by Adolf von Harnack in his *Die Lehre der zwölf Apostel, nebst Untersuchungen zur ältesten Geschichte der Kirchenverfassung und des Kirchenrechts* (TU 2/1–2; Leipzig: Hinrichs, 1884), and in *Die Mission und Ausbreitung des Christentums in den ersten Drei Jahrhunderten* (4th rev. ed.; 2 vols.; Leipzig: Hinrichs, 1924).

61. Klein, *Zwölf Apostel*, 50–52, 80–83.

62. Ibid., 52 (my trans.).

63. Here Schmithals (*Office of Apostle*, 179–80) appears to be right. Along with the discussion in the commentaries, cf. also the description of the history of early Christian heresy by H. Köster ("Häretiker im Urchristentum," *RGG*. 3:20).

64. Klein, *Zwölf Apostel*, 76–80.

65. Ibid., 75.

66. In addition to Paul's statements about his activity, cf. also Gal. 2:7–9; 1 Cor. 9:5; 2 Cor. 3:1; 11:4; the polemical fragments of 2 Cor. in general; Acts 13:1–3; 14:4, 14; *Didache* 11.2–6; and of course the tradition preserved in Matthew 10.

67. No other clear criteria than these may be inferred from the earliest texts, above all, none that are *exclusive* and *constitutive* for the "apostolate": neither being an eyewitness of the earthly life of Jesus nor being an eyewitness of the appearances of the resurrected Jesus is sufficient. Paul and Barnabas, e.g., were not companions of Jesus, and, on the other hand, not all the people mentioned in 1 Cor. 15:5–7 were apostles. In 1 Cor. 9:2 no *distinguishing sign* of an apostle is intended (cf. on this von Campenhausen, "Apostelbegriff," 113 n. 2). Even the commissioning by Christ was not peculiar to the apostles. The prophets, say, who were not always missionaries were also commissioned by Christ, as Matt. 7:22–23 and the Apocalypse in particular show. On the other hand, Paul does not expressly mention that he was appointed by Christ to be an *apostle*—which Sass (*Apostelamt*, 34–35) and von Campenhausen ("Apostelbegriff," 112 n. 2) rightly emphasize. Nor can miracles be associated only with apostles; rather, they were an attribute of pneumatics in general. After all, the gift of the spirit itself was already *eo ipso* a miracle. Apparently one only expected—as will be shown later—the apostles to give particularly impressive proofs of their possession of the spirit, which also brought with it an increase of authority. But this is explained well from the missionary context—which is presented in detail in

what follows. Cf. also von Campenhausen (ibid., 112–15) concerning the
absence of clear criteria for the apostolate. Even in his systematic presentation (pp. 119–30), von Campenhausen cannot for this reason come to a
clear result.
68. The passage in 1 Cor. 12:28, which pointedly mentions the apostles
first, is often adduced as evidence for the fact that the apostles (together
with the prophets and teachers) stand apart from the other officers and belong to the church as a whole. (Cf. on this esp. Harnack, *Zwölf Apostel*, 99
n. 12, 115; idem, *Mission*, 1:335, 349 n. 3; idem, *Entstehung und Entwicklung der Kirchenverfassung und des Kirchenrechts in den zwei ersten Jahrhunderten* [Leipzig: Hinrichs, 1910] 38–40, 63–76). But the Pauline
passage indicates that Paul sees the apostles lined up with the others named
and wants to consider them all charismatics (the intention of 1 Cor. 12 being
to ascribe the spirit to *all* members of the community in terms of the charismata bestowed on *all*, an emphatic contrast to an exclusive understanding
of the spirit). In general, the idea of an organized church, with tangible
structures, is not applicable to the situation in the first two or, indeed,
three generations of the early church. It should also be noticed that the catalogs of charismata in 1 Cor. 12:4–11 and Rom. 12:6–8 (21) do not mention
the apostles. They were therefore not downright exclusive or irreplaceable
in their importance and authority. I do not want to dispute that the "apostolate" and the gospel originally belonged together, precisely since the apostles were missionaries. For this reason, the establishing of new
communities also belonged to the mission of the apostle (cf. on this point
von Campenhausen, "Apostelbegriff," 110, and the literature cited there).
As a missionary, the apostle obviously does not belong only to one individual congregation. In spite of that, the apostle knows that he or she is directly bound, even responsible, to the congregations—not as a high and
remote religious officer but as a participating member (on this, cf. Eduard
Schweizer, *Church Order in the New Testament* [SBT 32; London: SCM,
1961] 100, 194–95). The apostles evidently belonged to the church as a
whole only in this way, by belonging to individual congregations. The correspondence of Paul shows that again and again (including Romans). It will
be shown that Paul supports this connection of the apostle with the individual congregation still more strongly than the opposing apostles do. I do not
mean that one can find with the apostles a comprehensive claim to authority
and representation or that the apostolate was considered independent of all
human instances, as von Campenhausen ("Apostelbegriff," 110–11) thinks.
Under no circumstance may 1 Cor. 4:3–4 be read apart from the general
precept in v. 5, for there Paul speaks of judgment in general. And should 1
Thess. 2:4–8 really pertain only to the "apostles"? That which is particular
here should pertain precisely only to the person of Paul, but that which is
general should refer to the proclaimers of Jesus on the whole, who are here
contrasted with other missionaries—as already Martin Dibelius (*An die*

Thessalonicher 1, 2, An die Philipper [3d ed.; HNT 11; Tübingen: Mohr, 1937]) and then esp. Günther Bornkamm (*Early Christian Experience* [trans. Paul L. Hammer; New York: Harper & Row, London: SCM; 1969] 6–7, 45 n. 22) have shown.

69. Paul is building up to the μετασχηματιζόμενοι κτλ. The opponents play a role that does not correspond to their own nature. That they feign something improper to them is already indicated in the first half of the sentence with the terms ψευδ- and δόλιοι. Not only ἀπμόστολοι (Χριστοῦ) but also ἐργάται are feigned roles which the opponents assigned to and claimed for themselves.

70. Schmithals, "Irrlehrer," 312–13.

71. Against Schmithals, ibid.

72. Cf. on this the essay by Adolf von Harnack, "κόπος, (κοπιᾶν, οἱ κοπιῶντες) im frühchristlichen Sprachgebrauch," *ZNW* 27 (1928) 1–10.

73. Matt. 10:10 and par. is, according to Rudolf Bultmann (*The History of the Synoptic Tradition* [trans. John Marsh; New York: Harper & Row, 1963] 103), a proverb which has been made by tradition into a word of the Lord. But it seems to me probable that taking over the proverb and transforming it into a Word of the Lord was already done with a view to missionary proclamation. In the saying Matt. 9:37–38 and par., texts which are younger in terms of the history of the tradition, harvest and mission are then characteristically made one. On these logia more will be said below (pp. 165–67) with the description of the early mission of the church.

For John 4:35–38, cf. Rudolf Bultmann, *The Gospel of John: A Commentary* (trans. G. R. Beasley Murray; Philadelphia: Westminster Press; Oxford: Blackwell, 1971) 196–200; and Ferdinand Hahn, *Mission in the New Testament* (SBT 47; London: SCM, 1965) 40–41.

74. For 1 Tim. 5:18, cf. Martin Dibelius, *The Pastoral Epistles* (4th rev. ed. by Hans Conzelmann; Hermeneia; Philadelphia: Fortress, 1972) 78–79.

For *Didache* 13:2, see Helmut Koester, *Synoptische Überlieferung bei den apostolischen Vätern* (TU 65; Berlin: Akademie, 1957) 212, 261. Koester asks the question whether the *Didache* already knows this saying as a Word of the Lord, whether or not perhaps here also the maxim is known as a proverb and is so used. But for our purpose it remains significant that the *Didache* applies this proverb to the proclaimer as well (even though no longer clearly to the missionary; but cf. also 13:1 and the previous chapters).

75. BAGD, "ἔργον," 2; Bertram, "ἔργον," *TDNT*, 2:635–52, esp. 638–39, 640.

76. According to Windisch (*2. Korintherbrief*, 342), ἐργάτης is an "established term of the mission" (my trans.).

77. It seems that this relationship has not been sufficiently noted in previous explanations of 2 Cor. 11:22–23.

78. Karl Georg Kuhn, *TDNT*, 3:368 (article *"Ἰσραήλ"* [*TDNT*, 3:356–91], written by Gerhard von Rad, Karl Georg Kuhn, and Walter Gutbrod).

79. For *Ἑβραῖος* and *Ἰσραηλίτης*, cf. *"Ἰσραήλ," TDNT*, 3:359–69 (Kuhn); 3:371–75; 3:382–91 (Gutbrod). For *σπέρμα Ἀβραάμ*, see below page 251 (cf. also Gutbrod, 3:390, on 2 Cor. 11:22: "a progressive loftiness of designation").

80. To date, a satisfactory investigation of Hellenistic-Jewish Apologetics has not been made. The work of Peter Dalbert (*Die Theologie der hellen-istisch-jüdischen Missionsliteratur unter Ausschluss von Philo und Josephus* [ThF 4; Hamburg-Volksdorf: Reich, 1954]) provides some information on the state of the sources, the questions of dating, and the secondary litera-ture. However, the problem of Apologetics has been insufficiently investi-gated and grasped by Dalbert. Jacob Freudenthal (*Alexander Polyhistor und die von ihm erhaltenen Reste jüdischer und samaritanischer Ge-schichtswerke* [Breslau: Skutsch, 1875]) is still very helpful for introductory questions. Most of the Apologetic fragments are treated here (Demetrius, two anonymous fragments, Cleodemus Malchus, Thallus, Theodotus, Eupolemus, Aristeas, Artapanus, Aristobulus). For the individual names, one may also consult vol. 3 of Emil Schürer (*Geschichte des jüdischen Volkes im Zeitalter Jesu Christi* [4th ed.; 3 vols.; Leipzig: Hinrichs, 1909]) and vol. 2, pt. 1 of Wilhelm Schmid (*Wilhelm von Christs Geschichte der Griechischen Literatur* [4th ed. rev. with Otto Stählin; Munich: Beck, 1920]). Individual Apologists are also treated in *RGG*. Interesting and in-structive for the critical reader is Moriz Friedländer (*Geschichte der jü-dischen Apologetik als Vorgeschichte des Christentums* [Zurich: Schmidt, 1903]) on the history of Jewish Apologetics. However, one must take into consideration that the definition of Apologetics is already blurred, and the source-critical differentiation is even less clear. The goal set and its execu-tion have been oversimplified and too strongly generalized. Adolf von Schlatter's *Geschichte Israels von Alexander dem Grossen bis Hadrian* ([3d rev. ed.; Stuttgart: Calwer, 1925] 70–90 and 184–221) and his interpreta-tions of Josephus, as well as the work of Paul Krüger (*Philo und Josephus als Apologeten des Judentums* [Leipzig: Dürr, 1906]), is to be noted too. Before I discuss the phenomenon further in the following pages, I should give a short definition of my understanding of Apologetics: it was the Jewish movement which argued with paganism about the Jewish faith using pagan genres and methods. In my opinion, the relevant sources (in chronological order) are: Demetrius, Philo the Elder, Eupolemus, Anonymus, Cleode-mus Malchus, Theodotus, Thallus (the latter four are perhaps Samaritans, but their basic tendency is in any case closely related to that of the Jewish Apologists), Ezekiel the Tragedian, Aristeas, the *Epistle of Aristeas*, Aristobulus, the *Sibylline Oracles*, Philo (in part), and Josephus. In addi-tion, the following (which are very difficult to classify chronologically) should be considered: pseudo-Hecataeus, pseudo-Aeschylus, pseudo-Soph-

ocles, pseudo-Heraclitus (the fourth and seventh letters), pseudo-Diog-
enes, pseudo-Phocylides, pseudo-Menander. 2 and 4 Maccabees are very
close to Apologetics also. The question whether Jewish Apologetics had
more than a merely literary character will also be discussed below.

81. The relationship of Hellenistic-Jewish Apologetics to wisdom literature is evident, for example, in the strong interest in sapiential motifs. Jewish and pagan "rationality" could meet each other here. Moreover, not only
the figure of Wisdom (Sophia) but also the typified image of the wise one
(and the righteous one) played a great role. The genuine tendency for Apologetic belongs exactly as little for the *Wisdom of Solomon* as for the
"genuine" Philo (the author of the allegorical commentary and of the questions); instead, it belongs to another branch of the wisdom movement:
Hellenistic-Jewish speculative mysticism, the later Gnosticism. Here the
goal is the mystical dissociation from history (even Jewish history) and from
the cosmos. Both the Wisdom of Solomon and Philo work with Apologetic
traditions but then depart far from them (cf., e.g., the relationship of Wisd.
of Sol. 13:16—14:31 to 13:1a and 15:1–3). And they both are interested in a
communion of Wisdom and wise ones beyond history and the world. The
piece *Joseph and Aseneth* also belongs to the realm of speculative mysticism. The Jewish magical papyri have their place between Apologetics and
speculative mysticism. The more strongly they present themselves as being
Jewish, the more they approach Apologetics (e.g., Paris Papyri 3009 and
Papyri Leid. J. 395); the more strongly pagan they become, the more frequently an inclination toward dualistic, acosmic mysticism can be established.

82. It seems to be a mistake of previous research to have considered the
texts in question mainly as apologetic and accommodating and never to
have discussed a serious theological intention. Even Dalbert's *Missionsliteratur*, despite its stated theme, does not earnestly examine and specify the
missionary purpose and method of the writings treated. This is not the case
in the research on Philo, although even here the apologetic parts elicit the
least interest from the researchers.

83. "Ἰσραήλ," *TDNT*, 3:365–67 (Kuhn) and 3:373–74 (Gutbrod).

84. Ibid., 3:367–68 (Kuhn) and 3:373–74 (Gutbrod).

85. Cf. the passages discussed below, pp. 43–45.

86. Against Kuhn, "Ἰσραήλ," *TDNT*, 3:367–68.

87. Eusebius, *Praep. Ev.* 13.12.

88. Felix Jacoby, *Die Fragmente der Griechischen Historiker* (3 vols.;
Leiden: Brill, 1954–64) 3:726.1 (Eusebius, *Praep. Ev.* 9.18.1).

89. "Ἰσραήλ," *TDNT*, 3:367–69 and 3:373–75.

90. Ibid., 3:367–68 and 3:373–75. Similarly also the Samaritan Apologist
Theodotus.

91. As is known, in Philo's work three large groups must be differentiated: the commentaries on the Mosaic laws *(Expositio Legis)* and related

tracts, the short commentaries on Genesis and Exodus *(Quaestiones)*, and the actual, allegorical commentary on Genesis. In the first group, the allegorical explanation is comparatively restrained. I would like to follow the opinion of many researchers who regard the intent of this group of writings to be the information of and the dispute with the pagans; this means that they belong to the Apologetic writings. More details on the origin of this group of writings and on their relationship especially to the allegorical commentary will be given below, p. 181 n. 59, in the section on the Jewish mission. I reckon the writings on the Essenes and the Therapeutae as also the writing on the eternity of the world and the political pamphlets and naturally also the proper apology, the *Hypothetica*, to this group.

92. This is often disputed by reference to the address in 4 Macc. 18:1 and the emphatically Jewish tone of the entire work. But form and style already speak against a purely Jewish character (a diatribe written in Greek and interspersed with many philosophical motifs—so I. Heinemann following Norden in "Makkabäerbücher [IV]" [PW 14 (1928) 800–805]) as well as the detailed introduction. Further reasons for the proximity to Apologetics are offered above.

93. Both the appreciation of the ancestral heritage and the motif of the exemplary model fit well into the Hellenistic world. Cf. below, pp. 131–37.

94. Already in the first three chapters and then, in inserted reflections, later on.

95. Not only in his tract against Apion but elsewhere as well, Josephus proves himself to be an Apologist, as his proëmia already show. Even if Josephus was a full member of a Pharisaic cooperative in Palestine, he does not show much of it in his work. Nevertheless, it is clear that he strongly depended on traditions. This, at least, Hölscher surely showed in his article "Josephus" (PW 9 [1916] 1934–2000). But Hellenistic-Jewish material and tendency predominate.

96. My trans.—the passage also in Gutbrod, "Ἰσραήλ," *TDNT*, 3:373 (cf. also 370).

97. Gutbrod (ibid.) does not do justice to the passages in Plutarch.

98. This passage is also in ibid., 3:373.

99. Weinreich, in particular, has demonstrated this in his essay on Alexander, the prophet of lies. For his view on the passage above, see Otto Weinreich, "Alexander, der Lügenprophet und seine Stellung in der Religiosität des 2 Jahrhunderts n. Chr.," *Neue Jahrbücher für das klassische Altertum* 47 (1921) 140–41. But he makes no contribution to the linguistic question.

100. It is unlikely that only "an incomprehensible language" is meant here (Gutbrod) or a language of fantasy. The narrator Lucian is, after all, of Syrian origin. When Lucian adds that the words were meaningless, that pertains to the content of the statements, not to the chosen language.

101. The propagandistic effect of these motives will be investigated more

closely, together with the description of the Jewish and Hellenistic mission below.

102. All this may be assumed on the basis of the original meaning of Ἑβραῖος, described above, pp. 41–46. Most of the commentators agree.

103. Cf. Haenchen (Acts, 260–62, 332) for these passages.

104. Especially the temples for the ruler cult in Samaria and Caesarea.

105. "Ἰσραήλ," TDNT, 3:359–63 (Kuhn).

106. Ibid., 3:363–69 (Kuhn) and 371–72 (Gutbrod).

107. Some Apologists may have preferred the designation Ἰουδαῖοι instead of Ἰσραηλῖται (or Ἑβραῖοι) because of the dispute with the Samaritans. Freudenthal writes: "Since the Samaritans did not want to be Ἰουδαῖοι but rather Ἑβραῖοι or Ἰσραηλῖται . . . , Eupolemus and Artapanus, who seems to be a contemporary of Eupolemus, ostentatiously use only the former name and never the latter ones; thereby, they also present their ancestors as true Judeans. On the other hand, the unselfconscious Demetrius speaks not of Ἰουδαῖοι but rather of Ἰσραηλῖται . . . , and likewise Philo and Josephus, for whom the differences with the Samaritans have again become less important, also use the names Ἑβραῖοι and Ἰσραηλῖται for the time before the Babylonian captivity" (Alexander, 101; my trans.). This may indeed have played a certain role.

108. Gutbrod, "Ἰσραήλ," TDNT, 3:372.

109. Jacoby, Fragmente, 3:722.1.7 (Eusebius, Praep. Ev. 9.21).

110. Jacoby, Fragmente, 3:722.10.

111. Cf. the passages in Carl Siegfried, Philo von Alexandria als Ausleger des Alten Testaments (Jena: Dufft, 1875) 269; cf. also Gutbrod, "Ἰσραήλ," TDNT, 3:372. In many of these passages one sees how Philo (going much further than the tendency of the Apologists) is out to give up all Jewish peculiarities in favor of a mystical unity (above all Deus 144; Sacr. 134; cf. Gutbrod, "Ἰσραήλ," TDNT, 3:372).

112. Josephus, Ant. 1.331–34.

113. Gutbrod overlooked this relationship in content ("Ἰσραήλ," TDNT, 3:372).

114. That is already clear from the introduction to the Antiquities, but likewise also from the writing against Apion.

115. The judgment of Gutbrod ("Ἰσραήλ," TDNT, 3:372) seems to contradict the purpose of Josephus: "It is not evident that the name Ἰσραήλ has any particular significance for Josephus as denoting the special religious situation of the Jewish people." Gutbrod can come to this judgment only because he understands the idea "religious" in a sense that is much too narrow for the understanding of the Jewish Apologists.

116. On this, cf. also the proof presented by Kuhn ("Ἰσραήλ," TDNT, 3:363–69) that Ἰσραήλ appears in Hellenistic-Jewish texts only in emphatically religious contexts, especially in liturgical contexts. Its presence in 4 Maccabees also supports the "heroic" ring of the designation.

117. Friedländer (*Apologetik*, 341–44) also refers to this passage.

118. With reference to the passages Lev. 19:9; Deut. 24:19; 25:4, 23, 25.

119. Contrary to what we know of rabbinical criminal law (cf. Str-B 3:527–30), the Apologist Josephus, who is very strongly influenced by tradition, takes the context of Deut. 24:19–22 so literally that he immediately interprets the lashing spoken of in 25:1–3 (which Paul suffered five times, according to 2 Cor. 11:25) as punishment for offenses against the commandment of assistance to the weak and the stranger.

120. On this, cf. Str-B 3:523. For the significance of the figure of Abraham in Judaism, cf. esp. Otto Schmitz, "Abraham im Spätjudentum und im Frühchristentum," in *Aus Schrift und Geschichte* (ed. Karl Bornhäuser; Stuttgart: Calwer, 1922) and Samuel Sandmel, *Philo's Place in Judaism: A Study of Conceptions of Abraham in Jewish Literature* (Cincinnati: Hebrew Union College, 1956).

121. 4 Macc. 16:20; cf. 14:20; 15:28; 17:6; further 13:12.

122. The example is mentioned in 4 Macc. 13:12; 15:28; 16:20; 17:6; and 18:20, 23; the validity is limited in 18:1.

123. Cf. also 4 Macc. 13:15–17.

124. The catalogs of trials of the Cynic-Stoic diatribe offer some examples (cf. Rudolf Bultmann, *Der Stil der Paulinischen Predigt und die kynisch-stoische Diatribe* [FRLANT 13; Göttingen: Vandenhoeck & Ruprecht, 1910]); Rosa Söder (*Die apokryphen Apostelgeschichten und die romanhafte Literatur der Antike* [Würzburger Studien zur Altertumswissenschaft 3; Stuttgart: Kohlhammer, 1932] 150–58) cites further examples from the Hellenistic novel. 4 Maccabees is particularly far removed from the Jewish and especially the early Christian concept of martyrdom (cf. Dörrie, "Märtyrer, I," *RGG*, 4:588). But the lack of a witnessing character does not argue for an absence of propaganda; on the contrary, the stories of suffering, persecution, and death from a Hellenistic provenance characteristically demonstrate for an audience.

125. W. L. Knox ("Abraham and the Quest for God," *HTR* 28 [1935] 57–60) must be credited with having shown the missionary character of the Hellenistic-Jewish legend of Abraham. This will be further developed below.

126. In both fragments (Jacoby, *Fragmente*, 3:724.1 and 2; Eusebius, *Praep. Ev.* 9.17.2 and 9.18.2). The fact that here and in the following the OT tradition is not exactly reproduced but is transformed by the use of pagan traditions (Freudenthal, *Alexander*, 92–96; cf. 90) must not yet argue against a Jewish and for a Samaritan origin of the anonymous fragments (contrary to Freudenthal). Only the assertion that Abraham stopped at Garizim and there received gifts from Melchizedek (frag. 724. 1.5) points to a Samaritan origin. The passage mentioned by Freudenthal (*Alexander*, 93) from the third book of the *Sibylline Oracles* (97–160, esp. 110–60) says something similar for the time of the giants. The related report of Thallos

(Theophilus, *Ad Autolycum* 3.29) is a different matter, since he must be the Samaritan mentioned by Josephus (*Ant.* 18.167); cf. Freudenthal, *Alexander*, 100–101, opposed by Jacoby, *Fragmente*, 2:256 and notes to 2:835–37).

127. In the second anonymous fragment (Jacoby, *Fragmente*, 3:724.2).

128. Josephus *Ant.* 1.109–19, esp. 113–16.

129. Ibid., 1.120–21.

130. For Cleodemus Malchus, see Jacoby, *Fragmente*, 3:214.7 and 727.1, and Josephus, *Ant.* 1.238–41. There the text itself is in 240–41, but the preceding seems to come from the same tradition. Cf. also Eusebius, *Praep. Ev.* 9.20.2–5. According to Freudenthal (*Alexander*, 130–36) Cleodemus Malchus is a Samaritan. His reasons are not very convincing (cf. below, p. 133).

131. Arabia, Libya (Africa), Assyria, and—this is not mentioned here since only the sons of Ketura are dealt with—the Jews, of course. The tradition taken up by Cleodemus Malchus is also reflected in the corresponding observations of Demetrius (Jacoby, *Fragmente*, 3:722.2; Eusebius, *Praep. Ev.* 9.29), Artapanus (Jacoby, *Fragmente*, 3:726.2.1), and the pagan Apollonius Molon (ibid., 3:728.1.2–3).

132. The actual text of Josephus (*Ant.* 1.239), which apparently goes back to the same tradition, reads, "He made all children and grandchildren colonists" (ἀποικιῶν στόλους μηχανᾶται; my trans.). Demetrius already said something similar (Jacoby, *Fragmente*, 3:728.2–3; Eusebius, *Praep. Ev.* 9.29): ". . . that Abraham sent (his) children to the East to settle."

133. "(Japhra, Sures, and Aphera— descendants of Abraham) [accompanied Heracles in his campaign against Libya and Anteus; and Heracles, who married Aphranes' (a descendant of Abraham) daughter (and thereby became a relation of Abraham), begot with her Diodorus. He begot Sophon because of whom the barbarians are called Sophacians]" (see above, n. 120). The lines which Freudenthal (*Alexander*, 133–35) draws to the cult of the Samaritans because of the mention of Heracles, who obviously then cannot be the Greek hero in person, are quite interesting but seemingly construed and not very convincing. Freudenthal also takes the view that Jews could not possibly have identified so extensively with pagan nature. Indeed, that is a *petitio principii* which is already untenable in the face of the works of Eupolemus and Artapanus (cf. what Freudenthal says about both of them in ibid., 105–30 [esp. 125–30] and 143–74 [esp. 162–69]). I am seeking to investigate here the reasons for this rapprochement with paganism. The assertion of Freudenthal that Cleodemus cannot have been a Jew because he was a prophet also does not stand the test. It rests upon the view that the Jews had no longer possessed true prophets since Malachi. But this is an orthodox fiction of later rabbis, with the same intent as the denial of Jewish syncretism. Evidence for the opposite will be offered below, pp. 103–9.

134. On this, cf. Erwin R. Goodenough, "The Political Philosophy of Hellenistic Kingship," *Yale Classical Studies* 1 (1928) 53–102.

135. Most of the manuscripts add Δαμασχοῦ, which fits the meaning.

136. *Ant*. 1.7, 2.159–60 (Jacoby, *Fragmente*, 2:90.19). A related tradition is found in the Roman historian Pompeius Trogus (Jacoby, *Fragmente*, 3:737, appendix, fragment 17c.2 [Justin's *Epitome* 36.1.10]): "For the Jews have their origin in Damascus, the principal city of Syria, from which also the Assyrian kings stem since Semiramis. The name has been given to the city by King Damascus. . . . After Damascus, Azelus and further Adores, Abrahames, and Israhel have been kings. But a happy harvest of ten sons made Israhel more famous than his forebears. Therefore, he left the people divided into ten kingdoms to his sons. He named all of them Judeans after the name of Judah, who had died after the partition, and he ordered that all should honor the name of the one whose share had come to all" (my trans.). Then the story of Joseph is narrated (here too a genealogical mistake is made: Joseph is the youngest son), followed by a description of the story of Moses and the exodus, which are similarly not exactly reproduced. Finally, a geographical description comes after the account of the history of the Jewish people (which is essentially a history of heroes).

137. A Jewish origin of these traditions of Nicolaus and Pompeius is likely for the following reasons (Theodore Reinach, *Oeuvres Complètes de Flavius Josèphe* [Paris: Leroux, 1900] n. 1, disagrees): The association of Nicolaus of Damascus with Jewish traditions is made probable by his capacity as friend and biographer of Herod; this impression is even strengthened by the fact that the Jew Josephus, to whom we owe this citation, actually uses the universal history of Nicolaus as one of his main sources. Finally, the indicated text itself argues for its proximity to Judaism. It not only reflects a friendly attitude toward Judaism but also reads like a recommendation of Judaism, indeed, as propaganda for Judaism. A Syrian origin for the thesis that Abraham, the heroic ancestor of the Jews, had been king of Damascus is highly unlikely; after all, the Syrians felt themselves to be superior to the Jews. The boasting remark that the descendants of Abraham, the Jews, were numerous would not stem from a Syrian source either; instead it conforms precisely to OT and Jewish self-understanding and propaganda. The concluding reference of the citation to a local tradition of Damascus must not argue against the Jewish origin of this note of Nicolaus; on the contrary, in Damascus there was a very old and very large Jewish diaspora community. In fact, the entire report probably originated with the justification and propaganda of this community toward its environment.

A similar origin for the tradition of Pompeius seems probable to me. It only becomes understandable when read as a statement of propaganda. The introduction to the above text argues for that already: the Jews are presented as a brave people. Only Antiochus Sidetes was able really to subjugate them. "Thereafter, they no longer tolerated any Macedonian king, and *they showed their own power of rulership by attacking Syria in great wars*." This introduction contradicts Pompeius's short note on the political fate of the Jews at the end of the entire description (Jacoby, *Fragmente*,

3:737, appendix, fragment 17c; 3:89). Here he reports that the Jews did not get away from Macedonian rule until the Roman period—but this is not entirely correct either, only insofar as the Maccabeans and the Hasmoneans respectively never attained *full* independence.

If the Jewish claim on Syria found in the tradition of Pompeius can be explained only from a Jewish source, then on the contrary the various mistakes of the present piece are to be explained as Pompeius's misunderstandings (perhaps already by his informants) of the Jewish source. The character of the original Jewish tradition as propaganda is betrayed even more clearly in the later portrayal (which is still to be treated below) of Joseph and Moses, in particular, as θεῖοι ἄνδρες (already prepared by the presentation of Abraham and especially of Jacob).

138. The different titles and attributes of the Hellenistic ruler (whether chosen by the latter or conferred on him by the philosophical royal ideology) already support this view. Some examples: σωτήρ, ἐπιφανής, εὐεργέτης, esp. also νόμος ἔμψυχος, incarnate Logos, incorporated stream of light. Cf. for all these titles and properties Goodenough, "Hellenistic Kingship." Contrary to Goodenough ("Hellenistic Kingship," 74–75), it seems that designation of the king as a sage does not clash with this ideology but belongs to it, even if this motif of the sage received a special nuance under Stoic influence. But the motif already belongs to the Platonic image of the king (cf., e.g., Kleinknecht, "βασιλεύς," *TDNT*, 1:564, and the literature indicated there). This idea was also widespread in the Jewish wisdom movement, and especially then in Apologetics as the tradition of Solomon as the wise king and then the *Epistle of Aristeas* show.

139. For the significance of astrology in late antiquity, cf. Franz Cumont, *Die orientalischen Religionen im römischen Heidentum* (Stuttgart: Teubner, 1975) 148–77; Rudolf Bultmann (*Primitive Christianity in Its Contemporary Setting* [trans. R. H. Fuller; Cleveland: World Publishing, Meridian Books, 1956; Philadelphia: Fortress, 1980] 146–55, and the literature indicated there). For the following, cf. esp. the essay on Abraham by Knox ("Abraham," 57–60).

140. This is clearly in the first of the two anonymous fragments (Jacoby, *Fragmente*, 3:724.1) and in Artapanus (ibid., 3:726.1; Eusebius, *Praep. Ev.* 9.18.1; vol. 8, pt. 2 of the Eusebius edition of the GCS, 191–95, esp. 193). It is presupposed in the pseudonymous Testament of Orpheus in the draft of Aristobulus (Eusebius, *Praep. Ev.* 13.12.5, ll. 5–10), probably also in Philo the Elder (Jacoby, *Fragmente*, 3:729.1.9–10; Eusebius, *Praep. Ev.* 9.20) and in Josephus, *Ant.* 1.154–68, esp. 158 and 167–68. Philo also seems to know this tradition and to polemicize against it. On Aristobulus, Philo the Elder, Josephus, and Philo, more below.

141. According to the second anonymous fragment (Jacoby, *Fragmente*, 3:724.2), Artapanus, Josephus, *Ant.* 1.167–68, and the tradition presupposed by Philo.

142. According to the first anonymous fragment, probably also Aristobulus and Philo the Elder. Knox ("Abraham," 56) compares with it the Berossus passage cited by Josephus, *Ant.* 1.158, and thinks that by citing the passage Josephus betrays that he knows the tradition of Abraham as the father of astrology.

143. Cf. the text-critical apparatus in Jacoby (*Fragmente*, on 1:20.678).

144. In the first fragment (ibid., 3:724.1.3).

145. δεινὸς ὢν συνιέναι τε περὶ πάντων καὶ πιθανὸς τοῖς ἀκροωμένοις.

146. τὴν περὶ τοῦ θεοῦ δόξαν, ἣν ἅπασι συνέβαινεν εἶναι, καινίσαι καὶ μεταβαλεῖν ἔγνω.

147. Cf. Knox, "Abraham," 57–58.

148. ἐκ γὰρ μεγέθους καὶ καλλονῆς κτισμάτων ἀναλόγως ὁ γενεσιουργὸς αὐτῶν θεωρεῖται.

149. This conception of the possibility of a natural knowledge of God (as presupposition for a sermon of judgment; cf. already 12:27) at a later stage (that of the final work) is changed into its opposite by the introductory phrase: it was not their false decision which did not allow the pagans to grasp this possibility but their nature; it was not knowledge which changed but ἀγνωσία (this term appears here for the first time in antiquity as the comprehensive description of human existence; then it appears more frequently in Gnosticism). The Greek text of 13:1a runs: μάταιοι μὲν γὰρ πάντες ἄνθρωποι φύσει, οἷς παρῆν θεοῦ ἀγνωσία.

150. That is especially to be noted in fragments of later Apologists and in the traditions used by Philo and Josephus. But the description of the special gifts of certain men in the older fragments also points in the same direction. These gifts, in fact, concern the secrets of cosmic events. More will be said on this subject in connection with the Apologists' understanding of spirit and miracles (see below, pp. 120–67). Here sapiential transformation of the OT faith in creation meets Hellenistic thought, namely, the Hellenistic view of the cosmos and cosmic religion. On the differences to the OT, cf. Bultmann (*Primitive Christianity*, 94–100); on cosmic religion, cf. the second volume of the work of André M. J. Festugière (*La révélation d'Hermès Trismégiste* [4 vols.; Paris: Librairie Lecoffre, 1944–54]) with the significant title "Le dieu cosmique." (See esp. the chapter on Philo's "La contemplation du monde" [ibid., 555–72], where the passages from the exposition of the laws destined for pagans clearly predominate, in which Philo is especially indebted to his Apologetic tradition.)

151. The dependence of "Christians" on Jewish Apologetics is known and has often been individually demonstrated, but a comprehensive analysis of form and content is still lacking.

152. Especially the later Jewish Apologists.

153. Rabbinic tradition also asserts that Abraham was the first missionary of Judaism. On that, cf. Str-B 3:195–96 and 215; Schmitz, "Abraham," 105–9; and Sandmel, *Philo's Place*, 77, 85. Sandmel and the others did not

notice that Hellenistic Judaism also saw Abraham as a missionary model, indeed, that the relationship of Abraham to paganism had been examined much more intensively here.

154. τήν τε ἀρετὴν αὐτῷ καὶ τὴν ἐπ᾽ αὐτῇ δόξαν ἐντεῦθεν ἐπιφανεστέραν συνέβη γενέσθαι. The term ἀρετή, which already came up in Ant. 1.155, means far more than only moral or philosophical virtue. The correlation with δόξα (cf. also the ἐπ᾽ αὐτῇ) shows that at least "praise" is meant. Indeed, the ἐπιφανεστέραν (in connection with what was mentioned previously about the *capabilities* of Abraham) seems to show that the meaning "divine power" is intended (respectively also the demonstration of force released by it). This important and essential meaning is widespread in Hellenism (cf. BAGD, "ἀρετή," 3, and the literature cited there). See below, pp. 120–67.

155. δεινὸς ἀνὴρ οὐ νοῆσαι μόνον ἀλλὰ καὶ πεῖσαι λέγων περὶ ὧν ἂν ἐπιχειρήσειε διδάσκειν.

156. Someone denying this relationship easily fails to notice that the Apologists wanted to present Abraham as a missionary. But looking around the Hellenistic world, one is soon struck by the close cooperation and overlap of cultural and religious mission.

157. A closer analysis of Hellenistic missionary activity will show that superiority is taken for granted both as the work of God and as a demonstration of an inner strength of spirit.

158. The legendary and novelistic descriptions have this very aim. More will be said on this later. We shall be especially occupied with the motif of rivalry.

159. I.e., on the earth, in the sublunary world (1. 3).

160. Eusebius, *Praep. Ev.* 13.12.5; here in the edition of the GCS 8, 2: 193.4–10. The Greek text of the portion given above in my translation is: Τέκνον ἐμόν, δείξω σοι, ὁπήνικα δέρκομαι αὐτοῦ ἴχνια καὶ χεῖρα στιβαρὴν κρατεροῖο θεοῖο. αὐτὸν δ᾽οὐχ ὁρόω· περὶ γὰρ νέφος ἐστήρικται λεπτὸν ἐμοί. (I would like to read the last two words with Christian August Lobeck [*Aglaophamus: Drei Bücher über die Grundlagen der Mysterienreligionen der Griechen, mit einer Sammlung der Fragmente der orphischen Dichter* (2d ed.; 2 vols.; Darmstadt: Wissenschaftliche Buchgesellschaft, 1961) 442 n. i.] instead of the transmitted λοιπὸν ἐμοί. To be sure, in his edition of the GCS Mras claims that this would be contradicted by what follows. I believe, however, that the following actually demands it. There the other persons are contrasted with Orpheus, who has already been shown in the introduction as a privileged receiver of mysteries. The purpose of the whole is to make it appear that the Jewish men of God stand far above Orpheus; he can only pass on a glimpse, but they can impart the full knowledge of the mysteries. The transmitted reading blurs this. The text goes on:) πᾶσιν (the reading στᾶσιν of Mras, shortened from ἑστᾶσιν—the clouds as subject—belabors the syntax and voids the meaning. The πᾶσιν suggested by

Lobeck (ibid.), following Hermann, seems justified, but not the δέκα πτυχαί) δὲ δεκάπτυχον ἀνθρώποισιν.

161. My trans. The text: οὐ γὰρ κέν τις ἴδοι θνητῶν μερόπων κραίνοντα, εἰ μὴ μουνογενής τις ἀπορρὼξ φύλου ἄνωθεν Χαλδαίων. This astounding parallel to John 1:18 is noted in Lobeck (ibid., 442 n. k.), following Grotius.

162. My trans. The text: ἴδρις γὰρ ἔην ἄστροιο πορείης καὶ σφαίρης κίνημ' ἀμφὶ χθόνα ὡς περιτέλλει κυκλοτερές τ' ἐν ἴσῳ, κατὰ δὲ σφέτερον κνώδακα. πνεύματα δ' ἡνιοχεῖ περὶ τ' ἠέρα καὶ περὶ χεῦμα νάματος· ἐκφαίνει δὲ πυρὸς σέλας ἰφιγενήτου.

163. My trans. The text: αὐτὸς δὴ μέγαν αὖθις ἐπ' οὐρανὸν ἐστήρικται χρυσέῳ εἰνὶ θρόνῳ· γαίη δ' ὑπὸ ποσσὶ βέβηκε (probably not to be translated as "to stride" with Riessler but rather as a good Greek assertion of existence; cf. LSJ, "βαίνω," A.2). χεῖρα δὲ δεξιτερὴν ἐπὶ τέρμασιν Ὠκεανοῖο ἐκτέτακεν· ὀρέων δὲ τρέμει βάσις ἔνδοθι θυμῷ οὐδὲ φέρειν δύναται κρατερὸν μένος. ἔστι δὲ πάντως αὐτὸς ἐπουράνιος καὶ ἐπὶ χθονὶ πάντα τελευτᾷ ἀρχὴν αὐτὸς ἔχων καὶ μέσσην ἠδὲ τελευτήν· (Abraham is allowed to see and to experience what is at first refused to the mystic: *the heavenly world* [cf. the lines which precede what is cited above from the Testament of Orpheus—193, ll. 2–3]. The text continues:) σὺ δέ κεν ῥέα πάντ' ἐσορήσω, αἴ κεν ἴδῃς αὐτόν· πρὶν δή ποτε δεῦρ' ἐπὶ γαῖαν. (Mras catches the meaning when he paraphrases: "If you were with God in heaven, you would easily overlook the universe; but before that [i.e., as long as you are still in the world] I want to show you his works, not him personally" [my trans.]. Distinctions are not made between lifetime and time after death, but rather between favored, not yet favored, and excluded. It is a part of the mysteries. At first, the mortal and the mystic have only the sublunar world. Then the Jewish man of God experiences the vision of the translunar, the divine world. The lines just cited and the ἴδρις γὰρ ἔην ἄστροιο πορείης seem to indicate that a heavenly journey is considered. A vision of the *essence* of God is not possible, according to the Apologists. See below, pp. 120–29).

164. "I want to announce it to those for whom there is authorization" (my trans.). For more on the introduction and the relationship between the ἱερὸς λόγος of the mystery, the νοῦς of the individual, and the mystical experience, see below, pp. 117, 143–48.

165. My trans. The text: ὡς λόγος ἀρχαίων (see pp. 124–25), ὡς ὑδογενὴς διέταξεν, ἐκ θεόθεν γνώμῃσι λαβὼν κατὰ δίπλακα θεσμόν.

166. It is improbable that simply the two tablets are meant, for the adjective δίπλαξ, as also the verb, means a *doubling* (something doubly placed, folded, or the like). But one cannot speak of a doubling of the law with the two tablets of the law; only the stones are doubled there, but not the law itself.

167. So also Riessler on the passage. Clearly the two forms should be related to one another. The question as to how that is to be understood will occupy us immediately (see also below, pp. 147–48).

168. My trans. The text: ἄλλως οὐ θεμιτὸν δὲ λέγειν· τρομέω δέ γε γυῖα, ἐν νόῳ·

169. My trans. and emphasis. The text: ἐξ ὑπάτου κραίνει περὶ πάντ᾽ ἐνὶ τάξει.

170. My trans. The text: (ὦ τέκνον,) σὺ δὲ τοῖσι νόοισι πελάζευ, γλώσσης εὖ μάλ᾽ ἐπικρατέων, στέρνοισι δὲ ἔνθεο φήμην.

171. Pp. 117, 143–48.

172. Friedländer, Apologetik, 305–7.

173. Ibid., 302–10.

174. My emphasis.

175. F. H. Colson in LCL on the passage. "μαθήματα, though often 'mathematics' in Philo, is here definitely restricted to astrology; cf. Mut. 71, 'The student of the nature of heaven, whom some call the μαθηματικός,' a passage which also illustrates Philo's regular assumption that Abraham before his call believed in Chaldaean astrology; cf. Abr. 69ff." (LCL, Philo 8.293).

176. My emphasis. The text: οὐδὲν ἔξω τῶν αἰσθητῶν αἴτιον ὑπολαμβάνοντες εἶναι.

177. My emphasis. The text: δι᾽ ἐπιστήμης τῶν πολλῶν καὶ δευτέρων καὶ γενητῶν εἰς ἀνεπιστημοσύνην ἰούσῃ (the soul) τοῦ ἑνὸς καὶ πρεσβυτάτου καὶ ἀγενήτου καὶ ποιητοῦ τῶν ὅλων καὶ διά τε ταῦτα ἀρίστου καὶ διὰ μυρία ἄλλα, ἃ διὰ μέγεθος ἀνθρώπινος λογισμὸς οὐ χωρεῖ;

178. My emphasis. The text: διὸ καὶ πιστεῦσαι λέγεται τῷ θεῷ πρῶτος, ἐπειδὴ καὶ πρῶτος ἀκλινῆ καὶ βεβαίαν ἔσχεν ὑπόληψιν, ὡς ἔστιν ἕν αἴτιον τὸ ἀνωτάτω καὶ προνοεῖ τοῦ τε κόσμου καὶ τῶν ἐν αὐτῷ. κτησάμενος δὲ πίστιν, τὴν τῶν ἀρετῶν βεβαιοτάτην, συνεκτᾶτο καὶ τὰς ἄλλας ἁπάσας, ὡς παρὰ τοῖς ὑποδεξαμένοις νομίζεσθαι βασιλεύς.

179. My emphasis. The text: ἀλλὰ τῷ περὶ τὴν ψυχὴν μεγέθει, φρονήματος ὢν βασιλικοῦ· καὶ δῆτα θεραπεύοντες αὐτὸν διετέλουν ὡς ἄρχοντα ὑπήκοοι τὸ περὶ πάντα μεγαλεῖον τῆς φύσεως αὐτοῦ καταπληττόμενοι τελειοτέρας οὔσης ἢ κατὰ ἄνθρωπον.

180. The difference is clear when one compares, e.g., what Philo says on Gen. 15:12 elsewhere: "'About sunset there fell upon Abraham an ecstasy,' that is what the inspired and God-possessed [ἐνθουσιῶν καὶ θεοφόρητος] experience is. Yet it is not merely this experience which proves him a prophet, but we have also the [letter fixed and recorded in the holy books . . . (Gen. 20:7). Now to every educated person (ἀστεῖος) the holy Word (ἱερὸς λόγος) assures the gift of prophecy]" (Her. 258–59). Here also the subject is the inspiration of Abraham; here too he becomes a prophet. What is said here is entirely in accord with that envisaged above, but the difference appears again immediately. Philo continues: "For a prophet (being a spokes-[person]) has no utterance of his own, but all his utterance [is foreign, belonging to somebody else], the echoes of another's voice (my emphasis). The [uneducated] may never be the interpreter of God, so that no worthless

person is 'God-inspired' (ἐνθουσιᾷ) in the proper sense. The name only be-
fits the wise, since he alone is a sounding instrument of God, smitten and
played by his invisible hand. Thus, all whom Moses (or Scripture) describes
as just are pictured as possessed and prophesying. . . ." (After the narration
of some biblical examples, Philo turns again to Abraham [263–65]:) "Admi-
rably then does he describe the inspired [ἐνθουσιῶν] when he says, 'about
sunset there fell on him [Abraham] an ecstacy.' 'Sun' is his name under a
figure for our mind [νοῦς]. For what the reasoning faculty [λογισμός] is in
us, the sun is in the world since both of them are light-bringers. . . . So
while the radiance of the mind [νοῦς] is still all around us, when it pours as
it were a noonday beam into the whole soul, we are self-contained, not possessed [ἐν ἑαυτοῖς ὄντες οὐ κατεχόμεθα]. But when it (the Nous) comes to
its setting, naturally ecstacy and divine possession and madness fall upon
us. *For when the light of God shines, the human light sets* (my emphasis);
when the divine light sets, the human dawns and rises. This is what regularly befalls the fellowship of the prophets. *The mind* (the Nous) [in us]
*is evicted at the arrival of the divine Spirit, but when that departs the
mind returns to its tenancy. Mortal and immortal may* [θέμις] *not share the
same home* (my emphasis). And therefore the setting of reason and the darkness which surrounds it produce ecstacy and inspired frenzy." Here and
elsewhere it is shown that the perfected ecstatic loses relationship
to him-/herself and to the world. One must differentiate here even more
strongly than Hans Jonas does (*Gnosis und spätantiker Geist* [2 vols.;
FRLANT NF 33, 45; Göttingen: Vandenhoeck & Ruprecht, 1954] 2: 70–
74); this problem can be better grasped tradition-critically than Jonas has.
Sandmel's book on Philo offers a good starting point because the figure of
Abraham is taken as the object of study and a differentiation is made between Philo's description of a "literal Abraham" and an "allegorical Abraham." But the conclusion Sandmel draws from this comparison seems to
neglect evident differences in content: "Philo's separation of the two Abra-
hams is no more than his literary device. It enables him to choose whether
to present a summary topic or, instead, exegetical details. . . . The Abraham
of the *Exposition* is exactly the same as the Abraham of the *Allegory*"
(Sandmel, *Philo's Place*, 187; cf. also 107, 189). (For the contrary, cf. perhaps *Abr.* 77 with *Det.* 159 or the interpretation of faith in *Abr.* 262–74
with corresponding passages in the allegorical commentary.) Certainly
there is not a total contradiction; certainly Philo understands both manifestations as supplementary, which the frequent overlapping in content and
form makes especially clear. But the differences must not be overlooked.
The differences, connections, and overlappings can best be understood if
one assumes that Philo reflects a tradition-critical development from ordinary Apologetics to an Apologetic (cosmic) mysticism to (individualistic, dualistic, acosmic) mystical speculation (cf. p. 181 n. 59). The concern of
Apologetics is too narrowly conceived by Sandmel. This allows him to move

the Abraham for non-Jews (the Apologetic Abraham) all too close to the Abraham for Jews (the allegorical Abraham). They are actually one concept for Sandmel's Philo (*Philo's Place*, 106–41). For the relation of Philo to the Hellenistic-Jewish legend about Abraham, cf., on the contrary, the short but important observations of Knox ("Abraham," 58–59). According to Knox, Philo comes upon an Abraham legend already determined in a missionary fashion.

181. My emphasis. The text: ὁπότε γοῦν κατασχεθείη, μετέβαλλε πάντα πρὸς τὸ βέλτιον, τὰς ὄψεις, τὴν χρόαν, τὸ μέγεθος, τὰς σχέσεις, τὰς κινήσεις, τὴν φωνήν, τοῦ θείου πνεύματος, ὅπερ ἄνωθεν καταπνευσθὲν εἰσῳκίσατο τῇ ψυχῇ, περιτιθέντος τῷ μὲν σώματι κάλλος ἐξαίρετον, τοῖς δὲ λόγοις πειθώ, τοῖς δ᾽ ἀκούουσι σύνεσιν. Thus the Philonic sketch of Abraham also does not conform to Sandmel's assertion (*Philo's Place*, 104, 200) that Abraham is not considered a missionary here, but only a proselyte.

182. My emphasis. The text: οὗτος ἅπασιν ἐπηλύταις εὐγενείας ἐστὶ κανών, δυσγένειαν μὲν τὴν ἐξ ἀλλοκότων νόμων καὶ ἐκθέσμων ἐθῶν, ἃ λίθοις καὶ ξύλοις καὶ συνόλως ἀψύχοις ἰσοθέους ἀπένειμε τιμάς, καταλιποῦσι, καλὴν δ᾽ ἀποικίαν στειλαμένοις πρὸς ἔμψυχον τῷ ὄντι καὶ ζῶσαν πολιτείαν, ἧς ἔφορος καὶ ἐπίσκοπος ἀλήθεια.

183. Str-B 2:523 (to John 8:33).

184. Str-B 2:574.

185. Cumont, *Oriental Religions*; Harnack, *Mission*; Reitzenstein, *Mystery-Religions*; Schürer, *Geschichte*, vol. 3; Paul Wendland, *Die hellenistisch-römische Kultur in ihren Beziehungen zum Judentum und Christentum* (4th ed.; HNT 2; Tübingen: Mohr, 1972). These works are singled out from the wealth of literature on the question touched on below. They offer the most detailed discussion—with a correspondingly abundant and sometimes exhaustive bibliography. Ulrich Kahrstedt (*Kulturgeschichte der römischen Kaiserzeit* [2d ed.; Bern: Francke, 1958] 305–8) has offered a good summary, unfortunately without examples and discussion.

2

Missionary Activity in New Testament Times

THE JEWISH MISSION[1]

The missionary successes of Judaism in late antiquity were impressive. One could find adherents of the Jewish faith in NT times in every part of the Roman Empire, as well as far beyond the imperial frontiers.[2] The density of the Jewish population was remarkably high in many places.[3] Harnack estimates that the number of Jews within the *Imperium Romanum* was more than four million;[4] Juster puts the figure even higher, at six or seven million.[5] The Jewish population in the diaspora of the Roman Empire was almost three times as large as the Jewish population of Palestine, the Jews accounting for approximately one-seventh of the total population of the empire.[6] The number of Jews living beyond the Roman frontiers can hardly be ascertained; however, there surely were important Jewish settlements in Babylonia and Media.[7]

The political and economic conditions of the six centuries prior to the Common Era alone cannot account for these figures. Among such conditions were the initial deportations of the Jews, their later voluntary settlement in colonies established by Persian and Hellenistic rulers, and finally, individual emigration from Palestine on account of the prevailing overpopulation and economic distress. The probably high growth of the Jewish population does not suffice as an explanation. The doubling of the Jews of Palestine since 700 B.C.E. contrasts with at least a fourfold, but more probably even a sixfold, increase of the total number of Jews in the empire.[8] In about two hundred years the Jewish population of Egypt and Asia Minor increased from almost nothing to a million each.[9] Whereas in this case one should take into account the vigorous colonizing effort of the Hellenistic rulers,[10] such an explanation does not apply to the growth of the community in Rome. During a period of somewhat more than one hundred years, a large number of Jewish congregations came into being in Rome.[11] Their total strength was at least forty thousand individuals.[12]

Therefore Harnack is completely correct in saying that the numerical strength of Judaism can be explained only if one takes into account, in addition to the no doubt significant natural increase of the Jewish population,[13] that pagans were won over to the Jewish religious community.[14] In my opinion, the numbers allow one to conclude that the increase due to conversion of the pagans was a much larger factor than the natural growth of the Jewish population. The spread of Judaism in the second and first centuries B.C.E. and in the first century C.E. thus compares quite favorably with the missionary successes of the early church. This is especially true when one considers that the mission of Jesus-believers, unlike that of Jews before them, received a soil already prepared. Indeed, the church came to inherit the successes of Judaism.[15]

The Organization of the Jewish Mission

Should one really suppose that this enormous expansion took place incidentally? To be sure, firsthand information about Jewish missionaries in the diaspora is mostly lacking; some exceptions will be duly noted.[16] Jewish missionary activity did not possess a central organization.[17] The large number of pagans who were won over to Judaism indicates that the Jews were strongly determined to recruit on behalf of their faith. This recruitment could not have been accidental and unpremeditated.[18]

Philo and Josephus make us aware that *the medium of Jewish propaganda was the synagogue worship and the exegis of the law presented there*.[19] Every pagan had free access since the *synagogue service* was a public event. One can also suppose that Jews encouraged the interest of pagans by invitations or similar means.[20] With a clear allusion to the Sabbath feast of *his own* time, Philo says the following about Moses (*Moses* 2.209–16, my ed.):

The prophet magnified the holy seventh day, seeing with his keener vision its marvellous beauty stamped upon heaven and the whole

world and enshrined in nature itself (209) . . . (211–12). Moses, great
in everything, determined that all whose names were written in his
holy burgess-roll and who followed the laws of nature should hold high
festival through hours of cheerful gaiety . . . [and specifically] by the
pursuit of wisdom only. And the wisdom must not be that of the systems hatched by the word-catchers and sophists who sell their tenets
and arguments like any bit of merchandise in the market, men who for
ever pit philosophy against philosophy without a blush, O earth and
sun, but the true philosophy which is woven from three strands—
thoughts, words and deeds—united into a single being for the attain-
ment and enjoyment of happiness . . . (215–16). It was customary on
every day when opportunity offered, and preeminently on the seventh
day . . . to pursue the study of wisdom with the ruler (ἡγεμών[21]) ex-
pounding (ὑφηγούμενος) and instructing (διδάσκων) what be said and
done in order to grow toward true life (καλοκἀγαθία) and to better morality and way of life. From that the practice results that even today the
Jews every seventh day occupy themselves with the philosophy of
their fathers, dedicating that time to knowledge and to the vision of
things which relate to nature (ἐπιστήμη καὶ θεωρία τῶν περὶ φύσιν).
For what are our places of prayer throughout the cities but schools
(διδασκαλεῖα) of prudence and courage and temperance and justice
and also of piety, holiness and every virtue by which duties to God and
people are discerned and rightly performed?

In *Spec.* 2.62–63 (my ed.) the Sabbath service is also presented as
training in philosophy (cf. also 2.61):

So each seventh day there stand wide open in every city innumerable
schools of good sense, sobriety, courage, justice and the other virtues,[22] in which the listeners sit in order quietly with ears alert and
with full attention, so much do they thirst for the sweet words, one of
special experience rises and sets forth (ὑφηγεῖται) what is the best and
sure to be profitable and will make the whole of life grow to something
better. But among the vast number of particular truths and principles
there studied, there stand out practically high above the others two
main heads (δύο τὰ ἀνωτάτω κεφάλαια): one with respect to God as
shown by piety and holiness, one with respect to humans shown by humanity and justice.[23]

One can see from the example of the Antiochene community (adduced by Josephus, *JW* 7.45) how successful the synagogue service
was: "Moreover, they were constantly attracting to their religious
ceremonies multitudes of Greeks, and these they had in some measure incorporated with themselves into their community."[24] The
self-assurance of the diaspora Jews increased accordingly. It ex-

pressed itself—far exceeding reality, to be sure[25]—for instance, thus in Philo (*Moses* 2.17–18):

> There is something surely still more wonderful[26]—even this: not only Jews but almost every other people, particularly those which take more account of virtue, have so far grown in holiness as to value and honor our laws.[27] In this they have received a special distinction which belongs to no other code. Here is the proof. Throughout the world of Greeks and barbarians, there is practically no state which honors the institutions of any other . . . (20–21). It is not so with ours. They attract and win the attention (ἐπάγεται καὶ συνεπιστρέφει) of all, of barbarians, of Greeks, of dwellers on the mainland and islands, of nations of the east and the west, of Europe and Asia, of the whole inhabited world (οἰκουμένη) from end to end.[28] For, who has not shown his respect for that sacred seventh day, by giving rest and relaxation from labor to himself and his neighbors, freemen and slaves alike, and beyond these to his beasts? . . . (23) Again, who does not every year show awe and reverence for the fast, as it is called,[29] which is best kept more strictly and solemnly than the "holy month" of the Greeks?[30] . . . (25) That the sanctity of our legislation has been a source of wonder not only to the Jews but also to all other nations is clear both from the facts already mentioned and those which I proceed to state.

Philo then turns to the discussion of the Septuagint translation (to be more precise, probably the Septuagint translation of the Pentateuch), in the course of which he keeps to the Apologetic tradition utilized in the *Epistle of Aristeas* (26–27).[31]

> In ancient times the laws were written in the Chaldean tongue, and remained in that form for many years, without any change of language, *so long as they had not yet revealed their beauty to the rest of mankind*.[32] But, in course of time, the daily, unbroken regularity of practice exercised by those who observed them (i.e., the laws) brought them to the knowledge of others, and their fame began to spread on every side.[33] . . . Then it was that some people, thinking it a shame that the laws should be found in one half only of the human race,[34] the barbarians, and denied altogether to the Greeks, took steps to have them translated.

With quite similar, probably traditional arguments, Josephus demonstrates (*Apion* 2.279–95) the spread of the Jewish law.[35] The example of the Jews makes it known everywhere, and it is imitated worldwide. Josephus employs here a very striking comparison: "As

God permeates the universe, so the law has found its way among all humankind."[36]

In the next section I shall demonstrate how such evidence shows that the Hellenistic Apologists regarded and proclaimed Judaism as the universal religion. But first one would investigate how these passages can document the actual propagandistic activity of the Jews in the Hellenistic world. These examples show in summary fashion (supported and complemented by many individual examples) that Judaism in the Hellenistic diaspora was held together most of all by the synagogue service, by its reading and exposition of the Pentateuch translated into Greek. In this way Judaism acquired and maintained its ability to attract converts.

To be sure, the edification of the synagogue congregation and the effort to win over Gentiles were kindred, indeed, nearly identical, tasks. The ever-present and powerful example provided by the piety of individual Jews also had a considerable propagandistic effect. Philo, above all, emphasizes this.[37] He is, however, only elaborating a *topos* often found in Apologetic literature,[38] one which surely corresponded to the actual state of affairs.[39] But Philo was not alone in wanting to extol the knowledge of the law on the part of individual Jews, who accordingly did not need to be given concrete legal directives.[40] A self-assurance widespread in Hellenistic Judaism manifests itself here.[41]

The contrast with certain contemporary Palestinian-Jewish spiritual currents is already clear-cut; this contrast becomes even more pronounced when comparison is made with the Pharisaic-rabbinic version of Judaism.[42] Yet Philo does not deny that the Jews were instructed through the exposition of the law provided in the synagogue service. On the contrary, he expressly tells us this.[43] After all, Philo's entire work is an interpretation of the law, and it must have been fundamentally intended for the purpose of edification at the synagogue service.[44]

The *exposition of scripture* in synagogue worship was decisive for the unity of spirit and life in the Diaspora. The lasting and widespread pagan respect for the Jews proved how strongly this unity was perceived by outsiders. A significant expression of the pagan recognition of Jewish unity is found in the legal and political treatment of the Jews by the Diadochi and above all by the Romans.[45] Individual pagan testimonies (including anti-Semitic ones) concerning Judaism also exist.[46] The unity of all Jews is not only presupposed but also often attacked. A widespread agreement among the pagan accounts can be recognized, provided one does not judge them by criteria obtained from the Pharisaic-rabbinical evidence.[47]

The unity of Judaism did not come from Jerusalem as an administrative or judiciary center.[48] To be sure, one should not underestimate the importance of Jerusalem as an ideal for the entire Jewish community. The Jews regarded Jerusalem, especially Mount Zion and the temple, as the center of the world. Evidence for this can be found throughout Apologetic literature.[49] This respect for the holy place expressed itself most visibly in the giant streams of pilgrims which flocked to Jerusalem, particularly at Passover.[50] In these pilgrimages the Diaspora Jews participated strongly.[51] Furthermore, one should mention the temple tax, paid also by Jews outside Palestine.[52] In addition, voluntary gifts were always being sent to Jerusalem.[53]

No Jewish institution possessed any central legislative, executive, or judicial authority over the Diaspora—at any rate not before the Jewish War.[54] Possibilities of intervention for Jerusalem institutions may well have existed, particularly in matters of advocacy and arbitration,[55] but these would have depended on moral authority, not on a judicial precedence of Jerusalem. It is not possible to prove that Jerusalem possessed a central doctrinal authority over the Diaspora community either. Goodenough has successfully demolished the old and widespread supposition that there was a central Jerusalem authority for the Diaspora, particularly in matters of doctrine.[56] At the same time, he has not satisfactorily investigated the question of why Judaism nevertheless did possess unity. This unity was surely anything but uniform and was not, strictly speaking, of an organized sort. Yet it existed and was effective. It could not merely have been an inner unity of conviction. Some outer framework must have persistently and successfully counteracted those centrifugal forces which as a matter of course affected the Diaspora community.

The synagogue worship by itself does not provide a satisfactory explanation. The persistent cohesion of all the Diaspora communi-

ties cannot be explained by the vitality of the individual Jewish congregations.[57] The continuous potential for interchange must have
existed, aided by the traveling proclivities of members of the Jewish
community.[58] How was such an interchange undertaken? What was
its intensity?

Philo and Josephus point to the *exegesis of scripture*. They do
not merely present their own insights and opinions. Research has
shown that both authors are heavily dependent on elaborate exegetical traditions.[59] Comparison of the two writers enables one to deduce communal traditions pointing to Jewish Apologetics.[60] The
other fragments of Jewish Apologetic literature which have been
preserved are also essentially exegetical in nature. Though I have
proceeded indirectly (the paucity of the sources allows no other
way), I feel compelled to conclude that one can recover *the scriptural exegesis of the Diaspora synagogue in Hellenistic-Jewish Apologetics*. In contrast to past scholarship, I believe that this Apologetic
literature worked heavily with tradition. This would imply that the
Hellenistic-Jewish Apologists were not private authors, but rather
exercised their activity in connection with the synagogue. Therefore, one cannot regard these texts as purely private compositions.[61] Although the Apologetic literature is preserved only in
fragmentary form, more has survived than other types of Jewish Diaspora literature. By itself this would not conclusively show that the
Apologists could be identified with the spirit of the majority of diaspora Judaism. But one can add the following observation to the fore-
going arguments: the various remnants of non-Apologetic,
non-Palestinian Jewish literature (and Palestinian documents devoted to the problems of the Diaspora)[62] are related to each other
insofar as they show similarities with or connections to Apologetic
writings.[63]

If the synagogue sermon was influenced by the spirit of Apologetics, then one can understand why the synagogue service was open
toward pagans and why the latter felt that they were directly addressed, for the continuing dialogue with paganism was then at the
heart of synagogue worship, in form as well as in content. The dialogue was a continuous pleading for understanding, a permanent
invitation—just as, conversely, it strove to make Judaism itself

more open toward the world. Regarded in this light, synagogue worship had the functions both of edification and of solicitation.

Thus the *Sitz im Leben* of Apologetic literature was, first of all, the synagogue service, more specifically, the exegesis of scripture therein. But the *Sitz im Leben* can be more accurately described on the basis of the way these works depended on each other, the existence of traditions, and similar considerations. On the strength of a source analysis of Philo's writings and Philo's various references to exegetical predecessors, Bousset postulated the existence of a Jewish academy in Alexandria.[64] But the hypothesis of one or a few distinct schools is not enough explanation, for several reasons. There is already much variety of motifs as well as genres in Philo, but much more so in the rest of Apologetic literature.[65] One can also point to the geographical dispersion of Apologetic activity.[66] Much more viable is a *common function or even profession which was not tied to a specific locality*. The exchange of traditions could then be explained by more or less widespread traveling of those people. Naturally, they must have received some training, though not necessarily always in the secluded sphere of schools. Training, especially of an advanced nature, in the *practice* of exegesis and the harmonization of exegetical opinions is conceivable in the context of exposure to a wide range of synagogue services. The travels of the novices could have begun very early. In addition, one can expect some formation of groups, which will be discussed presently.

When one views matters in this way, one gains new insight into a characteristic feature of synagogue organization. As I have already shown, although the exegesis of scripture was of decisive importance in maintaining the stability and cohesion of the synagogue, nevertheless the exegetes themselves were not synagogue officials.[67] The exegesis was carried out de facto by small groups of people.[68] The preceding arguments have shown that these special exegetes must have had contacts with each other. They appear only on the periphery of community organization, but this does not mean that their existence as such is doubtful but rather that they were not part of the administration and were—if not temporary volunteers —outside and above the framework of the individual congregations. I do not want to say that these individuals never settled down and were always traveling; Philo's own example is a case in point.[69] Moreover, there is a possibility that groups of these exegetes established themselves in particular localities. After all, Philo's work on the Therapeutae (though the situation there is very idealized and its historical core is difficult to grasp) speaks about people whose self-understanding and exegetical methods were often similar to those of the Apologists.[70] References for this will be given in the description of how Apologetics understood its own task.[71]

We possess hardly any direct evidence concerning the activity of the exegetes in Diaspora synagogues.

Some of the surviving texts *prima facie* seem to contradict the thesis presented here. I refer in particular to the above-mentioned passages from Philo on the Sabbath.[72] But the ἡγεμών in *Moses* 2.215 is Moses himself, whose hegemony surely served not as a model for the synagogue leaders as community officials, but rather for the Apologists. In *Spec.* 2.62 it remains quite uncertain who the "one of special experience" is. Where and how he gained his experience is unclear, as is his relationship to the local congregation. One thing that is certain is that the "experience" is supposed to signify that which elsewhere is described as "wisdom." But according to the ideal of the sage developed in the fourth and third centuries, a knowledge of the world (mainly acquired by traveling) belongs to "wisdom."[73] In Apologetic literature this ideal can be discovered at every turn. One cannot deny that this image of the sage was modified in speculative mysticism. But the Philo passage discussed here belongs to the Apologetic tradition. Finally, the passage from the *Hypothetica* (7.13) should be discussed in detail. According to this text, the prerogative to interpret scripture belongs to "one of the priests who happens to be present." Clearly no synagogue official is meant here (see the "who happens to be present" which—as shown by the sequel—is not always the case). One should take into consideration Philo's tendency to adapt the term "priest" to Hellenistic thought,[74] as well as his inclination to generalize the expression.[75] One should especially take into account his tendency to assimilate priests to prophets and sages.[76] Thus one can hardly suppose that here he has the Aaronic priesthood in mind. The simultaneous exercise of exegesis and of priesthood does not support this possibility. The interpretation of scripture does not acquire honor and significance through the priesthood, but conversely. The archaeological evidence from the diaspora also, in my opinion, refutes the hypothesis that the priests here necessarily belonged to the family of Aaron.[77] Thus the passage from Philo says that the interpretation of scripture was to be undertaken, as far as possible, by certain individuals not tied to the congregation. He calls them priests and probably means "priestly teachers." It is significant that a Roman funerary inscription is reported to have been erected for one who was regarded as a "priest and learned in the law" (*ἱερεὺς καὶ νωμύς; νομεύς* in the sense of *νομικός* is intended[78]).

One particular passage from Josephus is quite informative, especially when the parallel texts are also taken into account. I am thinking of *Ant.* 18.81–84. It runs as follows:

> There was a certain Jew (in Rome), a complete scoundrel who had fled (from his own country?) because he was accused of transgressing certain laws and feared punishment on this account. Just at this time he was resident in Rome, and played the part of an interpreter of the Mosaic law and its wisdom. He enlisted three confederates not a whit better in character than himself to the (Jewish) laws. Fulvia, a woman of high rank, [had come to them regularly and had become a proselyte] (*νομίμοις προσεληλυθυῖα τοῖς Ιουδαϊκοῖς*). They urged her to send purple and gold to the temple in Jerusalem. They, however, took the gifts and used them for their own personal expenses.[79]

Fulvia disclosed this to her husband, who, being a friend of Tiberius, apprised the latter of the whole affair. Thereupon the princeps ordered that the Jews be banished from Rome. In accordance with the command, four thousand Jews were called up and enrolled for military service in Sardinia.

This account teems with inaccuracies and improbabilities. How does Josephus know that the Jew in question had made himself liable to punishment? Which laws did this individual actually transgress, Jewish or pagan? The sweeping claim that the Jew was a scoundrel stands in contrast to the vague indication of his origin. Was his prior activity exercised in Palestine or elsewhere in the provinces? The Jews of Palestine maintained, as is well known, good contacts with the Jews in Rome. Did they then supposedly know nothing about the stay of this man in Rome, and thus did not accuse him before the Jewish community there? If, instead, the evildoer transgressed Roman laws, it is quite inconceivable that he could have avoided criminal prosecution in Rome.[80]

The criminal sought refuge in Rome, of all places, and in addition placed himself in the limelight of publicity! Josephus cannot help admitting that this refugee had success in Rome, though Josephus immediately adds that he falsely laid claim to certain functions. But he clearly was successful in doing this, and was even able to better his position by recruiting collaborators—naturally, according to Josephus, rascals of the same kind. In any case they were able to advertise quite successfully on behalf of the Jewish faith and the Jewish community; they even managed to win over one of the most distinguished Roman women, and it is intimated that she was not the only one.

Clearly these would not have been the first swindlers, and apparently Josephus wishes to present them as such. For this reason it is remarkable that Josephus, who is usually not at a loss for plain words, masks the accusation of ordinary swindlery in such involved phraseology, an accusation he clearly wants to make. Therefore this surely was not a cut-and-dried situation.

Josephus gets entangled in further difficulties in the subsequent part of his story. How did Fulvia discover the deception? Why is nothing said about Jewish legal proceedings against the three, who would indeed have committed nothing less than temple robbery? The community would have had a strong interest in punishing such an offense also because it would have damaged their public reputation. On the other hand, the crime of fraud of a few is no satisfactory reason for a decree of general banishment. If the Roman authorities had indeed wanted to punish in such a fashion all the pranks of foreigners, then the records would have registered more traffic leaving Rome than coming to Rome.

Tacitus's account is quite different:

> Another debate dealt with the proscription of the Egyptian and Jewish rites, and a senatorial decree directed that four thousand descendants of enfranchised slaves, tainted with that superstition and suitable in point of age, were to be shipped to Sardinia and there employed in suppressing brigandage: "if they succumbed to the pestilential climate it was a cheap loss." The rest had orders to leave Italy, unless they had renounced their impious ceremonial profane rites by a given date.[81]

According to this account, one is dealing with a large-scale action; the types of punitive measures also indicate this. The Jewish and

Egyptian cults were the victims; this probably means the members of the Isis cult in addition to the adherents of Judaism. There is no mention of our three friends and their patroness, nor of the crime which is described by Josephus. In any case, Tacitus's report of a joint conscription of members of both the Jewish *and* the Egyptian cults must be inaccurate. Not only the description of Josephus contradicts it, but also that of Suetonius. Suetonius recounts matters thus (*Tiberius* 36, my ed.):

> He abolished foreign cults, especially the Egyptian and the Jewish rites, compelling all who were addicted to such superstitions (*superstitio*) to burn the liturgical vestments together with all (cultic) vessels. Those of the Jews who were of military age he assigned to provinces of less healthy climate, ostensibly to serve in the army; the others of that same race or those who adhered to something alike he banished from the city, on pain of slavery for life if they did not obey. He banished the mathematicians, i.e. the astrologers as well,[82] but pardoned such as begged for indulgence and promised to give up their art.[83]

Here the astrologers appear together with the Egyptian and Jewish cults. Quite clearly the cults and practices themselves are in question, not only peripheral matters. Both the exercise of the cults and that of astrology are to be checked.[84]

The probable course of events was as follows: the increasing expansion of Judaism, of the Isis cult, and of astrology attracted the attention and concern of the princeps. Philo declares that Sejanus's hostility to the Jews also played a special role.[85] But the persecution must be seen within the larger framework indicated by the accounts of Tacitus and Suetonius. If the groups in question had simply maintained the status quo or grown through immigration, this reaction would hardly have been provoked. There must have been an aggressive expansion which transcended ethnic boundaries. Josephus's account may give a clue. The story is surely not in its entirety fabricated, since it actually creates great embarrassment for the narrator. That a woman from the most prominent Roman circles showed an interest in Judaism and was finally won over to it is probably historical.[86] It is also likely that the wife of Saturninus and the banishment of the Jews had something to do with each other—not because Fulvia was swindled but because she went over to the religion of Yahweh. Moreover, Josephus, because of his predilection for anecdotal narration, may have passed over the fact that Fulvia was only one of the more distinguished female proselytes; a hint of this, however, is still present. Only one of these ladies had Saturninus for a husband. His charge was the snowball which started the avalanche.

Josephus could hardly say that propaganda on behalf of the Jewish faith and, above all, the conversion of distinguished Roman women provided the grounds for persecution. The fact that Jewish missionary activity caused the suspicion of the princeps already had to be suppressed as far as possible; the fact that the conversion of Roman aristocrats to Judaism brought about the punishment of Jews had to be concealed completely. After all, Josephus was campaigning on behalf of Judaism with his literary activity, especially the *Antiquities*. Particularly important for him were the interest and the consent of aristocrats and intellectuals. Moreover, he was very much concerned with obtaining the favor of the princeps for himself and the Jewish religion in general.

Much less still could Josephus admit that Judaism and its representatives had been lumped together with adherents and missionaries of other religions. So Josephus had to doctor his narrative. With respect to the relationship of the Jewish mission to other missions, he employed the best tool for the manipulation of history, namely, silence. But total silence in face of the well-documented banishment of the Jews was impossible. So in this case he chose the second-best method, namely, moral disparagement. In order to avoid the danger that such moral turpitude would be quite generally attributed to all Jewish exegetes and missionaries, he presents it as an isolated case. Moreover, in the introduction he emphasizes that the Jews themselves were damaged the most by this behavior. A similar intent can be seen in the claim that Fulvia wanted to give a pious donation to the Jerusalem temple and that the three impostors prevented this. Comparison of Josephus's narrative with the accounts of Tacitus and Suetonius shows that Jewish missionary activity, just as that of the followers of Isis, was crowned with a degree of success which the Romans found eerie. Astrological practices probably increased along similar lines. Thus it is very likely that *the interpreters of the wisdom of the laws of Moses, depicted by Josephus, who were also active as missionaries, were not the only ones of their kind. They must be put into the wider context of a broad oriental missionary effort, wherein Isis worshipers, astrologers, and perhaps also others took part.*

Horace and especially Juvenal include the Jewish missionaries among the targets for their satirical mockery.[87] Thus propagandists for the Yahwistic faith must have been a typical feature of the capital already at the time of Augustus as well as in the subsequent period; this in turn presupposes that such missionaries must have been correspondingly numerous and assiduous. Juvenal confirms that which can already be found in Tacitus and Suetonius; he incorporates his caricature of the female representative of Judaism into a procession of oriental missionaries.[88] The Jewish mission formed part of the roundelay, so to speak, of Eastern cults with a missionary bent.[89] But first I would like to direct attention to Juvenal's description of the female propagandist of the Jewish religion, using it as a guide for a deeper understanding of the way Jewish missionary activity was organized and how it understood its own aims. The passage from Juvenal runs as follows:

> No sooner has that fellow departed than a palsied Jewess, leaving her basket and her truss of hay, comes begging to her secret ear; *she is an interpreter of the laws of Jerusalem, a high priestess of the tree, a trusty go-between of highest heaven.*[90] She, too, fills her palm, but more sparingly, for a Jew will tell you dreams of any kind you please for the minutest of coins.[91]

The pertinence of this passage to my previous arguments derives mainly from the first and most important of the titles given, namely, "interpreter of the laws of Jerusalem." But at first I would like to draw attention to some previously mentioned features. Juvenal has just described another conspicuous characteristic trait of Judaism, the sanctification of the Sabbath.[92] It is here indicated by the image of the basket filled with hay, a sort of haybox for the Sabbath dishes cooked on Friday.[93] But Juvenal also knows that the Sabbath is not only a sign of private piety but also the day for divine worship.[94] He is describing missionary activity which takes place outside the cult proper, and yet he is also referring to the latter.[95] To be sure, one should be wary in generalizing from this one detail. As part of his satirical technique, Juvenal is interested in the dramatic unity of place for the various missionary activities, namely, the bedroom of the aristocratic Roman lady. But other passages also show that under the catchword "sanctification of the Sabbath" *the differences between, as well as the common features of, the propagandistic activities of the Jews within and outside the cult itself* could be recognized.

The famous simile in Horace's *Satire* 1.4 (138–43) appears to presuppose this:

> As soon as I have leisure, I play with paper. This is one of those lesser frailties I spoke of, and if you should make no allowance for it, then would a big band of poets come to my aid—for we are the big majority—and we, like the Jews, will compel you to make one of our throng.

The comparison is concerned with conversion to leisure,[96] on the one hand to artistic leisure, on the other hand to Sabbath leisure. Naturally, the sanctification of the Sabbath is understood to be a communal characteristic of the Jews. *The recruiting activity is described as a movement*, its spread as a sudden attack. The one who has been overcome is drawn into the spell of the group and its customs and is entirely transformed. The swarming out of the Jews is already interpreted as a collective activity.

In Juvenal (14.96–106) the Sabbath also indicates the outermost as well as the innermost limits of Jewish missionary activity. That which on first sight appears to be but a single religious custom turns out to be the avenue to a different religion; the Sabbath establishes and maintains the bonds of common conviction.

> Some who have had a father who reveres the Sabbath, worship nothing but the clouds, and the divinity of the heavens, and see no difference between eating swine's flesh, from which their father abstained, and that of man; and in time they take to circumcision. Having been wont to flout the laws of Rome, they learn and practice and revere the Jewish law, and all that Moses committed to his secret tome, forbidding to point out the way to any not worshipping the same rites, and conducting none but the circumcised to the desired fountain.[97] For all which the father was to blame, who gave up every seventh day to idleness, keeping it apart from all the concerns of life.

The process of acculturation described here did not always take a whole generation (this particular length of time has its own satirical background) but was often more rapid. It is interesting that the law itself turns into a missionary by means of custom;[98] "law" here denotes the interpretation of the Jewish law. The triad "learning, practice, respect" is characteristic for a missionary practice geared to the interpretation of the law. The disparity between Jewish publicity and propaganda activity, on the one hand, and mystery-mongering, on the other, becomes even more obvious here than in *Satire* 6;[99] during the course of this work this will prove to be a paradox with great propagandistic effect.

A further important key word in the description of the Jewess in *Satire* 6 of Juvenal is *begging*. 3.13–14 and 292–301 also allude to it as characteristic for Jews; this is confirmed by Martial 12.57, 13. Cleomedes expressly says in the *Theoria Cyclica* (2.1) that one could find Jewish beggars in the proximity of the synagogue. In the portions of *Satire* 3 noted above, Juvenal also alludes to the connection of Jewish beggars with the synagogue. These texts are not talking about Jewish readiness to help needy fellow believers, nor about the relationship of poor Jews to their communities, but rather about Jewish importunity toward non-Jews.[100]

But if the Jewish synagogues were places where communal charity and help could be obtained, why were Jewish beggars who annoyed Gentiles tolerated in the neighborhood of synagogues?[101] Did not the synagogues thereby acquire an ill repute? Why did not the synagogue officials put an end to the activity of the beggars, which, after all, took place before their very eyes?

It is possible that poverty among Roman Jews increased during the reigns of Titus and Domitian because of the strong influx from plundered and impoverished Palestine as well as because of local political and economic pressures.[102] But I question whether this poverty increased to such an extent that outside help had to be solicited in the form of begging which became a proverbial nuisance. Had the Roman Jews become so poor since Cicero's time that they could no longer handle the distress in their own ranks, or at any rate check the abuse of pagans?[103] The Jewish community had long striven to maintain a good impression, to earn respect and influence, as well as to convert people of other faiths.[104] There is much in favor of the view that the Jews actually gained entrance to the distinguished and wealthy circles in Rome only after the Jewish War.[105] In the 70s not only the poor or the impoverished came from Palestine to Rome, but also the well-to-do and the influential, such as Agrippa and his sister Berenice[106] and Josephus.[107] To be sure, there was much internal distress to alleviate, and the Roman Jewish community was not overly rich. But a sudden impoverishment of the Roman Jews does not satisfactorily explain the nuisance of begging about which the pagans complained.

The real reason for the existence and toleration of Jewish beggars near (or in) the synagogues must be quite different. The best explanation for why the Jews did not hinder such activity can be deduced from the sixth satire of Juvenal. The female missionary here depicted employs her prophetic gift in exchange for a payment which she demands and in the end obtains. This interpretation involved essentially a religious value judgment; one could view the giving of this gift as done merely for the sake of material gain, or one could understand the solicitation of payment as a help to enable the present and future distribution of the gift. Naturally it called even more for a value judgment to decide whether the gift had worth at all, whether it justified or even necessitated a payment. The Jewish missionary and her followers surely judged matters otherwise than the satirist Juvenal; this is already indicated by the Jewess's titles which Juvenal transmits, as well as by the comparison to the other missionaries.

This so-called begging may well have been in reality the sign of a profession which intended to attract the attention of the pagans for the sake of the Jewish religion and its saving benefits.[108] If so, it could count on being able to elicit a resounding response to that which was offered and to be able to continue the missionary activity. When one looks at matters in this way, one can understand why the Jews, particularly the synagogue officials, did not drive out these beggars but allowed them to pursue their activity in the vicinity of the synagogues. One could even support this begging activity, since the community derived much advantage from it, despite all the difficulties which it could entrain. Surely it contributed more to an increase than a decrease in the number of visitors to the synagogue service and the number of community members, while the "beggars" themselves, through their activity, added life to the community worship.[109]

One does not go too far afield if one compares *the Cynic-Stoic*

wandering preachers to these Jewish propagandists, reviled as
beggars by their pagan Roman critics. The former also earned their
livelihood from what people gave them.[110] Quite generally, the
popular philosophers should be regarded as the models for preaching and missionary activity in late antiquity.[111] In many features of
Judaism the influence of the Cynic-Stoic begging philosophers and
of their views on life can be recognized.[112] Moreover, one can
easily see from Juvenal's general polemic against missionaries that
they all earned their livelihood from their propaganda. One should
reckon with a general pattern which was true for all pneumatics.[113]
Critics or grudgers understandably passed off this "livelihood" as
importunity, immorality, idleness, begging, cheating, and even
outright fraud. This criticism can be documented from very early
on,[114] and even today it is not entirely extinct. The criticism need
not always have been unfounded. A few bad examples were considered general proof.[115] Moreover, rivals here (as elsewhere) often
fought each other with similar critical and polemical arguments of a
moralizing sort.[116]

The very image of the beggar, as well as the parallels from the domain of Cynic-Stoic propaganda, indicate that the supposed Jewish
beggars were not sedentary but led a wandering life. There is archaeological evidence which shows that the synagogues provided
accommodations for travelers.[117] These structural features clearly
reflect a permanent and regular facet of synagogue life. It seems evident that these quarters were primarily intended for the lodging of
traveling teachers who participated in the synagogue service, and
were only secondarily meant for general philanthropy, which was
enjoined on individual community members or guests.[118]

Admittedly, we know very little about traveling undertaken by
Jewish teachers in the pre-Talmudic period. Nonrabbinical sources
yield only the following instances: the Jewish traveler with whom
Aristotle conversed;[119] the Jewish merchant in Adiabene, who
functioned as an honorary missionary, so to speak;[120] his Galilean
rival Eleazar;[121] and Fulvia's spiritual father, who is falsely accused
by Josephus of being a charlatan.[122] I suspect that one could also
include here the Jewish diplomat Eupolemus,[123] the unknown
founders of the Jewish community in Rome, who probably acted as

a united group,[124] and perhaps also a certain Agrius, for whom his colleague (!) Reginus erected a funerary stele in Rome on which the former is described as a meritorious εὐάγγελος.[125] At any rate, a general disposition to travel is quite well attested.[126]

Missionary activity of Jesus-believers, many of them even with original Jewish affiliations, deserves attention as indirect evidence too. The Lukan description of Paul everywhere establishing relations with the Jewish community and its synagogue worship serves the author's special aims[127] and thus has only limited usefulness in the actual reconstruction of the pattern of Pauline and, more generally, missionary activity of the early church. Nevertheless, it provides a recollection of the fact that missionizing Jesus-believers from time to time counted on the hospitality of friendly Jewish communities and occasionally were invited to give sermons.[128] Without some utilization of the Jewish communities as a base, the rapid expansion of missionary activity of the early church is inconceivable. The practice of hospitality which facilitated the work of the missionaries of Jesus and promoted their success[129] was inherited from Judaism.[130] The "possibilities" the "new" missionaries realized because of this practice worked with their models as well — as much as it helped the mutual transparency to continue.

How then did *the Jewish missionaries* operate? According to the Roman texts quoted, *first of all outside the synagogue, rather conspicuously and fairly obtrusively*. In my view, this means that *they employed all available spiritual talents*. In the Hellenistic world, where places of prayer were generally thought to be crowded with beggars,[131] the missionaries were also expected to show some tricks.[132] The transition between the religious and the pseudo-religious was fluid here. For example, the same term could designate both the professional buffoon and the sham priest.[133] In the oriental missionary religions the beggar priest became quite common.[134] Their image, like that of the Jewish missionaries, has been passed down to us nearly exclusively in caricature. But from these caricatures one can recognize that public attention was typically aroused by extraordinary, often ecstatic performances. The attention was directed not only at the missionaries themselves but also at the deity they represented. And they hoped not only for contribu-

tions but also for popular acclaim and conversions. Such was probably also the case with the Jewish missionaries.[135]

Jewish pneumatics existed in great variety. Josephus (*Ant.* 20.142)
mentions a Jewish magician Atomos (or Hetoimos)[136] who came
from Cyprus and was engaged by the procurator Felix, probably
as a court magician and counselor.[137] Luke knows of a Jewish magician and prophet in the service of the proconsul Sergius Paulus in
Cyprus (Acts 13:6–12) who is only a pseudo-prophet in Luke's
eyes.[138] In this respect the highly legendary report contains historically probable information, namely, about a common type and a
typical contest. That possibility is shown by the Josephus passage
discussed above, although it does not describe the same person, but
rather another version of a phenomenon which was most likely even
more widespread. One can recognize the influence these Jewish
pneumatics must have had, just as one can assume a relatively high
level of education and corresponding refinement among them, for
they knew how to treat royalty and people of high standing, including pagans.[139] Illiteracy and backwardness—in spite of the tendentious allusions of the pagan critics and satirists—are not necessarily
to be found among them, although they may have existed on occasion.

In *Ant.* 8.46–48 Josephus tells about the successful performance
of a Jewish miracle worker by the name of Eleazer for Vespasian and
his soldiers. By way of introduction, Josephus remarks that this
man, like many of his Jewish predecessors and contemporaries,
could appeal in his exorcism to Solomon, who not only had the same
talent but also handed down incantations to posterity. Many such
exorcists and texts must have existed in Josephus's time. Indeed,
Jewish magical texts and implements have survived until the present and invoke not only Solomon but also other Jewish heroes and
Yahweh or his angels as well. An examination of the magical papyri
proves that the influence of Jewish magic on pagans and Jesus-believers must have been enormous.[140]

But by the same token, the Jewish magicians also profited from
the pagan magicians. One cannot establish a clear-cut order of
precedence. There existed a continuous, mutual give-and-take
(especially between pagans and Jews). This problem of interconfes-
sionality will come up again below.

Juvenal's Jewish woman missionary is also a pneumatic. According to Juvenal, she is one of the numerous Jewish interpreters of dreams who practiced their art, which was generally known and esteemed in antiquity, for a paltry wage. Only someone following the criteria of later Jewish orthodoxy will find it strange that a *woman* is depicted with a spiritual gift and described as a Jewish functionary, even a high priestess. Female prophets and priests were familiar figures in Hellenistic times, and they were also expected to perform deeds worked by the spirit. The Jewish priestess mentioned in a Roman inscription could well have been a colleague of the one described by Juvenal.[141]

If one goes by such phenomena and not just by OT and Pharisaic-rabbinic criteria, one is not surprised when in Acts 19:13–20 miracle workers are described as sons of the Jewish high priest Sceva in Ephesus, although we know of no Sceva among the Jerusalem high priests of this period. A high priest in Hellenistic Judaism is no less improbable than the group appearance of exorcists.[142] This is not to call into question the legendary character of the Lukan narrative or its composition from several, originally disparate sources.[143] Nevertheless, the appearance of the sons of a (Hellenistic-Jewish) high priest as miracle workers seems no more fantastic than the remark in Acts 19:13 about wandering Jewish exorcists. Close examination reveals that these are fossils which do not fit the Lukan concept of a centrally oriented Judaism based on the Pharisaic-rabbinic orthodoxy just coming into its own in Luke's time.[144]

Hadrian's letter to Servianus is a good indication of how open to syncretism and its conceptions of pneumatics Judaism still was at the beginning of the second century. Hadrian writes about the situation in Alexandria:

> There those who worship Serapis are Christians, and those who call themselves bishops of Christ are worshipers of Serapis. There is no archisynagogue of the Jews there, no Samaritan and no Christian presbyter who is not a mathematician (astrologer), a soothsayer, or a quack.[145]

Pliny the Elder claims to know of a magical sect which traces itself back to Moses, Jannes, Lotapes, and the Jews.[146] Although the existence of this sect cannot be verified further and the information

about their heroes may be based on misunderstandings,[147] this notice presupposes at the very least the connection between Jews and
magic.

Hadrian and Juvenal are not the only pagan authors of the second
century C.E. who mention Jewish magic as a contemporary phenomenon: Apuleius,[148] Lucian, Celsus, and Numenius do so as
well.[149] In addition, there are the rabbinic and Christian attestations.[150] The church fathers' criticism of the Jewish magicians
shows that the latter's propaganda was still effective in later centuries. The famous passage in Origen, *Celsus* 7.8–10, demonstrates
the self-confidence of these miracle workers which became an interconfessional phenomenon.[151]

The pagan Celsus says that miracle men, mantics, and prophets
had been seen in Palestine and Phoenicia not only by him in his own
time (the second century), but also that they represented an age-old
phenomenon. Celsus mentions itinerant cultic preachers, pagans as
well as Jews,[152] as the most distinguished representatives of this
multibranched genre of pneumatics: "'There are many,' he says,
'who, although of no name, are moved without scruples and on the
slightest occasion, whether within or without the cultic places, ges-
turing like inspired persons;[153] they beg and roam in cities and
(army?) camps.'"[154] Thus there were quite a number of this breed.
Their namelessness indicates that they played down their individu-
ality for the sake of their pneumatic function, which agrees quite
well with some of the characteristics of the itinerant preachers described previously. They did not represent themselves, but rather
the respective sanctuaries. The distinction in the passage "whether
within or without temples" is easy to explain if one applies the above
analysis of the distinction in the Jewish mission between inner-
cultic and extra-cultic propaganda, with more or less the same propagandists. One could then assume that Jewish and non-Jewish cults
used a similar style of propaganda. The classification as beggars and
as itinerant prophets conclusively situates these people in the picture sketched above.

Celsus lists various expressions of the pneumatic consciousness of
such prophets (not spoken at the same time by the same persons): "I
am God or God's child or a holy spirit."[155] Such identifying ἐγώ εἰμι

formulae were common in Hellenism, and also in magic.[156] The following description of authoritative behavior as a "having come" is not limited to Gnosticism alone but is more generally found in oriental religions.[157] So also the Synoptic I-sayings of Jesus express the heavenly authorization of Jesus as "having come,"[158] and these sayings certainly did not originate in Gnosticism.[159] Likewise, there is talk of the coming of the prophets and the coming of God and of the messiah.[160] All of these passages have a more or less eschatological character. Gods are also often said to have come.[161] The prophets in Celsus then say:

> I have come, for the world is already passing away, and you, oh humans, because of [your] injustices, are coming to an end. But I want to save you, and you will see me returning again with heavenly power.[162] Blessed is the one who now worships me. But on all others I shall cast eternal fire, on cities and countries. And people who do not know their punishments will change their hearts in vain and moan. Those who have obeyed me I shall protect forever.[163]

This is certainly only one, probably stylized, example among many, which perhaps strengthens christological allusions for anti-Christian aims. In any case, prophets proclaiming an eschatological judgment and reciting soteriological-messianic statements certainly existed. I cannot detect any particular closeness to the apocalyptic concepts of history and the future, but perhaps there is a certain relationship with the judgment sermon of the Jewish Sibyl,[164] who in spite of all antipagan statements has a missionary intent;[165] she hopes to convert pagans of good will.[166]

An identification with the messianic statements of the Jewish Sibyl is possible only after an in-depth modification.[167] Nevertheless, such an identification would not totally contradict the Sibylline proclamation, for the Sibyl typically speaks of the messiah not only as a future phenomenon[168] but also as a past one.[169] This chronological vagueness is part and parcel of the messiah concept. The epiphany of a supernatural figure from heaven is, however, always clearly mentioned, although not *expressis verbis* a son of God. The extent to which the transcendental character of the messianic figure is emphasized can be seen in the fact that even historical figures are radically transformed.[170] Only in one passage, albeit an essential one, does the messianic action described have the character of a revelation decisive for salvation.[171] The tense is the imperfect! Conversely, the divine sons in Celsus are also royal figures, no matter how one understands ἐπανιόντα, for in any case they speak of their royal power.[172]

The prophets in Celsus are clearly identified as ecstatics.

> Whenever they have emitted such threats, they give off a series of unknown, insane, and totally unintelligible (utterances), whose meaning no one who possesses reason can discover, for it is obscure and worthless rubbish. But it gives every ignoramus (ἀνόητος) or charlatan (γόης) the opportunity (prized) above all things, to appropriate that which has been said in any way he or she wishes.[173]

With these last words Celsus calls attention to the fact that a state of dependence existed between the pneumatics, especially, of course, among those of the same confession, in fact, most probably a state of interdependence.

All of these examples prove the later "orthodox" assertion that the spirit had vanished from the Jewish communities with the last prophets of the Bible to be a tendentious construction.[174] In reality, one was familiar not only with numerous general charismatic phenomena but also with prophetic talents in particular, which one continued to take as a mark of spiritual distinction. The Jewish woman in Juvenal is also a prophetess, not just an interpreter of dreams.[175] Josephus cannot be used to support the Pharisaic-rabbinic thesis,[176] for in *Apion* 1.41 he never speaks of the spirit having abandoned Israel, but says only that the Jewish writings which had come into being since the Persian period are not on a par with those written previously because an "*exact succession* of prophets" (ἀκριβὴς διαδοχή) was lacking. What precisely this meant, and whether this exact succession ever existed, does not matter for this essentially ideological hypothesis. Josephus does not take it that seriously either. He reports elsewhere on various prophets up to his own time.[177] For the question I am pursuing it makes no difference if he terms them goëts, mantics, or prophets.[178] These terms reflect a personal value judgment, which, however, presupposes the existence of a divining capacity and activity among the persons concerned.

Our sources, including Josephus, do not show evidence of a

dearth of spiritual power, but quite the opposite. Josephus reckons the high priest Hyrcanus among the prophets.[179]

Thackeray correctly draws attention to the fact that Hyrcanus is thus characterized by the distinguishing mark of the ideal Hellenistic ruler.[180] These distinguishing marks were found in the Apologetic depiction of Abraham above and will be encountered below in the Apologetic representation of Moses.[181] Could it not be that some of the figures mentioned in what follows did embrace such ideals? In any case, some associated prophetic characteristics with messianic claims. A direct political and military aggressiveness was probably not always present, but was sometimes produced by the circumstances or subsequently added in the Romanophile presentation of Josephus and his tradition. The Essene Judas knew about all matters, especially, of course, about the future.[182] It is said of him that he had gathered a circle of disciples where one could learn prophecy.[183] The Essene Menahem was in possession of secret knowledge;[184] according to Josephus, this was common to more or less all Essenes.[185]

But there were prophets not only among the Essenes. Pharisaic prophets prophesied kingship to Herod's brother, Pheroras.[186] Judas the Galilean, founder of the party of the Zealots, probably possessed prophetic characteristics.[187] In the year 45 c.e., Theudas,[188] a Jew with a Hellenistic name (!) who was a prophetic miracle worker,[189] succeeded in gathering a huge crowd of people and in leading them to the Jordan together with all their belongings, where he promised a repetition of the miracle of the Jordan.[190] It is not stated in which direction the march proceeded. Was it too in the direction of the conquering Israelites?

Without giving the exact date, Josephus reports that before the Jewish War a band of men made their appearance in Palestine.[191] Probably because of their extraordinary deeds,[192] they were able to rouse a mass of people into a frenzy of enthusiasm ($\delta\alpha\iota\mu\sigma\nu\tilde{\alpha}\nu$)[193] and thereby to move them to march into the desert. Most likely this also was supposed to be a repetition of the exodus. In any case, one expected similar miracles to be worked by these prophets. That it was not a nationalistic or even an exclusively political group seems as clear as the fact that these people were, according to their own self-understanding and that of their enthusiastic public, genuine pneumatics, genuine prophets.[194]

It also seems doubtful whether this lively pneumatic activity was of apocalyptic provenance. The presence of eschatological hopes alone does not justify categorization as "apocalyptic." Similar expectations were shared by many groups within Judaism, even by Hellenistic ones.[195] One has to be more careful even before one claims that the hopes of the pneumatics described (including Theudas and his circle) were of an eschatological character. More than the conception of the exodus and of the time in the desert as a model for the present would be necessary to qualify for eschatological orientation because these concepts as such were not yet synonymous with such a perspective in those days. The prophets just mentioned seem to have been of Palestinian origin all the same.

Such is not the case with the prophet on whom Josephus reports immediately afterward.[196] He was a Diaspora Jew from Egypt, perhaps even a proselyte.[197] He too proved his pneumatic capabilities by successfully gathering thirty thousand people (certainly Jews; in Egypt?)[198] about himself. He marched with them through the desert and finally reached the Mount of Olives. One can imagine that this march also bore reference to the exodus tradition. When he promised that he would cause the walls of Jerusalem to collapse by a single word and thereby enable his troops to march into the city and occupy it, he could not have had in mind only the fulfillment of the prophecies of Ezek. 43:1–6 (cf. 11:23 and 44:1–4) or Zech. 14:4, for in both cases it is Yahweh who acts, whether in the entrance into the temple from the Mount of Olives or in the battle of the nations starting from the Mount of Olives. Since the march through the desert refers to the exodus, a possible parallel could be the taking of Jericho at the time of the conquest,[199] but that would mean that this prophet would be equating Jerusalem with the godless Jericho and the Jerusalemites with the Canaanites.

That one was thinking of a miraculous conquest of an unbelieving city could be reflected in the fact that Jerusalem Jews took part in the defense and massacre of this crowd of co-religionists, who can scarcely have represented a military threat.[200] Was this a conscious staging of the pilgrimage of the nations under a perspective slightly different from what the older prophets had had in mind? Was there behind this march the desire that diaspora Judaism, coming home from their dispersion, and including the proselytes as precursors of the great pilgrimage of the peoples, should wrest the holy city not only from the pagan Romans but above all from the unworthy Palestinian Jews, not by military aggression but in a miraculous spiritual assault? Could this be an extreme intensification of the occasional devaluation of the ethnic Jews vis-à-vis the proselytes in the Apologetic tradition of Philo?[201] But the brief descriptions of this peculiar episode do not permit more than these rather speculative questions.

At the very least, however, the story proves that the pneumatic phenomena reported by Josephus were not limited to Palestine, but rather that connections with the Diaspora existed. The frequent reports about such events in Palestine appear to represent but a selection, made by the historian to explain the genesis of the Jewish War. In my opinion, this view is supported by the observation of Josephus's tendency to more or less forcibly situate these phenomena within an immediate political context. Most of the evidence for the experience of spiritual power in Palestine would have resisted such a tendentious approach, even if it was as forced as Josephus's.[202] Events in the diaspora would give even less of a basis or reason for such form of interpretation and integration into the history of the Jewish rebellion because Jews of the diaspora took nearly no part in the first Jewish War and remained loyal to the Romans,[203] in contrast to the time of the second Jewish War.

Josephus himself also belongs to the Jewish prophets of the NT period.[204] In his prophecy before Vespasian, he terms himself a messenger sent by God who in his prophesying is concerned with God's will. The beginning of this prophetic saying reminds one of the self-portrayal of the prophet in Celsus:[205]

> You imagine, Vespasian, that in the person of Josephus you have taken a mere captive; *but I have come to you as a messenger of greater [things]*.[206] Had I not been sent before on this errand by God,[207] [then I would have known what the law of the Jews demands] and how it becomes a general to die.[208]

There follows the prophecy of the coming enthronement of Vespasian and also of his son, and the prophecy closes with the significant words "For myself, I ask for stricter custody, so that you can punish me if I have dared to trifle with the words of God."[209] It seems that Josephus understands his prophecy as a messianic one,[210] quite analogously to the prophecies of Jeremiah and Deutero-Isaiah concerning foreign rulers.[211] It appears to belong within the concept of Judaism as the universal religion, a concept which is discussed in more detail below.[212] For Josephus this testimony of his pneumatic gift, proven by the subsequent events, made possible his far-reaching missionary activity,[213] which was apparently quite successful.[214]

In surveying the pneumatic phenomena and especially prophecy of Judaism in late antiquity, one must also mention Philo.[215] First one must mention the passages in which Philo identifies prophecy with what is actually speculative mystical piety,[216] which is his main concern. These passages show that Philo wants prophecy to be seen as a present pneumatic phenomenon. We shall not, however, concern ourselves further with this passive, quietistic form of prophecy, which is bent on savoring God.[217]

Philo also knows another, more active form of prophecy going beyond older Hebrew scriptures. Its model is most of all the Apologetic depiction of Abraham and Moses. For this I would like to refer to the passage cited above, which argues for Abraham's missionary significance using his prophetic and royal importance as evidence.[218] The form of prophecy described there I find first in the description of the Septuagint translators.[219] One might be astonished at this thesis, but I have already pointed out that, according to Philo, translating the Torah into Greek meant breaking the limits of the law, which was in fact appropriate for the law because of the universal significance of the Mosaic work.[220]

Thus the Bible became its own first and most important missionary. Its missionary significance was proved precisely by the fact that a king was interested in it, commissioned its translation, and supported it.[221] The translators proved their wisdom, and thus their ability to translate, in conversations at the king's court.[222] Their ability had to correspond to the magnitude of their task. The difficulty came from their object's significance, which was of a universal nature not only by virtue of its being a royal text but also and above all because it was a prophetic text. One was "to translate laws which had been prophesied by oracles."[223] According to Philo, translating was an essential prophetic function, and thus the genesis of the original text was basically a process of translation too.[224] It is certainly not unintentional that Philo then also describes the translation activity of the seventy as a prophetic process.

Of further note is the fact that Philo places the translators in the cosmic realm, as it were:

Sitting here in seclusion with none present save the elements of nature, earth, water, air, heaven, the genesis of which was to be their first theme as hierophants, for the laws begin with the story of the world's creation, prophesying in ecstasy, as it were, and under inspiration, they wrote, not each several scribe something different, but the same nouns and verbs, as though dictated to each by an invisible prompter.[225]

Therefore, the seventy are not considered to be translators, but hierophants and prophets in pure thought, "whose sincerity and singleness of thought have enabled them to go hand-in-hand with the purest of spirits, the spirit of Moses."[226] The execution of the translation thus implied a certain coincidence of the translators with the author which presupposed and included a functional relationship.

A structural analogy to these processes of the genesis and handing down of the text is presupposed when Philo calls his exegetical predecessors "divine (i.e., divinely sounding) men" ($\theta\epsilon\sigma\pi\acute{\epsilon}\sigma\iota\iota$ $\check{\alpha}\nu\delta\varrho\epsilon\varsigma$).[227] They too are shown to be prophets in accomplishing their exegetical activity. Philo also depicts his own exegetical activity as prophetically inspired in four passages.[228] *The interpreters of the Bible, the exegetes, are therefore for Philo the prophets of the present.* They are capable of setting free the spirit bottled up in the composition of holy scripture (or in the exact succession of the prophets, according to Josephus). Insofar as they themselves did not create the text which is to be interpreted, the source of the spirit, they are subordinated to it. But insofar as the spirit speaks through their exegesis, they are quite equal to the prophets of old. The spirit has not vanished; it has merely modified itself. But with this very modification something like a return to the beginning occurs. I would like to analyze further this understanding of tradition shortly, but first I want to finish the survey of the activity of Jewish missionaries.

The circle is now complete. Philo's conception of the exegetes leads right back to the Jewish woman so impressively described by Juvenal. She too is both biblical interpreter and prophetess. Philo and some of his colleagues probably would not have liked to be compared with such a beggar priestess. After all, they strove for a nobler behavior and performance than that which this prophetess reveals—even if one takes the exaggerated caricature into account. Those Jews who, like Philo, had received more Greek education displayed a greater restraint toward miracles than others. In Jewish Apologetics, many gradations between belief in miracles and skepticism existed,[229] but these differences were not fundamental ones. In spite of varied evaluations of pneumatic details, there was a consensus that possession of the spirit was necessary and real,[230] and also that the interpretation of the law was the most important spiritual function.[231]

There was also a consensus on the efficacy of possession of the spirit,[232] including its effectiveness in propaganda.[233] What all these Jews had in common was the confidence that they possessed knowledge of forces which move and hold together the world, as well as the confidence that they could use this knowledge appropriately and effectively. One felt superior to the non-Jew on both points.[234] The self-confidence common to these people was no doubt rationalistic in its structure. But rationalistic arguments were only a thin veneer over a sense of reason which was totally transformed from what it had been in the classical Greek world; OT faith strengthened this thin veneer a little for a while. But under it a pneumatic rationalism had grown strong and philosophy proper devoted itself more and more to spiritual power. There seemed to be no way of stopping the triumphal procession of the pneumatics and with them of the belief in miracles, of whatever kind, past, present, or future.[235] Scriptures, cult, interpretation, reason, and spirit, now could interact freely.

All extracultic activity of the Jewish pneumatics was propaganda for the scripture-related cult itself as the locus where the individual pneumatic powers originated and were collected. One could experience even greater things in the cult than outside of it. It was here that one set eyes upon the source of the spirit, holy scripture. The seemingly so disparate evidence about the Jewish worship service, on the one hand speaking of scriptural interpretation throughout the whole service[236] and, on the other hand, speaking of a strong pneumatic activity,[237] easily leads to the conclusion that *the various spiritual manifestations within the cultic place and the worship service were different forms of scriptural interpretation.* The length of the worship service from early morning until afternoon provided sufficient time for a diversity of forms.[238] The many and varied genres of Apologetic literature, fragmentary as they are, impart a certain impression of this abundance of cultic forms. The idea that scriptural interpretation had to be strictly bound to one pericope is false; so is the idea that it needed to confine itself to one kind of expression alone.

Several other observations provide further evidence that the synagogue ceremony, determined by the duality of Scripture reading and scriptural interpretation, afforded an occasion for lively activity which was nothing short of theatrical.[239] First one should mention a third element that is not always mentioned because it is obvious, namely, prayer. It is closely related to scriptural interpretation.

Then there is the circumstance that numerous people were involved in the ceremony whenever possible. This further contributed to the variety of cultic life.[240] The majority of the assembled community participated more in an accompanying fashion, particularly through acclaiming applause.[241] The ceremony was thus in reality a performance before an audience, a spiritual theater.

This theatrical character of the worship service also revealed itself in synagogue architecture. In Epiphanius we find the following remark:

> There is a proseuche in Sichem, which is now called Neapolis, outside of the city on the plain, at about a distance of two milestones, built by the Samaritans, who imitate the Jews in all things, like a theater (θεατροειδής) in the open air and on a spot which lies free under the sky.[242]

It is true that this note dates from the fourth century and refers first of all to a Samaritan place of prayer. Nevertheless, Epiphanius, who had a certain familiarity with Palestine, expressly designates it as an imitation of Jewish models, thus alluding to an older Jewish custom. True, the reference here is to open structures, but the architecture of the closed Jewish synagogues also seems to indicate that the worship service was supposed to be a performance for an audience.[243] There was, after all, an open area extending from the front into the center, a kind of stage where the participants in the liturgy could act.

Thus the corresponding comments of Jerome and Chrysostom about the Jewish worship service do not seem to be simply polemical inventions.[244] In his commentary on Ezekiel, Jerome writes polemically about Jewish preachers, "They persuade the people that what they invent is true; then, in a theatrical manner, they invite applause and shouting *(in theatralem modum plausus concitaverint et clamores).*"[245] In Chrysostom one reads *(Homily against the Jews 1, 2)* that in the synagogues one played as if on stage (παίξουσιν καθάπερ ἐν τῇ σκηνῇ).[246] One can no more dispute here that for the sake of polemics a parallelism to the pagan theater was insinuated. Philo, on the other hand, had emphatically denied that in Jewish worship any theatrical performance was given.[247] But both points of view must have had a common point of reference in order even to conceive of such a comparison with the theater or of its rejection.[248]

Of course it was not pagan tragedies and comedies which were presented in the synagogue, but rather the worship services of those who believed in Yahweh, but this was precisely a well-organized presentation for an audience. The example of Ezekiel the Tragedian proves that there could even be theater performances in the narrower sense. Naturally, however, the presentation was essentially focused on the manifold variation of the art of the word. The immediacy of oral expression was probably preferred. A written fixation most likely only followed the presentation. It was used as teaching material and as a substitute for the live production in those cases where such free-lance artists were not personally available and also for purposes of study. The OT already considered art, especially of the word, as the sign of a God-given talent.[249] In this art, the representatives of wisdom thought excelled.[250] In the postexilic period the wisdom movement further developed this domain. The creative capability of the wise person was inspired.[251] Highly skilled performances in the sense just outlined must therefore have been looked upon as pneumatic demonstrations.

Considering what has been said above, and bearing in mind that since the days of Jesus ben Sirach the Jewish sage (the actual charismatic) was essentially an interpreter of scripture,[252] then one can say that the worship performances of the especially talented revealed and actualized the divine power contained in holy scriptures in manifold ways. The spirit portrayed and communicated itself essentially in the interpretation of the scriptures. But since this pneumatic process manifested itself in the ability of the individual charismatics, it thus appeared in a variety of forms and obviously invited a comparison between individual achievements. The natural result was that differences were noted and judgments passed. These judgments can hardly have been limited to the audience; the performers themselves must also have been influenced and determined by them, which probably created a competitive atmosphere.[253] However, this conjecture cannot be substantiated by direct evidence from our spurious knowledge about actual synagogue service. Indirect hints are given by the theological thinking of Apologetics, which will be discussed in the following. This way of thinking implies a competitive structure and is not stingy with comparisons and judgments.[254]

There is even less chance in satisfactorily clarifying the extent to which the liturgy of the Sabbath service had esoteric characteristics. On the whole, it was certainly oriented toward the public.[255] It is, however, undeniable that mysterious elements were characteristic of the Jewish service too. The tradition enunciated in the service possessed an ancient history. It also originally came from another linguistic realm. Also the existence of an actual cultic center like Jerusalem, which was, moreover, situated in the East, could have a mysterious effect, especially because here the ancient language was still spoken and used in the cult. Moreover, the Jews preserved peculiar liturgical (and private) customs. What underscored the mysterious character of the Jewish religion was that its essential aim was to withhold from general view the actual object of Jewish religious worship, the deity itself.[256] All this had entered into a strange alliance with syncretistic elements, whereby the latter—though widespread—contributed to an even stronger mystification, because they were the expression of a general yearning for the enchantment of the world (to deify humanity).

Any doubts about the existence of a fairly massive syncretism in the synagogues should have been dispelled at the very latest with the work of Goodenough.[257] In my opinion it is also beyond doubt that this syncretism betrays the closeness of the Jewish synagogues to the Hellenistic mysteries and to the philosophical schools which had come to behave more and more in accordance with the mysteries.

For all that, the synagogue service of a normal Jewish community did not thereby become a mystery performance.[258] Participation was not limited to the "initiated." This does not, however, exclude the possibility that a portion of the entire ceremony was set off by a special liturgical act as a mystery, namely, by excluding the uninitiated and by only then bringing the service to its mysterious climax.

In addition to the existence of mystery elements already mentioned, a basis for this thesis can be found in two already cited texts: the so-called Testament of Orpheus from the fragments of Aristobulus and vv. 96–106 of the fourteenth satire of Juvenal.[259] One could also add a number of passages from Philo in which there is talk of guarding an *arcanum* which must not be profaned.[260] Finally, one could mention that a Roman decree cited by Josephus refers to cultic meals of Jewish communities;[261] following the archaeological material provided by Goodenough,[262] one could interpret these as mystery meals. If these meals were constitutive parts of the normal service, a selection of participants was necessary anyway, for the circumcised were not allowed to eat with the uncircumcised. This argument would be strengthened by the Juvenal passage already mentioned, where circumcision is a sign of admission to certain mysteries. According to this thesis, then, it would be circumcision which conferred the right to participate in the full service.

It must, however, be noted that nowhere, not even in the passages cited, is there talk of a division of the normal Sabbath service. There is likewise not a single reference to a provision for common meals anywhere in the liturgy of the Sabbath celebration we know of. The mention of the baskets of the Jews would seem to indicate that one took care of one's own food supply for this long day. The common meals seem to have had their locus in special events and feasts, which were probably by special admission only, with circumcision the minimum requirement (for males). It is easy to imagine that such special events and festal ceremonies could much more easily be organized as actual mystery celebrations and that they could eventually also give rise to all manner of extravagance, just as to speculative mysticism of the type one finds in the allegorical commentaries of Philo.[263]

Since, however, the Apologetic biblical interpretation which was directed to the public (the Testament of Orpheus in its present form being an example of this exegesis) contained motifs partly mysterious and mystic, one could assume that a certain differentiation between the more exoteric and the more esoteric elements of the service was attained in a much simpler manner, which implied no basic division. The basic monistic structure of Apologetic exegesis would also, in my opinion, have resisted such a division in the liturgy. It is possible that a quite natural division resulted from the length of the service. One can hardly assume that all the participants continually paid attention for hours on end, or that all took part in the whole service. The level of participation and the ability to understand most likely themselves constituted a simple principle of selection. Accordingly, one could assume a natural progression from the general to the specific, from the simple to the sublime.

To the person only partially interested or encumbered by difficulties in understanding, the specific and the sublime would appear to be mysterious and concealed, and he or she would leave being bored or confused. For those who persevered and understood, and naturally all the more for those performing, the whole thing could appear to be a continuous process, an increasing clarification, a revelation of the essential and a progressive unveiling of the divine. A growing tendency toward the mystical, as well as toward the ecstatic, would have been in keeping with this. The difficulty for the listener and the viewer must have repelled and attracted at the same time.

But this can never be more than a hypothesis. That among the pneumatic phenomena introduced there existed decidedly mystical and ecstatic ones seems to be certain on the basis of the references in Apologetic literature. They evidently enjoyed special appreciation. It was the mental sinking into the cosmic mysteries and the ecstatic celestial migration, the residence in the astral world which certainly had the highest value,[264] namely objectively deepening all Apologetic theology. It was here that the pneumatics experienced the foundation and purpose of that which they advocated in their missionary work: the absolute superiority and closeness of the Jewish God.

The Theological Foundation of the
Jewish Mission

I cannot here present the theology of the Jewish mission in detail, for that would go beyond the purpose of this study. I shall only outline the essential theological motives of the Jewish missionaries.

THE TRUTH QUESTION

The Jewish missionaries were convinced that they could and should contribute to the solution of the truth question. Thus the author of the *Epistle of Aristeas* has the fictional writer of the epistle say right at the start:

> I perceive that you possess a yearning to know, a quality which is the highest possession of man—to be constantly attempting to add to his stock of knowledge and acquirements whether through the study of history or by actually participating in the events themselves. It is by this means, by taking up into itself the noblest elements, that the soul gains pure intention and having fixed its aim on piety, the noblest goal of all, it thus uses this as its infallible guide and so acquires a definite purpose. It was my devotion to the pursuit of religious knowledge that led me to undertake the embassy to the man I have mentioned (the Jewish high-priest). . . .[265]

What the *Epistle of Aristeas* has to offer as truth, even in matters explicitly religious, corresponds to the "love of learning." The horizon of experience is expanded, not transcended. There is no striving for a fundamental change, but for an improvement, in the sense of an augmentation effected by experiential learning. The answer to the truth question thus follows general criteria which are clear and valid for everyone. This emphasis on commonality, not only in the way of stating the question but also in presenting criteria for its answer, as well as the emphasis on general validity were essential concerns of the Jewish Apologists. Consequently, the debate with paganism about Jewish belief was conducted on the basis of pagan forms and with pagan methods.

Also characteristic of this attitude is the beginning of the *Antiquities* of Josephus. In this work Josephus certainly pursues a religious purpose, but that does not exclude the possibility that he intends his work to meet a Hellenistic thirst for education (1.5–9, esp. 8); it includes this. There is no break between this general Hellenistic interest in παιδεία and the religious interest of his pagan readers (Josephus takes the latter into account in 1.14–17); rather, there is a smooth transition. General knowledge and religious interest are closely associated not only for Josephus but also for his Apologist colleagues and the Hellenistic world in general.[266]

To judge by the beginning (1.1–4) and the conclusion (2.287) of his writing against Apion, Josephus sees in the critical objections of pagan readers to his presentation of the history of Jewish belief in the *Antiquities* an assault on truth itself. Josephus expresses the opinion at the end of his apology that he has clearly and unequivocally refuted these attacks. It is quite clear that the debate is conducted and concluded on a rationalist basis and that the rational assent of the readers is expected.

In taking up the general truth question and explicitly associating it with the contemporary aspiration for knowledge and culture, the Jewish missionaries were not guided by a superficial desire for some type of link to this aspiration. It was instead a fundamental concern connected with their understanding of God, which will be analyzed below.

Before I speak of this, I would like to point out that the self-understanding of the Apologists, which thought it could give an answer to the questions of the Hellenistic world, should not simply be confused with cheap boasting—at least insofar as we are dealing with the self-understanding of the authors and their concerns. What Josephus has to say also holds for the good faith of the other Apologists:

> Here I have alluded to them (Jewish laws and constitution) only so far as was necessary for my purpose, which was neither to find fault with the institutions of other nations nor to extol our own, but to prove that the authors who have maligned us have made a barefaced attack on truth itself (*Apion* 2.287).

When Josephus frequently reproaches and boasts in his apologia, he does it for the sake of the truth, not with a hostile purpose or contrary to his own better knowledge, but for the sake of the truth which is undivided and equally valid for all.[267] This conviction of Josephus and his Apologetic colleagues must be accepted. Our aesthetic judgments on the Apologists' mode of expression, which seems to be bombastic, must not become a judgment of the content of their work.

Since, in Apologetic thinking, truth was closely associated with rational proof, truth and fact became synonymous. Comparison and argumentation had only to bring to the fore what actually was the case. That may have been disguised, forgotten, or not yet known, but it was basically accessible to everyone. The introduction to the *Epistle of Aristeas*, as well as the first chapters of the *Antiquities* of Josephus, exemplify for all Apologetics that the Jewish mission saw itself as an enlightenment movement.

THE GOD QUESTION

Apologetics had learned from its predecessor, the skepticism of the wisdom tradition,[268] that the essence of God is beyond human observation.[269] However, in opposition to skepticism and in union with the older wisdom movement, interest focused ever more on the activity of God as an object of genuine and complete knowledge of the divine. It was held to be decisive that God encounters humans as one who acts. According to *Apion* 2.190–91, God is to be known on the basis of his works;[270] according to *Apion* 2.167, it is on the basis of his power (δύναμις). That the divine δύναμις is the way that the world and humanity encounter God is even more true for Aristobulus and for the *Epistle of Aristeas* than it is for Josephus.[271] It is important that in such contexts God's ἀρετή can be mentioned.[272] It thereby becomes clear that the ethical understanding of this concept has receded into the background and that now it can be used as a designation for divine power and significance. We must ask whether the anthropological use of this word in Apologetic texts is not to be understood first and foremost with this nuance.[273]

In all that has been said up to now, the OT concept of creation is paraphrased, but in a significantly modified form. True, the Apologetic texts contain some set phrases about the creator God and the act of creation,[274] but the real interest of the Apologists focuses on the continuing activity of God. The concept of creation is transformed by the idea of process.[275] In seeming contradiction to this is the fact that Josephus in the *Antiquities* explicitly presents the creation as the first of the Jewish antiquities (according to *Apion* 1.39,

the creation was almost three thousand years before Moses). In ac-
tuality, however, Josephus does not thereby refer, as does the Yah-
wist, to God's first act of salvation;[276] rather, he refers to primordial
time, the primordial past. The beginning is meant, that which is
prior and superior to delineated time, the ἀρχή as understood
by the Greeks. Whereas the OT belief in creation is completely
stripped of mythical features, the latter are again added in the account of Josephus. He uses both figures, which were for that time
fantastic, and a typifying presentation for this purpose.

This understanding remains constant — even in Josephus — in the
presentation of Jewish history. Characteristically, references to the
notion of covenant are lacking.[277] Even the accounts of the making
of the covenant are suppressed.[278] From the fact that the LXX had
translated the Hebrew ברית by διαθήκη, the Jewish Apologists
concluded more or less clearly that the covenant had become a testament.

In the OT account of creation and also elsewhere in the Old Testament, nature had become a component of history. Apologetics
now let history be absorbed by nature.[279] For the Apologists, even
the process of lawgiving was justified and explained by φυσιολογία.
That can be seen in the beginning of the *Antiquities* as well as in the
passage from *Apion* 2.190–92 which has already been cited. *Ant.*
1.18 reads:

> But, since well-nigh everything herein related is dependent on
> the wisdom of our lawgiver Moses, I must first speak briefly of him,
> lest any of my readers should ask how it is that so much of my work,
> which professes to treat of laws and historical facts, is devoted to
> φυσιολογία.[280] Be it known, then, that that sage deemed it above all
> necessary, for one who would order his own life aright and also legis-
> late for others, first to study the nature of God, and then, having con-
> templated his works with the eye of reason, to imitate so far as possible
> that best of all models and endeavour to follow it.[281]

God's nature shows itself in his works and thus provides the model
for a proper life. According to *Apion* 2.190–91, the aim of the first
commandment is the natural knowledge of God. In 193 there follows the reference to the *one* temple, which corresponds to the singularity of God. The singularity of the Jewish law and cult thus
mirrors the universality of the cosmos and its law. The law of nature
and the law of God are identical. In a way quite foreign to the OT,

the temple is presented as something intended for everyone, just as God is God for everyone.[282]

It corresponds to this view of God that the presence of divine power is attributed to all human beings in the form of the soul.[283] Thus there is a natural tie between humans and God. Important for the Apologetic view of God and the world is the opposition between two passages from Josephus's *Jewish War*, both of which speak of the divine character of the human soul. I refer to the difference between the two speeches on suicide in *JW* 3.361–82 and 7.344–88. According to the speech of Josephus in *JW* 3.361–82, although the soul is of higher value than the body because of its divine origin, it should not be arbitrarily separated from the body. Since the body, too, belongs to nature, it has a share in the expression of the divine will, for, as we have seen, the will of God and the law of nature are identical. The soul can separate from or unite with the body only when it conforms to the will of God—that is, in the natural course of events.[284] In the speech of Eleazar, soul and body are seen in opposition to one another. The soul is chained in the body as in a prison, and it yearns for the quickest possible release and return to its heavenly home. To conclude from this a religious merit of suicide is only logical.[285] The contrast between the two speeches shows that Josephus himself, despite his adoption of many Platonizing themes, has a monistic theology and anthropology which he steadfastly maintains against other opinions.[286]

A dualistic viewpoint was not possible for Josephus or the other Apologists.[287] As God is *one*, so too is the human being *one*.[288] Likewise the world is also *one*. Therefore dividing humans into two separate classes is impossible.[289] I am not trying to maintain that the Apologists had an undifferentiated view of the world and of humanity. They were well aware that the world is complex and that humans can change, but in the sense that the higher transfigures the lower, not that one cancels the other.[290]

PARTICIPANTS IN GOD (θεῖοι ἄνδρες) IN JEWISH TRADITION

In accordance with their image of God, the Apologists mention no visible appearances of God.[291] Such an appearance would have signified a manifestation of God's being and essence and a limitation in place and time of his all-present and always active eternal power. There was, however, no attempt to avoid reporting particular manifestations of this power. On the contrary, putting the understanding of God in such concrete terms was a central concern of the Apologists.[292] The OT references to the election of individuals from a larger community were for this reason further developed and were supplemented with additional names. Though the OT notion of covenant as such was no longer of any use,[293] it was still able to show the predisposition of a community for distinguishing some of its members. Potentiality and nascent stages were in the community, but it was a matter of the individual to actualize and strengthen it.[294]

This description of the relationship between the individual pneumatic and the community of Israelites was, in turn, a model for the understanding of all humanity. I have already referred to the fact that in the opinion of the Apologetic exegetes the human being possessed an organ for receiving the divine. As already mentioned, the notion of the all-present and ever-active power of God prevented the complete dissociation of an individual or group from the rest of mankind. For the Apologists, distinguishing an individual signified only a modular realization of the possibilities generally imbedded in human nature.[295] Discussing the privileges of individual human beings also did not mean abandoning the often expressed concern not to limit the divine power either spatially or temporally; that which took shape in an individual was the divine power already given to human beings in their nature. If God called a human being from the crowd, he actually called himself. If he elected a human being, he encountered himself. Those who were privileged were by no means unknown quantities; they had already demonstrated their competence, their ἀρετή,[296] which had emanated from the divine ἀρετή.[297] God's participation in the human and human participation in God is also described as partnership.[298] This synergism is forcefully formulated in *Ant.* 10.200: "(God), admiring Daniel's wisdom, made known to him both the dream and its interpretation."

Of what sort then were the special manifestations of God described by the Apologists? In accordance with their image of God (presented above), the Apologists let their conception of the constant nearness of God culminate in an enumeration of occasional divine epiphanies;[299] they did, however, avoid speaking of the visibility of such appearances.[300] If a material manifestation was projected at all, then it was with reference to the phenomena of voice and speech, which are much less tied to and bound by space and time. The divine voice and the divine word appear relatively frequently in the Apologetic texts.[301] Much more frequently, however, the divine spirit or other abstract entities are mentioned as forms of divine expression.[302] Those who were inspired were designated as ἔνθεος, "filled with God."[303] Correspondingly, the concept θεῖος ἀνήρ came to be used as a designation for the pious individuals chosen by God.[304] Occasional scruples against employment of this motif indicate that certain inhibitions due to OT beliefs still existed, but they do not signify a fundamental opposition to the direction or development of Apologetic theology.[305] It was difficult to raise a fundamental objection against the Apologists who were, after all, interpreting scripture. The θεῖοι ἄνδρες to whom they referred were not just any human beings, but first and foremost the great figures of history. They spoke in this way for the greater glory of Judaism and thus ultimately *ad maiorem gloriam dei*.[306]

One dealt with the manifestations of divine power in speaking (and then writing) about the great figures of the people. The attempt was made to do justice to the power which had manifested itself here, by seeking to combine these various figures into one.[307] Whoever was exalted by God was basically capable of great achievements in any sphere.[308] I can dispense with presenting a complete list of all the men of the Jewish past whom the Apologists held to be specially endowed. In any case, Enoch, Isaac, Jacob, Joseph, Elijah, Elisha, David, Isaiah, and Daniel belonged to that group. Above this select group, others towered still higher: Abraham,[309] Solomon,[310] and above all the θεῖος ἀνήρ par excellence, Moses.[311]

In the elaboration of the θεῖος ἀνήρ motif, Apologetics demonstrated once again its enlightenment character. According to Artapanus,[312] Moses is the teacher of Orpheus (Jacoby, *Fragmente*, 3: 3.4).[313] Moreover, his teaching is valid for all human beings. Not only does it consist of philosophy and religion, but the program of instruction encompasses "many things useful for human beings" (πολλὰ τοῖς ἀνθρώποις εὔχρηστα, 3: 3.4).[314] Philosophy and religion, of course, were also included. In this context, however, religious education is instruction not simply in Jewish religion but also in various forms of polytheism—even though we are dealing with a propaganda legend for Judaism which was to win people over to the Jewish belief of God.[315] Even pagan priests thus come into their own. The great educator can wait. His education goes from the less difficult to the more difficult.[316] This method of operation also testifies to the political capability of Moses. He knows how to bring into line the most diverse things and thus how to create a stable commonweal,[317] a monarchy, though not for himself but for Pharaoh. It is no wonder that Moses won the affection of the people.[318] The priests were quite justified in according divine honor to Moses (ἰσοθέου τιμῆς καταξιωθῆναι, 3: 3.6).[319] Moses had demonstrated a divine superiority. Therefore, in my opinion, it is not by chance that Artapanus speaks of the ἀρετή of Moses in the very next sentence (3: 3.7). This term summarizes all the preceding.

The superiority of the one who is similar to God must prove itself in all sorts of persecutions and adversities, and that in fact happens: the divine man is taboo.[320] This becomes even more clear when Moses has received the commission from the ruler of the world (ὁ τῆς οἰκουμένης δεσπότης) to save the Jews from Egypt (Jacoby, *Fragmente*, 3: 3.21–22). Pharaoh cannot prevent him from fulfilling this commission. The invulnerability and superiority of the man of God is further heightened through the use of the divine name.[321] Moses, who can also prove himself through further miracles,[322] can confidently enter into competition with the Egyptian priestly magicians.[323] In this competition his superior ability comes to light all the more, and Pharaoh has to let the Jews go.

Artapanus intends to show how superior knowledge generates superior ability and how both raise the one who is thus endowed above other humans. With his knowledge and ability, he shares in the powers that move the world. He comprehends the divine, which does not oppose the world but underlies and encompasses it. The work of Artapanus promotes the Jewish religion as the superior religion, superior because Moses (and, before that, Abraham and

Joseph) has shown that it imparts a lofty view of the world which allows one to act in a superior fashion.

In the background was a view of God, already described above, which equated the cosmic and the divine. However, God was not identified with the cosmos, for the essence of God was—as has been shown[324]—characterized as unknowable, thereby transcending the cosmos. What was equated was divine power and nature, as well as the natural order and the will of God. The cosmic process was seen as a manifestation of the power and will of God. The elect of God, the θεῖος ἀνήρ, had an essential share in this.

Ant. 3.180 nicely shows how God and nature collaborate in the θεῖος ἀνήρ:

> For if one reflects on the construction of the tabernacle and looks at the vestments of the priest and the vessels which we use for the sacred ministry, he will discover that our lawgiver was a θεῖος ἀνήρ and that these blasphemous charges brought against us by others are idle.[325] In fact, every one of these objects is intended to recall (ἀπομίμησις) and represent (διατύπωσις) the universe, as he will find if he will but consent to examine them without prejudice (ἀφθόνως) and with understanding.

This is an argument which today strikes us as peculiar but which was characteristic of Apologetics. The Apologists wanted to confront the charge of atheism,[326] not by merely refuting it but by demonstrating the religious superiority of Judaism and thereby its superiority in general. They wanted to show that the divine was expressed precisely in what was Jewish, hoping that unbiased and intelligent pagans would agree—an expectation characteristic of the focus of the Jewish missionaries on rationality. The decisive trump card was having a θεῖος ἀνήρ in one's own tradition. Josephus proves the divine quality of Moses with the cosmic character of the laws given by him. They reproduce something cosmic and lead to a cosmic piety.

This argumentation therefore presupposed that the nature of the lawgiver could be reflected in the law but that the nature of the lawgiver could capture the order of the process of nature and thereby the will of God as expressed in God's works.[327] Because this was realized in the fullest sense in Moses, he was held to be the most outstanding θεῖος ἀνήρ. We find the clearest expression of this in Philo.

He, however, has only given expression to what was generally the intention of the Apologetic tradition.

In Philo's *Moses* 1.155 one reads: (Because Moses gave up the wealth which was due as an adopted Egyptian prince, and thereby gave up ordinary human wealth in general),

> God rewarded him by giving him instead the greatest and most perfect wealth. That is the wealth of the whole earth and sea and rivers, and of all the other elements and the combinations which they form. For, since God judged him worthy to appear as a *partner* (κοινωνός; my emphasis) of His own possessions, He gave into his hands the whole world as a portion well fitted for His heir.

Moses thus won a share in God's universal dominion. Therefore the world too now stands at his disposal (156): *"Therefore, each element obeyed him as its master, changed its natural properties* (δύναμις), *and submitted to his command"* (my emphasis).[328] What is meant here is that it conforms to the changing will of the one who participates in God.

With the next figure of speech, Philo begins to discuss the performance of miracles by men of God (*Moses* 1.156–57, my ed.):

> *And this perhaps is no wonder* (θαυμαστός; my emphasis).[329] For if, as the proverb says, "what belongs to friends is common,"[330] and the prophet is called the friend of God,[331] it would follow that he shares also God's possessions, so far as it is serviceable. For God possesses all things, but needs nothing; while the *important man*, though he possesses nothing in the proper sense, not even himself, *partakes of the precious things of God* so far as he is capable.[332] And that is but natural, for *he is a world citizen* (κοσμοπολίτης; my emphasis), and therefore not on the roll of any city of the oecumene, rightly so because he has received no mere piece of land but the whole world as his portion.

Moses can exercise divine power because he shares in God's sovereign authority over the whole world. Here is a particular example of what holds true for the prophet, for the eminent person, in short, for the θεῖος ἀνήρ in general: the whole cosmos is assigned to him and thereby he is also given a share in God's power over the cosmos. Just like God, the θεῖος ἀνήρ has a right to change nature in such a way that the respective properties of individual things and individual phenomena accommodate themselves to his authoritative decision, and a transformation thus ensues. In short, his share in God's dominion and power enables the θεῖος ἀνήρ to perform miracles.

It must, however, also be mentioned that the Apologists' interest was fixed on the whole. The individual changes effected by the pneumatic in the Apologetic presentation simply express his abiding relationship to the world as a whole. Despite the changing of particulars, the whole is not changed at all. When the θεῖος ἀνήρ changes some particular thing on the basis of his sovereignty in the world, he is only demonstrating the constancy of the power bestowed on him and thereby the unity of his inheritance, the cosmos. Other texts also suggest that the Apologists advocated a sort of law of the conservation of energy which corresponded to their monistic understanding of God and the world.[333] The ambiguous relationship of the Apologists to miracles is thus explained: on one hand, vivid miracle stories, on the other hand—often in the same breath—a reserve toward miracles.[334] The miracle described on the one hand was not miraculous on the other, but quite natural.[335]

The range of perception of the miraculous varied and changed considerably. What appeared as impossible to one appeared as miracle to another. The vision the first of these persons had of the underlying forces of the world and of the divine power which moves it was still restricted or clouded. But for the other person this vision had become open. To a third one, however, who already possessed superior insight into the world, the event or phenomenon appeared as the actualization of one of many possibilities which were offered for the pneumatic to choose from and to appropriate. Breadth and depth of one's insight into the world would distinguish people. Miracles and reports of miracles could be understood as stimulus and aid to such a superior insight into the world.[336] Thus the fundamentally rationalistic structure of this pneumatic thinking betrays itself anew, joined as it is with a similarly monistic and universalistic tendency.

In the course of the discussion, I have already gone a bit beyond the text from Philo; the introduction to the underlying forces of the world is first made in the next sentence. But since this certainly does not contradict the previous remarks, but rather supplements and completes them, I was justified in anticipating some of these comments. Philo continues (158):

Again, was not the joy of his partnership with the Father and Maker of all magnified also by the honour of being deemed worthy to bear the same title?[337] *For he was named god and king of the [entire people], and entered, we are told, into the cloud where God was, that is into the unseen, invisible, incorporeal and archetypal essence of existing things.*[338] Thus he beheld (χατανοῶν) what is hidden from the sight of mortal nature.

A vision of the οὐσία of God is not reported here, only a vision of the οὐσία of existent things.

Here statements are made about Moses similar to those made about Abraham in the Testament of Orpheus.[339] There, too, God hid himself in the cloud. It could be penetrated by (or was nonexistent for) the person who could decipher the cosmic secrets of the starry heaven. That is equivalent to experiencing God's power and thus becoming certain of his existence. Abraham was, so to speak, allowed to experience the proof of God from natural theology. The cloud signifies that the Creator's essential secrets, as they stand over and behind the world, are hidden. On the other hand, penetrating the cloud and experiencing the cosmic secrets mean one and the same thing. Experiencing the cosmic secrets is actually equivalent to ascending to heavenly regions. Moses' journey to Sinai and into the cloud, as described by Philo above, is such an ascent. To judge from the parallels in Aristobulus, this disappearance into the cloud could be identical with the transcending of the boundaries between earthly and heavenly, with the disappearance of the separation between human and divine. Moses experiences the underlying forces of the world and thus shares God's omnipotence and majesty.

In the view of the Apologists the heightening of the faculties and of the significance of Moses over and beyond normal human and earthly boundaries, as well as his growing participation in the divine, first culminated in his ascent to Sinai. The exegesis emphasizes that in the OT report Moses was even deemed worthy of the designation God. Thus one could speak of a transcending of the boundaries of mortality. The θεῖος ἀνήρ now participated in the world's core and thereby in the divine secrets to such an extent that the realm of immortality was open to him.

The Apologists crowned this development with the death of Moses. Philo describes the departing Moses in the following way

(*Moses* 2.288): "He had to make his pilgrimage (ἀποικία) from earth to heaven, and leave this mortal life for immortality (ἀπαθανα-τίζεσθαι)." Death is here understood not as an end but as a journey on which the dying individual still retains his power to make judgments and decisions. It is a transition which the dying individual experiences as a transformation. Since he has previously experienced something similar, it is more correct to speak of a transformation that has already begun and is now being completed.

This process of transformation is then further presented as follows: "(God) *resolved his two-fold nature of soul and body into a single unity, transforming his whole being into mind, pure as the sunlight.*"[340] Somewhat later the text reads:

> For when he was already being exalted and stood at the very barrier, ready at the signal to direct his upward flight to heaven, the divine spirit fell upon him and he prophesied with discernment while still alive the story of his own death; told ere the end how the end came; told how he was buried with none present, surely by no mortal hands but by immortal powers; how also he was not laid to rest in the tomb of his forefathers but was given a monument of special dignity which no man has ever seen. . . .

In various ways it is suggested here that the death of Moses was not a death but a "translation," a transformation into something superhuman. Philo portrays this as a process which moves the world.[341] The death of Moses thus becomes an exaltation, a heavenly journey.[342] This upward movement which oversteps and transcends the boundaries of the human condition is anticipated through prophecy, which both formally and materially deprives death of its particular reality. Thus grave and sepulcher do not become ultimate signs of mortality, but symbols of immortality. It is also important that the cosmic powers undertake the burial, which certainly indicates that one has to see in the death of Moses a cosmic transformation.

According to the report of Josephus (*Ant.* 4.323–31), the final journey of Moses stands under the theme "He was going to the place from which he was going to disappear."[343] Shortly afterward the coming event is called a transformation (ἀπαλλαγή), then a departure (ἀπελ εῖν). This last earthly event in the life of Moses takes place on a high mountain (326). "And while he bade farewell to Eleazar and Joshua and was yet communing with them (πϱοσο-μιλῶν), all of a sudden a cloud descended upon him and he disappeared in a ravine."[344]

Regardless of how one interprets the intention of Josephus, his concluding remarks demonstrate that Hellenistic Jews discussed whether the report about the death of Moses spoke of his final divinization, and some interpreters probably had seriously adopted this view. Josephus writes (*Ant.* 4.326): "But he has written of himself in the sacred books that he died, for fear lest they should venture to say that by reason of his surpassing ἀϱετή he had gone back to the Deity." As explained above, Josephus's paraphrase of the end of Deuteronomy is anything but the account of a death. Moreover, the following references of Josephus to the greatness of the loss which the Israelites and the Jewish people generally had suffered indicate that, in the opinion of Josephus and his tradition, the ἀϱετή of Moses had burst through the boundaries of time and space, as confirmed by the Mosaic laws. It was maintained that by reading these laws one could relate to the past greatness of Moses (*Ant.* 4.331). This conception will be explored further in pursuing the Apologetic principle of tradition, but first the Apologetic version of the θεῖος ἀνήϱ must be presented in more detail. I shall therefore return once more to Philo's report on Moses' ascent of Mount Sinai.

In the passage cited (*Moses* 1.158), Philo related how Moses saw the very essence of existing things. That meant describing a vision of that which is invisible to mortals; however, not establishing an unbridgeable gulf between mortal and immortal but on the contrary—at least in the figure of Moses—establishing the possibility and giveness of a connection between the two. That no fundamental differentiation between Moses and the rest of humanity is intended in the reported translation of Moses is shown above all by the fact that the goal of this special experience of Moses is said to be its "publication" and "universalization" (*Moses* 1.158–59, my ed.):

He has set before us himself and his life as a well fashioned writing, and he presented a piece of work beautiful and godlike, a model for those who are willing to copy it.[345] Happy are they who imprint, or strive to imprint, that image in their souls.[346] For it were best that the mind (διάνοια) should carry the form of ἀρετή in perfection, but failing this, let it at least have the unflinching desire to possess that form.[347]

In the Apologetic view, God and the world were contained in the θεῖος ἀνήρ in order to bring about the right order of human existence. The θεῖος ἀνήρ was thought to properly articulate the will of God, which rules the cosmos. The passages adduced above which speak of the death of Moses (especially the account of Josephus) can show this. In his account of the Sinai event, Philo also says, just after the sentences already cited (*Moses* 1.162): "Perhaps, too, since he was destined to be a legislator, the providence of God which afterwards appointed him without his knowledge to that work, caused him long before that day to be the reasonable and living impersonation of the law (νόμος ἔμψυχος καὶ λογικός)."[348]

Moses, however, is not the only person of whom this can be said. He only epitomizes what had also been true of the heroes of the Jewish past who preceded him. In *Abr.* 5 Philo says of them: "For in these men we have laws endowed with life and reason (ἔμψυχοι καὶ λογικοὶ νόμοι)." The reasons which Philo adduces for the glorification (σεμνύνειν) of these men by Moses are important not only for the view of Philo and his tradition on the θεῖοι ἄνδρες as such, but also for the relationship which the Apologists saw between them and the written law, and thus also for the sense and significance of the law itself.

Here the first reason (*Abr.* 5): (Moses wished to show), "that the statutory laws (τεθειμένα διατάγματα) are not inconsistent with nature (τῆς φύσεως οὐχ ἀπᾴδει)." Quite simply that is because they do correspond to the rule which the patriarchs had lived without law, namely, the order of nature itself. In *Abr.* 6 it also says (in a striking conciseness which cannot be correctly reproduced in translation), "They were αὐτήκοοι δὲ καὶ αὐτομαθεῖς (they listened to no voice or instruction but their own)." That which determined their life was part of themselves, insofar as they "gladly accepted discipleship of nature (ἀκολουθίαν φύσεως ἀσπασάμενοι), holding that nature itself was, as indeed it is, the most venerable of statutes (πρεσβύτατος θεσμός), and thus their whole life was well ordered (ἅπαντα τὸν βίον ἠὐνομήθησαν)." Thus it is not surprising that in *Abr.* 3 the relationship between these prototypical men and the individual laws has been already described as that between originals with general significance (ἀρχέτυποι and καθολικώτεροι) to copies with particular significance (εἰκόνες and οἱ ἐπὶ μέρους).

Philo did not invent this corresponding relationship between nature (creation), the patriarchs, and the written laws, nor did he borrow it directly from paganism; rather, he took it from the Apologetic tradition. In the Testament of Orpheus in Aristobulus the sequence runs: nature, word of the ancients (previously exemplified in the figure of Abraham), and law of Moses. Josephus, in the introduction to *Antiquities* discussed above, makes a connection between nature and the law of Moses. The connection between the two is found in the *figure* of Moses.[349] Legislation presupposes the ordering of one's own life, and both presuppose the contemplation of nature, which leads to an imitation of this model (of φύσις) and to an emulation of it (οὕτως παράδειγμα τὸ πάντων ἄριστον μιμεῖσθαι, καθ' ὅσον οἷόν τε, καὶ πειρᾶσθαι κατακολουθεῖν). The lawgiver first imitates and emulates φύσις or the γνώμη θεοῦ (*Ant.* 1.14) in his own life and then conveys them to the law composed by him. That this is the appropriate interpretation of the sequence mentioned is made clear by the next sentence in *Ant.* 1.20. *Apion* 2.159–60 is also quite similar.

Thus the individual patriarchs are also pictured as prototypes for a life of ἀρετή. The depiction of Seth and his offspring (*Ant.* 1.68–71) and that of Abraham connect the ἀρετή of the heroes with cosmos and nature. Since they embody the universe and its order and are aware of this fact, they are truly θεῖοι ἄνδρες (as Josephus says explicitly in the passage cited, *Ant.* 3.180). They are thus also above the suspicion that they are charlatans and frauds, of which pagan anti-Semitism had accused Moses in particular.[350] The refutation was characteristically not a μετάβασις εἰς ἄλλο γένος, but a demonstration that the significance of Moses consists not in occasional, more-or-less doubtful practices but in the comprehensive and constant grasp of and domination over the whole (only a quantitative difference, actually).

The sequence seems to be transformed into its opposite through the fact that the idea of law's inspiration is found everywhere.[351]

Did the Apologists intend to say that the superior capabilities of the heroes, especially of Moses, were not themselves sufficient to provide a copy of their own existence? Why was it necessary to claim an immediate intervention of God? Was not the status of the law as a copy also denied by inspiration?

At *Ant*. 3.83–88, where—as mentioned—Moses descends from Mount Sinai like a son of the gods, he then says in an address to the Hebrews that God himself has *"dictated* for you rules for a blissful life and an ordered government."[352]

Then Moses emphasizes that he is speaking not in his own name but in God's name. He, Moses, is only a spokesperson (λέγων) for God. The ἀρετή and majesty of the divine author, who for the benefit of the people did not begrudge the spokesperson of the people his function,[353] can be recognized in these words.[354] But after this long introduction, Moses steps completely into the background, and God himself, in a special voice, proclaims the Decalogue to the people. On the one hand, Josephus is only following the biblical account, but on the other hand, he incorporates his own theological intention. This intention is in accord with Apologetic understanding of inspiration in general and of the significance of the Decalogue in particular. According to Philo (*Decal*. 32–35; cf. *Praem*. 2–3), a special divine sound was even created for this moment, a sound which guaranteed the immediacy of God's proclamation. At the same time, it prevented an anthropomorphic understanding of God that could have arisen from a reference to God's voice.

Precisely this peculiarity in describing the proclamation of the Decalogue reveals why the Apologists emphasized the direct divine intervention in the creation of the Jewish law, an emphasis which at first appears to contradict the θεῖος ἀνήρ motif. The Apologists were trying to remove all doubts about the law's divine character. According to Philo *Decal*. 19 (cf. *Praem*. 2), the words of the law which were given directly by God are especially those that lie at the basis of the law or that summarize it (νόμων τῶν ἐν μέρει κεφάλαια), in other words, the principles or summaries. The Ten Commandments, above all, fit this role. Josephus makes a similar judgment (*Ant*. 3.89). This immediate proclamation of God was to tell the Israelites what to do and to give some indication of the ἀρετή of the laws and of the divine lawgiver.[355]

However, this can and ought not remain one-sided. The law was not to be presented only as something divine. Here, too, mortals were allowed to appear as partners. The laws were understood to have been composed also by humans, especially by Moses. This is most obviously apparent in the fact that, when quoting scripture, Philo frequently names Moses (occasionally other "prophets" as well) as the author of the citation.[356] Moses is the legislator, he is the author of the law. The law is the law of Moses.[357] Questions were asked about his intentions in giving the law, as the introductions to Philo's *De Opificio Mundi (On the Creation)* and the *Antiquities* of Josephus have already illustrated. Moses and the law were more or less identified and the concept and the name were de facto frequently interchangeable.

All this was closely related to the oracular motif. It was used to greatest effect, of course, in phenomena such as the Jewish *Sibylline Oracles*. But Philo and Josephus also equated the word of God, especially the letter of the law, with oracle.[358] The synergistic element inherent in the oracle motif fitted quite well into Apologetic thinking.[359] Thus, too, the Apologetic conception of the law corresponded to the combination oracles presented of enigmatic strangeness and fixed and memorable formulation which could be variously applied. The oracles treated the relationship between the mysteriously divine and the actual situation as inherently dialectic: on the one hand, distant; on the other, direct and immediate. This dialectic was easily transferred to the problem of temporal distance, especially if—in applying this to the law—the oracles were understood as written, beginning with the Decalogue (Philo, *Moses* 2.97). The oracular motif thus became connected with the scriptural motif, and they complemented one another. What was fixed, and therefore also past, was at the same time that which one possessed, which could be spoken and which helped to gain a better understanding of the world. For the Apologists, the letters were, on the one hand, mysterious and not immediately accessible; therefore their knowledge and transmission was an object of divine activity. On the other hand, the γράμματα could also be taught, and their communication and dissemination were understood quite rationalistically as a cultural achievement. Eupolemus and Artapanus give examples of this, which have already been cited.

In the *Epistle of Aristeas*, things written in the Hebrew alphabet, which is peculiar and thus indicative of a special origin,[360] are called the precious and thus especially honorable Ἰουδαϊκὰ γράμματα (121).[361] We can see from the *Epistle of Aristeas* 311 how much the Apologists held as taboo the sequence of letters themselves, even those of the Greek translation. In conformity with Jewish custom (Deut. 4:2 and 12:32 are referred to), anyone is cursed who adds anything, changes anything, or removes anything from the text (τὰ γεγραμμένα).

In *Ant.* 1.17, Josephus shares the same viewpoint. "The precise details of our Scripture records (ἀναγραφαί) will, then, be set forth, each in its place, as my narrative proceeds, that being the procedure that I have promised to follow throughout this work, neither adding nor omitting anything." Josephus thereby gives his conception of scriptural exegesis, clearly based on traditional criteria. Important for the previous discussion are the motifs of "accuracy" and "document."

Scripture was understood as a collection of documents, which included also the idea of archival preservation. The lot of archival preservation was accorded first and foremost to the Decalogue. In the same breath with the story of God's special oral transmission of the Ten Commandments, Josephus mentions that Moses preserved the two tablets with their written form (δέκα λόγων οὓς Μωυσῆς ἐν ταῖς δύο πλαξὶ γεγραμμένους κατέλιπεν; *Ant.* 3.90).

The tablets Moses brought down from Mount Sinai underscored the authenticity of his report.[362] It is especially emphasized that they were written by the hand of God.[363] The tablets were thus a letter from heaven.[364] Heavenly letters are conspicuous not only for their content but also for their significance. The recipient and the owner of a heavenly letter are raised above the rest of the human crowd and themselves possess a form of taboo. The letter from heaven bestows happiness and blessing. With this must be related the remarks of Josephus, which are at first astonishing, that Moses had been on Mount Sinai in order to obtain that which would make possible for the people a happy life, a εὐδαίμων βίος.[365]

The tablets of the law were then—in conformity with the biblical account—preserved in the ark (*Ant.* 3.138; also cf. Philo, *Moses*

2.97). Thus they had, as it were, their own archive. Eupolemus (Jacoby, *Fragmente*, 3: 723.5.5; Eusebius, *Praep. Ev.* 9.39.5) shows that this document, a palpable bringer of happiness, was occasionally thought to have been preserved until after the destruction of Jerusalem by the Babylonians.

The accuracy which Josephus and others attributed to the Jewish documents was due not only to a concern for literary truth and legal reliability but also to the holy might and power of the texts. The letters were actually thought to convey power.[366]

Correspondingly, scripture as a whole is often designated as ἱερὰ γράμματα.[367] Philo uses the designation almost exclusively in his Apologetic work. The entire text has a divine character and is taboo. The *Epistle of Aristeas* especially emphasizes this.[368] The idea of the testament has become dominant. The Apologists thus combined the δύναμις motif with the conception of the *written* law and that of the θεῖος ἀνήρ. The divine man and the law, composed in letters and to be taken literally, were both understood as conveyers of power. The law was also occasionally conceived as personified.[369] Law and θεῖος ἀνήρ accordingly presented two different ways in which the same thing appeared. Both conceptions were nonetheless united—not just through the idea of the law written within— through the motif of the human lawgiver (also through the motif of the scriptural prophets).[370]

THE MEDIATION OF THIS PARTICIPATION THROUGH
EXPOSITION OF SCRIPTURES

The preceding analysis raises the question of whether the Apologists' connection of the θεῖος ἀνήρ concept to the concept of scriptures did not restrict the θεῖος ἀνήρ idea to the past, confining spirit and power to a scripture which was equated with tradition. One must also ask whether elevation of the written Jewish law did not result in a radical dissociation from the pagan intellectual and religious world. Both consequences would contradict the previous analysis of missionary practice and theory.

The answer to these questions is to be found not somewhere outside the Apologetic concept of law but only in a more precise analysis of the dialectic which is characteristic of this concept and which has been mentioned earlier. For this reason, I must once more examine a motif associated with the concept of law: the motif of the letters of the alphabet and the motif of antiquity, which is related.

According to the Apologetic viewpoint, the existence of something written, "official records written by the greatest sages," demonstrates how much a people has done "to let none of the events in their history be forgotten." The important thing is to possess "the oldest and most continuous historical tradition." Knowing the alphabet (the φύσις γραμμάτων) was an obvious prerequisite. All these criteria are listed by Josephus (*Apion* 1.8–10). The reference to letters and writing clearly makes it possible to draw parallels and thus to communicate.[371]

Josephus says that the Egyptians, Chaldeans, and Phoenicians all claimed that they had conformed to the criteria mentioned above. And in comparison with the Greeks, such assertions were justified. Yet Josephus tries to show that the Jews are the oldest people, since they have the oldest culture, and that they possess the most extensive reminiscences fixed in writing constitutes an essential factor in this demonstration. For proving this great antiquity, evidence of stability is always an appropriate part of the argument, and this too is an idea easily associated with the motifs of letters and writing. According to *Apion* 2.279, time is the best test for truth. According to the *Hypothetica* of Philo, the Jews have "for two thousand years not altered a single word of what was written by him (Moses)."[372] Precisely for this reason, according to *Moses* 2.12—14 Moses is "the best of all lawgivers" and "his laws are most excellent and truly divine (κάλλιστοι καὶ ὡς ἀληθῶς θεῖοι)," since his precepts (νόμιμα) "alone firm, unshaken, immovable, stamped, as it were, with the seals of nature herself, remain secure from the day when they were first enacted to now, and we may hope that they will remain for all future ages as though immortal, so long as the sun and moon and the whole heaven and universe exist."[373]

Even more forcefully than in the passages treated earlier, there is an expression here of the idea that the laws are divine because they are in writing, since their written form makes possible their unchangeableness. Unchangeableness, in turn, is a characteristic of nature, and ultimately of God himself.[374]

The previously established view that the letters of the alphabet carry power is thereby confirmed and considerably enhanced. For the Apologists the letter not only provided access to original principles—that is, to nature and to God himself—but the permanence and unchangeableness of the letter were also an image of nature and of God himself; like a road sign the letter showed the way to immutability and immortality. The letter became a means to break through and finally to transcend the boundaries of time (and space).

In this way we can understand Philo's wording in *Abr.* 5 (in connection with the statements quoted and commented upon earlier concerning the relationship between nature, inner law among the ancients, and statutory law): "So . . . one might properly say that the [statutory] laws (νόμοι τεθέντες) are nothing else than memorials of the life of the ancients (ὑπομνήματα βίου τῶν παλαιῶν), [dealing in an antiquarian fashion] (ἀρχαιολογοῦντες) [with] their actual words and deeds."[375]

Preserving past achievements in the statutory laws and in writing in general did not, in the opinion of the Apologists, shrivel and eradicate a living quantity, but rather had the opposite effect. Eternal values in this way received an appropriate form which preserved them for posterity. Therefore, the reference of the Apologists to antiquity[376] and the reference to the patriarchs and their legacy was synonymous with the praise of the living and eternal powers of Judaism.[377] Looking back into antiquity actually meant looking forward into the future and into eternity. That which had been ratified by God and the heroes had surpassed time.

The sacred past came to be understood as a quantity which transcended itself because of the eternal power stored up in it. Thus, we read in *Ant.* 3.317–19: "But the admiration in which that hero (Moses) was held for (his) ἀρετή and (his) marvelous power of inspiring faith in all his utterances were not confined to his lifetime: they are alive today." Every Hebrew respects the law just as though the lawgiver were still alive.[378] "There are many other proofs of his superhuman power (τεκμήρια τῆς ὑπὲρ ἄνθρωπόν ἐστι δυνάμεως αὐτοῦ)." Josephus mentions two of these, and between them interjects the comment "So surely has that legislation, being believed to come from God, caused this man to be ranked higher than his own nature" (320). Even unbelievers are impressed by the authority of this legislation: "To this very day the writings left by Moses (τὰ κατα-

λειφθέντα ὑπὸ Μωυσέος γράμματα) have such power that even our
enemies admit that our constitution was established by God himself, through the agency of Moses and his ἀρετή" (322).[379]

Although the Apologists' understanding of scripture did indeed
place importance on the fixation and delimitation of sacred letters,
texts, and collections of texts, still these limits could also be blurred.
Sometimes only scripture appears as tradition; elsewhere the two
are distinguished from one another.

Josephus knows a fixed canon with a selection of writings, which
is defined by the precise and delimited succession of prophetic
authors. I have already quoted the relevant passage,[380] as well as
his proclamation of faithfulness, to the Jewish records, that is, the
canon.[381] But the *Antiquities* do not follow these principles. The
time period which is described there stretches far beyond that of the
canonical scriptures, into Josephus's own time. Moreover, any careful reader of the *Antiquities* is struck by the fact that Josephus actually sticks very little to his introductory rule about being faithful
to scripture; rather, he harmonizes, selects, expands, and omits.
Schlatter comments that Josephus does not quote scripture, but
only paraphrases it.[382] This is also the case with the other Apologists. Only Philo's Apologetic work adheres somewhat more strictly
to scripture, yet compared with his allegorical commentary, scripture is only infrequently quoted.

All this points to a characteristic freedom on the part of the
Apologists with respect to the text and its limits, and the simplest
explanation for this nonchalance may be that it was nurtured by the
confidence in the power of the letter, which precisely because of its
fixed character was capable of transcending itself. The respect for
scripture seems to have produced the proliferous tradition, but in
that process scripture became a part of the tradition, with tradition
towering over everything. Josephus's work shows how in this way
one was easily capable of reaching into and including the present.[383] The movement starting from scripture was allowed to
sweep in every direction. The great minds of paganism and the individual soul were included in it and were made proclaimers of eternal truth.[384]

It is not surprising that finally the Apologetic expositors of scripture also felt themselves drawn into this powerful current. The way

in which the Apologists treated scriptures already proves that they certainly felt on a par with them. It has already been pointed out that Philo and Josephus drew a parallel between their own activity and that of the translators of the OT. And legend had reported something extraordinary about those translators. They represented, according to the *Epistle of Aristeas* and the tradition used by Philo and Josephus, the extraordinary abilities which had been bestowed on the Jewish people because of their possession of the law. I have already pointed out that Philo and Josephus had even put themselves on the same level with the OT prophets.[385]

The exposition of scripture was understood as the point of contact between the divine power speaking from the text and encompassing the text. This may be concluded from Aristobulus's work. According to him, statements found in the biblical tradition (ἐκδοχαί) are to be accepted according to the reality they reflect (πρὸς τὸ φυσικῶς λαμβάνειν).[386] Accepting the meaning which accords with reality is identical to the act of exposition. The process of understanding is powered and directed by the wisdom of Moses, his inherent divine "pneuma," which is identical to his thinking and imagination. The exegete wants to find the truth, and the truth is what was conceived (νενοημένα) by the lawgiver. If the exegete does not find it, he himself is to blame, not the lawgiver. As scripture interprets itself, it is ultimately nature reflected in scripture which uncovers itself. But since the exegete as well as his audience is part of nature, exegesis completes the circle and gives nature its full strength and power.

This becomes even clearer in *Ant*. 1.18–26, mentioned earlier.[387] The legislation can be understood only by someone who is able and willing to see how nature is reflected in the lawgiver and then in the law.[388] *Ant*. 1.23 reads: "Our legislator, on the contrary, having shown that God possesses the very perfection of ἀρετή, thought that men should strive to participate in it, and inexorably punished those who did not hold with or believe in these doctrines." The following statement shows that Josephus equates his own purpose directly with that of Moses (my ed.):

> I therefore entreat my readers to begin their investigation from this point of view (ὑπόθεσις).[389] For, to those who investigate in this spirit, nothing will appear unreasonable, nothing incongruous with the majesty of God and his love for humans; everything, indeed, is set forth

> here in keeping with the nature of the universe; some things the law-
> giver shrewdly veils in enigmas, others he sets forth in solemn alle-
> gory; but where ever straightforward speech was expedient, there he
> makes his meaning absolutely plain.

The astonishing notion that one has all the necessary tools to explain
everything is both rationalistic and optimistic. Truth in its entirety
can reach and influence the person with understanding.

Yet this rationalistic optimism did not remain entirely unclouded.
The passage just quoted from Josephus hints at this. Although the
process of exposition was for the Apologists a natural self-disclosure,
this did not deny that understanding was not given to everyone. The
literal wording of the text could be experienced as incomprehensible or enigmatic; it could conceal the true meaning of a text and,
taken by itself, lead to completely false conceptions.

Aristobulus distinguishes between the letter of the text, which,
when taken alone, inevitably leads to mythical and human conceptions, and the real (φυσικός) meaning. However, it is also clear that
for Aristobulus and thereby for all persons of understanding there is
no contradiction between the two, that the literal wording actually
points (σημαίνω) to the deeper meaning. Since cooperation between the divine and the human appears frequently in Apologetic
literature, it is not surprising that exposition of scripture is perceived on the one hand as divine self-disclosure, but on the other
hand is made the object of discriminating reflection and gives rise to
an interpretative method modeled on Hellenistic philosophy.[390]

Philo also makes a distinction between the literal sense and the
true meaning of the text. The literal sense is called ἡ ῥητὴ καὶ
φανερὰ ἀπόδοσις, ἡ ἐν φανερῷ καὶ πρὸς τοὺς πολλοὺς ἀπόδοσις.[391] φανερός here is used without emphasis to mean "obvious,
evident."[392] Other expressions of this sort in Philo are αἱ ῥηταὶ
γραφαί, ἡ ῥητὴ διήγησις, or simply τὰ ῥητά.[393] With these one can
compare the designations σύμβολα, αἰνίγματα, and μεταφοραί.
αἰνίττεσθαι occurs with particular frequency, along with its synonyms.[394] With all these designations Philo makes it clear that the
individual words and individual statements of sacred scripture point
beyond themselves to a unified whole which is truly essential. But
only the wise are capable of understanding the meaning of these
enigmas and symbols.

The allegorical method is practiced by the Therapeutae.[395] These people, who were a paradigm for a βίος θεωρητικός, are described as follows: They possess "knowledge and [vision of the matter of] nature (πράγματα τῆς φύσεως) following the truly sacred instructions of the prophet Moses" (*Cont.* 64). Philo informs us in detail about their exegetical practice: "The interval between early morning and evening is spent entirely in spiritual exercise (ἄσκησις)" (*Cont.* 28). According to both general and Jewish custom, asceticism is a preparation for the ecstatic or mystic vision. "They read the holy scriptures and seek wisdom from their ancestral philosophy by taking it as an allegory." In literature from this period, the word φιλοσοφία should not be exaggerated. The word refers to all types of wisdom, but especially the higher wisdom of a divine character.[396] The ἱερὰ γράμματα used by the Therapeutae probably signify the OT, which here is identified as tradition.

Allegorical writings of an older period are mentioned first in the next paragraph. Philo continues, giving the reason for the allegorical interpretation: ". . . (They interpret allegorically) since they think that the words of the literal text are symbols of something whose hidden nature is revealed by studying the underlying meaning."[397] For this purpose, the Therapeutae have "writings of men of old, the founders of their [school], who left many memorials of the form used in allegorical interpretation.[398] These they take as a kind of archetype (ἀρχέτυπος) and imitate the method (which corresponds to) the intention (of the founder)."[399] The tradition is clearly expanded here in the sense discussed above. Scripture is joined by those writings of the ancients which interpret scripture and stimulate further interpretation. These writings form, together with scripture, the tradition of the sect.

The ancients are a model not only for the exposition of scripture in the technical sense but also for fully utilizing and embedding it in one's thought and religious life. Connecting with a significant ὥστε to the paradigmatic scriptural exposition of the ancients, fixed in written form, Philo continues: "[Thus they not only have visions,] but also compose [psalms and hymns] to God. . . ."[400] Thus the art of scriptural exposition handed down from ancestors is understood as a vision, and it is associated with expressions of worship, which were commonly viewed in antiquity as projecting beyond the realm of ordinary earthly activity. This shows that the expository method, which initially seems merely formal and methodological, could be understood in a very realistic way. The transcending from a literal to an allegorical sense could be seen as carrying over into another realm, defined by pneumatic powers expressing themselves in the "elevated" speech of psalms and hymns.

Just how far this realistic understanding of the allegorical exposition can be taken is shown *Cont.* 78, where again exposition as a part of worship (here, during the holy days) is being discussed:

> The [exegeses] of the sacred scriptures [take place through contemplative exposition in the form of allegories] (δι᾽ ὑπονοιῶν ἐν ἀλληγορίαις). For to these people the whole [legislation] seems to resemble a living creature with the literal ordinances for its body and for its soul the invisible mind laid up in its wording. It is in this mind that the rational soul (λογικὴ ψυχή, which probably means the "pneuma" of the allegorical exegete) begins to [behold] (θεωρεῖν) [in a distinct manner] the things akin to itself (τὰ οἰκεῖα).[401]

Thus the pneumatic attains the vision (θεωρία) through allegory. The comparison which follows is especially important for our further discussion.

> [(In doing so, it, i.e., the rational soul) beholds as though through the mirror of the terms (ὥσπερ διὰ κατόπτρου τῶν ὀνομάτων; the reference is to the ῥηταὶ διατάξεις, the λέξεις, or one could also say the γράμματα)] the marvelous beauty of the concepts [which step into view], and unfolds and removes (διαπτύξασα καὶ διακαλύψασα) the [symbols], [so that it] brings forth the thoughts and sets them bare to the light of day for those who need but a little reminding (ὑπόμνησις) to enable them to [envision the invisible by means of the things which are visible].[402]

It is therefore the task of the interpreter of allegory to grasp the ψυχή of the λέξεις, the πνεῦμα which is both hidden and delineated by the γράμμα. But in order to do this, the interpreter of allegory must possess the λογικὴ ψυχή. With its help the ὀνόματα then become the κάτοπτρον of the νοῦς and the letters turn into the mirror of the spirit. The veil of the symbols disappears in this way, or it becomes transparent; it no longer hinders the true vision, but rather enables it.[403]

In the truest sense of the word, the method here becomes the way; it begins a process which is completed only in the further course of the worship,[404] in the succeeding hymns and responsories (including ones which are danced), in the communal meal, and finally in the vigil with its ecstatic dances, which dramatically recreate and recast the Red Sea miracle, including the songs of praise connected with it.[405] Hence, the vision involves far more than merely intellectual knowledge. Intended is the mystical vision of the underlying essence of individual phenomena, the θεωρία φύσεως (*Cont*. 90). To me, it is no accident that this worship of the Therapeutae concludes with a prayer facing the rising sun, the hands stretched out to heaven. The cosmic background and objectives of the whole practice are underscored by this.

The concluding words of Philo about the Therapeutae, people previously designated as paradigmatic expositors of scripture and as models of piety, sound like a summary characterization of the Hellenistic-Jewish Apologists:

> . . . [(the Therapeutae) have taken into their hearts the [vision of nature, and live in it and the soul alone,][406] citizens of heaven and the world, [genuinely recommended] to the Father and Maker of all by [. . .] ἀρετή, [which] has procured for them God's friendship and added a gift going hand-in-hand with it, true excellence of life (καλοκἀγαθία), a boon better than all good fortune (εὐτυχία) and rising to the very summit of felicity (εὐδαιμονία).[407]

From here one can look back to the beginning of the treatise on the Therapeutae. In *Cont*. 2 they are defined because of their name as persons who have mastered an art of healing which cures souls; this is superior to the art of physicians, which treats the body. Their name also identifies them as persons who, because of nature and the sacred laws (ἐκ φύσεως καὶ τῶν ἱερῶν νόμων), worship the true Being (τὸ ὄν), "who is better than the good, purer than the one (ἕν), and more primordial than the Monad." That nature and sacred laws are classified together is just as interesting as the fact that both are named as the source (ἐκ) of truly pious worship and the fact that the object of worship is consequently designated as neuter.[408]

We have here again the physico-theological approach, not only to the knowledge of God but also to the worship of God. In *Cont*. 11 this is described as a soaring flight:

[The race of the truly pious (τὸ θεραπευτικὸν γένος) are] always taught from the first to use their sight, and should [(therefore)] desire the vision of the true Being], and [should] soar above the [perceptible] sun, and [should (therefore)] never leave [this order] which carries them to perfect happiness.

It cannot be denied that Philo's description of these people contains features which are characteristic of the mysteries. Immediately following the sentence just quoted, the aspiration of the Therapeutae to a heavenly vision is portrayed as a Bacchanalian rapture. The next sentence reports their efforts to dissociate themselves from bourgeois life, which of course finally led to the cloisterlike organization by the Mareotic Lake. However, this seclusion does not mark a hatred of the world; instead it contributes—as the whole description reveals—to a higher and more encompassing insight into the world.[409] This more intensive insight into the world is clearly portrayed as an upward movement toward a better knowledge of God, which in turn should lead to a more profound cosmic vision.

The true knowledge of God is said to be achieved by going beyond the sun, but this does not mean opposing the natural order represented by the sun (and the other heavenly bodies). The sun is clearly a station along the path to knowledge: the source of this path, according to *Cont.* 2, is nature. Thus the term τάξις in *Cont.* 11 does not oppose the order the senses discern in visible nature, but complements it instead. *Τάξις* means the order which encompasses everything. For this reason I have translated it as "order" and have understood the last καὶ to have summarizing and interpretative function, in the sense of "and therefore." Perfect happiness (τελεία εὐδαιμονία) does not differ from the things of the world, but rather fulfills them. This understanding of happiness is the same as that of other Apologetic texts. It is an expression of the salvation propagated by Jewish missionaries: a vital consciousness which transcends the limits of the day-to-day world, literally bursts through. This happiness is experienced as an extension and intensification of nature beyond common human measure.[410] In *Cont.* 11 Philo means a guidance given by the all-encompassing order to those who follow their evolving discernment as they ascend the natural order.

This confirms the assumption first made when analyzing the

Abraham motif and repeated several times since then,[411] namely, that astrology enjoyed the particular esteem of the Apologists because they stressed the connection between the vision of the world and the vision of God. The association between astrology and the understanding of vision was a point of departure for the heavenly journey.[412] At first, human life as a whole was seen on this ascending line, with the lives of the patriarchs, especially of Moses, as paradigms. But then individual paradigmatic events in the lives of the patriarchs led to the expectation that one could actually experience anticipatory illustrations of this ascent during one's life.

The passages quoted, especially the wording "because of nature and the sacred laws," indicate that the exposition of scripture also belongs in this context. This exposition was correlated to the knowledge and the experience of nature, and it helped to raise the self. For this reason I would assume that exegesis could induce and support concrete mystical experiences. (Exactly how it did this cannot be determined.) Such concrete experiences could confirm and deepen a much greater whole, for in principle the contemplation of natural things was tied to intellectual knowledge and the knowledge of God in a vast and multifaceted relationship that included both natural and mystical experience. The declared goal in any case was to heighten vital consciousness beyond human limits, using the most diverse and at the same time intensive methods.

The presentation up to this point should have demonstrated that the motif of the enigmatic character of the written letter did not fall outside the Apologists' otherwise monistic self-understanding and understanding of scripture, any more than did the necessity of an allegorical exposition of scripture. The notion of scripture as an archive of the spirit became more prominent, and the concept of exegesis as a self-exposition of scripture was reinforced.

In both cases there were also synergistic factors. The divine aspect of scripture was, of course, enhanced by the enigmatic character; the Apologists were probably conscious of this and emphasized it accordingly.[413] Aristobulus claims that Moses received the law in two forms, an exoteric form and an esoteric form.[414] Therefore, it was God's will that the true meaning of scripture was not always immediately clear, but was frequently shrouded in enigma. The enigmatic character of the written letter was not a mark of inferiority but a mark of divinity, and thus could stimulate persons of good will to listen more closely to the exposition.

One could speak of a progression, and finally even of an evolution. In their encounter with the text, the Apologetic exegetes could not help but experience the increasing proximity of the divine and sense themselves transformed as a result. This experience also elevated them above their environment and its everyday quality. It was not only Philo and Josephus who, through close association with the prophets, themselves became prophets. The intensive observation of the θεῖοι ἄνδρες in the tradition transformed the observers into θεῖοι ἄνδρες themselves. The *Epistle of Aristeas* illustrates this with respect to the delegates sent by Eleazar, who are supposed to translate the law. Because they are entrusted with the tradition in this way, they turn out to be superior human beings.

Hence, the silence of the Apologetic texts with regard to the Apologists' own missionary achievements probably did not derive merely from a general pressing interest in the tradition. It probably was based on the fact that one discovered oneself in the tradition to the same degree that the tradition in its self-exposition applied to one. When one spoke of θεῖοι ἄνδρες of the past, one was speaking of oneself. Just as much as one was conscious of being molded by the tradition, one also, on the other hand, probably introduced one's own self-understanding into the tradition. Therefore, we must take into account the fact that Apologetic portrayals of history are encoded self-portraits. The marked tendency of Apologetic texts to typify and to provide paradigms would also suggest this. We are dealing here with pattern books. In addition, these texts include legendary and novelistic features. When adapted to the present, these features call for imitation, as shown by the parallels of form criticism.[415]

JUDAISM AS UNIVERSAL RELIGION

In the previous sections, I have already pointed out that the Apologists tended to understand Judaism as the universal religion. The Apologetic exposition of scripture was aligned with cosmic religiosity; the final goal was to help humanity find a common piety.[416]

The ultimate hope was cosmic peace.[417] The enmity between

human and beast, a sign of the disorder of nature, would then be eliminated. And the effect of nature back in its proper balance would be noticeable also in human affairs. War, strife, and other disruptions of the human community would have disappeared.[418] This fusion of natural and human order fits just as precisely into the Apologetic world view analyzed above as does the fusion of natural and human disorder.[419]

I have mentioned the tendency, especially of Josephus, to see the happy life as a consequence of piety; corresponding to this tendency, the future was described as a condition of general well-being.[420] One expected that all the powers of nature would work together to promote the well-being not only of the individual but also of the whole community.[421] Not only an inner well-being was thought of, but also external prosperity, wealth, many children, even a long life, which would eventually pass over into immortality.[422] In their picture of the future, the Apologists painted humanity in full bloom. This was supposed to express the fact that God's salvation, indeed, God himself,[423] would finally live among the people.

The archetype of an ideal humanity, like the one offered by the Sethites or the Jewish patriarchs,[424] was then to be imitated to an even greater degree. Thus it was also understandable that future happiness was earmarked first of all for pious persons and the pious nation. The concepts of Zion and Jerusalem as the center of the world, and the Jewish people as the focal people, had been taken up into the Apologetic vision of the future. Taken up also was the hope of an eschatological return of the Jews from the diaspora.[425] But one cannot speak of nationalistic narrowness. This is already evident in the fact that proselytes were counted among the pious without further ado;[426] indeed, now and then they were held up for special consideration.[427] Even the future expectation of the *Sibylline Oracles* is, on closer inspection, not as nationalistic as it is usually said to be. The distinguished people of the end time is not mentioned by name and not restricted to biological boundaries. I am certain that the band of the elect is meant to include all who will have joined the pious up to the appointed day.

The depictions of the future also show that the Apologists assigned a permanent superiority to those who had proven themselves

prior to the appointed day. To the pious, the Apologists assigned
the full authorities and abilities and the significance which the OT
prototypes had ascribed to the eschatological king, the Messiah.[428]
However, this increased and exponentially enlarged judicial, royal,
and prophetic authority was to be exercised on the behalf of all, to
bring happiness to all.[429] The ἀρετή of the pious, individually and
as a whole, was to help all of humanity and transform it.[430] That is,
the good example of the elect was expected to be an effective stimulus for the rest, so that they would eventually join with the pious in
confession and praise, and before the one God would stand one humanity with one faith.[431] The unity of the human race envisaged in
principle and in practice by the Apologetic missionaries was finally
to be realized.[432]

As promising tokens of this development, the Apologists could
produce the image of their own ideal past and traces of an intellectual and cultural influence upon the past of other nations[433] and
could point to present evidence as well. The extensive Jewish mission served not only as such evidence but also as its penetrating
force. This force expressed itself in direct, numerical success, and in
the indirect influence on customs and thought.[434]

Thus the Jewish mission was a preparation for and in a certain respect an anticipation of the future. Still, the latter was to be distinguished from its preparation in history and in the spread of Judaism
by this: in the future, the competition with paganism would cease.
This competition had previously determined the development of Judaism and its situation. The honors of the future would have, so it
was believed, a conclusive character. That which had proved itself
would have to be proved no longer. The superiority of Jewish piety
would then be recognized generally and unequivocally. Those who
had proved themselves up to that time would then take up the leadership over humankind.[435]

From all this it can be seen that the hope for the future played a
role in Apologetics which was not insignificant. The universal claim
and the universal importance of the Jewish mission were emphasized in this way, yet it also is just as clear that the future of the individual and of the whole community lay in the further development
of the present[436]—the transfiguration into glory of the pious.[437]
One can speak of an end time only in a very figurative sense, for an

actual end, a clear limit, was not at all set.[438] The hope was that all limits would blur and cease. Even the judgment proceedings and punishments with all of their drastic detail, as one finds especially in the *Sibylline Oracles*, did not depict an actual end, but rather gave strong pedagogical perspective. Not only the *Sibylline Oracles* but also *On Rewards and Punishments (Praem.)* count on divine judgment to reform a majority.[439]

Thus, the Apologetic missionaries described the future by pointing to a development whose beginning and outcome could already be seen clearly and whose course was well in hand. They were certain not only of their cause but also of their ability, potential, and prospects. They knew that the powers which accompanied piety were strong enough to overcome all difficulties that stood in the way; they were not overwhelmed by adversity. If necessary, they were also prepared to endure suffering, but this perseverance—in accord with the entire disposition of Apologetic theology—was understood as a heroic achievement.[440] Heroic deeds could be dared, since they knew that the boundary of death did not really exist at all, but had faded away for the pious. They knew that this life, however severe it might be, passed over into immortality.[441] There were plenty of signs that immortal powers existed and were present, for they witnessed the manifestations of the divine spirit and also produced them themselves. Eventually this demonstrated and successful superiority of the pious would be recognized by the whole world, and their leadership over the world would dawn.

In the future, the glory of God and the glory of the pious would finally unite for the salvation of the whole world.[442] This was the goal of the Jewish missionary effort. Indeed, the splendor of this glory already shone from their work.

THE PAGAN MISSION

Mission as Competition[443]

The investigation has thus shown that the Jewish mission continuously and deliberately related to Hellenism and understood this relation as competition. Indeed, inner superiority and outer penetrating force were gained from this competitive comparison.

In turning now to the pagan competitors of the Jewish missionaries, I am unable to offer a detailed description of their activity. For this, I refer to the works of Franz Cumont and Arthur Darby Nock.[444] I see myself all the more unable to clarify the historical connections between the Jewish and the Hellenistic mission. The reciprocal relationship between Judaism and Hellenism took many forms; it was the goal of Jewish history and the history of pagan thought and religiosity. In the NT period the Jewish mission is part of an intellectual and religious expansion movement that embraced the entire Mediterranean world and the Near East.

In NT times not only the cult places, but also the alleys and markets of the ancient cities, as well as the rest areas on the more important long-distance and rural roads, were full of the noise and bustle of the most diverse religious and philosophical recruiters.[445] The oldest propagandists of the Hellenistic world were the philosophers, who served as missionary models in Hellenistic times. This was especially true of the Cynic-Stoic popular philosophers, whom I have already treated above.[446] In addition, there were the neo-Pythagorean philosophers, who are difficult to date and locate precisely.[447]

The oriental cults were carried to other places by oriental immigrants and subsequently also by some Greek and Roman converts. In addition, these cults had itinerant preachers. Their work was supported by the local recruiting of the cults as they became settled.

Begging was characteristic of the philosophical and religious converting activity of many missionaries.[448] We have already encountered it in the investigation of Jewish missionary activity,[449] and I have attempted to show that this asking for financial support could not have been merely a sign of widespread parasitism and widespread superstitious fear.[450] Instead, begging must have been a generally recognized religious phenomenon. The pleading for support by itinerant pneumatics who recruited for their deity or their philosophical beliefs must have been part of that.[451]

Healings and exorcisms were offered as exceptional deals,[452] as well as magic arts, astrological knowledge and practices, oracles, and more. Not to be forgotten is rhetoric, which not only clothed the achievements of the deity and its messengers in the right words but also obtained the appropriate publicity. Literary recognition and commemoration going beyond the immediate oral word were also sought, and this recognition was a financial one also.[453]

All these attractions for the eye and ear, which in many cults were supplemented with large public performances such as processions, public ceremonies, and the like,[454] served to stimulate participation in the act of divine worship.[455]

Not much more can be reported about the relation between propaganda outside of divine worship and the act of divine worship itself. The sources are meager. Some missionary cults did permit nonmembers to attend some, if not all, cultic performances.[456] To what extent that was also true of the philosophical schools and the real mystery cults is difficult to determine.[457] As far as the philosophical schools are concerned, I should point out that their recourse to mystery motifs and elements is not always to be taken literally or to be given an immediate sociological significance. Often a merely figurative and purely literary usage must be assumed. Parallels occur in classical Greek philosophy, especially in Plato.[458] The fact that the younger oriental mysteries continued or imitated the old Greek ones with regard to organization should be investigated further, as well as the fact that these religions all tended to occupy an essential place in public life, in analogy to the oldest mysteries, the Eleusinian ones.[459] In this way, arcane discipline and the desire to communicate and to influence the public stood in tension with each other.[460]

In general, all religions of Hellenism that took up mission and set out into the world adopted various elements of the Greek mysteries, although they did not necessarily become mystery religions. The philosophical schools also adopted mystery elements as they took up worldwide propaganda.

Certain sociological and legal factors were behind this development. Besides the already mentioned desire to communicate and to influence the public, there were Hellenistic laws on associations and clubs. Analogous to the existing mystery associations, a propagandizing religion or philosophy could strive for recognition as an association. Moreover, the older Dionysiac mysteries offered a model for combining universal expansion with the forming of small mystery associations. These associations exhibited uniform features, and they probably also had contact with each other.[461] On the whole, what Nock wrote on pages 57–58 applies to the oriental missionary religions: "The cult was for the majority of its worshippers not a mystery cult, and in many places in the Hellenistic period proper it was not a mystery cult at all. The uninitiated devotee might attend the public worship, might pray for help, might make his vows in sickness and pay them in health, might have sacrifice offered by the priest, might wear a ring with representations of the gods as an amulet, might put up private shrines or join in a cult association, might dine "at the god's couch. . . ."

The frequently cited sixth satire of Juvenal (521ff.) gives an impression of the groups and the intensity of their recruitment. Here the most disparate missionaries are introduced: those of Cybele, of Attis, of the Jewish God, and finally also magicians and astrologers. Juvenal quite drastically describes the ways and means in which these diverse people attempted to arouse attention and to impress. This striving for effect was the common trait in their diversity.

Judging by Juvenal's report, the missionaries tried to demonstrate the extraordinary character of their message by the most extraordinary means at their disposal. Whoever engaged in such public performances would have to reckon with competitors and adapt to the situation. The public would judge the performances of the missionaries (and thereby also their respective religions) according to something like an international and interconfessional scale of values for the divine. This judgment led more-or-less directly to a ranking of the religions, as Juvenal's presentation seems to indicate. The order he gives clearly reflects a value judgment. The achievements become more impressive, more comprehensive, and also more effective. The final sequence, Jewish woman missionary, then magician, then astrologer, suggests a value-laden inquiry and assessment based on individual demonstrations. The degree of manifest knowledge of nature and cosmos and the control of their powers were the criteria.

The stylized biographic sketches of certain individuals point out this competition of different salvation messages.[462] These truth seekers sampled assorted religious and intellectual groups and schools and decided in favor of the one that proved itself to be clearly superior.

The convincing demonstration of the power of a specific deity could then be praised and acclaimed as εἷς θεός[463] (followed by the name of the particular deity) over other defeated deities; the veneration of that particular deity was thereby declared as binding. Such acclamations responded to and competed with similar declarations of other cults expressed by their propagandists and acclaimed by their believers and converts. Acclamations as ratifying responses to wondrous manifestations of the deity played an important role in Hellenistic cults and their expansions.[464] The pneumatic demonstrations of the missionaries were among those manifestations, and the propagandists looked for the corresponding reaction of their observers and listeners.

The missionary groups and cults of Hellenism presumably shared common motives and standards, similar to a lingua franca and an international currency. Influenced by these common conceptions and ways of judgment, which were constituted from Greeks, oriental, and newer Hellenistic elements, individual missionaries followed the prevailing fashion and adopted certain standards of conduct and expression. They were fully conscious of the meaning and effect of their repertoire.[465] The example of Alexander of Abonuteichus, which Weinreich has analyzed in an investigation that is informative for the reconstruction of the entire religious propaganda of the Hellenistic world,[466] shows the deliberate and successful use of all the components of recruiting advertisement available to religious propaganda. The trend toward world mission is substantiated here, not only by the personal activity of Alexander but also by the assignment of disciples to mission and by the firm intention to establish a foothold in Rome, the world capital. Jews and Christians thus also encountered many competitors in their worldwide activity.

The θεῖος ἀνήρ Motif[467]

The personality and the capability of the missionary played a decisive role in the debate of the missionary groups. The success of a message depended on the missionary's ability to express the divine in his or her performance. A passage in Dio Chrysostom of Prusa shows that in NT times the public really waited for people who could demonstrate the divine in human form. Clearly, such appearances were not simply products of literary imagination. In his first Tarsic speech, Dio first wonders why the Tarsians allow him to speak, and then suggests that he is being confused with certain other people:

> It seems to me you have often heard divine human beings (θεῖοι ἄνθρωποι) who say they know all things and (they are able) to speak about all things regardless of which way they are ordered and what kind of nature they possess, (that is) about humans and demons and, indeed, about gods, further about earth, heaven, and sea, about sun, moon, and the other stars, yes, about the entire cosmos, even about its destruction and origin and ten thousand other things.[468]

The following sentence suggests that their rhetorical capability corresponds to their tremendous knowledge. Whoever claims to be on the tracks of the world and its mysteries and can demonstrate it appropriately is applauded by the masses and is considered a θεῖος ἄνθρωπος.

Dio dissociates himself from this type of divine human being. Yet the role he assumes, that of the true—essentially Cynic—philosopher is not so far removed from the ideal of the θεῖος ἄνθρωπος. It has already been shown in the analysis of the διάκονος concept that the missionary consciousness of the Cynic-Stoic popular philosophers superseded by far the boundaries of the normal.[469] They saw themselves as personifications of the ideal wise person, who conspicuously demonstrated his superiority over material things.[470] In this they emulated the founders of Cynic philosophy, who already knew themselves to be superior to other human beings and who had manifested their superiority in their appearance.

These forerunners had already outlined their godlike function with, among others, the expression κατάσκοπος.[471] In *Diss*. 1.24, Epictetus takes the dispute of a member of the school to Rome as the occasion for a diatribe. The mission of the Cynic envoy is outlined in this way: "And now we are sending you to Rome as a scout."[472] The use of the concept κατάσκοπος shows that this is not an insignificant journey, nor simply a mission in the name of the philosophical school, but rather the assumption of a function similar to that of Diogenes and the other great Cynics, namely, to represent the Cynic way of life and mission. The designated one goes forth as a propagandist of the school. Otherwise, it would also be unintelligible why this mission is the subject of the description of the Cynic's proving himself in the particular difficult circumstances (περιστάσεις). περίστασις is a technical term of the Cynic-Stoic diatribe. The first sentence of the diatribe reads, "The περιστάσεις are those which show what men really are."[473] Only someone who proves himself in all περιστάσεις can be sent as a missionary. "No one sends a coward as a κατάσκοπος." These words certainly indicate that the envoy is not sent on a business trip: this κατάσκοπος, though sent by human beings, is reminded of the model of Diogenes,[474] "Diogenes, who before you, was sent as κατάσκοπος" (*Diss* 1.24.6). If this divine messenger is placed directly before the eyes of the disciple and given the very same title, that signifies that the disciple's mission has a corresponding authority; actually, he is going to Rome under God's commission.[475] Therefore, he must exert all his energies for this assignment. The equipment described in *Diss*. 1.24.11 is a sign of this and of the proper attitude which is supposed to be propagated.

For the discussion between Paul and his opponents presented below, it is important to note that the περιστάσεις, according to the conception of the Cynic-Stoic diatribe, prove to the missionary *his own* divine power and thus support his propaganda.

The example of Peregrinus Proteus shows to what degree such demonstrations could become miraculous in character with less intellectual representatives of Cynic-Stoic popular philosophy.[476] He allowed himself to be burned and thereby proved his power to be superior to human weakness and limitations. His disciples and missionaries proclaimed his "apotheosis," which they proclaimed not as something completely new but as the culmination of what had gone before. I am certain that the proclamation of the disciples and the intention of their master showed a continuity.

This propensity for the miraculous and the course of Peregrinus's life in general clearly show how far Cynic-Stoic popular philosophy had opened itself to philosophical and religious syncretism and thereby had blurred the differences in content.

Among the philosophers, this was especially true of the Neo-Pythagoreans. As a result, they gained a decisive influence on subsequent philosophical and religious developments. The most important and effective Neo-Pythagorean philosopher in NT times was Apollonius of Tyana.[477] His extensive traveling and recruiting activity is not the product of later legends but rather forms their basis in fact. It is probably also historical that Apollonius linked his presentations of profound philosophical teachings with various impressive manifestations of unusual capabilities, beginning with rhetorical ones. This gave his opponents and those of his disciples (beginning with the apostatical Euphrates) an occasion to reproach him with being a magician and enchanter, which was to say, a charlatan and cheat.[478] This was probably also the basis for his trial, certainly historical, under Domitian which, as a side note, made him a comrade of fate and suffering of Jewish and "Christian" missionaries and converts. He then had the opportunity to personally prove the

views on suffering and death which he had articulated in the probably genuine fifty-eighth letter.[479] He thought that human life,
continuously nourished by the powers of the cosmos and thereby
constantly raised above its limitations, would completely transcend
all limits at death and be absorbed into the universe.

The Apollonius legend subsequently linked this general view of
the master to his own death and presented it—in the same way as
the Jewish Apologists presented the death of Moses—as a disappearance (in the sense of a cosmic exaltation and generalization).[480]
Apollonius doubtless understood himself as a proclaimer of this ele-
mental and effective presence of divine-cosmic power in the human
world. He presented himself as an example, not as an exception but
as a clarifying and enlightening indication of what was real and possible for everyone. So there is no reason why Philostratus should
have been the first to bestow the predicate θεῖος on Apollonius.[481]
As an impressive and stimulating symbol, this self-designation made
a great deal of sense with the fifty-eighth letter in the background.[482]

It seems that the Serapis cult was characteristic for the propaganda of missionary religious groups.[483] It needed strong propaganda to free itself of the suspicion that it was merely an artificial
religion. This suspicion gave it a disadvantage in relation to older religions. The method it used to succeed against its competitors and
manifest its missionary claim must have had these characteristics
which were necessary for catching on with the public. Against the
myths of older cults the Serapis cult set an endless number of aretalogies diligently drawn and collected.[484] What counted were the
ἀρεταί of the deity, which the myths also enumerated.[485]

The power of the deity tangibly entered the life of the individual
believers; it distinguished them and enabled them to recruit for
their god and his or her worship. According to a letter preserved on
papyrus,[486] Serapis appeared to Zoilos around 258/7 B.C.E. in several dreams and warned and pushed him with ominous sickness (and
marvelous healing). This induced Zoilos to petition the Egyptian
minister of finance, Apollonius, for permission and the means to
construct a Serapis temple and establish a Serapis cult in Zoilos's
present place of residence. These dream apparitions showed signifi-

cant parallels to the official cult legends;[487] they paralleled Zoilos with cult founders.[488] Together with the other experiences from a divine source, these apparitions certify him as the authorized representative of the deity to all the townspeople and the minister of finance. They even identify him with another missionary of the same god as the preferred one at this place.[489]

According to Delian inscription from the third century B.C.E.,[490] a Serapis believer named Apollonius was deemed worthy of a divine dream oracle and was thereby called on to build a temple for Serapis, who had been worshiped only in the family circle since his grandfather's (an Egyptian) arrival, to enable the god's public recognition and worship. Apollonius obeyed. The site was procured, the temple was built. But on that account a legal action was brought against Apollonius. This misfortune befell not only him (and the few other believers) but also, as it is said twice, the deity. This identification of the fate of the deity with that of his missionary (and then also of the other believers) also becomes perceptible in the dream's words of consolation, for Serapis says, "*We* shall triumph." The subjects of this and the next sentence overlap because of the intimate union of god and human being. The next sentence reads, "Now that the trial is ended and *we* have triumphed in a manner suitable to the god, *we* praise the gods through the fact that *we* render suitable thanks." A hymn follows which assigns this newest miracle to the countless others wrought by Serapis and Isis. The previously cited dream oracle is now presented as a divine response to the (effective) prayer of Apollonius, and the same holds true for the divine help at the trial. It is a divine answer to a human petition. The deity itself renders the opponents speechless in court. But the glory of this miracle falls on the representative of the deity, for the conclusion of the chorus says, "And the entire crowd on this day was astonished at your might, and you brought your servant great glory. . . ." God and a human being had worked together, but it was difficult to determine whether the deity or the human being had effected the extraordinary. Indeed, the individual act had no miraculous power of the deity. The individual miracle manifested what was known from antiquity, and the glorification of the individual deed made it timeless.[491] That brings in the motif of tradition.

The Motif of Tradition

The Greeks had already shown a certain predilection for archaic things before the Hellenistic era, but during this time the antiquarian interest and efforts, especially for and in things coming from the East, became tremendous.[492] In the discussion about whether and where to find universal and eternal truth, it was suggested that the *answer* lay in temporal and spatial distance.[493] The general principle was that the older and more eastern things were, the more divine and credible they were. Human beings had been closest to the gods in ancient times.[494] Since the temples and the traditions were older in the East, the wisdom of the East must be more eternal and divine. In the East, mysterious traditions were anxiously guarded. The language was mysterious because it was unintelligible; even the sounds of the language (because they were strange and because the relation between verbal expression and living reality was not understood) seemed to radiate a mysterious and magical power. At the same time, it was debated who the oldest wise people were and where the best hoard of divine wisdom might be found. The results of this debate varied widely.

Berossus and Manetho, then Apion, among others, and the Jewish Apologists showed that they had understood the signs of the times. They met the questions of the West and North halfway and were able—in their own interest—to reinforce them. Inevitably, these people competed with each other.

How did the concept of tradition express itself in propaganda? The Hellenistic philosophers emphasized the past founding period and oriented themselves to the founders of their schools, who increasingly enjoyed divine veneration. The one who received it first was Epicurus. This shows in Lucretius's glorifying him in the impressive poem "De Natura Rerum."

In Cynic-Stoic popular philosophy, the great philosophers of the past were imitated, and even the mythical hero Heracles was taken as a model.[495] The Stoic school developed an expanded interest in the past, which is noticeable in Posidonius.

The Neo-Pythagoreans oriented themselves to the past even more strongly than the Stoics and the Cynic-Stoic diatribe. "Here (in the small Neo-Pythagorean groups) the wisdom of Pythagoras was transmitted as secret teaching in alleged unbroken tradition, especially the magical and astrological practices reportedly handed down from him." And, "As the most essential task the Neo-Pythagoreans took up the imitation of the life of Pythagoras; that is, they derived the guiding principles which were acknowledged as binding from the biography of Pythagoras that was circulating in different refractions."[496]

Thus, the θεῖος ἀνήρ motif was oriented to the tradition both for the Cynic-Stoic popular philosophers and for the Neo-Pythagoreans — as in Jewish Apologetics. Indeed, among the Neo-Pythagoreans the conflation went so far that for modern historians the contours are completely blurred. As in the case of the Jewish Apologists, their individual self-understanding entered the description of the models in such a way that their individual identity was concealed in these models.

The flowering Pythagoras legend had already made him into a great traveler.[497] Egypt, Persia, Assyria, Babylonia, India, and other lands became stations of his legendary travels, in which he mixed with various and sundry priests, holy people, and sages. The purpose was no longer to own wisdom but to gain a comprehensive "Weltanschauung." This, of course, became the declared goal of the Neo-Pythagoreans, following and developing on older legends. They could reach back to a tradition saturated with wisdom and holiness and refer to it in this successful propaganda. This tradition had already attained written form, although it continued to grow.

In the mission of the cults the age motif was utilized no longer primarily for legal reasons,[498] but rather for propaganda purposes.[499] Here the scriptural motif played a vital role, for which a few examples will be given.[500] The letters of the alphabet, once the holy signs of priesthood, had in the meantime become instruments of mystery and magic because the letter was thought to carry power.[501] This belief was strengthened as the expressions of the mysterious and the divine multiplied. The knowledge of the letters was considered to be a gift imparted by the gods. The Isis aretalogy of Andos, which characteristically refers to a stele of Isis in the temple of Ptah-Hephaestus in Memphis, puts one of her most significant ἀρεταί in the following words: "The hidden and found letter symbols of wise Hermes I have inscribed for the devotees, thus, engraving an awe-inspiring ἱερὸς λόγος."[502]

The oracle of Poitiers strictly maintains the fiction of divine inspiration.[503] In his trance, the prophet dictates the oracle to the scribe (ἱερογραμματεύς) in the presence of king and priests. Thereupon this work is deposited in the holy archives of Heliopolis so that all can investigate it there.

Ptolemy's report in the Tetrabiblos is also interesting.[504] Ptolemy is making propaganda for astrology. Allegedly, he had found a part of his astrological teaching in a very old and badly damaged book. Because of its poor condition the book was very difficult to understand. This fiction of Ptolemy is intended to enhance the credibility of his teaching. Although this is a literary convention, it may be assumed that Ptolemy also subjectively thought that his teaching rendered the sense of the old, above all, that it communicated divine truth.

As a sign, holy writings were frequently described as being concealed and discovered in temples.[505] This emphasized their ancient, divine, and mysterious character, which is partly underlined further by other features, such as foreign script. The *Kore Kosmou* says,

> (Hermes) saw the whole and when he had seen it, he understood; and when he had understood, he was able to reveal and to show. He also engraved that which he had understood; and after he had engraved it, he concealed it, since he considered it to be better to remain silent about most of it than to speak of it, so that every generation born subsequent to the world should seek it. (*Kore Kosmou* 5; also cf. 7)[506]

About a magic book it is said, "This book itself, belonging to the twelve gods, was found in Aphroditopolis (in the vicinity) of the greatest goddess Aphrodite, the heavenly one who embraces the All."[507]

These mysterious, concealed, and rediscovered writings with their holy signs are a variation on the heavenly letters documenting divine revelation.[508] In this way, something specific is traced back to the distant myths of primordial times in order to ensure its power and authority. In the long run, the written texts can take the place of the cult myth, as has already been shown for the Serapis cult. An aretalogical text reads, "The ἀρετή (miraculous deed) is recorded in the library of Mercury."[509] Here the individual text functions as a record or document.[510] Aretalogies were preserved in large numbers in the archives of cult sanctuaries.[511] The multitude of texts and their anonymity could stimulate the antiquity necessary for the cult myth. An impressive abundance and an indeterminable antiquity of these testimonies was valued. It was necessary to show the omnipresent might of the god in all its multiplicity.[512] Simultaneously, the superiority over other cults had to be proven, thus the tradition recruited and testified for its representative.[513] Therefore, in Hellenism the motif of the θεῖος ἀνήρ and the motif of tradition did not have to be mutually exclusive. Rather, they could supplement each other as a twofold expression of the omnipresent power of the deity. In this way, both motifs could complement each other in recruitment.[514]

The invocation of antiquity was supposed to bestow universal validity on the competing Hellenistic cults and creeds. The ancestors were not appealed to out of fear or awe. Rather, one was sure of oneself and counted on the dissemination of one's teaching, proven to be divine by its mysterious origin. The written fixation of this literature and corresponding reports testifies that dissemination was intended. Even the reference to the necessity of allegorical interpretation of the old texts did not necessarily contradict this.[515] On the contrary, it could work as propaganda and incite people to also work with these obviously mysterious texts and their probably divine content, guided at first, of course, by those already accustomed to and practiced in them.[516]

As an example of the final phase of this whole development, I would like to offer the accounts of the *Book of Elkesai*.[517] Hippolytus reports, "Alcibiades . . . came to Rome and brought a book with him, pretending that a certain righteous man, Elkesai, received it from the Serers of Parthia and then handed it over to a certain Sabiai, but it was communicated by an angel (χρηματισθείς)."[518] The mysterious book therefore was inspired; the transmission is kept in the dark. It comes from the East and is very old. In the following the tension that has been cited and that is characteristic for the

Hellenistic tradition motif becomes clear. Although Alcibiades is interested in the dissemination of his teaching, he nevertheless emphasizes the mysterious character of the book very strongly. "He regarded it to be unreasonable that these great and unspeakable mysteries would be trampled under foot or handed over to many, indeed, he counselled these to be guarded as precious pearls, since he says, 'Do not read this discourse to all human beings, and guard these injunctions carefully, for not all men are reliable and not all women are sincere.'" (Hippolytus, *Refutatio omnium haeresium* 9.17—my trans.)

THE MISSION OF THE EARLY CHURCH

Mission as an Announcement of God's Rule

Through their self-designations, the opponents of Paul revealed not only that they were missionaries but also in whose footsteps they planned to tread: in those of the Jewish missionaries, who had held and were holding their own in the missionary competition of the Hellenistic world. These footsteps have now been followed and have led us to certain conceptions of the spirit, the models and the standards which the opponents of Paul appealed to and by which they were to be measured. This, however, has not yet covered the opponents' entire area of competition. The opponents' pride in their Jewish heritage and its universal mission was, after all, combined with the claim to be Jesus-missionaries. Indeed, they claimed—and were believed by many—to be better missionaries than Paul. They had the right, which could hardly be disputed by Paul, to bear the title of διάκονοι Χριστοῦ.[519]

Since there is no doubt that much of Paul's understanding of mission and missionaries was colored personally to a certain degree,[520] the question could arise whether the opponents of Paul did not represent the early church's general understanding of mission, which therefore could be seen entirely in the context of Jewish Apologetics. In the discussion of the opponents' designation of function, it proved difficult to gain a job description for the functions of "deacon" and "apostle" from the early texts.[521] This could strengthen the temptation to equate the description of the missionaries opposing Paul with the image of Jesus-missionaries in general. But the third traditional title used by Paul's opponents for the Jesus-missionaries, the term "worker,"[522] argues against this. It also occurs in a text which reveals a concept of mission entirely different from the one developed by Jewish Apologetics and presupposed by the opponents of Paul,[523] even though the text was contemporaneous with Paul's opponents and not dependent on Paul. I am thinking of Matthew 10 and its parallel in Luke.

The mission discourse in Matthew 10 is a collection of sayings composed by Matthew.[524] Yet the Sayings Source (Q) appears to have given a certain support to this composition, for one part of the Matthew tradition (Matt. 10:5–16) is preserved in Luke 10:1–16 in a similar version. A briefer and changed version of this mission discourse is found in Mark 6:7–13 and Luke 9:1–6.[525] The best evidence for a double tradition is the twofold account of Luke.

Synoptic comparison further shows that the connection between Matt. 10:5–16 and the pericope of the call of the disciples (Matt. 10:1–4) is secondary. The other two evangelists report the call of the disciples separately (Mark 3:13–19;[526] Luke 6:12–16). Luke 10:2–16 (the sending of the *seventy*) proves moreover that the twelve also did not belong to the mission discourse of Q. How could Luke, who so strongly emphasizes the apostolate of the twelve elsewhere,[527] have eliminated the twelve from the mission discourse?[528] By using the ἑτέρους in v. 1, he links the narrative with the tradition of the twelve.[529] In all the Synoptic pericopes mentioned,[530] the verb ἀποστέλλειν generally appears. Only Matt. 10:2 and Luke 6:13 utilize ἀπόστολος.[531] The text of Matt. 10:2, however, is suspect,[532] and Luke is the only evangelist who also employs the ἀπόστολος concept as a title elsewhere (cf. also Luke 17:5; 22:14; 24:10). The primarily missionary character of the sending thus is again underlined.

The missionary character shows itself especially clearly in the Q version of the mission discourse and the following sayings on discipleship in Matthew. Early church tradition is expressed here. This is supported by the completely eschatological perspective in these logia. The eschatological character of the concept of mission is especially evident in the content of commissioned proclamation: ἤγγικεν ἡ βασιλεία τοῦ θεοῦ (Luke 10:9, 11; cf. Matt. 10:7; 9:2). But the comparison of the envoys with sheep among the wolves (Matt. 10:16; Luke 10:3) also speaks for an older tradition.[533] The other sayings on discipleship in Matt. 10:17–41 are of the same severity. In this discourse Matthew has combined not only sayings of similar content but also sayings of similar origin.

The missionary concept and practice of the Q tradition used by Matthew still reflects an immediate expectation of the parousia. The view represented here is very similar to the proclamation of Jesus himself as it is probably mirrored in the sayings on discipleship or Matt. 10:34–39.[534] In spite of their detailed "technical" instructions and aside from the brief notice about the proclamation of the nearness of the βασιλεία, the sayings on discipleship in the mission discourse contain nothing of the proclamation's content. Apparently, therefore, these messengers did not proclaim the life of Jesus, not even so much the person of Jesus, but rather the coming of God's rule. These people were not in demand as eyewitnesses but as messengers of the coming one. The equipment offered to them and the conduct demanded of them point to the urgency of their commission.

The concept of miracles expressed in Luke 10:2–20 and Matt. 10:5–8 (15) is also noteworthy. No special authority to work miracles is granted here. The miracles of the disciples do not flow out of a mana conferred upon them. Luke 10 and Matthew 10 do not say, You are going to work miracles. In place of the expected indicative stands an imperative (Luke 10:9 and Matt. 10:8), both times in immediate conjunction with the demand to announce the nearness of the kingdom.[535]

The missionaries of the early church spoken of in the tradition underlying Luke 10 and Matthew 10 are not the first messengers of the imminent βασιλεία. Luke 10:16 stands as the conclusion of the mission discourse to the seventy. This saying similarly appears in Matt. 10:40. In Luke's version it reads, "Whoever hears you hears me, and whoever despises you despises me. But whoever despises me despises the one who sent me." In Matthew's version the saying reads, "Whoever receives you receives me, and whoever receives me receives the one who sent me."[536] A parallel which is somewhat older because of its proverbial character[537] says, "The disciple is not above (his) teacher and the slave is not above (his) master. It is enough for the disciple to be like his teacher and the slave like his master. If they have called the master of the house Beelzebub, how much more his household" (Matt. 10:24–25). The disciple is like his teacher, the slave like his master. In terms of the proclamation, that means they suffer the fate of the Lord as his representatives. It makes no difference whether or not this is an original saying on discipleship of the earthly Jesus. In any case the early church related it to the fate of its proclaimers. Like Jesus himself, they were messengers of the end time, for the proclamation of Jesus also began with the call ἤγγικεν ἡ βασιλεία τοῦ θεοῦ (Mark 1:15; cf. Matt. 4:17).

What differentiated these missionaries of the early church from Jesus was that they identified him as the coming Messiah (later as the one who has come) and proclaimed his parousia. They knew that they were representatives of Jesus; this probably led them to transfer the Jewish concept of the apostle to themselves. The essence of the Jewish concept of the apostle has been paraphrased as שְׁלִיחוֹ שֶׁל אָדָם כְּמוֹתוֹ. But the intention, the proclamation of the end time, of the parousia of Christ, existed before the title of apostle and did not necessarily entail it, as the indicated texts show.[538]

Mission as Pneumatic Demonstration

An entirely different picture is encountered in the mission discourse of Mark 6. Here the eschatological tension has almost completely vanished. The nearness of the βασιλεία is no longer mentioned. In the conclusion (Mark 6:12–13) only the proclamation of repentance and miracle activity are referred to, for the preaching of repentance can also be understood in an uneschatological sense. Apart from the "technical" details, Mark reports that the disciples have received the ἐξουσία for the journey. The revisions of the call of the Twelve which have been preserved speak of this pneumatic authority. The missionary, the apostle, no longer proclaims the imminent end but the present power. With this the proximity to the Jewish missionaries is indicated and with it also a certain material dependence on these predecessors.

This picture of the missionary is also found in the older Antio-

chean tradition utilized by Luke.[539] Stephen distinguishes himself
as a miracle worker and thereby legitimizes himself as a missionary
(Acts 6:8–10). The climax of his miraculous authority is found in his
oratorical capability (Acts 6:10). It is interesting that a transfiguration of Stephen is referred to in Acts 6:15. One thinks immediately
of the picture of the θεῖος ἀνήρ sketched above.[540]

In reporting on the mission of Philip, Acts 8:6–8 says, "The masses gave credence unanimously to what Philip had said when they
heard (him) and saw the signs which he did.[541] For many who had
unclean spirits were liberated of these, for they came out crying
with a loud voice,[542] and many who were paralyzed or lame were
healed; so there was much joy in that city." Here miracles have an
essential tie to reality and are not merely signs of continuation. The
theological content of Philip's proclamation is briefly summarized:
"He proclaimed Christ to them" (Acts 8:5). Miracle activity takes the
spotlight from proclamation.

An account of the confrontation between a missionary of the early
church and a proclaimer of another salvation teaching follows. The
dispute is less over the different messages than over the different capabilities and results. In reality the confrontation is a competition of
the proclaimers. The competitor is defamed in the sharpest manner
in the description. But this polemical caricature must still acknowledge the miraculous power of Simon and the imminent danger arising from it. The opponent is not ignored, but he is not convinced by
the arguments either; he is won over by the greater but basically
similar ability of his competitor. When Simon is called a magician,[543] he is given a rebuke which was frequently employed in polemics but was always a sign of basic equality with the critic.[544]

The summary which reports the activity of Simon has the same
style as the summary of Acts 8:6–8. Simon pretends "to be something great" (Acts 8:9). "And all, from children to old folk, gave credence to him and said, 'This is the power of God which is named the
Great'" (v. 10). That which was stated previously, "The masses
unanimously gave credence to what Philip had said" (Acts 8:6), is
now formulated "All gave credence to him (Simon)" (v. 10; also cf. v.
11); but afterward it is said, "However, when they believed Philip"
(v. 12). This is an account of a confrontation between two pneumat-

ics of different denominations. It cannot be said that one only demonstrates his personality, the other, in contrast, the authority standing behind him. Both do both! The demonstrations correspond to the respective realities behind them. Eventually the stronger one wins. For the crowds who are called on to judge, it means that the reality of one representative is stronger.

In the passage at hand, the competitor acknowledges his defeat. His conversion characteristically is described in a very superficial way. Certainly a part of what follows must be attributed to Luke and his desire to defame this competitor.[545] But such conversions were common, apparently called for by such kind of theology and the corresponding missionary practice. One need only compare how superficial the conversion of Apollos appears in Acts 18:24–25.[546]

Paul's confrontation with the Jewish prophet Barjesus (or Elymas) is narrated in Acts 13:6–12.[547] Of course, this man is identified as a false prophet (v. 6) and magician (v. 8).[548] Barjesus is a confidant of the governor (corresponding to the oriental counselors who were sometimes kept by members of the upper class)[549] now competing with Paul for the governor's favor. Faith is spoken of only incidentally. It is chiefly the story of the confrontation of the two men, in which story the greater pneumatic, the stronger miracle worker, triumphs. The miraculous punishment then leads the governor to faith.[550]

In Acts 14:8–18 Paul and Barnabas are venerated as gods who have become human on the basis of their miracle. This polytheistic view of God is completely rejected. But the concluding phrase of 14:18—"They scarcely restrained the people from offering sacrifice to them"—nevertheless serves *ad maiorem gloriam apostolorum*. Polytheism is indeed strongly rejected, but not the concept of the θεῖος ἀνήρ.[551] Tendencies similar to those expressed in this tradition can be found in Acts 15:11–12.

The miracle recounted in Acts 19:11–12 is among the most powerful of the entire NT. The miracle is so impressive that Jewish exorcists try to lay hold of Paul's miraculous power using the ὄνομα he uses. They swear, "I adjure you by the Jesus whom Paul preaches" (v. 13). The kerygma, therefore, is essentially a paraphrase of the miracle-working name. The demon drastically demonstrates that the name and with it also the kerygma may not be separated from the person of the miracle-working missionary. Non-"Christians" may not use this decisive tool. The difference between it and the old pericope of the strange exorcists in Mark 9:38–40 is clear. The missionary has become a medium of the power of Jesus (Acts 19:13, 15). The concept of Jesus-faith proclaimed here would apparently be abandoned if the union between name and proclaimer were denied. An obviously powerful reality stands behind the proclaimer, but only behind him. In the following verses, the conversion of the magicians is probably decisive, but magic is replaced only by the belief in a greater and mightier miracle-working power (cf. v. 20). The triumph in the competition is the real content of the account.

Christology as an Aid in
the Competition

This concept of mission and the accompanying practice have their basis in a change of christology. It was no longer the coming of the Christ which was decisive, but rather his might in the past and present.[552] This change had already occurred before the writing of the Gospel according to Mark. The concept of miracles changed due to the change of christology. This change is recognizable in the miracle stories of the Synoptic tradition. Of course, these short pieces at first served only as edification. But the miracle accounts then tend to show a new interest in the person of the miracle worker. In many stories he is not a messenger of the end time but the present donor of divine power. The dialogue of Jesus with the demon in Mark 1:23–28 is one example.

The concluding chorus is also significant. It emphasizes the singularity or newness of such deeds (Matt. 9:33). In Mark 2:12 the conclusion of the story of the paralytic reads, "We never saw anything like this!" The person of Jesus is very strongly featured in the preceding narrative. For the community from which this text originated, the testimony of the imminent end was not essential, but rather the testimony of present power. The account's emphasis on the power of Jesus indicates an audience that knew of similar mighty deeds of other divine human beings. The emphasis on the uniqueness of Jesus' performance is in fact relative to those experiences previously made.

The change in the early church's proclamation of Jesus Christ becomes still clearer in the miracle stories of distinct novelistic character, which are called "novellas" by Dibelius.[553] These stories are not strictly focused on an explanatory saying, but rather narrate in a broader manner. Whenever the deeds of Jesus are reported, the intention to demonstrate his superiority is clearly evident (Mark 4:35–41; 6:45–52). The stories want to prove his superiority over any other benefactor (also cf. Mark 5:1–20; 5:21–43; 6:35–44). Essentially, the novelistic miracle story blurs the boundaries between God and the envoy of God.[554]

When the early church made itself conscious of the superiority of its Lord, it thereby simultaneously justified its own practice.[555] The miracles of Jesus in these novelistic miracle stories are, of course, exemplary miracles, and the faith in these miracles concomitantly has an exemplary character (Mark 7:32–37; 8:22–26; 9:14–29).

In the sketch of their respective Gospels, Mark and Luke follow this christological conception. The miraculous character of the Christ is emphasized at every turn. It is interesting that Matthew does not follow this tendency.[556] The proclamation of the early church went different ways in spite of its similar material.

When the disciples themselves are depicted as bearers of ἐξουσία, as miracle-working missionaries, it corresponds to the picture of Jesus as a superior miracle worker. The consequences are evident in the account of the return of the seventy. Luke himself probably wove it around the very old logion of 10:18.[557] Little can be said about its original meaning.[558] In the context of Luke, this logion apparently explains the assertion of the disciples in v. 17 and the ἐξουσία described in v. 19. The latter goes very far and is corrected by v. 20. The entire pericope parallels the disciples with Jesus. They are the representatives of Jesus in the present. Luke certainly did not invent the parallelism as such. It already belongs to the theology of the oldest tradition. Nor was Luke the first to attach this concept of miracles to the portrayal of the disciples. Mark 6:37–44 and its parallels showed the same thing. Moreover, Luke 10:1–16 reveals that here the evangelist followed the given tradition. The stylistically not completely smooth introduction of 10:1 already attests to that, but also the fact that it is the seventy, not the twelve, who are paralleled to Jesus seems to indicate the use of older material, for elsewhere Luke is concerned about the precedence of the twelve. Similar assertions about the authority of all believers are found in the spurious ending of Mark (16:17–18). So it may also be assumed that the frequent parallels between the apostles and Jesus in the Acts of the Apostles did not originate with Luke.

The christological variations of the preceding investigation lead not only beyond the story of Jesus but also back behind it. The narrative of the transfiguration (Mark 9:2–8) relates the figure of Jesus to Moses and Elijah. Hahn has attempted to prove that an original Palestinian version may be reconstructed here.[559] At the same time, however, he also works out the Hellenistic character of the version known to Mark. Here a transfiguration is truly reported, a transformation into a divine being. The eschatological character of the original story has disappeared. In Hahn's opinion, this also affects the role of Moses and Elijah in the story, whom Hahn sees incorporated in the original version already as people who bear witness to the imminent arrival of the time of salvation.[560] But the original function of the two figures in the text still seems unclear. In any case, the two great figures of the OT no longer have an eschatological function in the latest version before Mark. However, their significance does not yet seem to be sufficiently marked when Hahn says that "Elijah and Moses are merely witnesses of the fulfillment which has become event in the bodily appearance of the son of God."[561] Here the function of the heroes of the past in Hellenistic Judaism, especially in Apologetics, has not been considered. Moses and Elijah are for Hellenistic-Jewish tradition two of the most significant θεῖοι ἄνδρες, as mentioned above.[562]

Moses as well as Elijah count as great miracle workers—as now also Jesus. Moses and Elijah each had a vision of God on a mountain. Above all, tradition also ascribes an ascension—that is, a transfiguration—to each of them.[563] Now they appear to Jesus in his transfiguration and communicate with him. He is taken up in their circle, but over against even them he is distinguished by the heavenly voice. The allusion to Deut. 18:15 in the heavenly voice (Mark 9:8) thus can no longer be understood eschatologically but must reflect the Hellenistic-Jewish conception of the prophet (prophet equals bearer of power). Different θεῖοι ἄνδρες seem to be paralleled here, with precedence given to the youngest among them.

At the same time, however, the church of believers participates in this event with the presence of the disciples. Both the esoteric feature and the transfiguration motif are noteworthy in this pericope joining Jesus to the bearers of OT tradition.[564]

Hahn has also investigated the Moses typology elsewhere in the NT.[565] One can agree with his ascription of the core of the discourse of Acts 7 to a pre-Lukan, Hellenistic tradition. The Moses typology was central to this original tradition. But here again Hahn has skirted from a full religio-historical determination of origin. The following motifs belong to the Hellenistic-Jewish conception of θεῖος ἀνήρ and are also to be found in the Jesus tradition. Right away, Acts 7:20 says of Moses, "He was pleasing to God (as ἀστεῖος)."[566] Parallel to that Luke 2:52 reads, "And Jesus increased in wisdom, age, and grace with God and human beings." These conceptions arose from the wisdom teachings of Hellenistic-Jewish Apologetics. That the Egyptians appear as guardians of wisdom is also traditional.[567] The legend of the flight into Egypt in the prologue of Matthew could be connected to this.

Of Moses, educated with divine help and with Egyptian wisdom, it is said in Acts 1:22, "He was mighty in his words and deeds." Luke 2:40, 52, and especially Luke 24:19, are comparable.[568] In this last passage it is said of Jesus (the προφήτης!), "He was a prophet mighty in deed and in word." In Acts 7:35 the titles ἄρχων and λυτρωτής are attributed to Moses, according to the LXX predications of God. λύτρωσις appears as a typical messianic word in the formula reflecting old traditions in Luke 24:21: "But we had hoped that he was the one to liberate Israel." λύτρωσις, in addition, emerges two times in the Lukan prologue, which also reproduces old tradition. Luke 1:68 (cf. 2:38) reads, "God . . . has prepared a liberation for his people (cf. "for those who awaited the liberation of Jerusalem"). The glorification of Moses is ultimately carried so far in Stephen's speech that actually everything appears as his work. So also with the miracles (7:36).

The obscure passage on the giving of the law (Acts 7:38) at least says that Moses received the law from the hand of an angel and is himself the mediator of the divine message. If the commandments are called λόγια ζῶντα, they are thereby characterized as oracles and Moses as the announcer of oracles,[569] a well-known conception from Hellenistic-Jewish typology.[570]

It would correspond to the Hellenistic-Jewish conception of the role of the θεῖος ἀνήρ if this comparison of Moses to Jesus did not remain confined to the two individual figures but received a more general character.[571] The Moses-Jesus typology lends an exemplary character to the whole.[572] There is also a Moses typology in Acts 3:13–16 which was not sponsored by the model of the θεῖος ἀνήρ. This also holds true for other texts which Hahn cites. But Matthew's childhood story of Jesus, briefly treated by Hahn, shows some areas of contact with the Hellenistic-Jewish legend of Moses. "In Matt. 2:13–23, the concluding part of the Nativity Narrative, the childhood of Jesus is related in analogy with the story of the youth of Moses, a complex of tradition already met with in this form."[573] The Magi narrative, which associates the child with the representatives of the highest education and deepest wisdom, also appears to originate from this same Hellenistic-Jewish world. This association with the wisdom of the world is also characteristic of Moses, although no Magus story is narrated for him.

Both the Aramaic-speaking and Greek-speaking parts of the early church tended to fill their picture of Jesus with essential features from the Moses legend. This parallelism of Moses and Jesus started a chain into which other figures of Jewish tradition could eventually also be incorporated. A series of successions arose; at their end always stood the present believers. They were linked to the flow of God's power, which had penetrated the world and was to continue to do so. A special significance should be attributed to the glorified form of Jesus.

These sketches of some of the tendencies and changes in the early church's conception of mission have been able to establish a determining influence of Hellenistic-Jewish Apologetics on the development of the early church's mission. *The opponents of Paul in 2 Cor. were therefore no singular figures but representatives of a large group of missionaries of the early church, perhaps indeed representatives of a majority.*

NOTES

1. See Karl Georg Kuhn ("προσήλυτος," *TDNT*, 6:727–744) for a detailed review of the literature. More recent material in Hans Joachim Schoeps, *Paul: The Theology of the Apostle in the Light of Jewish Religious History* (London: Lutterworth, 1961) 220–29; Eduard Lohse, "Jüdische Mission," *RGG*, 4:971–73; Hahn, *Mission*, 21–25. The account which follows has

many points of contact with Rosen and Bertram (Georg Rosen, *Die Juden und Phönizier: Das antike Judentum als Missionsreligion und die Entstehung der jüdischen Diaspora* [rev. and expanded by F. Rosen and G. Bertram; Tübingen: Mohr, 1929]); unfortunately their work is marred by the curious "Phoenician" hypothesis. A critical examination of the evidence shows only that the Jewish mission often had its start among people speaking a Semitic language, and perhaps its successes there were relatively frequent. But one cannot speak globally of a "conversion of the bulk of the Phoenician as well as of the Aramaic-Syrian population to Judaism" (as Rosen and Bertram do [ibid., 4]). The Phoenician and Syrian colonies also held their own in the diaspora, alongside the Jewish settlements. The Syrian cults in particular were characterized by great propagandistic zeal, and a corresponding success (cf. Cumont, *Die orientalische Religionen*, 94–123).

The proposition of Rosen and Bertram seems to be correct: there existed among the Jews a widespread missionary awareness and a corresponding missionary activity. Moreover, much of what they say about missionary motivation and thinking, especially about the significance of the Septuagint, is noteworthy (*Juden und Phönizier*, 22–27); the analysis of the relationship of the mission to the OT is, however, oversimplified. The problems of the postexilic period and their assimilation in the OT are not discussed in earnest. The relationship of the Jewish missionary conception in late antiquity to the Israel of preexilic and exilic times (especially to the prophetic proclamation) is much more complex than the presentation in Rosen and Bertram makes it out to be. If this relationship can, in fact, be analyzed already, then it should be the object of a separate comprehensive investigation. In my view, such an investigation ought to include detailed preliminary studies (using archaeological data) of the relationship between the Jerusalem community and the various diaspora communities and Samaria, as well as the relationships between the diaspora communities themselves. One can make no progress here by merely repeating old propositions. For this reason I have almost entirely avoided confronting these problems in the account which follows; that would be beyond my competence. The absence of a sufficiently detailed investigation of the supporters and methods of the Jewish mission is another weakness in the presentation of Rosen and Bertram. Thus their main message, namely, the emphasis on the missionary drive of Judaism, remains a postulate and hypothesis and never really acquires historical contours.

2. The best survey is in Jean Juster (*Les Juifs dans l'Empire Romain: Leur condition juridique, économique et sociale* [2 vols.; Paris: Geuthner, 1914] 1:179–212), but see also Emil Schürer, *Geschichte des jüdischen Volkes im Zeitalter Jesu Christi* (4th ed.; 3 vols.; Leipzig: Hinrichs, 1909) 3:1–188. The Samaritans likewise had a relatively strong diaspora; see Colpe, "Samaria 3," *RGG*, 5:1355 (Galilee, Judea, Transjordan, Syria, Babylonia, Egypt, Arabia, Rome). Various connections with the Jewish diaspora ex-

isted there. The This suggests that the problems of the Jewish and the Samaritan diasporas were not far removed from each other, which in turn explains the phenomenon that the surviving remnants of the Samaritan Apologetic literature are apparently related to Jewish Apologetics.

3. Especially in Alexandria, Antioch, Damascus, Cyprus, Cyrene, and Rome.

4. Adolf von Harnack, *Die Mission und Ausbreitung des Christentums in den ersten drei Jahrhunderten* (4th ed.; Leipzig: Hinrichs, 1924) 1:13.

5. Juster, *Les Juifs*, 1:209–12. These figures are confirmed by Salo W. Baron (*A Social and Religious History of the Jews* [2d rev. ed.; New York: Columbia University Press, 1952] 1:167–79), even though he breaks them down in a different fashion. According to G. Ernest Wright (*Biblical Archaeology* [2d ed.; Philadelphia: Westminster; London: Duckworth, 1962] 242), the population of Palestine was at least two million in NT times. Juster's (*Les Juifs*, 1:210 n. 2) figure of five million is too high; he interprets *JW* 2.280 and 6.422 incorrectly. Philo (*Flacc.* 43) reports that the Jewish population of Egypt came to one million. But according to Josephus's report (*JW* 7.43), the Syrian diaspora appears to have been the largest, i.e., it must have been larger than the Egyptian diaspora. So for Syria we should assume a figure of more than one million. With some justification, Juster also conjectures a similar figure for Asia Minor (*Les Juifs*, 1:210); Antiochus had settled a considerable number of Jews there (2,000 families according to Josephus, *Ant.* 12.149, i.e., at least 20,000 persons) and many Jews could be found in the port cities. (Cf. also the detailed compilation of the accounts by Schürer, *Geschichte*, 3:12–24.) Large Jewish colonies and communities must also have existed in Cyprus and Cyrenaica (Juster, *Les Juifs*, 1:211 n. 4; and Schürer, *Geschichte*, 3:52–53, 56). The Jews in the city of Rome and a large number of other towns and regions must be added. The figures given by Josephus (*JW* 2.280; 6.425) for Palestinian and diaspora pilgrims can be more easily accepted in the context of six million Jews in the Roman Empire and a large number in the diaspora beyond the eastern frontiers. Josephus's figures do not appear to be overly exaggerated.

6. See the preceding note for determination of the first of these ratios; the second ratio is given by Juster (*Les Juifs*, 1:210 n. 3), following Harnack.

7. Specifics in Schürer (*Geschichte*, 3:5–10) and Juster (*Les Juifs*, 1:199–203). The Parthian satellite state of Adiabene, in which Judaism gained a firm foothold after the conversion of the royal house, also lay to the east of the Roman frontiers (see p. 100).

8. Wright, *Biblical Archaeology*, 242, for Palestine; for the empire, cf. above, n. 5.

9. Compare above, note 5. The Jewish colony of Elephantine in Egypt is known to us from the pre-Hellenistic period. However, settlements of this sort cannot be compared with the later size of the Jewish population of Egypt. The vigorous expansion of Judaism in Egypt as well as in Asia Minor

probably was connected with the course of events during the period of the Diadochi and also with the renewed strength of Palestinian Judaism. The real upswing probably only dates from 200 B.C.E.

10. The Seleucids as well as the Ptolemies pursued a broadly conceived policy of settlement, which affected not only the Greeks but also other nationalities. They either arranged forced deportations, as did earlier rulers in antiquity, or else settled reliable groups in localities which were important or exposed to danger. (During certain periods, the Jews were considered one of these reliable groups.)

11. According to Valerius Maximus (1.3.3), Jewish missionaries were banished from Rome in 139 B.C.E. (on the passage, see below, p. 189 n. 124). But many influential Jews lived in Rome already at the time of Cicero (*Pro Flacco* 66–69; on the passage, see below, pp. 98–99).

12. According to Josephus (*Ant*. 18.84), Tiberius drafted 4,000 able-bodied Jews as a punitive measure. This means that the total strength of the Jewish colony can be considered ten times as high. The figure 4,000 mentioned by Josephus is confirmed by Tacitus (*Annals* 2.85), but Tacitus assigns it to adherents of the Jewish *and the Egyptian* communities in Rome. However, it is likely that Tacitus made an error in this matter, since Suetonius (*Tiberius* 36), who mentions no specific number (against Juster, *Les Juifs*, 1:209 n. 12), confirms the statement of Josephus that the recruits were Jews. He also says that it was the *iuventus*, which is supported by Tacitus's *"qui idonea aetas."* The whole computation would become void if one could trust Tacitus's remark that "those who were tainted with that superstition" were pressed into military service. This could signify that 4,000 proselytes were conscripted, and, as one can conjecture from the wording, specifically those who belonged to the class of freedmen. (The followers of the Egyptian cult may be omitted here, as stated above.) If all this were true, one would arrive at a truly astronomical figure in the appraisal of the total strength of the Jewish population. For this reason I suggest that there is another error here. The figure of 50,000 to 60,000 Jews, as assumed by Juster (*Les Juifs*, 1:209), is too high, while the figure of 12,000 to 15,000, which Harnack conjectures (*Mission*, 1:12), is too low. (The English translation based on the 2d ed. has 10,000.)

13. In the form of a wise forecast put on the lips of Moses, Philo mentions the overpopulation of Judea, which is said to have led to the sending out of colonists and the founding of colonies everywhere (cf. *Moses* 2.232). In *Spec*. 1.133 and 141 he also speaks of a large population, although it is not said specifically that the statement pertains to Palestine alone. What Philo says about marital ethics (on this, cf. Isaak Heinemann, *Philons griechische und jüdische Bildung: Kulturvergleichende Untersuchungen zu Philons Darstellung der jüdischen Gesetze* [1932; reprint, Hildesheim: Olms, 1962] 261–92) is likely to have been a view widespread in Hellenistic Judaism. It is astonishing that Heinemann does not investigate the relationship of this

view to the OT Jewish wisdom tradition. This latter tradition seems to be the primary source of Philo's views, views which, by the way, contradict his speculative mysticism. Neo-Pythagorean influence may also have played a role. On the rapid multiplication of the Jews, cf. Tacitus, *Histories* 5.5.

14. Harnack, *Mission*, 1.13.

15. The Book of Acts is exaggerating on dogmatic grounds when it has Paul always start in the synagogue. However, the connection which is asserted as existing between the synagogue service and the Christian mission is not entirely fictitious, particularly not for the non-Pauline Christian mission.

16. See below, pp. 100–101.

17. The problem of the central organization of the diaspora is discussed on pp. 88–89.

18. Seen correctly by Rosen and Bertram (*Juden und Phönizier*) in particular.

19. Moriz Friedländer in particular has drawn attention to this (*Apologetik*, 223–30; here one also has the passages cited below).

20. This is supported by Josephus (*JW* 7.45), Horace (*Satire* 1.4, 143), and Juvenal (14.96–106). The passages are treated in more detail above pp. 85–86, 97 and 98.

21. This is Moses himself. On Moses as ruler, cf. Erwin R. Goodenough, *By Light, Light: The Mystic Gospel of Hellenistic Judaism* (New Haven, Conn.: Yale University Press, 1935) 184–90.

22. The parallelism to the previously cited passage from Philo's *Moses* is striking. I doubt that this is a private opinion of Philo. Rather, he seems to be using current expressions.

23. The double commandment is here clearly understood as the summary of the law, and at the same time it is viewed as the fundamental statute governing the exposition of the law and synagogue worship. The various NT versions of the double commandment as well as of the attempts to summarize the law are usually compared with their rabbinical parallels in recent exegetical literature; a comparison with the Hellenistic-Jewish understanding of the law would be just as rewarding.

A further passage dealing with synagogue worship is *Hypothetica* 7.13: ". . . And indeed they do always assemble and sit together, most of them in silence except when it is the practice to add something to signify approval of what is read. But some priest who is present or one of the elders reads the holy laws to them and expounds them point by point till about the late afternoon, when they depart, having gained both expert knowledge of the holy laws and considerable advance in piety." I shall discuss this passage later, p. 180 n. 40, p. 198 n. 238.

24. Josephus surveys a very long period here. It stretches from the successors of Antiochus IV to the Jewish War.

25. Philo, as well as Josephus, starts with a correct observation also made by Juvenal (14.96–106), namely, that pagans imitate Jewish customs. Cf.

also Seneca in Augustine, *City of God* 6.10. But this observation is then generalized, and every similarity is taken for an imitation. On the following, cf. Friedländer, *Apologetik*, 193–248.

26. Something more wonderful than the miraculous permanence of the Jewish laws and the Jews' undeviating observance of these laws.

27. My emphasis.

28. The Jewish laws themselves are represented here as missionary forces, as missionaries active on their own behalf.

29. The Day of Atonement is meant; cf. Colson (LCL, Philo 6.460 n. a).

30. Colson comments on the passage: "Or 'holy season.' A vague term (not indicating necessarily a whole month) for the periods varying with different Greek states, in which hostilities or legal processes were forbidden" (LCL, Philo 6.460–61 n. b).

31. Since Philo's account differs in some respects from that in the *Epistle of Aristeas*, it is probably not based on the *Epistle of Aristeas* directly but rather on a tradition common to both (or on a tradition which grew from *Ep. Arist.*). The *Epistle of Aristeas*, as well as Philo and Josephus, restricts the legendary translation of the seventy to the Pentateuch. The *Epistle of Aristeas* and Aristobulus reveal that other translations already existed before this one. Thus the legend recounted in the *Epistle of Aristeas* is propaganda, meant to raise the Alexandrian translation of the Pentateuch above the others. In my view it is not yet settled the extent to which these other translations survived elsewhere. One must reckon with even greater variations in the translations of the other parts of the OT, where the non-Alexandrian versions probably held their ground for a longer time, or even supplanted the Alexandrian versions. But the Pentateuch appears to have acquired and retained a decisive role in shaping the exegesis and theology of the diaspora. The Prophets and the Psalms played only a minor or nonexistent role. The situation of the wisdom literature was different. Since the beginning of the second century B.C.E., it was joined with the law and thus enhanced the importance of the Pentateuch all the more. (Jesus ben Sirach already considered the law the essence of wisdom.) This is a good reason to question whether the prophetic preaching can really explain the vitality of the Jewish mission; the growth of the wisdom movement was certainly more important.

32. My emphasis. Here again the law has a clearly universal character.

33. The correct observers of the law thus acted in accordance with the character and concerns of the law.

34. If the translation of the OT was called for because of the immediate requirements of the Jewish Diaspora communities (the *communis opinio* of LXX research today), then the translation was no doubt soon utilized for propaganda purposes. In several studies Bertram has in fact convincingly demonstrated that in the LXX itself one can see a concern for and a positive attitude toward the Gentiles. The passage from Philo previously cited, and to a certain degree, even the *Epistle of Aristeas,* show that afterward the

translation was regarded by Diaspora Jews as being prompted and influenced by missionary concerns.

35. *Apion* 2.279–95; cf. esp. 282.

36. Ibid., 284.

37. E.g., in the passages cited above.

38. It will become clear that the individual and his example provided a very important theme in Apologetic literature; in this one can observe the survival and broadening of tendencies found in later wisdom literature, and at the same time the influence of Hellenistic thought.

39. The relevant passages are in Schürer, *Geschichte,* 3:156, 164–72; Friedländer, *Apologetik,* 193–98, 209–31; cf. also Tacitus, *Histories* 5.5.

40. Following the passages from the *Hypothetica* cited above (p. 178 n. 23), Philo continues in 7:14: "And so they do not resort to persons [who give instructions ($\theta\varepsilon\sigma\mu\psi\delta\sigma\acute{\iota}$)] with questions as to what they should do or not do, nor yet by keeping independent transgress in ignorance of the law, but any one of them whom you [approach] with inquiries about their ancestral institutions can answer you readily and easily." In commenting on Philo's statement that these individuals though independent are not self-willed (in Greek, $o\grave{v}\delta\grave{\varepsilon}\ \varkappa\alpha\theta$' $\dot{\varepsilon}\alpha\upsilon\tau o\acute{v}\varsigma$), Colson says: "Lit. 'relying on themselves,' i.e. they learn from each other" (LCL, Philo 9.453 n. b). This strengthens the argument previously presented.

41. The *Epistle of Aristeas* is in this respect significant; cf. also *Sib. Or.* 3.591–95 and Josephus, *Apion* 2.173–81. It is interesting that Philo can cite Deut. 30:10–15 to show the familiarity of Jews as well as proselytes with the law (*Virt.* 183–84; *Praem.* 80–81; cf. *Post.* 84–88; *Mut.* 236–39; *Somn.* 2.180). Paul does the same (Rom. 10:8) in a section devoted to the essence of missionary preaching. Clearly Philo and Paul interpret the passage in different, indeed contradictory, ways. But Philo's exegesis provides a background for Paul's declaration that Christ is the end of the law. Nor should one overlook that both Paul and Philo expound their respective conceptions of the divine covenant in this context. It is noteworthy that Philo, as well as Josephus (in the passage mentioned earlier), shows a knowledge of Jer. 31:31–34, though they interpret it in the sense of a deepened understanding of the law. In the next two sections the modifications of the covenant idea as interpreted by the Apologists will be investigated in more detail.

42. Cf. the passages quoted by Str-B (1:909–10) on the teaching authority of the rabbis.

43. In the previously quoted passages on synagogue worship, esp. *Moses* 2.209–12, 215–16, and *Spec.* 2.61–63, as well as *Hypothetica* 7.13.

44. Cf. the treatment of Hartwig Thyen (*Der Stil der jüdisch-hellenistischen Homilie* [FRLANT NF 65; Göttingen: Vandenhoeck & Ruprecht, 1955]) and the literature there indicated. For a discussion of this problem, see below, p. 181 n. 59.

45. Cf. Juster, *Les Juifs*, 1:129–79; 2:93–214.

46. The most detailed collection of pagan statements about Jews in Greco-Roman antiquity is in Théodore Reinach's *Textes d'auteurs grecs et romains relatifs au judaïsme* (ed. and trans. T. Reinach; Paris: Leroux, 1895). This material has been thoroughly examined by F. M. T. de Liagre-Böhl ("Die Juden im Urteil der griechischen und römischen Schriftsteller," in *Opera Minora: Studies en bijdragen op Assyriologisch en Oudtestamentisch terrein* [Groningen: Wolters, 1953] 101–33).

47. The latter is almost always done in secondary literature, either explicitly or implicitly; as a result, the pagan sources are not given their proper due. This is also the case for Liagre-Böhl ("Die Juden").

48. This is the *communis opinio* of scholarship; for a contrary view, see Erwin R. Goodenough (*Jewish Symbols in the Greco-Roman Period* [13 vols.; Bollingen Series 37; New York: Pantheon, 1953–69]).

49. Eupolemus and Philo the Elder, passim; pseudo-Hecataeus (Josephus, *Apion* 1.197–99); *Ep. Arist.*, esp. 83–120; *Sib. Or.* 3.573–85, 702–23, 772–95; 5.403–7. For Philo's views, *Spec.* 1.73 is significant. Josephus's veneration of Jerusalem and the temple can be seen throughout his work.

50. Juster, *Les Juifs*, 1:357.

51. Philo, *Spec.* 1.69.

52. Juster, *Les Juifs*, 1:377–85.

53. Ibid., esp. 378.

54. Although this is generally asserted (also by Juster), there is no convincing evidence for it.

55. According to Philo (*Spec.* 4.190–92), the Jerusalem tribunal functioned as a court of last appeal in the adjudication of doubtful cases. But as Heinemann shows (*Philons Bildung*, 181–82), this passage does not manifest a very good acquaintance with actual conditions in Jerusalem; it probably owes more to Philo's knowledge of the Bible than to the real state of affairs. See also *Spec.* 3.53 (on this, cf. Heinemann, *Philons Bildung*, 22).

56. Goodenough, *Symbols*, 1:3–32.

57. The pagan sources talk about this in particular.

58. On this, see Juster, *Les Juifs*, 2:302–5.

59. It is today almost universally recognized that Philo's and Josephus's views were conditioned by tradition; only the more precise determination and context of these traditions are matters of controversy. For further orientation on Philo and Josephus, see Jean Daniélou (*Philon d'Alexandrie* [Paris: Fayard, 1958]) and Antonie Wlosok (*Laktanz und die philosophische Gnosis: Untersuchungen zu Geschichte und Terminologie der gnostischen Erlösungsvorstellung* [AAWH 2; Heidelberg: Winter, 1960]) on Philo, and Henry St. John Thackeray (*Josephus: The Man and the Historian* [New York: Jewish Institute of Religion, 1929]).

The style of Philo's writings shows an *affinity with orally delivered lec-*

tures, edificatory ones in particular. Of course, the extant version of all the tractates was revised for literary publication. The connection to the Hellenistic-Jewish homily should not be restricted to the allegorical commentaries (which is not Thyen's intention). On the other hand, the tractates do manifest differences of composition and method despite their stylistic unity; this has already been mentioned.

The older view, that the several subgroups within the Philonic corpus reflect different stages of Philo's life, did not prevail. This view, while it pointed to affinities and contrasts among the individual subgroups, provided no convincing explanation for the changes (even *Spec.* 3.1–6 is not pertinent in this respect). Moreover, scholars came to entirely opposite conclusions concerning the sequence of the writings.

The view becoming more and more widespread today is that the several sets of writings were composed more or less at the same time (so, e.g., Goodenough and Daniélou), a more realistic view closer to the evidence of the texts. The differences among the several writings are now explained by the diversity of the audiences addressed. But I cannot adopt Erwin Goodenough's opinion (set forth in particular in his "Philo's Exposition of the Law and His *De Vita Mosis*," *HTR* 26 [1933] 109–25, and shared by Daniélou) that Philo's presentation of the Mosaic law (including that in the *Vita Mosis*) was destined for Gentiles. This hypothesis does not explain the close affinity of the *Expositio Legis* to oral delivery. Moreover, this view can be sustained only if one detaches the piece *De praemiis et poenis* (a work which belongs to this category, judging by the introduction). At the very least, one must set aside the long closing section 79–172 (so Goodenough, "Exposition," 119–21) with its eschatological passages, where the nationalistic Jewish expectations are obvious. Here of course, Jews are being addressed, but the discourse also mentions proselytes (152). Conversely, the Jews themselves were also addressed previously (esp. in *Virt.* 175–79 —the section on true nobility has been discussed above, pp. 56–59).

All these difficulties disappear when one assumes that *both Jews and Gentiles* are being addressed throughout. (Colson already tends to favor this explanation in his introduction to volumes 6–8 of his LCL edition of Philo, 6:ix–xviii, but not forcefully enough.) This must have been the normal situation in Jewish Diaspora worship. This "popular group" of Jews, to use Goodenough's expression (*An Introduction to Philo Judaeus* [New Haven, Conn.: Yale University Press, 1940] 54), was composed of the regular visitors to the synagogue, accustomed to the presence of Gentiles.

Goodenough quite correctly says that the allegorical commentary was intended "for another group of Jews, the group whom he [Philo] called the 'initiates'" (*Philo*, 55). This, however, would imply special services for a particular group; since there were many synagogues in Alexandria, such a situation is easily conceivable. The *Quaestiones* could be thought of as educational tracts meant for those who wished to be accepted into this select group. It should be noted immediately that this community is not to be identified with the circle (or circles) of exegetes to be mentioned presently, for the latter, despite their mysticism, retained ties with the world, whereas the exegesis in the allegorical commentary has as its fundamental postulate a freeing from the world. The Therapeutae, with similar ties to the world, thus cannot have been the group which initiated the allegorical exegesis either.

The coexistence of works of differing tendencies in the Philonic corpus shows that Philo himself, and probably also the majority of his mystically disposed hearers, wanted no break between their own special group and the Jewish community at large, although the basic differences were in reality unbridgeable. The history of religions, including that of Christianity, provides many other instances of such inconsistencies.

Josephus's works are intended for the literary market much more directly than Philo's. Yet the *Antiquities* primarily utilize *traditional material which owed its development and dissemination to synagogue worship*. Moreover, the literary product retains an expressly edificatory character and pointedly presents itself as exegesis. Josephus is even presumptuous enough to compare his own work to that which produced the Septuagint, and he draws a parallel between the aims of the two enterprises. Finally, it is significant sociologically that Josephus intended his writings, especially the *Antiquities*, primarily for a circle of readers sympathizing with Judaism.

60. Josephus did know Philo (see *Ant.* 18.29–30), although not personally. Thus while he may have been acquainted with Philo's work a literary dependence cannot be proved. The examples adduced by Thackeray in favor of literary borrowing (LCL, Josephus 4:xiii, and the passages noted there) are hardly convincing (cf. Sandmel, *Philo's Place*, 59–77). But even if in one or another instance Josephus really did use Philo, this is without any real significance when one views the matter in the context of the extensive corpus of the two writers. Thackeray fails to ask the question What did Josephus *not* borrow from Philo? It is at any rate significant that the contacts to which Thackeray points are always from Philo's *Expositio*, i.e., his Apologetic work. I would therefore like to suppose a dependence on the part of both Philo and Josephus on a common Apologetic tradition. Cf. Adolf von Schlatter, *Geschichte Israels von Alexander dem Grossen bis Hadrian* (3d rev. ed.; Stuttgart: Calwer, 1925) 199, 424–25.

61. The literary character of the surviving documents is of course not to be denied entirely. The synagogue sermon was already intended for public consumption. The tendency which one observes in the work of Philo and Josephus to make the sermon accessible to the "book trade" and thus to an even wider public is not without precedent.

62. The Book of Jonah (probably of Palestinian origin, but devoted to diaspora problems); the story of the three pages in the Greek 1 Ezra (originally a Persian legend, taken up and transformed in the diaspora); the Daniel legends (narratives connected to the previous diaspora story, but of Jewish origin); the *Story of Ahikar* (an adapted Babylonian wisdom narra-

tive); the Book of Tobit (likewise eastern diaspora); the Wisdom of Solomon (Hellenistic Diaspora of Egypt or, more probably, Syria); *Joseph and Aseneth* (Egyptian diaspora); the additions to Esther and Daniel (whose place of origin cannot be exactly determined, but which surely is non-Palestinian). The place and time of origin are also difficult to determine for the Letter of Jeremiah, the various parts of Greek Baruch, and the *Biblical Antiquities* of pseudo-Philo, but a non-Palestinian origin for these is not impossible.

63. The prehistory of Apologetics, which unfortunately cannot be traced here, includes the Book of Jonah, the story of the three pages, the *Story of Ahikar,* the Daniel legends, and probably also the Book of Tobit. All these are products of wisdom thinking. Ecclesiasticus (Wisdom of Sirach) should also be mentioned here; after all, the work was translated in Egypt into Greek. Unlike Robert Henry Pfeiffer (*History of New Testament Times with an Introduction to the Apocrypha* [New York: Harper & Bros., 1949] 371), I can find no anti-Hellenistic tendencies in it. On the contrary, in spite of his fidelity to the law, the offspring of Sirach is very open to the world (see, e.g., what is said in 39:4 about the wise man). I even maintain that for him the revelation of Wisdom in the law is not supposed to be restricted to Israel. Rather, its temporary restriction to Israel is to be the beginning of its expansion into the world, with the teacher of Wisdom playing a prominent part. Support for this interpretation comes not only from what is said about Wisdom in the first part of Sirach 24, but also from the second part (vv. 23–34), at first in a more pictorial fashion, then in a direct fashion.

The Wisdom of Solomon and *Joseph and Aseneth* both presuppose the tradition of Apologetics. Apologetic methods seem to be employed in the additions to Daniel and Esther (not to speak of 2, 3, and 4 Maccabees, which are close to Apologetics anyway). In this connection one can also mention the Letter of Jeremiah, the second half of Baruch, and pseudo-Philo.

64. Wilhelm Bousset, *Jüdisch-christlicher Schulbetrieb in Alexandria und Rom: Literarische Untersuchungen zu Philo und Clemens von Alexandria, Justin und Irenäus* (FRLANT NF 6; Göttingen: Vandenhoeck & Ruprecht, 1915); Philo references are on pp. 8–14, respectively, 8–154.

65. On Philo, see above, note 59. The Apologetic writers use the modes of chronological, epic, pathetic, legendary, and novelistic styles of historiography; the genres of tragedy, probably comedy, the literary epistle, proverbial poetry, the literary testament, the philosophical edificatory diatribe (throughout the tractate), simple commentary as well as that of prophecy.

66. Palestine (at least Eupolemus), Alexandria and Egypt, Damascus and Syria. That the pagan Alexander Polyhistor (who lived mostly in Rome) gathered Apologetic fragments seems to presuppose an even wider dispersion. Finally, one should think of the Samaritan Apologists.

67. Juster, *Les Juifs,* 1:455–56.

68. Thus the passages from Philo given below.

69. However, aside from his trips to Jerusalem and Rome, practically nothing is known about the course of his life. Second, as has already been pointed out, his final intention is quite different from that of the Apologists.

70. See Paul Wendland, "Die Therapeuten und die philonische Schrift vom beschaulichen Leben," *Jahrbücher für classische Philologie* Supp. 22 (1896) 695–770.

71. See above, pp. 145–47.

72. See above, pp. 84–85.

73. Sirach 34 (31):11; 39:4. According to Josephus, one of these Jewish sages met Aristotle during his travels (*Apion* 1.176–82). He must have been a predecessor of the Apologists.

74. Heinemann, *Philons Bildung*, see index under Priester.

75. Ibid., see index under Priestertum des jüdischen Volkes.

76. The relevant passages are provided by ibid., 59–62, 182.

77. Two other Roman inscriptions in which the priestly title appears to be not necessarily associated with Aaronic descent have been preserved. In one case a priest who was the son of an archisynagogus is mentioned. The second mentions a priestess (*ἱερισσα*). For references, see Juster, *Les Juifs*, 1:453 n. 8. In my opinion, Juster still tries to maintain not very convincingly, the Aaronic descent of these two individuals also.

78. References in Juster, *Les Juifs*, 1:453 n. 8.

79. The Greek here seems to be contorted and cautious: λαβόντες ἐπὶ χρείας τοῖς ἰδίοις ἀναλώμασιν αὐτὰ ποιοῦνται.

80. Josephus recounts something which the Jews and Romans themselves did not discover. What is his source of information?

81. *Annales* 2.85. On Tiberius's measure, see Reitzenstein, *Mystery-Religions*, 126, 142–43.

82. This is the usual meaning of the plural "mathematics." Similarly, the word μαθηματικός in Greek is occasionally used to designate an astrologer; μαθήματα can mean "astrology" (see above, p. 80 n. 175).

83. *Tiberius* 36. The close connection of Isis and Serapis cults in those days may mean that the latter was included in the reference to the former.

84. Liturgical vestments and instruments are to be burned, the "art" of astrology must be abandoned.

85. Philo, *Leg. Gai.* 159–61.

86. The narrative is already difficult enough for Josephus. How would it have looked without this detail? Can one really imagine the story without it?

87. Horace 1.4, 142–43; Juvenal 6.542–47. The passage from Juvenal in particular has been often discussed. I shall have to express my disagreement specifically with Reitzenstein's interpretation (*Mystery-Religions*, 176–77).

88. Juvenal 6.511–91. This procession will be analyzed in the section on pagan missionary activity (p. 80 n. 175).

89. Reitzenstein (*Mystery-Religions*, 176–77) in particular has drawn at-

tention to the syncretistic character of this description, but I cannot agree with the way in which he proceeds to depict this phenomenon. Syncretism, mysteries, mysticism, and Gnosticism are not one and the same thing.

90. (My emphasis; the text:) "interpres legum Solymarum et magna sacerdos arboris ac summi fida internuntia caeli."

91. Juvenal 6.542–47.

92. See the passages provided by Reinach *(Textes)* under "Sabbat" in the index, esp. Ovid, *Ars Amatoria* 1.75, 415; Horace, *Satire* 1.4, 138–43; 9, 60–69; Persius 5.184; Juvenal 3.14; 6.156–60; 14.96–106; Seneca in Augustine, *City of God* 6.10; Tacitus, *Historiae* 5.4. Strangely enough, the Sabbath is often viewed as a day of fasting (for references, see Reinach, *Textes*, "Sabbat").

93. Similarly, Juvenal 3.14; see Ludwig Friedländer's commentary on this passage *(D. Junii Juvenalis Saturarum libri V: Mit erklärenden Anmerkungen* [2 vols. in 1; Leipzig: Hirzel, 1895]).

94. Juvenal 6.156–60; 14.96–107.

95. See above, pp. 84–88.

96. Horace also mentions the Sabbath as a day of strict rest, on which one cannot even carry on a conversation, a day of rest which even the uncircumcised observed, awed by the Jews *(Satire* 1.9, 67–72). This awe, just as in the example from Juvenal's *Satire* 14, which will be noted presently, could be the first sign of an impending conversion to Judaism: "Surely you said that there was something you wanted to tell me in private"—"I mind it well, but I'll tell you at a better time. Today is the thirtieth Sabbath. Would you affront the circumcised Jews?"—"I have no scruples ('nulla mihi religio'),'' say I—"But I have. I am a somewhat weaker brother, one of the many. You will pardon me, I'll talk another day." (So Horace, at the place referred to above.) The much-disputed question of what the thirtieth Sabbath means here is most simply answered if one takes this to be a shortened form of a date: the thirtieth of the month, a Sabbath (so also Fairclough, commenting on the passage in LCL).

97. "Judaicum ediscunt et servant ac metuunt ius, tradidit arcano quodcumque volumine Moyses, non monstrare vias eadem nisi sacra colenti, quaesitum ad fontem solos deducere verpos."

98. Or, rather, Moses himself. The law is in fact equated with the lawgiver. It is Moses himself who gives commands and prohibitions; see text in previous note.

99. I have in mind the *arcanam in aurem* of 6.543.

100. The passages run as follow:

Juvenal 3.13–16: "Now the holy fount and grove and shrine are let out to Jews, who possess a basket and a truss of hay for all their furnishings. For as every tree nowadays has to pay toll to the people, the Muses have been ejected, and the wood has to go a-begging." Friedländer says in his commentary on this passage: "The grove . . . the trees of which now have to bring profit to the aerarium is filled completely with a begging rabble, and thus itself has become a beggar" (*Juvenalis*, my trans.).

Juvenal 3.292–96. A drunkard interrogates the poet, as he is going somewhere at night: "Where are you from?" "Whose vinegar, whose beans have blown you out? With what cobbler have you been munching cut leeks and boiled [sheep's head]? (I.e., the drunkard suspects that the poet has been stuffed with food of more or less inferior quality at someone else's place.) What, no answer? Speak out, or take that upon your shins! Where is your stand? In what prayer-shop (synagogue) shall I find you?"

Martial 12.57, 13 (in an enumeration of diverse disturbers of the peace): "Nor the Jew taught by his mother to beg."

Cleomedes, *Theoria Cyclica* 2.1 (2d cent. C.E.): "It is said that some of these [i.e., Epicurus's expressions] stem from brothels, others are similar to (utterances) of the celebrating women during the feasts of Demeter, still others come from the house of prayer [synagogue] and from those who beg there [or even "in them"], Jewish gibberish, baser than anything that creeps on the ground" (my trans.).

101. Samuel Krauss (*Synagogale Altertümer* [Berlin and Vienna: Harz, 1922] 191) asserts that alms were given in synagogues. Landauer, as cited by Friedländer apropos Juvenal 3.296, disputes the view that alms were distributed in the synagogue and holds the opinion that the passage can well be explained by the fact that the synagogue provided lodging for the poor and, above all, for teachers.

102. To show this, e.g., is the opinion of Hermann Vogelstein and Paul Rieger (*Geschichte der Juden in Rom* [Berlin: Mayer & Müller, 1896] 1:20).

103. Cicero speaks about the multitude of the Jews and their influence, which cannot be explained if they had no financial means (*Flacc*. 66; cf. also 28).

104. By Cicero's time they have gained strong influence (*Flacc*. 66–69).

105. This is the main intention of Heinrich Graetz (*Die jüdischen Proselyten im Römerreiche unter den Kaisern Domitian, Nerva, Trajan und Hadrian* [Breslau: Jahresbericht des jüdischen-theologischen Seminars Breslau, 1884]).

106. Suetonius, *Titus* 7; Dio Cassius 66:15.18.

107. See Dio Cassius 66.15, in addition to Josephus's own statements.

108. Of course, not every begging activity of the Jews is included, nor should it be disputed that there may well have existed professional beggars. But did Martial's Jew (12.57, 13; see above n. 100), who was taught by his mother to beg and thus had received job training, really have begging as his profession?

109. On this, see further pp. 101–6, 112–17.

110. Kahrstedt (*Kulturgeschichte*, 308–13) provides a striking description. Cf. also below, pp. 152, 155–57.

111. André Oltramare (*Les origines de la diatribe romain* [Geneva: Im-

primeries populaires, 1926] 40) informs us about the significance of Cynic-Stoic diatribe in the first century B.C.E. Cf. Wendland (*Kultur*, 75–96) on the influence of Cynic-Stoic diatribe on propaganda in this period. Norden (*Beiträge*, 392) says: "Since this [Cynicism] was an ἀγωγὴ βίου tied to no firm doctrines, it was possible that philosophers of other persuasions could agree with it in matters of morality; one can think of the Platonist Nigrinus or the Neoplatonist Julian" (my trans.). Cynicism survived in the monastic movement, long after the decline of the Peripatetics and the Neoplatonists. Written evidence for Cynic influence is not always easy to find, since these popular philosophers primarily employed oral means of propagating their ideas, in addition to their mode of life, which itself was already a form of propaganda. For this reason, I can agree with Norden's observation (ibid., 342) that the written sources show no connection between the Cynics of the late classical period and the wandering philosophers who again became numerous in the first century C.E., but I do not want to erect this into an argument from silence. Cf. what Oltramare (*Origines*, 21) says about the Cynic epistles.

112. See on this Thyen, *Homilie*; Paul Wendland, "Philo und die kynisch-stoische Diatribe," in Paul Wendland and Otto Kern, *Beiträge zur Geschichte der griechischen Philosophie und Religion* (Berlin: Reimer, 1895); and esp. Heinemann, *Philons Bildung*, index under Kyniker, Jüdische, and Kyniker.

113. See above, p. 155.

114. This is already found in Plato; for references, see Windisch, *2. Korintherbrief*, 100.

115. This is the situation, e.g., in the cases of Peregrinus and the prophet Alexander in Lucian, although probably neither was quite as unscrupulous as Lucian's caricatures make them out to be.

116. One example is the way in which the Greek philosophical schools criticized each other. Other instances are the arguments over the terms "magician" and "sorcerer" or over "superstition," which Judaism and Christianity, on the one hand, and paganism, on the other, used to describe each other.

117. Esp. the Greek Theodotus inscription (Jerusalem, first century C.E.): "Theodotus, (son) of Vettenus, priest and archisynagogus, son of an archisynagogus, grandson of an archisynagogus, has built this synagogue for the reading of the law and for instruction in the commandments, as well as the guest room and the chambers and the water vessels, to lodge those coming from abroad, who have need for such (the synagogue), the foundations whereof were laid by his fathers, and the elders, and Simonides" (CIJ 2.232–35 [my trans.] with further literature indicated, of which the article by Samuel Klein should be singled out). Surely we are dealing with a Hellenistic synagogue in Jerusalem. Such means of lodging were available also outside Jerusalem—else one could explain the phenomenon simply as one

occasioned by the needs of the festal pilgrims from the diaspora. In a third-century Aramaic inscription from Er Rama, a similar synagogue hostel is attested (CIJ 2.163). The synagogues of Capernaum and Hamman Lif seem to have had quarters for strangers. The numerous chambers in other synagogue remains also show that these were intended as quarters for accommodation, since the synagogue was not, strictly speaking, a dwelling house. Goodenough (*Symbols*, 1.182, 2.90) skeptically discusses the whole question, but his tendency to interpret all architectural peculiarities as having been designed for the purposes of a mystery cult seems to be too arbitrary. On Jewish travel, see Samuel Krauss (*Talmudische Archäologie* [3 vols.; Leipzig: Fock, 1910–12]) 2:316–82; there rabbis are mentioned as travelers too.

118. Gustav Stählin, "ξένος," *TDNT*, 5:1–36.

119. Josephus, *Apion* 1.176–82.

120. Josephus, *Ant.* 20.24–42.

121. Ibid., 20.43–48.

122. Ibid., 18.81–84.

123. Freudenthal (*Alexander*, 105–30, esp. 123–25) has made it very plausible that the diplomat mentioned in 1 Macc. 8:17 and 2 Macc. 4:11 was identical with the Eupolemus who wrote an Apologetic historical work. Schürer (*Geschichte*, 3:474–77), e.g., also accepts this hypothesis.

124. Valerius Maximus 1.3. The original of the text is lost, and it is preserved only in the form of two excerpts. As far as methodology is concerned, Reitzenstein (*Mystery-Religions*, 123) is right, against Schürer, to maintain that the two extracts mutually complement each other; in both cases we are dealing with abbreviated versions, which single out only what the excerpters found interesting. The text describes an expulsion of the Jews, along with the Chaldeans, from Rome in 139 B.C. In the excerpt of Julius Paris, it runs as follows: "The same person (i.e., the consul named) compelled the Jews who had tried to taint Roman morals with the cult of Sabazius Jupiter, to return home" (my trans.). In Nepotianus's excerpt one has the following: "The same Hispalus also banished from the city the Jews who had tried to transmit to the Romans their sacred customs, and he removed *their private altars* from public places" (my trans. and emphasis). That we are dealing with a group is shown by the expression "who . . . tried" (*conati erant*) common to both texts. The extraneous origin of the group is demonstrated by Julius Paris's "compelled [them] to return home" (*repetere domos suas coegit*). Regardless of how one solves the problem of Jupiter Sabazius, the people banished were evidently Jews. On the Sabazius question, see below, p. 197 n. 237.

125. In CIJ 1:145–46 one should so correct the word ευαγγεδω, which certainly is misspelled. The word εὐάγγελος signifies "messenger of good tidings," especially the one who conveys news of victory. Here it functions not so much as a sobriquet but rather, in light of what follows, as a designa-

tion of function. It does not designate one of the synagogue officers but rather a missionary preacher. The script is Greek, but the text is Latin; for this reason, I do not see why κολληγα should be something other than the Greek transcription of the Latin word for "colleague." For secondary literature on this inscription, see Jean Baptiste Frey (CIJ 1.145–46).

126. Juster, *Les Juifs*, 2:303 n. 6.

127. Hans Conzelmann, *The Theology of St. Luke* (trans. G. Buswell; New York: Harper & Row, 1960; Philadelphia: Fortress Press, 1982) 157–69.

128. Luke 4:16–21; Acts 13:15.

129. On hospitality, see Stählin, "ξένος," *TDNT*, 5:1–36; Donald W. Riddle, "Early Christian Hospitality: A Factor in the Gospel Transmission," *JBL* 57 (1938) 141–54. Following Harnack, Riddle in particular has demonstrated the dependence of the importance of hospitality for the missionary activity of the early church.

130. Against Stählin and Riddle.

131. Artemidorus writes, "(When seen in a dream:) A place of prayer: beggars, vagabonds, loafers, wretched people pleading for alms mean grief, anxiety, and afflictions of the soul for both men and women. For, on the one side nobody goes to a place of prayer who is not concerned about something, and on the other side beggars are ugly, helpless and entirely unhealthy and still, they get in the way intentionally. This is so universally and inevitably" (*Oneirocriticon* 3.53, my trans.). Bauer ("προσευχή," BAGD, 713) is right in saying that this does not refer to synagogues in particular. On begging at sanctuaries, cf. Hendrik Bolkestein, *Wohltätigkeit u. Armenpflege im vorchristlichen Altertum: Ein Beitrag zum Problem "Moral und Gesellschaft"* (Utrecht: Oosthoek, 1939) 209, 384–85.

132. Bolkestein, *Wohltätigkeit*, 209.

133. βωμολόχος (in Artemidorus, *Oneirocriticon* 1.1, together with γόης and the προίκτης of 3.53). Also of interest are μάγος and πλάνος.

134. Bolkestein, *Wohltätigkeit*, 210–14, 384–85.

135. Juvenal 6.511–634 suggests this; cf. also Apuleius, *Metamorphoses* 8.24–30; 9.4 and 8–10. See p. 152.

136. On the textual problem, cf. the end of note 2 in Haenchen, *Acts*, 398–99. (Cf. p. 169).

137. Arthur Darby Nock in F. J. Foakes-Jackson and Kirsopp Lake, eds., *The Beginnings of Christianity* (5 vols.; New York and London: Macmillan, 1920) 5:164–88; and Kahrstedt, *Kulturgeschichte*, 306–8 (on the philosophical house chaplains). On pagan pneumatics, see pp. 151–59.

138. "Pseudo-prophet" is a judgment on the theological value of his performance, not on the reality of his achievements (Haenchen, *Acts*, 397–98). Jewish magic is treated in ibid., 397 n.5, and in the literature cited there; further by Ludwig Blau, *Das altjüdische Zauberwesen* (Strasbourg: Trübner, 1898); cf. also n. 140).

139. As did Clearchus's Jew (p. 189, n. 119) and Jesus ben Sirach.

140. The relationship between Judaism and paganism in magic has been examined by Goodenough, *Symbols*, 2:153–295.

141. See above, p. 185, n. 77.

142. Cf. Luke 11:19 for Jewish exorcism.

143. Haenchen, *Acts*, 397–98.

144. More on this passage, pp. 169–70.

145. My trans.; the text according to Emil Schürer, *Die Gemeindeverfassung der Juden in Rom in der Kaiserzeit* (Leipzig: Hinrichs, 1879) 26.

146. Pliny, *Natural History* 30.1, 11. An interesting text-critical problem is posed by Reinach (*Textes*, 282) as to whether ΛΟΤΑΠΗΣ or ΛΟΤΑΠΑΙΟΣ in the text is an error for ΑΡΤΑΠΑΝΟΣ, the Apologist with a strong propensity for syncretism; according to Freudenthal (*Alexander*, 173), the story of Jannes and Jambres should perhaps be attributed to him.

147. According to Jewish legend, Jannes is an Egyptian, not a Jewish magician. However, cf. the references collected by Schürer (*Geschichte*, 3:292–94), which suggest a Jewish apocryphal work that seems to reckon with the repentance of Jannes and Jambres.

148. Apuleius, *Florida* 1.6.

149. Lucian, *Tragoedopodagra* 173; Origen, *Celsus* 1.26; Numenius in Eusebius, *Praep. Ev.* 9.8.

150. The rabbinic passages are in Blau (*Zauberwesen*) and then esp. in Goodenough (*Symbols*). The Christian ones can be found in Krauss (*Synagogale Altertümer*, 190, 225) and in *JQR* 6:237–38.

151. This passage has been discussed frequently. Cf. Richard Reitzenstein, *Poimandres: Studien zur griechisch-ägyptischen und frühchristlichen Literatur* (Leipzig: Teubner, 1904) 222–26; Gillis P. Wetter, *Der Sohn Gottes: Eine Untersuchung über den Charakter und die Tendenz des Johannesevangeliums* (FRLANT NF 9; Göttingen: Vandenhoeck & Ruprecht, 1916) esp. 4–26; Eduard Norden, *Agnostos Theos: Untersuchungen zur Formengeschichte religiöser Rede* (4th ed.; Darmstadt: Wissenschaftliche Buchgesellschaft, 1956) 188–90; cf. also Harnack, *Mission*, 364 n. 1; Walter Schmithals, *Die Gnosis in Korinth: Eine Untersuchung zu den Korintherbriefen* (FRLANT NF 48; Göttingen: Vandenhoeck & Ruprecht, 1956) 126–27; idem, *Office of Apostle*, 165–68. My trans.

152. They come from Palestine and Phoenicia. One can ask if Phoenicia does not simply mean Palestinian borderlands here and thus refers also to representatives of the Syrian diaspora.

153. Or does it mean "they move as prophets?"

154. My trans. στρατόπεδον, if meant in a military sense, then not as a mass of tents or barracks but in Roman fashion, as an (army) village or town with many more than mere military installations and people.

155. My trans. Schmithals (*Gnosis in Korinth*, 126–27; *Office of Apostle*, 165–68) attaches great importance to these prophets.

156. Some references in Bultmann, *John*, 225 n. 3, no. 3.

157. Against Schmithals, *Gnosis im Korinth*, 126–27; and idem, *Office of Apostle*, 165–68. Also against Heinz Becker (*Die Reden des Johannesevangeliums und der Stil der gnostischen Offenbarungsreden* [FRLANT NF 5/50; Göttingen: Vandenhoeck & Ruprecht, 1956] 15–16), who wants to present this prophetic discourse as a typically Gnostic revelation discourse.

158. Mark 1:28 par.; 2:17; Luke 5:32; 12:49, 51–53; Matt. 10: 34–35; Matt. 5:17; 10:45 par.

159. Bultmann (*Synoptic Tradition*, 152–56) tries to present at least Luke 12:49–50 as a saying which could possibly be determined by Gnosticism, but he is not particularly convincing here.

160. Matt. 6:10; Luke 11:2; Matt. 11:14; 17:10–12; 27:49; Matt. 11:3. Cf. Bultmann, *Synoptic Tradition*, 156 n. 3. See also above, p. 109.

161. Cf. Bultmann, *Synoptic Tradition*, 156 n. 3, esp. the supplement to 156 n. 3 on p. 409.

162. One could also translate "ascend again" or "come again." Norden (*Agnostos Theos*, 188–90) chooses the first; Schmithals (*Gnosis in Korinth*, 126–27) and most others choose the second. Most likely an ambiguous term was consciously chosen. Therefore I also attempted an ambivalent translation.

163. My trans.

164. The close connection between judgment and revelation in the Sibyllines could already be characteristic (Dalbert, *Missionsliteratur*, 113). There is also talk of general sinfulness and general judgment, and this is demonstrated with a variety of examples. Israel, however, is usually excepted from this, although not always (*Sib. Or.* 3.276–80). The concepts of messiah and judge are interconnected (*Sib. Or.* 3.46–56, 286–87, 652–56; 5.108–10, 414–33). Just as with the prophets in Celsus, the judgment is often described as a fire (*Sib. Or.* 3.287, 689–92, 761; 4.173, 176–80; 5.177–78, 274, 377; see Dalbert, *Missionsliteratur*, 119). According to *Sib. Or.* 5.512–31 (cf. also 5.210–13), there is even talk of a universal conflagration (as the result of a cosmic war).

165. On this, cf. esp. Friedländer, *Apologetik*, 31–54; and Dalbert, *Missionsliteratur*, 106–23.

166. *Sib. Or.* 3.556–61, 564–67, 583, 616–31, 654, 716–23; 4.162–70; 5.276–85, 357–59, 428–33, 493–503. Cf. also the proëm which Theophilus (*Ad Autolycum* 2.36) cites.

167. *Sib. Or.* 3.46–56, 286–87, 652–56; 5.108–9, 256–59. (The wording was revised by Christians, but it was already messianically phrased in the original Jewish version, which has Moses and Joshua in mind); *Sib. Or.* 5.414–33.

168. *Sib. Or.* 3.46–56, 286–87, 652–56; 5.108–9, 256–59,

169. *Sib. Or.* 5.414–33. At least in *Sib. Or.* 3.286–87 and 5.256–59, it is chiefly figures of the past which are being considered. The transformation

into future figures cannot be explained simply by referring to the fictive location of the Sibyl in the distant past. What about all the events narrated in
the imperfect or the aorist, among others those in *Sib. Or.* 5.414–33?

170. Cf. the previous note.

171. *Sib. Or.* 5.414–33.

172. This is not to contest the fact that the prophets in Celsus have some
essential characteristics for which there is no equivalent in the pre-Chris-
tian parts of the *Sibylline Oracles*. But the *argumentum e silentio* is of limited value for the Jewish Sibylline literature, because the extant oracles
only reflect a much more extensive tradition which was formed, dissemi-
nated, and collected orally.

173. My trans. Despite her polemics against pagan-pneumatic practice
(esp. in *Sib. Or.* 3.221–33), the pneumatic phenomenon is actually not
alien to the Sibyl; first of all, the Sibyl is herself an ecstatic prophetess, and
second, the Jewish people are portrayed as a community of pneumatics: all
of them will be prophets (*Sib. Or.* 3.582–93; cf. 3.194–95).

174. The passages in Str-B 1:125–34 do not describe facts, but arguments
against specific claims, e.g., against non-"orthodox" pneumaticism. However, the Pharisaic rabbis could not sustain it, if only because they, too,
were dependent and intent on the living authority of the present. On this,
cf. the passages mentioned in Str-B 2:128–34. Even the passages in 1 Maccabees 4 and 8 about a prophet to come have either apologetic or polemical
intent. Origen, later on in his discussion with Celsus, can make good use of
the Pharisaic-rabbinic construction concerning the ceasing of the spirit, but
he has to make one small adjustment: in the classical spiritual desert he has
to leave an oasis for Jesus and the apostles, and this has remained the Christian way of adopting and adapting the Pharisaic-rabbinic position (and historicizing claim).

175. "*Summi fida internuntia caeli.*" For a further interpretation, see below, p. 197, n. 237.

176. As is usually done.

177. On the prophets in Josephus, cf. Erich Fascher, ΠΡΟΦΗΤΗΣ: *Eine
sprach- und religionsgeschichtliche Untersuchung* (Giessen: Töpelmann,
1927) 161–62; on the Jewish prophets in general, cf. Harnack, *Mission,*
1:344; esp. Rudolf Meyer, *Der Prophet aus Galiläa: Studie zum Jesusbild
der drei ersten Evangelien* (Darmstadt: Wissenschaftliche Buchgesellschaft, 1970); and "προφήτης," *TDNT,* 6:823–27.

178. "Goët" tends to be used more for the delusive miracle worker,
"mantic" for the fraudulent soothsayer. In addition, the term "pseudo-
prophet" is used. In almost all these cases the existence of extraordinary
phenomena is presupposed. It is just that it appears to Josephus's preju-
diced taste mostly as demonic, as a devil's art.

179. Josephus, *Ant.* 13.300; 1.69. Totally without basis Thackeray maintains, "It should be noted that Josephus (or his source) does not use 'proph-

ecy' in the biblical sense" (Josephus, *Ant.* [LCL] 7.378–79 n. a). What is "prophecy in the biblical sense?" The phenomenon of prophecy in the OT should not be confined to the self-understanding of the great biblical prophets. Moreover, one must distinguish between what the great prophets thought about themselves and their function, and what people like Josephus took it to mean. I would like to suggest that precisely those prophetic phenomena which the great prophets presupposed and against which they fought outlived them and even contributed to coloring the image of the great prophets themselves.

180. Josephus, *Ant.* (LCL) 7.378 n. a.

181. See pp. 50–59 and below, pp. 124–37.

182. Josephus, *JW* 1.78–80; *Ant.* 13.311–13.

183. Josephus, *Ant.* 13.311–13.

184. Ibid., 15.373–79.

185. Ibid., 15.379; cf. also *JW* 2.159; 2.112–13 (*Ant.* 17.345–48) and Otto Bauernfeind and Otto Michel, ed. & trans. (*Flavius Josephus, De bello Judaico: Der jüdische Krieg* [Bad Homburg: Gentner, 1960] 439 n. 83; hereafter referred to as *Josephus JW*).

186. Josephus, *Ant.* 17.41–46, esp. 43–44.

187. Josephus mentions Judas in *JW* 2.118, 433; 7.253; *Ant.* 18.4–10, 23–24; 20.102 (Acts 5:37). On the prophetic gift, cf. Eduard Meyer, *Ursprünge und Anfänge des Christentums* (3 vols.; Stuttgart: Cotta, 1962) 2:404. On the question of the identity of this Judas with the son of the "robber" Ezechias, cf., on the one hand, Meyer (ibid., 2:403 n. 1) and, on the other hand, Sigmund Mowinckel (*He That Cometh* [trans. G. W. Anderson; Oxford: Blackwell, 1959] 284). Mowinckel notes something which is also important for the above context, namely, that the famous Hillel took Ezechias to be the messiah. Thus Hillel and Ezechias appear as pneumatics.

188. Josephus, *Ant.* 20.97–99. Bibliography in Haenchen, *Acts*, 252 n. 4.

189. γόης τις . . . προφήτης γὰρ ἔλεγεν εἶναι.

190. Haenchen, *Acts*, 252. Meyer, *Ursprung*, 2:404, refers to the analogy to Elijah and Elisha.

191. Josephus, *JW* 2.258–60; *Ant.* 20.167–68. Cf. also *Ant.* 20.188.

192. According to Josephus, *JW* 2.258–61, they refer to their θειασμός; according to *Ant.* 20.167–68, they are "goëts." *Ant.* 20.188 also speaks of "goëts."

193. Josephus, *JW* 2.259.

194. This is especially clear in Josephus, *Ant.* 20.167–68.

195. In addition to the *Sibylline Oracles*, it is above all Philo's tractate *Praem.* which indicates this.

196. Josephus, *JW* 2.261–63; *Ant.* 20.169–72. Bibliography in Haenchen, *Acts*, 619.

197. That he was of the Jewish faith can be seen in his undertaking and in the response to it.

198. The geographical situation would then be the most plausible. Moreover, it would be hard to imagine that an Egyptian Jew could gain such a following among a Palestinian population. Finally, one must bear in mind that the enmity of his co-religionists lashed out at this prophet from Jerusalem in particular.

199. Joshua 6.

200. Apparently only his bodyguard was armed (δορυφόροι, Josephus, *JW* 2.262). When Josephus infers from the presence of these people the threat of an armed attack and a surprise takeover of the Antonia fortress, it simply is due to his tendency to downplay all these movements. He contradicts himself in his parallel report, where he reports on the prophet's announcing the miracle of the falling of Jerusalem's walls.

201. Especially clear in Philo's tractate on true nobility (*Virt*. 187–227) and in his eschatologically influenced *Praem*. 152.

202. The striking phenomenon that Josephus—despite his strong Galilean and Judean experiences and contacts, his good information about the diaspora, and his stay in Rome—said nothing about Jesus or early church may be explained that way.

203. Only after the Jewish War did disturbances in Alexandria and Cyrene arise because of Sicarii who had been driven out of Judea. Josephus tells about them at the end of his report on the Jewish War. As a matter of fact, it is even questionable whether the events in Cyrene really had anything to do with the Sicarii, for they were provoked by a weaver who had fled from Judea, Jonathan (Josephus, *JW* 7.488), who—like the prophets described above—also knew how to gather a crowd by promising miracles in the desert. There he also marched with them. It is expressly noted that these people were poor and the crowd unarmed. I cannot go any further here into the social background of this undertaking or the intrigues which were connected or linked up to it.

204. Josephus's summarizing comment about Josephus himself in *JW* is important, "He was an interpreter of dreams and skilled in divining the meaning of ambiguous utterances of the Deity; a priest himself and of priestly descent, he was not ignorant of the prophecies in the sacred books" (*JW* 3.352–54). One should compare also the continuation which indicates something of his technique: "[When,] at that hour, he was [immersed by them (the holy writings) into God's mystery and aroused in himself] the dreadful images of his recent dreams, he offered up a silent prayer to God. . . ." (In the prayer itself we read among other things, ". . . since thou hast made choice of my spirit to announce the things that are to come . . ."); cf. also the German translation of that passage by Bauernfeind and Michel (*Josephus JW*) and their notes on this. Scriptural erudition, visionary dreams, and interpretations of dreams form a partnership in Josephus resulting in a quite lively and actualizing pneumatic interpretation of Scripture. This is an important reference for the connection of scriptural interpretation to pneumaticism. On dreams, cf. also Josephus, *Life* 208–9.

205. Above, p. 104. The text here is Josephus, *JW* 3.400. On the translation, cf. again also Bauernfeind and Michel (*Josephus JW*).

206. ἐγὼ δὲ ἄγγελος ἥκω σοι μειζόνων, Josephus, *JW* 3.400. That active formulation is remarkable after what has already been said.

207. μὴ γὰρ ὑπὸ θεοῦ προπεμπόμενος, ibid. 3.400.

208. Ibid., 3.400.

209. Ibid., 3.403.

210. In my view, the statements of Josephus mentioned above (n. 204) already support this. However, this is not the place to speak about Josephus's conception of εἱμαρμένη and τύχη (although especially the latter would deserve attention). A discussion of Adolf von Schlatter's interpretation in *Die Theologie des Judentums nach dem Bericht des Josephus* (BFCTh 2/26; Gütersloh: Bertelsmann, 1932) 32–34 and in idem, *Wie sprach Josephus von Gott* (BFCTh 14/1; Gütersloh: Bertelsmann, 1910) 55 and throughout would be necessary, together with an analysis of Josephus's concept of history and its place in Apologetics. I discuss this above in the context of Jewish mission theology, pp. 121–22, 124–37, 139–48.

211. Jer. 27:6–11; Isa. 41:2–3, 25; 44:28–29, and other passages which talk about Cyrus, above all the prophecies mentioned earlier by Josephus (*JW* 3.352).

212. Above, pp. 148–51.

213. For his pneumatic performances he received an honorarium. That the broader public also knew about this is shown by the passages cited in Bauernfeind and Michel (*Josephus JW*, 461 n. 96). By virtue of his fortunate lot, Josephus was able to live with relatively few cares, to devote himself totally to his work, and to expect a widespread sympathetic response, precisely also in non-Jewish circles. That he is thinking of this is proved not only by his dedications but also by the express and implicit propagandistic aim of his work, especially of the *Antiquities* and the apology *Against Apion*. On the "mission" of Josephus, cf. Graetz, *Proselyten*, 26 (following Bruno Bauer). Unfortunately this question has not been further examined in recent times.

214. His continuous connection with the circle of Epaphroditus is not the least of the arguments in favor of this. According to Eusebius (*Hist. Eccl.* 3.9), the Romans even set up a statue to him and included his works in the public library.

215. Naturally Philo's understanding of spirit and his own relationship to pneumaticism cannot be discussed in any detail here. From the extensive literature on this problem, one should mention the works of Hans Leisegang, *Der heilige Geist: Das Wesen und Werden der mystisch-intuitiven Erkenntnis in der Philosophie und Religion der Griechen* (vol. 1, pt. 1; Leipzig: Teubner, 1919); Goodenough, *Light*; Hans Windisch, *Paulus und Christus: Ein biblisch-religionsgeschichtlicher Vergleich* (UNT 24; Leipzig: Hinrichs, 1934); Hans Lewy, *Sobria Ebrietas: Untersuchungen zur*

Geschichte der antiken Mystik (BZNW 9; Giessen: Töpelmann, 1929); Hans Jonas, *Gnosis und spätantiker Geist* (2 vols.; FRLANT NF 33, 45; Göttingen: Vandenhoeck & Ruprecht, 1954); Wlosok, *Laktanz und die philosophische Gnosis;* further, Harry A. Wolfson's *Philo: Foundations of Religious Philosophy in Judaism, Christianity, and Islam* (2d ed.; 2 vols.; Cambridge, Mass.: Harvard University Press, 1948) 2:3–72, esp. 2:22–54, should be referred to.

216. Jonas, *Gnosis*, 2:109–11, 117–19.

217. On this, cf. ibid., 2:111, 118–19.

218. Pp. 57–58, above.

219. Philo, *Moses* 2.31–40.

220. Pp. 86–87, above.

221. Philo, *Moses* 2.28–30.

222. Ibid., 2.33.

223. My trans. the text: θεσπισθέντας νόμους χρησμοῖς διερμηνεύειν (Philo, *Moses* 2.34).

224. On the problem of the relationship between προφητεία and ἑρμηνεία, cf. Goodenough, *Light*, 193, esp. n. 170 and Wolfson, *Philo*, 2:40–43. I would agree with Goodenough, against Wolfson, that in Philo the two concepts are basically synonymous. Wolfson systematizes too much here.

225. Philo, *Moses* 2.37 (my ed.).

226. Ibid., 2.40.

227. Philo, *Spec.* 1.8; cf. the mention of the "worthy and excellent men" (*Q. Gen.* 1.10) or of the φυσικοὶ ἄνδρες (*Abr.* 99; *Post.* 7), most likely interpreters interested in cosmology.

228. Philo *Mig.* 34–35; *Cher.* 27; *Somn.* 2.252; *Spec.* 3.1–6.

229. On this, cf. Dalbert, *Missionsliteratur*, 132. In my view, however, Dalbert does not correctly evaluate the problem. See pp. 118–51, esp. pp. 127–37.

230. The question here is not how often the term "spirit" occurs. Very often the term δύναμις, which is synonymous with πνεῦμα, expresses the same content (cf. the selection of the passages in ibid., 131–34).

231. In addition to the passages cited from Philo, Josephus, and Juvenal, this is proved by the fact that Apologetic literature is characteristically an interpretation of scripture.

232. Which is attested again and again, sometimes quite drastically.

233. Apologetic praxis is the strongest argument in favor of this.

234. To establish this as well as the following is the whole object of Apologetics.

235. Attestations from Hellenism, pp. 151–59.

236. Cf. the passages from Philo above, pp. 84–91.

237. On this, cf. the passages given above, pp. 103–4 and 111–12. One should also refer to the Roman measures which brought the Jews together with syncretistic groups (pp. 92–96). Even if the Romans did treat the

new forms of pneumatically oriented syncretism according to the analogy of the Bacchanalia trial, this in no way signifies that they were always mystery cults, especially not orgiastic ones. Even if it is stated in the passage cited (p. 189 n. 124) that those Jews who had been expelled together with the Chaldeans were threatening to corrupt Roman morals, this still does not imply orgiastic activities (against Reitzenstein, *Mystery-Religions*, 119–22). A connection to the Sabazius cult of Asia Minor, to which the phrase "Sabazi Jovi cultu" alludes, is out of the question because in 139 B.C.E. it is not possible that the Sabazius cult was already so filled with Jewish elements that its representatives abroad could unequivocally appear to be Jews. It is much more appropriate to look for similarities between the Jews and the simultaneously expelled Chaldeans. The suspicion that the Jews would corrupt Roman morals could be an allusion to the seductive power of the Jewish ethos (above all, the Sabbath celebration), which was a common complaint, at least in later times. Philo's explanation of the Sabbath, a non-Jewish explanation as established by Heinemann (*Philons Bildung*, 110–18), indicates that Hellenistic-Jewish Apologetics linked cosmological speculations with the Sabbath, which could suggest at least to outsiders a comparison with the astrological speculations and practices of the Chaldeans (cf. Tacitus, *Histories* 5.4). Perhaps this explains the "Sabazius Juppiter" in the Valerius text, unless it is a later addition of a copyist. During the reign of Tiberius, the Jews and astrologers were again simultaneously expelled (see pages 93–94). This could show that the suspicion of certain common points remained firm. The relationship between the titles of the Jewish woman in Juvenal, "*magna sacerdos arboris*" and "*summi fida internuntia caeli,*" seems to indicate something similar. Connecting the tree with the mysteries of Attis (Reitzenstein, *Mystery-Religions*, 176) is much less to the point than connecting it to Jewish speculation on the tree of life. In Prov. 3:18, wisdom is already termed the tree of life; later readers at least must have noticed that the cosmic function of wisdom is mentioned immediately afterward. In Sir. 24:12–22 the cosmic meaning and the soteriological function of Wisdom is represented in detail with the image of the tree of life. That later interpreters then formed the equation tree of life = wisdom = law, is proved by 4 Macc. 18:16. Philo quotes the cosmological interpretation of Wisdom as the tree of life as traditional (Apologetic) in *Q. Gen.* 1.10–11. Juvenal's description of the Jewish woman as a prophetess of the highest heavens can then be easily linked with this equation of tree, tree of life, and wisdom as well as with the cosmological interpretation of this relationship. The cosmological speculations of Jewish Apologetics will be discussed in greater detail below.

238. This length is referred to by Philo in the *Hypothetica*; see above, p. 178 n. 23. Cf. also Josephus, *Apion* 1.209 (quotation of Agatharchides about the Sabbath in the temple).

239. Krauss (*Synagogale Altertümer*, 135, 170–71) refers to the varied

program of the Sabbath ceremony, which even needed something like a stage manager.

240. Ibid.

241. Ibid., 171, following I. Elbogen.

242. Epiphanius, *Haereses* 80.1; my trans. See the passage in Krauss, *Synagogale Altertümer*, 344. Carl Watzinger and Heinrich Kohl (*Antike Synagogen in Galiläa* [Leipzig: Hinrichs, 1916] 175) oversimplify the problem.

243. Examples in Krauss, *Synagogale Altertümer*; Watzinger and Kohl, *Antike Synagogen*; Goodenough, *Symbols*.

244. The passages in Krauss, *Synagogale Altertümer*, 225.

245. Jerome and Ezekiel 34:1.

246. Chrysostom, *Hom. c. Jud.* 1.2, 247.

247. Philo, *Moses* 2.211.

248. Krauss (*Synagogale Altertümer*, 56) points out that the synagogue, as the meetinghouse of the community, could definitely be compared with the theater of a city. In this connection, however, he is thinking of community gatherings in the broader sense of the term, that is, gatherings of the Jewish community of the city. Krauss did not actually carry the closeness between synagogue and theater beyond intimations. On the contrary, he says at the end of his work that the synagogue was "a place of prayer which was marked by order and governed by divine tranquillity" (ibid., 408), and he is of the opinion that "one could hardly have heard inordinate shouting at the common worship service" (ibid., 409). All the same, this is not a real argument against the thesis developed above.

249. The artisan displays artistic capability in the sense of a charismatic gift (Exod. 28:3; 31:3; 35:31; cf. also Sir. 9:17). Yet strictly speaking, "Israel's artistic charisma lay in the realm of narrative and poetic portrayal" (Gerhard von Rad, *Old Testament Theology* [trans. D. M. G. Stalker; 2 vols.; New York: Harper & Row, 1962–65] 1:364). On the same page, von Rad also points out that there was no interest in theoretical aesthetics, but oratorical, narrative, and poetic ability was indeed valued and cultivated. Von Rad had previously noted that ancient Isreal had already taken over the art of rhetoric from the Egyptians and had perfected it to a surprising degree (ibid., 1:54–56). However, this reference to the so-called "Solomonic Enlightenment" already denotes the transition to Israelite-Jewish wisdom, which will be the topic of discussion below.

250. On this, in addition to the "Solomonic Enlightenment" (mentioned in the previous footnote) and its manifestations, cf., e.g., Prov. 15:23; 18:4; 20:15; 24:16.

251. Sir. 9:17; 37:20, 21 (negative), but above all Sir. 38:34—39:11 and again 39:6–11.

252. This becomes evident above all in Sir. 39:6–10.

253. Speech contests seem to have been cultivated by the Jewish wisdom

movement, as the Elihu speech in the Book of Job shows (Paul Volz, *Hiob und Weisheit: das Buch Hiob, Sprüche und Jesus Sirach, Prediger* [Schriften des Alten Testaments 3/2; Göttingen: Vandenhoeck & Ruprecht, 1911] 94–95). Cf. also the contest of the pages in 3 Esdras 3–4.

254. See pp. 122–37, 149–51. See also pp. 53–54, 56–59, 101–9, 151–55, 158–59, 167–70.

255. See above, pp. 84–88. Even the use of Greek argues in favor of that.

256. Cf. also above, pp. 41–45, 54–58, 96–98.

257. The passages cited above (pp. 41–46 and 58–60) argue in favor of this, especially the presentation in Juvenal's sixth satire. It has already been stated that we are dealing here with normal expressions of Hellenistic Judaism and not exceptional phenomena (see above, pp. 87–91 and 92–99; cf. also 197 n. 237).

258. On this point Goodenough has himself contributed to the unclarity in the religio-historical and phenomenological statement of the problem, above all because his approach is too strongly history of ideas and psychology of religion; he does not give sufficient consideration to the concrete historical possibilities and facts. The definition of the terms "mysteries" and "mysticism" remain too general.

259. See above pp. 54–56 and 96–97.

260. Philo, *Sacr.* 60; *Q. Gen.* 4.8 and the parallel fragment printed therein, *Quaestiones* (LCL, Philo supp. 2.214, no. 8b); cf. also the fragment in ibid., (LCL, Philo supp. 2.262, no. 20). On the texts, cf. Goodenough, *Light*, 260–63; idem, *Symbols*, 6:206–17; and each book's bibliography.

261. Josephus, *Ant.* 14.213–16. On this, cf. Schürer, *Geschichte*, 3.143, and Goodenough, *Jewish Symbols*, 6.206.

262. Goodenough, *Symbols*, vols. 5 and 6.

263. The reference to circumcision in Juvenal 14.104 could also be taken as referring not to the entire preceding statement, but only to the admission to the secret spring mentioned in this very verse. This source could refer, in turn, to proselyte baptism, which was, of course, undertaken only after the circumcision (Friedlander's commentary on 14. 104).

Furthermore, it should be noted that we know very little about the legal situation in the diaspora synagogue, and almost nothing about the legal significance of proselyte circumcision. From Philo and Josephus it can be ascertained only that the proselytes were looked upon as full Jewish citizens and full members of the community. Which rights they possessed in contrast to the uncircumcised cannot be precisely determined. I would like to suggest that full membership was distinguished, in addition to table fellowship and admission to the Jerusalem temple cult, also by the right to vote and to participate fully in the constitutional life of the community, which included the enjoyment of Roman privileges.

264. Cf. the references, pp. 51–52, 54–56, 84–87, 103–4, 110–11, 197

n. 237, 129–34, 144–47, 216 n. 424, 153–54.

265. *Epistle of Aristeas* 1–3 (*APOT*, 2:94).

266. Cf. what was said above, pp. 111–12, on pneumatic rationalism; and below, pp. 127–28.

267. That is important for the problem of "boasting" (and also of "judging"), which was at the center of the Corinthian discussion.

268. Von Rad (*OT Theology*, 1:453–65) deals with sapiential skepticism in details. In my estimation, the significance of sapiential skepticism for the further development of the Jewish wisdom movement cannot be overestimated. Apocalypticism, Apologetics, and speculative mysticism all equally presuppose it.

269. Cf. Dalbert, *Missionsliteratur*, 130–37. It is well known that this is quite frequently said in Philo and also in the Apologetic parts of his work. For Josephus, reference may be made to *Apion* 2.167 and 2.190–91. In Aristobulus (Eusebius, *Praep. Ev.* 13.12.5 [GCS, Eusebius 8, 2:193, ll. 15–17]) there is also no report of a vision of the essence of God.

Consistently, Apologetics includes no real revelation (in contrast to Apocalypticism and to speculative mysticism), which speaks for the immediate influence of skepticism. Schlatter (*Theologie des Judentums*, 28) points out that Josephus avoids the concepts "revelation" and "to reveal" since the essence of God is not revealed. Dalbert (*Missionsliteratur*, 130–37) distorts the facts by presenting them under the heading "spiritualized revelation" and by frequently referring to "revelation." An appearance or a manifestation is not yet a revelation.

270. Schlatter, *Theologie des Judentums*, 28.

271. The passages from Aristobulus and the *Epistle of Aristeas* are cited in Dalbert, *Missionsliteratur*, 131–32. It seems that Philo's theory of the powers, which has been much discussed, has its immediate prehistory in the view of the Apologists. Of course, for the Apologists the very fact that the LXX can call the heavenly hosts δυνάμεις was significant (the passages are cited in Wolfson, *Philo*, 1:219–20). On the other hand, it cannot be disputed that there were non-Jewish influences both on the Apologists and on Philo. The literature on δύναμις has been collected by E. Mary Smallwood, ed., *Philonis Alexandrini Legatio ad Gaium* (Leiden: Brill, 1961) 156.

272. E.g., Philo, *Spec.* 1.209; *Cont.* 26; Josephus, *Ant.* 1.23; 17.130; 18.266. Cf. Bauernfeind, "ἀρετή," *TDNT*, 1:460, who includes the OT passages in which תהלה is translated by ἀρετή (cf. 1 Pet. 2:9, which repeats missionary theology).

273. Selected passages in Bauernfeind, "ἀρετή," *TDNT*, 1:458–59 (although they are treated by Bauernfeind primarily in a moral sense).

274. The passages are cited in Dalbert, *Missionsliteratur*, 124–25.

275. That is expressed most strongly in the designations which place God in a genetic relationship to the world: γενεσιάρχης (Wisd. of Sol. 13:3), γενεσιουργός (Wisd. of Sol. 13:5), γενετήρ (*Sib. Or.* 3.296, 726), παγ-

γενέτωρ (*Sib. Or.* 5.328), παγγενέτης (*Sib. Or.* 3.555); cf. Dalbert, *Missionsliteratur*, 126. Both passages from Wisdom of Solomon are from an Apologetic section.

276. Von Rad, *OT Theology*, 1:136–39.

277. Schlatter (*Theologie des Judentums*, 47) notes this. Elsewhere, too, in the Apologetic literature the covenant notion falls quite into the background. Wisd. of Sol. 12:19–22, part of a missionary hymn, is an exception. Wisd. of Sol. 18:21–25 and 15:1–3 belong to the speculative mystical reworking of originally Apologetic tradition integrated into the final edition of this book.

278. Schlatter, ibid. Further passages are cited in Behm, "διαθήκη," *TDNT*, 2:126–29. On this subject, see below, pp. 131–37.

279. This is true at least of the treatment of history in the fragments of Apologetic literature and in Philo. However, the following passages from Josephus just cited indicate that he too stands in this tradition.

280. Thackeray's translation is "natural philosophy" (LCL, Josephus 4.11).

281. The parallels to the *De opificio mundi* of Philo are clear, but an actual dependence of Josephus on Philo does not exist, despite many claims to the contrary. No literary dependence of either text on the other can be proven. Their commonality consists in the dependence on a common Apologetic tradition. I have mentioned the text of Josephus, in particular, since here the distance from the historical thinking of the OT is particularly clear, despite the aim of Josephus to write history in the tradition of OT historiography.

282. This leads to the theme of "Judaism as universal religion," which is treated above, pp. 148–51.

283. Cf. Schlatter, *Theologie des Judentums*, 18–19.

284. Further passages on the conception of the immortality of the soul in Josephus are adduced in Bauernfeind and Michel, *Josephus JW*, 461 n. 88.

285. The speech of Eleazar is surely not historical, neither in its wording nor in its content. It is not conceivable that a Sicarius of all people is to have had such a dualistic theology and anthropology. I would think that Josephus puts a heterodox speech of this sort on the lips of the hated leader of the Sicarii in order to disqualify fully the Judaism of this patriot.

286. Philo's position in his allegorical work is different. There the anthropology is dualist in conformity to the rest of the theology.

287. Nor can dualism be ascertained in Aristobulus, not even in the fragment which contains the Testament of Orpheus (Eusebius, *Praep. Ev.* 13.12.5–6). Both the testament itself and its context are monistic in orientation. It is striking that a citation from Aratus is attached to the testament. Aristobulus does not establish oppositions, but only differences (between what is lower and what is higher).

288. Here Apologetics differs from speculative mysticism. This difference

appears most clearly in the contrast between the final redaction of Wisdom of Solomon 1–2 and 13 and the Apologetic tradition which has been utilized.

289. On this division of humanity into two different classes, which is characteristic of speculative mysticism and later Gnosticism, cf. Reitzenstein, *Mystery-Religions*, 323–24, 368, 401, 405–7, and Jonas, *Gnosis*, 1:212–14 and 2:113–15. The passages from Philo which speak of a division into heavenly and earthly human beings are found, characteristically, in the allegorical commentary (*Cher.* 42; *Deus* 142–44, 179–83; *Her.* 76).

290. I have given examples of this above in discussing the figure of Abraham. I might mention in addition that the ignorance which Abraham (Philo, *Abr.* 70–80) had to overcome in his conversion is not of a fundamental sort. Here no metaphysical opposition is overcome, but only a defect which temporarily blocks a generally present possibility. The actual process of conversion is presented as a deed of Abraham, "Then opening the soul's eye as though after profound sleep, and beginning to see the pure beam instead of deep darkness, he followed the ray and discerned what he had not beheld before" (Philo, *Abr.* 70.) The further passages on ἄγνοια in the Apologetic parts of Philo's work seem to have a less fundamental character than those in the allegorical commentary. (Quite clear is the character of ἄγνοια as a defect also in *Spec.* 4.188–92. Here the priest, who is at the same time a prophet—thus, in brief, the pneumatic—can intervene to help).

291. Dalbert, *Missionsliteratur*, 130–31.

292. Examples in ibid., 131–36.

293. See above, pp. 120–21.

294. Dalbert is correct in saying, "Upon closer examination we will, however, always find that these figures are representatives of the people of God. What is said about their capabilities, deeds, and miracles, always serves its honor" (*Missionsliteratur*, 138; my trans.). That does not deny the fact that these are "stories of heroes," for the people of God here is no longer that of the OT. Whenever Israel is viewed as a collective entity, it appears as a community of pneumatics, at least as a potential one. On this, cf. the passages cited by Dahl (*Volk Gottes*, 100–103), esp. *Sib. Or.* 3.234–64, 580; 5.155–61; *Ant.* 4.114; *Praem.* 66, 93, 114. *Sib. Or.* 4.24–34 should be mentioned, and the Apologetic midrash used in Wisdom of Solomon 11–19. In this heavily edited passage, the people of God is a taboo, but that means it is a bearer of "pneuma."

295. Cf. what was said above on Abraham.

296. This is generally the case, even if the ἀρετή concept is not always used. *Ant.* 12.281 may be especially mentioned, where it says that God watches the ἀρετή of the pious.

297. Especially clear is *Ant.* 1.23: "Our legislator, on the contrary, having shown that God possesses the very perfection of ἀρετή, thought that men should strive to participate in it."

298. Esp. in Josephus. The passages are in Schlatter, *Theologie des Jud-entums*, 31–32.

299. Passages in ibid., 53–54 (ἐπιφάνεια) and 30–31 (παρουσία).

300. Dalbert (*Missionsliteratur*, 130–31) rightly emphasizes this (similarly Schlatter, *Theologie des Judentums*, 53–54).

301. Dalbert, *Missionsliteratur*, 131, 134–35.

302. Note the compilation in ibid., 131–37.

303. In *Sib. Or.* 5.263 all Jerusalem is described as filled with the spirit of God; in *Sib. Or.* 3.295 the song of the Sibyl is described thus. The notion appears frequently in Philo and Josephus. On the latter, cf. *Ant.* 9.35 and *JW* 3.353. For particulars, see Schlatter, *Theologie des Judentums*, 60.

304. Ludwig Bieler (Θεῖος Ἀνήρ: *Das Bild des "göttlichen Menschen" in Spätantike und Frühchristentum* [2 vols.; Vienna: Höfels, 1935]) has collected the essential ancient texts on the phenomenon of the θεῖος ἀνήρ. The Jewish texts are found in his work at 1:16–19, 32; 2:1ff. (LXX), esp. 2:24–26. Also important is Windisch, *Paulus und Christus*, 24–28; the Jewish passages are on pp. 89–92 and esp. 101–14. Hans Dieter Betz (*Lukian von Samosata und das Neue Testament: religionsgeschichtliche und paränetische Parallelen* [TU 76; Berlin: Akademie-Verlag, 1961] 100–105) provides a comprehensive collection of pagan texts and an interpretation of the passages in Lucian, as well as further literature. See above, pp. 155–59.

The term θεῖος ἀνήρ appears in Jewish texts in: Philo, *Virt.* 177 (the sinless man as θεῖος ἀνήρ); Josephus, *Ant.* 3.180 (Moses) and 10.35 (Isaiah). In *Moses* 1.158 Moses is termed θεῖος. In Artapanus (Jacoby, *Fragmente*, 3:726; Eusebius, *Praep. Ev.* 9.18) Egyptian priests deem Moses worthy of divine honor (ἰσοθέου τιμῆς καταξιωθῆναι 3, 6). In the *Epistle of Aristeas* 140 the Jews are called ἄνθρωποι θεοῦ by the Egyptian priests (a weakening of the tradition used by Artapanus). In *Ant.* 8.34 Solomon is spoken of as one who possesses divine understanding (θεία διάνοια); also cf. *Ant.* 10.268: Daniel has πίστις καὶ δόξα ὁμοῦ θειότητος.

305. Characteristic of this is the passage from the *Epistle of Aristeas* mentioned in the previous note, as well as the usage of Philo. On that topic, Windisch, *Paulus und Christus*, 101–4; and Bieler, Θεῖος Ἀνήρ, 2:24–36.

306. Not without basis, Bieler and Windisch (see above, n. 305) mention that the OT prepared for the Hellenistic-Jewish interpretation by its portrayals of men of God (not least of all in the Elijah and Elisha legends). Above all, however, the wisdom literature can be referred to, and especially late Jewish wisdom. It is symptomatic for the disappearance of the boundaries between God and man. The general interest was to magnify the power of God.

307. Thus Demetrius, Eupolemus, and later also Justus of Tiberias (about whom not enough is known to classify him clearly among the Apologists) pretend to write on the Jewish kings, although they treat much that has

nothing to do with the title. Philo the Elder entitles his work, which devotes a good deal of attention to the patriarchs, "On Jerusalem" (similarly Theodotus entitles his work "On Shechem").

308. This view already came to light in the description of Abraham (above). Cf. also the description of Moses by Philo in *Moses*, with Moses as king, lawgiver, high priest, and prophet, or also the previously mentioned reference from *Ant*. 13.299, which states that God deemed Hyrcanus worthy of a threefold honor, that of rule over the people, the high priesthood, and prophecy.

309. He was already treated above.

310. Confirmed by the tradition developed in Wisdom, by Eupolemus, and Josephus (*Ant*. 7.377–82 and 8.1–60).

311. Heinemann, "Moses," PW 16: 359–75, esp. 365–75; Jeremias, "Μωυσῆς," *TDNT*, 4:848–73, esp. 850–64. Both articles have detailed bibliographies. Interesting but hardly useful because of its one-sided and forced thesis (that there was a substantial, indeed decisive influence on Judaism and early Christianity via the legend of Pythagoras) is the work of Isidore Lévy (*La Légende de Pythagore de Grèce en Palestine* [Paris: Champion, 1927]; on Moses, see pp. 137–38). But early Neo-Pythagoreanism unquestionably influenced Judaism, at least Hellenistic Judaism. Heinemann (*Philons Bildung*, index under "Pythagoras") has treated this topic reliably, quoting passages from the Apologetic tradition of Philo. On Neo-Pythagoreanism, cf. Martin P. Nilsson, *Geschichte der griechischen Religion* (2 vols.; HAW 5/2; Munich: Beck, 2d ed. of vol. 1, 1955, 1st ed. of vol. 2, 1950) 2:396–99; Dörrie, "Neupythagoreer," *RGG*, 4:1432–33, and above, pp. 157–58, 160–61.

312. Jacoby, *Fragmente*, 3:726.3.1–4; Eusebius, *Praep. Ev*. 9.27.

313. Moses comes from a people whose ancestors were distinguished by their superior endowment. Abraham is presented in the first fragment (Eusebius, *Praep. Ev*. 9.18.1) as a teacher of astrology. According to the second fragment (9.23.1–4), Joseph surpassed his brothers in understanding and insight and then later became the blessed administrator of Egypt. He newly divided the land, added fertile fields, and did not omit the priests in distributing the land (and even allied himself with them by marriage); last but not least, he discovered measurements. He was an ideal founder of culture, in other words, one who was clever and inventive, endowed with superior insight, and therefore also tolerant.

314. Abraham as a founder of culture was discussed above, pp. 50–55.

315. Otto Weinreich, *Gebet und Wunder: Zwei Abhandlungen zur Religions- und Literaturgeschichte* (Stuttgart: Kohlhammer, 1929) 298–309.

316. In this tolerance (cf. n. 313) Artapanus goes the furthest of all the Apologists, but he does so in conformity with their enlightenment principle. His aim was to convert people to Judaism, as shown by the story of Moses' stay in Ethiopia. Moses brings circumcision to the Ethiopians.

317. I have referred above (pp. 53–54) to the same feature also in the description of Abraham. This feature belongs to the picture of the royal man, which is more or less identical with that of the θεῖος ἀνήρ. The royal man gives rules to the community through his presence and behavior.

318. As did Abraham (above, pp. 58–59). Respect, honor, and affection of the masses for the divine man generally play a great role. This is discussed more or less clearly for all the figures named.

319. The name of the god Hermes, the messenger of the gods, was even granted to Moses because he was able to interpret the sacred writings. For Eupolemus (Jacoby, *Fragmente*, 3:723.1.ab; Eusebius, *Praep. Ev.* 9.25.4; Clement of Alexandria, *Stromateis* 1.153.4), Moses is also the first of the sages, who gave humanity (first the Jews and then through them the Phoenicians and the Greeks) the art of writing (γράμματα according to Eusebius, γραμματική according to Clement; cf. on this Dalbert, *Missionsliteratur*, 41). On the interpretation of words and writing, see pp. 133–42, 144, 161–64.

320. The notion of taboo along with the motif of persecution and suffering is closely connected with the θεῖος ἀνήρ problem. This is presented in the most detailed way in the long midrash assimilated in *Wisdom of Solomon* 11–12 and 16–19, although in the original, Apologetic version it is related to the whole people of Israel and not only to individuals. This collective variant of the taboo notion is also present in the descriptions of Israel's miraculous preservation at the Exodus (Ezekiel in Eusebius, *Praep. Ev.* 9.29.14; Artapanus in Jacoby, *Fragmente*, 3:726.3.22–39, esp. 31–33; cf. also Aristobulus in ibid., 3:726.3.20: corresponds to Eusebius, *Praep. Ev.* 9.27, with the same paragraph numbers as in Jacoby). The first part of *Wisdom*, which speaks of the suffering of the righteous individual, goes even further. Here, however, the speculative-mystical reworking of the tradition (wherein suffering and death have a fully docetic character) is carried through in a much stronger way.

Pseudo-Hecataeus (Josephus, *Apion* 1.190–91) must also be mentioned, as well as the legends of Daniel, especially their further development in the Greek additions to the Book of Daniel, and the Book of Esther, and especially the Greek additions to it. Finally, I want to point to 2, 3, and 4 Maccabees. In all these texts, threat and suffering are eclipsed by the triumph of the chosen one(s), either because their salvation is reported or because their suffering and death is heroicized. In most cases the enemies meet an evil end (this has the character of a necessary reaction of nature more than that of a real act of judgment). The mention of threat, suffering, or death serves in the cases mentioned only as background which underscores the superiority of those designated by God. All the opposing forces can only underline more strongly what is involved in the men of God and the people of God. Cf. also pp. 50, 156–57.

321. Jacoby, *Fragmente*, 3:726.3.24–25. The king is paralyzed by the

name of the Jewish God whispered in his ear by Moses (then he is restored by Moses). A priest who tries to efface the divine name from a tablet dies in convulsions.

322. Ibid., 3:726.3.26–27. The Apologists like to understand miracles as a way of legitimizing the pneumatic. Josephus, *Ant*. 10–28, reads (when King Hiskia, because of the severity of his illness doubts Isaiah's assurance that he would become well within three days, although Isaiah appeals to God's command): "And so he asked Isaiah to perform some sign or miracle (σημεῖόν τι καὶ τεράστιον) in order that he might believe in him (πιστεύσῃ) when he said these things, as in one who came from God. For, he said, things that are beyond belief (παράλογα) and surpass our hopes are made credible (πιστοῦται) by acts of a like nature." R. Marcus here adds an interpretative comment: "That is, incredible statements can be accepted only when supported by equally incredible acts." Cf. also *Ant*. 6.91.

323. Jacoby, *Fragmente*, 3:726.3.30–31. I have already referred to the motif of the demonstrative proof in a contest in analyzing the Apologetic tradition of Abraham (p. 53). See below, pp. 153–55.

324. See above, pp. 120–22.

325. Literally, ματαίως ἡμᾶς ὑπὸ τῶν ἄλλων τὰς βλασφημίας ἀκούοντας.

326. Tacitus, *Histories* 5.5. Further passages may be found in Liagre-Böhl, *Opera Minora*, 119–20.

327. Thus Moses (or the prophets generally) can be conceived of as God's translator, as mentioned above (p. 110). In *Ant*. 3.83 Moses is returning from Mount Sinai behaving like a god. He lets the name and the majesty of God appear in his rendering of the commands of God. Moses himself only translates (87). See pp. 134–36, 256–57.

328. My emphasis. τοιγαροῦν ὑπήκουεν ὡς δεσπότῃ τῶν στοιχείων ἕκαστον ἀλλάττον ἦν εἶχε δύναμιν καὶ ταῖς προστάξεσιν ὑπεῖκον.

329. Philo is obviously alluding to the concept of θαῦμα (miracle). The change of tense should also be noted. Philo no longer tells of something in the past, but instead is using the timeless present.

330. The proverb was already used in Philo, *Abr*. 235.

331. According to Exod. 33:11. On the expression φίλος θεοῦ, cf. the literature cited by BAGD, "φίλος" 2.a α and β, esp. that of Peterson and Dibelius (pp. 153, 161–62). Note, too, Schlatter, *Theologie des Judentums*, 39 (also referring to the parallel concept θεοφιλής; again cf. BAGD). The use of this concept is symptomatic of the synergism between God and humans, especially in the Apologetic texts.

332. My emphasis. The Greek text: ὁ δὲ σπουδαῖος ἄνθρωπος . . . τῶν δὲ τοῦ θεοῦ κειμηλίων . . . μεταλαγχάνει.

333. This is conveyed in a brief formula in the *Epistle of Artisteas* (210): "God works and knows everything with the help of everything (πάντα διὰ παντὸς ὁ θεός ἐνεργεῖ καὶ γινώσκει)." Aristobulus supports this view in a particularly clear way. His decisive concept is δύναμις θεοῦ (θεία δύναμις),

and the first fragment (Eusebius, *Praep. Ev.* 8.10.1–17) already shows that with this concept he wants to include the OT testimony of God's miraculous acts. These statements on divine power are accompanied by similar ones on God's establishment of an unchangeable world (ibid., 8.10.9–11) and on his omnipresence (ibid., 8.10.12–15). An analysis of the second fragment (ibid., 13.12.1–4) confirms this. In a further example, the literal biblical text is followed (as opposed to the intended meaning) when divine words and divine deeds are identified (ibid., 13.12.3–4), divine deeds and divine activity already being considered as one. Thus the activity of God is unmistakably a natural process, manifesting similarity in change. The fact that the word, activity, and power of God are synonymous simply means that God's will manifests itself as the law of the cosmic process. Ultimately, power is also order and law. In what follows, Aristobulus retains his interest in that which is permanent in the cosmic process; he thereby sees the possibility of comprehending something divine (as the interpretation of the Sabbath command shows). His allegorical interpretation in general aims at grasping what is natural (the φυσικαὶ διαθέσεις) and attempts a real comprehension in the sense of a natural comprehension (τὸ φυσικῶς λαμβάνειν).

The riddle of the conclusion of *Wisdom of Solomon* is explained by the very fact that Apologetic tradition is used here (19:18–21), but a redactional exposition which could have united this statement with the intent of the work as a whole has either broken off accidentally or is left out intentionally (to keep the work open-ended). The fragmentary character of the conclusion is emphasized by Karl Siegfried in Emil Kautzsch et al. *Die Apokryphen und Pseudepigraphen des Alten Testaments* (reprint; Hildesheim: Olms, 1962) 476–507. In Siegfried's translation (note also his explanation) the verses read: "For the elements changed places with one another, as on a harp the notes vary the nature of the melody (?), while each note remains the same. This may be clearly inferred from the sight of what took place" (ibid., 507, my trans.). The following list of miraculous events becomes meaningful only after this introductory statement.

334. The wording of Josephus clearly shows this reserve: "But on these matters let everyone decide according to his fancy" (*Ant.* 1.108, after mentioning the longevity of the patriarchs). At *Ant.* 3.81 (the theophany on Sinai) Josephus joins to a similar remark the characteristic addition "For my part, I am constrained (ἐμοὶ δὲ ἀνάγκη) to relate (ἱστορεῖν) them as they are recorded in the sacred books." The style of non-Jewish historiography, especially that of Josephus's model, Dionysius of Halicarnassus, may have influenced these remarks. Thackeray (*Josephus: The Man*, 57–58; also his note in Josephus, *Ant.* [LCL 4] 1.108) and others here see a rationalistic trait in Josephus. Thackeray considers this intention of the Apologist, based on Josephus's frequent rationalization of the text of the Bible (identified by him and by Julien Weill, trans., *Oeuvres Complètes de Flavius Josèphe* [ed. Theodore Reinach; Paris: Leroux, 1900] 98). This position, however, does

not take account of the fact that just as many of Josephus's legendary and novelistic expansions of the text of the Bible and of Jewish tradition can be characterized as miraculous. Thus we hear the words of Moses (*Ant*. 2.270): "To mistrust, O Lord, thy power (δύναμις), which I venerate myself and know to have been manifested to my forefathers, were madness too gross, I trow, for my prudence to conceive." The so-called rationalistic traits, just as the traits indicating a belief in the miraculous, can without a doubt be found already in the tradition used by Josephus. Similarly, Artapanus first adds a rationalistic interpretation—from the lips of unbelievers—to his report of the miracle of the Red Sea and then gives an interpretation indicating a belief in the miraculous. The two appear side by side in Philo. Cf. above, pp. 111–12 and pp. 118–20.

335. So-called rationalism and the belief in miracles can be reconciled. For the Apologists it is not a case of contradictions, but of different aspects of the same thing.

336. This differentiation also offered tactical advantages. On the one hand, accounts of pneumatic demonstrations, which were so important for successful propaganda, could be given. On the other hand, by flirting with an attitude of distance, it was possible to keep open a way to the skeptical rationalists, who were also present, and to prepare for a missionary dialogue with this position.

337. Philo has once again chosen the Aorist.

338. My emphasis; the Greek text: ὠνομάσθη γὰρ ὅλου τοῦ ἔθνους θεὸς καὶ βασιλεύς. εἴς τε τὸν γνόφον, ἔνθα ἦν ὁ θεός, εἰσελθεῖν λέγεται, τουτέστιν εἰς τὴν ἀειδῆ καὶ ἀόρατον καὶ ἀσώματον τῶν ὄντων παραδειγματικὴν οὐσίαν.

339. Above, pp. 54–55.

340. My emphasis; the Greek text: ὃς αὐτὸν δυάδα ὄντα, σῶμα καὶ ψυχήν, εἰς μονάδος ἀνεστοιχείου φύσιν ὅλον δι' ὅλων μεθαρμοζόμενος εἰς νοῦν ἡλιοειδέστατον.

341. ὅλον δι' ὅλων μεθαρμοζόμενος.

342. No differentiation is made between exaltation and heavenly journey.

343. πορευόμενος ἔνθεν οὗ ἔμελλεν ἀφανισθήσεσθαι. ἠφανίσθη is also used of Elijah (*Ant*. 9.28). *Ant*. 4.323–31 (my ed.).

344. The ravine comes from the biblical account. The two parallels cited by Thackeray (LCL, Josephus 4.632 n. b) of Dionysius of Halicarnassus show, however, the actual tendency of Josephus. On Aeneas, *Ant*. 1.64.4 (in Thackeray's trans.) reads: "But the body of Aeneas could nowhere be found and some conjectured that he had been translated to the gods." On Romulus, ibid., 2.56.2 reads: "The more mythical writers say that as he was holding an assembly (ἐκκλησιάζοντα) in the camp darkness descended upon him from a clear sky and . . . he disappeared, and they believe that he was caught up by his father Ares." In both cases a *deification* is recorded. The same phrase, ἀναχωρεῖν πρὸς τὸ θεῖον, which Josephus, *Ant*. 4.326, attenu-

ates, is used in *Ant*. 1.85 quite unabashedly for the death of Enoch, and of Enoch and Elijah (*Ant*. 9.28) it is also said that no end to their lives in the proper sense (τελευτή, θάνατος) is known. The shortening of the account of the disappearance of Elijah has thus not led to a rationalization in the usual sense of the word (against Thackeray, LCL, Josephus 6.17 n.*c*).

345. My emphasis.

346. καθάπερ τε γραφὴν εὖ δεδημιουργημένην ἑαυτὸν καὶ τὸν ἑαυτοῦ βίον εἰς μέσον προαγαγὼν πάγκαλον καὶ θεοειδὲς ἔργον ἔστησε παράδειγμα τοῖς ἐθέλουσι μιμεῖσθαι. εὐδαίμονες δ᾽ ὅσοι τὸν τύπον ταῖς ἑαυτῶν ψυχαῖς ἐναπεμάξαντο ἢ ἐσπούδασαν ἐναπομάξασθαι.

347. Again the ἀρετή concept is much broader than simply a moral idea. Its meaning reflects all the divine qualities which were accumulated in Moses.

348. It is incorrect to translate νόμος ἔμψυχος, as does Goodenough (*Light*, 186 and elsewhere), with "incarnate law." Something intrinsic or inherent is certainly meant, yet it does not refer to body or flesh, but to the soul. On νόμος λογικός Goodenough (ibid., 186 n. 36) convincingly says: "The translation of νόμος λογικός by 'vocal law' is justified by the common Hellenistic notion that the king's business was to make articulate the divine realm and will into which he could penetrate."

349. Josephus, *Ant*. 1.18; see above, p. 121.

350. γόης καὶ ἀπατεών. So Apollonius Molon and Lysimachus, according to Josephus, *Apion* 2.145. The answer of Josephus which has already been paraphrased is found in *Apion* 2.161. Philo says something similar in *Hypothetica* 6.2. There the accusation is given as γόης καὶ κέρκωψ and subsequently refuted.

351. Heinemann (*Philons Bildung*, 477) deals explicitly with the problem of the juxtaposition of divine and human authorship of the law; his solution—Philo was not really concerned with the question—is unsatisfactory.

352. βίον τε ὑμῖν εὐδαίμονα καὶ πολιτείας κόσμον ὑπαγορεύσας. On the text, see above, p. 207 n. 327 and below, pp. 211 n. 365, 256.

353. ἐπὶ συμφέροντι τῷ ὑμετέρῳ πρὸς ἐμὲ μὴ φθονήσαντος εἰπεῖν (*Ant*. 3.85).

354. There then follows a lengthy description of God as the one who brings salvation to Israel as well as a promise of a happy life (εὐδαίμων βίος). This promise explains the understanding of salvation for those who will follow the commandments. A reference to Moses' encounter with God follows, probably to underscore the reality, the extent, and the permanence of the proven and promised care of God for the Jewish race (οὕτως ἐκείνῳ τοῦ γένους ἡμῶν καὶ τῆς τούτου μέλει διαμονῆς. *Ant*. 3.88). On this, cf. also pp. 136, 148–51.

355. Josephus here goes so far as to make a taboo of the literal wording of the Decalogue, which was not to be communicated to unauthorized persons. His view, however, conflicts somewhat with the practice of Apolo-

getic exegesis, which treats the literal text as something freely available that conceals the real meaning, while Josephus maintains that the meaning could be freely communicated.

356. On this, compare Thyen, *Homilie*, 70–71. The criticism of Michel's explanation is correct; it can be supplemented by the pertinent considerations presented above. Who is more concerned with the participation of human beings in the divine than Philo and the other Apologists?

357. Schlatter, *Theologie des Judentums*, 62–64.

358. For Philo, see *Moses* 2.188; *Decal*. 15; *Spec*. 2.188; *Praem*. 2; *Leg. Gai*. 210, and elsewhere; cf. Heinemann, *Philons Bildung*, 475–78. For Josephus, see *Ant*. 3.212; *JW* 6–301, 311; cf. Schlatter, *Theologie des Judentums*, 65ff.

359. Esp. clear in Josephus, *Ant*. 3.212.

360. The *Epistle of Artisteas* 98 speaks of ἅγια γράμματα in the description of the clothing of the high priest. Ἑβραϊκὰ γράμματα appears in the *Epistle of Aristeas* 3, 30, 38. See above, pp. 42–43, on Ἑβραῖος. On the motif of letters, see also pp. 137–44, 161–64, 206 n. 319.

361. In the *Epistle of Artisteas* 155 and 168 they are called γραφή.

362. "Having so said, he showed them two tablets on which were graven the ten words, five on either of them (ταῦτ᾽ εἰπὼν δύο πλάκας αὐτοῖς ἐπιδείκνυσιν ἐγγεγραμμένους ἐχούσας τοὺς δέκα λόγους, ἐν ἑκατέρᾳ πέντε)" (Josephus, *Ant*. 3.101).

363. καὶ χεὶρ ἦν ἐπὶ τῇ γραφῇ τοῦ θεοῦ (*Ant*. 3.101).

364. On the motif of the heavenly letter, cf. Röttrich, "Himmelsbrief," *RGG*, 3:338–39, and the literature cited there, especially the works of Stübe; cf. also pp. 162, 246, 248–50.

365. Josephus, *Ant*. 3.75: "Moses [. . .] told them that he himself was departing to Sinai, intending to commune with God and to receive something [useful] from Him. (τι λαβὼν παρ᾽ αὐτοῦ χρήσιμον. The reading χρήσιμον is a simplification, although reference is certainly made 'de facto' to the hoped for word of God, actually to its significance)." In *Ant*. 3.77 the hope of the people is also mentioned: Moses will return from God "with that promise of blessings which he had led them to expect (μετὰ τῆς ἐπαγγελίας τῶν ἀγαθῶν, ἣν προύτεινεν αὐτοῖς)." In *Ant*. 3.78 the Israelites ask God "to grant Moses a gift which would promote their happiness (Μωυσεῖ δοῦναι δωρεάν, ὑφ᾽ ἧς εὖ βιώσονται)." According to *Ant*. 3.85, the speech of God took place for the benefit (συμφέρον) of the Israelites. Reference has already been made to the fact that in *Ant*. 3.88 an εὐδαίμων βίος is promised in return for obedience. This happy life is painted in very earthy colors (a fruitful earth, a calm sea, an abundance of children, strength of war). Just as the θεῖος ἀνήρ himself enjoys the fullness of life, so too others receive vital energy from the νόμος which he brought. Cf. p. 134, and pp. 146, 148–51, 256–57.

366. An obvious example from Artapanus has already been mentioned

above, p. 206 n. 321.

367. The passages are in Schrenk, "γράφω," *TDNT*, 1:761–64. Also cf. below, pp. 162–64.

368. The following passages are given in Dalbert (*Missionsliteratur*, 137, 141). The law is of divine origin in *Epistle of Aristeas* 15, 31, 240 (here appears quite clearly the cooperation between the divine and the human lawgivers, which has already been observed), 313. It is holy (31, 171, 313). It is full of wisdom (31). To it belong the same titles of respect that are due to God himself (177–79). It is taboo. Anyone who makes an unauthorized translation is punished (313–16).

369. Passages from Philo and Josephus may be found in Schlatter (*Theologie des Judentums*, 64).

370. Although in Apologetic evaluation and exegesis the Pentateuch is dominant, Moses and the prophets are assimilated to one another. The writings of the prophets also belong to the ἱερὰ γράμματα (Josephus, *Ant.* 10.210, on the Book of Daniel). Conversely, Moses is also counted among the prophets. No proofs of this need to be adduced here because of the abundance of passages. Josephus (*Apion* 1.37, 41) can claim that the canon as a whole was written by the prophets. On the problem, cf. Schlatter, *Theologie des Judentums*, 59 and 54–55.

371. This is already clear with Eupolemus and Artapanus, for according to them, Jewish heroes conveyed the knowledge of letters to other nations. The Apologists also stress the fact that the law is in written form, in order to be able to compare it with other traditions.

372. Eusebius, *Praep. Ev.* 8.6.9 (my ed.).

373. τὰ δὲ τούτου μόνου βέβαια, ἀσάλευτα, ἀκράδαντα, καθάπερ σφραγῖσι φύσεως αὐτῆς σεσημασμένα, μένει παγίως ἀφ᾽ ἧς ἡμέρας ἐγράφη μέχρι νῦν καὶ πρὸς τὸν ἔπειτα πάντα διαμενεῖν ἐλπὶς αὐτὰ αἰῶνα ὥσπερ ἀθάνατα, ἕως ἂν ἥλιος καὶ σελήνη καὶ ὁ σύμπας οὐρανός τε καὶ κόσμος ᾖ (*Moses* 2.14).

374. Since the law is *written*, the image of sealing with the seals of nature can be employed, as these confer upon the law a cosmic character (this is declared in the conclusion of the passage quoted above). When the νόμιμα are designated βέβαια, ἀσάλευτα, and ἀκράδαντα because of their written form, this is an allusion to divine epithets which indicate eternity and immortality. The *written* law reflects the eternity of God and the world. On the other hand, the proximity to the concept of testament is also clear.

375. Colson (LCL, Philo 6.7) correctly translates the phrase οἷς ἐχρήσαντο, which refers to the works and deeds, with "actual."

376. This has come up before. Its importance is clearest in the apology of Josephus. Cf. also Heinemann, *Philons Bildung*, 473–75.

377. For a selection of passages on the patriarchs and their legacy from Josephus, see Schlatter, *Theologie des Judentums*, 59; Gottlob Schrenk, "πατρῷος," *TDNT*, 5:1014–15. On Philo, cf. Heinemann, *Philons Bildung*, 470–73.

378. It is significant that here there is a reference to "Hebrews" even in the present.

379. Similarly *Ant.* 11.6 says, "When Cyrus read them, he wondered at the divine power and was seized by a strong desire (ὁρμή) and ambition to do what had been written (τὰ γεγραμμένα)." Cyrus was reading with astonishment the prophecy of Deutero-Isaiah (44:28). This reveals for one thing that for Josephus the prophets also belong to the γεγραμμένα, and for another that according to Josephus's conception prophecy operates in such a way that the intended person reads it and is thereby compelled to act in accordance with what is written.

380. See above, p. 106.

381. See above, p. 136.

382. Schlatter, *Theologie des Judentums,* 67–68.

383. Admittedly the introduction to the *Jewish War,* written earlier than the *Antiquities,* contains a certain discrepancy to what has been said up to this point, for here (*JW* 1.16) necessary interest in the new and the contemporary is stressed. The Greek historians are criticized because they write about past events. Moreover, Josephus believes that he is able to forego an archaeology of Judaism, since there were already enough such works. However, the introduction to the *Antiquities* resolves the discrepancy by showing that an interest in the present does not exclude the active interest in the past, but rather includes it, and by showing that an interest in the past must reach all the way into the present. In *JW* 1.18, Josephus had already said that he was beginning his account where the prophets and the earlier writers had left off. He thus places himself and his presentation on that same level and sees his work as a worthy continuation.

384. This is clearest in Aristobulus.

385. See above, pp. 109, 111–12.

386. Eusebius, *Praep. Ev.* 8.10.2.

387. See above, pp. 121–22.

388. The law understood in this way becomes the παίδευμα in *Ant.* 1.21.

389. When they read the *Antiquities.*

390. Cf. page 163. This is not the place to treat the allegorical method of Apologetics in detail. The question here is what self-understanding is expressed by the use of this method.

391. Siegfried, *Philo,* 163.

392. Obvious for everyone.

393. In the Latin translation we also have the expression *litera (litera haec; litera haec complectitur; ac literam sic habet),* Siegfried, *Philo,* 163. In *Deus* 6 (to be sure, a passage from the allegorical commentary), a passage from the Pentateuch can be introduced in this way: κατὰ τὸ ἱερώτατον Μωυσέως γράμμα τοῦτο.

394. Odo Casel, *De Philosophorum Graecorum Silentio Mystico* (Giessen: Töpelmann, 1919) 79. Cf. also Hans Leisegang's index to the Cohn and Wendland edition of Philo (Leopold Cohn und Paul Wendland,

214   *The Opponents of Paul in Second Corinthians*

eds., *Philonis Alexandrini: Opera Quae Supersunt* [7 vols.; Berlin: De Gruyter, 1926] vol. 7).

395. On the Therapeutae, see above, p. 183 n. 59 and p. 91; the essential information and discussion is in the pioneering work on the Therapeutae by Wendland ("Therapeuten") and in Heinemann, "Therapeutai," PW, 2d ser., 51:2321–46. Also cf. Lewy, *Sobria Ebrietas*, 31–34; Émile Bréhier, *Les idées philosophiques et religieuses de Philon d'Alexandrie* (3d ed.; Paris: Vrin, 1950) 321–24. For Festugière (*Révélation*, 1:31) the portrayals of the Essenes and Therapeutae by Josephus and Philo are only *"peintures romantiques,"* but in them *"on sent bien l'esprit du temps."*

396. On the significance of the word φιλοσοφία in Hellenism, cf. Günther Bornkamm, *Das Ende des Gesetzes: Gesammelte Aufsätze 1* (2d ed.; BevTh 16; Munich: Kaiser, 1958) 143 n. 12.

397. *Cont.* 28. The Greek text: ἐπειδὴ σύμβολα τὰ τῆς ῥητῆς ἑρμηνείας νομίζουσιν ἀποκεκρυμμένης φύσεως ἐν ὑπονοίαις δηλουμένης.

398. Ibid., 29. The Greek text: συγγράμματα παλαιῶν ἀνδρῶν, οἳ τῆς αἱρέσεως ἀρχηγέται γενόμενοι πολλὰ μνημεῖα τῆς ἐν τοῖς ἀλληγορουμένοις ἰδέας ἀπέλιπον. (On the translation of ἰδέα, cf. Colson, LCL, Philo 9.129 n. c.)

399. Ibid., 29. The Greek text: οἷς καθάπερ τισίν ἀρχετύποις χρώμενοι μιμοῦνται τῆς προαιρέσεως τὸν τρόπον.

400. Ibid., 29. The Greek text: ὥστε οὐ θεωροῦσι μόνον, ἀλλὰ καὶ ποιοῦσιν ᾄσματα καὶ ὕμνους εἰς τὸν θεόν. . . .

401. Ibid., 78. The Greek text: αἱ . . . ἐξηγήσεις τῶν ἱερῶν γραμμάτων γίνονται δι᾽ ὑπονοιῶν ἐν ἀλληγορίαις. ἅπασα γὰρ ἡ νομοθεσία δοκεῖ τοῖς ἀνδράσι τούτοις ἐοικέναι ζῴῳ καὶ σῶμα μὲν ἔχειν τὰς ῥητὰς διατάξεις, ψυχὴν δὲ τὸν ἐναποκείμενον ταῖς λέξεσιν ἀόρατον νοῦν, ἐν ᾧ ἤρξατο ἡ λογικὴ ψυχὴ διαφερόντως τὰ οἰκεῖα θεωρεῖν.

402. Ibid., 78. The Greek text: ὥσπερ διὰ κατόπτρου τῶν ὀνομάτων ἐξαίσια κάλλη νοημάτων ἐμφαινόμενα κατιδοῦσα καὶ τὰ μὲν σύμβολα διαπτύξασα καὶ διακαλύψασα, γυμνὰ δὲ εἰς φῶς προαγαγοῦσα τὰ ἐνθύμια τοῖς δυναμένοις ἐκ μικρᾶς ὑπομνήσεως τὰ ἀφανῆ διὰ τῶν φανερῶν θεωρεῖν.

403. On the mirror vision, see below, p. 264; on the hiddenness, see above, pp. 42–45, 54–56, 97–99, 115–17, 127–29, 133–42, 146–48, 162–64.

404. The words συνηδομένων εἰς τὸ ἔτι ἑψόμενον (sec. 79) suggest this.

405. Wendland may be right in thinking that Philo presents a heavily stylized account. Nevertheless, the stylization is no heavier here than in the rest of the work, and there is nothing to show why the dramatic recreation of the Red Sea miracle should be a Philonic invention.

406. The Greek text here reads: . . . θεωρίαν ἀσπασαμένων φύσεως καὶ τῶν ἐν αὐτῇ καὶ ψυχῇ μόνῃ βιωσάντων. Colson unnecessarily complicates matters in his translation: ". . . who have taken to their heart the contemplation of nature and what it has to teach, and have lived in the soul alone. . . ."

Then he discusses in a footnote what the possible significance of the τῶν ἐν αὐτῇ might be, and first proposes that the phrase turns the meaning toward "the theological side of physic," and certainly not toward the content of the natural world. Then he proposes that the τῶν be omitted and the phrase be translated "lived in it and the soul alone." But the expression τῶν . . . βιωσάντων can be understood very simply as a clause coordinated with the ἀσπασαμένων and whose antecedent is the θεραπευτῶν which introduces the whole sentence.

407. *Cont.* 90.

408. Philo generally prefers the personal ὁ ὤν. Colson's translation, "the Self-Existent," is incorrect (LCL, Philo 9.115).

409. It should not be overlooked that even the course of the actual acts of worship is described in considerable detail—in a writing intended for outsiders.

410. Cf. above, p. 211 n. 365.

411. Cf. p. 200 n. 264.

412. The protest of the Sibyllines and of Philo against *pagan* astrology is directed against deification of heavenly bodies, not against a knowledge of the biblical God which has been gained or confirmed by natural perception or experience.

413. The intensification of the enigmatic element in connection with the motifs of letter and of writing and the emphasis on a special method of exposition surely had propagandistic motives as well. An obscure and enigmatic description excited curiosity. The Apologists surely erected such fences to arouse a desire to climb over them. It has already been shown (above, pp. 97–99, 115–17) how little the secrecy motif reflected fundamental principles and sociological distinctions. The separation of exoteric and esoteric factors must instead signify a viewpoint tied to the nature of the understanding of scripture, as the explanations above attempt to demonstrate.

414. Eusebius, *Praep. Ev.* 13.12.5 (GCS 8, 2:194, ll. 5–6). Cf. also above, p. 55.

415. On this, cf. Martin Dibelius, *From Tradition to Gospel* (New York: Scribner's, 1965) 75–78, 81–89, 92–96; and below, pp. 158–59, 160–61, 170–73.

416. As in previous sections, I certainly do not intend nor am I able to provide a detailed and definitive description. I can only attempt to give what are in my opinion the most essential features of the Apologetic vision of the future. Much less am I able to discuss and clarify in full the relationship of the Apologetic vision to that of the rest of Judaism and the OT. Numerous such connections obviously exist. It would be particularly interesting (and important for the classification of Apologetics) to study further the relationship of several motifs to corresponding ones from the earlier and contemporary wisdom movement, as well as to analyze their further history in the later development of the wisdom movement.

An important concern in the following discussion will be to show that the Apologists had not simply taken over or advocated a nationalistic Jewish eschatology. The one-sidedness of the portrayals of Bousset and Gressmann, and Volz, will be avoided. I am concerned less about isolated viewpoints (which can also be found elsewhere) than about the dominant self-understanding.

417. *Sib. Or.* 3.781–95; *Praem.* 85–97. Clearly in these passages Isa. 11:6–10 serves as the model (see the evidence in the case of *Praem.* given by Colson [LCL, Philo 8.364–65, 455–56]); in the case of Philo, Lev. 26:6 is also a model.

418. In addition to Philo, *Praem.* 85–87, cf. *Sib. Or.* 3.367–80, 571–91, 616–19, 740–55, 767–71.

419. However, precisely in these passages it is particularly clear that we are dealing with interpretations and further developments of OT prophetic statements. In addition to Isa. 11:6–10, also cf. Hos. 10:12; Joel 2:23; Isa. 32:16–20; 45:8; 48:18–19; Jer. 31:23; and the commentary on these passages in von Rad, 1:373–74, and Horst, "Gerechtigkeit Gottes, II," *RGG*, 1:1404. The further evolution of the understanding of righteousness found among the Apologists, compared with these OT passages, clarifies the connection with the wisdom movement. This explains well what follows.

420. Cf. above, pp. 134, 136, 146. Also important in this connection is Philo, *Praem.* 98–117.

421. Of course, even before this one can talk about individual happiness; but cf. also *Praem.* 118–26.

422. *Praem.* 98–114 is especially characteristic. Accordingly, immortality was preferred to resurrection. The conquest of want and death was to take place by means of a rapidly increasing vitality.

423. *Sib. Or.* 3.787.

424. According to *Ant.* 1.68–71, Seth had lived a life in ἀρετή, and his descendants became his imitators. "These . . . inhabited the same country without dissension and in prosperity (ἀστασίαστοι . . . εὐδαιμονήσαντες), meeting with no untoward incident to the day of their death" (sec. 69). It is significant for the high value placed by Apologists on astrology that directly after this description of an ideal humanity comes, still in sec. 69, the remark "They also discovered the science of the heavenly bodies and their orderly array." To preserve this information for humanity—even through the deluge—it was written on stone. Also Cf. *Ant.* 1.104–8. The other patriarchs might compare; cf. what is said above, on 50–59 and 124–27, about the relationship of Abraham and Moses to foreigners, or the statements of Eupolemus on the construction of the temple. In *Sib. Or.* 3.218–47, the people of the righteous is depicted as an ideal humanity.

425. *Sib. Or.* 3.573–91, 702–6, 767–80; Philo, *Praem.* 115–17, 162–67.

426. See above, pp. 49–60, 83–102.

427. *Praem.* 152.

428. *Sib. Or.* 3.582–91, 781–85; *Praem.* 79–97, esp. 85–97.

429. *Sib. Or.* 3.582–600, 781–94. *Praem.* 79–84, esp. 85–97.

430. *Praem.* 93, 107, 114–17.

431. This is found very clearly in *Sib. Or.* 3.582–90, 616–19, 715–26, 755–60, 767–76.

432. In the Jewish *Sibylline Oracles* (*Sib. Or.* 3.247, 261) the statement appears that God has given the earth to all humans in common. Josephus also sees humanity as a unity and knows of a world age characterized by unity (Schlatter, *Theologie des Judentums,* 72–73 and 242).

433. See above, pp. 49–60 and 118–48, and esp. 124–33.

434. See above, pp. 85–87.

435. Developed in detail in *Sib. Or.* 3.767–76; *Praem.* 84, 91–97, 113–14, 162–67.

436. This is quite clear in Philo's presentation. But the *Sibylline Oracles,* which speak more about God's intervention in the course of history, also closely parallel the primordial time, present, and end time of the nation of the righteous (3.219–47, 573–91, 767–80).

437. See above, p. 216 n. 422. The descriptions on pp. 129–34 of the fate of the greats of the past served as models in this regard.

438. Therefore an actual eschatological consciousness was not present—on the contrary.

439. *Sib. Or.* 3.556–63, 611–18, 624–28, 693–97, 732–43, 761–66.

440. According to Philo (*Praem.* 4–6) the period of lawgiving is followed by the period of testing in a gigantic spectacle with many contests, which are depicted as athletic ἀγῶνες. Colson (LCL, Philo 7.314 n. b.) is probably correct in thinking that Philo wants to describe the history of Jewish people with this image. Nevertheless, his interpretation becomes conclusive only when we remember that this image is placed at the beginning of the tractate and relate the following rewards and punishments to this introductory thought. On the other hand, Colson's objection that this image is not referred to again is less significant.

441. This is shown above all by 4 Maccabees. See above, pp. 49–50; cf. pp. 125, 129–32.

442. This is especially impressive in *Sib. Or.* 3.767–95.

443. Cf. above, p. 200 n. 254.

444. Cumont, *Oriental Religions;* Arthur Darby Nock, *Conversion: The Old and the New in Religion from Alexander the Great to Augustine of Hippo* (Oxford: Clarendon, 1933), to which I am heavily indebted. Also to be mentioned are Wendland, *Kultur;* Reitzenstein, *Mystery-Religions;* Karl Prümm, *Religionsgeschichtliches Handbuch für den Raum der altchristlichen Umwelt: Hellenistisch-römische Geistesströmungen und Kulte mit Beachtung des Eigenlebens der Provinzen* (Freiburg im Breisgau: Herder, 1943). Other references to secondary literature in Werner Förster, *Neutestamentliche Zeitgeschichte,* vol. 2, *Das Römische Weltreich zur Zeit*

des Neuen Testaments (Hamburg: Furche, 1955–56) 2:108–259, esp. 159–83.

445. A graphic picture is given by Kahrstedt, *Kulturgeschichte*, 353–54.

446. Pp. 28–29 and 99–100. Also cf. above, pp. 156–57, 160 n. 61. In addition, the factual propaganda of these people is noted by Oltramare, *Origines*, 155–57 (Sextius), 158–61 (Papirius Fabianus, cf. p. 181).

447. Cf. Dörrie, "Neupythagoreer," *RGG*, 4:1432–33.

448. Cf. Nock, *Conversion*, 75–76, 82–83, 97–98; Bolkestein, *Wohltätigkeit*, 210–14, 384–85.

449. Above, pp. 98–101.

450. As is maintained by Nock, *Conversion*, 75–76, 82–83, 97–98.

451. This is plainly evident in the sixth satire of Juvenal. A characteristic picture of a begging preacher, which also conveniently shows the influence of the Cynic-Stoic itinerant philosophers on the portrayal of Hellenistic missionaries, is given by the inscription from Kefr Havar, presented by Adolf Deissmann (*Licht vom Osten: Das neue Testament und die neuentdeckten Texte der hellenistisch-römischen Welt* [4th rev. ed.; Tübingen: Mohr, 1923] 87); cf. also Hugo Gressmann, "Heidnische Mission in der Werdezeit des Christentums," *ZMR* 39 [1924] 23). Rengstorf ("ἀποστέλλω," *TDNT*, 1:398 n. 9) denies a missionary consciousness to this begging priest because the term ἀποστέλλειν is employed in the text instead of πέμπειν. But this argument is too formalistic. In addition, why differentiate between commercial and religious authorization when interpreting the matter at hand: a representative being sent by a goddess? For the begging clergy as a whole, also cf. Michaelis, "πῆρα," *TDNT*, 6:119–21.

452. Nock, *Conversion*, 83–91, 101–5.

453. Gressmann, "Heidnische Mission," 18–22; Carl Clemen, "Die Missionstätigkeit der nichtchristlichen Religionen," *ZMR* 44 (1929) 230–31; K. Kerényi, *Die griechisch-orientalische Romanliteratur in religionsgeschichtlicher Beleuchtung* (2d ed.; Darmstadt: Wissenschaftliche Buchgesellschaft, 1962) passim; Nock, *Conversion*, 89–91. These phenomena parallel the described Jewish procedure.

454. Nock, *Conversion*, 80–83.

455. This could be demonstrated by the description of the Isis mission in Juvenal's sixth satire. Also cf. above, pp. 96–106, 112–17.

456. This problem has been examined by Nock (*Conversion*, 56–58). His observations prohibit following the kind of one-sidedness found especially in Reitzenstein (*Mystery-Religions*), that is, to categorize all oriental missionary cults as mystery religions on the basis of the presence of mystery elements (or, in the long run, to attribute them all to Gnosticism). For the problem of the mysteries, esp. the growing interest in the mysteries, cf. Nock (*Conversion*, index under Mysteries, esp. 102–6), Cumont (*Orientalische Religionen*, passim), Hopfner ("Mysterien," *PW* 16:1209–1350), Johannes Leipoldt (*Von den Mysterien zur Kirche:*

Gesammelte Aufsätze [Hamburg: Reich, 1962] 5–50; idem, "Mysterien," *RGG*, 4:1232–36; cf. esp. bibliography).

457. The nonmissionary mysteries of Eleusis, Andania, Pheneos, and Samothrace are of no interest here. The mystery cults in question are above all the Dionysiac, the Orphic, the Isis (Serapis), the Attis, and the Mithras mysteries, and in the second century the mysteries of Alexander of Abono-teichus. A multitude of mysterylike private circles appeared in NT times as well. These also bore a more-or-less philosophical stamp, either Neo-Pythagorean or Hermetic in character. Here, just as in an endless number of magic clubs, one followed Gnosticizing ideas. All these little groups did not display actual missionary character, although they were signs of the times, which they in turn also influenced, especially with their literary products. They were not identical with the Gnostic movement, only off-shoots of it.

458. A thorough presentation by Wlosok, *Laktanz und die philosophische Gnosis*, 12–16, 33–37, 118–21, 134–42, 248–49.

459. The approach of Ptolemy IV apparently speaks for a corresponding tendency in the Dionysiac mysteries (Cumont, *Orientalische Religionen*, 193–94). This is known of the Mithras mysteries. The cults of Serapis, Isis, Cybele, and Attis, as well as the mysteries attached to them (particularly those mysteries reserved for the privileged), obviously tried to become publicly accepted and thus often reached their goal.

460. Cf. above, pp. 112–17.

461. Leipoldt, *Aufsätze*, 12–20. Regarding the missionaries, the example followed was perhaps that of the widespread and generally recognized associations of Dionysiac artists. After all, the Dionysus mysteries had appropriated the motif of a recruiting god from the Dionysus myth. Dionysus was his own first missionary; as his believers identified with him, they emulated his actions. The same holds true for Attis (Gressmann, "Heidnische Mission," 23–24).

462. There are examples in the Menippus tradition, the Letter of Thessalus, the Pseudo-Clementines, Justin, Augustine, Cyprian, and Philostratus's *Life of Apollonius of Tyana*. Cf. Nock, *Conversion*, 107–12.

463. On this formula, cf. Otto Weinreich, *Neue Urkunden zur Sarapis-Religion* (Tübingen: Mohr, 1919) 17–18, 24–25; and Peterson, *ΕΙΣ ΘΕΟΣ*.

464. Cf. Weinreich, *Urkunden*, 17–18, 24–25. The extant stories are partly fictional in character. Nevertheless, they do express an existing self-understanding. And these manipulated and stylized texts also bear the characteristics of models. They are supposed to incite corresponding actions (of miracle workers and believers). Weinreich, *Urkunden*, 24–25; Dibelius, *Tradition*, 76–78, 81–83, 93–96.

465. This explains the accommodation of Jewish Apologetics to Hellenism.

466. Otto Weinreich, "Alexander" 129–51.

467. Cf. above, pp. 122–37. In the following, the frequently discussed literary θεῖος ἀνήρ motif (cf. the works cited above, p. 204 n. 304) will be examined less than its actual manifestations (as far as they can still be recognized).

468. Dio Chrysostom, 33.4; my trans.

469. See above, pp. 27–32. Rengstorf in *TDNT*, 1:399, argues quite correctly that in the Cynic-Stoic diatribe ἀποστέλλω appears almost as a technical term for religious and moral authorization, and he suspects that this is but a reflection of a more general usage in philosophical religiosity. The Cynic is empowered by the deity as God's envoy (ibid.). Cf. ibid., 408, further about the missionary consciousness of the Cynic; in addition, Kurt Deissner, "Das Sendungsbewusstsein der Urchristenheit," *ZSTh* 7 (1929–30) 782–87.

470. The theme of the Cynic-Stoic wise person in the diatribe is briefly summarized by Oltramare (*Origines*, 57–60, esp. no. 58 and nos. 67–73; also cf. index under Sage.

471. According to an anecdote, Diogenes assumed this title as he was being questioned about his commission. Cf. Norden, *Beiträge*, 377. (In the third century, Kerkidas finds in Διογένης the origin of Diogenes: he is the heavenly offspring of Zeus (διογένης). Ζανὸς γόνος οὐράνιός τε κύων, true θεῖος and ἄνθρωπος at the same time.) This concept appears in the title of two writings of Antisthenes: "Lord or Beloved" (κύριος ἢ ἐρώμενος) and "Lord or the Scouts" (κύριος ἢ κατάσκοποι, Diogenes Laertius 6.18; Norden, *Beiträge*, 373–85. Hicks in LCL reads κύρος both times. The fact that proper names appear also in other titles of the tenth volume of writings could speak for that). Thus, the Cynic is simultaneously κύριος. According to a note of Stobaeus (3.63), as a Cynic is on the verge of being sold in Corinth and is asked what he can do, he replies, "To rule over human beings (ἀνθρώπων ἄρχειν)." Thereupon the herald sneeringly offers him for sale as a κύριος. "Lord, Messenger, and Scout (κύριε, ἄγγελε καὶ κατάσκοπε)" are the epithets Epictetus employs as forms of address for Cynics in *Diss.* 3.22, 38. Norden (*Beiträge*, 375) also cites *Diss.* 3.22, 49: "But how do I encounter those whom you hold in respect and in awe? Not as slaves? Who, when he sees me, does not believe that he sees his king and master (τίς με ἰδὼν οὐχὶ τὸν βασιλέα τὸν ἑαυτοῦ ὁρᾶν οἴεται καί δεσπότην)?"—my trans. Also cf. the Philo parallels cited by Norden, *Beiträge*, 375 n. 3.

472. καὶ νῦν ἡμεῖς γε εἰς τὴν ῥώμην κατάσκοπον πέμπομεν (Epictetus, *Diss.* 1.24, 3).

473. My trans.; the Greek text: αἱ περιστάσεις εἰσὶν αἱ τοὺς ἄνδρας δεικνύουσαι. For the Cynic-Stoic catalogs of circumstances, cf. Bultmann, *Paulinischen Predigt*, 19. See also above, pp. 73 n. 124, 125, 150–51.

474. Norden (*Beiträge*, 382): "The youth who is to be sent to Rome as a scout is exhorted not to show himself as a δειλὸς κατάσκοπος and not to bring back foolish reports or insignificant things, but to imitate Diogenes, for he was οἷος δεῖ κατάσκοπος" (my trans.).

475. Every Cynic is a servant of Zeus. The emperor and his governor mean nothing to him, only "the one who has sent him and whom he serves, Zeus" (*Diss*. 3.22, 56, my trans.; also in the following quotes from Epictetus in this note). The Cynic is: "messenger, scout and herald of the gods" (*Diss*. 3.22, 69). He is "a messenger sent from Zeus" (*Diss*. 3.22, 23: ὅτι ἄγγελος ἀπὸ τοῦ Διός... ἀπέσταλται); (Cf. Rengstorf, "ἀποστέλλω," *TDNT*, 1:399). The assignment of the Cynic is ἀπαγγεῖλαι ταληθῆ (*Diss*. 3.22, 25). Cf. the countertype, the bad κῆρυξ of the mysteries, given by Epictetus, *Diss*. 3.21, 16. Cf. Schniewind, "ευαγγείζω," *TDNT*, 1:69 and the passages cited there. How the missionary consciousness shapes the philosopher's personality can be seen in *Diss*. 3.22, 23: "As a messenger he is sent from Zeus and to human beings in order to inform them about good and evil, that they have gone astray. . . ." However, the deity does not merely send; the relationship between deity and envoy is more intimate. In Enoch 15, the identity of the wise person and the deity is put into words: "But if you do not take these things, especially when they are placed before you, but despise them, then you will not only be a co-diner with the gods, but also a co-ruler. For so does Diogenes, and also Heracles and those like them and they were rightly divine and called so." Rengstorf (*TDNT*, 1:409–10) describes well how this dissociated self-consciousness is the Cynic's motor behind his kerygma, his responsibility, and his mission in general.

Seneca also depends somewhat on the Cynic-Stoic ideal of the wise person. *Dialogus ad Serenum* reads, "The wise is a neighbor and relative of the gods; he is, excluding immortality, like God" (8.2 [my trans.]; the entire dialogue is interesting in this respect). A divine power has descended to the earth in the wise person; he is possessed by a heavenly power (*Epistle* 31, 11). Seneca's relationship to Cynic-Stoic popular philosophy is investigated by Oltramare, *Origines*, 252–55. What Seneca says about the propaganda of the wise person is especially important. Ibid., 284–85, nos. 68 and 68a; cf. also the themes Oltramare has put together from Seneca on the wise person, ibid., 282–84, nos. 55–57.

476. For a bibliography on Peregrinus Proteus, see *Lucian de Samosata: Philopseudès et de morte Peregrini* (introd. and comments by Jacques Schwartz; Textes d'Études 12; Paris: Société d'Editions, 1951). Betz (*Lukian von Samosata*, 121–23) offers a valuable interpretation of Lucian's description of self-immolation.

477. A satisfactory historical-critical investigation of the biography by Philostratus does not exist. Bibliographical notes in Hempel, "Apollonius," *RGG*, 1:476.

478. Philostratus, *Life of Apollonius* 1.2; 4.18; 5.12, 37; 7.17, 20; 8.5, 7; Lucian, *Alexander the False Prophet* 5; Dio Cassius 77.18.4; Eusebius, *Against Hierocles*.

479. For the authenticity of the letter, cf. Norden, *Agnostos Theos*, 337–38; and Gross, "Apollonius," *RAC*, 1:529–33, esp. 531.

480. Philostratus, *Life of Apollonius* 8.29–31.

481. Philostratus, *Apollonius* 1.2; 2.17, 40; 5.24, 36; 7.21, 31, 38; 8.5, 7 (7), and elsewhere.

482. The evident parallels to the Jewish understanding of the θεῖος ἀνήρ, as described above, really demand a more thorough investigation of the relationship between Neo-Pythagorean philosophy and the Jewish wisdom movement. Yet in view of the completely unclarified situation of the sources, that is presently impossible.

483. For the Serapis cult, cf. Weinreich, *Urkunden,* and Gressmann, "Heidnische Mission," 17–18, 20–21; Cumont, *Orientalische Religionen,* 68–74; Dibelius, *Tradition,* 70–74, 92–97; and esp. Nock, *Conversion,* 45–47.

484. Weinreich, *Gebet und Wunder,* 119–20; idem, *Urkunden,* 10–11; see above, pp. 162–63. Further literature on the Isis and Serapis aretalogies in Cumont, *Orientalische Religionen,* 241 n. 44; On p. 80, Cumont evaluates the significance of the wonders and the aretalogies more skeptically than I do.

485. Nock writes: "While a miracle did not necessarily attract all who saw it to a new worship, the principle was fully accepted that miracle proved deity. 'I make you a god in his eyes: I tell of your *virtues* (which can mean virtues or miracles),' says a character in the *Adelphi* of Terence (535–36), and a curious papyrus catechism includes, 'What is a god? That which is strong. What is a king? He who is equal to the Divine'" (Nock, *Conversion,* 91). And on pp. 83–84, Nock writes, "There was another means of winning adherents. . . . I refer to the supposed miracles done by these gods and the literary propaganda which made them known and enhanced their value. These miracles would be largely miracles of healing but were not limited to that. Aristides, who tells us at length elsewhere about the various divine graces bestowed on him in his illnesses, says in his prose hymn to Serapis . . . 'Who the god is and what nature he has may be left to the priests and the learned among the Egyptians to say and know. Our praise will be sufficient for the moment if we tell of all the varied blessings which he is shown to bring to men, and through these very things his nature can be seen.'" The parallel to the Apologetic understanding of God and miracles seems evident to me (see above, pp. 120–33).

486. *Papiri Greci e Latini,* 4 (1917) 435, quoted by Deissmann, *Licht vom Osten,* 121–28. Also cf. Nock, *Conversion,* 49–50.

487. Nock, *Conversion,* 50.

488. Cf. what has been said above about the parallels between Jewish heroes and Jewish missionaries (p. 148).

489. He therefore even shows himself superior in the competition with a fellow believer, a very essential parallel for understanding the opposition against Paul.

490. *Inscriptiones Graecae* 11.4.1299; Weinreich, *Urkunden,* 19–20, 31–33; cf. Gressmann, "Heidnische Mission," 18; Cumont, *Orientalische Religionen,* 74, 238 n. 21; Nock, *Conversion,* 50–55.

491. The Jewish parallels, see above pp. 102, 104, 107–11, 122–37, 148, 150–51.

492. Hecateus, Posidonius, Alexander Polyhistor, Varro, Apion, Chaire-mon, Nicolaus of Damascus, Dionysius of Halicarnassus, Pallas, Eubulus, and Plutarch are a few of the many examples. They also show that the East participated in this active antiquarian interest.

493. Very well presented by Festugière, *Hermès*, 1:1–18, 19–44.

494. "Ces prophètes auraient d'autant plus d'autorité qu'ils seraient plus éloignés—'maior e longinquo reverentia.' Plus éloignés dans le temps, car, plus on remonterait dans le passé, plus on se rapprocherait de cet âge d'or où les dieux venaient ici-bas converser avec les hommes, s'unissaient à des mortelles, engendraient dans demi-dieux doués d'une sagesse surhumaine. Plus éloignés dans l'espace, et, dans ce cas, on irait chercher vers l'Orient, chez ces peuples, 'qui sont les premiers à voir se lever le Soleil' et auxquels il se communique d'une façon plus pure et plus immédiate, en ces pays aux temples millénaires dont les prêtres gardaient jalousement des secrets mer-veilleux et parlaient une langue dont les sons mêmes avaient de l'efficace, exerçaient un pouvoir magique dès là qu'on les prononçait" (ibid., 1:14). Also cf. Dahl: "Age in and of itself means greatness and dignity for the Hel-lenists" (*Volk Gottes*, 99; my trans.).

495. See above, pp. 156–58.

496. Dörrie, "Neupythagoreer," *RGG*, 4:1432–33, my trans.

497. For the Pythagoras legend, cf. Festugière, *Hermès*, 1:24–25.

498. Until the second century B.C.E., the age of a culture was essentially a legal problem (see above, page 158). In order to be legally recognized, a cult and its tradition had to have a certain age. If they dated back to an in-definite, mythical time, so much the better. This legal factor did not disap-pear completely in the following centuries; it played a role in confrontations with the state, as the history of Christianity since its second and third gen-erations shows.

499. Leipoldt (*Aufsätze*, 24–31) has nicely shown how the oriental mys-tery religions on the one hand adapted in many ways to general Hellenistic taste for the sake of intelligibility, but on the other hand also extolled their own esoteric customs, bolstered by their distinctive traditions in order to retain their peculiar propagandistic power.

500. Further examples in Festugière, *Hermès*, 1:15–18, 19–20, 230 n. 6, 319–24; Franz Boll, *Aus der Offenbarung Johannis: Hellenistische Studien zum Weltbild der Apokalypse* (Leipzig: Teubner, 1914) 7–8; Johannes Lei-poldt and Siegfried Morenz, *Heilige Schriften: Betrachtungen zur Reli-gionsgeschichte der antiken Mittelmeerwelt* (Leipzig: Harrassowitz, 1953).

501. Franz Dornseiff, *Das Alphabet in Mystik und Magie* (Leipzig: Teub-ner, 1922).

502. Werner Peck, ed., *Der Isishymnus von Andros und verwandte Texte* (Berlin: Weidmann, 1930) 15 (text), 31–33 (interpretation). Cf. Fes-tugière, *Hermès*, 1:320; Boll, *Offenbarung*, 7. The Greek text: δειφαλέω

δ'Ἑρμᾶνος ἀπόκρυφα σύνβολα δέλτων εὑρομένα γραφίδεσσι κατέξυσα, ταῖσι χάραξα[ς] φρικαλέον μύσταις ἱερὸν λόγον. For Hermès's association with letters, see above, p. 206 n. 319.

503. According to Festugière, Hermès, 1:320.

504. Ibid., 1:320; Boll, Offenbarung, 7.

505. Festugière, Hermès, 319–24; Boll, Offenbarung, 7.

506. Festugière, 1:324, my trans.

507. PGM, 7:864–70; cf. also PGM, 8:41; "Your true name stands written on the holy column in the sanctuary at Hermupolis"; and PGM, 24a:4–5: "Copy of a holy book that was found in the treasure chamber of Hermès," all my trans. For all these, cf. Festugière, Hermès, 1:323–24.

508. Boll, Offenbarung, 7. Cf. above, p. 136, and below, pp. 246–47, 248–50.

509. Oxyrynchus Papyri 9 (1915) 235, 1382, my trans. This text is interpreted by Weinreich, Urkunden, 13ff. and Peterson, ΕΙΣ ΘΕΟΣ, 215–19. Cf. above, p. 158.

510. This is also true of the speeches of Aristides (Weinreich, Urkunden, 15; Nock, Conversion, 83–85, esp. 90–93). For further examples, see Peterson, ΕΙΣ ΘΕΟΣ, 217–20.

511. Peterson, ΕΙΣ ΘΕΟΣ, 218–19.

512. The number and antiquity of the testimonies are decisive, which is why the archives are stressed. The deposit in the temple archive and the discovery in the temple are related motifs in accrediting religious teaching and knowledge (against ibid., 219). For that, cf. the introduction of Zosimos cited by Peterson. The opponents of Ignatius (ibid., 219–20) were also hardly concerned about a specific legal certification of this or that miracle. They wanted a general confirmation that the present reappeared in the texts of the holy past, that their teaching was therefore effected by the spirit.

513. This is why the Roman senate first seized the holy books (ἱεροὶ λόγοι) of the forbidden mysteries (Livy 29.1.12; 39.16.8). Cf. Franz Altheim, A History of Roman Religion (London: Methuen, 1938) 316.

514. Cf. above, pp. 133–37.

515. On allegorical interpretation in antiquity, cf. esp. Franz Cumont, Recherches sur le symbolisme funéraire des Romains (Paris: Geuthner, 1942) 3–8.

516. Cf. above, pp. 141–48.

517. On the Book of Elkesai, cf. Festugière, Hermès, 1.19; and Wilhelm Brandt, Elchasai: Ein Religionsstifter und sein Werk: Beiträge zur jüdischen, christlichen, und allgemeinen Religionsgeschichte (Leipzig: Hinrichs, 1912) 9–12, 67–68, 72–73, 76–77, 99–100; pp. 76–81 also have the accounts of the Elkesaite mission.

518. Hippolytus, Refutatio Omnium Haeresium 9.13, my trans.

519. Above, pp. 27–32.

520. Above, pp. 33–34.

521. Above, pp. 27–32, 32–33.

522. Above, p. 40.

523. For the early church's understanding of mission, cf. Hahn, *Mission*. Here I can forego a debate with Hahn's reconstruction of the development of the early church's conception of mission. I will only sketch two non-Pauline missionary types of early Christianity. The question whether the circle around Stephen represents another distinctive type and whether it is the oldest missionary type of the early church cannot be discussed here; the sources demand their own investigation.

524. According to Bultmann (*Synoptic Tradition*, 145), the discourse was originally regarded to be the mission discourse of the exalted one (cf. also ibid., 158, on Matt. 10:16a and Luke 10:3). There is a detailed analysis in Hahn, *Mission*, 42–46.

525. Cf. Bultmann, *Synoptic Tradition*, 145–56, 325.

526. According to Bultmann (ibid., 341), this is a redactional piece of Mark. The English translation of *The Synoptic Tradition* then mistranslates Bultmann's reasoning. The German text says here that *Mark motivates* with this piece the continuous accompaniment of the twelve and their being sent out.

527. Cf., e.g., von Campenhausen, "Apostelbegriff," 104, 115–19. Also cf. above, p. 33.

528. On the institution of the twelve and its original character, cf. Julius Wagenmann (*Die Stellung des Apostels Paulus neben den Zwölf in den ersten zwei Jahrhunderten* [ZNWSup 3; Giessen: Töpelmann, 1926]); Klein (*Zwölf Apostel*); von Campenhausen ("Apostelbegriff," 104–5; and idem, *Ecclesiastical Authority*, 14–22). I regard the twelve to be an institution of the early church, but not for missionary purposes. A distinctly missionary activity is later reported only of Peter.

529. According to Bultmann (*Synoptic Tradition*, 325), Luke offers the exact Q tradition, while Matthew combines the accounts of Q and of Mark. So also Hahn, *Mission*, 41–42.

530. Cf. von Campenhausen, "Apostelbegriff," 104–6.

531. In addition also Mark 6:30 in the pericope on the return of the disciples not mentioned above. Von Campenhausen ("Apostelbegriff," 105) rightly believes "that also in this passage no Christian title but only the general Jewish authorization is to be found" (my trans.).

532. Cf. ibid., 104, and the scholars cited there.

533. Cf. n. 524.

534. On the eschatology of Jesus, cf. Günther Bornkamm, *Jesus of Nazareth* (trans. Irene and Fraser McLuckey with James M. Robinson; New York: Harper & Row, 1960) 64–95; Hans Conzelmann, "Jesus Christus," *RGG*, 3:641–46; Rudolf Bultmann, *Das Verhältnis der urchristlichen Christusbotschaft zum historischen Jesus* (2d ed.; SHAW. PH 3 [Heidelberg: Winter 1961]) 15–17.

535. In Rom. 15:19, the σημεῖα καὶ τέρατα (σημεῖα καὶ τέρατα καὶ δυ-

νάμεις in 2 Cor. 12:12; Acts 2:22 [2 Thess. 2:9]; and Heb. 2:4) are also according to the context, to be understood eschatologically (in this respect
nothing can be derived from 2 Cor. 12:12). That wonders, divine as well as
demonic, would multiply in the end time is said (sometimes invoking Deut.
12:2–4) in Matt. 24:24, Mark 13:22, Rev. 13:13, and *Didache* 16:4. The
wonders of Satan are counterparts to the wonders of the Messiah.

536. An older Jewish saying on charity to the little ones is probably present in Matt. 10:40. It was reinterpreted at the latest in Q to refer to behavior toward Jesus-messengers (but cf. Mark 9:37, 41; Matt. 10:42). Behind
the messenger stands the risen one. Concerning the complexity of these
verses and their transmission, cf. Bultmann (*Synoptic Tradition*, 142–43).
According to Bultmann, Luke 10:16 is older than Matt. 10:40, and the corresponding Q saying goes back to Jewish usage. He cites Str-B 1:590: "The
man's envoy [i.e., his representative or plenipotentiary] is the same as himself" (my trans.).

537. Cf. Bultmann, *Synoptic Tradition*, 75, 86, 103, 107, 168.

538. A later echo of this concept of the apostle is found in *Didache* 11:4,
"Everyone who comes to you should be received as the Lord."

539. For this, cf. Hahn, *Mission*, 61–63, esp. 61 n. 1. That Luke utilized
older traditions in Acts 6:1–6, 8–15; 7:54–58; 8:2; 8:4–13, 26–39; 11:19–
30; 12:25; chaps. 13 and 14; and 15:1–33 seems certain to me too. But with
that the question of Paul's missionary journeys has not yet been resolved.
The text of chaps. 13 and 14 seems to describe a model mission. Apart from
the introduction (Acts 13:1–3), the novelistic element is especially pronounced in both chapters and the typifying features are conspicuous. It appears that the famous missionaries of the Antiochene community had
turned into exemplary types themselves; thus their names do not seem to
bear the weight of the story, but rather serve as secondary labels, in my
opinion, secondary even in a literary sense.

540. Above, pp. 129–37, 156–58.

541. Here προσέχειν means "believing," better still, "offering credence"
(against Haenchen *Acts*, 300, 302; with Foakes-Jackson and Lake, *Acts*,
4:89, on Acts 8:6).

542. On exorcism as a means of propaganda, cf. Harnack, *Mission*,
1:155–70. There the competition with the pagan conjurers is treated, as
well as the practice of the Christian exorcisers. Also cf. above, pp. 102–4,
152. On missionary confrontation, cf. further the passage from Tertullian
cited in ibid., 1:162–64. Also cf. the passages listed above, p. 200 n. 254.

543. On the double use of the term "magician" (on the one hand, in the
sense of the Persian fire priest, on the other hand, in the sense of the
conjuring charlatan and goët), see in detail Foakes-Jackson and Lake, *Acts*,
4:164–67. Also cf. above, pp. 106–7.

544. Cf., e.g., Richard Reitzenstein, *Hellenistische Wundererzählungen*
(Leipzig: Teubner, 1906) 35–37.

545. Is the conclusion of the story really intended to imply the final con-

version of Simon? Probably not. (Against Foakes-Jackson and Lake, *Acts*, 4:94.)

546. Concerning the minimal expectation we may place on the faith of the first generation of newly converted Jesus believers, cf. Harnack, *Mission*, 1:115.

547. For the two names, cf. above, p. 102; in detail Foakes-Jackson and Lake, *Acts*, 4:143–44.

548. Cf. ibid., 5:182–88.

549. Cf. ibid., 5:183–84. Cf. above, p. 102.

550. The content of the sermon is not decisive in itself. Significant above all is "The teaching proves able to work miracles." Haenchen, *Acts*, 400. Cf. above, pp. 103–12, 118–37, 151–59.

551. A very similar feature is found in the episode of Acts 28:2–10.

552. On this, cf. Ferdinand Hahn, *The Titles of Jesus in Christology: Their History in Early Christianity* (trans. Harold Knight and George Ogg; New York: World; London: Lutterworth, 1969) 288–307.

553. Cf. the detailed exposition and evidence in Dibelius, *Tradition*, 70–103; cf. above, pp. 148, 158–59, 160–61.

554. Ibid., 96 and elsewhere.

555. Ibid., 103 and elsewhere.

556. Cf. Heinz Joachim Held, "Matthew as Interpreter of the Miracle Stories," in Günther Bornkamm, Gerhard Barth, and Heinz Joachim Held, *Tradition and Interpretation in Matthew* (Philadelphia: Westminster; London: SCM, 1963) 165–299.

557. Perhaps an original account of a vision (cf. Bultmann, *Synoptic Tradition*, 108, 161, 163). But the following verses, Luke 10:19–20, are probably creations of the pre-Lukan community (ibid., 111, 158, 163). Bultmann asks if the transition to the Hellenistic conception has not already taken place here.

558. Cf. ibid., 111, 158, 163.

559. Hahn, *Titles of Jesus*, 334–37.

560. Ibid., 335–36.

561. Ibid., 336. Above is my own translation instead of the slightly incorrect approved one: "Elias [*sic*] and Moses are merely witnesses of the fulfillment which with the bodily manifestation of the Son of God has already taken place."

562. See above, pp. 124–27.

563. See above, pp. 129–33.

564. Cf. the esoteric feature of the motif of the selection of the disciples and the picture of the cloud. For the cloud motif, however, cf. what was said above on pp. 129 and 130–31 about the transfiguration of Moses, and cf. as well the ascension pericope in Acts 1. For the transfiguration motif of Mark 9:2–8, it should be mentioned that the conclusion of v. 2 belongs to the Hellenistic version (Hahn, *Titles of Jesus*, 336, 343 n. 22).

565. Ibid., 372–88.

566. Compare Philo, *Moses* 1.9, 18; in addition, Josephus, *Ant.* 2.7, 9.

567. To speak about the wisdom of the Egyptians seems to have been proverbial (Foakes-Jackson and Lake, *Acts*, 4:75).

568. Ibid.

569. Ibid., 4:78.

570. Above, pp. 134–37.

571. Above, pp. 122–31, 137–42, 155–58, 160–61.

572. Therefore, Haenchen's (*Acts*, 275–90) characterization of the discourse can be adopted without gratification (against Hahn, *Titles of Jesus*, 374, 400 n. 165).

573. Hahn, *Titles of Jesus*, 386.

3

The Self-Understanding of the Opponents[1]

THE SELF-CONSCIOUSNESS OF THE OPPONENTS

The analysis thus far has taken its departure from the fragment 2 Cor. 10—13 and tried to gain a picture of the opponents by starting with their self-designations. The question remains whether the understanding gained thus far can be transferred to the fragment 2 Cor. 2:14—7:4, which was written a short time before. Is the polemic directed against the same opponents?

The Identity of the Opponents in 2 Cor. 10—13 and in 2 Cor. 2:14—7:4

There are many indications that the opponents in 2 Cor. 10—13 are the same as those in 2:14—7:4. The subject of debate is the same, namely, the appropriate conduct of the apostle and the values it communicates. διάκονος and διακονία are key words in 2 Cor. 2:14—7:4;[2] they recall the important functional designation διάκονος discussed above. The designations of origin in chaps. 10—13 intimate the role of tradition in the missionary proclamation of the opponents. This corresponds to the importance which Paul attaches to the discussion of the understanding of tradition in chap. 3.

The concept of "pneuma" is essential for both fragments (2 Cor. 3:3, 6, 8, 17, 18; 4:13; and 6:6 on the one hand—2 Cor. 11:4; 12:18; and 13:13 on the other hand; in 11:4 it is integrated into a short summary of the proclamation of the opponents). 2 Cor. 11:4 indicates the central importance of the christological question. The passages 13:4; 10:1, 7; 12:8–9; and 13:3 all correspond to that, as well as 4:5, 10–12; and 5:16; in addition, there are 2:14–15; 3:3, 14, 17–18;

4:4–6; 5:6–10; and 14:21. Especially noteworthy is the repetition of the simple Ἰησοῦς in chap. 4, corresponding to the importance of the single Ἰησοῦς in 11:4.

As both fragments discuss the appropriate conduct of the apostle, they have to establish the proper criteria for a comparison. This brings up the problem of recommendation, particularly also that of self-commendation (2 Cor. 3:1; 4:2; 5:12; 6:4; 10:12, 18; 12:11) and the issue of boasting (5:12; 7:4; 10:8, 13–17; 11:10–23, 30; 12:1–10). The catchword λογίζεσθαι prominently appears in 2 Cor. 3:5 as well as in 10:2, 7, 11; 11:5; and 12:6. The problem of remuneration is discussed not only in 2 Cor. 11:7–12 and 12:13–18 but also in 2:17. This list of similarities could be increased further, but these examples show well enough that both fragments debate very much the same subjects in similar situations.

This unity in the situation of both fragments appears even stronger if one notes the most glaring differences from the discussion in 1 Cor.: the question of factions has disappeared, and the understanding of "gnosis" and the Gnostic savior-myth are no longer attacked. On the contrary, Paul shows a positive attitude toward them in 2 Cor. 3:3, 13–14, 17–18; 4:4–6; 5:1–10; and 11:2–3, 6, 13–15. And in the christological discussion, docetism is no longer an issue (1 Cor. 12:2 contradicts 2 Cor. 11:4).

The polemic against libertinism has disappeared in 2 Cor., with the exception of the very stereotypical formulation in 12:21. The context of that formulation will be discussed below, p. 237. The most important new feature of the polemic in 2 Cor. is its direction toward missionaries coming from outside Corinth and their close association with and boasting of Jewish tradition. The opponents of 1 Cor. did not carry any particular Jewish traits. And contrary to 1 Cor., the OT becomes a topic of 2 Cor.

Therefore it appears permissible to use the fragments of 2 Cor. 2:14–7:4 and 10–13 together in order to improve on the picture of the opponents. There are some nuances, but the opponents and the problems are the same.

The Opponents as θεῖοι ἄνδρες

How did the opponents of Paul in 2 Cor. realize the contemporary ideas of mission? Paul almost constantly draws the picture of

the opponents in contrast to his own.[3] In 2 Cor. 2:14–17 he speaks
first of his own preaching activity as he sees it, then suddenly brings
his opponents into the debate.[4] Why does this happen so abruptly?

THE ἱκανότης

The transition from 2:16a to 16b is particularly abrupt. Paul has
spoken of the proclamation before. Now he asks, πρὸς ταῦτα τίς
ἱκανός; thus he raises a question of principle: who is enabled for
such great tasks? Before that he had spoken of himself, and in the
subsequent sentence the subject is "we," too.[5] Does this mean that
Paul considers himself able?[6] The question of the text remains without answer. Should this break be attributed to a sudden change of
mood on the part of Paul, which cannot be identified today?[7] But a
psychological answer to the difficulty of the text is no answer. Pre-
suming a pause in dictation is a makeshift solution.[8] The context
helps to answer the problem.

Paul had spoken of proclamation as a demonstrative procession.
He had been speaking of himself. When he then does not answer
the sudden question about the qualification for this function, he intimates that he has doubts about his own qualification for proclamation. But when he compares himself with the opponents after that
unanswered question, his critical statement about the opponents
must relate to this questionable ability.[9] In his own positive characterization in v. 17b, Paul appears to indicate the reasons for *his*
ἱκανότης. But he does not enumerate here, as we would expect,
certain qualities; instead he speaks of the relations existing in his
proclaiming activity.[10] The ἱκανότης with respect to the act of proclaiming is circumscribed with ὡς ἐξ εἰλικρινείας. It is worth noting
that ὡς ἐξ εἰλικιρνείας is parallel in construction to ὡς ἐκ θεοῦ. Does
this mean that εἰλικρινεία here is a divine attribute too, just as it has
to be assumed for 2 Cor. 1:12?[11] In any case, the ὡς ἐκ θεοῦ sees
the proclamation in a certain relationship to the essence of God.[12]

In 2 Cor. 3:5 Paul returns once more to the ἱκανότης.[13] He says:
οὐχ ὅτι ἀφ᾽ ἑαυτῶν ἱκανοί ἐσμεν λογίσασθαί τι ὡς ἐξ ἑαυτῶν. Here
Paul denies his own ability point-blank.[14] This confirms that Paul in
2:16–17 does not want to speak simply of his qualification. According to 3:5, the ἱκανότης is the ability λογίσασθαί τι ὡς ἐξ ἑαυτῶν.[15]
The faculty of judgment of the preacher is under scrutiny, that is,

his ability to assess a preacher's potential, both his own and that of others.[16] Paul puts against this faculty the πεποίθησις, that is, his confidence about having been empowered by God, or rather Christ, for his task.[17] ὡς ἐξ ἑαυτῶν seems to refer back to ὡς ἐξ εἰλικρινείας in 2 Cor. 2:17, and thus also to ὡς ἐκ θεοῦ.[18] This reference back to 2:17 is supported by the continuation of 3:5: ἀλλ' ἡ ἱκανότης ἡμῶν ἐκ τοῦ θεοῦ.[19] This expression of confidence on the basis of being enabled by God also recalls 2:17. Paul denies having the ability to preach with his own power. His qualification comes from God, and ownership and control remain with God.

The issue of λογίζεσθαι is treated similarly in 1 Cor. 4:1.[20] Paul demands that "people should assess us in such manner: assistants of Christ and stewards of the mysteries of God." Little judgment is left with the audience, since according to the context the criteria for judgment are taken away from the viewer. 1 Cor. 4:3 could be a good circumlocution of what Paul means in 2 Cor. 2:16–17 and 3:4–6: "It is of absolutely no matter to me whether I am judged by you or by any (other) human tribunal."[21] Judgment by others is the issue, but not alone. Paul's confidence goes one step further in 1 Cor. 4:3b, 4: "I don't even judge myself, for I am not conscious of anything." But Paul then relativizes this statement: "But in that I am not justified; the one who is judging me is the Lord" (1 Cor. 4:4).

The real content of Paul's πεποίθησις is that the judgment is with the Lord, his eschatological tribunal (v. 5b). Paul ascribes the λογίζεσθαι to God also in other passages. This means that Paul in 2 Cor. 2:16–17 wants to state first of all that he does not want to arrogate any divine faculties but that he expects everything for the judgment of God.

This becomes still clearer (and so does the real aim of Paul's argumentation) if one follows the suggestion of Windisch, who points to the similarity with the question καὶ τίς ἔσται ἱκανὸς αὐτῇ; in Joel 2:11.[22] According to LXX, the text asks for the ability to face divine judgment.[23] The Joel text does not give an answer to this question either. Implied is a negative answer, at least as far as the direct question is involved. The ἱκανότης is given only through the eschatological miracle of conversion. This is intimated by the imperative in v. 12 (ἐπιστράφετε πρός με . . .).

In 2 Cor. 2:15 relationship to eschatological judgment is hinted at too.[24] Here the proclaimer of the gospel is described as mediator of judgment. If one sees Joel 2:11 as a conscious parallel, then by not giving an answer to his question Paul is saying in 2 Cor. 2:16: if nobody can face divine judgment, how can a human being become mediator of such a judgment? I understand this question, as in Joel 2:11, as a question of resignation.[25] The answer did not disappear.[26]

Since Paul afterward suddenly becomes polemical and compares himself with his opponents, one must conclude that the opponents *had* an answer for such a question and that their answer was positive. The opponents must have said: ἱκανοί ἐσμεν. Paul counters their self-assured claim with his critical question. He wants to show that it is impossible to adorn oneself before judging God with things which befit only God. Paul's allusions to qualities and activities of God might be easily explained if the opponents had spoken with strong assuredness about their abilities and had claimed divine qualities.[27] Paul sees their lack of restraint as caused by an absence of eschatological perspective, a perspective which would give them the right measure.

In 2 Cor. 2:14–16 Paul presents his proclamation as a revelatory event using Gnostic and Apocalyptic motifs.[28] One may conclude that Paul wants to tell his strongly Gnostic community that the opponents did not really know of the true character of proclamation, namely, that revelation happened in it, efficacious and decisive, effecting life and death. This could imply the further reproach that the opponents did not know anything at all about revelation, or at least did not show much interest in it. Instead of revelation the opponents offered self-assurance. They demonstrated their ability to assess themselves and others, their gift to evaluate and to exploit their own divine potentials. But Paul wants to say that the proclamation of Christ as revelation cannot be delivered through the development of superhuman qualities, but only through the miracle of divine intervention.

It seems that Paul's intention comes out in 2:14–16. In his apologia, he is trying to show the Corinthian community that the opponents' theology and proclamation do not fit the Corinthians' own presuppositions or answer their questions. The Corinthians should be on Paul's side rather than on that of his opponents.[29]

THE ORIENTATION TOWARD COMPETITION

The audacity of the opponents to pass judgment on themselves and others is described by Paul in 2 Cor. 2:17 as "bartering away" the Word of God.[30] καπηλεύειν is frequent in philosophical polemic.[31] Plato, for instance, says in *Protagoras* (313 CD): "Can it be . . . that the Sophist is really a sort of merchant or dealer in provisions on which [the] soul is nourished? . . . And in the same way, those who take their doctrines the round of our cities, hawking them about to any odd purchaser who desires them." Plato does not blame the Sophists for going from place to place, although this provides the basis for their reproachable attitude. Plato dislikes most that the Sophists offer wisdom like wares, thus acting like peddlers. They expose wisdom to the fluctuation of supply and demand. This betrays their disinterest in the evidence of the subject matter. It is exposed to other criteria, the laws of the market. That is further clarified in the subsequent description that they sell, "and there may well be some of these too . . . who are ignorant which of their wares is good or bad for the soul."

It is not the mind or, in NT terms, the spirit that decides, but superficial things. The teaching is offered like wares in a market-oriented competition. Success alone decides the value of the substance of proclamation and the preacher's worth. Yet the uncritical person might see mind or spirit manifested in those demonstrations.

Lucian describes this competition in the dialogue *Hermotimus or Concerning the Sects* with colorful words, saying, "I certainly cannot say how in your view philosophy and wine are comparable, except perhaps at this one point that philosophers sell their lessons as wine-merchants their wines—most of them adulterating and cheating and giving false measure" (*Hermotimus* 59). For the sake of success in the competition, wisdom is falsified.[32]

Paul is using καπηλεύειν to describe the opponents as peddlers of missionary preaching; they treat their preaching as wares which they expose to competition and promotion in the marketplace. He is of the opinion that they have been tempted to promote sales of themselves and of the Word of God.[33] If they give themselves a false appearance for the sake of success,[34] then they falsify the message. The tendency of Paul's argumentation is to accuse the opponents of a swindle. This can be seen clearly in 2 Cor. 4:2.[35] While 2:17 portrayed Paul as not being like those who "hawk the word of God," he says in 4:2 that he does not belong with those "who go about in falsehood" and "who falsify the word of God." καπηλεύοντες and δολοῦντες are used by Paul as synonyms, both related to the λόγος τοῦ θεοῦ. Paul accuses the opponents indirectly of πανουργία in 11:3, and 12:16 also proves that this question was debated in Corinth.[36]

Paul misses in the opponents' attitude the right relationship to the cause they represent. They preferred the face value of "appearance." This can be concluded from Paul's polemics in chaps. 10—13 in particular.[37] Here the term λογίζεσθαι appears again and therefore reveals itself as a slogan of the Corinthian discussion.[38] The opponents believed that they could judge not merely themselves but also others. The result of their self-assessment was that they belonged to Christ, meaning that they participated in Christ (2 Cor. 10:7; cf. 1 Cor. 1:12).[39]

The result of their judgment about Paul was that he did not belong to Christ, that he did not participate in him, that he was "unskilled in speaking" (ἰδιώτης τῷ λόγῳ; 2 Cor. 11:6).[40] They claimed that they were skilled in free pneumatic speech; 12:6 is interesting in this context. Paul fears that someone could credit his boasting to him (εἰς ἐμὲ λογίσηται)[41] and therefore could attribute something to him which would exceed his everyday existence (ὃ βλέπει με . . .).[42] To transcend the everyday was the intent of the opponents, the subject of their boasting.[43] Whereas the Corinthians looked in vain for the δοκιμή of the Christ speaking in Paul, the opponents apparently could demonstrate it in a verifiable manner.[44]

Paul also mentions the opponents' τολμᾶν (11:21–29). Their brazenness, together with their frequently cited boasting, proves that the opponents produced explicit propaganda to their advantage.[45] They made a name for themselves and thus impressed a majority of their audience. Although Paul does not speak of their propaganda before pagans, we can compare them with the many pneumatics who wandered about in those days not only advertising their cause but also recruiting for it. I have attempted to show in the case of the method and the appearance of the preachers that the boundaries between church and world were fluid. It appears that the opponents saw the essence of proclamation in competition, and the competition was over the λόγος τοῦ θεοῦ, the missionary preaching.[46]

THE PROOF OF WORTH IN COMPETITION

It appears that the opponents considered it necessary to prove their worth in the missionary competition. In this competition they sought standards for a proper assessment of persons and issues[47] and conducted comparisons (cf. 2 Cor. 10:12).[48] Paul refuses to do such comparing.[49] His standard is removed from common comparison.[50] It is given to him by God in the form of the congregation in Corinth, founded by Paul's preaching. Paul's renouncing comparison with others must have been proof for the opponents and the community that Paul was not a true pneumatic, which means they questioned his qualifications as a preacher. According to 1 Cor. 2:13, συγκρίνειν is a gift of the pneumatic. Paul has to deny himself the public exercise of this gift. Therefore, the opponents accused Paul of comparing himself only with himself; he concedes that here.

In 2 Cor. 10:12–13, where the Western text is to be preferred,[51] Paul reproaches the opponents for boasting without measure and conducting unrestrained propaganda.[52] His own μέτρον, his κανών, rests on what God has done for him.[53] But this is also God's deed for the community, namely, that they have come to believe and thus can become the basis for the continuation of Paul's preaching (10:13–16). Paul has to forego any immediate competition and any validation arising from it.

Paul does not renounce the σημεῖα τοῦ ἀποστόλου (2 Cor. 12:12),[54] but even in this respect Paul seems to lag behind the opponents. Their signs and wonders must have resembled those of the Hellenistic-Jewish and Hellenistic θεῖοι ἄνδρες.[55] Paul does not want to follow suit.[56] He ascribes to his signs only a symbolic meaning.[57] Käsemann has correctly reminded us of the relationship of 12:12 to its context.[58] The preceding verses spoke of anything but the external glory and power of apostolic existence.[59]

For their comparison the opponents used the pneuma as standard and not their own opinion,[60] just as one would expect from pneumatics of the Hellenistic age. I have in mind the Philo quotation given above, in which the θεῖος ἀνήρ Abraham is presented as κανών.[61] There is also all the evidence which has been given on the νόμος ἔμψυχος.[62] It was the pride of the opponents that they could prove the pneuma as active. They could demonstrate the δοκιμή of the Christ speaking in them, that is, the δοκιμή of the pneuma. The question was who was δόκιμος and who ἀδόκιμος (2 Cor. 13). Paul in turn demands of the Corinthians δοκιμάζειν (13:5).

According to 2 Cor. 10:18, the person who recommends himself—and that means the pneumatic who makes propaganda with his performance—is not recommended by the Lord God.[63] He is ἀδόκιμος instead (cf. 13:5–7). But this is the opinion of Paul. That particular person would have considered himself δόκιμος, would certainly not have accepted Paul's charge that he was not recommended by the Lord. On the contrary, he would have understood his own self-commendation as an exhibition of divine spiritual gifts.

The catalog of vices preceding chap. 13 (2 Cor. 12:20–21) shows the consequences of unrestrained competition in the eyes of Paul.[64] This is not merely a collation of conventional formulae. The catalog of vices is divided. In the first part, the words only describe strife in its various forms.[65] In the second part, clearly distinguished from the first, appear the moral failures which are typical for a catalog of vices.[66] One can conclude that the condensed formulation in v. 20 alludes to the deplorable state of affairs in Corinth caused by the competition of the opponents. Before the second part of the catalog of vices, Paul uses missionary terminology (προαμαρτάνειν and μετανοεῖν in 12:21, and the former again in 13:2), concepts he uses nowhere else.[67] Perhaps this is an allusion to the previous pagan life of the Corinthians and their subsequent coming to faith in Jesus.[68]

If that was intentional, then Paul would be stating very bluntly that the Corinthians in reality never had become Jesus-believers. That Paul can talk this way is proven by 1 Cor. 3:3.[69] For drawing such conclusions Paul would need very strong reasons. They seem to be given by the pneumatic competition, the consequences of which are attacked in the first part of the catalog of vices. In Paul's opinion, the competition exposed the essentially faithless attitude of the Corinthians (and naturally also of the opponents).

Thus Paul would have correctly seen the fact that the opponents and their admirers did nothing else than what propagandists and believers of Judaism and of paganism practiced everywhere.[70] The opponents in turn would have believed that their conduct not only impressed the community of faith but also advertised the Jesus-faith in their pagan environment.[71]

The Opponents and the Community

THE REMUNERATION

It has been shown above that καπηλεύειν (2 Cor. 2:17) alludes to the substantial difference between Paul's conduct and that of the opponents.[72] I do not want to claim, though, that in using this verb Paul attacks the remuneration of the opponents as such. Already in the philosophical polemic the attack did not go so much against financially compensating the popular philosophers. Most philosophers took money.[73] Monetary gain was attacked only if it went out of bounds and started to condition method and content.

The Corinthian opponents took money for their preaching too. Whenever Paul mentions this in our fragments, he blames the opponents not for taking money but for using the receipt of the money to strengthen their self-confidence. 2 Cor. 11:7–11 and 12:13–15 show that the opponents had received money in Corinth.[74] The opponents took money in order to claim the same authority as Paul (11:12).[75] They wanted to put themselves on the same level as Paul and prove that they possessed the same rights. It is significant that Paul does not counter their attempt by alluding to moral perversion or referring to his own office, but only by referring to his practice.

The argumentation of the opponents appears foreign to us—at least at first sight. We cannot imagine that the meaning and right of a spiritual mandate could be derived from the receipt of money, but these seemingly strange ideas are explained by 1 Cor. 9:6–18. It is the right of the apostle to receive money and to be supported by the communities.[76] The frequency of the monetary question in various passages of the Corinthian correspondence, but also in 1 Thessalonians and in Philippians, proves that this problem was important in Paul's time.[77] Paul never attacks this claim of the apostles morally. On the contrary, he even justifies it with some difficulty in 1 Cor. 9.

This entire chapter deals with the ἐξουσία of the pneumatics, especially that of the preacher. It is first of all the right not to work (1 Cor. 9:6). The meaning is that the apostle is not to be dependent on a paying (secular) profession. For all apostles, and Paul includes himself, it is true that the mediation of "spiritual goods" is to be honored by "earthly goods," as in the relationship of sowing to harvesting (v. 11). The subsequent question intimates that all other proclaimers have actually done that (v. 12).[78] This right of the preacher of the gospel is a spiritual privilege associated with an authority to administer spiritual goods. 1 Cor. 9:14 says even more pointedly, "Thus the Lord ordained for those who proclaim the gospel that they should live off the gospel." This remuneration therefore is nothing else than a recognition of the achievement of the proclaimer in his or her administration of the spiritual goods.[79]

2 Cor. 11:8 mentions such remuneration too. Paul is speaking of the support he had received from other communities and gives the meaning of this compensation.[80] It is not merely a financial requital or a simple confirmation of achievement; it is assistance for the pursuit of the mission to the Corinthians (πρός τὴν ὑμῶν διακονίαν 11:8).[81] Accepting money demonstrates the superiority of the proclaimer over the congregation as well as the importance of the congregation for his or her missionary task.

Paul employs the strong term συλᾶν for accepting remuneration. It is obvious that he uses that word with the subsequent description of the opponents' conduct in Corinth in mind (cf. further the terms καταναρκᾶν [2 Cor 11:9; 12:13–14], ἀβαρής [11:9], καταβαρεῖν [12:16]). The opponents exercised the authority mentioned and understood it as an opportunity to prove their claim (cf. 11:12). The merit of Paul, instead, is, as he states almost ironically, that he has received no money in Achaia.[82]

Paul again speaks of the boasting of the opponents in 11:18–23. The words he uses here recall the language employed for the previous ironic description of his accepting gifts of support. This leads to the conclusion in 11:18–23 that Paul is attacking the superior conduct of the opponents in Corinth. He continuously uses concepts which describe the way a despot keeps at a distance from the common people.[83] A similar audacity of Jewish beggars who proved to be Jewish missionaries was described above.[84] I would presume that the Corinthian opponents must have achieved full success because the community had rewarded their work plentifully and thus confirmed their ἐξουσία.[85]

It is understandable why the Corinthians complained that Paul accepted no money from them. They assessed his attitude as a failure to prove his love, even as an injustice (12:13).[86] Paul excuses himself ironically for showing "consideration," but he intimates, too, that his consideration has been judged by the Corinthians as a lack of esteem for them (12:13).[87] When the proclaimer receives remuneration, it is a sign of recognition for the preacher but also an honor for the community.[88]

But Paul foregoes any financial support from the community he happens to work for at the time.[89] He does allow other congregations to help him, yet apparently only those who understand the giving of such support as a demonstration of interpersonal relationship. The organization of the collection is meant to improve and document this mutual participation, not only between the Pauline communities and Jerusalem but also among the Pauline congregations and their missionaries and with the sister communities founded by them.[90]

The ideas in question can perhaps be better understood if we draw upon a passage from the other fragment relevant to this study. The terms "injustice" (2 Cor. 12:13) and "taking advantage" (12:17–18; cf. v. 14) recall 2 Cor. 7:2.[91] There Paul writes: "We have done injustice to no one, we have not destroyed anyone, we have not taken advantage of anyone." Rather the apostle has opened his heart to the Corinthians, and he has bound himself closely to them not by his action but by his suffering. Now he expects as a sort of remuneration (ἀντιμισθία!) that they open their heart to him (6:11–13; 7:2–4). Paul has taken all of his communities into his suffering and thus into a living spiritual relationship with him (11:28–29). In contrast, one would have to see the opponents as being mainly interested in having their spiritual performance recognized and honored. Their interest in the community was secondary to that, and they had no interest in personal communion with its members. Only in representing the divine or cosmic rule was the pneumatic's activity intended for the community.[92]

Paul, even in his intended new visit to Corinth, does not want to claim his right to support by the Corinthians (2 Cor. 12:14). As he did not attach great importance to his signs of apostleship, he also foregoes acknowledgment of his privilege by the Corinthians.[93] This acknowledgment would express itself in their gifts, which were expected by other apostles according to Cor. 9:12: ἄλλοι τῆς ὑμῶν ἐξουσίας μετέχουσιν. In contrast to his opponents, Paul is interested in their gifts (12:14; cf., besides 7:2–4, also Phil. 4:17). Paul's remark οὐ γὰρ ζητῶ τὰ ὑμῶν ἀλλὰ ὑμᾶς wards off the reproach frequently uttered against philosophers and migrant preachers of those days that they were fraudulent "goëts."[94] Paul is certainly alluding to the conduct of his opponents.

It is curious that Paul does not strengthen his general argument with a reference to the *spiritual* communion existing between him and the Corinthians. He likes this motif, as we know from elsewhere in the Corinthian correspondence from 1 Thessalonians and from Philippians, and it would have suggested itself easily here too. Instead Paul moves the subsequent debate to the field of *lex naturae* in using the image of the caring parents.[95] This makes for a double difference from 1 Cor. 9. Paul there argues first for the *right* of the proclaimer to receive support, then uses his *personal commission*, his very own task, to explain why he renounces this right.

The different reasoning behind Paul's conduct in 2 Cor. 12 could be explained easily if, in clear contrast, the opponents followed the example of Jewish Apologists and understood the individual appearance, conduct, and intention of the pneumatic as representing the νόμος ἔμψυχος (pp. 131–33), as a rule which tied the community together. This νόμος ἔμψυχος was identical with the *lex naturae*. In his counterargument, Paul would be saying that true *lex naturae* was the principle of community expressed in continuous human relationships, not the self-confident will of the pneumatic projected into the cosmos.

The wordplay δαπανήσω-ἐκδαπανηθήσομαι possibly denotes the difference between Paul and his opponents too, implying polemically that they let others make sacrifices but were not willing to sacrifice themselves; they held sway.[96]

Paul understands his renunciation of his spiritual right as proof of his greater love (2 Cor. 12:15), but the Corinthians respected only the person who would show them his or her love by accepting their money. According to Paul's question in 12:15, accepting remuneration was the sign for the congregation that the proclaimer was ready to give all the πνευματικά.[97] The οὐ κατεβάρησα of v. 16a also shows that Paul renounces the privilege of the pneumatic.[98]

In v. 16b Paul compares himself ironically with his opponents. He reproaches them with fraudulent intention elsewhere too. The comparison suggests that, in the opinion of the Corinthians, Paul had staged a deception even more clever than that of the opponents.[99] Paul apparently was blamed because, on the one hand, he renounced the acknowledgment of his proclamation by way of a direct remuneration yet, on the other hand, indirectly requested such acknowledgment by sending the brothers for the collection.[100] ἀλλὰ ὑπάρχων πανοῦργος δόλῳ ὑμᾶς ἔλαβον cannot simply refer to a charge of embezzlement.[101] It appears that the Corinthians' complaint about being taken advantage of referred to the meaning of the collection. Paul thought the monetary contribution to the collection should witness to the unity of the church.[102] But it seems that the Corinthians had understood Paul's request to participate in the collection as an indirect demand for acknowledgment. What he did not dare to request directly he tried to get indirectly.

The charge then would be not one of financial embezzlement but one of charlatan deception. What, then, is the meaning of v. 18c? Like Paul, Titus wants to have nothing to do with a pneuma which encourages one to rule, as it did the opponents.[103] An abundant display of spiritual power and its financial acknowledgment by the Corinthians were proof for the strength of the spirit in the eyes of the opponents and the congregation.[104] In the eyes of Paul they are proof of self-glorification and unmitigated exploitation, signs of the highest form of discord.[105]

THE LETTERS OF RECOMMENDATION

Of course, neither the opponents nor the Corinthians saw things that way. This comes out clearly in the discussion about letters of recommendation.[106] The relationship of the two questions in 2 Cor. 3:1 is hard to define.[107] The first question cannot be a self-correction of Paul. In such a case a polemical question to the opponents would hardly follow as immediately as it does here. The ἤ μή introducing the second question would not be explained sufficiently if the first question quoted a charge of the opponents and the second question gave Paul's polemical answer, rebutting the charge by ironically leading it *ad absurdum*. In such a case, καί or ἀλλά would have been more suitable.

συνιστάνειν obviously refers to the debate in Corinth. Word statistics show this. συνιστάνειν occurs sixteen times in the NT; thirteen references are found in the authentic Pauline letters. The transitive meaning occurs here only. Eight of the thirteen Pauline attestations are found in 2 Cor. 2:14—7:4 and 10—13. These are also the only NT passages (with the exception of Rom. 16:2) where συνιστάνειν means "recommend." Thus συνιστάνειν is a slogan in the Corinthian debate. In the eight references of the fragments under scrutiny, συνιστάνειν appears six times as συνιστάνειν ἑαυτόν, and the two other occurrences relate to that. It may be that Paul was accused of συνιστάνειν ἑαυτόν. The πάλιν in 3:1 hints at that.[108] But the transition to the ἤ of the second question becomes understandable only if the first question already implies a polemic against the opponents. 2 Cor. 5:12 reveals that self-commendation and self-glorification (in the eyes of Paul) are characteristic for the opponents.[109] 2 Cor. 10:12 and 10:18 bring decisive proof.[110]

This term is one further concept of the adversaries' competing propaganda in Corinth;[111] it fully manifests the peculiar nature of the debate. It has been shown that the opponents did not recommend their secular ἐγώ. Self-commendation in the true sense of the term was considered too much in bad taste, at least in philosophical circles.[112] It has also become apparent that the opponents were pneumatics who demonstrated not so much *their own* deeds as the powerful deeds of the *spirit*. If they recommended themselves at all, then it was, in the wider sense of the term, by recommending the spirit given to them. In that modified sense of self a close interaction of letters of recommendation and self-commendation is easily imaginable. The letters of recommendation and the use of the concept of the spirit proved that the adversaries did not intend to impose *themselves*.

The custom of writing letters of recommendation and of presenting them was widespread in those days.[113] Paul himself gives some examples. In Jewish communities, letters of recommendation were authorizations too.[114] The earliest evidence for that is found in Acts 9:1–2 (cf. 22:5). Letters of recommendation are credentials there. They legitimize Saul as the delegate of the high priest. The assumption that the opponents of Paul in Corinth had understood their letters of recommendation as an authorization by Jerusalem is disproved by the fact that they asked for letters of recommendations from the Corinthians too.[115] They were interested in letters of recommendations from the congregations in general.

Other communities were supposed to learn from the epistles carried by the opponents who the bearers were and what they were able to do.[116] Paul's reference to the congregation as his letter seems to allude to that. But that does not yet completely interpret 2 Cor. 3:2.

It appears that 2 Cor. 12:11 resembles such a recommendation by the community.[117] Paul reproaches the congregation for not having recommended him. That means he presupposes that it is the community's task to recommend their proclaimers. The following sentence says, "I do not fall short of the 'superapostles' in any way although I am not anything. The signs of an apostle were worked among you in all patience and through signs, and proofs of miracle and power" (12:11–12). Paul has not been inferior in anything which commends an apostle of Jesus, which is what the congregation ought to have recognized and reported.

I have shown before that Paul did not put much emphasis on apostolic signs. Nevertheless those signs had served as a recommendation of the superapostles. It appears that Paul's adversaries asked that those recommendations be written up for them.[118] Their conduct revealed that it was far from them to let any of their achievements be forgotten. The letters of recommendation thus were something like chronicles of the deeds of pneumatic power performed by the adversaries of Paul. The demonstrations of such power, the remuneration, and the letters of recommendation all confirmed their active possession of such gifts.[119] The opponents' presentation of such chronicles listing manifestations of pneumatic energy could explain why Paul inserted more catalogs of circumstances in the two fragments under discussion than anywhere else (2 Cor. 4:8–9; 6:4–10; 11:23–33; 12:10).[120]

It should be noted that the terms διάκονος or διακονία appear in all those catalogs (except in 2 Cor. 12:10). In 4:8–9 it is to be inferred from 4:1, since the context is an elaboration of the true διακονία as indicated in 4:1, and before that in 3:6.[121] Since the opponents understood themselves as διάκονοι Χριστοῦ, Paul had reason to use the term in the passages mentioned. The reader is reminded that Jewish-Hellenistic and Hellenistic missionaries understood themselves and their conduct as a παράδειγμα for their message. They considered themselves intimately associated with their proclamation and its fate, and they demonstrated that. Analysis of the term has shown that διάκονος could be used in this way.[122]

Now the succession of the two questions in 2 Cor. 3:1 can be understood. Self-commendation and identification by way of letters of recommendation need not exclude each other, but could go together. Both witnessed to the effect of divine δύναμις on the preacher.

Therefore it is not necessary to see the opponents as inspectors from Jerusalem. Those points which connect them to traditional concepts (the terms ἀπόστολος, διάκονος, ἐργάτης, their understanding of pneuma, the relationship to the community) show that these people were not representatives of an *institution* and did not want to be. The opponents were interested in the possession and proof of the spirit. They did not derive their possession of the spirit from an institutionally secured right. It was the present and controllable possession of the spirit which claimed particular privileges. Paul argues against the market orientation and competitiveness of their methods and character.[123]

For them, their spirit guaranteed their right, not their right their spirit. But with that I have already anticipated what is still to be analyzed below. The task now is to ascertain the opponents' understanding of their theological base.[124] Following the direction of 2 Cor. 2:14—7:4 suggests itself, since that passage has already been in the center of consideration. This means turning now to 3:1–18, where the view goes beyond the previously treated motifs of self-commendation and letters of recommendation to even more basic theological statements.

THE TRADITION OF
THE OPPONENTS

The Tradition Motif

THE RELATIONSHIP BETWEEN
SELF-COMMENDATION AND
TRADITION

The succession of questions in 3:1, which we have already discussed, is not the only thing that is noteworthy in 2 Cor. 3:1–18. The subsequent sequence of thoughts and motifs has also continued to puzzle the exegetes.[125] It is easy to understand why Paul should designate the community he himself founded as his "letter of recommendation" in v. 2a. This dramatic statement is characteristic of the Pauline understanding of the relationship between apostle and community. It strengthens and sharpens the rejection, implied in the polemic question in v. 1b, of the opponents' practice of dealing in letters of recommendation.[126] What *is* strange, however, is the further thought that the community is written on Paul's heart as a letter of recommendation.[127] That this is what Paul actually means —that a group could serve as a public recommendation because it was written on the heart of the person being commended—is confirmed by the supplementary phrase "to be known and read by all people." What is this supposed to mean?

The strangeness only increases when the community is described as a letter of Christ,[128] through which the concept of the heavenly letter enters the picture.[129] The expression "written in our hearts" appears to be completely neutralized by the phrase διακονηθεῖσα ὑφ' ἡμῶν.[130] So it is surprising to find the phrase "written on [the] hearts" later. Now the hearts are clearly those of the community;[131] *here* is where one must look for the letter. At the conclusion of v. 3 there is not only the contrast between ink and spirit (which fits well with vv. 1–3a, and all the more so if the καρδία of the apostle were being discussed). It is surprising to find also the contrast between tablets of stone (not papyrus, e.g.) and tablets of flesh (in the form of hearts).[132] The "tablets" certainly refer to the tablets of the Decalogue,[133] but the allusion is complicated by the fact that two further OT motifs are introduced.[134] The first is the contrast between the law written on tablets and that written on the heart;[135] the second is the new spirit, which will be given to humans in their heart.[136]

The thoughts introduced in 2 Cor. 3:3 are taken up again only in v. 6 (v. 4 is an intrusion which refers back to 2:16–17).[137] In v. 6 the motif of the New Covenant, alluded to in the OT reference at the end of v. 3, is introduced explicitly. However, contrasts appear in v. 6b which have not been prepared for by the OT references in v. 3 and their development.[138] These are the contrasts between letter and spirit and between giving life and killing.[139] Why should Paul mention the tablets of the law, and the figure of Moses in the first place? The introduction of this material is just as surprising as the fact that neither Moses nor Scripture nor even the covenant is mentioned after 4:1.

For this reason the section has been thought to be a midrashic insertion.[140] But from 2 Cor. 2:16 on, Paul has been pursuing a powerful polemic. And in some manner 3:3—which prepares for v. 6—does show that Paul wants to connect the discussion of Moses with this polemic. This becomes crystal clear with the polemical "insertion" of vv. 4–5, which look back to 2:16–17 and, as has already been pointed out, can easily be related to the rest of Paul's conflict with his opponents.[141]

Through references to the preceding material, the contentious formulations in 2 Cor. 3:4–6 also establish a connection between the statements about Moses and the covenant, and the broader conflict.[142] Finally, the OT exposition itself is sharply formulated in antitheses, lending itself to pointed expression in a discussion. A midrash would look quite different.[143]

Paul wanted the text from 2 Cor. 3:1 on to be understood as a whole, not as a collection of aphorisms or loose-leaf pages. From 2:16 on, Paul frequently turns to his readers and opponents. In order for the polemic to make sense, he must have been able to count on his readers' understanding the connections and the critical references. Precisely because a direct, polemical style is used to some extent, the next step must be to examine the opponents' theology, for its presupposed coherence, and to see Paul's "jerky" argumentation as a critical engagement with it. [144]

One might be inclined to suppose that Paul's opposition lies in a Judaizing movement; the representatives of the Judaizer hypothesis find their strongest support in this text. [145] But a confrontation with nomism is not to be found in 2 Cor., as is made clear by a comparison with Galatians. The label διάκονοι δικαιοσύνης in 2 Cor. 11:15 is to be understood positively. [146] The fact that the concept of νόμος is wholly lacking from 2 Cor. 3 argues against a conflict with Jewish nomism.

Above all, the Judaizer hypothesis fails to explain Paul's abrupt shifts and his succession of motifs. On the other hand, the development of thoughts in the text rules out the possibility that the Jewish elements are mere digressions which do not really belong to the discussion.

A different approach to the analysis of this part of Paul's polemic can reconstruct a complete set of motifs standing over against Paul's. [147] The hypothesis that the opponents' spiritual origin was in the world of Hellenistic-Jewish Apologetics is useful here too.

This background has helped to explain the relation between self-commendation and the letters of recommendation, from which the motif of the heavenly letter is not so far removed. [148] Hellenistic-Jewish Apologetics used it when describing the origin and significance of its tradition, just as did Hellenistic religious propaganda in general. [149]

It has been shown that the Decalogue was a heavenly letter for the Jewish missionaries. They wanted the special source and center of the Jewish religion to be understood as a recommendation for Judaism. This naturally had the effect of recommending the missionaries themselves. In examining the coherence of Paul's text, the special origin of the Decalogue should not be seen in *opposition* to (a) the rest of the law, (b) the figure of the lawgiver, or (c) individual piety, particularly the Moses-veneration of the pneumatics. All these motifs were interdependent.

The Decalogue was described as being imparted directly to the people in God's voice. Then again it was described as being handed down in the form of stone tablets, which God himself wrote.

All the same, the intent in emphasizing the divine origin and significance of the Decalogue was not to show its total otherness from that which is human. Instead, the Word of God was also seen as intrinsic to humans. The commandments reflected both the world order and the intrinsic structure of human existence. That which was written on the tablets did not contradict that which was written within human beings; both showed the mighty will of God, which empowers and controls the world. It has already been shown that the Apologists did not see God's order and God's power (or spirit) in opposition to one another, but understood them as synonymous.

Thus what was written within human beings and what was written on stone tablets could complement each other because of the conception of the Decalogue as a heavenly letter and the inclusion of the spirit motif. All this could be used as a recommendation and could be integrated with pneumatic displays. These manifestations (and the chronicles of pneumatic deeds) reflected the relationship between God and humanity in the double form of the outer law and the inner law. In light of the missionary intent of these Jewish pneumatics, it is not surprising that they emphasized publicity, as Paul mentioned.

Thus I have been able to summarize results from the history-of-religions investigation by closely following the slogans handed down by Paul in 2 Cor. 3:1–3. In the process, I have given a preview of 3:4–18, and I now want to begin with a renewed focus on the pneumatic factor in this section.[150]

The Apologists' respect for the letter of the tradition and their pneumatic self-confidence were not mutually exclusive but belonged together. This correlation between letter and spirit guided their cultic and missionary practice and led to a systematic exposition of Scripture. They employed the allegorical method. It was characterized by a tension between elements which appeared to be irreconcilable only at first glance. On one side were the recognition and glorification of that which was given, the letters which had been handed down. On the other side was the bold advance beyond the given, beyond the letter of tradition, through the expositor's spiritual power. Actually, one element called for the other. The necessity for allegory arose precisely from a lasting, even elevated, respect for tradition. But this respect led in turn to an interpretation which crossed the boundaries to the present. Letter and spirit did not stand in opposition to one another, but demanded one another. An essential mark of God-given perfection was the ability to see this connection.

If this point of view was the opposing position to 2 Cor. 3:6, then the connection of this verse with the preceding material is thoroughly logical, and the following material connects nicely as well.[151]

THE FORM OF THE TRADITION

Up to this point, only the Decalogue has been identified with the γράμμα. But the decisive expressions in 2 Cor. 3:6 make it clear that more than the Decalogue is involved in Paul's discussion with his opponents. As so frequently happens, the Decalogue stands for a larger whole, of which it is the most prominent part. This larger whole includes the law. The concept of the law is broadened, as it was in Judaism, by the fact that Moses is presented not only as the mediator but also as the representative of the law. Indeed, he is finally identified with the law. This identification goes beyond the authority of the lawgiver to the figure of Moses himself. Since Moses and the γράμμα are equated, γράμμα clearly means more than that which is commanded. The sudden introduction of the Moses figure, which has puzzled the exegetes, is most readily explained if the opponents place it at the focal point of their proclamation.

παλαιὰ διαθήκη appears as a further synonym of γράμμα and Μωυσῆς in 2 Cor. 3:14. In Paul this concept appears only here.[152] Since Paul does not explain the term further—despite its obvious importance—but presupposes it as familiar to his readers, the opponents must have introduced it into the discussion. This agreement, together with the previous investigations, suggests that the παλαιὰ διαθήκη were the collected, sacred scriptures of Judaism,[153] the ἱερὰ γράμματα.[154]

But the understanding of γράμμα goes still further. Paul uses γράφειν (and γράμμα) as thematic words in the chain of associations in 3:1–3 (commendation, letter of recommendation, heavenly letter, law, scripture in general). If the chain of associations came from the opponents, then it is most likely that they had also handed down the associated catchword, γράμμα. They would have broadened the Greek concept to include the present communication of the tradition. The opponents thus made this concept the leitmotif of a programmatic claim unifying past and present. Given their relationship to Jewish Apologetics (as described above), that is hardly surprising. It has been shown that holy scriptures, tradition in general, and the pneumatic self-consciousness of the bearers of the contemporary tradition all united in Jewish Apologetics to form a vigorous and magnetic consciousness of tradition.[155]

Paul's opponents combined a firm loyalty to scripture with a very broad understanding of tradition; they demonstrate this by linking their pride in their Jewish heritage with their missionary claims. I am thinking of the relation between the opponents' designations of origin (Ἑβραῖοι, Ἰσραηλῖται, and σπέρμα Ἀβραάμ) in 2 Cor. 11:22 and the following designation διάκονοι Χριστοῦ (11:23).[156]

Before I examine 2 Cor. 11:22–23 more closely, I wish to turn once more to the connection between chaps. 3 and 4. The christological statements in 4:4–6, which have a strongly polemical orientation, are formulated antithetically to the statements about Moses (and tradition) in 3:7–18,[157] with 4:1–2 (and 3) forming the connecting link.

But the two text units are not only related by antitheses. The analysis of 2 Cor. 3:1–4:2 has shown that the opponents' relationship to tradition corresponded to their understanding of the apostolate.[158] In 4:3–15 a corresponding relationship between christology and apostolic understanding can be recognized in Paul's own statements.[159] The references are not surprising, for the entire fragment 2:14—7:4 is an apology for the apostolate which confronts a different concept. The polemical character of 4:1–15 is underlined by the tenor of the whole fragment, especially by vv. 1–2, 3a, and 5. That means that one can expect from the opponents a definite but different conception of the relationship between christology and the understanding of the apostolate. From the connections between the polemical chaps. 3 and 4, one can in addition draw conclusions about the opponents' corresponding complex of traditions. They will have related apostolate to tradition, apostolate to christology, and thereby tradition to christology.

The text mentioned above, 2 Cor. 11:22–23, reinforces this supposition. The listing of the opponents' self-designations begins with their designations of origin and reaches its climax in the designation of function, διάκονοι Χριστοῦ. As implied by the concept of διάκονος, this designation of function establishes a close connection between the designated missionaries and the Χριστός, that is to say, their image of Christ. This is underscored by the opponents' claim, cited by Paul in 2 Cor. 10:7, that they belong to Christ. One may conclude from the succession of concepts in 2 Cor. 11:22–23 that the opponents' understanding of tradition culminated in their relationship to Christ. This meant that the Christ of the opponents belonged to the tradition represented by the apostles.

2 Cor 5:16–17 further illustrates how the opponents developed their christology in connection with their understanding of tradition and linked this with the explication of their apostolic self-understanding. Verse 16, which has been hotly disputed in the history of exegesis,[160] is—as Bultmann has shown—part of the train of thought from 5:11 to 6:10. Schmithals's effort to eliminate the verse as a gloss is clearly a regression from Bultmann's analysis.[161] The context is that of a critical comparison between the conception of genuine apostolic works held by Paul and that held by the opponents. The key word, "self-commendation," appears right at the beginning of the section.

Paul rejects the opponents' approach, which judges the genuineness of an apostolate from pneumatic displays (at 2 Cor. 5:13, ecstasy is given as an example).[162] Paul cannot place himself in the limelight and prove his own legitimacy and that of his cause in a theatrical performance. This would be a case of ἐν προσώπῳ καυχᾶσθαι (5:12) that leads nowhere.

The following verses show that such an approach has been abandoned and something new has begun; such demonstrations, together with their corresponding thoughts and judgments, are disqualified as "sarcic." Verse 16a implies that the judgment of men is no longer pursued in the manner of the σάρξ.[163] In light of vv.

12–13, this can only mean no longer according to one's visible merits.[164] This is clarified in v. 16b, where it is extended to the most extreme case:[165] it applies even to the understanding of Christ.[166] The method of argument brings v. 16b very close to 5:12–13; the phrase γινώσκειν κατὰ σάρκα Χριστόν is set parallel to the phrase ἐν προσώπῳ καυχώμενος. Those who value pneumatic displays are labeled in v. 16a as those who judge "sarcicly." They are thus identical with the representatives of that christology which Paul hypothetically presents as "the most extreme example" in v. 16b.[167] Together with the corresponding habits of judgment and action, this christology belongs to the ἀρχαῖα (v. 17b).[168]

In 2 Cor. 5:17 (just as in 3:6–18) Paul wants to show the radical contrast between "then" and "now." He does this by using an apocalyptic scheme from his tradition.[169] The text becomes more sharply defined, and its connection with the preceding polemic becomes clearer, if τὰ ἀρχαῖα was a positive slogan of the opponents which referred to their religious tradition, from the recent past back to primordial times. This would be similar to the use of ἀρχαῖος and its derivatives in Hellenistic-Jewish Apologetics and in Hellenistic propaganda. It would be what Josephus understood by his ἀρχαιολογία (compare the fundamental statements in *Ant.* 1.5–6 and 20.259–60).[170] Of course, the opponents would not write history as such, only express their powerful sense of tradition.

In this context it would not be surprising if the story of a recent hero who was important for their propaganda were to be included among the ἀρχαῖα, even if he had been active only a few decades earlier. In this way recent events were connected with those of antiquity, and the power residing in the tradition proved its continuing effectiveness.

Thus Paul's expression gains pungency, just as in 2 Cor. 3. The opponents spoke of a continuity which gave an aura of divinity to antiquity; Paul speaks of a radical break as the decisive divine deed. He declares antiquity and tradition, the apparent guarantees of divinity, to be at an end, thus deliberately renouncing an essential element of missionary competition in the Hellenistic world. In the eyes of the opponents and their colleagues of differing persuasions, this was a frivolous and supremely *un*clever thing to do.[171] But now I want to discuss the advantages which the opponents expected from their tradition, paying closer attention to the content of the tradition itself.

The Moses Tradition

2 Cor. 3:7–18 dovetails well with Paul's polemic if it opposes a "heretical" Moses-tradition.[172] If praise of the Jewish tradition could be linked with pride in being a διάκονος Χριστοῦ, then a positive conception of the διακονία of Moses was likely.[173]

MOSES AS θεῖος ἀνήρ

The opponents would not have understood Moses' *diakonia* as a representation of death. It probably represented divine power and might, similar to that of a θεῖος ἀνήρ in Hellenistic-Jewish Apologetics.[174] According to the few surviving Hellenistic-Jewish texts presenting an interpretation of the wandering in the wilderness,[175] Moses' repeated sojourn on Mount Sinai quite understandably distinguished him personally and conferred divine character and appearance on him. Examples of this have already been mentioned.[176]

One can see how the opponents may have understood this pericope (Exodus 33 and 34) from Philo's presentation in *Moses* 2.69–70.[177] Philo puts Moses' ascent of Sinai under the rubric προφητεύειν καὶ θεοφορεῖσθαι. The fasting spoken about in the text is understood as a superhuman feat which underscores the qualities of Moses:

As for eating and drinking, he had no thought of them for forty successive days, doubtless because he had better [nourishment on the basis of contemplation (θεωρίαι)], through whose inspiration, sent from heaven above,[178] he [improved], first of mind, then of body, [through] the soul,[179] and in both so advanced in strength and wellbeing that those who saw (him) afterward could not believe (their eyes).[180] For [(we read)] that by God's command he ascended an inaccessible and pathless mountain, the highest and most sacred in the region, and remained for the period named, taking nothing that is needed to satisfy the requirements of bare sustenance. Then, after the said forty days had passed, he descended with a countenance far more beautiful than (at the time) when he ascended, so that those who saw him were filled with awe and amazement.[181] *They were unable to en-*

dure with (their) eyes any longer because of the assault of the sun-like brilliance that flashed from him.[182]

This text, and one from Josephus to be introduced shortly, exemplifies the synergism between divine and human, already described above as characteristic of Apologetics. Thus it clarifies the role of Moses' glorification in the propaganda of Paul's opponents (2 Cor. 3:7).

According to Philo's presentation, the superhuman capabilities of Moses, which developed in the interplay between divine inspiration and human spiritual powers, grew from the inside toward the outside. The result was that finally the external appearance revealed the inner development, the θεῖος ἀνήρ. External strength and well-being are signs of the same inner phenomena.

At first glance, strength and well-being may appear to be plebian categories, but just the opposite is meant: something special, something aristocratic, is to be represented. Strength and well-being are placed in opposition to human weakness and human misery, which are seen as limiting factors, as opposed to human existence. Strength and well-being are found, in a real and true sense, only in the divine sphere. Philo speaks about them first.

Philo uses these concepts to describe the spiritual and physical consequences of Moses' sojourn in the vicinity of God. Moses' beauty, which is impressively illustrated at the end of the text referred to, and his overpowering radiance are identical with the strength and well-being which assert themselves outwardly.[183] But this is not all. The text describes the appearance—not just striking, but even terrifying—of a man who is strange and uncanny to his fellow beings because he has become divine. Moses has become a θεῖος ἀνήρ. ἰσχύς and εὐεξία belong to the *reality of the divine sphere*.[184] But at the same time, these thematic concepts show a *relationship with the human world*, for they really are not so distant from the human sphere. More precisely, Moses' distinction is presented as a possibility for other humans. The "terror" of the people is only temporary, not final. Philo can disregard it in the continuation of the text.[185]

This attempt to use the transfigured Moses as proof that the reality of the divine is also available to humans can be recognized in

Josephus's interpretation of the pericopes concerning Moses' sojourn on Sinai.[186] Josephus was surely influenced by tradition in interpreting this material. The portrayal of the first stay on Mount Sinai (*Ant*. 3.75–82) emphasizes the remarkable fact that Moses does not perish in the presence of the divine. Moses' return is like that of a divine youth: "Moses appeared (ἐπιφαίνεται), radiant and high-hearted (γαῦρός τε καὶ μέγα φρονῶν)" (*Ant*. 3.83).

The return here means an end to terror and a new hope for the future, surely not only because the people can look forward to retaining an excellent leader and thus hope to bring their journey to a happy end. The hope here is more fundamental. Moses had experienced divine reality and was not destroyed. Therefore a possibility is opened up for humanity to come into contact with the divine and survive. The passage must be explained this way because the portrayal of the Jewish hopes, which are contrasted with the "terror" described previously, leads immediately to the statement "The air too became serene and purged of its recent πάθη on the arrival of Moses" (*Ant*. 3.83).[187] The alteration of the peoples' inner situation is externalized; divine reality, which moves both the objective world and the individual's inner being, has made its appearance in the figure of Moses and becomes a possibility for humanity.[188]

The reference to the second descent from Mount Sinai, which links Exodus 32 and 34, is very weak in comparison with the text in Exodus (*Ant*. 3.99–100). It is said in retrospect that Moses took no nourishment in the human sense. Here too the appearance of Moses drives the previous fear away and creates sheer joy. However, the content of the following short speech shows that nothing so simple as the return of a friend from abroad is being portrayed. Rather, the person who returns has been chosen to converse with God, lead the people, and found the cult, and moreover is supplied with documents written in God's own hand.

Distinction and equality are the two decisive features of a further passage in the *Antiquities*. This is *Ant*. 3.212–13 (cf. also 3.222–23), on which Exod. 34:32–33 (together with Num. 7:89) has clearly had its impact. At first glance the text seems to be almost an antithesis to the pericope about Moses' transfiguration. Without a doubt this impression was intended. According to this text, Moses renounces every honor that the people want to bestow on him and dedicates himself wholly to the service of God.

But the text continues: "He now desisted from further ascents of Sinai and entered the tabernacle and there received oracles on all things which he besought from God" (my trans.). Moses is an extraordinary human being because he can pose questions to God and receive oracles.[189] Similarly, the conclusion of the section notes that Moses wrote the constitution and the laws of the people under divine dictation.[190]

On the other hand, however, Moses is "dressed in everyday fashion and conducts himself in all things as a completely normal commoner, who desired in nothing to appear different from the crowd."[191] The sole thing dividing him from the people—and this is consistent with his prophetic function and capability—is that he is mindful of the interests of all.

Something like an ideal leader of the people is being described here, one who can afford to renounce those things which pertain only to his personal position and worth and who distinguishes himself from the people only where the people as a whole are affected. Josephus does not mean an ἰδιώτης in the literal sense—in the sense in which the opponents in Corinth had reproached Paul (2 Cor. 11:6).

The short passage itself expresses well enough how manifestly important Moses is; the description of Moses and his tradition in Josephus had already sufficiently glorified his outstanding characteristics and capabilities. The reader who has followed the presentation of the *Antiquities* to this point knows that no ordinary man lurks beneath the ordinary clothing, or behind the modest and common man appearance which links Moses with the people.[192] Rather, there is a divine personality.

The θεῖος ἀνήρ text in *Ant.* 3.180 is not being corrected or invalidated.[193] On the contrary, the reader of Josephus already knows that those with whom Moses compared himself are by no means ἰδιῶται, but persons who stand close to the divine. They are at the upper, not the lower, limits of humanity; they represent the positive potential of human existence. This is shown in this passage by the goal of the Jewish constitution (the leading of a life pleasing to God) and similarly by the motif of Moses' becoming like the people, for if he is becoming like the people, that means that the people are becoming like *him*.

The context of this paragraph should be noted carefully. It is no accident that Josephus relates this text to the preceding descriptions of the ascents of Mount Sinai by Moses. The descriptions are no longer necessary, but they are presupposed. If the three texts which have been cited are placed side by side, the distance between Moses and the people, which results from his deification, dwindles as the people become more and more like him.

Judging from the relatively slight remainders of the tradition, the biblical accounts of Moses' glorification, especially Exod. 34:29–35,[194] lent themselves well to the full presentation of the Apologetic conception of the θεῖος ἀνήρ. The deification of the individual could be presented as a synergistic process. One could show how this transfiguration removed the θεῖος ἀνήρ from the mass of his admirers, not in a fundamental sense but to portray the possibility to the believer more vividly. The divine superiority of the θεῖος ἀνήρ should not oppress the others but elevate them, first in an inward and then in an outward manner. Thus they would participate concretely in the divine powers of life, externalizing the divine radiance as unlimited power and well-being. Behind this stood the hope that this was a way of escaping the limitations of human existence, that is, of conquering death.

Moses lost his biographical identity and became a type. The investigation of the self-understanding of the Jewish missionaries has shown that the present representatives of the Jewish tradition identified themselves with those of the past. They in turn could then develop into models, so that the process I have described would repeat itself, from the initial transfiguration and dissociation from the public to the final assimilation and identification with it. The opponents of Paul would have followed this concept as well. This is confirmed by the fact that they spoke not only of the figure but also of the *diakonia* of Moses. I have already drawn attention to the connection between the opponents' designation of function, διάκονοι, and the διακονία of Moses himself.

THE OLD TESTAMENT AS THE ARCHIVE OF THE SPIRIT

A close connection and correlation between pneumatics of the past, tradition in the narrower and broader sense, and pneumatics of the present has been found both in Hellenistic-Jewish Apologetics and in the discussion in 2 Cor. 2:14—3:6 which had been begun by the pneumatics and then continued critically by Paul. This close connection and correlation also appears in the development of 2 Cor. 3:7–18, especially if vv. 8–12, which quite markedly betray Paul's style, are set aside.[195] The description of Moses' transfiguration is followed not only by the mention of the covering but also by the thought that the παλιαιά διαθήκη is holy scriptures constantly read (v. 14). The latter is clearly paralleled by the figure of Moses.[196] The πνεῦμα concept is then introduced explicitly in v. 17. Finally, the representatives of the present generation are mentioned in their relation to the past (v. 18). This line of interpretation attempts a continual opening of the past to the present; the thoughts and observations which depart from this interpretation bear the characteristic marks of Paul's theology.[197]

The fact that the interpretation is limited to Exod. 34:29–35 seems to emphasize the thought of continuity between the past and the present. The exegetical models of Hellenistic-Jewish Apologetics already seem to avoid or conceal the thematic context of Exod. 34:29–35, namely, Exodus 33—34. That theme is *the renewal of the broken covenant.*[198] Instead, the text of the veil is interpreted as a *description of the climactic point of the Mosaic experience of God, and the ultimate foundation for the experience of God in general.* The bond between the privileged one and his many subordinates and followers was seen in the lasting reality of Moses' transfiguration and in the tablets he brought with him. Above all, these tablets served as a pledge of the continued efficacy of the power transforming Moses, as a testament of God and then of Moses as well. The figure and the significance of Moses lived on in the law; thus Moses could continue spreading the power which had transformed him. This power could transform others via tradition.

In reviewing the Apologetic conception of the relationship between θεῖος ἀνήρ, tradition and the present, which was presented in detail above, I have already described the line of thought which remains in 2 Cor. 3:12–18 if the explicit polemical statements and the genuine Pauline concepts are disregarded. One factor that still needs to be explained is the κάλυμμα motif, which is of decisive significance for Exod. 34:29–35 and all the more so for 2 Cor. 3:12–18.

It has frequently been recognized[199] that the κάλυμμα motif appears again in 2 Cor. 4:3, where it is unmistakably connected with the motif of spiritual "hardening." As in 3:12–18, the covering is here expressly connected with the proclamation. Paul shows further that, *in his opinion*, the misunderstanding and obstinacy related to it are the true "veiling." The digressions about the covered thoughts, or hearts, of the Israelites disturb the train of thought in 3:12–18. In 4:3 these motifs are signs of *Paul's* special interest. But the leading thought in the earlier interpretation of the Exodus pericope did not seem to be this covering of the hearts. It was rather the shining of the δόξα on the face of Moses, and the intentional veiling of this face.

A study of word frequency shows that the motifs of concealment and revelation are extremely significant in this context. Paul uses καλύπτειν only in 2 Cor. 4:3. In 4:2 we have a synonym, namely, κρυπτός. Paul speaks emphatically: "We renounce the secrecy of shame." This phrase ἀπειπάμεθα τὰ κρυπτὰ τῆς αἰσχύνης is restated positively as "by the open statement of the truth we establish ourselves." φανεροῦν, which appears thirteen times in Paul's letters, is found seven times in 2 Cor. 2:14—7:4 and once in 11:6. Outside of the text in question, the substantive φανέρωσις appears only in 1 Cor. 12:7. Generally speaking, the concepts of revelation, openness, sight, and insight accumulate in 2 Cor. 2:14—7:4 and 10–13; the antithetical concepts are abundant too.

Thus ὀσμὴ τῆς γνώσεως appears in 2 Cor. 2:14 (cf. 2:16), and γνῶσις also appears at 4:6, 6:6, 10:5, 11:6; εὐωδία 2:15; (συνιστάνειν), γινώσκειν and ἀναγινώσκειν 3:2; ἀτενίσαι 3:7, 13; (δόξα), παρρησία 3:12, 7:4; ἐλευθερία 3:17; ἀνάγνωσις 3:14, ἀναγινώσκειν 3:15; ἀνακαλύπτειν 3:14, 18; κατοπτρίζεσθαι 3:18; αὐγάζειν 4:4; φωτισμός 4:4, 6; κηρύσσειν 4:5, 11:4; φῶς (λάμπειν) 4:6; περιφέρειν 4:10; φανερωθῆναι 4:10–11; τὰ βλεπόμενα and τὰ μὴ βλεπόμενα 4:18; εἰδέναι and γινώσκειν 5:16; πρεσβεύειν 5:20 (cf. θριαμβεύειν 2:14); λόγος ἀληθείας 6:7; ὡς ἀγνοούμενοι καὶ ἐπιγινωσκόμενοι 6:9; ἀνοίγειν 6:11; πλατύνεσθαι 6:11, 13; ἀλήθεια 11:10 (and 13:8); οὐ ψεύδομαι 11:31; βλέπειν and ἀκούειν 12:6. Compare also κάλυμμα 3:12–18; ποροῦν 3:14; τυφλοῦν 4:4.[200]

Paul interprets "the secrecy of shame" as a περιπατεῖν ἐν πανουργίᾳ and as δολοῦν τὸν λόγον τοῦ θεοῦ in 4:2, and contrasts with this the revelation of God's truth. Therefore we must view the concepts πανουργία and δολοῦν as synonyms for κάλυμμα and καλύπτειν. Finally, I wish to refer to the motif of the disguise of Satan and his emissaries (11:14–15).

The accumulation of all these concepts in 2 Cor. 3:7–18 is especially striking because Paul uses them here and elsewhere in connection with his proclamation or that of his opponents. In 4:2 Paul says that the openness and public nature of his proclamation is essential. But then what does εἰ δὲ καί mean in 4:3? The key lies in its connection with the term ἡμῶν. εὐαγγέλιον ἡμῶν is an infrequent term in Paul, but the ἡμῶν is specifically emphasized (not the term κεκαλυμμένον) by the phrase εἰ δὲ καί. This phrase probably alludes to a slogan of the opponents,[201] but hardly to a slogan of anti-Pauline polemic.[202] Paul does not want to say that his gospel is *also* *veiled*, but that *even his* gospel is veiled.

But if the polemic of the opponents is being alluded to here, then they must not have maintained that Paul's gospel was veiled but theirs was not.[203] Paul had already dissociated himself from (the opponents') fraudulent proclamation in 4:2. The text makes more sense if the opponents had spoken positively about the veiling of their proclamation.[204] This is the basis for understanding the polemic in 4:2. Whether the opponents put Paul on the same level with themselves, and then took up this assertion through the εἰ δὲ καί only to tear it down, or whether (and this is more likely) Paul attacked their own claims without feeling that he himself was subject to reproach—in any case *Paul* does not understand the κάλυμμα motif as being positive.

The opponents, then, had introduced it into the Corinthian debate. They apparently used it to refer to one of the essential points of their message. Indeed, to judge from the style of Paul's polemic, they could use it to describe their entire presentation. The discussion in 2 Cor. 3 shows that the example of Moses in the pericope Exod. 34:29–35 was their basic point of reference.[205] Apparently the veil was understood just as much as the stone tablets as an essential mark of the Mosaic ministry. A superficial glance at the narrative could lead to the presumption that the veil was supposed to protect the Israelites, who were not able to look upon the *doxa*, from being blinded.[206] But the OT text says instead that the covering was put on when Moses stopped speaking to the people, and remained on his face until he went into the tent and had the encounter with God.

The opponents could have used the phrase εἰς τὸ τέλος to interpret further the tension-filled OT statements about the function of the covering;[207] the veil would have prevented the Israelites from "seeing the goal." This "goal" could only have been the perfection of the Mosaic experience of God, namely, turning to the Lord, as mentioned later, which caused the veil to disappear, and the further process of transfiguration. The covering would thus be the barrier between the complete experience of God as achieved by the perfect θεῖος ἀνήρ and the experience of the others.

But this barrier—at least from the point of view of Hellenistic-Jewish Apologetics—cannot be a fundamental one. Josephus (*Ant.* 3.212–13)[208] is obviously applying the κάλυμμα motif when he says that, on the one hand, Moses' clothing and conduct misrepresented the true nature and function of the divine man but that, on the other hand, with his clothing and conduct, Moses is able to establish and maintain contact with the people. Thus his true function can aid the people and help them, with the transmission of the law, to lead a life pleasing to God. The disguise therefore is not a hindrance, but a bridge and a help. It has a pedagogical function and points to the richness and power of its bearer, but it also distinguishes the recipients. The veil becomes a sign of glory especially because it hints at whom and what it conceals and the goal this leads to. The pedagogical help stimulates the people to follow the exemplary leader and to participate in his power and his experience.

It is then clearly stated—after a parenthetical comment from Paul—that the same covering covered the *Old Testament* (2 Cor. 3:14). If this thought came from the opponents, then for them the covering of the OT performed the same function as that of Moses and simultaneously hindered and helped along the way to an insightful existence and experience.

The Apologists saw the experience of Moses as being typical; in other words, it was constantly repeatable.[209] They readily interpreted the turning of Moses to God and the removal of the veil as a continual change occurring in the OT text itself, a continual unveiling but engaging the proper reader also.[210] This reader/interpreter who was enabled to see this process of turning within the texts would recognize the cause and force behind this process and thus become aware of the explosive and infinitely expansive dimensions of this experience. 2 Cor. 3:17a turns out to be an exegetical gloss explaining the word κύριος in 3:16. It indicates that the κύριος in the OT text in question is to be identified with the πνεῦμα. The goal and power which the proper reader will see is the spirit, the force behind the continuous self-unveiling of the text in the experience of the spiritual reader/interpreter.

According to the Apologetic model, πνεῦμα must be understood essentially as divine δύναμις.[211] Applied to the OT, that meant that the text turned to the spirit again and again, resulting in a constant unveiling. Again, not only was the spirit the goal, but it also gave the necessary strength for the process of transformation. This unveiling must have been identical in meaning with the increasing illumination of the true nature of the text, which was described above (pp. 136–38) as the self-exposition of the tradition.

But the knowledgeable audience should not be forgotten. The statements about the covering have already pointed to it, though only in a negative way. Now the concept of the spirit is added, and v. 18 speaks explicitly about a deeply moved and participating audience. The contrasts between all these thoughts must have been drawn by Paul for a polemical purpose.

The opponents, then, must have equated the covering first with the letters of the text and then with its literal sense, for according to contemporary Apologetics and that of late antiquity in general, the literal sense concealed the essential reality of the text, its spiritual content and its spiritual power.[212] At the same time, the letters, like the covering discussed above, could point to the essential meaning of the text. One had only to apply correct spiritual method, namely, allegory; that meant letting the spiritual power of the text itself work and turn the text.[213]

The assumption expressed on pp. 249–50, following the series of associations in 2 Cor. 3:1–6 and Apologetic thinking, is confirmed: the opponents brought the letters into immediate connection with the spirit. In the letters one could see the spirit and express it verbally. The spirit did not stand in opposition to the letters. The letters only veiled the spirit, thus showing—to those who understood—the way to its uncovering. This was in essence a self-exposition of the spirit, so that it was possible that the opponents claimed that the spirit could give life to the letters (in contrast to Paul's opinion in 3:6). At the same time, the essence of the text was identical with the essence of the exegete, namely, the divine power which was at work within and upon him or her. The process of interpretation was not only a self-exposition of the spirit but also the interpreter's recognition of himself or herself *in* the text.

In connection with the presentation of the Apologists' scriptural exposition, I referred to a passage from *Cont.* 78 (pp. 144–45, above). According to the passage, the literal statement of the text can serve the allegorizer as a mirror of the spirit, thus giving him or her the ability to "see" true visions and to gain an essential position in the continual process of transformation. In 2 Cor. 3:18 Paul seems to allude to similar thoughts on the part of his opponents. Here too a mirror is being viewed.[214] To judge from the context, the opponents must have used "mirror" to mean first the face of Moses and then the OT text, which turned to the Lord just as did Moses' face and was thereby unveiled. The result was that the text, like the face of Moses, reflected the splendor of the Lord and was able, by virtue of the spirit which powered this process, to work on the expositors so that they became increasingly transformed in the course of the (allegorical) exegesis. The phrase ἀπὸ δόξης εἰς δόξαν points to a process; the phrase ἀπό . . . πνεύματος points to the transforming power.

Thus the emphasis on the special and the concealed could imply a universal possibility. It could also serve as an incentive to trust in the leadership of these capable persons, who knew the way to a special spring which poured forth the most primal power of all, a power whose influence could be felt everywhere and always. When the opponents made the motif of concealment a sustaining and characteristic motif of their proclamation, they were acting not contrary to their missionary intentions but in conformity with them. They used "the special" as a category of encounter, and thus could be certain of having both an audience and a clientele. The particular Jesus orientation then meant that one claimed on the basis of the inclusion of Jesus into the line of Jewish θεῖοι ἄνδρες a better understanding of the OT, to experience its power more intensively and to be able to impart it more effectively.

Excursus: Literary Critical Analysis
of 2 Cor. 3:7–18

The reconstruction of the string of thoughts used and taken apart by Paul in 2 Cor. 3 has shown that they followed not only the theology of the opponents but also the latter's exegesis of Exod. 34:29–35. This leads to the question whether this exegesis was available to Paul as a literary unit. I want to pursue this question further, even though the answer will remain hypothetical. In the process, I shall have to repeat some things said earlier to complete my argument. A literary critical analysis of 2 Cor. 3:7–18 can also clarify Paul's argumentation further, but not within the scope of this study. What I do here can be but preparation for a more exact presentation of Paul's intentions.

Windisch and Schulz in particular have uncovered the difficulties which stand against a coherent reading of the text.[215] Verses 7 and 8 are meant as comparison, but the first part of that comparison is disproportionately longer than the second.[216] Verse 7 also contains several elements which have no basis in the OT report, in addition to the rephrasing of the OT text. The phrases διακονία τοῦ θανάτου, ὥστε μὴ δύνασθαι ἀτενίσαι, and τὴν καταργουμένην do not occur in the Exodus text, nor does anything similar. One could argue that ὥστε μὴ δύνασθαι interpreted at least the intent of the OT pericope, but διακονία τοῦ θανάτου and τὴν καταργουμένην are total reversals of the meaning of the passage.[217] One has to pay particular attention to τὴν καταργουμένην, because the verb καταργεῖσθαι occurs four times in different forms in 2 Cor. 3:7–18.

A new comparison begins in v. 9. In contrast to the previous one, the first half of the comparison now is unexpectedly short. Even the predicate of the sentence is missing. Whereas in v. 7 Paul stuffed the sentence with explanations, he now uses a laconic brevity. The explanation in v. 10 is given a very elliptic form;[218] the reference of ἐν τούτῳ τῷ μέρει is a *crux interpretum*.[219] The entire verse attempts to bring the preceding line of argument, structured in the form of the Jewish *Qal wachomer*, to a preliminary formulaic conclusion. Although this sentence is meant to give cause and justification to the argument, it is not yet conclusive, for it needs to be supplemented by a further γάρ sentence. The argumentation changes as the contrast τὸ καταργούμενον–τὸ μένον is emphasized.

The sentence begun in v. 12 is not continued in v. 13. There is an *aposiopesis*, a sudden interruption.[220] Paul does not make any attempt to clarify it afterward. On the contrary, after καθάπερ in v. 13 he continues as if in a main clause.[221] The comparative sentence contains a direct phrase from Exod. 34:33,[222] but it is not entirely a verbatim quote. The order of the object and the prepositional phrase are reversed. Instead of the compound ἐπιτιθέναι (περιτιθέναι in Exod. 34:35), the simplex form is chosen; the imperfect tense occurs instead of the (historicizing) aorist. But the phrase adopted from Exodus 34 is only brief. τοῦ καταργουμένου turns the intent of the OT passage on its head,[223] especially if the Pauline text is claiming a conscious deception by Moses.[224]

2 Cor. 3:14a does not make real sense as a simple and immediate continuation of the preceding argument,[225] especially since τὸ αὐτό (v. 14) directs the reader back to the κάλυμμα of Moses in v. 13. ἀλλά here describes a contrast or opposition to the entire previous statement.[226] A mere correction would have had to refer to an action or intention of the previous subject (Paul/we or Moses).

Verse 14b leaps from the hardened hearts of the Israelites to the reading of the OT in the present, in a way leading back to v. 13. The statement about the veiling of the OT is parallel to the earlier description of the veiling of the face of Moses.

The referent of μὴ ἀνακαλυπτόμενον in v. 14c is a real puzzle.[227] It is difficult as well to decide what the ὅτι phrase relates to.

In v. 15 the same problem is found as in v. 14a. Again the veil is interpreted as an "inner" blinding,[228] although v. 18 speaks once more of a veiling of the face. The introduction of the sentence with ἀλλά is strange.[229] One would expect a real contrast to the preceding sentence to follow, but that is not the case.

Only once in his letters does Paul use the name of Moses for the OT; the term παλαιὰ διαθήκη in v. 14 is also unique. The strong verbal resemblance of v. 14 and v. 15 makes for some stylistic harshness. The second verse seems to interpret and repeat the first one.[230]

The meaning of v. 16 is equally hard to define in the context. The subject of this sentence should be Μωυσῆς, judging from the preceding; the OT passage would call for that too.[231] But Paul does not want to speak of a conversion of Moses. He aims instead at the πάντες in v. 18.

The OT text has been altered in v. 16.[232] The imperfect has been replaced by the aorist or the present tense. Instead of εἰσεπορεύετο, the text has ἐπιστρέψῃ, ἄν has become an ἐάν, and ἔναντι κυρίου has turned into πρὸς κύριον.[233]

The referent of v. 17a is not easy to define.[234] An exegetical gloss has been suspected here.[235] This indicates that the Pauline text may be better explained by assuming different textual seams and components.

κατοπτρίζεσθαι in v. 18 means "view in a mirror," which conflicts with ἀνακεκαλυμμένῳ προσώπῳ. It should be clear that one can look only with an unveiled face. Why then does the text state this obvious matter? But this is not the only difficulty. Paul clearly relates the ἀνακεκαλυμμένῳ προσώπῳ to the Jesus believers. But the veiled face had referred to Moses before. The interpretation of the metaphor in v. 14b then applied the veil motif to the reading of the OT. When the text spoke of the veiling of other persons, it referred to their νοήματα (v. 14a) or their καρδία (v. 15). This veiling and unveiling of minds and hearts is hinted at again in v. 17b, when Paul mentions ἐλευθερία. Thus the metaphorical use of the veil motif applied to the inner nature of the listening crowd. One would expect something similar in v. 18.

The question of where the δόξα κυρίου can now be seen arises. According to v. 13, to which the ἀνακεκαλυμμένῳ προσώπῳ of v. 18 refers, the face of Moses is the place of δόξα. But in v. 18 the unveiled faces do not bear the δόξα themselves. They see the δόξα first on someone else. In order to ease that difficulty, exegetes had incorrectly used the translation "reflect in a mirror." After the preceding verses the reader will not easily understand what the mirror of the δόξα for the Jesus believers is or who the εἴκων (τὴν αὐτὴν εἰκόνα) is.[236]

I suggest that the textual difficulties can easily be resolved by assuming that the opponents had put their tradition in writing and that Paul based his refutation on this text. A rebuttal in the form of a persiflage is common in the ancient world; the Bible provides many examples. The tradition or text of the opponents would have contained their exposition of Exod. 34:29–35. In reconstructing this postulated text, I shall follow the principle that all obviously critical and persiflating statements in 2 Cor. 3:7–15 come from Paul, while the positive statements—if recoverable at all—go to the account of the opponents.

The εἰ δέ introducing 2 Cor. 3:7 seems to indicate that Paul is quoting (cf. also 4:3).[237] The leap from v. 6 to v. 7 would be more easily explained that way. Without the introductory εἰ δέ and the problematic τοῦ θανάτου, there remains a simple exposition of Exod. 34:30 that could be attributed to the opponents. τοῦ θανάτου corresponds to Paul's critical interpretation of the Moses covenant.[238] It influences the two subsequent verses as well. They present in a condensed form important elements of Paul's understanding of justification by faith. They can be credited to Paul. The postponed τὴν καταργουμένην in v. 7 has no basis in the OT text. It appears to be a Pauline gloss too. It expresses his tendency to stress that the old is past, in contrast to the eschatological καινός. For Paul the old is transitory, ephemeral;[239] for the opponents the age of tradition demonstrates spiritual continuity. After striking the reference to the transitory as Pauline, a rather positive statement about the function of Moses remains (as one would expect it from the opponents).

These contradictory tendencies explain the quantitative disproportion between v. 7 and v. 8. What was said about Moses' ministry was not intended for a comparison but was simply meant to state that Moses had δόξα.

In v. 10 a few deletions (καί . . . οὐ . . . τούτῳ τῷ μέρει εἴνεκεν) and changes (of the genitive τῆς ὑπερβαλλούσης δόξης into a dative) turn the sentence into a smooth clause which would correspond to the intentions of the opponents. It would explain well the inability of the Israelites to see the δόξα of Moses and thus would support the emphasis on the δόξα of Moses. On the other side, the embellishments that complicate the sentence would serve the critical intention of Paul (as an abstract foundation for the Qal wachomer, which Paul has introduced himself).

Paul's words in v. 11 bring this argumentation to its climax. The conclusion of v. 12, which in turn introduces a new thought, is also from Paul's hand. His intention, expressed many a time in 2 Cor. 2:14—7:4 (and then in chaps. 10—13), here is condensed to a brief formula.

The comparative element in v. 13 appears to be an artificial addition and can be ascribed to Paul. Μωυσῆς begins a new sentence. It is based on the opponents' emphasis on the mysterious basis of their message.[240] Perhaps it was they too who read the πρὸς τὸ μὴ ἀτενίσαι into the OT text. But τοῦ καταργουμένου,[241] again added on, seems to come from the same hand that had supplied τὴν καταργουμένην in v. 7, namely, Paul's. He (and not the opponents) wanted to talk of the transience of the old (cf. 5:17). εἰς τὸ τέλος would not stand alone without the attribute τοῦ καταργουμένου. It could be understood in a positive sense, as already shown above (p. 261).

In v. 14a Paul again shows his own objective. The concept of the hardening of hearts is hardly that of the opponents. Instead it has a firm place in Pauline proclamation.[242] Verse 14a would thus prepare the polemical thesis of Paul in vv. 4:3–4 that the gospel is hidden only to the obdurate ones.

On the other hand, v. 14b would follow v. 13 well because the main thought is continued. The veil which covered the face of Moses covers the reading of the OT as well. It has been shown that the motif of the παλαιὰ διαθήκη and the motif of hiddenness both fit well into the teaching of the opponents, since both can explain the concept of allegorical interpretation of scriptures. The basic problem of such interpretation is mentioned in v. 14b and the subsequent passage.

It is obvious that this suggested Vorlage of v. 14 makes the connecting phrase ἄχρι γάρ difficult to explain. But if one takes γάρ as an added copulative—Paul could not leave v. 14a and b unrelated—and if one ignores it for the Vorlage, then v. 14b connects well with v. 13. The repetition of σήμερον appears to be superfluous to the opponents' tradition. Perhaps one of them was added by Paul. The ἕως of v. 15 does have a foundation in the Exodus text.

The μὴ ἀνακαλυπτόμενον in v. 14c prepares the ὅτι sentence.[243] The usual claim is that this participial phrase refers back to κάλυμμα because it is grammatically congruent. But instead, some roughness in the syntax can be expected if the text has been worked over. A glossatory postposition of the καταργεῖσθαι phrases has been noticed before. The previous phrases referred not to the veil but to the δόξα of Moses (vv. 7, 13) and something more fundamental in v. 11 (the ministry of Moses or even the Old Covenant). In addition, the μὴ ἀνακαλυπτόμενον in v. 14c is far removed from its alleged referent κάλυμμα. "Uncovering the veil" is also a curious expression; usually not a veil itself but an object covered by a veil is uncovered. ἀνακαλύπτεσθαι and περιαιρεῖσθαι are not complete synonyms, as the common reading of v. 14c would require. If μὴ ἀνακαλυπτόμενον is understood as an absolute accusative and the following ὅτι sentence as a declarative clause ("that . . ."), the phrase would correspond to Paul's other descriptions of the end of the old (here the abolition of the OT/Old Covenant) in Christ; it must be a Pauline gloss. The reason he makes this statement here and not after v. 16 may be found in the context: v. 16 alludes to a conversion of the Jews, and a reference to the abolition of the OT/Old Covenant might have been out of place there.

Heinrici correctly understands v. 15 as a gloss. It would, however, be a gloss of Paul's, since "veiling" and "hardening" are equated here.

The original subject of v. 16 seems to have been Μωυσῆς.[244] In v. 18 the (uncovered) veil is thought of as having rested on the face, and that means for v. 16 on the face of Moses.[245] Verse 16 no longer narrates like v. 13. The change of tense shows that something lasting and universally valid is meant.[246] In an abbreviated allegorical interpretation, the experience of Moses is identified with the fate of the OT/Old Covenant.

Perhaps ἡνίκα ἄν in v. 15 originally belonged to v. 16. The ἀλλά of v. 15 would then be an interpreting appendage to v. 14b with the meaning "it does not remain that way but ἕως σήμερον. . . ." The message of v. 16 in the original version of the opponents would have been: despite the veiling, until this day Moses' (the OT's) veil will always be removed again whenever Moses (the OT) turns to the Lord. The passive becomes significant,[247] especially with the exegetical gloss in v. 17a. This gloss would fit well into the version of the opponents. Further observations on the importance of these statements have already been made above.[248]

The approach taken thus far with respect to the "original" meaning of vv. 13–17 would also explain τὴν δόξαν κυρίου κατοπτριζόμενοι in v. 18. The opponents would have said that the δόξα of the Lord could have been seen in the mirror of the face of Moses had he not put the veil over it. The same would be true for the OT. The Moses veil would continue to cover the OT and the (Lord's) δόξα until the (recurring) turn to the Lord. What was intimated in v. 16 and v. 18b would then follow: the uncovering of the δόξα of the Lord/Spirit and the transformation.

πάντες in v. 18 is based on Exod. 34:32: καὶ μετὰ ταῦτα προσῆλθον πρὸς αὐτὸν πάντες οἱ υἱοὶ ᾿Ισραήλ. Exod. 34:35 explicitly says: καὶ εἶδον οἱ υἱοὶ ᾿Ισραὴλ τὸ πρόσωπον Μωυσῆ ὅτι δεδόξασται. The opponents would hardly have emphasized the πάντες and said that *all* believers already saw the δόξα κυρίου. They would merely have pointed out the basic possibility for everyone. Paul would have had a greater interest in emphasizing the πάντες.

Verse 18 connects to the preceding with δέ. That implies an antithesis to the experience of Moses, which is contrasted with the experience of the Jesus-believers.[249] The secondary nature of the ἀνακεκαλυμμένῳ προσώπῳ has already been noticed. These two words seem to assure the contrast between Moses and the Jesus-believers in the sense of "the one" and "the many."[250] *All* the believers are already like Moses. This is a typical Pauline emphasis. It appears, therefore, that it was Paul who added πάντες together with ἀνακεκαλυμμένῳ προσώπῳ in order to bring to bear an essential point of his polemic. This would fit his antielitist democratizing tendency.

The teaching and self-understanding of the opponents included the ideas of transformation by the power of the spirit. But τὴν αὐτὴν εἰκόνα as well as κυρίου appear to come from Paul.[251] The two phrases overload the sentence; both agree with Paul's interest in contrasting his own christology and that of his opponents. The ideas of revelation, sovereignty, and rule are central to Paul's christology.

On the basis of the previous arguments, I would like to propose the following reconstruction as the text which came from the opponents and was used by Paul for his polemical criticism. The suspected Pauline glosses and modifications are underlined, and the important concepts of Pauline theology and polemics are not underlined:

ἡ διακονία [τοῦ Μωυσέως (or τῆς παλαιᾶς διαθήκης)] τοῦ θανάτου ἐν γράμμασιν ἐντετυπωμένη λίθοις ἐγενήθη ἐν δόξῃ, ὥστε μὴ δύνασθαι ἀτενίσαι τοὺς υἱοὺς ᾿Ισραὴλ εἰς τὸ πρόσωπον Μωυσέως διὰ τὴν δόξαν τοῦ προσώπου αὐτοῦ τὴν καταργουμένην, πῶς οὐχὶ μᾶλλον ἡ διακονία τοῦ πνεύματος ἔσται ἐν δόξῃ; εἰ γὰρ ἡ διακονία τῆς κατακρίσεως δόξα, πολλῷ μᾶλλον περισσεύει ἡ διακονία τῆς δικαιοσύνης δόξῃ. καὶ γὰρ οὐ δεδόξασται τὸ δεδοξασμένον ἐν (or διὰ) τούτῳ τῷ μέρει εἵνεκεν τῆς ὑπερβαλλούσης δόξης. εἰ γὰρ τὸ καταργούμενον διὰ δόξης, πολλῷ μᾶλλον τὸ μένον ἐν δόξῃ.

ἔχοντες οὖν τοιαύτην ἐλπίδα πολλῇ παρρησίᾳ χρώμεθα, καὶ οὐ καθάπερ Μωυσῆς ἐτίθει κάλυμμα ἐπὶ τὸ πρόσωπον αὐτοῦ, πρὸς τὸ μὴ ἀτενίσαι τοὺς υἱοὺς Ἰσραὴλ εἰς τὸ τέλος τοῦ καταργουμένου. ἀλλὰ ἐπωρώθη τὰ νοήματα αὐτῶν. ἄχρι γὰρ τῆς σήμερον ἡμέρας τὸ αὐτὸ κάλυμμα ἐπὶ τῇ ἀναγνώσει τῆς παλαιᾶς διαθήκης μένει, μὴ ἀνακαλυπτόμενον ὅτι ἐν Χριστῷ καταργεῖται. ἀλλ᾽ ἕως σήμερον ἡνίκα ἂν ἀναγινώσκηται Μωυσῆς κάλυμμα ἐπὶ τὴν καρδίαν αὐτῶν κεῖται· ἡνίκα δὲ ἐὰν ἐπιστρέψῃ πρὸς κύριον, περιαιρεῖται τὸ κάλυμμα. ὁ δὲ κύριος τὸ πνεῦμά ἐστιν· οὗ δὲ τὸ πνεῦμα κυρίου, ἐλευθερία. ἡμεῖς (οὖν) δὲ πάντες ἀνακεκαλυμμένῳ προσώπῳ τὴν δόξαν κυρίου κατοπτριζόμενοι τὴν αὐτὴν εἰκόνα μεταμορφούμεθα ἀπὸ δόξης εἰς δόξαν, καθάπερ ἀπὸ κυρίου πνεύματος.

The Jesus Tradition

JESUS AS A θεῖος ἀνήρ

In the section on the form of the tradition, I have shown that Paul's argumentation presupposes that the opponents' understanding of tradition included a particular christology. In addition, they must have paralleled Moses and Christ. This parallel was also a part of other christological traditions of the early church, although it was not always drawn with the same intention. I concluded that the opponents were mainly interested in the earthly existence of Jesus as a figure comparable to Moses.

An internal argument gleaned from the fragments under discussion is the unusual frequency of the simple name Ἰησοῦς. Elsewhere Paul does not use this name without a title very often, but the usage in other Pauline writings confirms the initial impression left by the occurrence of the simple name.[252]

In 1 Thess. 4:14 Paul explicitly refers to something "known" and uses the simple Ἰησοῦς twice. Ἰησοῦς ἀπέθανεν καὶ ἀνέστη obviously refers to the earthly Jesus, as does the formulaic statement τὸ πνεῦμα τοῦ ἐγείραντος τὸν Ἰησοῦν ἐκ νεκρῶν in Rom. 8:11. The fact that the second Jesus reference in 1 Thess. 4:14 speaks of the parousia seems to be a contradiction. But Paul is using the simple name Jesus in the second case to emphasize the relationship of the returning Jesus to the earthly Jesus. This corresponds to the use of the name Jesus in the kerygmatic formula of 1 Thess. 1:10, which is trying to state that the risen and returning son is the same as the earthly Jesus. Similarly, the earlier references to death and resurrection or resurrection alone connect the earthly Jesus to the present one.

Phil. 2:10 names Jesus in the second stanza of the hymn; the first stanza (2:6–8) had spoken about Jesus' life but had not mentioned his name. The name appears only in the second stanza (which describes the heavenly exaltation of the Christ) to intimate that the fate of the earthly Jesus is continued in the "heavenly" phase, that both stanzas speak of the same person.[253]

In Rom. 3:26 Paul seems to have chosen the name Jesus to secure the connection of πίστις to the saving death of Jesus in the previous tradition (3:25–26). The phrase στίγματα Ιησοῦ (Gal. 6:17) is probably a traditional wording, since it is used only once by Paul. It clearly refers to the suffering of the earthly Jesus, which is transferred to the person of Paul.

Thus the simple name Jesus in Paul always points to the earthly Jesus. Invariably, it also alludes to the problems of continuity and identity.[254] The low frequency of the term in the authentic Pauline correspondence and the fact that it occurs often in immediate proximity to traditions and traditional formulae indicate that Paul is reacting to a matter discussed in the early church, which he does not bring up on his own in the same fashion.

That is different with the opponents of 2 Cor. They seem to have a major stake in this discussion. 2 Cor. 11:4 shows that the simple name Jesus appeared in their program, of course with a clear theological intention. Thus, Paul was able to dissociate himself from their use of the name Jesus with one adjective (ἄλλος).

Paul says in 2 Cor. 11:4: "If anyone comes along and proclaims another Jesus whom we did not proclaim, or you receive another spirit whom you had not received, or another gospel which you had not accepted, you bear it all right."[255] Today there is general agreement that ὁ ἐρχόμενος does not refer to a single person, such as an imaginary envoy from Jerusalem.[256] Paul is here generalizing about the opponents who have intruded on the congregation (cf. τις [2 Cor. 10:7] or ὁ τοιοῦτος [10:11]).[257] In 2 Cor. 11:4 he states the basic difference between his proclamation and that of the opponents.[258] As opposed to Gal. 1:6, here more than a different gospel is at stake.[259] In 2 Cor. 11:4 Paul defines the difference to the opponents more precisely and radically than in the passage from Galatians.[260]

The difference appears most of all in the christology.[261] ἄλλος Ἰησοῦς does not merely refer to the extreme possible consequences of a suspected contrast; it means a real difference.[262] It could not have been a Gnostic christology; the simple Ἰησοῦς already speaks against that.[263] It will be observed later that the opponents could also use the Χριστός title. But since Paul is suggesting a basic antithesis between his and the opponents' proclamation by using the name of Jesus, the difference must have consisted mainly in a different understanding of the earthly Jesus, an issue not essential for Gnosticism.[264]

Paul writes in 2 Cor. 4:5, "We do not preach ourselves," which means we do not preach our pneumatic self like the opponents do in their demonstrations of power, "but Christ Jesus as Lord." Paul strikingly emphasizes the κύριος through postpositioning.[265] This is further underlined by the continuation of the sentence: the authentic preachers make themselves the subject of their proclamation only insofar as they become slaves of the congregation, in contrast to the spiritual agitators.[266] This argumentation of Paul demonstrates that he sees the rule of the exalted one being neglected by the lordly demeanor of the opponents.[267]

They neglect, in the opinion of Paul, something else as well: *the true respect for Jesus,* the earthly one. Only the preachers who show self-denying commitment to their community recognize truly the rule of the exalted one. Only this congruence happens "for the sake of Jesus."[268]

The close relationship of δουλεία and διὰ Ἰησοῦν, as well as Paul's use of Ἰησοῦς and κύριος, confirms the result of the previous analysis, namely, that the simple name Jesus refers primarily to the earthly Jesus. The critical intent of the context of the διὰ Ἰησοῦν further clarifies the meaning of ἄλλος Ἰησοῦς in 11:4. *Paul is attacking another understanding of the earthly Jesus,* one that must have had central importance for the opponents.

Their understanding of Jesus was not defined by an equation of δοῦλος and 'Iησοῦς, nor did it correspond to the Pauline interpretation that the rule of Christ Jesus was achieved by *exaltation*. Instead, it was connected with an articulated doctrine of tradition and an emphatic doctrine of the spiritual self.[269] The latter suggests that the opponents' christology presented Jesus as an extraordinary pneumatic, as a θεῖος ἀνήρ. This must have made it easy for the opponents to draw parallels between Jesus and the θεῖος ἀνήρ Moses.

The passage 2 Cor. 4:7–16 confirms that Paul had to fight a completely different understanding of the essence and meaning of the earthly Jesus. Paul directs the attention of his readers to the preachers' fragile earthly existence, based on and anticipated by the human fate of Jesus.[270] In 4:10–11 Paul speaks about the "killing of Jesus" and about "being given into death for the sake of Jesus."[271]

According to Paul, apostolic existence is tied to the earthly past of Jesus,[272] and this tie is brought about by the exalted one. As a result, the apostle must not flee the workaday world, the realm of human frailty, but turn to it. The opponents seem to have held a contrary opinion. They demonstrated their spiritual power in the belief that it needed to be verified.[273] The fact that Paul discusses the necessary human frailty of an apostle together with the name Jesus in a polemical context reveals that the opponents' concept of objective demonstration of spiritual power grew out of their understanding of Jesus.

The use of the phrase ζωὴ 'Iησοῦ shows the degree to which Paul is responding to slogans and arguments of his opponents. This phrase occurs only in these two sentences of his writings. A close parallel is found in Rom. 5:10: "For if we *were* reconciled with God by the death of his son when we were still enemies, how much more *will* we be saved by his life as reconciled ones."[274] But the difference from 2 Cor. 4:10–11 is obvious. In Rom. 5:10, life and death are *life and death of the son*, and they refer to *two different time periods following each other*. A temporal differentiation in the depiction of the consequences corresponds to that. Life here definitely means a new epoch. This is also the case for Pauline language elsewhere.[275] He always connects life to the life of the resurrected one (unless simple biological activity or temporal existence is meant), and he speaks of eternal life, which already affects the present but is heavily determined and directed by the future.

This is not so in 2 Cor. 4:10–11.[276] The genitive Ἰησοῦ indicates Jesus' earthly existence, as mentioned above. If ζωή were meant in a future sense,[277] then 4:10–11 would have to speak of a *new* body. But this is not the case.[278] Nor can ἐν τῷ σώματι be translated simply as "corporal" to say that the life after resurrection was corporal like earthly life.[279] In that case, ἐν τῷ σώματι would have to be stressed, which it is not. On top of that, the parallel ἐν τῇ θνητῇ σαρκί makes such an interpretation absurd.[280] The subjunctive φανερωθῇ, which occurs twice, could be making a statement with a future meaning. In Paul's use, however, this verb never indicates a simple act, but instead a public revelation. In a future statement God would have to be the observer. But God is the logical subject of the sentence, and according to v. 12 the congregation is the audience. Paul is saying that the manifestation in front of the congregation is happening *now*.[281] Thus ζωή, like νέκρωσις Ἰησοῦ, refers not only to the earthly existence of Jesus but also to a mode or potential of the earthly Jesus.[282]

This way of expression, which is unique in Paul, seems to have come from his opponents. The phrase ζωὴ Ἰησοῦ was probably one of their slogans. It referred to the sensational power of life demonstrated by the θεῖος ἀνήρ Jesus in the past, which could be reproduced by his messengers since.[283] For the opponents, this manifestation of the divine was unambiguous. The dialectic relationship of "death" and "life" in 2 Cor. 4 must be Paul's.[284] It corresponds to Paul's way of thinking and arguing and to the tendency of his polemic as observed thus far. He uses the dialectic here as elsewhere to reverse the expressions and intentions of his opponents. Paul is saying the same thing here as when he speaks of the believer's suspenseful eschatological existence in other passages.

The two final clauses in 2 Cor. 4:10–11 say the same thing as the final clause in v. 7. Only someone taking human weakness and frailty seriously can experience the power of God, the vigor of Jesus, not as a glorious spectacle but as the miracle of the divine "nevertheless."[285] The powerful deeds of a θεῖος ἀνήρ do not substantiate and legitimize the appearance and preaching of Jesus' missionaries. Instead, the frailty of Jesus as it is mirrored in his proclaimers alone marks their legitimacy. God's divinity is expressed only through his preachers' mortality, for their weakness is the sign of his majesty, just as in the case of Jesus. This is exactly how Paul elsewhere characterizes the revelation. I would like to point to his statements on the revelation in the cross in Gal. 3:1, 6:12–14, and 1 Cor. 1:17—2:6, as well as to his gloss in the pre-Pauline hymn at Phil. 2:8. This theology also follows the tendency of a pre-Pauline tradition.

The christology attacked by Paul in 2 Cor. 4 differs from the one he adopts in Phil. 2:6–11 as well as from his own. The emphasis on Jesus as a θεῖος ἀνήρ rather brings to mind the christology of certain layers of the Synoptic tradition of which I spoke above.[286]

The continuation of the train of thought in 2 Cor. 4:12–16 shows that Paul is very much interested in leading his congregation away from the temptation of a false understanding of spirit and power. Paul emphasizes that the vigor appearing in his proclamation against a background of suffering and death is meant for the congregations and not for him (4:12). Death works in the preachers for the sake of life in the communities of faith. The proclaimers have become the slaves of their congregations (4:5).[287] This is directed against the manifestation of divine superiority through pneumatic performances, a proclamation which dissociates the spiritual performer from the audience and their workaday world despite a professed interest in the weal of the public.[288]

The passage 2 Cor. 5:16 has now become clearer by way of a detour. It has already been shown that Paul connects his polemics against the pneumatic propaganda of the opponents with an attack on the underlying christology.[289] We can now define it more precisely as a glorification of the earthly Jesus.[290] This prejudices already the much-debated κατὰ σάρκα as referring to the objective reality of the earthly Jesus. The opponents thought that this was an unambiguous and verifiable reality; they claimed that this reality could therefore be immediately understood.

The trend of vv. 5:11–21, already observed above,[291] together with the first "intuitive" impression of v. 5:16a, supports Plummer's thesis:[292] "They (who relate the κατὰ σάρκα to οἴδαμεν) make κατὰ σάρκα subjective, qualifying the view of the person who estimates: whereas κατὰ σάρκα is objective, qualifying the aspect of the person who is estimated."[293] In my opinion, this is confirmed by v. 5:16b, although at first sight the order of the sentence could lead to the opposite opinion. But the postposition of

Χριστόν, which initially appears to separate κατὰ σάρκα from the object and to refer to the preceding predicate ἐγνώκαμεν, actually emphasizes the object.[294] The postposition thus supports the function of the conditional clause in describing the extreme.[295] This function of v. 5:16b and its entire content would be absurd if κατὰ σάρκα referred to the verb. In that case Paul would not have had to form a conditional clause or speak in a hypothetical realis.[296] A declarative statement would have been appropriate instead. The fleshly knowing of the Christ would then be the unbeliever's relationship to Christ. To describe this relationship, Paul would have chosen a declarative statement and μέν-δέ, not εἰ καί-ἀλλά. In addition, he probably would have added οὕτως or a similar adverbial phrase to οὐκέτι γινώσκομεν.[297]

Schmithals thinks that such a statement would be impossible in *Paul*, for "how are we to imagine that Paul intends to know no one anymore in his morally neutral, psychical-physical appearance? How should one avoid this? What would be reprehensible about it? Surely Paul is not a Gnostic!"[298] And at the same place he writes: "Further, and above all, this interpretation is not possible because the Χριστὸς κατὰ σάρκα of v. 16b is of decisive significance in the salvation-history for Paul."

The qualification "morally neutral" is misleading. Schmithals also overlooks the fact that in Paul's opinion the appearance and objective reality of the object of knowledge do not determine the knowledge of faith. On the contrary, the resurrection of Jesus and the reality of the new creation are also the noetic presuppositions for the believer's understanding of existence prior to and outside the existence of faith, even for the knowledge of the earthly Jesus and his cross.

In Rom. 1:3 and 9:5 the Χριστὸς κατὰ σάρκα as such is not the point of departure or even the sole object of knowledge. Nowhere in Paul is Jesus as such immediately accessible for the knowledge of faith. In passages like Gal. 1:13–16, Phil. 3:4–11, and Rom 7:7–25, Paul indicates that a human being's objective reality prior to and outside faith does not reveal its true essence or its true meaning by itself. A radical cut between crucifixion and exaltation is always necessary, and the believer must acknowledge the miraculous identity of the exalted with the crucified one. These are the prerequisites for truly understanding reality. Objective reality looked at as such does not yield anything.

THE PRESENCE OF JESUS

The self-understanding of the opposing pneumatics and their basic understanding of Jesus as an objective pneumatic performer is rejected in 2 Cor. 5:16, as it had been before. One should note that the opponents did not limit themselves to the use of the Jesus name but employed the Christ title as well, probably also for the earthly Jesus. But that title may have been used to blur the line between heavenly Lord and earthly Jesus, to point out that the potential of the earthly Jesus reached beyond the limits of his human existence and broke them.

I have already shown the importance of continuity in the theology of the opponents and have referred to 2 Cor. 5:16–17.[299] According to 5:12, the opponents boastfully commended their own selves by praising their pneumatic gifts and experiences, while in 5:14 Paul's polemical intent is to point out that the death of Jesus has put an end to all human existence.[300] A new possibility of life is not the result of human will or authority.[301]

The opponents apparently did not perceive the death of Jesus as a turning point. They fancied that the life of Jesus was still directly accessible. They did not see that such access required their integration into the break which is defined by the cross and the resurrection. The absence of a sharp dividing line between the earthly life of Jesus and his exaltation seems to have characterized their christology.

According to 2 Cor. 13:3, the Corinthians were looking for proof that the Christ was speaking in Paul. The approach and the example of the opponents seems to have instigated their demand. The Corinthians had experienced the mighty deeds of the opponents as proof that the Christ was speaking in them.[302] The miracles of the opponents legitimated the presence of Christ.

The motif of Christ speaking in his envoys here is connected with people who emphasize the necessity of objective proofs of legitimacy in pneumatic performances. This brings to mind that the $\theta\varepsilon\tilde{\iota}o\varsigma$ $\dot{\alpha}\nu\dot{\eta}\varrho$ concept was similarly connected with the motif of tradition, as I have shown above using Jewish and Hellenistic examples: the divine man of the past entered the tradition, the storehouse of spiritual power, because he overcame the limits of his humanity. Through the tradition's mediation he communicates himself and his powers to the pneumatics of subsequent generations on the basis of an inner relationship.[303]

In 2 Cor. 13:4 Paul meets this demand and the implied criticism of the opponents with a brief interpretation of the saving events,[304] thus countering the christological arguments behind their demand.[305] Paul polemicizes against the pride reigning in Corinth and relates his own weakness to the fate of Christ.[306] In this text as elsewhere Paul sees crucifixion and exaltation as two different modes of existence of Christ, primarily in succession to each other.

Paul speaks of ζωή here too, but here he means the resurrected and not the earthly Jesus. Because of the cross, weakness is still a visible reality for the believers. The reality of resurrection, the ζωή, will be visible to us only in the future. It is present now only as faith in the resurrected one.[307] This implies that the people in Corinth already believed themselves to be in clear possession of life *now* because they did not want to know of the deeply *dividing* function of the cross and therefore did not distinguish between the earthly Jesus and the exalted Lord. The ζωή already conferred by them to the earthly Jesus was seen as continuing.

This ζωή expressed itself in the powerful deeds of Jesus and continued to reveal itself in the deeds of the present. Therefore one spoke of the δύναμις of Jesus or Christ as a continuous spiritual power. The fact that past and present could be subsumed under the common concept of power is an example for the negation of temporal differences; it is identical with the denial of two modes of existence of Christ and the claim of only one instead. The opponents may have spoken of transfiguration as a transition from the human to the divine sphere, from the temporal to the supertemporal. This would agree with the Apologetic understanding of Moses and the reports about the end of the life of Apollonius.[308] Jesus apparently was presented as a pneumatic who was continuously triumphant.

The argumentation of Paul in 2 Cor. 11:23–33 demonstrates the extent to which the image of Jesus and the concrete appearance of the opponents conformed to each other. Paul says in his counter-propaganda: "I am (even) more (than the opponents)," namely, more than they, a διάκονος Χριστοῦ.[309] I have already noted that διακονία in Hellenistic times frequently meant responsible, fateful representation.[310] The question in 2 Cor. 11:23–33 is whether the activity of Paul or that of the opponents correctly represents Christ.[311] Paul justifies his own authority by enumerating his sufferings. He is not using this chronicle to say "I am more of an envoy of Christ than the opponents because I suffer more than they." What he means instead is "I am more than they an envoy of Christ because *I can boast*—in contrast to them—*of my sufferings.*" Whereas Paul boasted of his sufferings, the opponents were proud of their spiritual experiences and powerful deeds. In their opinion (but not Paul's) these attested to the authenticity and vividness of their representation of Christ. While Paul claims that the power of the Christ comes to its completion in weakness (2 Cor. 12:9), they must have believed that the power of the Christ was present in the mighty deeds of his messengers. Paul presents his fate not only as the fate of Christ but also as a representation of the Christ; the opponents seem to have done the same. Paul responds to their power-oriented representation of Christ with the catalog of circumstances in 11:23–33. This appears to counter a corresponding positive enumeration with which the opponents justified their claim (cf. the discussion of the letters of recommendation above, pp. 242–46). Their list probably was christologically oriented, like the Pauline rebuttal.[312]

The opposing pneumatics felt close to the divine men of the past who had transcended the limits of humanity. This feeling must have been especially strong in the ecstatic experiences they had. A special closeness to the fate of Jesus, who was thought to have overcome the limits of humanness and death, was probably experienced and then expressed by the opponents. It is no accident that Paul comes to speak of the ecstasies of the opponents in a passage with a strongly christological orientation, and simultaneously debates the christology of the opponents (as demonstrated above). I am thinking of the context of 2 Cor. 5:13.[313]

Paul wants to rebuff the opponents, who are putting themselves into the public spotlight. Apparently he wants to concede that the opponents can give the congregation a pretext for their boastfulness. I have shown above that this ἀφορμή of the opponents must have been mighty deeds of the spirit and spiritual experiences.[314] Paul argues that he does not want to demonstrate his ecstasy to the Corinthians in public (5:13).[315] Ecstasy is meant for God alone. Paul can show the Corinthians only his σωφροσύνη, because it is meant for them.[316] Since this sentence substantiates the previous one, ecstasy in particular must have belonged to the repertory of the opponents' boasting ἐν προσώπῳ.

Further evidence for ecstatic experiences of the opponents is found in 2 Cor. 12:10.[317] Here too boasting is the subject.[318] The description of Paul's ecstatic experience is a climax in this fragment's train of thought. Paul had previously countered the opponents' achievements and their christological orientation with his catalog of circumstances (11:23–33) and thereby attacked their spiritual self-understanding.

2 Cor. 12:11–15 picks up this thought again and applies it to the Corinthian situation. But in between, Paul explicitly debates the problem of ecstasy. The phrase ἐλεύσομαι δὲ εἰς ὀπτασίας καὶ ἀποκαλύψεις κυρίου proves that Paul has now reached a certain point in the series of questions the opponents had raised.[319] The missing article of ὀπτασίαι and ἀποκαλύψεις and their plural form show that the subsequent paragraph will discuss a theme and not merely narrate a Pauline experience.[320] The subject of this paragraph is not only a certain vision of and revelation to Paul but visions and revelations in general. In the next paragraph, Paul is speaking of his own miracles and mighty deeds but also of more general phenomena that characterize apostles and the opponents in particular (12:12).[321]

I do not want to discuss the peculiarity of the Pauline report.[322] One should not use Paul's description of his experience to deduce the exact sequence of the opponents' experiences, but one can say that the opponents also related their ecstatic experiences to Christ, because the genitive κυρίου in 2 Cor. 12:1 belongs to the theme.

But the opponents must have ascribed a higher importance to this particular christological relationship, a higher and more positive importance than Paul did. Paul does not return to the peculiar christological relationship between ecstatic experiences and Christ in the subsequent report.[323]

Because of Paul's allusions to different heavens and especially because of corresponding parallels in Hellenistic-Jewish Apologetics, I suspect that the visions of the adversaries were expressions of a cosmic mysticism.[324] In a polemical allusion to the experiences of the opponents, Paul defines the receiving of ἄρρητα ῥήματα as the climax of his ecstasy.[325] They belonged to the repertory of motifs of Hellenistic mysticism. Paul claims that—in contrast to himself —his opponents had not done justice to the unsaid and inexpressible character of those heavenly words. No human being was allowed to make them known, yet they apparently communicated them. Paul, on the contrary, keeps a distance from that experience. His peculiar style is partly related to the arcane and private nature of the experience.[326]

The opponents boasted of their experiences and made them the subject of their propaganda, as Paul's polemic in 5:12–13 has shown.[327] It would be wrong to assume that they gave their spiritual performances just for their own sake. They wanted to proclaim the spiritual power given to them and thereby confirm their relationship to Christ and justify their apostolic existence.

The relationship of 2 Cor. 5:13 and 12:1–10 to their respective contexts shows that the opponents viewed their ecstatic experiences as the temporary climax of their spiritual ability, or—integrating their concept of tradition—as the bubbling over of the power of the spirit, coming from the depths of history and increasingly actualizing and communicating itself. It would correspond to the opponents' concept of continuity if their intensified spiritual experience can be interpreted not only as a confirmation of the connection to the past but also as a bridge to the future.

I would like to remind you once more of the ideas of transformation and transfiguration in 2 Cor. 3:18.[328] I also want to point out that Paul frequently uses intensifiers in describing the self-understanding and activity of the opponents, especially many compounds with ὑπέρ, starting with ὑπερλίαν ἀπόστολοι (2 Cor. 11:5; 12:11). There are corresponding terms and allusions in 2 Cor. 10:14–16; 11:20–21, and further in 12:7; 3:10; 4:7, 15, 17, and to a degree also in 7:4. These passages do not support the idea that Paul is attacking an escapist, world-denying, dualistic attitude but an intensified feeling of life. The dualistic moment is part of the criticism of Paul. The other side reminds us instead of the monistic and evolutionary tendencies of Apologetics.[329]

The polemics of Paul disclose that the adversaries claimed and hoped for an individual increase of life (beyond the spatial and temporal limits of human existence), not a collective increase of life like that of Hellenistic-Jewish Apologetics. But since the opponents' demonstrations of superior spiritual power swept people along, one may ask whether there was not also a collective aspect in the background. This could mean that the opponents had adopted not only the missionary conception and method of Apologetics but also its missionary goals.

This would be supported by the fact that the opponents' treatment of the past did not concentrate merely on individuals but also included collectives.[330] If one assumes that the same ideas also applied to their hope for the future, one can better understand why Paul frequently made critical remarks about the necessity of a lively relationship between the proclaimer and the congregation, a relationship full of mutual consideration and sharing.[331] That means that he was not addressing religious ostentatiousness alone but was denying that that eschatological expectation had a community-building potential, contrary to the intentions of the antagonists. Their hope for a meeting and mutual enrichment of individual and collective happiness was thus given an abstract character by Paul.

Paul's polemics reveal time and again that in his opinion the adversaries had no real understanding of the eschatological character of a life of faith.[332] If one relates Apologetic eschatology to the left-over traces of the opponents' expectations, then it is clear why Paul cannot agree with this concept of eschatology.[333] Paul is demanding what his foes reject: an acknowledgment of real limits, a real end and a real beginning.[334]

NOTES

1. The discussion of this description of the self-understanding of the opponents in scholarly literature has resulted in a good deal of misunderstanding. Therefore I took the opportunity in this translation to bring out my points more precisely, and the English text here is more of an improvement on the German text than the translation has been thus far. This is most strongly the case in the translation of pp. 274–305 of the German edition, below, pp. 264–83.

2. διάκονος in 2 Cor. 3:6; 6:4; διακονία in 3:7, 8, 9; 4:1; 5:18; 6:3; δια-κονεῖν in 3:3.

3. Käsemann ("Legitimität," 34) says: "We learn the accusations leveled against Paul from the catchwords of the Pauline response" (my trans.). On

the basis of those catchwords, Käsemann deduces not only the individual charges of the opponents but also their self-understanding, although with a result different from the one I shall come up with. This method is used by Bultmann and Schmithals too. It can be developed further if one pays more attention to the alleged leaps of thought and pauses of dictation.

4. οἱ πολλοί (again at 2 Cor. 11:18). Is οἱ πολλοί a technical term in the polemic? Could the opponents have used it to indicate their agreement with the majority of missionaries? Given the Jewish background of the adversaries' understanding of mission and the exemplary role of Jewish missionaries for those of the Jesus-faith, this conjecture is not far-fetched.

5. The question is surprising, because Paul had already spoken of his fulfillment of that task. Cf. Windisch, *2. Korintherbrief*, 99.

6. So Lietzmann, *Korinther*, 109; Philipp Bachmann, *Der zweite Brief des Paulus an die Korinther* (3d ed.; KNT 8; Leipzig: Deichert, 1918) 136; cf. Windisch, *2. Korintherbrief*, 100.

7. Lietzmann (*Korinther*, 109) bases this hiatus of thought on the psyche of Paul and the situation. Allegedly both can no longer be fully identified, only that Paul "had reason to defend his personal adequacy" (my trans.).

8. Against Windisch, *2. Korintherbrief*, 99.

9. Windisch (ibid., 108, on 2 Cor. 3:5) also presumes that ἱκανός was a "key word of the opponents" (my trans.).

10. Cf. Bachmann, *2. Korinther*, 136–37 on ὡς. According to Windisch (*2. Korintherbrief*, 101), this is a way to state innocence.

11. Windisch (*2. Korintherbrief*) and Kümmel (in Lietzmann, *Korinther*) on 2 Cor. 1:12.

12. Paul means more than "divine sanctioning of the execution of the apostolic office" (against Windisch, *2. Korintherbrief*, 101; my trans.).

13. Lietzmann, *Korinther*, 111.

14. Cf. 1 Cor. 15:9. 2 Cor. 3:4–6 is not "a kind of self-recommendation" (as claimed by Windisch, *2. Korintherbrief*, 107; my trans.). Paul particularly emphasizes the impossibility that one is able to stand on one's own before God. Paul sees this happening only as a possibility of faith.

15. Cf. below, n. 18.

16. Windisch, *2. Korintherbrief*, 108; Bachmann, *2. Korinther*, 147–48.

17. Cf. 2 Cor. 10:2. According to Bultmann, πεποίθησις here means "the specific self-awareness of the apostle" (*TDNT*, 6:8). Bultmann compares it with παρρησία in 2 Cor. 3:12. Bultmann understands the τοιαύτην as comprising 3:1–3 altogether (for these verses, cf. above, pp. 242–43 and pp. 246–49). Bultmann surmises that πρὸς τὸν θεόν is not directly dependent on πεποίθησις but on the entire sentence and "corresponds to κατέναντι θεοῦ in 2:17, 2:19 and ἐνώπιον τοῦ θεοῦ in 4:2" (*TDNT*, 6:8 n. 2). I could add that it indicates the eschatological aspect of the entire statement.

18. ὡς ἐξ ἑαυτῶν thus is most probably not "only a repetition of ἀφ᾽ ἑαυτῶν caused by dictation" (as claimed by Lietzmann, *Korinther*, 111; my

trans.). It contrasts λαλεῖν ἐκ θεοῦ with λογίσασθαι ἐξ ἑαυτῶν. I relate it, with Windisch (2. *Korintherbrief*, 108), to λογίσασθαι.

19. The parallels from Philo quoted by Windisch (2. *Korintherbrief*, 108) speak more of a missing talent. Paul here speaks of vocation instead (v. 6a). Further, it has to be noted that Paul can speak of the ἱκανότης ἐκ θεοῦ only because of the πεποίθησις πρὸς τὸν θεόν (cf. κατέναντι θεοῦ 2:17). The οὐχ ἱκανός is thus not an "expression of the religious language of humility" (ibid., 108; my trans.); instead, the following shows that it is the attitude in face of the eschatological judge. In addition, the term διάκονος (see above, pp. 27–32) speaks against this language of humility claimed by Windisch. (Note also the relationship of that term to the office of Moses in 2 Cor. 3.)

20. The term here means "ascribing a title to oneself, usurping a position" or, as paraphrased in 2 Cor. 3:5, "to ascribe to oneself the qualification and authorization for apostolic service and try to prove these personal qualities from one's successes" (ibid., 108; my trans.; Windisch also refers to 10:2, 12:6, and 1 Cor. 4:1).

21. That is the way Lietzmann (*Korinther*, 18) translates the passage (in my trans.).

22. Windisch, 2. *Korintherbrief*, 100.

23. The Hebrew text reads מִי יְכִילֶנּוּ . It thus asks: "Who is able to stand?" LXX derives the יְכִילֶנּוּ (hiphil of כּוּל) incorrectly from יכל, "being able, can," and then translates it with an adjective. Such a translation has its own weight.

24. Windisch has overlooked this correction.

25. Windisch, 2. *Korintherbrief*, 100.

26. Against Windisch, ibid. Schlatter interprets this question correctly as "No to oneself" (*Paulus*, 498; my trans.).

27. ἱκανότης could mean a divine quality too. ἱκανός in the LXX frequently renders the שַׁדַּי of the Hebrew text (Rengstorf, "ἱκανός," *TDNT*, 3:294). Rengstorf also gives references to Josephus, Plato, and others. Cf. also Plummer, 2 *Corinthians*, 85. There is an obvious similarity to what I discussed above, pp. 122–37, 155–59.

28. Gnostic motifs are (1) the universal character of revelation (perhaps θριαμβεύειν is a revelatory term too); (2) pleasant odor as an indication of revelation and a sign of λογικὴ λατρεία; (3) identification of the event of revelation and of proclamation; (4) revelation as fate; (5) dualistic motifs; (6) idea of determination in v. 16 (ἐκ-εἰς). Apocalyptic motifs are (1) Χριστός-title; (2) the contrasting pair σωζόμενοι-ἀπολλύμενοι (to be understood in a future sense).

29. The opponents perhaps provided Paul with the term θριαμβεύειν, but Paul understood it in the sense of worldwide revelatory activity, whereas the adversaries took it to mean the triumph of the pneumatic (cf. Bornkamm, *Vorgeschichte*, 30 n. 114).

30. ὁ λόγος τοῦ θεοῦ most often means missionary proclamation, if and

where such activity can be spoken of (this meaning is especially frequent in Luke and Acts). Cf. Harnack, *Lehre der zwölf Apostel*, 240–41; Windisch, *2. Korintherbrief*, 101; *TDNT*, 4:115–17.

31. For the following, see Windisch, *2. Korintherbrief*, 100, and *TDNT*, 3:603–5.

32. Further references in Windisch, *2. Korintherbrief*, 100, and *TDNT*, 3:606–7.

33. The proclamation of the opponents "no longer puts the listener in front of God but binds him to whatever the teacher is and wants" (Schlatter, *Paulus*, 499; my trans.). Strachan (*2 Corinthians*, 79) gives a good interpretation of the passage. He emphasizes that Paul polemizes here more against the promotion of their personalities and their alleged abilities than against their earning money as such.

34. Schlatter writes on the mode of operation of the adversaries, "The accommodation to others, the syncretism which acquires Jewish as well as Greek elements, proves to be the necessary mode of operation which guarantees success" (*Paulus*, 500; my trans.).

35. Lütgert (*Freiheitspredigt*, 77–78) and Windisch (*2. Korintherbrief*, 100–101) also compare 2:17 and 4:2. The false teaching of the rivals expresses itself in their conduct.

36. Cf. also the sharp invectives of Paul in 11:13–14 and their analysis by Käsemann ("Legitimität," 37) and Windisch (*2. Korintherbrief*, 341).

37. Käsemann ("Legitimität," 55) also connects the discussion on ἱκανότης in 2:12–3:6 with the debate in chaps. 10—13 and its slogan.

38. Stated cautiously by Windisch (*2. Korintherbrief*, 295).

39. On the self-assessment of the antagonists, see Lütgert (*Freiheitspredigt*, 68–73) and Käsemann ("Legitimität," 36–41). On the charges of the opponents, see Bultmann (*Probleme*, 24) and Schmithals (*Gnosticism*). The slogan "belonging to Christ" was not a catch-phrase of the so-called Christ party. It was no party motto but an individual expression of self-understanding; as used by the opponents, it must have meant that they had a special relationship to Christ (cf. also 2 Cor. 11:23 and below, pp. 251–52). Schmithals (*Gnosticism*, 196–209, and esp. 124–41) understands the relationship to Christ differently from the way I do. Schmiedel (*Briefe*, 272–73) notes that the Χριστοῦ εἶναι has to be seen together with ἐξουσία in 10:8 (because of the τε γάρ). The arrogant ἐξουσία of the opponents destroys (cf. 11:8 and 12:19). The personal acquaintance with Jesus cannot have been the decisive reason for this imagined special relationship to Christ. The καθώς . . . οὕτως καὶ ἡμεῖς in 10:7 speaks against that. Cf. the further good interpretation Bachmann (*2. Korinther*, 350–53) gives of the passage in question. He shows the connection of Χριστοῦ εἶναι with ἐξουσία and, based on that, the decisive difference between Paul and his adversaries.

40. Cf. 10:10. See Käsemann, "Legitimität," 35; Schlier, *TDNT*, 3:217;

Bultmann, *Probleme*, 24; Schmithals, *Gnosticism*, 176–79. Cf. also above, pp. 256–57.

41. Windisch, *2. Korintherbrief*, 380–81.

42. Windisch (ibid., 381) similarly disagrees with those who see this as a cautious expression to prevent complaints and distortions from the opposite camp and avoid statements which cannot be checked by others (e.g., Lietzmann, *Korinther*, 155).

43. Cf., further, Käsemann, "Legitimität," 67, and the analysis of 12:2–10 pp. 281–82. On boasting, see pp. 118–20, above.

44. On Paul missing out in this respect, see 13:3 (Käsemann, "Legitimität," 35; Bultmann, *Probleme*, 24; cf. also below, p. 278). On the appearance of Paul, cf. also Bultmann, *Probleme*, 30–31. Cf., further, Windisch, *2. Korintherbrief*, 417. The fool's speech in chaps. 11 and 12 (ibid., 315–98) is a persiflage on the self-glorifying practice of the opponents. Paul is playing the role of the bragging mimus (esp. 11:16—12:10). Here we also see—although in negative formulation—the criterion which Paul uses against his opponents: when he himself engages in competitive propaganda like his adversaries, he no longer speaks κατὰ κύριον (11:17).

On the opponents' ability to prove themselves, see Windisch, *2. Korintherbrief*, 315, 417. According to Käsemann ("Legitimität," 35 and 35 n. 16), Paul was "caused to defend his ἐξουσία" (my trans.); cf. 2 Cor. 10:8, 13:10. Cf. Bultmann, *Probleme*, 24, and above, p. 285 n. 20.

θαρρεῖν, τολμᾶν, λογίζεσθαι, and πεποίθησις could also have belonged to the repertory of the opponents (Käsemann, "Legitimität"). The adversaries charged Paul with weakness, with lack of pneumatic power; this would express itself in attitudes and actions expressed by those terms ("ἐξουσία and πνεῦμα are interchangeable terms" [my trans.]; Käsemann, "Legitimität," 35). Cf. also Schmithals, *Gnosticism*, 230–37. Windisch (*2. Korintherbrief*, 417 [on 13:3]) refers correctly to the parallels of "demanding of signs" in the Gospels.

45. Cf. Bultmann, *Probleme*, 25.

46. Schlatter (*Korinthische Theologie*, 104) believes that the opponents stressed the work in the Corinthian congregation more than missionary preaching, their real task, but he bases this hypothesis on the postulate (presupposed by him as well as by others, but never proven) that the opponents of 2 Cor. had already caused the abuses attacked in 1 Cor. I have shown above, too, that one must not distinguish between missionary work and service within a congregation. On the competition motif, see above, p. 200 n. 254.

47. On μέτρον τοῦ κανόνος, see esp. Käsemann, "Legitimität," 56–61. Paul's μέτρον and his δοκιμή are placed in doubt. The real question is what μέτρον and κανών are. That determines the understanding of 10:12–18 and of 3:1–6. Bultmann (*Probleme*, 22) correctly contradicts Käsemann, who understands this measure as "instruction for duty" (cf. Windisch, *2. Korin-*

therbrief, 310) or "installation in a vocation" ("Legitimität," 59; my trans.).
It is the measure given by the spirit in competition. A "tradition principle"
in a legal sense cannot be found with the adversaries. μέτρον is the extent of
the πνεῦμα. κανών here is the "standard of judgment" (Beyer, *TDNT,*
3:599–600; Käsemann, "Legitimität," 59; Kümmel in Lietzmann, *Korinther,* 209; my trans.). This standard "does not consist of a geographically defined missionary district, but rather of the missionary mandate proven by
missionary success" (my trans. of Kümmel in ibid., 209, against Lietzmann
[ibid., 143]). Cf. above, p. 59.

Galatians 1 and 2 do not parallel the passages in 2 Cor.; the claimed
agreement between Pauline theology and the *church,* one of the arguments
of Galatians, is absent in 2 Cor. 10:12–18 (against Käsemann, "Legitimität,"
51). The opponents of Paul in 2 Cor. were no Jewish-Christian missionaries
either, no *legal* representatives of the early church in Palestine, no שליחים
(against Käsemann, ibid., 51).

48. Käsemann, "Legitimität," 56–57; Bultmann, *Probleme,* 21. It follows
from these companions (with Käsemann, against Bultmann) that the opponents believed that they possessed a μέτρον as much as Paul did (although a
different one). The adversaries miss the "verifiable definiteness" in Paul
(Käsemann, "Legitimität," 50; my trans.). This stands against Schlatter's interpretation too (*Paulus,* 623).

49. Usually the irony of the sentence 10:12 is not felt. It follows from the
relationship to v. 11 and is emphasized by the γάρ. Paul's ἔργον is not to enter into a competition. When he then does it after all, he does it only as a
πάρεργον, as it were. Cf. above, p. 287 n. 44.

50. On Paul's dialectic understanding of μέτρον, see Käsemann, "Legitimität," 59–60.

51. Ibid., 56–57. Cf. Bultmann, *Probleme,* 21, and Windisch, *2. Korintherbrief,* 309. Against that, Kümmel in Lietzmann, *Korinther,* 208, and
Schmithals, *Gnosticism,* 186. In this matter the outside agitators behave
like the indigenous pneumatics attacked in 1 Cor. (one reason for the misinterpretation of Schmithals). The antagonistic pneumatics of 2 Cor. do not
evade evaluation and judgment; they expose themselves to it, but their
measure and proof was the manifestation of the spirit. Käsemann on Paul's
differing attitude: "Because he understands his apostolate as a gift of grace,
he cannot and must not expose it to human beings . . . , he stands outside of
the 'sarcicly' found possibilities of comparison and judgment" ("Legitimität," 58; my trans.).

52. See also Käsemann, "Legitimität," 59. Boasting without measure and
going beyond one's competence seem to have been discredited by both
parties.

53. "However, both . . . calling and blessing are the canon of the apostle
in such a fashion that they remain a function of divine grace, not becoming
available and manageable objects of the 'sarcic' sphere" (ibid., 59; my
trans.).

54. On the σημεῖα τοῦ ἀποστόλου, cf. Windisch, *2. Korintherbrief*, 396–97, and Käsemann, "Legitimität," 35, 61–71. Käsemann presupposes that Paul defends himself against an accusation. According to Käsemann, the opponents have made this concept a key term of the debate. Käsemann says, with reference to 1 Cor. 1:22, that some people opposed to Paul must have seen the performance of miracles as proof of possession of the spirit. It is improbable that the opponents thought of the first apostles only in this respect (against Käsemann, ibid., 61). The opponents must have reported miracles of their own too.

55. Signs legitimized the Hellenistic missionary because they proved the spirit, not because of any general legal requirement (cf. pp. 101–11, 122–37, 151–59). This modifies Käsemann's thesis ("Legitimität," 61–62) and his interpretation of the opponents' understanding of pneuma as "force of the principle of legitimizing which operated by divine right" (ibid., 50; my trans.).

56. Ibid., 62–63.

57. This real sign of apostleship is his continuous effort for his congregation (ibid., 70–71).

58. Ibid., 62–63.

59. This makes the apostolic existence of Paul suspicious (ibid., 50–51), according to the criteria of all Hellenistic pneumatics, including the pagan ones.

60. Therefore they accused Paul of fleshly conduct (2 Cor. 10:2). This charge refers in the context first to Paul's conduct as proclaimer and only secondarily to his existence as such. Thus this accusation is not specifically Gnostic. The opponents' reproach is a "judgment that is supposed to brand Paul as an apostolic impostor who in 'sarcic' wisdom . . . pursues all the 'sarcic' motives and uses all the tricks that Paul has already enumerated and dismissed in 1:12, 2:17, 4:2, and coherently in 1 Thess. 2:3–7" (Windisch, *2. Korintherbrief*, 295; my trans.). That means the opponents had accused Paul of being a "goët" (ibid.). Since they saw Paul as a competitor, they ranked him below themselves with those accusations. Paul does not refute the denunciations directly. He does not present a competitive counterpicture. Instead Paul tries to analyze the charge theologically, thus bringing the discussion to a fundamental level.

61. See above, p. 59.

62. See above, p. 131–33.

63. Cf. Käsemann, "Legitimität," 59 on 10:18: the δοκιμή of Paul, in contrast to that of his opponents, is not "a controllable fact" (my trans.). This makes Käsemann's hypothesis of an authorization of the opponents by Jerusalem questionable. "For it is apparent what the opponents assessed as proofs of δύναμις. It is the effective performance which does not appeal to a legitimizing legal body but convinces by itself, which impresses by powerful deeds" (Bultmann, *Probleme*, 24; my trans.).

64. See Windisch, *2. Korintherbrief*, 408–9 (but cf. p. 412). Bultmann

supposes a concrete reference to this catalog of vices too: "This then would present the 'specific Hellenistic motif of the pneumatics' liberty' which Käsemann ("Legitimität," 40) misses, not as a theme but as an allusion" (Bultmann, *Probleme*, 24; my trans.). Bultmann sees in Corinth a "congregation agitated by the competitors" (ibid., my trans.), which misses in Paul the impressive appearance of the pneumatics. I doubt that one can explicitly describe the opponents as libertinists based only on the second part of the catalog of vices (Schmithals, *Gnosticism*, 222–24). The stereotypical expressions of this part of the catalog are very different from the tactics of Paul in his concrete and elaborate discussion of Corinthian libertinism in 1 Cor. Cf. below, n. 70.

65. Windisch, *2. Korintherbrief*, 408; Lietzmann, *Korinther*, 160.

66. Sexual excesses and aberrations (Windisch, *2. Korintherbrief*, 411; Lietzmann, *Korinther*, 160).

67. Windisch, *2. Korintherbrief*, 410–11. Windisch (ibid., 415) wants to add καὶ μετανοήσασιν to τοῖς προημαρτηκόσιν in 13:2 too. But in 13:2 Paul does not talk as generally as in 12:10–11. Here the same differentiation is found as in the letter of reconciliation (2 Cor. 2:1–11 and 7:5–13). Yet this cannot mean that only a small group was critical of Paul (cf. also v. 3 and ibid., 417).

68. So Schlatter, *Paulus*, 674–76. Lietzmann (*Korinther*, 160) opposes this interpretation, claiming that for Paul those sins were removed by baptism. But 1 Cor. 3:3 shows that Paul does not think that magically.

69. Cf. 2 Cor. 13:3.

70. The hypothesis that Paul attacked libertinism here and fought Judaizers elsewhere in 2 Cor. does not make sense to me. In the introduction, I have shown why I cannot see 2 Cor. 6:14—7:1 as an authentic part of Paul's Corinthian correspondence (p. 12). Cf. also above, n. 64.

71. The opponents did not consciously cross the borders to paganism (against Lütgert, *Freiheitspredigt*, 80–87). 2 Cor. 6:14—7:1 does not contribute to this question (see previous footnote).

72. This puts the οἱ πολλοί into right light. Then it is not possible to agree with Windisch, who says, "Thus in the judgment of Paul most preachers of the gospel are avaricious and unauthorized, fraudulent people. He and his own are the few authentic, honest, selfless workers in the kingdom of God" (*2. Korintherbrief*, 101; my trans.). In referring to Luke 18:11, Windisch proves that he has not understood at all the point of Paul's criticism. Cf. above, p. 284 n. 4.

73. For documentation on 1 Thess. 2:7, see Dibelius, *Thessalonicher, Philipper*. In 1 Thess. 2:7 Paul sets off his activity against that of other migrant preachers. Cf. the continuation of this discussion, for instance, in *Didache* 11:3—12:4; *Hermas, Mandate* 11, and Lucian, *The Passing of Peregrinus* 13.

74. 11:7–11 and 11:12—12:18 belong together (as already shown by

11:1–6), although the opponents are not explicitly mentioned in 11:7–11 and Paul instead discusses reproaches coming from the Corinthians themselves. Paul directs his critical address beyond the Corinthians to the intruders who had helped to revive the resident criticism of Paul. The transition from v. 6 to v. 7 is explained by the fact that Paul claims in v. 6 to have given the most important thing, namely, his gnosis of Christ. No transitional thought has dropped out, as many commentators believe. Paul has not looked for an approbation of this gnosis which he gave openly. A remuneration would have functioned as such an approbation. For the sake of God, Paul could not allow any secret in his proclamation, and he would not permit others to honor him as a divine man. The terms ταπεινοῦν and ὑψωθῆναι are clear enough and do not need extensive elaboration (as in Windisch, *2. Korintherbrief*, 334, or Lietzmann, *Korinther*, 147).

75. Windisch, *2. Korintherbrief*, 335–40; Kümmel in Lietzmann, *Korinther*, 210–11; Schlatter, *Paulus*, 645.

76. Cf. Harnack, *Mission*, 1:183–84.

77. Munck (*Paul*, 181) claims that the Corinthians had not recognized a right of the apostles to financial support before the intrusion of the opponents. He gives no good reasons. 1 Cor. 9 speaks against Munck's hypothesis. Munck uses 2 Cor. 11:7–12 and 12:13–18 as evidence, but these texts point toward a more general and older practice.

78. Von Campenhausen ("Apostelbegriff," 112) understands this as the ἐξουσία not only of the apostle but also of everyone serving in the community. Following Lietzmann (*Beginnings*, 187), that specifically includes apostles, preachers, prophets, and teachers, i.e., everyone who because of his or her task had no time to earn money.

79. ὀψώνιον is not a set and fixed salary, as one might presume (cf. Heidland, *TDNT*, 5:591). In renouncing the ὀψώνιον, Paul understands it "comprehensively for any support in cash or kind" (ibid., 592 n. 7).

80. Schlatter (*Paulus*, 650) compares such support with the customs of the rabbis. The great difference between 2 Cor. 11:8 and Phil. 4:15, as well as 1 Cor. 9:15–18, should not be overlooked (cf. Windisch, *2. Korintherbrief*, 336, and his reference to 1 Thessalonians).

81. Cf. Windisch, *2. Korintherbrief*, 335.

82. Windisch (ibid., 338) misses this ironic paradox aimed at the opponents' boasting about fees. "The meritorious aspect consists in the fact that in Achaia he took upon himself the additional burden of a sideline occupation" (my trans.).

83. This is the strongest evidence for the aggressive, even importunate, character of Paul's antagonists, especially if λαμβάνειν means "lay hands on," i.e., a violent grasping in order to carry someone away. Cf. Kümmel in Lietzmann, *Korinther*, 211, against Munck, *Paul*, 178–79.

84. See above, pp. 97–100; cf. p. 152.

85. This does not mean that all the Corinthian believers had intentionally

and completely turned away from Paul (Windisch, *2. Korintherbrief,* 329), but the writer makes them realize that possibility. To judge from v. 14 that Paul had had no success at all in Corinth is too much (against Kümmel in Lietzmann, *Korinther,* 209).

86. Paul had refused them their right to pay and so to assess the pneumatics. But while staying with them, he had (in their opinion) granted that right to other congregations.

87. It appears that the Corinthians interpreted his conduct as not having mediated to them *all* of the πνευματικά. Cf. the reaction of Paul 12:11–18. They reproached Paul in addition for having renounced all recognition. In the judgment of the Corinthian believers, this attitude of Paul's called into question the authenticity of the foundation of the faith community in Corinth and cast doubt on the individual calling of the believer. Cf. Windisch, *2. Korintherbrief,* 390–91; Lietzmann, *Korinther,* 157–58. Also cf. above, pp. 241–42, and esp. below n. 97.

88. Cf. above, p. 239.

89. Windisch, *2. Korintherbrief,* 336. The congregation misinterpreted this renown of Paul (11:7–12), and the striving of the outside agitators for the same ἀφορμή as Paul's incited further criticism. Thinking of these intrigues of the intruders probably instigated Paul to the sudden outburst in 11:13–15.

90. More about that in Georgi, *Kollekte.*

91. Lietzmann, *Korinther,* 158.

92. This was the case with the Hellenistic-Jewish Apologists (see above, pp. 122–37).

93. On the contrary, he aspired with this renunciation a ἐμαυτὸν ταπεινοῦν (2 Cor. 11:7). Cf. also the charge in 10:1 and 12:21 (on 12:21, cf. Bultmann, *Probleme,* 30–31). People apparently inferred the failure of Paul from Paul's attitude to the question of remuneration. Cf. Lietzmann, *Korinther,* 147, on 2 Cor. 11:8.

94. Windisch, *2. Korintherbrief,* 399.

95. Ibid., 399–400; Lietzmann, *Korinther,* 158.

96. The νόμος ἔμψυχος is essentially the right of the ruler (above, pp. 76 n. 138, 131–33, 241.

97. "It had been made clear to the Corinthians that their congregation was inferior because it was founded by a 'false' apostle" (Lietzmann, *Korinther,* 158; my trans.). Cf. above, n. 87.

98. ἔστω means "granted" (Windisch, *2. Korintherbrief,* 402). The Corinthians had to concede that Paul had not burdened them, but that does not say anything about the real problem, namely, the right and recognition of the pneumatics. Paul cannot answer the question of the Corinthians as they put it to him.

99. Cf. Lietzmann's translation (*Korinther,* 158). Windisch, (*2. Korintherbrief,* 402) sees the difficulty of the passage and its contradictions, but

his solution is unsatisfactory because it does not really connect the issues of financial support and of the collection.

100. Cf. δόλῳ ὑμᾶς ἔλαβον in 2 Cor. 12:16 and εἴ τις λαμβάνει in 11:20 (see above, p. 291 n. 83). For a rhetorical question the formulation would be too complicated (against Lietzmann, *Korinther,* 159). On the charge, see Schmithals, *Gnosticism,* 228 n. 152.

101. Against Munck, *Paul,* 173. Käsemann translates with "premeditated wile," "greed" ("Legitimität," 36; my trans. from the German).

102. Cf. Georgi, *Kollekte.*

103. Thus 2 Cor. 12:18 does not speak against separating chaps. 10—13 from 8:6—7 (against Jülicher, *Einleitung,* 98).

104. The relationship of charismata and the unity of the church is no longer discussed the same way as in 1 Cor. (esp. chap. 12); Käsemann, "Legitimität," 40; cf. also what he says about Paul's renunciation (ibid., 58–59).

105. On the relationship of Paul to the community (mutual dependence), cf. Käsemann, "Legitimität," 60–61. Munck (*Paul,* 171, 181–82) suspects, curiously enough, that the amount earned by the opponents endangered the collection which was so important for Paul.

106. I cannot see a parenthesis in 3:1–3 (against Strachan, *2 Corinthians,* 79, and others). Paul immediately continues his discussion with the opponents.

107. 2 Cor. 3:1 does not interrupt the train of thought (against Windisch, *2. Korintherbrief,* 102). Paul addresses a conduct of his opponents similar to that categorized by καπηλεύειν.

108. So most exegetes; cf., e.g., Lietzmann, *Korinther,* 109. But the opponents turned the term into a slogan, not Paul. Now both parts accuse each other of the same thing: *self*-glorification without *measure*.

109. ἀνθρώπους πείθομεν, according to Bultmann (*Probleme,* 13), already proves polemical intention; cf. Lietzmann, *Korinther,* 123. Bultmann sees πείθειν as a slogan of the adversaries. The opponents seem to have accused Paul of wheedling people because he possessed no proof for the authority of his proclamation. Paul's further phrase θεῷ δὲ πεφανερώμεθα does not pick up a charge of the adversaries (secretiveness and insincerity of Paul). This statement polemicizes directly against the practice of the opposition (against Bultmann, *Probleme*).

110. On 2 Cor. 10:12, see Käsemann, "Legitimität," 58. The adversaries want to get their hands on something. ἀφορμή, according to Windisch (*2. Korintherbrief,* 177), is the material or means for boasting.

111. This speaks against Hausrath's suggestion of seeing in 3:1 opponents different from those in chaps. 10—13 (*Paulus,* 432—38). Self-recommendation and letters of recommendation did not mean to exclude each other.

112. Windisch, *2. Korintherbrief,* 102–3.

113. Ibid., 103–4; Lietzmann, *Korinther,* 110.

114. On Jewish letters of recommendation, see Str-B, 2:689 n. 1 (Acts 9:2).

115. Käsemann ("Legitimität," 44–45) and Strachan (*2 Corinthians*, 79–80) make that assumption about Jerusalem letters, disproven by Bultmann (*Probleme*, 22). Schmiedel (*Briefe*, 225) tries to explain ἢ ἐξ ὑμῶν as a transition to v. 2, with insufficient reasons: here the idea of the Corinthians as a letter of recommendation is said to presuppose the Corinthians as authors of that metaphorized letter. But the διακονηθεῖσα in v. 3 speaks against that.

If the intruders had been recommended by Jerusalem, what would such a legal institution and authorization (Käsemann, "Legitimität," 46) mean to a congregation of Gnostics? If the principals in Jerusalem had been illegitimate figures, Paul would have had an easy response.

116. Käsemann does not ask at all what stood in the letters. On the content of letters of recommendation in general, see Clinton W. Keyes, "The Greek Letter of Introduction," *AJP* 56 (1935) 28–44.

117. Windisch (*2. Korintherbrief*, 104) refers to this parallel of 3:1.

118. Schlatter's argument that the adversaries would not have worked such signs because they were false apostles is a *petitio principii* (*Korinthisches Theologie*, 110–11). And merely because the intruders had not founded the Corinthian congregation, it does not mean that they had founded no other congregation.

119. Windisch (*2. Korintherbrief*, 178) also suggests a connection between the opponents' letters of recommendation and their spirit-filled boasting.

120. On the Pauline catalogs of circumstance, see Bultmann, *Paulinischen Predigt*, 71–72. Also see Windisch, *2. Korintherbrief*, and Anton J. Fridrichsen, "Zum Stil des paulinischen Peristasenkatalogs 2. K. 11:23ff.," *SO* 7 (1928) 27–29. On the content, see above, pp. 156–57.

121. Schlatter (*Paulus*, 570–71) demonstrates with a reference to 2 Cor. 6:4 that Paul does not discuss διακονία in general but polemicizes about the authentic διακονία.

122. On the propagandistic nature of the catalogs of circumstances (esp. 2 Cor. 11:23–33, which uses the style of the royal *res gestae* and aretalogies), cf. Fridrichsen, "Stil des Peristasenkatalogs," and idem, "Peristasenkatalog und Res Gestae: Nachtrag zu 2. K. 11:23ff.," *SO* 8 (1929) 78–82. Paul's καύχησις is highly dialectic, but he had simpler prototypes. Fridrichsen unnecessarily psychologizes in seeing a "tension in his [Paul's] character between human self-consciousness and Christian self-denial" ("Stil des Peristasenkatalogs," 29; "Peristasenkatalog: Nachtrag," 81; my trans.). It is easier to presume an ironical imitation of the opponents' self-portrayal.

123. Not against representation of a claim by Jerusalem "of authentic transmission and interpretation of holy tradition" (Käsemann, "Legitimität," 52; my trans.).

124. In addition to the intimation thus far of contacts between the image of the opponents and the Hellenistic-Jewish motif of νόμος ἔμψυχος, one could ask whether the mention of συνείδησις (and its surprising communal reference) in 2 Cor. 4:2 and 5:11 could not be a polemical allusion to the opponents' conceptions of the law dwelling in the pneumatic and its relationship to the community and to the law at large. The close connection to the discussion of tradition and Christology could underline that. But the peculiar formulation of Paul does not allow any inference on the opponents' understanding of συνείδησις.

125. For this passage, cf. esp. Windisch, *2. Korintherbrief*, but also Plummer, *2 Corinthians*; Lietzmann, *Korinther*; and others.

126. On the phrase "you are our letter," cf. 1 Cor. 9:2, "for you are my apostolic seal (σφραγίς μου τῆς ἀποστολῆς) in the Lord."

127. The reading ὑμῶν for ἡμῶν tries to smooth over these difficulties. A few interpreters have even seen the expression as an interpolation (they are identified in Windisch, *2. Korintherbrief*, 105).

128. Lietzmann writes, "Here two images are mixed together" (*Korinther*, 110; my trans.).

129. Seen correctly by Windisch, *2. Korintherbrief*, 105; Lietzmann, *Korinther*, 110; and others.

130. This phrase has consistently been perceived as difficult by commentators.

131. Windisch, *2. Korintherbrief*, 107.

132. The difficulties have always been recognized. Attempts were made early to remove them by textual "improvements." Windisch, *2. Korintherbrief*, and Lietzmann, *Korinther*, report on modern textual alterations.

133. According to all the commentaries.

134. Cf. Windisch, *2. Korintherbrief*, 106.

135. Jeremiah 31 (38):33; cf. also Prov. 3:3, 7:3.

136. Ezek. 11:19, 36:26.

137. For this reason Windisch understands 3:1–3 as "a short apologetic insertion" (*2. Korintherbrief*, 107; my trans.).

138. Seen correctly by Windisch, ibid., 110.

139. "Giving life" corresponds to the OT chain of motifs indicated here, but "killing" does not.

140. Ibid., 112.

141. See above, pp. 231–32.

142. διακονία (cf. 3:7–9); τὰ κρυπτά and κεκαλυμμένον (cf. 3:12–18); περιπατοῦντες ἐν πανουργίᾳ (also 3:12–18); φανέρωσις τῆς ἀληθείας (cf. 3:14c, 16, 17b, 18); 4:4 (cf. 3:18).

143. More is said about this above, pp. 254–71.

144. Siegfried Schulz, in his noteworthy treatise ("Die Decke des Moses: Untersuchungen zu einer vorpaulinischen Überlieferung in II Cor. 3:7–18," *ZNW* 49 [1958] 1–30), also points out that Paul's argumentation in 2

Cor. 3 presupposes a specific Jewish-Christian opposing position which might be recovered from 3:7–18. This thesis signifies a decisive advance in the interpretation of the third chapter.

145. Cf. what was said above about Baur and his followers (in the Introduction, pages 2–3). A different argumentation is in Lütgert, *Freiheitspredigt*, 48–62; Bultmann, *Probleme*, 25; Schmithals, *Gnosticism;* in somewhat modified form, Käsemann, "Legitimität," 39–40; Schlatter, *Korinthische Theologie* and *Paulus*. Schlatter does not succeed—one sees that precisely in his handling of 2 Cor. 3:6–18—in showing the opponents as pneumatics and at the same time adherents of the Jewish tradition. Strachan (*2 Corinthians*, xii, xxvii), who calls attention to the connection with Philo, also sees the opponents as representatives of "Jewish legalism." That the opponents were hypocrites who obscured their true Jewish opinions is a threadbare theory which has been repeated since Baur (see, e.g., Schmithals, *Gnosticism*, 208 n. 128; cf. 208). Lütgert (*Freiheitspredigt*, 48–62) and Käsemann ("Legitimität," 39) argue correctly against this theory.

146. Seen correctly by Lütgert, *Freiheitspredigt*, 48–49; Bultmann, *Probleme*, 25 n. 28. Cf. above, pp. 27–28, 32.

147. Schulz ("Decke") does point out that Paul's argumentation is tied to opposing statements coming from another theological position, but he shies away from identifying this as the position of Paul's opponents. He establishes certain connections between the two and maintains that the opponents had made the Jewish-Christian tradition which stands behind 3:7–18 their own. But the Pauline discussion proves that the connections are much closer, so close that they can be untangled only through assumption of a uniform counterposition. This fault in Schulz's investigation is connected with his failure to investigate closely the religio-historical background of the tradition glossed in 2 Cor. 3; he also does not try to draw a profile of Paul's opponents from the history of religions.

148. See above, p. 136.

149. See above, p. 162.

150. The position taken by Paul in 2 Cor. 3:7–18 can be understood only if one presupposes that his opponents connected the γράμμα- and the πνεῦμα-motifs with the motif of Moses. Schulz ("Decke") has not noticed this. On this more is said above, pp. 263–64.

151. Cf. pp. 254–64.

152. Schulz ("Decke," 11–12) therefore assigns it to the pre-Pauline tradition. The best remarks on the concept are found in Windisch, *2. Korintherbrief*, 121.

153. "παλαιὰ διαθήκη, undoubtedly conceived of as written documents" (Windisch, *2. Korintherbrief*, 121; my trans.). The parallel to the following term, Μωυσῆς, leads Windisch to limit παλαιὰ διαθήκη to the Pentateuch. But this is too mechanical. The identification is explained by the fusion of the motif of the law with the θεῖος-ἀνήρ motif in Apologetic theology (as de-

scribed above, pp. 131–37). The world order is captured in the divine man, just as the divine power is captured in the law. Therefore the divine man can stand for the law, and the law for the divine man. The confinement of the divine within definite boundaries (whether those of a person or of a specific piece of writing) in both cases emphasizes the limitless power which is being represented here. The inheritance has become a dynamic testament. Schulz paid too little attention to the immediate connection between παλαιὰ διαθήκη and ἀνάγνωσις and the analogy with the tablets of law (which is stressed). Thus he interprets διαθήκη as "covenant," just as he generally understands the OT pericope in terms of the pre-Pauline tradition and its concept of the covenant. He does this even though the wording of 2 Cor. 3:7 offers no support, but suggests completely different motifs. Indeed, the limitation of text observation to the insertion, which itself no longer centers on the thought of the covenant, argues for a dissociation from the covenant motif. See p. 259.

154. On this concept, see above, p. 137.

155. Above, pp. 122–48. The spirit or power of God was seen as the uniting element.

156. Cf. above, pp. 27–32, 40–60.

157. The *doxa* which appears on the face of Christ is defined in a completely different manner from that which appears on the face of Moses. Not only are the origin, permanence, and effectiveness different, but also the locus of the radiance: it is the Christ, the *eikon* of God, even the *kyrios* in person (4:4, 5).

158. Above, pp. 246–50.

159. The verses 4:5b, 10–11, and 15 point to this. See above, pp. 273–77.

160. The literature on 2 Cor. 5:16 is legion. The earlier discussion is compiled well in Windisch, *2. Korintherbrief*, 186–89. The biographical interpretation, which dominated earlier, has retreated into the background today. What Bultmann wrote in *Probleme*, 12–20, is decisive. One should consider, in addition, Otto Michel, "Erkennen dem Fleische nach," *EvTh* 14 (1954) 22–24; Walter Schmithals, "Zwei gnostische Glossen im Zweiten Korintherbrief," *EvTh* 18 (1958) 552–73, later integrated into his book *Gnosticism*, 302–25. In the following, I first want to show that Paul is actually dealing with the Christology of the opponents in 5:16–17 and then find its place in the framework of the opponents' theology. The details of their christology are discussed on pp. 276–77.

161. Schmithals, *Gnosticism*, 218 n. 140, 302–15.

162. Bultmann, *Probleme*, 14; cf. pp. 280–81. In view of this opinion, which is also shared by Schmithals (*Gnosticism*, 188–92), it is not clear why "glorying ἐν προσώπῳ" should not be "boasting of outwardly visible advantages" (Schmithals, *Gnosticism*, 305). Schmithals *(Gnosticism)* himself shows clearly that Paul's opponents were concerned with proving their pos-

session of the spirit. The alternative proposed by Schmithals (*Gnosticism*, 304) for the phrase ἐν προσώπῳ καυχᾶσθαι, either "boasting externally visible qualities" or "the false, unfounded boasting of the 'old man,'" is a false alternative between two aspects of the same thing. The second is Paul's theological qualification of the first, whereas the first clearly alludes to the propaganda of the opponents (cf. on this Bultmann, *Probleme*, 14–16). The misunderstanding of the phrase ἐν προσώπῳ καυχᾶσθαι and its significance in its context appears to be a decisive handicap of Schmithals's interpretation (in "Glossen") of the progression of thoughts in 2 Cor. 5:11–21. To this is related a lack of understanding (which has already shown itself in Schmithals' *Gnosticism*) of the dialectical character of the Pauline argumentation, as Bultmann has convincingly worked it out.

163. Bultmann, *Probleme*, 16–17.

164. Ibid., 14–15. To this one must also compare what Bultmann says about *sarx* in his *Theology of the New Testament* (New York: Scribner's, 1951–55) 1:232–46 about the concept of σάρξ, and in *TDNT*, 3:648–52 about the Pauline understanding of καυχᾶσθαι. Bultmann is correct in using "givenness" as the unifying concept between the neutral and the negative usages of σάρξ in Paul (as well as in the transition from the more neutral attributive usage of κατὰ σάρκα to the mostly negative, adverbial usage of this formula). Bultmann also points out that for Paul the (sinful) σάρξ makes itself known especially in καυχᾶσθαι (*Theology*, 242–43; *TDNT*, 3:649–50) and that the phrase ἐν προσώπῳ καυχᾶσθαι in 2 Cor. 5:12 is parallel to κατὰ σάρκα καυχᾶσθαι in 2 Cor. 11:18 (*Theology*, 234–35; *TDNT*, 3:650 n. 39). Schmithals's criticism (*Gnosticism*, 305, 311) of Bultmann's concept of "worldly givenness" (*Probleme*, 15, 17) overlooks the detailed exegetical grounding which Bultmann gives it in the passages mentioned above. Yet it cannot be denied that an unsuitable idealistic—and, related to that, also an individualistic—component has entered Bultmann's exegesis of these concepts and this text. This was due to his inclusion of the opposition between "visible" and "invisible," based upon the strongly gnosticizing expression of 2 Cor. 4:18. This idealistic and individualistic component does not do justice to the "spatial" and "epochal" statements in 2 Cor. 5:14, 17.

165. Bultmann, *Probleme*, 17.

166. "In context, the question is how a person should be understood and judged" (ibid., 16; my trans.). This is extended even to Christ. The relationship of the κατὰ σάρκα in v. 16 has been discussed and clarified further on pp. 276–77.

167. For the hypothetical statement, see Georg Heinrici, *Der zweite Brief an die Korinther* (8th ed., MeyerK 6; Göttingen: Vandenhoeck & Ruprecht, 1900) 206–10; Lietzmann, *Korinther*, 125. The premise, however, is a concession to the partner in the discussion. The following conditional and concessive clauses of a polemical character are found in the fragments under discussion: 2 Cor. 3:7 (see above, pp. 245–55); 4:3 (see

above, pp. 260–61); 5:3 (cf. Bultmann, *Probleme*, 8); 10:7; 11:6, 16; 13:5; finally, compare also 11:4 and 11:20. These are partly direct quotations and partly allusions to statements made by the opposing side.

Bultmann (*Probleme*, 17) interprets v. 16b as "the most extreme example," but he does not see this statement as quoting a christology of the opponents.

The value of 5:16b as evidence is improved by this concrete reference, for at first glance a truism appears to be expressed here. If it were actually intended in this way, one would expect this statement with the main and subordinate clause in inverted order and with v. 16b as the presupposition. But Paul actually has a completely different christology in mind, with which he hypothetically identifies himself. Precisely by carrying this christology to a (hypothetical)-past, which he qualifies by using the phrase κατὰ σάρκα, he keeps his critical distance, which then becomes manifest in the following main clause.

168. This christology is dealt with in detail on pp. 271–83.

169. Cf. the parallels collected by Windisch, *2. Korintherbrief*, 189–90. Rom. 7:6 (just as much as Rom. 2:27, 29) presupposes the discussion of 2 Cor.

170. Also see above, pp. 118–19, 121, 136–37.

171. The style of Paul's argumentation and that which can be extracted (partly in reflection) of the opponents' theology do not support the view that the opponents and those of the same mind had planned and advocated an annulment of the "Old Covenant" (against Schulz, "Decke," 13–16, 18–19, 21–23). They did differentiate themselves from other Jewish missionaries and theologians. *But they differentiated themselves by an excess of tradition* (cf. pp. 172–74). Precisely on this account they could consider themselves and their propaganda superior, giving themselves out to be the better exponents of the Mosaic tradition and therefore the true representatives of Judaism.

172. Schulz ("Decke") establishes the fact that Paul is critically glossing another tradition by demonstrating tensions and contradictions in 2 Cor. 3:7–18 itself.

173. On pp. 27, 229, I pointed out the noticeable accumulation of the concepts διάκονος and διακονία in the passages under investigation. These concepts, together with the opponents' designation of function, διάκονος Χριστοῦ, played a special role in the proclamation of the opponents. Schulz ("Decke," 28) thinks that Paul's opponents must have designated themselves servants of Moses, but he does not relate this to 3:7. For him, the tradition used by the opponents comes in only at 3:7b. But 3:7b is closely linked with 3:7a by Paul's syntax and the context. The statement ἐγενήθη ἐν δόξῃ is as essential a prerequisite as the image ἡ διακονία ἐν γράμμασιν ἐντετυπωμένη λίθοις. After all, the consecutive clause requires a larger theme.

This can be seen in the OT text as well. Exod. 34:29–35 describes Moses' presentation of the tablets of the law as the decisive basis for the relationship to God and for serving God. 2 Cor. 3:7b has meaning only in connection with 3:7a. The reference to the powerlessness of Israel must likewise be understood differently from Schulz, not as *ad malam partem Israel* but as *ad maiorem gloriam Mosis*. The opposition (observed also by Schulz) of this exaltation of Moses to the following Pauline line of argumentation, with its climax in 3:10, and the complete reversal of the OT thought in 3:13, then becomes even more pronounced, while the τοῦ θανάτου in v. 7a and the τὴν καταργουμένην appear as extraneous elements. This was Paul's correction. He does not simply deny majesty to the role of Moses, but rather he assigns to it a radically different "majesty," the majesty of death. Paul does not develop this course of thought in isolation, *ab ovo*, but with reference to a wholly different direction of interpretation.

174. Above, pp. 122–37.

175. In Philo and Josephus. The corresponding sections, which undoubtedly existed, have been separated from Eupolemus and Artapanus. In the preserved fragments, Aristobulus deals only with the first ascent. The Wisdom of Solomon does depict the wandering in the wilderness, but not Moses' theophanies on the mountain. The midrash assimilated here is interested more in the destiny of the people of Israel.

176. Above, pp. 128–33.

177. Moses is described as becoming φιλόθεος and θεοφιλής in *Moses* 2.67. The synergism noted above in the θεῖος-ἀνήρ view shows in the following passage: "Inspired by heavenly love (καταπνευσθεὶς ὑπ' ἔρωτος οὐρανίου), he honored in an exceptional way the Lord of all and was honored in return by him" (*Moses* 2.67; my trans.). Exodus 33 must have been of special significance for Judaism. This text was often interpreted, as can be seen in the Apologetic tradition which is to be discussed here, as well as in the allegorical commentary of Philo. In my opinion, John 1:18 refers to such traditions.

178. ἄνωθεν ἀπ' οὐρανοῦ καταπνεόμενος.

179. The soul power of the θεῖος ἀνήρ is meant, which on the basis of the interaction of individual qualities and spiritual inspiration is now able to work from the inside outward, thus actively intervening in God's functions. Colson tones the text down when he translates "He grew in grace." (ἐβελτιόντο).

180. "In both" means in thought as in body. ἐπιδιδόναι is used intransitively here to mean "advance."

181. The translation must be weaker than the Greek. The astonishment and horror in the presence of a divine appearance is meant.

182. Emphasis mine; the Greek text: κατέβαινε πολὺ καλλίων τὴν ὄψιν ἢ ὅτε ἀνήει, ὡς τοὺς ὁρῶντας τεθηπέναι καὶ καταπεπλῆχθαι καὶ μηδ' ἐπὶ πλέον ἀντέχειν τοῖς ὀφθαλμοῖς δύνασθαι κατὰ τὴν προσβολὴν ἡλιοειδοῦς φέγγους ἀπαστράπτοντος.

Windisch (2. *Korintherbrief*, 114; my trans.) refers to this passage in Philo and concludes: "Thus Paul relies on Jewish tradition." But Windisch neglects to consult the Philonic context, and thus he does not see the extent and significance of the tradition. Paul's own relationship to this tradition is also too direct in Windisch. The mediation of the tradition seems to have been brought about through the *opponents*. Windisch also refers to Acts 22:11 and 1 Tim. 6:16. Schulz ("Decke") neglects to investigate the passage in Philo as well.

183. Cf. the γάρ introducing *Moses* 2.70. The interpretation of the text precedes a text paraphrase which justifies and explains.

The interpretation of δόξα given here one must assume also on the part of Paul's opponents, for it corresponds to the Apologetic theology described above (pp. 210 n. 354; 136; 146; 148–51).

184. In Philo's account the inability of the Israelites to endure the radiance is also set in opposition to the transfiguration of Moses. Just as in 2 Cor. 3:7, however, no opposition between Moses and the people is being developed; the contrast serves *ad maiorem gloriam Mosis* (cf. the reference to Schulz above, p. 299 n. 173).

185. This Philonic parallel explains the connection between the position attacked in 3:7–18 and the self-understanding opposed in 2:14—3:3 and in the fragments in general. Cf. pp. 258–64.

186. He condenses the pericopes into two in order to be able to leave out the episode of the golden calf. It is characteristic that Exod. 34:29–35 has influenced both depictions. Cf. also above, p. 259. For the following text also, see above, p. 207 n. 327; 134; 136 n. 365.

187. Reinach (*Josèphe*) translates πάθη with "perturbations," Thackeray (LCL, Josephus) with "disturbances." In my opinion, the concept was chosen because it can be employed in the sense of external events or inner developments, and obviously the objectifying of the latter is being described. Hence the best translation is "bad experiences."

188. Shortly afterward an important example is given of how the possibility becomes a reality, namely, in the peculiar transmission of the Decalogue, *Ant*. 3.89–101 (see p. 134, above).

189. See above, p. 135.

190. See above, p. 134.

191. My trans.; the Greek text: ἰδιωτεύων καὶ τῇ στολῇ καὶ πᾶσι τοῖς ἄλλοις ἄγων ἑαυτὸν δημοτικώτερον καὶ μηδὲν βουλόμενος τῶν πολλῶν διαφέρειν δοκεῖν (*Ant*. 3.213).

192. The relationship of this aspect of the presentation to the κάλυμμα motif is discussed on pp. 261–62.

193. See above, p. 126.

194. The passages interpreted above, pp. 127–33, must not be overlooked, especially those that speak about the final glorification of Moses (pp. 129–33; cf., in addition, pp. 148–51).

195. Here the *difference in content* of the two διακονίαι is the *prerequi-*

site for the proof of the superiority of the New Covenant. Thus the δόξα, which at first had appeared to suggest a common structure, is assigned not only differing strengths (3:10) but also differing function and nature (3:11, as well as the following). The author of Galatians 3 and 4 is speaking here. For more on the tensions and differences, see below, pp. 264–71.

196. There is a parallel between v. 13 and v. 14, and the figure of Moses is again referred to in vv. 15 and 16.

197. The emphasis on the transitory nature of δόξα and of the OT (2 Cor. 3:13 and 14c; cf. the earlier vv. 7 and 11), as well as the praise of hope and freedom (vv. 12 and 17b), both express central thoughts of Paul's proclamation. They polemically oppose a theology which is tied to the process of tradition and is enslaved to the individual self. (As for v. 17b, which reads like a summary of Gal. 4:21—5:1, I consider it absurd to deny Paul's authorship and assign it to a Gnostic glossator, as does Schmithals [*Gnosticism*, 315–16, 319–25]. The tension with the context is more simply resolved by assuming a conflict between the opponents' theology and Pauline polemic.)

The references to the "hardening" in 2 Cor. 3:14 and 15 are also genuinely Pauline (cf. 1 Thess. 2:16; Gal. 3:19–25; 4:21–31; Romans 2—3; 7; 9—11), while they radically oppose Apologetic theology. Schulz ("Decke," 12–18, 21–27) interprets those references as elements of the Jewish-Christian tradition which Paul had to struggle against. But the frequent attestation in other Pauline texts makes the proof of non-Pauline authorship more difficult, especially since then the antagonism would lose its sharp edge to the point that one could question the existence of a tradition with which the opponents criticized Paul and against which he had to polemicize.

Why should Paul have rejected a strongly critical exposition of the OT, an exposition that dissociated itself from Jewish tradition to such an extent that it spoke about an abolition of the Old Covenant (Schulz, "Decke," 13, 22–23)? Such an exposition would have developed the same relationship to the OT law as Paul in Gal. 4:21–31 (the motif of the παλαιὰ διαθήκη is discussed above, p. 250, and further, pp. 262–71, 305 n. 228). Schulz also did not consider all the difficulties which arise from the threefold transfer of the veil motif from the covered object to the observing subject (3:14a, 15, 18a —simultaneously internalized in 3:14, 15) and the respective returns to the object (3:14b, 16, 18). Conversely, the πνεῦμα concept as such cannot be denied to the opponents (above, pp. 231–34, 246–50; further, pp. 262–64).

198. For the actual message of Exodus 33—34, cf. Klaus Baltzer, *The Covenant Formulary: In Old Testament, Jewish, and Early Christian Writings* (trans. David Green; Philadelphia: Fortress, 1971) 39–43. It is significant that in context Exod. 34:29–35 appears to be an "insertion."

199. Windisch, *2. Korintherbrief*, 121; Lietzmann, *Korinther*, 115; Peter Corssen, "Paulus und Porphyrius (Zur Erklärung von 2. Kor. 3:18)," *ZNW* 19 (1919–20) 10; Schulz, "Decke," 27–30. Lietzmann (*Korinther*, 115) asks

whether Paul's polemic against his opponents (2 Cor. 4:3) has not led him to use the picture of the κάλυμμα. The only question is whether it is a reproach against the opponents or their own theology that is being cited in 4:3–4. Schlatter (*Paulus*, 525) and Plummer (*2 Corinthians*, 95, 109–18) were preoccupied with the fact that the κάλυμμα motif appears again in 4:3. Plummer writes: "In these six verses as in the preceding chapter St. Paul is sometimes answering charges which had been brought against himself, and sometimes indirectly bringing charges against his Judaizing opponents by hinting that they do what he declares that he himself does not do; and we cannot always decide which of the two he is doing" (ibid., 110).

200. According to Windisch (*2. Korintherbrief*, 135), this is linked to vv. 13–14a, 15, and 18 of the preceding chapter.

201. With Lietzmann (*Korinther*, 115) and Kümmel (in Lietzmann, *Korinther*, 201) against Windisch (*2. Korintherbrief*, 134); see Klöpper, *Kommentar*, 81.

202. As claimed by Lütgert, *Freiheitspredigt*, 74–75; Lietzmann, *Korinther*, 115; Kümmel in Lietzmann, *Korinther*, 201. Kümmel also discusses the interpretation advanced by Fridrichsen. Schlatter (*Paulus*, 525) tries to understand the passage in a nonpolemical sense.

203. As claimed by Lütgert, *Freiheitspredigt*, 74–75. According to Lütgert, the opponents proclaimed the public nature of the δόξα. But this notion gives Lütgert no help in interpreting 2 Cor. 4:2.

204. Neither Bachmann (*2. Korinther*, 180–81) nor Plummer nor Klöpper asks why Paul would have accused the opponents of secretiveness and what positive self-understanding the opponents must then have had. The opposing Judaizers in Galatia strongly attacked Paul's proclamation. If the Corinthian opponents are guilty of fraud, why are they then reproached for secretiveness, or even for concealment of the gospel? It cannot have been a concealment of the "final consequences" which Judaizers otherwise drew from Judaism, i.e., a radical nomism (see above, p. 248). Nor can one reproach Paul's opponents for intruding—in fact, Paul never does that.

205. Schulz, "Decke," 27–30.

206. Ibid., 8, 12.

207. On the difficulties of the OT text, cf. the works of Alt, Eissfeldt, Noth, Holzinger, and Rudolph mentioned by Baltzer (*Covenant Formulary*, 39 n. 1 and 41 n. 12). Cf. also Johannes Goettsberger, "Die Hülle des Mose nach Ex. 34 und 2. Kor. 3," *BZ* 16 (1922) 1–17, and Schulz, "Decke," 7 n. 28.

208. Cf. above, pp. 256–57.

209. Cf. above, pp. 131, 139–42, 148–51.

210. This interchangeability of Moses and the OT seems to have affected the formulations of Paul, who in v. 15 can speak without hesitation of Moses' being read aloud (a form of expression not otherwise observed in Paul) and in v. 16 again refers directly to the Moses of the OT pericope.

The reader has to supply the subject of the sentence from the previous remark, which had related to the OT. More on this on pp. 266–67, 269.

211. Cf. above, p. 197 n. 230 (cf. pp. 140–42, 144–45). This conception of the spirit as the divine miracle-working power, the power that changes people when they encounter the tradition, appears to stand behind the reference to the spirit in v. 18 (καθάπερ ἀπό; see below, p. 264).

212. See above, pp. 142, 162–63.

213. See above, pp. 142–48, 163–64. In Clement of Alexandria (*Stromateis* 5.56) there is a very good parallel for this and the following, which according to Casel (*De Philosophorum Graecorum*, 62–66; cf. 51–72) surely could have come from an ancient Neopythagorean source. On pp. 63; 107 n. 1; 113; 145–46; and 154 it is παραπέτασμα; on pp. 135–36 it is κάλυμμα; and on p. 92 n. 1 it is συγκάλυμμα.

214. Richard Reitzenstein (*Historia Monachorum und Historia Lausiaca: Eine Studie zur Geschichte des Mönchtums und der frühchristlichen Begriffe Gnostiker und Pneumatiker* [FRLANT 24, NF 7; Göttingen: Vandenhoeck & Ruprecht, 1916] 244–55) brought the translation of κατοπτρίζεσθαι by "to see in a mirror" back into favor. Similarly also Windisch (*2. Korintherbrief*, 127–28), Lietzmann (*Korinther*, 113), and Kümmel (also in Lietzmann, *Korinther*, 200). Corssen's objections ("Paulus," 2–10) don't hold. The parallels adduced by Reitzenstein (*Historia*, 244–55; cf. also idem, *Mystery-Religions: Their Basic Ideas and Significance* [Pittsburgh: Pickwick, 1978] 402–4, 454–59, and earlier) show that the view of the mirror and the resultant transformation (as, in general, the thought of a magical-mystical transformation) were not limited to the so-called mystery religions (nor indeed to the Gnostics) but were widespread. I think, in opposition to Schulz ("Decke," 18–19), that v. 18 also can be explained from Jewish presuppositions.

215. Windisch, *2. Korintherbrief*; Schulz, "Decke." Cf. also Corssen, "Paulus," 8–10; Schulz also discusses the problem of the *hapax legomena*.

216. Windisch, *2. Korintherbrief*, 112–13; Schulz, "Decke," 3–6.

217. How τὴν καταργουμένην could solve the aporia of v. 7 (Windisch, *2. Korintherbrief*, 114) is impossible to understand. Instead the aporia is increased by this phrase. Nor does the text allow the claim that the transitory nature of the δόξα of Moses consisted in its character as a reflection. Cf. Schulz, "Decke," 3–4.

218. The connector καὶ γάρ is already difficult. Windisch says, "Only the εἵνεκεν τ. ὑπερβ. δ. makes the connection with v. 9 clear" (*2. Korintherbrief*, 117; my trans.). Windisch (ibid., 116) wants καὶ γάρ to indicate the random connection of a new idea with the preceding statement. But that is not enough.

219. Ibid., 117.

220. Ibid., 119.

221. On the difficulties of v. 13, see ibid., 119–20.

222. Neither here nor elsewhere in the midrash do we have quotes as such. The OT words, whether directly taken over, paraphrased, or alluded to, are completely integrated into the exposition.

223. The various readings for εἰς τὸ τέλος τοῦ καταργουμένου show how soon this sentence was misunderstood (also cf. Lietzmann, *Korinther*, 112).

224. πρὸς τὸ μή expresses a purpose. Cf. the discussion of Schmiedel with Heinrici (Schmiedel, *Briefe*, 228). This argument is also given by Bachmann, *2. Korinther*, 161; Windisch, *2. Korintherbrief*, 120; Friedrich Blass and Albert Debrunner, *A Greek Grammar of the New Testament and Other Early Christian Literature* (trans. and rev. by Robert W. Funk; Chicago and London: University of Chicago Press, 1962) no. 402,5 (where the possibility of a consecutive translation is considered too). Windisch (*2. Korintherbrief*, 120) discusses the attempts of commentators to interpret away the text's reference to a conscious deception by Moses (e.g., Bachmann, *2. Korinther*, 163). See also Schulz, "Decke," 10–11.

225. Windisch (*2. Korintherbrief*, 120) attempts a paraphrase; similarly Schlatter (*Paulus*, 514) and Lietzmann (*Korinther*, 113). But these attempts to smoothen the text do not succeed. The difficulty remains.

226. Correctly Schmiedel, *Briefe*, 229.

227. Cf. the discussion in Windisch, *2. Korintherbrief*, 122; Schulz, "Decke," 12.

228. The most probable understanding of v. 14c as speaking of the end of the παλαιὰ διαθήκη (Bachmann, *2. Korinther*, 169), supported by the heavily emphasized καταργεῖται does not make the transition to v. 15 and the repetition of the idea there any easier to explain.

229. Just as in v. 14a. See Windisch, *2. Korintherbrief*, 122; Schulz, "Decke," 11.

230. Heinrici (*2. Korinther*, 131) therefore considers v. 15 to be an addition. Cf. Windisch, *2. Korintherbrief*, 122–23.

231. According to Goettsberger ("Hülle") and Corssen ("Paulus"). Here Moses becomes the "model of everybody who turns to the Lord with determination" (Corssen, "Paulus," 10; my trans.). Windisch (*2. Korintherbrief*, 124), however, correctly argues that Paul would have had to fully develop such an interpretation of the OT text. The reading of Corssen is also contradicted by the fact that Paul intends v. 16 to continue v. 15 directly; i.e., he means to speak of the Jews and the readers of the παλαιὰ διαθήκη. Nor could the text be saying that *Moses* is converting Israel (Windisch, *2. Korintherbrief*, 124).

232. "The use Paul is making of this text appears to be amazingly arbitrary" (Windisch, *2. Korintherbrief*, 123; my trans.); cf. Schulz, "Decke," 15–16.

233. λαλεῖν αὐτῷ has dropped out.

234. Lietzmann, *Korinther*, 113.

235. Kümmel in Lietzmann, *Korinther*, 200.

236. Furthermore τὴν αὐτὴν εἰκόνα is freely constructed; cf. Windisch, *2. Korintherbrief*, 128, and Blass and Debrunner, *Grammar*, no. 195,4. On the difficult construction ἀπὸ κυρίου πνεύματος, see Windisch (*2. Korintherbrief*, 127) and Lietzmann (*Korinther*, 113); also Blass and Debrunner, *Grammar*, no. 474,4.

237. See above, p. 298 n. 167 and esp. pp. 254–58.

238. If the genitive τοῦ θανάτου is dropped, the otherwise difficult integration of ἐν γράμμασιν (cf. the commentaries on that) becomes much easier.

239. τὴν καταργουμένην then prepares the Pauline addition in v. 8; cf. also Windisch, *2. Korintherbrief*, 114.

240. Plummer paraphrases the transition well: "Unlike our opponents, we have nothing to conceal" (*2 Corinthians*, 93). But the opponents are not hiding Jewish legalism.

241. It does not mean the law but the δόξα (against Goettsberger, "Hülle," and Schlatter, *Paulus*, 514).

242. See above, p. 302 n. 197.

243. μὴ ἀνακαλυπτόμενον would then be an absolute accusative, and the ὅτι sentence would be a declarative clause.

244. Corssen, "Paulus," 10. The scruples of Windisch (*2. Korintherbrief*, 124) are answered by the solution proposed.

245. Against Windisch, *2. Korintherbrief*, 127.

246. Windisch (ibid., 123) suggests a future sense for ἐπιστρέψῃ and περιαιρεῖται. That means that the text speaks of *the conversion of the Jewish people as something hoped for*. This would be the opinion of Paul, the glossator, and would correspond to his eschatology.

247. The change seems to stem from the opponents.

248. Above, pp. 262–64.

249. The exegesis of most commentators would require a concluding οὖν here (the alleged conclusion from v. 16). With δέ, the sentence in fact becomes an antithesis to v. 13. Although the Jews are not yet converted, the eschatological people of God—the people of the καινὴ διαθήκη—has already become a reality and remains open for the people of God of the Old Covenant. Thus Paul reverses the scriptural proof of his adversaries with his polemical redaction. It is not true that Paul "somehow proved too much" (Lietzmann, *Korinther*, 115; my trans.). Only by integrating himself completely into the community of the eschatological people of God can Paul argue for the truth of his apostolate against the prototype of the opponents, Moses.

250. Not only apostles and "professional" proclaimers of the Jesus-faith, but also all believers, are contrasted with Moses. Cf. also Windisch, *2. Korintherbrief*, 127; Plummer, *2 Corinthians*, 105.

251. Cf. above, p. 267.

252. Cf. the excursus in Schmithals, *Gnosticism*, 130–32.

253. See Dieter Georgi, "Der vorpaulinische Hymnus Phil. 2,6–11," in *Zeit und Geschichte: Dankesgabe an Rudolf Bultmann zum 80. Geburtstag* (ed. Erich Dinkler; Tübingen: Mohr, 1964) 263–93, esp. 285, 288–289.

254. Windisch states it this way: "'Jesus' in Paul is the name for the 'whole' Christ" (*2. Korintherbrief*, 138; my trans.).

255. This passage has been used frequently to assess the christology of the opponents. For the meaning of the "if" clauses as statements of fact and for the text-critical questions of the verse, see Lütgert, *Freiheitspredigt*, 63–67; Windisch, *2. Korintherbrief*, 325; Käsemann, "Legitimität," 37–41; Lietzmann, *Korinther*, 145; and Kümmel, ibid., 209–10.

256. Käsemann ("Legitimität," 37–39) provides good arguments (in debating Schlatter [*Paulus*, 631–35] and Hausrath [*Paulus*, 423–24 and elsewhere]). Paul is fighting against a real danger, not only an imminent one (against Munck, *Paul*, 176–78). Otherwise Paul would not claim that the congregation was being overcome by Satan.

257. Bultmann (*Probleme*, 27–28) illustrates the coherence of 2 Cor. 11:1–6 well (esp. against Käsemann's separation of vv. 4 and 5 ["Legitimität," 44]). 11:1–6 is paralleled by the concrete polemic of 11:18–23. Also cf. Windisch, *2. Korintherbrief*, 317–18, 328–33, 347–49; Lietzmann, *Korinther*, 145; Klöpper, *Kommentar*, 418, 428. Good also is Holsten, *Paulus*, 1:203.

258. Paul here uses the terminology of missionary preaching; cf. Windisch, *2. Korintherbrief*, 325–29; Schniewind, *TDNT*, 1:69. On the so-called missionary terminology, see also Albrecht Oepke, *Die Missionspredigt des Apostels Paulus: Eine biblisch-theologische und religionsgeschichtliche Untersuchung* (Leipzig: Hinrichs, 1920) 40–76.

259. With Lütgert, *Freiheitspredigt*, 53. The triad is not only rhetorical (against Windisch, *2. Korintherbrief*, 327).

260. The main charges of Paul's adversaries in 2 Cor. were theological. If Paul is speaking in an abbreviated fashion, it is not because the polemic against him was merely moralistic (against Windisch, *2. Korintherbrief*, 329).

261. If it is possible to extricate from Paul's polemic the christology of the opponents, then Windisch's questions (*2. Korintherbrief*, 325–26) regarding ἀνέχεσθε are resolved.

262. Lütgert, *Freiheitspredigt*, 64–65, 67–68.

263. Cf. Windisch, *2. Korintherbrief*, 328, against Lütgert (and then Schmithals).

264. If the adversaries had not been interested in the earthly Jesus, then Paul could not have said that they were interested in another *Jesus*. He would have had to say that they did not care for the earthly Jesus (if they had been Gnostics). This against Schmithals, *Gnosticism*, 132–35.

265. Windisch, *2. Korintherbrief*, 138; Schlatter, *Paulus*, 528. On textual criticism, see Windisch, *2. Korintherbrief*.

266. That is not servility (against Windisch, ibid., 138).

267. On the κύριος title in Paul, see Bornkamm, "Paulus," *RGG*, 5.184.

268. διὰ Ιησοῦν alludes to the unity of Jesus' suffering and death. Cf. Plummer, *2 Corinthians*, 129–31, 219; Schlatter, *Paulus*, 529, 534.

269. See above, pp. 236–37, 246–49.

270. Plummer, *2 Corinthians*, 119, 130–32.

271. My analysis of this passage will differ from that of Schmithals in the interpretation of the opponents' christology, even though Schmithals (*Gnosticism*, 163) also associates the frequent use of the name Jesus in this passage with the polemic of Paul. νέκρωσις means "killing," not "being dead" (Windisch, *2. Korintherbrief*, 145).

272. 4:10–11 has to be seen not only in connection with 4:7 but also with 4:5.

273. See above, pp. 236–46.

274. ἐν τῇ ζωῇ αὐτοῦ may even mean "in his sphere of life."

275. Cf. Bultmann, "ζάω," *TDNT*, 2:868–70.

276. Plummer, *2 Corinthians*, 130–31.

277. Lietzmann, *Korinther*, 115–16; Schlatter, *Paulus*, 533. Against the interpretation which sees a future statement here, see also Schmiedel, *Briefe*, 234, and Bachmann, *2. Korinther*, 197–98.

278. Against Lietzmann, *Korinther*, 116; Schlatter, *Paulus*, 533–34. Verses 10a and 10b mean the same body. "The double use of ἐν τῷ σώματι shows that both phases of the process are exhibited by the same object" (Windisch, *2. Korintherbrief*, 144–45; my trans.).

279. Against Lietzmann, *Korinther*, 116.

280. Plummer, *2 Corinthians*, 130–31. Schmithals (*Gnosticism*, 161) also argues against a future sense of the passage.

281. Verse 12 is not surprising at all (against Windisch, *2. Korintherbrief*, 147). One is reminded of 2 Cor. 2:14–17 especially because of περιφέρειν, πάντοτε, and ἀεί. "περιφέρειν frequently is used of a possession or a state that oneself bears constantly" (ibid., 145; my trans.).

282. Windisch (ibid., 145–46) also understands the parallel ἵνα clauses in a present sense. But the parallel naming of Jesus indicates more than an identity between the earthly and the resurrected Jesus, which leads to a double reference to the believers' ἐν τῷ σώματι. Paul wants to say more. The stressed ἐν τῇ σαρκί in the second ἵνα sentence proves that Windisch's interpretation is insufficient.

283. It is no accident that 2 Cor. 11:5 is used as an argument for the staying power of the false preachers. Paul characterizes their feeling of superiority sarcastically with the adverb ὑπερλίαν. But their pneumatic vocation had been tested and verified (cf. 12:11–12); therefore their christology, the basis for their self-confidence, must also have been right in their eyes and the Corinthians' eyes. The λογίζομαι of Paul seems to be modeled on that of the adversaries (pp. 231–35).

284. The weakness, suffering, and death of Jesus could only have had a

secondary importance for the opponents. If they were mentioned at all, then it was only in a heroic sense, i.e., as part of an unequivocal verification of the superiority of Jesus (cf. pp. 156–57).

285. On the Pauline understanding of ζωή, also cf. Bultmann, *Probleme*, 13.

286. Pp. 170–74. In developing his christology, Paul did not ignore the material and the tendencies of the evolving Jesus tradition. He was fully aware of them and consciously rejected a certain tendency and justification of the formation of the Jesus tradition. He opposed the attempts to portray Jesus' life as an unambiguous manifestation of the divine, which in his eyes would hide the scandal of the cross and the humanity of Jesus and would replace the eschatological revelation of God with historically tangible "proofs of God."

287. Also cf. Bultmann, *TDNT*, 3:20–21. The strictly eschatological view contradicts the opponents' understanding of christology and proclamation.

288. According to Paul, the preacher of the Jesus-faith should not spread his or her knowledge about Jesus but rather take up Jesus' fate. This is not the grandiose fate of a θεῖος ἀνήρ, but weakness, suffering, and dying. In a true contemplation of Jesus' life one is not edified by legendary power displays of Jesus. Paul thinks that someone taking Jesus' fate seriously has to obediently tie his or her own humanity to the exalted Lord and has to accept Jesus' humanity with all its weakness. In emphasizing Jesus' weakness, Paul takes the earthly fate of Jesus much more seriously than his antagonists do. He takes it so seriously that he dares to adopt Jesus' fate as his own. Paul does not report on Jesus' earthly life because Jesus has become his *kyrios*; the earthly life of this *kyrios* has become the fate of Paul. "In refusing to make Jesus of Nazareth the hero of a tradition, Paul conserved the power that would perpetuate that tradition as a living faith" (Strachan, *2 Corinthians*, 112, on 5:16).

289. Pp. 252–54, above.

290. Cf. also Schlatter, *Paulus*, 563–64.

291. Pp. 252–54.

292. The "intuitive" impression of v. 5:16a in Schmithals, *Gnosticism*, 309.

293. Plummer, *2 Corinthians*, 176.

294. Windisch, *2. Korinthians*, 185; Schmithals, *Gnosticism*, 309.

295. Cf. on this above, p. 253.

296. Again cf. p. 253 above. A similar argument is in Schmithals, *Gnosticism*, 309–10.

297. More on the relationship of κατὰ σάρκα to its context in Bultmann, *Theology*, 234, and idem, *Probleme*, 16. Bultmann decides to associate κατὰ σάρκα with the object. Michel ("Erkennen," 23) contradicts that without a sufficient argument. Seen abstractly, Windisch could be correct in writing, "In my opinion, both versions boil down to the same motivation,

and a distinction is impossible: if "sarcic" conditions assert themselves in a judgment, they will usually appear with the subject as well as the object; therefore, just as in καυχῶνται κατὰ σάρκα the modality and content of comprehension cannot really be distinguished" (2. *Korintherbrief*, 185; my trans.). But I would argue that the text calls for a differentiation.

298. Schmithals, *Gnosticism*, 310.

299. Pp. 246–50, 252–54.

300. On the polemical intent, see Bultmann, *Probleme*, 13–15; cf. Michel, "Erkennen," 22. Windisch (2. *Korintherbrief*, 186) opposes this interpretation with insufficient arguments. The death of Jesus is not seen as a turning point for Paul if one interprets vv. 14–15 as a mystical or ethical statement (ibid., 182–83). Paul is not giving a differentiation of personal piety in these verses, and v. 16 does not refer to the personal experience of conversion (against Windisch). The entire historic existence of the human race is meant. Lietzmann (*Korinther*, 129) also does not see the full implications of the text in question when he makes πάντες ἀπέθανον an ancillary thought and v. 16 an idea on the side. On the polemics of vv. 12 and 14, cf. Schlatter, *Paulus*, 557–60.

301. νῦν means the beginning of the new eon in a fundamental and general sense; cf. Bultmann, *Probleme*, 17, and Kümmel in Lietzmann, *Korinther*, 205.

302. I assume that the opponents are behind the Corinthian demand quoted by Paul because the intruding agitators had brought about the new conflict. Their claimed possession and demonstration of the spirit played an important role in the conflict, particularly in their criticism of Paul. See the next note too.

303. See above, pp. 129–33, 137–48, 155–64, 167–74. Hellenistic-Jewish Apologetics saw the great persons of the past as representatives of the spirit in the present and as contributors (through their life's work) to the tradition as a treasure house of the spirit. Based on this accumulated treasure, the divine men of the present could pursue their own spiritual career. They would represent the spiritual tradition and power at large but not any great person of the past in particular. Pagan Hellenism also thought that particular *persons* of the past could be reincorporated in divine men of the present. The most impressive examples are the figures of Pythagoras and Alexander the Great. Reitzenstein discusses how Hellenistic paganism represented the spiritual past in the present and how that related to Judaism, but he narrows it all down to the context of mysticism. In fact, this is a much wider phenomenon of Hellenism in which Hellenistic Judaism shares in its own way. Gnosticism participates in this phenomenon as well, but again in a particular fashion. It certainly is not the only representative (against Schmithals, *Gnosticism*, 193–96).

304. Käsemann ("Legitimität") questions whether Paul in 13:4 quotes a fixed formula (against Windisch, 2. *Korintherbrief*, 418).

305. Cf. Schlatter (*Korinthische Theologie*, 88), although 2 Cor. 13:4 does not attack the same position as 1 Cor. 1:25 and 28.

306. "The earthly frailty is but a component of what Paul calls weakness" (Käsemann, "Legitimität," 53; my trans.). "His ἀσθένεια clarifies his Χριστοῦ εἶναι in the sense of discipleship of the crucified one." ἀσθένεια appears "at the same time as an attribute of humanness and of revelation" (ibid., 55; my trans.).

307. Ibid., 55–56.

308. For the Apologetic understanding of Moses, see pp. 126–33, 149, 172–74. For Apollonius, see Philostratus, *Life of Apollonius* 8.28–29. Also above, pp. 157–58.

309. Perhaps one could add "and thus the *right* superapostle." The passage is definitely a persiflage of the self-understanding of the opponents.

310. Above, pp. 27–32.

311. On the Pauline christology, see Käsemann, "Legitimität," 53–56.

312. Perhaps 2 Cor. 11:32–33 responds to a use of the Abraham tradition mentioned above, p. 51.

313. I have already shown that 5:13 is polemically oriented (above, p. 282). ἐξέστημεν in 5:13 is not describing a charge by the adversaries that Paul is "irresponsible" (Käsemann ["Legitimität," 36 n. 36; my trans.] and Lietzmann [*Korinther*, 124] contemplate that). The word does not have the same meaning as the ἀφροσύνη Paul is reproached with, according to 11:16; cf. Windisch, *2. Korintherbrief*, 179; Kümmel in Lietzmann, *Korinther*, 204. Neither does 2 Cor. 5:13 quote a charge of the opponents (against Schlatter, *Paulus*, 557–58).

314. P. 293 n. 110.

315. Paul's ἀφορμή is everything that he writes in his letters (Bultmann, *Probleme*, 14), esp. something like 2 Cor. 6:4–10. Nothing intimates here that Paul would have to answer a charge that he had made false use of his ecstatic experiences (against Windisch, *2. Korintherbrief*, 179–80).

316. Käsemann, "Legitimität," 67; Bultmann, *Probleme*, 15.

317. Cf. Lütgert, *Freiheitspredigt*, 71–73; Schlatter, *Korinthische Theologie*, 83; Käsemann, "Legitimität," 63–66; Bultmann, *Probleme*, 14–15, 25. Yet Käsemann ("Legitimität," 40) has his doubts with respect to the interpretation of the passage just presented. On the text criticism of 12:1, see Windisch, *2. Korintherbrief*, 367; Lietzmann, *Korinther*, 152; Kümmel in Lietzmann, *Korinther*, 212; and Schmithals, *Gnosticism*, 209–10. Lietzmann is the most convincing.

318. 2 Cor. 12:1, 5–6. On the relationship of 12:1–10 to 3:6, see Strachan, *2 Corinthians*, xxv–xxvi, with a reference to Philo. Strachan sees the visions and ecstasies of the opponents "as authenticating their teaching. Paul is reluctantly compelled to meet them on their own ground" (ibid., 30).

319. Käsemann ("Legitimität," 63–66) disregards 12:1 completely. On

ἐλεύσομαι as the sign of a transition to a new topic, see Windisch, *2. Korintherbrief*, 369, and BAGD, "ἔρχομαι."

320. Against Windisch (*2. Korintherbrief*, 368–69), who draws the opposite conclusion from the missing article.

321. It is impossible to claim that Paul here wants to emphasize an advantage which his opponents did not have (against Klöpper *[Kommentar]* and Schmiedel *[Briefe]*); after all, Paul is speaking only of *one* vision of his own. Further support for the assumption that Paul is here addressing the ecstatic piety of his opponents in Schmithals, *Gnosticism*, 209–18.

322. Windisch (*2. Korintherbrief*, 369–80) notes many religio-historical parallels. On the theological issue, consult Käsemann, "Legitimität," 63–71 (includes a discussion of secondary literature).

323. Neither for Paul nor for his adversaries is a vision of Christ reported here. The κυρίου in 2 Cor. 12:1 is not an objective but a subjective genitive, in the case of Paul certainly an author's genitive. Kümmel (in Lietzmann, *Korinther*, 212) brings further arguments against Schlatter's (*Paulus*, 658) opinion that Paul here wanted to describe a vision in which Christ was the object. κυρίου does not mean God but Christ (against Strachan, *2 Corinthians*, 30). Perhaps the adversaries understood κυρίου in the sense of a possessive genitive and meant exemplary experiences of Jesus (similar to the transfiguration).

324. For the parallels in Hellenistic-Jewish Apologetics, see above, pp. 146–48.

325. Käsemann, "Legitimität," 63–64.

326. Ibid., 67. It is a σημεῖον for "eschatological events that have not yet occurred" (ibid., 68; my trans.). But Paul is thinking less of a unique experience than of a private experience (against Käsemann, "Legitimität," 64, 66). This is proven by the fact that Paul here compares his experience with those of others. He discusses contemporary ideas, and he próves that he understands the syncretistic terminology of his antagonists very well (against Schmithals, *Gnosticism*, 210–13, and frequently elsewhere). But in a masterful way he dialectically refutes the conception behind the terminology. Whereas Schmithals describes the Pauline intentions well, his description of the background of the opposing position is questionable. In particular, I do not accept Schmithals's claim that the discussion in 2 Cor. 12:1–10 presupposes the Gnostic myth. In this passage there is nothing to be found that is not already there in the multifarious pneumatic, mystical, and ecstatic movements of Hellenism, Gnostic and non-Gnostic movements alike. There is nothing specifically Gnostic in the passage, nothing that could be explained only on a Gnostic basis. The passage 2 Cor. 5:1–10 does not bear on 12:1–10 at all. (See Georgi, "Rez. v. W. Schmithals").

327. The point of the text is missed if one assumes that it wants to underline the superiority of *Paul* (against Lietzmann, *Korinther*, 153, and others).

328. Pp. 262–64.

329. Above, pp. 122–29, 148–51.

330. Like Israel (see above, pp. 40–60, 246–50, 254–58).

331. Cf. the passages mentioned above, pp. 238–46, 270, 272–76, especially the fact that Paul applies this type of mutual relationship to future existence too (2 Cor. 4:14; 13:4).

332. Already in 2 Cor. 2:14–17. Then in 3:3, 8–12, 16; 4:14–18; 5:1–10; 5:14–21, and so on.

333. On eschatology of Jewish Apologetics, see above, pp. 148–51.

334. Especially clearly in 2 Cor. 4:5–6 and 5:16–17.

Conclusion

THE RELATIONSHIP OF PAUL
AND HIS OPPONENTS

The study has shown that the epistolary fragments 2 Cor. 2:14—
7:4 and 2 Cor. 10—13 attack the activity of migrant preachers of
Jewish origin who were working for the early church. They had arrived in the Corinthian Jesus-community after the letter 1 Cor., and
they were successful in winning over a majority of the believers.
These missionaries came from the world of Hellenistic-Jewish Apologetics, and they successfully entered on the inheritance of Jewish
mission. In so doing they followed a trend in the missionary development of the early church. Those intruders had already gained
great prestige through their readiness and ability to compete with
Jewish and pagan pneumatics and missionaries before they entered
Corinth. They certainly were willing to compete with other agents
of the Jesus-faith too, as their attitude toward Paul proves. In Corinth they built on their prestige to further their own work and to dis-
mantle Paul's influence, which in their opinion was destructive for
the church and the Jesus-faith.

Imitating the Jewish missionaries, the opponents advertised their
Jewish particularities as a critical potential vis-à-vis their competitors and as propagandistic attractions. This had brought them great
success among believers and nonbelievers. The opponents combined an elaborate concept of tradition with a pronounced self-understanding. An essential link was provided by the θεῖος ἀνήρ
christology. Through retrospective views of the past, demonstrations of the power of the spirit in the present, and ecstatic break-
throughs into the future and the beyond, they augmented their

present existence. They apparently anticipated a glorified future. The aim of their missionary efforts was probably to let people participate in that future. Their peculiar appearance and their theology did not contradict the scale of religious values operative in the Hellenistic world; instead, they were related to that scale and were therefore promising and attractive.

Paul sees his very existence threatened by these intruders, for they attack his function as a missionary, the center of his life. Paul answers to the opponents' reproach that he disregards the glory of God as it is available in the tradition and in the present, that he is blocking it instead of assisting it in its increasing success, as would be appropriate for a missionary. Paul describes apostolic existence and the life of faith in general as conditioned by the "now" of God, by the eschatological moment. The presence of the Lord is meant, not the overbearing presence of the pneumatic who is trying to deify himself and humanity.

The past is not simply the time before, leading into and out of the present, but it is the opposite of the present. The Lord through his triumph has elevated the present and has turned the time before it into the ἀρχαῖα. The preacher should not advertise continuity as the program of faith and as a proof of God's power. The proclaimer must not repristinate the past in the message for today; he or she must let the past become and remain the past and recognize its everyday and profane character. There is no reason to glorify or to hide the past. After discovering that the past is human, the preacher can profess to relive it.

Paul's thinking is always based on the presence of the Lord, and his hope remains centered on him. Consequently, he does not need to prove and demonstrate the spirit of God on the basis of the course of history. He criticizes any spiritually glorifying falsification of what has happened and what is happening. His criticism is motivated by the presence of the crucified and exalted Lord. Paul knows that he stands at the end of history as well as at its beginning. This radical eschatological orientation has taught him to see the secularity of history which liberates him from historical relationships. The present existence of Paul is molded by the true past of Jesus of Nazareth. It is also conditioned by the fate of his congregations and by his missionary activity.

It should not be overlooked that Paul was forced to reflect again on the essence of a life of faith, and missionary existence in particular, by representatives of the universalistic traditions and tendencies of Judaism, merely modified by a Jesus perspective. Paul thus was challenged to reexamine the relationship to his Jewish tradition and thoroughly scrutinize the legitimacy of the proclamation of Jesus and the founding of Jesus communities in the face of the claims and demands raised by the word of the OT and its tradition.

In the Epistle to the Romans, written a few months after these fragments, Paul gives a final account about his reflections. What he says in Romans appears to be formulated in the face of a liberal and universal Judaism with an enormous missionary impulse. The first three chapters of Romans already demonstrate that. The interpretation of Romans would have to recognize that the most "Protestant" form of Judaism provided the foil for Paul's critical argumentation in his last letter.

THE RELATIONSHIP OF PAUL AND
HIS OPPONENTS TO THE
CORINTHIAN CHURCH

The thesis presented states that the opponents of Paul in 2 Cor. were of a religio-historical formation and theology different from the indigenous Corinthian believers with whom Paul had to wrestle in 1 Cor. The difference between the discussions of the first and the second letters to the Corinthians, as well as the references of 2 Cor. 3:1 and 11:4 to a foreign provenance of the adversaries, has led to this thesis. The final picture distinguishes these adversaries more clearly from the opponents in 1 Cor. who were residents of the community. Both groups believed in Jesus Christ, but the adversaries in 1 Cor. were Gnostics, and those of 2 Cor. were shaped by Hellenistic-Jewish Apologetics.

How was it possible for the intruders to gain the support of the residents against Paul? Both Hellenistic-Jewish Apologetics and Jewish speculative mysticism, which later turned into Gnosticism, were parts of or at least indebted to the Jewish wisdom movement. Corinthian Gnosticism either originated in Jewish Gnosticism or was connected with it through some pagan links. In any case there were relationships between Apologetics and Gnosticism.

These common features were strengthened by the generally used language of Hellenistic syncretism. Both the intruders and the residents valued the immediacy and intensity of the possession of the spirit as well as the demonstrations of its superiority (especially in the form of ecstatic phenomena).

Nor can it be denied that the θεῖος ἀνήρ concept, despite its emphasis on historical reification, carried a certain docetic component which expressed itself in a tendency to glorify reality. This tendency may have been noticed more easily by a Gnostic, even more strongly than actually intended.

Although Gnostics were not strongly interested in the concept of continuity as such, they were familiar with the concept of the primeval religion and could appreciate the idea of tradition as an archive of the spirit. The Gnostics were also acquainted with the allegorical exegesis of texts. In addition, they were faced with the impressive appearance and offering of the intruders. They were not only imposing, but apparently also convincing, and they had already been acknowledged and recommended by other congregations. The intruding apostles could further strengthen their position if they were able to reawaken and strengthen the opposition against Paul which Paul and Timothy had silenced before. In that they were successful.

Paul attempts (2 Cor. 2:14—7:4) to drive a wedge between the congregation and the intruding opponents. He shows that the opponents do not really understand revelation or salvation and therefore have no real eschatology. He argues that they have a very different relationship to history and the world than the Corinthian Gnostics. Paul points out that the christology of the intruders should not suit the Corinthians at all, given their presuppositions.

Whereas Paul occasionally took an anti-Gnostic line in 1 Cor., he does not hesitate to use a good number of Gnostic concepts in 2 Cor. They are part of his Jewish theological inheritance. He employs them now to make it clear to the Corinthians that if they considered their own theological presuppositions they would have to be on his side, not on that of the migrant preachers opposing Paul. This Gnosticizing approach of Paul finds its climax in 2 Cor. 5:1–10. I have discussed that elsewhere.[1]

It is surprising that Paul's tactic was not successful. The letter represented by the fragment 2:14—7:4 did not strike home despite its clever approach and its rich theological content. Instead it is the subsequent letter in which Paul risks his apostolic existence and makes a fool of himself—of which we have a fragment in 2 Cor. 10—13—that breaks the spell.[2] The effort of Titus contributed too.

Contemplating the fate of Pauline theology and missionary work and the later Christian development, one is at first inclined to consider the victory of Paul in Corinth merely a retarding element within a history which the spiritual relatives of Paul's opponents increasingly dominated. In the form of the Lukan writings, they even became the executors of Paul. In the second century they influenced the destiny of the church and its theology to a considerable degree.

But history is not that simple and continuous. A glance at the NT discloses a variety of theologies and their effects. Mainly because of Luke, Paul's voice was not forgotten, whereas the name and the work of the opponents of Paul in 2 Cor. were not preserved. History in its inconsistency has also brought it about that our only knowledge of those important and influential theologians of the first generation comes not from their kindred author Luke but from Paul.

NOTES

1. In Georgi, Review of W. Schmithals, *Die Gnosis in Korinth*.
2. See above, pp. 16–18.

Bibliography 1

Altheim, Franz. *A History of Roman Religion* (New York: Dutton, 1937; London: Methuen, 1938).

Bachmann, Philipp. *Der zweite Brief des Paulus an die Korinther* (3d ed.; KNT 8; Leipzig: Deichert, 1918).

Baltzer, Klaus. *The Covenant Formulary: In Old Testament, Jewish, and Early Christian Writings* (trans. David E. Green; Philadelphia: Fortress, 1971).

Baron, Salo W. *A Social and Religious History of the Jews* (2d rev. ed.; New York: Columbia University Press, 1952).

Bauer, Walter. *Die Briefe des Ignatius von Antiochien und der Polykarpbrief* (HNT Supp. vol. 2; Tübingen: Mohr, 1920).

———. *A Greek-English Lexicon of the New Testament and Other Early Christian Literature* (trans. and ed. William F. Arndt, F. Wilbur Gingrich, and Frederick W. Danker; Chicago: University of Chicago Press, 1979).

———. *Orthodoxy and Heresy in Earliest Christianity* (ed. Robert A. Kraft and Gerhard Krodel; Philadelphia: Fortress, 1971).

Bauernfeind, Otto and Michel, Otto, trans. and ed., *Flavius Josephus, De bello judaico: Der jüdische Krieg* (Bad Homburg: Gentner, 1960).

Baur, Ferdinand C. "Die Christuspartei der korinthischen Gemeinde," in *Ausgewählte Werke in Einzelausgaben* (ed. Klaus Scholder; Stuttgart and Bad Cannstatt: Fromann, 1963) 1:1–146.

———. *Paul the Apostle* (London and Edinburgh: Williams & Norgate, 1875–76).

Becker, Heinz. *Die Reden des Johannesevangeliums und der Stil der gnostischen Offenbarungsreden* (FRLANT 68, NF 50; Göttingen: Vandenhoeck & Ruprecht, 1956).

Betz, Hans D., *Lukian von Samosata und das Neue Testament* (TU 76; Berlin: Akademie, 1961).

Bieler, Ludwig. *ΘΕΙΟΣ ΑΝΗΡ: Das Bild des "göttlichen Menschen" in Spätantike und Frühchristentum*, 2 vols. in 1 (Darmstadt: Wissenschaftliche Buchgesellschaft, 1967).

321

Blass, Friedrich, and Debrunner, Albert. *A Greek Grammar of the New Testament and Other Early Christian Literature* (trans. and rev. Robert Funk; Chicago: University of Chicago Press, 1961).

Blau, Ludwig. *Das altjüdische Zauberwesen* (Strassburg: Trübner, 1898).

Bolkestein, Hendrik. *Wohltätigkeit und Armenpflege im vorchristlichen Altertum: Ein Beitrag zum Problem "Moral und Gesellschaft"* (Utrecht: Oosthoek, 1939).

Boll, Franz J. *Aus der Offenbarung Johannis: Hellenistische Studien zum Weltbild der Apokalypse* (Leipzig: Teubner, 1914).

Bornkamm, Günther. *Early Christian Experience* (trans. Paul Hammer; New York: Harper & Row, 1969).

———. *Das Ende des Gesetzes: Gesammelte Aufsätze 1* (2d ed.; BEvTh 16; Munich: Kaiser, 1958).

———. *Jesus of Nazareth* (trans. Irene and Frazer McLucky and James M. Robinson; New York: Harper & Row, 1960).

———. *Studien zu Antike und Urchristentum: Gesammelte Aufsätze 2* (BEvTh 28; Munich: Kaiser, 1958).

———. *Die Vorgeschichte des sogenannten Zweiten Korintherbriefs* (SHAW. PH 2, 1961. Heidelberg: Winter, 1961). Reprinted in *Geschichte und Glaube 2: Gesammelte Aufsätze 4* (BEvTh 53; Munich: Kaiser, 1971) 162–94.

Bousset, Wilhelm. "Gnosis," PW 7 (1912) 1502–34.

———. *Hauptprobleme der Gnosis* (FRLANT 10; Göttingen: Vandenhoeck & Ruprecht, 1907).

———. *Jüdisch-christlicher Schulbetrieb in Alexandrien und Rom* (FRLANT 23, NF 6; Göttingen: Vandenhoeck & Ruprecht, 1915).

———. *Die Religion des Judentums* (3d rev. ed. by Hugo Gressmann; HNT 21; Tübingen: Mohr, 1966).

———. "Der zweite Brief an die Korinther," in Wilhelm Bousset and Wilhelm Heitmüller, eds., *Die Schriften des Neuen Testaments* (Göttingen: Vandenhoeck & Ruprecht, 1917) 2:141–90.

Brandt, Wilhelm. *Elchasai, ein Religionsstifter und sein Werk: Beiträge zur jüdischen, christlichen und allgemeinen Religionsgeschichte* (Leipzig: Hinrichs, 1912).

Bréhier, Émile. *Les idées philosophiques et religieuses de Philon d'Alexandrie* (3d ed.; Paris: Vrin, 1950).

Bultmann, Rudolf, *Exegetische Probleme des zweiten Korintherbriefes* (SyBUSup 9; Uppsala: Wretman, 1947).

———. *The Gospel of John: A Commentary* (trans. G. R. Beasley-Murray; Philadelphia: Westminster, 1971).

———. *The History of the Synoptic Tradition* (trans. John Marsh; New York: Harper & Row, 1963).

———. *Primitive Christianity in Its Contemporary Setting* (trans. Reginald Fuller; Cleveland: World Publishing, Meridian Books, 1956).

――――. *Der Stil der paulinischen Predigt und die kynisch-stoische Diatribe* (FRLANT 13; Göttingen: Vandenhoeck & Ruprecht, 1910).

――――. *Theology of the New Testament* (trans. Kendrick Grobel; New York: Scribner's, 1951–55).

――――. *Das Verhältnis der urchristlichen Christusbotschaft zum historischen Jesus* (SHAW. PH 3, 1960; Heidelberg: Winter, 1961).

Calvin, John. *Commentary on the Epistles of Paul the Apostle to the Corinthians* (Calvin's Commentaries 20; Grand Rapids: Baker Book House, 1981 repr.).

Campenhausen, Hans von. *Ecclesiastical Authority and Spiritual Power in the Church of the First Three Centuries* (trans. John Baker; Stanford: Stanford University Press, 1969).

――――. "Der urchristliche Apostelbegriff," *StTh* 1 (1947) 96–130.

Casel, Odo. *De Philosophorum Graecorum Silentio Mystico* (Giessen: Töpelmann, 1919).

Chrysostom, John. *Homilies on the Second Epistle to the Corinthians* (trans. J. B. Morris; Library of the Fathers 8; Oxford: Oxford University Press, 1841).

――――. *Homilies on the Epistles of Paul to the Corinthians* (NPNF ser. 1, vol. 12; Edinburgh: T. & T. Clark, 1889).

Clemen, Carl. "Die Missionstätigkeit der nichtchristlichen Religionen," *ZMR* 44 (1929) 225–43.

Cohn, Leopold, and Wendland, Paul, eds. *Philonis Alexandrini opera quae supersunt* (7 vols.; Berlin: De Gruyter, 1926).

Conzelmann, Hans. *The Theology of St. Luke* (trans. Geoffrey Buswell; New York: Harper & Row; London: Faser, 1960).

Corssen, Peter. "Paulus und Porphyrius (Zur Erklärung von 2. Kor. 3: 18)," *ZNW* 19 (1919–20) 2ff.

Cumont, Franz. *The Oriental Religions in Roman Paganism* (New York: Dover, 1956). German: *Die orientalischen Religionen im römischen Heidentum* (Stuttgart: Teubner, 1975).

――――. *Recherches sur le symbolisme funéraire des Romains* (Paris: Geuthner, 1942).

Dahl, Nils A. *Das Volk Gottes: Eine Untersuchung zum Kirchenbewusstsein des Urchristentums* (Darmstadt: Wissenschaftliche Buchgesellschaft, 1963).

Dalbert, Peter. *Die Theologie der hellenistisch-jüdischen Missionsliteratur unter Ausschluss von Philo und Josephus* (ThF 4; Hamburg: Reich, 1954).

Daniélou, Jean. *Philon d'Alexandrie* (Paris: Fayard, 1958).

Deissmann, Adolf. *Light from the Ancient East* (trans. Lionel R. M. Strachan; New York and London: Hodder & Stoughton, 1911). German: *Licht vom Osten: Das neue Testament und die neuentdeckten Texte der hellenistisch-römischen Welt* (4th rev. ed.; Tübingen: Mohr, 1923).

Deissner, Kurt. "Das Sendungsbewusstsein der Urchristenheit," *ZSTh* 7 (1929–30) 772–90.

Dibelius, Martin. *An die Thessalonicher 1, 2, An die Philipper* (3d ed.; HNT 11; Tübingen: Mohr, 1937).

————. *From Tradition to Gospel* (trans. Bertram Lee Woolf; New York: Scribner's, 1935).

————. *The Pastoral Epistles: A Commentary* (4th rev. ed. by Hans Conzelmann; trans. Philip Buttolph and Adela Yarbro; Hermeneia; Philadelphia: Fortress, 1972).

Dornseiff, Franz. *Das Alphabet in Mystik und Magie* (Leipzig: Teubner, 1922).

Elbogen, Ismar. *Der jüdische Gottesdienst in seiner geschichtlichen Entwicklung* (3d ed.; Frankfurt am Main: Kauffmann, 1931).

Fascher, Erich. *ΠΡΟΦΗΤΗΣ: Eine sprach- und religionsgeschichtliche Untersuchung* (Giessen: Töpelmann, 1927).

Festugière, André-Marie Jean. *La révélation d'Hermès Trismégiste* (4 vols.; Paris: Lecoffre, 1944–54).

Foakes-Jackson, F. J., and Lake, Kirsopp, et al., eds. *The Beginnings of Christianity* (5 vols.; New York and London: Macmillan, 1920–65).

Foerster, Werner. *From the Exile to Christ: A Historical Introduction to Palestinian Judaism* (trans. Gordon E. Harris; Philadelphia: Fortress, 1964).

Freudenthal, Jacob. *Alexander Polyhistor und die von ihm erhaltenen Reste jüdischer und samaritanischer Geschichtswerke* (Breslau: Skutsch, 1874–75).

Fridrichsen, Anton J. *Le problème du miracle dans le christianisme primitif* (Strasbourg and Paris: Istra, 1925).

————. "Zum Stil des paulinischen Peristasenkatalogs 2. Kor. 11:23ff.," *SO* 7 (1928) 25–29.

————. "Peristasenkatalog und Res Gestae: Nachtrag zu 2. Kor. 11.23ff.," *SO* 8 (1929) 78–82.

Friedländer, Ludwig. *D. Junii Juvenalis Saturarum libri V: Mit erklären-den Anmerkungen* (Leipzig: Hirzel, 1895).

————. *Darstellungen aus der Sittengeschichte Roms in der Zeit von Augustus bis zum Ausgang der Antonine* (9th and 10th ed. by G. Wissowa; 4 vols.; Leipzig: Hirzel, 1919–21).

Friedländer, Moritz. *Geschichte der jüdischen Apologetik als Vorgeschichte des Christentums* (Zurich: Schmidt, 1903).

Gaster, Moses. *The Samaritans: Their History, Doctrines, and Literature* (London: Milford, 1925).

Georgi, Dieter. Review of W. Schmithals, *Die Gnosis in Korinth*, in *VF* (1958–59) 90–96.

————. *Die Geschichte der Kollekte des Paulus für Jerusalem* (ThF 38; Hamburg: Reich, 1965).

————. "Der vorpaulinische Hymnus Phil. 2,6–11," in *Zeit und Ge-*

schichte: Dankesgabe an Rudolf Bultmann zum 80. Geburtstag (ed. Erich Dinkler; Tübingen: Mohr, 1964) 263–93.

Goettsberger, Johannes. "Die Hülle des Mose nach Ex. 34 und 2. Kor. 3," *BZ* 16 (1922) 1–17.

Golla, Eduard. *Zwischenreise und Zwischenbrief: Eine Untersuchung . . .* (*BS* 20/4; Freiburg: Herder, 1922).

Goodenough, Erwin R. *By Light, Light: The Mystic Gospel of Hellenistic Judaism* (New Haven: Yale University Press, 1935).

————. *An Introduction to Philo Judaeus* (New York: Barnes, 1963).

————. *Jewish Symbols in the Greco-Roman Period* (Bollingen Series 37; New York: Pantheon, 1953–69).

————. "Philo's Exposition of the Law and His De Vita Mosis," *HTR* 26 (1933) 109–25.

————. "The Political Philosophy of Hellenistic Kingship," *Yale Classical Studies* 1 (1928) 53–102.

————. *The Politics of Philo Judaeus* (New Haven, Ct.: Yale Univ. Press, 1938).

Graetz, Heinrich. *Die jüdischen Proselyten im Römerreiche unter den Kaisern Domitian, Nerva, Trajan und Hadrian* (Breslau: Jahresbericht des jüdischen-theologischen Seminars Breslau, 1884).

Gressmann, Hugo. "Heidnische Mission in der Werdezeit des Christentums," *ZMR* 39 (1924) 10–48.

Haenchen, Ernst. *The Acts of the Apostles: A Commentary* (trans. Bernard Noble and Gerald Shinn; ed. Hugh Anderson and Robert McLachlan Wilson; Philadelphia: Westminster, 1971).

Hahn, Ferdinand. *Mission in the New Testament* (SBT 47; London: SCM, 1965).

————. *The Titles of Jesus in Christology: Their History in Early Christianity* (trans. Harold Knight and George Ogg; Cleveland: World Publishing, 1969).

Harnack, Adolf von. *Entstehung und Entwicklung der Kirchenverfassung und des Kirchenrechts in den zwei ersten Jahrhunderten* (Leipzig: Hinrichs, 1910).

————. *Die Lehre der zwölf Apostel, nebst Untersuchungen zur ältesten Geschichte der Kirchenverfassung und des Kirchenrechts* (TU 2/1–2; Leipzig: Hinrichs, 1884).

————. "κόπος, κοπιᾶν (οἱ κοπιῶντες) im frühchristlichen Sprachgebrauch," *ZNW* 27 (1928) 1–10.

————. *The Mission and Expansion of Christianity in the First Three Centuries* (2d ed.; trans. and ed. James Moffatt; New York: Putnam, 1908). German: *Die Mission und Ausbreitung des Christentums in den ersten drei Jahrhunderten* (4th rev. ed.; 2 vols.; Leipzig: Hinrichs, 1924).

Hausrath, Adolf. *Der Apostel Paulus* (Heidelberg: Bassermann, 1872).

————. *Der Vierkapitelbrief des Paulus an die Korinther* (Heidelberg: Bassermann, 1870).

Heinemann, Isaak. *Philons griechische und jüdische Bildung: Kulturvergleichende Untersuchungen zu Philons Darstellung der jüdischen Gesetze* (Breslau: Marcus, 1932; Hildesheim: Olms, 1962).

Heinrici, Georg. *Der zweite Brief an die Korinther* (8th ed.; Meyer K 6; Göttingen: Vandenhoeck & Ruprecht, 1900).

Held, Heinz J. "Matthew as Interpreter of the Miracle Stories," in Günther Bornkamm, Gerhard Barth, and Heinz J. Held, *Tradition and Interpretation in Matthew* (Philadelphia: Westminster; London: SCM, 1963).

Holl, Karl. *Gesammelte Aufsätze zur Kirchengeschichte* (Tübingen: Mohr, 1921–28).

Holsten, Carl. *Das Evangelium des Paulus* (2 vols.; Berlin: Reimer, 1880).

Jacoby, Felix. *Die Fragmente der griechischen Historiker* (3 vols. in 15; Leiden: Brill, 1954–64).

Jeremias, Joachim. *Jerusalem in the Time of Jesus: An Investigation into Economic and Social Conditions During the New Testament Period* (trans. F. H. and C. H. Cave; London: SCM, 1969).

———. *Jesus' Promise to the Nations* (Franz Delitzsch Lectures for 1953; SBT 24; London: SCM, 1958).

Jonas, Hans. *Gnosis und spätantiker Geist* (2 vols.; FRLANT NF 33, 45; Göttingen: Vandenhoeck & Ruprecht, 1954).

Jülicher, Adolf. *Einleitung in das Neue Testament* (7th rev. ed.; ed. Erich Fascher; Tübingen: Mohr, 1931).

Juster, Jean. *Les juifs dans l'empire romain: Leur condition juridique, économique et sociale* (2 vols.; Paris: Geuthner, 1914).

Käsemann, Ernst. "Die Legitimität des Apostels: Eine Untersuchung zu II Korinther 10–13," *ZNW* 41 (1942) 33–71.

Kahrstedt, Ulrich. *Kulturgeschichte der römischen Kaiserzeit* (2d ed.; Bern: Francke, 1958).

Kautzsch, Emil, et al. *Die Apokryphen und Pseudoepigraphen des Alten Testaments* (reprint; Hildesheim: Olms, 1962).

Kerényi, K. *Die griechisch-orientalische Romanliteratur in religionsgeschichtlicher Beleuchtung* (2d ed.; Darmstadt: Wissenschaftliche Buchgesellschaft, 1962).

Keyes, Clinton W. "The Greek Letter of Introduction," *AJP* 56 (1935) 28–44.

Klein, Günther. *Die zwölf Apostel: Ursprung und Gehalt einer Idee* (FRLANT NF 59; Göttingen: Vandenhoeck & Ruprecht, 1961).

Klöpper, Albert. *Kommentar über das zweite Sendschreiben des Apostels Paulus an die Gemeinde zu Korinth* (Berlin: Reimer, 1874).

Knox, Wilfred L. "Abraham and the Quest for God," *HTR* 28 (1935) 57–60.

Koester, Helmut. *Synoptische Überlieferung bei den apostolischen Vätern* (TU 65; Berlin: Akademie, 1957).

Krauss, Samuel. *Talmudische Archäologie* (3 vols.; Leipzig: Fock, 1910–12).

————. *Synagogale Altertümer* (Berlin and Vienna: Harz, 1922).

Krenkel, Max. *Beiträge zur Aufhellung der Geschichte und der Briefe des Apostels Paulus* (Braunschweig: Schwetschke, 1890).

Krüger, Paul. *Philo und Josephus als Apologeten des Judentums* (Leipzig: Dürr, 1906).

Kümmel, Werner G. *Kirchenbegriff und Geschichtsbewusstsein in der Urgemeinde und bei Jesus* (Sy BUSup 1; Göttingen: Vandenhoeck & Ruprecht, 1968).

Kuhn, Karl. G., "Die Schriftenrollen vom Toten Meer," *EvTh* 11 (1951–52) 72–75.

Lake, Kirsopp. *The Earlier Epistles of St. Paul* (London: Rivingtons, 1927).

Leipoldt, Johannes. *Von den Mysterien zur Kirche: Gesammelte Aufsätze* (Hamburg: Reich, 1962).

Leipoldt, Johannes, and Morenz, Siegfried. *Heilige Schriften: Betrachtungen zur Religionsgeschichte der antiken Mittelmeerwelt* (Leipzig: Harrassowitz, 1953).

Leisegang, Hans. *Der heilige Geist: Das Wesen und Werden der mystisch-intuitiven Erkenntnis in der Philosophie und Religion der Griechen* (vol. 1, pt. 1; Leipzig: Teubner, 1919).

Lévy, Isidore. *La légende de Pythagore de Grèce en Palestine* (Paris: Champion, 1927).

Liagre-Böhl, F. M. T. de. "Die Juden im Urteil der griechischen und römischen Schriftsteller," in *Opera Minore: Studie en Bijdragen op Assyriologisch en Oudtestamentisch terrein* (Groningen: Wolters, 1953) 101–33.

Liddell, Henry G.; Scott, Robert; Jones, Stuart. *A Greek-English Lexicon* (Oxford: Clarendon Press, 1925–40); *Supplement*, ed. Barber, E.A. (1968).

Lietzmann, Hans. *An die Korinther I, II* (4th ed. supp. by W. G. Kümmel; HNT 9; Tübingen: Mohr, 1949).

————. *The Beginnings of the Christian Church* (trans. Bertram L. Woolf; New York: Scribner's, 1937).

————. "Zur altchristlichen Verfassungsgeschichte," *ZwTh* 55 (1913) 88–153.

Lobeck, Christian A. *Aglaophamus; sive, De theologiae mysticae Graecorum causis libri tres* (Darmstadt: Wissenschaftliche Buchgesellschaft, 1961).

Lohmeyer, Ernst. *Die Briefe an die Philipper, an die Kolosser und an Philemon* (10th ed; MeyerK; Göttingen: Vandenhoeck & Ruprecht, 1954).

Lütgert, Wilhelm. *Amt und Geist im Kampf* (BFCTh 15/4, 5; Gütersloh: Bertelsmann, 1911).

————. *Freiheitspredigt und Schwarmgeister in Korinth: Ein Beitrag zur Charakteristik der Christuspartei* (BFCTh 12/3; Gütersloh: Bertelsmann, 1908).

————. *Gesetz und Geist: Zur Vorgeschichte des Galaterbriefes* (BFCTh 22.6; Gütersloh: Bertelsmann, 1919).

————. *Die Irrlehrer der Pastoralbriefe* (BFCTh 13/3; Gütersloh: Bertelsmann, 1909).

————. *Die Vollkommenen im Philipperbrief und die Enthusiasten in Thessalonich* (BFCTh 13/6; Gütersloh: Bertelsmann, 1909).

Meyer, Eduard. *Ursprünge und Anfänge des Christentums* (3 vols.; Stuttgart: Cotta, 1962).

Meyer, Rudolf. *Der Prophet aus Galiläa: Studie zum Jesusbild der drei ersten Evangelien* (Darmstadt: Wissenschaftliche Buchgesellschaft, 1970).

Michel, Otto. "'Erkennen dem Fleische nach,'" *EvTh* 14 (1954) 22–29.

Moulton, James H. and Milligan, George, *The Vocabulary of the Greek Testament Illustrated from the Papyri and Other Non-Literary Sources* (London: Hodder & Stoughton, 1914–29).

Mowinckel, Sigmund. *He That Cometh* (trans. G. W. Anderson; New York: Abingdon, 1954; Oxford: Blackwell, 1959).

Munck, Johannes. *Paul and the Salvation of Mankind* (trans. Frank Clarke; Atlanta: John Knox, 1977).

Nilsson, Martin P. *Geschichte der griechischen Religion* (2 vols.; HAW 5/2; Munich: Beck, 2d ed. of vol. 1, 1955; 1st ed. of vol. 2, 1950).

Nock, Arthur D. *Conversion: The Old and the New in Religion from Alexander the Great to Augustine of Hippo* (London: Oxford Clarendon, 1933).

Norden, Eduard. *Agnostos Theos: Untersuchungen zur Formengeschichte religiöser Rede* (4th ed.; Darmstadt: Wissenschaftliche Buchgesellschaft, 1956).

————. *Beiträge zur Geschichte der griechischen Philosophie* (Jahrbuch für Klassische Philologie, Supp. 19; [1893]).

Oepke, Albrecht. *Die Missionspredigt des Apostels Paulus: Eine biblisch-theologische und religionsgeschichtliche Untersuchung* (Leipzig: Hinrichs, 1920).

Oltramare, André. *Les origines de la diatribe romain* (Geneva: Imprimeries populaires, 1926).

Peek, Werner, ed. *Der Isishymnus von Andros und verwandte Texte* (Berlin: Weidmann, 1930).

Peterson, Erik. *ΕΙΣ ΘΕΟΣ: Epigraphische, formgeschichtliche und religionsgeschichtliche Untersuchungen* (FRLANT NF 24; Göttingen: Vandenhoeck & Ruprecht, 1926).

Pfeiffer, Robert H. *History of New Testament Times, with an Introduction to the Apocrypha* (New York: Harper, 1949).

Plummer, Alfred. *A Critical and Exegetical Commentary on the Second Epistle of St. Paul to the Corinthians* (ICC 34; Edinburgh: Clark, 1915, many reprints).

Prümm, Karl. *Diakonia Pneumatos: Der zweite Korintherbrief als Zugang zur apostolischen Botschaft* (Rome, Freiburg, and Vienna: Herder, 1960–62).

————. *Religionsgeschichtliches Handbuch für den Raum der altchristlichen Umwelt: Hellenistisch-römische Geistesströmungen und Kulte mit Beachtung des Eigenlebens der Provinzen* (Freiburg im Breisgau: Herder, 1943).

Rad, Gerhard von. *Old Testament Theology* (trans. D. M. G. Stalker; New York: Harper & Row, 1962–65).

Reinach, Theodore. *Oeuvres complète de Flavius Josèphe* (Paris: Leroux, 1900).

————. *Textes d'auteurs grecs et romains relatifs au judaïsme* (Paris: Leroux, 1895).

Reitzenstein, Richard. *The Hellenistic Mystery-Religions: Their Basic Ideas and Significance* (trans. John E. Steely; Pittsburgh Theological Monographs 15; Pittsburgh: Pickwick, 1978).

————. *Hellenistische Wundererzählungen* (Leipzig: Teubner, 1906).

————. *Historia Monachorum und Historia Lausiaca: Eine Studie zur Geschichte des Mönchtums und der frühchristlichen Begriffe Gnostiker und Pneumatiker* (FRLANT 24, NF 7; Göttingen: Vandenhoeck & Ruprecht, 1916).

————. *Poimandres: Studien zur griechisch-ägyptischen und frühchristlichen Literatur* (Leipzig: Teubner, 1904; Darmstadt: Wissenschaftliche Buchgesellschaft, 1966).

Rengstorf, Karl H. *Apostolate and Ministry: The New Testament Doctrine of the Office of the Ministry* (trans. Paul D. Pahl; St. Louis: Concordia, 1969).

Riddle, Donald W. "Early Christian Hospitality: A Factor in the Gospel Transmission," *JBL* 57 (1938) 141–54.

Rohde, Erwin. *Psyche: The Cult of Souls and Belief in Immortality Among the Greeks* (trans. W. B. Hillis; New York: Harper & Row, 1966).

Rosen, Georg. *Juden und Phönizier: Das antike Judentum als Missionsreligion und die Entstehung der jüdischen Diaspora* (new ed. by Friedrich Rosen and Georg Bertram; Tübingen: Mohr, 1929).

Sandmel, Samuel. *Philo's Place in Judaism: A Study of Conceptions of Abraham in Jewish Literature* (Cincinnati: Hebrew Union College, 1956; New York: Ktav, 1971).

Sass, Gerhard. *Apostelamt und Kirche: Eine theologisch-exegetische Untersuchung des paulinischen Apostelbegriffs* (Forschungen zur Geschichte und Lehre des Protestantismus 9/2; Munich: Kaiser, 1939).

————. "Die Apostel in der Didache," in *In Memoriam Ernst Lohmeyer* (ed. Werner Schmauch; Stuttgart: Evangelisches Verlagswerk, 1951) 233–39.

Schlatter, Adolf von. *Geschichte Israels von Alexander dem Grossen bis*

Hadrian (3d rev. ed.; Stuttgart: Calwer, 1925).

————. *Die korinthische Theologie* (BFCTh 18/2; Gütersloh: Bertelsmann, 1914).

————. *Paulus der Bote Jesu: Eine Deutung seiner Briefe an die Korinther* (Stuttgart: Calwer, 1934).

————. *Die Theologie des Judentums nach dem Bericht des Josephus* (BFCTh 2/26; Gütersloh: Bertelsmann, 1932).

————. *Wie sprach Josefus von Gott?* (BFCTh 14/1; Gütersloh: Bertelsmann, 1910).

Schmid, Wilhelm. *Wilhelm von Christs Geschichte der griechischen Literatur* (4th ed. rev. with Otto Stählin; Handbuch der klassischen Altertumwissenschaft 7; Munich: Beck, 1920).

Schmiedel, Paul W. *Die Briefe an die Thessalonicher und an die Korinther* (2d ed.; HKNT 2/1; Freiburg: Mohr, 1892).

Schmithals, Walter. *Gnosticism in Corinth: An Investigation of the Letters to the Corinthians* (trans. John E. Steely; Nashville: Abingdon, 1971). German: *Die Gnosis im Korinth: Eine Untersuchung zu den Korintherbriefen* (FRLANT NF 48; Göttingen: Vandenhoeck & Ruprecht, 1956).

————. "Die Irrlehrer des Philipperbriefes," *ZThK* 54 (1957) 297–341.

————. *The Office of the Apostle in the Early Church* (trans. John E. Steely; Nashville: Abingdon, 1969).

————. *Paulus und die Gnostiker: Untersuchungen zu den kleinen Paulusbriefen* (ThF 35; Hamburg: Reich, 1965).

Schmitz, Otto. "Abraham im Spätjudentum und im Frühchristentum," in *Aus Schrift und Geschichte: Festschrift Adolf Schlatter* (ed. Karl Bornhäuser et al.; Stuttgart: Calwer, 1922) 99–123.

Schoeps, Hans J. *Paul: The Theology of the Apostle in the Light of Jewish Religious History* (trans. Harold Knight; Philadelphia: Westminster, 1961).

Schürer, Emil. *Die Gemeindeverfassung der Juden in Rom in der Kaiserzeit, nach den Inschriften dargestellt* (Leipzig: Hinrichs, 1879).

————. *A History of the Jewish People in the Time of Jesus Christ* (trans. John Macpherson, Sophia Taylor, and Peter Christie; New York: Scribner's, 1891). German: *Geschichte des jüdischen Volkes im Zeitalter Jesu Christi* (4th ed.; 3 vols.; Leipzig: Hinrichs, 1909). Note also new English version: *The History of the Jewish People in the Time of Jesus Christ (175 B.C.–A.D. 135)* (rev. and ed. Geza Vermes, Fergus Millar, Pamela Vermes, and Matthew Black; Edinburgh: Clark, 1973–) 2 (of 3) vols.

Schulz, Siegfried. "Die Decke des Moses: Untersuchungen zu einer vorpaulinischen Überlieferung in II Cor 3:7–18," *ZNW* 49 (1958) 1–30.

Schwartz, Jacques, ed., *Lucian de Samosata: Philopseudès et de morte Peregrini* (Strassburg Université, Faculté des lettres, Textes étude 12; Paris: Les Belles Lettres, 1963).

Schweizer, Eduard. *Church Order in the New Testament* (SBT 32; London:

SCM, 1961).

Siegfried, Carl. *Philo von Alexandria als Ausleger des Alten Testaments* (Jena: Dufft, 1875).

Smallwood, E. Mary, ed. *Philonis Alexandrini Legatio ad Gaium* (Leiden: Brill, 1961).

Söder, Rosa. *Die apokryphen Apostelgeschichten und die romanhafte Literatur der Antike* (Würzburger Studien zur Altertumswissenschaft 3; Stuttgart: Kohlhammer, 1932).

Stählin, Otto. "Die hellenistisch-jüdische Literatur," in *Wilhelm von Christs Geschichte der griechischen Literatur* (ed. Wilhelm Schmid; HAW 7/2/1; Munich: Beck, 1920) 535–656.

Strachan, Robert H. *The Second Epistle of Paul to the Corinthians* (MNTC; London: Hodder & Stoughton, 1935).

Strack, Hermann L., and Billerbeck, Paul. *Kommentar zum Neuen Testament aus Talmud und Midrasch* (7 vols. in 6; Munich: Beck, 1922–61).

Thackeray, Henry St. J. *Josephus: The Man and the Historian* (New York: Jewish Institute of Religion, 1929).

Thyen, Hartwig. *Der Stil der jüdisch-hellenistischen Homilie* (FRLANT 65, NF 47; Göttingen: Vandenhoeck & Ruprecht, 1955).

Vogelstein, Hermann, and Rieger, Paul. *Geschichte der Juden in Rom* (Berlin: Mayer, 1896).

Volz, Paul. *Die Eschatologie der jüdischen Gemeinde im neutestamentlichen Zeitalter* (Hildesheim: Olms, 1966).

―――. *Hiob und Weisheit: Das Buch Hiob, Sprüche und Jesus Sirach, Prediger* (Schriften des Alten Testaments 3/2; Göttingen: Vandenhoeck & Ruprecht, 1921).

Wagenmann, Julius. *Die Stellung des Apostels Paulus neben den Zwölf in den ersten zwei Jahrhunderten* (ZNWSup 3; Giessen: Töpelmann, 1926).

Watzinger, Carl, and Kohl, Heinrich. *Antike Synagogen in Galiläa* (Leipzig: Hinrichs, 1916).

Weill, Julien. *Oeuvres complètes de Flavius Josèphe* (ed. Théodore Reinach; Paris: Leroux, 1900).

Weinreich, Otto. *Antike Heilungswunder: Untersuchungen zum Wunderglauben der Griechen und Römer* (RVV 8/1; Giessen: Töpelmann, 1909).

―――. "Antikes Gottmenschtum," in *Römischer Kaiserkult* (ed. Antonie Wlosok; Wege der Forschung 372; Darmstadt: Wissenschaftliche Buchgesellschaft, 1978) 55–81.

―――. *Gebet und Wunder: Zwei Abhandlungen zur Religions- und Literaturgeschichte* (Stuttgart: Kohlhammer, 1929).

―――. *Neue Urkunden zur Sarapis-Religion* (Tübingen: Mohr, 1919).

―――. "Alexander der Lügenprophet und seine Stellung in der Religiösität des II Jahrhunderts n. Chr.," *Neue Jahrbücher für das klassische Altertum* 47 (1921) 129–51.

Wendland, Paul. *Die hellenistisch-römische Kultur in ihren Beziehungen zum Judentum und Christentum* (4th ed. by Heinrich Dörrie; HNT 2; Tübingen: Mohr, 1972).

————. "Philo und die kynisch-stoische Diatribe," in *Beiträge zur Geschichte der griechischen Philosophie und Religion* (ed. Paul Wendland and Otto Kern; Berlin: Reimer, 1895).

————. "Die Therapeuten und die philonische Schrift vom beschaulichen Leben," *Jahrbücher für klassische Philologie* 22, supp. (1896) 695–772.

Wetter, Gillis P. *Der Sohn Gottes: Eine Untersuchung über den Charakter und die Tendenz des Johannesevangeliums* (FRLANT 26, NF 9; Göttingen: Vandenhoeck & Ruprecht, 1916).

Windisch, Hans. *Der zweite Korintherbrief* (Meyer K 6; Göttingen: Vandenhoeck & Ruprecht, 1924).

————. *Paulus und Christus: Ein biblisch-religionsgeschichtlicher Vergleich* (UNT 24; Leipzig: Hinrichs, 1934).

Wlosok, Antonie. *Laktanz und die philosophische Gnosis: Untersuchungen zu Geschichte und Terminologie der Gnostischen Erlösungsvorstellung* (AAWH 2; Heidelberg: Winter, 1960).

Wolfson, Harry A. *Philo: Foundations of Religious Philosophy in Judaism, Christianity, and Islam* (Cambridge, Mass.: Harvard University Press, 1948).

Wright, George E. *Biblical Archaeology* (2d ed.; Philadelphia: Westminster; London: Duckworth, 1962).

Epilogue

INTRODUCTION

Since this book, a reworking of a 1958 dissertation, appeared, discussion of matters touched on in it has progressed to varying degrees.[1] Therefore, a review approach to the discussion would provide an uneven, fragmented, and unsatisfactory picture. Spicing it with polemic and praise could not make up for that, and a jury approach or scoreboard method, especially in a situation of uneven research, would not further scholarly discussion. For these reasons, I will here present a series of suggestions concerning the more important questions, intimating some new insights, developments, tendencies. My interest is in suggesting what can and should be done in the future. This will continue the self-understanding I had when I worked on this book, which showed in the various versions of it, in 1955, 1958, 1964. I saw my task not as one of making a definitive statement but as one of conducting an experiment offering experimental models of integration for a whole range of observations made by myself and others.[2]

First, a few general observations are in order. In the scholarly community and elsewhere, we have increasingly been convinced that biblical texts are not flat phenomena coming out of the writing press fed by an author's mind. Biblical texts participate in the ups and downs and tos and fros of human history, personal as well as collective, and thus they have the third dimension of depth and the fourth dimension of time too. In other words, they participate in the historical process, some more extensively and dramatically than others. This process is especially lively where texts are dialogical by nature, as in letters, especially letters that are part of an ongoing correspondence, as with 1 and 2 Corinthians.

The option of seeing a certain ancient document as one primary
unit is one of many options the exegete and historian has to try, certainly the first in a series of probabilities but not the only, and certainly not the paramount, one. An undue degree of respect is given
to the primacy of larger textual units. In fact, though, the discussion
of biblical texts has proven that this respected assumption is the
least probable of all, certainly in the area of the OT. But even in the
New Testament the "unity is primary" option has lost in the case of
the Gospels, which represent extensive collections. In the Pauline
correspondence, critical questions with respect to the original unity
of the Philippian and Corinthian correspondence, and also of 1
Thessalonians and Romans, are numerous and strong. And in the remaining parts the debate about original unity is intense in the case
of the Johannine correspondence and the Book of Revelation too.
All this amounts to more than two-thirds of the NT.

Literary criticism in the sense of source criticism bore the major
burden of critical investigation before World War I, but after the
1920s form criticism added its powerful voice. Following World
War II, redaction criticism, a child of form criticism, came along and
is now trying, unsuccessfully, to stand on its own feet in rejection of
its heritage. In recent years conservative voices have become
stronger again, and even redaction criticism is often used as a conservative tool. But this conservative criticism—and criticism it is,
despite denials—makes three important points that no historical
critic should forget. First, analysis should not become the all-in-all
of criticism. There is no analysis without synthesis (although there is
no synthesis without analysis either, including historical-critical
analysis). If it were so, decomposition would occur quickly indeed.
The second important point is that history should not deteriorate
into data collection. No doubt, in the name of historical criticism, a
gypsy-moth-like approach is not uncommon in NT studies and related fields, where fact after fact and reference after reference are
devoured with obvious results. This kind of digestion is no historical
understanding at all. The third argument of conservatives emphasizes the peculiar character of religious quests and issues. I agree
that a number of prayers is different from a number of warships. But
despite all this justified criticism, the historical-critical perspective

has to be kept alive strongly and unequivocally. It will have to differentiate as well as integrate.

THE IMMEDIATE TEXTUAL BASE

A variation of the aforementioned dialectic of analysis and synthesis with which historical criticism is faced is that of differentiation and generalization. In that dialectic 2 Cor. has suffered from an imbalance in the direction of generalization. The letter, or its fragments, have been taken very much as an appendix to 1 Cor. but meanwhile the texts of 2 Cor. have forced themselves upon the exegetes and have called for recognition of their particular character as to text and situation.

The Fragmentary Character
of 2 Corinthians

2 Corinthians has proven to be more fragmented than scholarship before the 1950s recognized. Now a new consensus seems to be taking shape. This is no wonder, because the seams in 2 Cor. 2:13/14 and 7:4/5 are the best examples in the entire NT of one large fragment secondarily inserted into another text, and in my opinion 6:13/14 and 7:1/2 provide as good a basis for a literary-critical operation, seeing 6:13 and 7:2 as originally connected but secondarily separated by a text added by a later editor. The splits in 2:13/14 and 7:4/5 (also in 6:13/14 and 7:1/2) are so basic, and the connections between 2:13 and 7:5 (and in 6:13 and 7:2) are so obvious, that the burden of proof lies now with those who defend the unity of the present texts, and they have not brought any good new arguments to support their claims.[3] The lack of integrity with respect to chaps. 7—9 is not quite as obvious; it is more striking with regard to the connection between chaps. 9 and 10. There are strong indications that there was a secondary collation of fragments.[4]

Form-Critical and Rhetorical-Critical
Possibilities

Since this study is focusing on the opposition against Paul, the historian could be tempted to look merely for the relevant references and to extract the necessary historical information from them and from their contexts. But the textual base is not merely a quantity of words; it is also formed in particular arrangements, primarily and secondarily. More recent form-critical observations on Pauline epistles in light of Hellenistic epistolography have not yet been sufficiently applied to the elements of epistolary bodies and frameworks of the existing individual fragments of 2 Cor. or 2 Cor. at large with regard to what is left and what might have been lost.[5]

It might come out, in fact, that little of the two letters most relevant for this study (2 Cor. 2:14—7:4 [6:14—7:1 excepted] and chaps. 10—13) has been lost. Some doubt has been raised with respect to the possibility that 2 Cor. 2:14–17 is the thanksgiving portion of the so-called Apology in 2:14—7:4.[6] All of Paul's letters start with personal references to himself, be they within a thanksgiving section or without. This would be the case in 2:14–17 also. That Paul does not give thanks for the addressees as usual in his letters is not surprising in this case, given the degree of conflict already existing.

If 2:14–17 is the thanksgiving section of the subsequent letter, then those four verses would present a summary of the content of the letter too, here the distinction of the "us" from the "them" being that of those who belong as victims to the triumphal procession of the corporate Christ from those whose milieu is the marketplace.

2 Cor. 6:11–13 and 7:2–4 could represent the last personal remarks with which Paul usually concludes his letters. So also at the end of this fragment not much of the original might have been lost, just a final greeting. This, together with the missing address, would not have accounted for a large quantity.

The last four chapters of 2 Cor. contain the end of the severe letter anyway. But there does not seem to be much missing from the beginning either. Again we have a long passage that concentrates on the person of the writer and on his relationship to the addressees, a presentation to be expected at the beginning of a letter. It is not surprising that this angriest of all surviving communications of Paul would not have a thanksgiving at all, and so correspond to Galatians (the other major polemical letter), all the more, since the later epistle, that of reconciliation (1:1—2:13 and 7:5–16), still has reverberations of the conflict in its veiled and delayed thanksgiving in 1:11 at the end of the introductory passage, which started with a blessing of God instead of with the thanksgiving customary for Paul.

Additional help might come from an approach related to the form-critical one: the rhetorical-critical method. Hans Dieter Betz, in particular, has recently shown how fruitful this methodological perspective can be.[7] Before he applied it to Galatians in his Hermeneia commentary, he tried it out on 2 Cor. 10—13. That study by Betz showed also that his categories need still more discussion.

The understanding of the formal dimensions of chaps. 11 and 12 can gain greatly from more attention to the genre of "fool's speech," which is used here, and to its background in the ancient "mimus."[8] The study of J. Zimijewski has brought new insights into Paul's own style of argument and communication, but the model of the genre "fool's speech" remains practically unused.

The usefulness of the severe letter for collecting data on the opponents has been proven since the time of Baur, although with varying results, but it can be better assessed if considerations of the peculiarities of the genre used for chaps. 11 and 12 are included. From the characteristics of the genre "fool's speech" and its particular application to an apology, we could learn more about the nature of the polemics used here, of irony and sarcasm, all with respect to the decision on how much schemes and stereotypes are used and how much concreteness and pointedness are intended on the other side. Thus better control of the data can be achieved. In addition, ancient rhetoric had great experience in the area of polemics. Rhetorical methods and examples of old can provide criteria for the distinction between fictitious and concrete attacks (or defenses) and between stereotypical and factual references.

The rhetorical nature of 2 Cor. 2:14—7:4 has not yet been explored much.[9] I presume that the rhetorical genre of the political speech, the γένος δημιγορικόν or συμβουλευτικόν was the model.[10] An interesting question is also what kind of rhetoric the opponents preferred, and which rhetorical genres. Research that investigates the rhetorical dimensions of the Jewish wisdom movement, its Gnostic as well as Apologetic versions, will help here, because the definite difference between Paul's choice of forms, genres, and rhetorical devices in 1 Cor. and 2 Cor. is influenced by the correspondents.[11] In 2 Cor. they represented the Apologetic form of Jewish wisdom. Wisdom of Solomon, Philo, and Josephus present good examples and give indications of rhetorical consciousness, wisdom, sophistication, and differentiation, apparently produced by training and also giving models for it. The question how much of this was merely a copy of Hellenistic rhetoric and how much was independent growth within the wisdom movement with further diversification in its various branches is an intriguing one. That rhetoric was an issue in the Corinthian debate is clear from 2 Cor. 11:6 anyhow.

The investigation of rhetorical issues has been too much set against form-critical inquiry, and vice versa. A combination of form criticism, redaction criticism, and rhetorical criticism is more promising in Pauline studies, especially if a historical perspective is kept in mind for all of them.

WIDENING OF THE TEXTUAL BASE

Another dimension of the issue of textual base is the question whether the two fragments 2 Cor. 2:14—7:4 (with the exception of 6:14—7:1), and in 10:1—13:13 are the only texts to be used for the construction of the opposition. Should the other fragments of 2 Cor. be included? Should the base be extended to include 1 Cor. also?

The scholarly discussion of the last two decades has proven that it makes sense to look at the fragments of 2 Cor. not just as an appendix to 1 Cor. but also separately. It has shown that the fact that the entire correspondence is directed to the same addressees cannot be taken as an a priori argument for the unity of the situation. The fragmentation of the correspondence, and the existence of very different, often conflicting data, could not be reasonably dealt with in a harmonizing approach.[12]

Paul's Intermediate Reaction

The fact that Paul brings so much new information in 2 Cor. 2:14—7:4 and in chaps. 10—13, information which contradicts major features of the situation in 1 Cor. and of the opposition there, and the observation that this new information is concentrated in these fragments have been the major reasons for focusing on this textual base. It is also quite obvious from the literature that nobody has been willing or able to deal with all parts of the Corinthian correspondence equally in trying to deal with the opponents in both letters. The dictate of equal attention is as impossible as it is unnecessary.

But there is no doubt that the other fragments of 2 Cor. hold more information on the new situation in Corinth than my book acknowledged. In the case of the letter of reconciliation and in the two fragments on the collection, the conflict of Paul with his opposition can be seen from its decline, from its receding and disappearing side. The history after the fact and of the effect here might help to discover a trajectory which can be followed backward.[13]

There is the debate about travel plans in 2 Cor. 1. The nature and force of that debate as a matter of conflict have yet not been explored enough. The issue does not appear to be merely a pragmatic one for the Corinthians. Psychological and moral factors like courage and dependability do not seem to be sufficient cause for the upset. But what kind of ideological issue could be behind it? Was it induced by the opponents?

A thorough stylistic and form-critical analysis of the peculiar discussion Paul presents in 2 Cor. 1:12–22 is still missing. If that format were to relate itself not only to general patterns, habits, and functions but also to particular circumstances, it might assist in illuminating the latter more. Also, reasons for the terminology used here, which is unusual in the context of the Pauline correspondence at large, might intimate peculiar signals not just about the issue at stake but also about its relationship to the overall conflict.

I do not foresee that the results of such more detailed inquiry could have Paul's adversaries in 2 Cor. come out any more Gnostic than elsewhere in the fragments of 2 Cor. which I concentrated on initially. Gnostics did not pay much attention to something as "fleshly" as itineraries; even less did they see spiritual qualifications or disqualifications in them. A more this-worldly orientation seems to be behind the argument, which would correspond to my picture of the opponents generally. But this general observation does not suffice as yet.

The problem of the ἀδικήσας in 2 Cor. 2 and 7 may yield more information too. I had been prematurely satisfied with the indirect support Paul's discussion of this problem gives to the understanding of the opponents as outsiders because the reduction of the heat of debate and of the number of people involved suggests that the real source of the previous conflict is no longer present and that only a relatively weak remainder is of local nature.

Paul's preceding negative experience, a painful visit (2 Cor. 2:1–4), is commonly understood as being an insult. But the style and form of communication are remarkable too. Paul's "evasive" approach by way of circumlocution needs to be more carefully analyzed. The results of that analysis may further clarify the conflict itself.

The uniqueness of the inverted "thanksgiving" in 2 Cor. 1:3–11 has been observed many times (especially by Paul Schubert),[14] but it has not been exhaustively studied. Its relationship to and bearing on the situation and on the character of the debate has been touched on only superficially. The psychological explanation that Paul's anger lingers on is not satisfactory in the light of the very sophisticated phrasing of the whole passage.

In my book on "the collection" I pointed to some allusions in chap. 8 to the conflict as a past affair. But since 2 Cor. 12:14–18 intimates that the collection may have played a significant role at the height of the exchange, the allusions in the collection fragments deserve further scrutiny in order to extract more information about the dispute itself from its aftershocks in subsequent events and reflections.

Paul's Long-Range Reaction

One aspect of the conflict between Paul and his opponents in 2 Cor. has dawned on me only recently, and that is the light the Epistle to the Romans casts on the earlier conflict. Romans was written from the very Corinth where the opponents had worked only a year before. There is a tremendous missionary zeal and universalism in all of Romans, a stunning optimism, almost triumphant in chaps. 10—15, an activism which seems to stand in considerable tension to the concept of justification by grace of the first chapters, at least as usually interpreted, namely, as a kind of quietism.

Should Paul have had some second thoughts with respect to the opponents of 2 Cor.? There are precedents for that kind of "revisionism" vis-à-vis previous forms of opposition in Paul's correspondence. The fragments of 2 Cor. show this with respect to major tenets of the opposition of 1 Cor. I have described the major aspects of that revision in my book.

Already in the fragments of Philippians, Paul had "rethought" some major theses of 1 Cor. which he had developed there in a polemical situation, particularly with respect to the understanding of community and of eschatology. In Philippians 1 and 3 we see an approach that is more personal, whereas 1 Cor. 12 and 15 are more collectively oriented. In 1 Cor. 15 the future dimension is heavily emphasized, but in Philippians 3 the present experience is emphasized, stressing its process character. Philippians 1 gives a particular eschatological importance to the personal experience of death. In all these changes in Philippians 1 and 3, Paul comes closer to Gnostic ideas.

But Philippians 3 shows some interesting modification with regard to the position taken earlier against the Galatian opposition. The opposition Paul has in mind in Philippians 3 does not seem to be wholly different from that attacked in Galatians. But although the language against these new Judaizers now is even more stern than in Galatians, at least in Phil. 3:2, 7–8, and 18–19, there appears to be some revision, which takes into account concerns the Galatian opponents seemed to have had. Besides the concept of existentializing, even in the form of transformation, which integrates Gnostic concerns expressed by the Corinthian opposition *and* the Judaizing Gnostics in Galatians, Philippians 3 now stresses ideas of ethical activism and of modular responsibility not foreign to the Galatian rivals. The use of the testament form in Philippians 3, inherited from Jewish wisdom, suggests some similar interest in continuity despite Paul's prevailing opposition to the saving dimensions of the law and works of the law. Of course, it is all presented in dialectical fashion in Philippians 3, but still Philippians 3 represents a considerable change compared with Galatians 3 and 4. Romans and 2 Cor. 2:14—7:4 will present some new critical variations of the concept of continuity, but in light of the variant in Philippians 3.

1 Cor., not only in chaps. 12 and 15 but also in chaps. 1—4 and

10, proves that Paul is not as thoroughly opposed to speculation as his polemics in Galatians could make us understand. And the statement "a Jew to the Jews" in 1 Cor. 9:20 shows that the anti-Judaizing arguments in Galatians cannot be translated into an anti-Jewish ideology or stance.

These are but a few examples to show that it is impossible to take Paul as representative for theology as the combination of doctrine and *Weltanschauung*. Arguments and statements by Paul cannot be read as if they were informative pieces to be projected into a system of thought. Even less can Paul be seen as somebody who had a finished theological theory of which he used individual fixed parts on individual occasions, going to his bookshelf as it were, and pulling a particular volume necessary to deal with the question at hand. Paul's use of the form of epistolary correspondence is no accident; it is called for by his understanding of theology and theological communication as dialogue. Openness to exchange and experiment and to integration of experience and expectation characterizes the letters as well as the theology expressed. Paul's letters demonstrate how he integrates the practice of his faith and that of others into his power of imagination; they are fed not only by his own ingenuity but also by that of many others, including his opponents. Even his most "theoretical" letter, the Epistle to the Romans, demonstrates this style of experimental theologizing in form as well as in content.

There are overwhelming signs of a continuous trend in the seven authentic letters which prove that Paul's theology cannot be dissolved into a relativistic phenomenon steered by individual situations, reactions, and other whims. It is impossible also to isolate and minimize Paul's polemical passages as more or less erratic, if not irrational, psychologically conditioned outbursts or as doctrinaire statements; on the contrary, they are essential parts of Paul's theological momentum, of his openness to the dialectic of practice and theory.[15]

Some further rethinking of Pauline and early "Christian" communications must be done with respect to internal relationships in the church and to the dialogue between the various branches of the church and the contemporary scene. Denominational and general Christian triumphalism and imperialism still dictate the consciousness, or at least the subconscious, of us scholars.

After Paul

Jean-François Collange's intriguing suggestion about the usefulness of 2 Cor. 6:14—7:1 for our understanding of Paul's adversaries has already been mentioned. I have expressed my skepticism about a possible integration of this fragment into the context of Paul's authentic correspondence, but even though 6:14—7:1 does not yield any direct information about Paul's understanding of the opponents, it can help us with regard to the history of the effect of Paul's own polemical letters. If it were merely telling us something about the reading habits of the Corinthians after Paul—in case the final editor had found this fragment in the Corinthian archives and did not bring it personally from elsewhere, which is less probable because there is no trace of this peculiar theology elsewhere in the editorial tendencies of the redactor—this inauthentic fragment would tell us more about milieu and climate in Corinth after the conflict was over. For the fight and its solution had become an element in this further development, reflected in later habits.[16]

Can the history of the redaction of the fragments of 2 Cor. contribute more than merely insight into later developments in Corinth and the early church? Is it possible to learn anything about the trajectory of the various Corinthian opponents, and thus more about the start and evolution of the trajectory, from the "canonical" end product? Günther Bornkamm has told us the fascinating story of the redaction of the fragments of 2 Cor., but the history of redaction has yet to be integrated into an understanding of the fragments of 2 Cor. that is more differentiated as to the textual base and evolution of historical situations.

If Bornkamm is correct, the Corinthian church was successful in neutralizing the issue of conflict and then externalizing it. A major reason for that conclusion seems to have been that the editor(s) of 2 Cor. were not willing or able to identify the opponents as present because the opponents were too similar to the editors themselves. In other words, the opponents of Paul in 2 Cor. had been successful in the long run and had gained control of the branch of the church responsible for the redaction of 2 Cor.

The use of the letter of reconciliation as a frame, and the postponement of the severe letter, prove that the trajectory of the edition of the fragments points away from the Gnostics, not toward them. Had the Gnostics taken control of the fragments, they would have given 2:14—7:4 more prominence, perhaps dramatically juxtaposed it with chaps. 10—13. The letter of reconciliation would have been of less use to them, as the two fragments on the collection would have been too, perhaps with the exception of the first half of chap. 8 and the second half of chap. 9. The insertion of the inauthentic 6:14—7:1 makes a Gnostic history of redaction of the fragments finally impossible. Marcion received the letter already as an edited one. The hypothesis that 2:17 and 5:16 are Gnostic margins completely contradicts the traceable history of the fragments and their redaction.[17]

Further Methodological Observations and Considerations

The discussion of the sequence of events in my study of the opponents was a predecessor to my later work on the collection, where the importance of the interplay between events, particularly the sequence of events, and theology is stressed.[18] This awareness of the interplay between the succession of events and theology seems to be similar to the old interest in the development of personalities and of individual theologies which was especially strong before World War I, but this similarity is only in appearance. Whereas in those days the interest was in evolution, and this as a psychological and biographical phenomenon, now the interest is more in the interplay between situation, personality, community, environment, and theology. It is therefore a multifaceted and comprehensive dialogue, its conditions as well as its consequences an *interacting continuum*. More could be done with respect to comprehending the impact of Paul's theology and strategy and their exchange—including the critical dialogue with opposing forces—on the subsequent history of church and theology. This might in retrospect give further clues about the character, importance, and integrity of the opponents in 2 Cor.—a semicircular argument, no doubt, but I hope not a full circle.

My study on the opponents of Paul in 2 Cor. belongs to that branch of scholarship which explores the richness of the dialogue in the Mediterranean during NT times. In so doing I see Judaism, the early church, and then also the NT documents as intimately related to that interchange. Barriers between phenomena like the Greek-speaking world and Judaism, "Christianity" and paganism, orthodoxy and heresy, religious and secular, appear now as secondary artificial constructs of later generations, often in religious apologetics or on behalf of religious and political domination—antitheses and categories all too quickly picked up in modern times by scholars, allegedly for easy historical classification.

As in any historical study worth a reader's attention, there is a certain tendentiousness in my book. Some of it I now regret; some of it I hold on to still. I remain excited about the theology and practice of Paul, and I confess to a continual strong theological aversion to the practice and theory of Paul's adversaries in 2 Cor. and also to their later and modern successors. But what I regret is a certain theological defensiveness which expresses itself in a doctrinaire attitude extolling orthodoxy and denouncing heresy. The book would have to be completely rewritten to repair that. I can point to some remedial features in the original work which could make up for such traces of Christian imperialism on my part. I could refer here to my at least marginal emphasis on the antielitist and antiinstitutional tendencies of Paul or to the opponents of Paul as predecessors of main-line Christianity. I discuss why the adversaries—in a Jesus context—could consider themselves right and Paul wrong. I come even closer to presenting the integrity of that position when I portray their Jewish background, Jewish Apologetics, as possessing a serious theology of its own instead of being a sellout to Hellenistic thought and life, as it is most often denounced to be.

But still, as I worked on this book, I was under subconscious pressure to show that Paul's opponents had no class, an old trick in the polemical depiction of "heretics," with the difference that later theology, doctrine, and then theological and historical scholarship gave that polemics the appearance of "objective" description and judgment.

My book added to the number of studies that moved beyond the slogan of "normative Judaism," a term brought into common use by the first Frothingham Professor at Harvard University, George

Foote Moore.[19] My predecessor in my former chair had also argued
in his criticism of Wilhelm Bousset's "Die Religion des Judentums
im neutestamentlichen Zeitalter" (1903) against this scholar's use of
sources to which "so far as we know, Judaism never conceded any
authority." But to whom was this Judaism entitled to concede, or
withhold, authority? What were its active organs, its voice, its influence? In fact what Moore has in mind is but one of many forms of
Judaism. Moore claims for NT times a general Jewish decision and
agreement as to center and periphery, correct and incorrect, which
overlooks the entire Jewish literature written during the time of origin of the documents of the NT.

This opening up of traditional frontiers is certainly true also for
the borderline between so-called "Christianity" and Judaism. One
of my major claims about the relationship of the opponents of Paul
to Judaism is that these Jesus-believers propagated the concept of
continuity, integrating Jesus into Judaism and relating Judaism directly to themselves. As they made propaganda for a Jesus-related
Judaism, they set themselves apart from other Jewish propagandists
who would advocate a Judaism without Jesus. But for Paul's adversaries in 2 Cor. the advocacy of Jesus did not mean establishment of
a religion other than and opposed to Judaism. Why not a different
version of Judaism, one more among many others? Variety was the
name of the game in Judaism as well as in Hellenism at large. That
would not necessarily mean a bland relativism. A sometimes aggressive competitiveness appears to have been more the order of the
day, oriented toward the goal of a more successful achievement as
well as toward a larger ideal. Indeed, one could advertise one's particular engagement and version as the most authentic and best representation of that ideal, for instance, of Judaism as world religion.

But would the concept of eschatological novelty not set at least
Paul apart? This is the customary view, and it is amazing that almost
always this theological category is immediately translated into social
and institutional terms, allowing people to speak of a new and different religion, more or less organized as a separate entity. But that
does not necessarily follow, not even from Paul's reference to Judaism in the context of his Damascus experience in Gal. 1:13. This is
often taken to be a conversion experience, but Paul never does de-

scribe it as such in his own letters, contrary to Luke. He sees it as a vocation experience, a vision of calling, a prophetic calling for that matter, like Jeremiah's. Did Jeremiah confess and convert to a new religion, or did he start one? He did not, despite his polarizing description of his mission and his endless attacks on Israel, her institutions, and her people. Compared with Jeremiah's polemic, that of Paul appears tame.

In his last surviving letter, the Epistle to the Romans, Paul considers himself still an Israelite (Rom. 11:1), and that is, according to the context, particularly vv. 3–5, a member of the living Jewish people. This means that Paul consciously remained a Jew to his life's end. He still distinguishes himself and other Jesus-believers from "the Jews" in Romans, but this distinction is never developed into a sociological one, certainly not in the sense of one's own faith being a new institution, a new religion. On the contrary, the concept of the holy remnant is used in Romans 9—11, particularly in chap. 11. This concept of continuity despite entire discontinuity is a radical dialectic which Israel's prophets used at least since Amos.

Not even the development of varying social conceptualizations and their concrete implementation are new in the biblical-Jewish world. Centralization was secondary in Israel anyhow, and it did not succeed too well after Josiah's reform either, nor after Ezra, as the continuing polemic against other sanctuaries and the building of other temples and cultic centers outside Jerusalem prove.[20] There are the Qumran and the Essene communities, the community of the Therapeutae that Philo writes about, and the synagogue as a pluralistic religious institution. There are also wisdom schools as religious centers, apocalyptic and Gnostic groups, and so on and so on, none of them intended as the start of a new religion different from Israel-Judaism.

It is amazing that the term "Christian" appears for the first time not only all of a sudden but also frequently in literary documents between 90 and 120 C.E.[21] This is the period when the Pharisaic rabbinate increasingly succeeds in purging Judaism of non-Pharisaic elements and when Jesus-believers start to create problems for the Romans, as the correspondence of Pliny the Younger proves. It is interesting that both Tacitus and Suetonius, our other earliest Roman sources of the term "Christiani," relate to Pliny.[22] Both claim that the term existed already during the Neronian persecution.[23] If this is true, it should be noted that this incident was local only.[24] Even Luke indicates local character for the name Χριστιανός originally.[25] His suggestion that the term was used for early Jesus-believers in Antioch is indirectly refuted by Paul, an Antiochean missionary of more than a dozen years. He never uses the term; apparently he did not know it yet. Thus "Christian" cannot be used for the description of the self-understanding of the early church during the first two generations. The earliest "Christian" authors using it, from the third generation most of all Luke, are interested in interpreting the church of Jesus as a new religion different from the Jewish religion.[26]

It cannot be proved that Paul or any of his contemporary Jesus-believers had any thought of representing or founding a new religion. Rather, they considered themselves related to Israel's holy writings and thought they were continuing, improving, or radically renewing Israel's covenant with God, bringing about its real potential in some way.[27] They were often less radical than Apocalyptic or Gnostic Jews who did not believe in Jesus, and there is no reason to separate those who believed in Jesus from the crowd of those who wanted to interpret and promulgate the revelation of God given to Israel in her scriptures.

Paul thinks of the end of the law within the context of scriptures, as Romans 10 dramatically demonstrates. He sees this actually born out of scriptures. As Romans 9—11 proves, Paul understands his separation from his fellow Jews only as a temporary one, for some years at most, to be corrected by the eschaton at hand. The institutionalizing of Paul's and other Jesus-believers' eschatological radicalism and the interpreting of their actions as having founded a new religion do injustice to them.

Following these observations, I have made semantic changes in the translation at hand. I have avoided the terms "Christians" and "Christianity" as far as the description of phenomena of the first generations of Jesus-believers is concerned. Instead I used concepts like "early church," "Jesus-believers," "community of faith." With this I tried to follow the historical reality where Paul and fellow believers present their audiences with a new, often radical perspective on an old tradition. The missionary perspective of this is not denied at all; on the contrary, the various Jewish groups advertised their own respective causes first among themselves. Those, who went also to Gentiles in order to make propaganda for Judaism, like Apologists and Gnostics, did not give up on addressing their fellow "Jews" either, as the "Hellenists" in Acts 6 prove, for instance.

BIBLIOGRAPHY 2

William **Baird**, "Letters of Recommendation," *JBL* 80 (1961) 166–72. David L. **Balch**, "Background of 1 Cor. 7: Sayings of the Lord in Q: Moses as a Theios Aner in 2 Cor.," *NTS* 18 (1972) 351–64. Michael L. **Barre**, "Paul as Eschatological Person: A New Look at 2 Cor. 11:29," *CBQ* 37 (1975) 500–526. C. K. **Barrett**, "Christians at Corinth," *BJRL* 46 (1964) 269–97; "῾Ο ΑΔΙΚΗΣΑΣ (2 Cor. 7:12)," in Otto Böcher and Klaus Haacker, eds., *Verborum Veritas: Festschrift für G. Stählin* (Wuppertal: Brockhaus, 1970) 149–57; "ΨΕΥΔΑΠΟΣΤΟΛΟΙ (2 Cor. 11:13)," in A. Descamps and R. P. A. Halleux, eds., *Mélanges Bibliques en hommage au R. P. Béda Rigaux* (Gembloux: Dulcot, 1970) 377–96; "Paul's Opponents in II Corinthians," *NTS* 17 (1971) 233–54; *A Commentary on the Second Epistle to the Corinthians* (New York: Harper & Row, 1973). William **Bates**, "The Integrity of II Corinthians," *NTS* 12 (1965–66) 56–69. Horst **Baum**, *Mut zum Schwachsein—in Christi Kraft: Theologische Grundelemente einer missionarischen Spiritualität an Hand von 2 Kor.* (Stud. Institut, Missiol. S.V.D. 17; St. Augustin: Steyler, 1977). Klaus **Berger**, "Die impliziten Gegner: Zur Methode des Erschliessens von 'Gegnern' in neutestamentlichen Texten," in Dieter Lührmann and Georg Strecker, eds., *Kirche: Festschrift für G. Bornkamm* (Tübingen: Mohr, 1980) 373–400. Hans Dieter **Betz**, *Der Apostel Paulus und die Sokratische Tradition: Eine exegetische Untersuchung zu seiner Apologie (2 Kor. 10—13)* (BHT 45; Tübingen: Mohr, 1972). Frederick F. **Bruce**, *First and Second Corinthians* (London: Oliphants, 1971). Rudolf **Bultmann**, *Der zweite Brief an die Korinther erklärt* (ed. Erich Dinkler; Göttingen: Vandenhoeck & Ruprecht, 1976). Jean-François **Collange**, *Énigmes de la Deuxième Épitre aux Corinthiens* (SNTSMS 18; New York and Cambridge: Cambridge University Press, 1972). John N. **Collins**, "Georgi's 'Envoys' in 2 Cor. 11:23," *JBL* 93 (1974) 88–96. Arthur **Dewey**, "Spirit and Letter in Paul" (diss., Harvard University, 1982). William G. **Doty**, *Letters in Primitive Christianity* (Philadelphia: Fortress, 1973). James D. G. **Dunn**, "2 Cor. 3:18—The Lord Is the Spirit," *JTS* 21 (1970) 309–20. Jost **Eckert**, *Der Apostel und seine Autorität: Studien zum Zweiten Korintherbrief* (diss. Habilitation., Munich, 1973). Franz **Ehgartner**, *Astheneia: Schwachheit als Grundprinzip apostolischer Wirksamkeit: Bibeltheologische Untersuchung zum paulinischen Apostolatsverständnis* *nach 2 Kor.* (diss., Graz, 1979). Earl E. **Ellis,** "Paul and His Opponents: Trends in the Research," in Jacob Neusner, ed., *Christianity* (Bibliography 3), 264–98. Francis **Fallon,** *2 Corinthians* (Wilmington: Glazier, 1980). Erich **Fascher,** "Die Korintherbriefe und die Gnosis," in K. W. Tröger, ed., *Gnosis und Neues Testament* (Gütersloh: Mohn, 1973). Gerhard **Friedrich,** "Die Gegner des Paulus im 2 Korintherbrief," in Otto Betz, Martin Hengel, and Peter Schmidt, eds., *Abraham, unser Vater. Festschrift O. Michel* (AGJU 5; Leiden and Cologne, 1963) 181–215. Issac I. **Friesen,** *The Glory of the Ministry of Jesus Christ: Illustrated by a Study of 2 Cor. 2:14—3:18* (diss. 7; Basel: Reinhardt, 1971). Dieter **Georgi,** "Corinthians, First Letter to the" and "Corinthians, Second Letter to the," IDBSup, 180–86. Robert **Grant,** *The Letter and the Spirit* (London: SPCK, 1957). Erhardt **Güttgemanns,** Review of D. Georgi, *Die Gegner des Paulus,* in ZKG 77 (1966) 126–31; *Der leidende Apostel und sein Herr: Studien zur paulinischen Christologie* (FRLANT 90; Göttingen: Vandenhoeck & Ruprecht, 1966). M. **Harada,** *Paul's Weakness: A Study in Pauline Polemics (2 Cor. 10—13)* (diss., Boston University, 1968). Murray J. **Harris,** *2 Corinthians* (Grand Rapids: Zondervan, 1976). Colin J. A. **Hickling,** "The Sequence of Thought in 2 Cor., Chapter 3," NTS 21 (1975) 380–95. Philipp E. **Hughes,** *Paul's Second Epistle to the Corinthians* (Grand Rapids: Eerdmans, 1962). Niels **Hyldahl,** "Die Frage nach der literarischen Einheit des Zweiten Korintherbriefes," ZNW 64 (1973) 289–306. Jacob **Jervell,** "Der schwache Charismatiker," in Johannes Friedrich, ed., *Rechtfertigung: Festschrift für E. Käsemann* (Tübingen: Mohr, 1976) 185–98. Robert **Jewett,** *A Chronology of Paul's Life* (Philadelphia: Fortress, 1979). Sherman E. **Johnson,** "A New Analysis of Second Corinthians," ATR 47 (1965) 436–45. Peter R. **Jones,** *The Apostle Paul: A Second Moses According to 2 Cor. 2:14—4:7* (diss., Princeton Theological Seminary, 1973). Edwin A. **Judge,** "Paul's Boasting in Relation to Contemporary Professional Practice," AusBR 16 (1968) 37–50. Walter C. **Kaiser,** Jr., "The Weightier and Lighter Matters of the Law: Moses, Jesus, and Paul (2 Cor. 3:1–17)," in Gerald F. Hawthorne, ed., *Festschrift Merrill C. Tenney* (Grand Rapids: Eerdmans, 1975) 203–12. Heinrich **Karpp,** "Christennamen," in RAC, 2:1114–38. Alexis **Kniazeff,** "Quand le Christ a fait disparaître le voile (2 Cor. 3:14)," in *Eulogia: Festschrift B. Neunheuser* (Rome: Anselmiana, 1979) 203–12. Werner G. **Kümmel,** *Introduction to the New Testament* (Nashville: Abingdon, 1975). A. T. **Lincoln,** "Paul, the Visionary: The Setting and Significance of the Rapture to Paradise in 2 Cor. 12:1–10," NTS 25 (1979) 204–20. Gerd **Lüdemann,** *Paul, Apostle to the Gentiles: Studies in Chronology,* trans. F. S. Jones (Philadelphia: Fortress Press, 1982). Dieter **Lührmann,** *Das Offenbarungsverständnis bei Paulus und in den Paulinischen Gemeinden* (WMANT 16; Neukirchen: Neukirchener, 1965). Christian **Machalet,** "Paulus und seine Gegner: Eine Untersuchung zu den Korintherbriefen," *Theokritia* (1970–72) 183–203. George W. **MacRae,** "Anti-Dualistic Polemic in 2 Cor. 4:6," *Studia*

Evangelica 4/1 (1968) 420–33. Thomas W. **Manson,** "2 Cor. 2:14–17: Suggestions Towards an Exegesis," in Jan N. Sevenster, and W. C. van Unnick, eds., *Studia Paulina* in Honor of J. de Zwaan Septenarii (Haarlem: Bohn, 1953) 155–62. Gerald G. **O'Collins,** "Power Made Perfect in Weakness: 2 Cor. 12:9–10," *CBQ* 33 (1971) 528–37. F. **Ogara,** "Ministri Christi sunt? ut minus sapiens dico: plus ego," *VD* 18 (1938) 33–42. Stanley N. **Olson,** *Confidence Expressions in Paul: Epistolary Conventions and the Purpose of 2 Corinthians* (diss., Yale University, 1976). Derk W. **Oostendorp,** *Another Jesus: A Gospel of Jewish-Christian Superiority in 2 Cor.* (Kampen: Kik, 1967). Karl **Prümm** (see Bibliography 1). Matthias **Rissi,** *Studien zum Zweiten Korintherbrief: Der Alte Bund—der Prediger—der Tod* (ATANT 56; Zurich: Zwingli, 1969). Peter L. **Schmidt,** "Epistolographie," *Der kleine Pauly,* 2:324–27. Walter **Schmithals,** "Die Korintherbriefe als Briefsammlung," *ZNW* 64 (1973) 263–88. Paul **Schubert,** *Form and Function of the Pauline Thanksgivings* (BZNW 20; Berlin: Töpelmann, 1964). John H. **Schütz,** *Paul and the Anatomy of Apostolic Authority* (SNTSMS 26; New York and Cambridge: Cambridge University Press, 1975), esp. 165–86. I. da Conceicão **Souza,** *The New Covenant in the Second Letter to the Corinthians: A Theological Investigation of 2 Cor. 3:1—4:6 and 5:14–21* (diss., Gregorianum, Rome, 1977). Gerd **Theissen,** *The Social Setting of Pauline Christianity: Essays on Corinth,* trans. and ed. John H. Schütz (Philadelphia: Fortress Press, 1982). Stephen H. **Travis,** "Paul's Boasting in 2 Cor. 10—12," *Studia Evangelica* 6 (TU 112; Berlin: Akademie, 1973) 527–32. H. **Ulonska,** "Die Doxa des Moses: Zum Problem des Alten Testaments in 2 Kor. 3:1–16," *EvTh* 26 (1966) 378–88. W. **van Unnick,** "'With Unveiled Face,' an Exegesis of 2 Cor. 3:12–18," *NovT* 6 (1963) 153–69. Christos S. **Voulgaris,** *"ΕΙ ΚΑΙ ΕΓΝΩΚΑΜΕΝ ΚΑΤΑ ΣΑΡΚΑ ΧΡΙΣΤΟΝ, ΑΛΛΑ ΝΥΝ ΟΥΚΕΤΙ ΓΙΓΝΩΚΟΜΕΝ:* 2 Cor. 5:16: The Problem of St. Paul's Opponents in Corinth," *Theologia* 46 (1975) 148–64; *ΝΕΑ ΘΕΩΡΗΣΙΣ ΤΩΝ ΕΡΙΔΩΝ ΤΗΣ ΑΠΟΣΤΟΛΙΚΗΣ ΕΚΚΛΗΣΙΑΣ ΤΗΣ ΚΟΡΙΝΘΟΥ ΚΑΙ ΤΩΝ ΕΝ ΑΥΤΗ ΑΝΤΙΠΑΛΩΝ ΤΟΥ ΑΠΟΣΤΟΛΟΥ ΠΑΥΛΟΥ* (Athens: Theological School of Athens University, 1976). Ronald A. **Ward,** "The Opponents of Paul," *Restoration Quarterly* 10 (1967) 185–95. Joseph **Zimijewski,** *Der Stil der paulinischen 'Narrenrede': Analyse der Sprachgestaltung in 2 Kor. 11:1—12:10* (BBB 52; Cologne and Bonn: Hanskin, 1978).

EPILOGUE NOTES 1–27

1. In general, my book has been well received, particularly in the United States. The only two entirely negative critics were W. Schmithals and E. Güttgemanns. The amazing thing was that they overlooked the real weaknesses of my book, which I shall point out in this epilogue.

The hermeneutical and methodological differences between Schmithals,

Güttgemanns, and myself are very strong and have increased since their critiques appeared. Only an elaborate essay could deal with that, but it would rob essential space for the pursuit of the goals I have set for myself in this epilogue.

New attempts at portraying the opponents of Paul in 2 Cor. have been made by various scholars since my book appeared, most of all by R. A. Ward, G. Friedrich, C. K. Barrett, C. Voulgaris, G. Lüdemann (see also the earlier study of F. Ogara, which had escaped me). They have challenged me into studying further the interplay between Judaism, Hellenism, and the earlier church, and also the development of the latter. This epilogue will report on that research of mine and on my further suggestions.

K. Berger has presented an interesting attempt to develop a methodology of opponent research. He tries to overcome the basic difficulties such generalizing confronts: the vast differences of the particulars as well as the high degree of arbitrariness which the historian's or theologian's presumption about the existence and the character of opposition possesses. The range of actual differences already observed in intertestamental and early Christian literature is greater than Berger's method can handle. This is even more true as soon as hypothetical possibilities are discussed. Each case will still have to be dealt with and judged individually, and the methods will have to fit the cases.

A not unsympathetic criticism of my book was expressed by J. N. Collins. There is, indeed, insufficient treatment of Thucydides 1.133 and Pollux 8.137 in the text above. But in neither case is the meaning "messenger" really refuted by Collins, and my primary point is that διάκονος/διακονία means more than "servant/service" as "waiter/waiting on tables." In fact, Collins gives more support to my argument that there is a trend in the Greek language to emphasize the being sent as a messenger as a particular and prominent side of διάκονος/διακονία. It is not the status but the function that is the major issue for me here.

As to Epictetus the philosopher, there is *a particular* mission. Epictetus deals with that. This mission is a representative and communicative mission. It clearly has a persuasive intention, in this much also a missionary interest (including the inviting into one's own philosophical school). Collins's limiting of the meaning of διάκονος/διακονία in Epictetus to "servant/service" is completely unjustified. But this downplaying of the associative horizon of a certain term (here clearly showing in the other terms Epictetus uses in conjunction with the one in question) is still very common in the context of a term analysis where Kittel's conceptual Platonism is still alive and an ideal term is seen as reality: when the term does not exist, the subject-matter does not exist. The widening of term analysis into motif analysis and into tradition criticism should have helped overcome this Platonism, especially if those further steps are open to phenomena of social history.

2. The notes reflect this more suggestive approach. The five bibliographies interspersed hint at the wide range of research and discoveries ongoing, of which this book, particularly its epilogue, is part. The traditional confusion of the *theological entity* of the biblical canon with the *historical reality* of Judaism is being overcome. The studies listed prove that it is increasingly recognized that not only Hellenism but also Judaism and "Christianity" within it were pluralistic phenomena and that they were interrelated with one another in many different ways too. Part of the confusion on the part of us theologians had been conditioned by our interest in identifying *normative* Judaism and "Christianity"—artificial constructs and not historical—with religious (and social) propriety claiming high class for our canonical phenomena and disregarding contradicting phenomena or denouncing them as base or even nonsensical. But unobserved by much of professional theology and exegesis, the "heretical," "superstitious," and "perverse" practices, experiences, and reflections, in the context of the first- and second-century C.E., nevertheless have been and are being researched. They deserve our attention because they were of great interest to Jews and Jesus-believers. The bibliographies of this epilogue (Bibliographies 2–6) therefore contain many studies on such allegedly subreligious and other more worldly matters.

It should be emphasized that the present book neither did nor does intend to deal with Paul's own theology directly, but only with the context of it. In doing so, it prepares the way for my further commenting on Paul's own practice and thought as it will happen in my commentary on 2 Cor. in the Hermeneia series. F. Fallon has shown in his brief but lucid commentary that my view of the opponents of Paul can illuminate the exposition of 2 Cor., and how.

3. The best argument is that of J.-F. Collange, but only through conceding the un(pre)-Pauline character of 6:14—7:1 in the first place. He has offered an ingenious suggestion understanding that passage as a fragment which Paul himself included in one of his two editions of the end of the fragment 2:14—7:4. This fragment with 6:14—7:1 was intended for different recipients than the other one without it. The fragment which included 6:14—7:1 was meant for the opponents and their collaborators. Therefore, it can yield for Collange additional information about Paul's image of the adversaries. The tone Paul used against them would then be much more radical than my portrait of them would allow. Collange points to the first verses of chap. 4, esp. 4:3–4, and to 2:15 and identifies the ἀπολλύμενοι and the ἄπιστοι as the opponents. This possibility is worth considering, but the statements in these verses all appear to be too general to make them that pointed. And the collation of two different editions at the end of chap. 6 and chap. 7 increases the complexity of the situation unnecessarily.

4. There is recent discussion of the letter's unity or disunity by C. K. Barrett, W. Bates, N. Hyldahl, S. Olson, and M. Rissi. People who defend the unity of 2 Cor. have not disappeared. A combination of interesting

theologizing as well as psychologizing suggestions for the sake of such defense can be found, e.g., with K. Prümm (1:72–77, 370–87, 503–5, 529–31, 547–62), more on the theologizing side; with W. Bates, more on the psychologizing side; and with W. G. Kümmel and F. F. Bruce, more in between the two. Scholars like C. K. Barrett defend merely the unity of the first nine chapters.

The common conservative argument that the unity of the present textual arrangement would make "more sense" than the assumption of an earlier fragmentation of a later collation can be countered with another conservative point of emphasis, that of the unity of scriptures. Communities which were able to endure and enforce apparent massive discrepancies caused by the collection of multifarious documents of frequently contradictory information and mutually excluding points of view (e.g., the Pentateuch, the prophets, and the wisdom books in the "Old Testament," and then the four Gospels and the Epistles of Paul and James in the "New Testament") could stomach a lot, thus being able to suffer or even to encourage experiments in collating on the smaller scale of individual documents.

5. On Greek and Hellenistic epistolography, see P. Schmidt and W. G. Doty.

6. So J. F. Collange.

7. H. D. Betz, *Der Apostel*.

8. On which H. Reich has presented such a fascinating study that it is yet unreplaced (see Bibliography 4).

9. A first major step in this direction is made by the dissertation of A. Dewey.

10. On this genre, see G. Kennedy (see Bibliography 5).

11. On attempts to see *Wisdom of Solomon* and its tradition in this way, see J. Reese and D. Georgi, "Weisheit Salomos" (both in Bibliography 3).

12. New things could happen any day without preparation, as the Antiochean incident in Galatians 2 or the eruption of the Galatian conflict shows. The critical discussion about the Philippian correspondence actually started from the observation that 3:2—4:3 deals with a conflict that Philippians 1 and 2 know nothing about yet. But still the fragment Phil. 3:2—4:9, with the exception of 4:4–7, was written a few weeks after chaps. 1 and 2.

13. The concept of *trajectories* as developed by H. Koester and J. Robinson (see Bibliography 3), in combination with H. G. Gadamer's notion of *Wirkungsgeschichte*, can and should be used much more in the context of exegesis and reconstruction, both not to be isolated from the hermeneutical task and process but to be essential parts of it.

C. K. Barrett (*2 Corinthians*, 10–21) has suggested that 2 Cor. 10—13 be understood as the last fragment of the Corinthian correspondence and that chaps. 2 and 7 be seen as an all-too-optimistic reaction of Paul to an all-too-optimistic report from Titus about Corinth. The conflict instead exploded afterward, and 2 Cor. 10—13 was Paul's response to it, together with a visit, his last to Corinth, alluded to in Acts 20. Barrett argues that 2 Cor. 10—13 cannot have been the letter of tears because the issues discussed in chaps. 2 and 7 and in chaps. 10—13 of 2 Cor. do not correspond (incident of ἀδικήσας, false teaching and the practice of superapostles). But this question turns back against Barrett (and even more against those holding on to the original unity of the entire letter), namely, why the very serious conflict dealt with in chaps. 10—13 (particularly the fact that invaders from the outside were responsible for it) would not even be hinted at in 2:1–13 or in 7:5–16. It is impossible to believe that Titus and Paul should have been so deceived about the danger of the activity of the invaders that the optimism of chaps. 2 and 7 could occur. In addition, the ἀδικήσας appears to be a member of the congregation, a Corinthian, not one of the invaders. Finally, why would 2 Cor. 10—13 not mention at all these ups and downs, particularly the apparent reconciliation of chaps. 2 and 7? Had such an explosive and successful flare-up happened again, as Barrett assumes, Paul would certainly have addressed himself in particular to the issue of the ἀδικήσας, according to Barrett the leading superapostle, in chaps. 10—13 again, for whose reinstatement Paul would have pleaded so strongly in chaps. 2 and 7.

14. P. Schubert, 46–50.

15. Experimental and dialogical theology was the style of much if not most theologizing and reflection, as well as communication, in the early church, including "Gnostics and Judaizers." This style of theology was abandoned—and not even that in one day—only when theology became state ideology and, to a degree, state law, at least in the victorious branch of the church. The many examples of experimental theology in the early church when it still was free prove that experiment does not exclude firmness, does not mean reactive meandering, does not imply a rubberlike constitution.

16. This is an essential part of the methodologically difficult but nevertheless inevitable question of how the exegete and historian is to use the events and communications *after* the fact for the understanding of the fact itself, without using an inappropriate hindsight technique. The traditional answer of historical-critical exegesis that the historian and exegete can and must ignore the *history after the fact and of the effect* completely, and that this part of history belongs at best in the area of curiosities, can no longer be maintained.

17. See W. Schmithals, 304–25. It is true that *1 Clement* presupposes an increase of the Gnostic character of the Corinthian congregation, but that development is in accord with Paul's own shift from 1 Cor. to 2 Cor. 2:14—7:4. In this entire passage, not just in 3:17 and 5:16, Paul has strengthened his Gnostic inclinations. Thus he himself is an accomplice in the growth of the tendencies Clement complains about. The alliance of Paul with the Corinthian Gnostics finally had isolated, quashed, or driven away the opponents of 2 Cor. Clement gives no indication that the Corinthian

Gnostics used 2 Cor. (with or without 3:17 or 5:16). But why should they have left out such a document if they knew of its existence? They did not know about it and therefore could not have amended it. On the contrary, the attacks of *1 Clement* seem to have restored or reintroduced an element that resembled the opposition attacked in 2 Cor., an element that later should win out not only in Corinth but also in much of the church.

18. Recently, the increasing interest in Pauline chronology, particularly in the works of G. Lüdemann (*Studien zur Chronologie*) and R. Jewett, documents the importance of viewing Paul's practice and theology as a dialogical process in which the various situations and their forces play an active part. My book on the collection has taken this approach too.

19. The reader certainly will have noticed my total silence about G. F. Moore (Bibliography 3) in the book above. It is not that I had not read the famous study, but I remember still my utter frustration when I started collecting material for my dissertation and learned that Moore in an all too sovereign fashion had dictated one form of Judaism to be *the* Judaism of the first three centuries of the Christian era, ignoring almost completely intertestamental Jewish literature. It was only later that I overcame my frustration and started to appreciate Moore's work for what it was, an introduction to the theology of Pharisaic rabbinic literature, quite remarkable for a Protestant historian.

20. The Jews of Elephantine built a temple for Yahweh. The Tobiads possessed a Yahweh temple in East Jordan, and a Yahweh temple existed on Mount Garizim until John Hyrcanus destroyed it 128 B.C.E. Well known is the Jewish temple at Leontopolis, Egypt, founded by Onias IV after he had been driven out of Jerusalem.

21. There are the NT references in Acts 11:26 (on the disciples in Antioch), 26:28 (ironically used by Agrippa), and 1 Pet. 4:16 (on suffering/persecution), and then there are the passages in *Did.* 12:4 and Ign., *Eph.* 11:2 (the believers); *Magn.* 4:1 (exhortation to be a Christian not merely by name); Ignatius, *Rom.* 3:2; *Pol.* 7:3 (the Christian in God's school); cf. also *Trall.* 6:1; Polycarp, *Phil.* 3:2; *Martyrdom of Polycarp* 3:2; 10:1; 12:1–2. Ignatius and Polycarp use the term Χριστιανισμός too. There are further Latin references: Tacitus, *Annals* 15.44; Suetonius, *Nero* 16.2 (for the Neronian persecution), and, further, Pliny the Younger (see next note).

22. *Epist.* 96 and 97.

23. Both are friends of Pliny the Younger. On Tacitus, cf. Pliny, *Epist.* 7.20.3 and 4; on Suetonius, see Pliny, *Epist.* 1.18.24; 3.8; 5.10; 9.34; 10.94, 95. Tacitus and Pliny both served as Roman magistrates in Asia Minor, at about the same time, Tacitus from 112 to 113, as proconsul in the province Asia (inscription of Mylasa, 487 *Orientis Graecae inscriptiones selectae*), Pliny the Younger, ca. 110–112, as legatus Augusti (see besides his own letters the inscription *Corpus inscriptionum Latinarum*, 5:5262).

24. The reference of Suetonius (see above, n. 21) appears to be more fac-

tual. The reference in Tacitus (see above, n. 21) is loaded with interpretation, clearly reflecting Tacitus's own opinion on the "Christians," completely out of touch with what is reported and with our general knowledge of the size of the Jesus-community and of its importance at that time.

25. Neither Suetonius nor Tacitus hints that the Roman authorities tried to go beyond the limits of the city of Rome, contrary to the procedures followed in squelching the Dionysiac mysteries in 186 B.C.E., the precedent for the handling of foreign "superstitions."

26. Acts 11:26.

27. There are some interesting coincidences. Tacitus and Suetonius report the name *Christiani* for Rome. The friend of Tacitus and Suetonius, Pliny, is first magistrate in Rome, then "legatus Augusti" (with consular power) in northern Asia Minor (since ca. 110 C.E.). Roughly a year later, Tacitus takes over a procuratorship in the central province of Asia Minor. Suetonius seems to have stayed with Pliny in Asia Minor. Luke, who most probably wrote his two-volume work in Asia Minor (Ephesus?), claims that the term *Christiani* (he uses a Greek transcription of an entirely Latin term) was first used in Antioch. His dating appears to be wrong, but the fact that the term *Christiani* may have been known and used by Antiochean Jesus-believers during Luke's time is perhaps supported by Ignatius's use of the term (and of the further, now Hellenized, derivative Χριστιανισμός). But the Ignatian correspondence in which this appeared originated in Asia Minor. Polycarp relates to Asia Minor too. And then there is 1 Peter writing to Asia Minor from Rome. So roughly between 90 and 120 C.E. we see a line drawing itself from Rome to Antioch via Asia Minor. In each case there is indication of more local than worldwide use of the term *Christiani*, and the Latin flavor remains very strong; so also a legal perspective. A heavier use can be stated only for Asia Minor, and this merely since the 90s.

It is important to note that the majority of the many "Christian" writings stemming from this period between 90 and 120 do not as yet use the term *Christianus* or the derived form Χριστιανισμός: *1 Clement* and Hermas (Rome), John and Matthew (Syria), Hebrews, Barnabas, *2 Clement* (Egypt?), 2 Thessalonians (Greece?); not even the Apocalypse of John, which originated in Western Asia Minor, knows of the term(s) yet. Even more striking is the absence of the term(s) from the somewhat later pastoral epistles, which may have been written in Asia Minor too. Thus the term "Christian" ("Christianity") has no general circulation around the turn of the first century to the second century, not even during the first part of the second century.

The increase in use of the term "Christian" (the individual designation precedes the communal designation, and this in Latin!) appears to coincide with the growing rearrangement and realignment of the identity of the Jewish communities impressing itself slowly on the Diaspora too, after the end of the "synod of Jamnia." Pliny and his friends show that the Roman authorities increasingly felt forced to discern, distinguish, and discriminate, partly out of legal considerations, those who called Jesus the Christ. But that distinction as a sociopolitical and legal one was not of the church's conscious intention and making. It evolved, heavily influenced by outside forces. The three "Christian" authors who appear to have an interest in something like a social (and cultural) distinctiveness of "Christianity" are Luke, Ignatius, and Polycarp. With them dates the real origin of the Christian religion, particularly with Luke. He offers anti-Judaism as an essential ingredient of the ideological base with the simultaneous complete usurpation of the biblical tradition. The Apologetic as well as the polemical prescription proved successful with him, increased by his successors, the Apologists. It paved the way toward the political and cultural victory of that branch of the church. Cf. further discussion and literature in H. Karpp.

ORGANIZATIONAL AND SOCIOLOGICAL DIMENSIONS

Cohesiveness and Expansion

I had first studied the missionary functions of the opponents of Paul in 2 Cor. and their relationship to the early church. In the meantime, the sociological dimensions of preaching and mission of the early church have been analyzed more, but the underlying general pattern of preaching, teaching, and missionary activity has not yet been explored, nor have the structuring and organizing dimensions of that pattern. My original study and similar studies have also not investigated the interplay between Hellenistic missionary activity and communal order, local, regional, or universal—as in the case of Judaism, Dionysiac mysteries, the Isis and Serapis cults, and other mystery religions—or—a most fascinating competitive phenomenon—the interplay with cultural and political propaganda of Hellenistic and Roman communities and states.

JUDAISM

The question of why the Jews survived as a worldwide religion and community despite the absence of a central authority, even of regional centralization, has not yet been sufficiently studied, let alone explained. The usual answer that initially Temple and Torah, and later Torah, Mishnah, Tosephtah, and Talmud, kept the Jews together is not true, at least not as to the presupposition of that answer. It presupposes homogeneity and consistency where they did not exist. The body of literature mentioned presents a startling variety, and this increases as soon as one moves beyond those writings. Reference to the institution of the rabbinate does not help either. It appears to help only those who directly or indirectly confuse the rabbinate with something like the Roman Catholic clergy and its function and organization. But this analogy is not true, not even for the time of the triumph of the Pharisaic version of the rabbinate.

The reference to the rabbinate, however, touches upon the most essential factor of the actual cohesiveness, that of Jewish interpretation. Interpretation of earlier tradition is already an essential and continuous part of biblical and intertestamental literature. At that time interpretation was unwritten as well as written, clearly with equal standing for both. This massive phenomenon of continuous interpretation, although multifarious and colorful, had always been a central part of Israelite life and remained the major structuring and organizational device in postexilic Judaism. Postexilic literature shows clearly that, with the exception of the final redaction of the Pentateuch, legal exposition and discussion represent a minority. The kind of literature which later was called haggadic dominates —and in fact does so already in the Pentateuch, where the nonlegal material provides the hermeneutical frame for the legal material, and not vice versa. The interpretative treatment of the law found in two documents of postexilic literature which claim considerable authority for themselves, Sirach and *Jubilees*, is clearly haggadic. The legal documents among the Qumran writings are exceptional in post-Pentateuchal literature, and it is symptomatic that they are produced by a circle closely related to the priesthood.

Three further features appear to confuse the picture completely, at least at first sight, none of them as yet sufficiently registered in the discussion of the character, nature, and strength of Judaism. First there is the observation that wisdom played a strong as well as an independent part in Israel and that its importance increased tremendously in the postexilic period.[28] Second, the fact that Jesus ben Sirach is the first Jewish scribe known to us outside the temple and that his kind of wisdom not only is surviving in the oldest Mishnah tractate, *Pirke Aboth,* but also penetrates rabbinic literature even in its "halachic" portions demonstrates sufficiently that the scribes/rabbis have their origins in the wisdom represented by Jesus ben Sirach. The third and most confusing feature is the fact that the first extensive legal discourse known to us after Qumran is Philo's exposition of the law, a venture of Hellenistic-Jewish Apologetics, of all things. But although involved in legal discussions to a high degree, the "haggadic" dimensions of Philo are very strong indeed.

No attempts were made before the first Jewish War to centrally regularize and organize those multifarious interpretations, and not before the beginning of the second century did the centralizing efforts of the Pharisaic branch of the rabbinate reach beyond Palestine.[29] A far-ranging literary production, including interpretations of legal texts, flourished in Palestine and even more in the diaspora until the second Jewish War outside of Pharisaic and Pharisaic rabbinic circles.[30] The historian is well advised to count the Jesus-oriented interpretative efforts of those decades among the literary activity of Judaism too.

This productivity of Jewish interpretations of older traditions, at least in the form of written literature surviving, decreased considerably after the second Jewish War outside of Pharisaic rabbinic circles, in particular after the codification of the Mishnah with "Christianity" starting to establish its own literary identity after the split with Pharisaic Judaism during the second century. But even Mishnah, Tosephtah, and Talmud still show a far-ranging diversity of styles and interpretations, in fact, a lively debate and exchange, frequently unsettling as well as unsettled.

Thus neither office nor official text(s) can present themselves as explanations of this amazing cohesiveness within and despite extreme diversity and expansion. The basic reason instead lies simply in the collective and individual willingness of all adherents to Judaism to apply Israel's tradition, however perceived, ever anew. The interpretations were not only the live presence of tradition but also the renewed revelation of Israel's God, in fact, the expression of God's continuous relationship with the people of the covenant.[31] The Pharisaic rabbinic version of interpretation was but one among many. Only by historical accident did it succeed and prevail over other forms, and the history of Judaism proves that this success remained but partial.

The interpretation of Israelite-Jewish traditions by the Jewish diaspora was at least an equal factor in all this, deep into the second century C.E., and it did not cease then either. The possibility that Hellenistic-Jewish hermeneutics had an impact on rabbinic hermeneutics will be discussed below, as well as the fact that diaspora Judaism had need for more intensive hermeneutical considerations and activity earlier than the earlier Palestinian rabbinate.

Hellenistic-Jewish interpretation remained flexible. The interpretations spread, and the interpreter often traveled. Interpretation and mission interacted intensely. A closer look at the practice of "pagan" Hellenistic missionary activity should have made me aware that in Hellenistic Judaism as well the missionary activity, communal order, and worldwide cohesiveness of the religion in question were interdependent and interactive also. That the Jewish religion and community survived as a worldwide community despite the absence of a central authority for at least four hundred years, that is, at least from 300 B.C.E. to 100 C.E., is neither a miracle nor unique.[32]

HELLENISTIC PATTERNS IN GENERAL

Hellenistic mystery-religions and associations like the Dionysiac *technitai* give parallels for the Jewish phenomena mentioned. Migrants kept Hellenistic missionary religions and associations of more than local provenance together, not necessarily "professional" missionaries, priests, teachers, prophets, and artists alone, but also "ordinary" people—travellers, traders, sailors, soldiers, job seekers, and the like.

This worldwide phenomenon, a paradox for our experience, has not yet been studied enough. It is important for the sociology of religions, of religious associations, even of secular associations. It has been and still is more common to take the individual phenomenon of the Roman Catholic Church, its historical success, and even its criteria for and description of "sects" as a generalizable case and yardstick.[33] It has also been used in more general areas, like political science, for assessing the life-expectancy of groups and of organizational structures, with devastating political consequences.[34] This point of view has produced the almost automatic conclusion (usually claimed to be the only realistic one) that more flexible, particularly more horizontal, decentralized, "anarchic" structures, and more participatory phenomena have no chance to endure, grow, and survive.[35]

Besides the Roman version of the Catholic Church, the Marcionites and the Manicheans were the only centrally organized religions or associations in the entire Hellenistic world,[36] with the Manicheans being the least tightly organized of the three. The Marcionite church was the first to present this model and put it into reality; the Catholic Church, and in particular its Western version, copied many elements of it, most of all the idea and reality of an exclusive canon of holy scriptures.[37] Initially the Marcionite church was much better organized than the Catholic Church, but nevertheless the Marcionites "disappeared" after two hundred years. The Manicheans did not survive either, although they lasted for at least one thousand years.[38]

The vast majority of Hellenistic religions did not develop centralized, hierarchical structures, not even the missionary religions which expanded over the entire Mediterranean and beyond, with the exception of those mentioned above.[39] But most of them survived for a considerable time, some for more than five hundred years (Dionysus, Isis/Serapis, and the Great Mother, at least), Judaism until today, and they did so often under extreme adversity. And the other religions that did not survive mostly died not from their own fault either but because of aggressive and politically sanctioned activity, often on the part of the Christian church. That kind of extreme force was responsible, too, for the final elimination of the Marcionite church and of the Manicheans, in the latter case in unorganized cooperation with Eastern political powers.

Common myth and rite also provided part of the unity of the various Hellenistic groups and religions, but not in a too-rigid fashion. They could vary greatly from town to town, region to region.[40] The major cohesive and unifying force was a mobile infrastructure, centrally undirected and uncontrolled. These various groups and religions reflected the basic structure of Hellenistic culture and political life, missionary phenomena themselves of great force and success. Even the Romans made themselves part of that culture and organized themselves according to Hellenistic principles, at least with respect to their outreach. The Romans of the first century C.E. did not possess a centralized and hierarchical structure for their empire. The Roman Empire under and after Augustus remained for a long time what the Hellenistic empires before had been, "a commonwealth of self-governing cities."[41]

Much of the cohesiveness of Hellenistic culture and also of its political structures, including the Roman one, was achieved and supported by ideological propaganda and exchange. The military presence of the political power was not pervasive. In the Roman Empire of the first century C.E., it was concentrated at the borders. Contrary to common perception, hierarchical centralization grew but slowly in the Roman Empire.

It is interesting to note that only the Marcionite, Catholic, and Manichean churches imitated this tendency of the later empire. None of the other religions did, nor did the other branches of the "Christian" church, or Judaism either. The fact that the Roman Empire finally adopted as a state religion that religious organization which structurally and ideologically assimilated itself to the state the most was not sociologically necessary; it represented a convergence of ideological and political opportunities.[42]

The co-optation of the Catholic Church by Constantine helped the political system but made the Catholic Church lose much of its identity and integrity, structurally and theologically. This was the final result of a counterrevolution which had started in the second century in the form of a growing accommodation to the Roman state and society, particularly as they were moving away from the Hellenistic heritage. The sometimes catastrophic development in the Roman Empire during the second and third centuries proves that the moving away from pluralism and the horizontal organizational structures inherited from Hellenism, and the experimentation with hierarchically and centrally structured conformism and uniformity, was not necessarily beneficial but could be destructive. Only when political, administrative, cultural, and religious conformism were brought together, and this by force, as under Constantine, could this counterrevolution succeed, with the help of the extreme good fortune that between 274 and 325 the empire experienced sudden relief at its borders and therefore was not challenged or tested severely to the degree it had experienced in the fifty years before.[43]

PAUL AND HIS OPPONENTS

I have gone into some detail about the sociological and political dimensions of the development of Hellenistic religions because interdependence of mission and horizontal organizational structure have thus far been little observed as stabilizing factors and because the importance of that structural model for a world culture like Hellenism has been more or less overlooked. Not only has its general availability and usefulness been neglected, particularly in Jewish and Christian studies, but also its success and survival rate. The latter actually has been denied almost universally, and therefore this form of organization has not been taken seriously at all.

Despite all differences in theology and organizational detail, both Paul's concept of church organization and that of his opponents in 2 Cor. were variations of the basic concept of horizontal and mobile infrastructure as means of a worldwide organization, with propaganda not as peripheral to it but as its very core and motor. Paul differs with his opponents on the importance of the market in all this. For the opponents as for most other Hellenistic propagandists, the market provided the major milieu for communication, with performance and achievement in competition as means of persuasion. Here I understand "market" in its double sense (as used in Hellenism too): literally as the marketplace but also metaphorically as the idea of trade of whatever kind and of exchange, mostly under competitive pressure and evaluation.

The phenomenon and the motif of the Hellenistic market in their importance for religious and other propaganda and for establishing and maintaining regional and universal organization have not been researched yet. Scrutiny here will yield various new perspectives on the nature of Judaism and the early church in their different branches. The organization of Paul's congregations will also be seen in a clearer context and thus be better understood. The independence and interdependence of religious communities within their immediate religious affiliations, but also across the religious borders, will become clearer. Trust in survival may have possessed a more secular side, too, than usually realized.

Paul's attitude toward the marketplace was clearly mixed. He apparently used it physically. He appreciated, shared, and emphasized the open dimension of the market as a physical and an ideal phenomenon. Although he took to its challenge too, nevertheless he refrained from its competitive dimension and from its achievement orientation, particularly also its judgmental function. It would be wrong to interpret this as a more transcendental, less concrete orientation. Paul's insistence upon the human dimension of Jesus, of his own office, and of the believer's existence would defy this "spiritualizing" interpretation often given in the name of an eschatological perspective.

It was also a mistake on my part—in its pro-Pauline romanticism (and liberal Protestant imperialism)—to arrive too quickly at a condemnation of the opponents' intentions and position as too this-worldly and as too immanent. Paul and his opponents went together quite a bit longer in their orientation toward the Hellenistic *agora* (market). The opponents' elitism clearly was not hierarchical, and like Paul they were committed to a horizontal structuring of the individual community of faith as well as of religion universal. A detailed study of the social and religious functions of the marketplace will help describe that similarity between Paul and his opponents, and also the impact of the fact and idea of the market on organizational concepts and practices. This would bring out the true line of distinction between the two opposing positions more clearly and fairly and less romantically.

The degree of social integration of the Pauline congregations can be judged better than has been done thus far as soon as the sociology of Hellenistic missionary movements is analyzed. The various contradictions between (a) Paul's independent work, (b) his nevertheless unmitigated interest in the unity of the church universal, (c) his own authority, (d) the independence of his congregations, (e) his interest in collaboration, (f) his condemnation of his opponents' working on his mission field, and (g) his interest in coming to Rome may appear to be contradictions only for our modern logic, and they may not exist any longer as soon as the actual social features and ex-

pectations of the Hellenistic scene are considered. We might understand better, too, how much the degrees of social integration in the
religious marketplace could be exploited and manipulated in the
propagandistic contest. How much or how little Paul's ideals and actual tactics differed (evolved?) might show too, and we would learn
whether this would cast any new light on the conflict between Paul
and his opponents. This would make possible a more informed discussion about the dependence and independence which religious
communities possessed vis-à-vis other communities, but particularly also vis-à-vis missionaries, be they their founders or traveling
and competing visitors.

Hellenistic-Jewish Consciousness and Practice

THE INTEGRITY AND CONFIDENCE OF DIASPORA JUDAISM

In the still-understudied area of nonrabbinic Judaism,[44] particularly of Hellenistic Judaism, the concept and function of Jewish
consciousness have to be perceived more clearly. The authenticity
of this version of Judaism has not yet been recognized enough. In
this case too, I should better use the plural and speak of the various
versions of diaspora Judaism and their authenticity. Since there was
no central teaching authority or a similar administrative or
disciplinary force at the center of this form or forms of Judaism, at
least not before the second century C.E., their authenticity is best
described as active attention and orientation toward Israel's tradition, and the communal acceptance of that intent.

Scholarship on Hellenistic Judaism must free itself completely
from the spell of the alternative with which diaspora Judaism allegedly was confronted: continuation and appropriation of "authentic"
(or "normative") Judaism, that is, that of the Palestinian Pharisaic
kind; or accommodation, which usually means losing out, to Hellenism, a Hellenism which is too often identified with Greek culture,
even in an ethnic sense.

The phenomenon generally called Apologetic Judaism is improp-
erly so named.[45] It is neither defensive nor conformist. The posi-

tive and original nature of this form of Judaism will be seen more clearly as its function within and its relationship to the Israelite Jewish wisdom movement is studied, for it is a part of that movement. All the various remains of Apologetic Judaism prove that it was confident that its particular understanding of the Israelite Jewish tradition was appropriate. This understanding appears peculiar or strange only for someone who uses the yardstick of *one* form of Judaism alone and from that perspective caricatures the options which Hellenistic Judaism in general and Jewish Apologetics in particular represent.

The strength of the confidence of the Jewish Apologists is proven by their theology and by their missionary inclination. This theology is a positive and constructive one based on a strong consciousness of Israelite Jewish tradition, of course understood according to the vision of these interpreters. In this difference they are original and distinguishable from other Jewish options, but also from any number of other pagan options, not the least because of their clear claim of Jewishness, the definition of which we have to entrust first of all to their judgment.

This Apologetic theology is certainly very open to Hellenistic culture and exists in a lively and integrative dialogue with its non-Jewish environment. Ridiculing their intent and approach to dialogue, or their Jewish integrity, would not be proper hermeneutical or historical-critical tools of inquiry. Legendary as they may be, some of the narratives in Apologetic writings, for instance, in the *Epistle of Aristeas*, are not any "stranger" than a good bit of historical or geographical lore in either Herodotus or Strabo, to choose just one Greek and one Hellenistic example.

The particular identity of Jewish Apologetics will show more clearly if it is compared carefully with similar writings of non-Jewish authors like Berossus, Manetho, Hecataeus, Heliodorus, or the Ninus romance, unfortunately all surviving only in fragmentary form. Particularly valuable examples for this comparison are found in Alexander Polyhistor, who had combined Jewish Apologetic writings of a romance type with similar writings from other branches of Hellenism. Moses Hadas has made the first steps in the direction of such comparison.[46]

I would want to count the Alexander romance among those pagan apologetic writings[47] too; it could give clues to the potentially critical political dimensions and tendencies of such literature, particularly if read with the eyes of M. Braun.[48] There appears to be an emancipatory potential in this kind of literature not really observed yet in my book. This dimension could be just latent, but occasionally it could be subversive if not altogether aggressive. Readers who have often complained about the "arrogance" of this literature may see it with different eyes if looked at from such perspectives. There is at least no lack of confidence in those writings, whatever the difference of intention or tendency. And with confidence integrity is usually also associated.

THE MISSIONARY INTENTION OF JEWISH APOLOGETICS

The arrogance or, better, confidence of Jewish Apologetic writings is often of a propagandistic and outright missionary nature. There is no proof for the relatively common assumption that this so-called Apologetic literature was meant for insiders alone. Josephus definitely has a non-Jewish public in mind. In the case of Philo, it can be assumed also, although in neither case was it exclusively a direction toward the outside. The very fact that we know of much of this literature only through fragments quoted by non-Jewish authors proves further that this literature was read by non-Jews, and not by chance but because the authors meant it for them.

I had presented positive evidence for a strong missionary activity of Judaism in my work, but in much of scholarship the old legend continues that Judaism propagated itself mainly through biological means and that its offspring had spread themselves over the world, with the off-balanced result that the ratio between motherland and diaspora became roughly 1 to 3 in favor of the Mediterranean diaspora, not to speak of the many Jews beyond the borders of the Roman Empire. The result of the continuation of this legend is obvious: the idea of Judaism as a basically ethnic, if not racial, entity. The myth of ancient and medieval Judaism as monolithic continues too.

What is most surprising is that Erwin Goodenough's monumental work, especially his volumes on *Jewish Symbols in the Greco-Roman Period* are treated as if they had made no difference, as if they had only the importance and impact of a small paperback. There are some doubts about details of his inquiry and his method, but they are not such that they could wipe out his gigantic collection of evidence (a) for diaspora Judaism as having an identity and integrity of its own and (b) that diaspora Judaism was open to the dialogue with paganism without any fear of losing itself.

Strongly influenced by Goodenough, my work added to the number of studies which moved beyond the concept of "normative Judaism,"[49] a term brought into common use by the first Frothingham Professor at Harvard University, George Foote Moore, although the idea is much older. But Moore gave it particular fascination through the unmistakable stamp of his combination of unmatched erudition and astounding clarity. However, his concept of normative Judaism does not hold up well. His selection and his interpretation as well are particularly fascinating because of their representative character, representative of a certain influential kind of history of ideas—of religion and theology.[50] But this orderly world has gone, and it may never have existed, certainly not in New Testament times.[51]

In much of the criticism against Goodenough, scholars object to his advocacy of Jewish mysticism. Again, Goodenough's terminology and method may have some defects. He may not have mentioned enough the presence of mysticism among Pharisaic rabbis, but he did not forget it. And why did the official rabbinic tradition marginalize or even suppress the mysticism present even in its own circles? Through Gershom Scholem's work this mystical rabbinic Judaism has gained notice.[52] It has made us aware how vast the range and amount of Jewish mysticism was in Palestine. This calls all the more for a comparison with Hellenistic-Jewish and Gentile-Hellenistic phenomena. Morton Smith's work has presented enough data to challenge the common restraint and reservation as adherence to a modern bourgeois concept of "propriety."[53] It is not improper but rather appropriate and even necessary to include in our observations phenomena usually classified as "magic." This classification is often identical with denunciation, bracketing, elimination.

Certainly not everything is the same, and to look for Helena in every woman would be a boring enterprise. Variety and difference occur in the area of mysticism too, not only in general but also in Jewish mysticism. There is not merely one-way traffic either, that is, from Hellenism in general to Judaism in particular. On the contrary, there is mutual influence.[54] Goodenough's mistake is not that he found too much Jewish mysticism but that he overlooked its richness, diversity, and complexity, both on Palestinian soil and in the diaspora.

Further studies in the area of biblical and Jewish wisdom always open to the international and interreligious scene will increase our awareness of the width and depth of that variety and exchange. The basic theses of Goodenough appear to be vindicated more and more, not the least by the finds at Nag Hammadi.[55] Gnostic and Jewish studies will have to communicate more with each other. Then the particular identity of Apologetic Judaism will come out more clearly too, as a special branch of the Jewish wisdom movement, not really recognized by Goodenough in its peculiar identity.

Archaeological finds in the Mediterranean have given further support to our knowledge of the pluralism of Judaism in NT times.[56] The spade has dug up a great variety of architectural forms of synagogues and many variations among other Jewish remains. But within all that variety one can make many general observations about identity and continuity. All the people acquiring, building, or modifying those structures which served as synagogues had been confident of being authentic Jews despite the diversity they ended up with. There is no sign that people worshiping in those buildings were interested in surrendering the identity and integrity of Jewish religion, in selling out to paganism, but the Judaism they adhered to demonstrated in their various enterprises an explosive richness, which was certainly one of its major attractions.

There is no evidence that this Jewish identity was ethnic, was felt as ethnically "foreign" or as peculiarly "Palestinian," that is, as isolated, segregating from the Hellenistic culture people came from and lived in. On the contrary, the archaeological remains demonstrate physically that one could live very consciously within the surrounding culture and as part of it. Thus "strangeness" or even "foreignness" and "being at home," "being apart" and "being part," difference and familiarity, distinction and participation, with respect to the general Hellenistic culture existed in a positive dialectic relationship. It is important to note that this variety and this dialectic continued to exist into the "Christian" period, that is, into a time when Mishnaic Judaism had formed and had started to exercise greater influence on diaspora Judaism, partly under greater pressure from outside, even more so when Church and state coalesced.

These Jewish people were also very pragmatic from the start and made the local situation an important part of their considerations. They had no cultic prejudice against private or public buildings, not even against a former gymnasium, as in the case of Sardis, where the building converted to a synagogue still remained within an environment dedicated to sports so offensive to a major part of the Jewry in Jerusalem around 170 B.C.E. Decidedly cultic restrictions and changes occurred, but late in synagogue architecture and practice.[57]

The variety of synagogue locations, from the center of town to places outside the wall, shows that there was no requirement as to where a synagogue should be situated, and even the provision of a building instead of an open place appears to have been more a matter of convenience, availability, and financial resources than one of necessity. However, there is no evidence of any ghettolike seclusion or a templelike isolation, not even in the case of large complexes acquired by Jews, as in Sardis. Instead, many of the synagogues found are parts of city blocks, some of public and some of residential nature. It is interesting that little if any evidence has been found for Jewish residential areas around the synagogues, although we know of that from the literature, mostly from Philo.[58] But the residential area inhabited by Jews in Alexandria was not ghettolike, in the later sense of the term.

The synagogue remains of the diaspora do not show provisions for an entirely open access or exit to and from the building—like freestanding structures with colonnades outside and/or several large entrances. But in no case, not even at Dura, do the synagogues show any signs of barring entry to the public, as a hidden or extremely small entrance would, and more still a mazelike structure. This is all the more interesting since some of the buildings were originally private houses. Although one might at first sight judge the later Dura-Europos arrangement to be this kind of maze, the sizable width of the door and its position in relation to the street speak for openness, certainly also in the case of the older synagogue there. From Apologetic Jewish sources we know that individuals were addressed in those synagogue homilies, and individual decisions and responsibility were called for. Therefore, the indiscriminate openness of a public showcase would have been as inappropriate as a cagelike or cavelike structure.

The diaspora synagogues found thus far were open to individual visitors. Dura demonstrates how little this could be misread for a privatistic approach. In Dura, often understood as a structure interested in seclusion, the peristyle court speaks of a concern for public appearance.[59] Its presence, its later relocation and enlargement, and the growing tendency to put it more prominently before the entrance wall in an axial fashion are as remarkable at Dura as elsewhere. It proves that the Jewish community responsible was interested in the Hellenistic appearance of their place of worship, and increasingly so. Furthermore, it demonstrates the public nature of the building because the frontal peristyle court in Hellenistic architecture, although derived from the private house, emphasized the monumental and representative, most of all the public, dimension of the building, whereas the private peristyle court would move to the center of the building, in this case *surrounded* by rooms, which is not the case at Dura. Still another important point is that the frontal peristyle court was a decidedly secular feature, not a cultic one. Therefore the ever-stronger interest in its prominence shown by some Jewish synagogues challenges some common assumptions about the strength of the interest in cultic isolation of the local Jewish place of worship, of its taking the place of the Jewish temple.[60] That the adoption of the peristyle court had anything to do with the Torah procession, in and of itself still an unclarified feature, has not been proven.[61]

As visitors entered the synagogue complex, they did not find any discriminating provisions, nothing comparable to the different courts and portions of the Jerusalem temple, no gradations of holiness, no signs of any segregation, even of sexes. There is no evidence of women's galleries—even the Galilean evidence often quoted for this is ambiguous at best.[62] Other evidence cited for such segregation, like the presence or absence of footrests at Dura, is entirely spurious. The argument that the building itself, that is, the existence of the assembly hall, provided the separating device—men inside, women outside—is most literally an argument from silence, an ideological proposition. The obvious possibility that no segregating devices were found because no segregation of whatever kind existed appears to be the most natural and plausible.

My earlier treatment of the reference in Juvenal to the Jewish woman priest therefore stands in the wider context of new observations which make it necessary to reconsider the nature, dimension, and function of purity in the synagogue, particularly its worship, and especially also the role of women. The status of women and their possibilities within the Jewish community, cultic and secular, may have been more emancipated than usually believed, including their inclusion in the ranks of leadership, which Juvenal hints at.[63] Lack of any kind of social, sexual, or ethnic segregation would put the Jewish communities into the same situation with the communities of mystery religions, where the absence of such means of segregation has long been observed as a major reason for their attraction.[64] The whole dialectic between openness and restriction, its range and its function in missionary competition, needs further study.

Inscriptions and papyri of Jewish content, or those found in the context of Jewish buildings, also prove that the Jewish communities did not discriminate on ethnic grounds. There are many Greek names and some Latin ones, even of donors or synagogue officials.[65] In the cases of double, Hebrew/Aramaic and Greek/Latin, names or of a change of a Semitic name into Greek or Latin, the direct or indirect Mideastern origin is obvious. For the opposite change, from Greek/Latin to Hebrew/Aramaic, I do not know of any evidence, although the possibility should be considered for converts. In most cases we possess the non-Semitic name only. Why should one assume that all or the majority of these names were those of people who had immigrated from Palestine or of their de-

scendants? We do know of assimilations, particularly also of the ac-
quisition of citizenship of Greek or Roman communities.[66] But we
have the actual cases of double names; we know about Jewish pride
in family ties and also about the power of tradition. Therefore it
would be a tour de force to assume that all the non-Semitic names,
or even most of them, were expressions of secondary assimilation of
people of Palestinian descent. Probability points in the opposite direction, to the absence of ethnic connection in most cases. This is
particularly true for the so-called *theophoric* names, not only the
formations with *theos*. More striking even are those that point to pagan deities in particular. It appears more probable that the majority
of these people were converts or descendants of converts.

If we were to infer the characteristics of Judaism from those diaspora remains, we would never suspect that it was a religion first and
most of all interested in cultic purity. Even less would we be able to
infer anything like Pharisaic piety or Pharisaic rabbinic legislation,
although the actual comparison finds some similarities.[67] The few
provisions for ablution found or suspected would not distinguish
these synagogues from any other religious establishment in the
Mediterranean, old or new.[68]

On the other side, none of the literally colorful evidence found in
the Jewish diaspora could have been anticipated from the Pharisaic
rabbinic sources. There is, in fact, much contradiction between rabbinic law and lore as to synagogues and worship, on the one hand,
and the architectural evidence of the diaspora, on the other. This is
true especially with respect to location, equipment, use of images,
and most of all pagan symbols, although the evidence of the diaspora
has led to some new readings of the rabbinic sources and to the discovery that they were not always that "kosher," that they were in
fact more liberal, tolerant, and experimental than usually believed.[69]

Therefore, the Mishnaic and Talmudic sources do not appear to
be good instruments for identifying and explaining the features of
diaspora finds. They tend to lead more to unnecessarily confusing
and obfuscating harmonizations. Literary sources of diaspora Judaism and pagan references deserve more attention and use in this respect.

Nothing of the table found in the midst of the Sardis synagogue—its size and prominent position, the eagles supporting it, the two lions on either side—fits into the ideas of worship given by biblical writings or rabbinic sources. Neither the form nor the size of this table excludes the possibilities of sacrifice and/or sacred meals, which the pagan Hellenistic environment would naturally infer from the equipment. The question of use remains an open one. Torah shrines have been claimed for several synagogues, but unambiguous evidence exists only for Dura because of the paintings surrounding the niche. Even here, however, the arrangements of benches on the side and in front of the niche leave open some questions as to their use.

Conscious cultic orientation has not been proven for any of the diaspora synagogues found.[70] Even the Torah niche at Dura, remarkably placed into a broad side of the room not into a small side, points more to Sidon or Tyre, whereas one of the smaller sides would have been physically closer to Jerusalem, although not pointing precisely in that direction either. In fact, in all cases the position of the synagogues, including that of their later versions, was and remained defined by local streets. Why not assume that the inside arrangements were also conditioned and defined by local conveniences, among which we would have to count the local understanding of liturgical necessities?

These are just a few examples which show that the new finds have not documented any sense of legal or ideological conformity in diaspora Judaism, let alone a dependence on Palestine, and in particular not dependence on the Pharisaic rabbinate. The people who built and maintained those structures proved, too, that they were confident about being Jewish. They seemed to be in constant exchange with fellow Jews, as the existence of guestrooms proves.[71] But the great variety of finds shows that the local Jewish communities were able to judge for themselves what was necessary for them and that, as much as they dialogued with their Jewish tradition and fellow Jews, they were also ready to communicate with their pagan environment without fear. The many changes in buildings and equipment demonstrate that they were ready and able to constantly redefine themselves.[72] How far-reaching and confident the dialogue with the pagan environment was is seen in the use of pagan symbols, images, and features which from a "biblical perspective" would appear idolatrous. Goodenough has presented enough evidence for that, and Morton Smith has pointed to the connection even with magic.[73]

By chances of soil, climate, and history, the Dura synagogue has come to preserve the most spectacular ancient pictorial find outside Italy and Egypt. The Dura paintings belong stylistically in the context of Hellenistic and Roman art and have by chance become a major demonstration piece for it. The relationship to the contemporary pagan environment shows in content as well as in style.[74] Thus we have a variation of pagan art and ideology as well as a variation of Jewish life and religion. These imaginative interpretations of biblical tradition and their inspired integration of "foreign" pagan elements should not surprise the student of biblical tradition which a closer look lets appear as less purist and puritan, allowing us instead to surmise a vast base of popular religion even more unashamedly "syncretistic" than the Old Testament literature surviving. The historian of religion might even start to ask—and the remains of the diaspora synagogue would contribute to this trajectory—whether one of the marks of identity not just of Jewish but also of Israelite (and then also of "Christian") religion was the readiness for syncretistic integration and amalgamation.[75]

This syncretism cannot be judged as a sign of weakness—on the contrary. One does not merely receive, one radiates too. I cannot go much into the influence of the biblical religion on its environment; that is an assignment for further research. During the Hellenistic era, when Judaism took its place and role in this pluralistic world culture with ingenious courage and enthusiasm, Jews started to play a very active part in it, in varying ways for a long time.[76] The missionary activity of the Hellenistic Jews, their interpretation of scriptures, their concept of the divine man, and their idea of their religion as a world religion with eschatological dimensions may have had the most dramatic influence possible, if the many indications that the ideology of the Augustan reform had connections with that propaganda prove to be correct. Many hints and parallels in the literature of Augustan "theology," most of all Horace, Vergil, and

Livy, seem to intimate that. This is a fascinating field for intense studies, which would be all the more breathtaking if even Posidonius would have to be seen in this sphere of influence and if he too had functioned as a powerful mediator, as Moses Hadas has suggested.[77]

Before I go any further into the theology of Jewish Apologetics, I want to conclude that as the evidence for assuming a strong missionary intent and activity of Judaism has increased since my book appeared, so has proof for the central and stabilizing function of this propagandistic activity, its major contribution to the cohesiveness of Jewish religion. The content of this contribution, its interpretation of the scriptures, has been the focus of attention in much of my book and will be discussed further (below).[78] In the present consideration of the sociological dimensions of my inquiry, I want to touch on some remaining problems worth further research, problems that deal with the form of synagogue worship and with the issue my book has been most of all associated with, that of the θεῖος ἀνήρ.

BIBLIOGRAPHY 3

Barbara **Aland**, "Marcion, Versuch einer neuen Interpretation," *ZThK* 70 (1973) 420–47. Shimon **Applebaum**, "The Legal Status of the Jewish Communities in the Diaspora," in Safrai and Stern, eds., *Jewish People*, 1:420–63; "The Organisation of the Jewish Communities in the Diaspora," in Safrai and Stern, eds., *Jewish People*, 1:464–503. J.P.V.D. **Balsdon**, *Romans and Aliens* (Chapel Hill: University of North Carolina Press, 1979). Elias **Bickerman**, "Symbolism in the Dura Synagogue," *HTR* 58 (1965) 127–51. François **Blanchetiére**, "Juifs et non-juifs: Essai sur la diaspora en Asie-Mineure," *RHPR* 54 (1974) 367–82. Richard **Brilliant**, "Painting at Dura-Europos and Roman Art," in Gutmann, ed., *Dura-Europos*, 23–30. Bernadette **Brooten**, *Women Leaders in the Ancient Synagogue* (Brown Judaic Studies 36: Chico, Calif.: Scholars Press, 1982). Philippe **Bruneau**, *Recherches sur les cultes de Délos à l'époque hellènistique et à l'époque impériale* (Bibliothèque des écoles françaises d'Athènes et de Rome 217; Paris, 1970). Klaus **Bussman**, *Themen der paulinischen Missionspredigt auf dem Hintergrund der spätjüdisch-hellenistischen Missionsliteratur* (Europ. Missionsschr. 23.13; Bern: Lang, 1972). Marilyn J. S. **Chiat**, "First Century Synagogue Architecture: Methodological Problems," in Gutmann, ed., *Ancient Synagogues*, 41–60; *Handbook of Synagogue Architecture* (Brown Judaic Studies 29; Chico, Calif.: Scholars Press, 1982). Carsten

Colpe, "Manichäismus," *RGG*, 4:714–22; "Synkretismus," *Der kleine Pauly*, 5:1648–52. Gaalyaha Cornfield, *Daniel to Paul: Jews in Conflict with Graeco-Roman Civilization* (New York: Macmillan, 1962). William D. Davies, *Christian Origins and Judaism* (London: Darton, Longman, Todd, 1962). Charles H. Dodd, *The Bible and the Greeks* (London: Hodder & Stoughton, 1954). Samuel K. Eddy, *The King Is Dead: Studies in Near Eastern Resistance to Hellenism, 334–331 B.C.* (Lincoln: University of Nebraska Press, 1961). Otto Eissfeld, "Dura-Europos," *RAC*, 4:358–70. Louis H. Feldman, "Josephus as an Apologist of the Greco-Roman World," in Schüssler-Fiorenza, ed., *Aspects*, 68–96. Henry A. Fischel, *Rabbinic Literature and Greco-Roman Philosophy* (SPB 21; Leiden: Brill, 1972); "Story and History," in Fischel, ed., *Essays*, 443–72; (ed.) *Essays in Greco-Roman and Related Talmudic Literature* (New York: Ktav, 1977). Jean B. Frey, *Corpus Inscriptionum Iudaicarum* (New York: Ktav, 1975). Harald Fuchs, *Der geistige Widerstand gegen Rom in der antiken Welt* (Berlin: De Gruyter, 1964). Leo Fuchs, *Die Juden Ägyptens in ptolemäischer und römischer Zeit* (Vienna: Roth, 1924). John G. Gager, *Kingdom and Community* (Englewood Cliffs: Prentice Hall, 1975). Dieter Georgi, "Weisheit Salomos," in Kümmel, ed., *Jüdische Schriften aus hellenistisch-römischer Zeit* 3/4 (Gütersloh: Mohn, 1980); "Das Wesen der Weisheit nach der Weisheit Salomos," in Jacob Taubes, ed., *Gnosis und Politik* (Paderborn: Schöningh, 1984) 66–81. Jocelyn Godwin, *Mystery Religion in the Ancient World* (San Francisco: Harper & Row, 1981). Michael Grant, *The Jews in the Roman World* (London: Weidenfeld & Nicholson, 1973). William S. Green, ed., *Approaches to Ancient Judaism* (Brown Judaic Studies 1, 9, 11; Chico, Calif.: Scholars Press, 1978, 1980, 1981). Ithamar Gruenwald, *Apocalyptic and Merkavah Mysticism* (AGJU 14; Leiden: Brill, 1980). Joseph Gutmann, ed., *The Dura-Europos Synagogue: A Reevaluation* (Religion and the Arts 1; Missoula, Mont.: Scholars Press, 1973); (ed.), *Ancient Synagogues: The State of Research* (Brown Judaic Studies 22; Chico, Calif.: Scholars Press, 1981); (ed.), *The Synagogue: Studies in Origins, Archaeology, and Architecture* (New York: Ktav, 1975). Moses Hadas, *Hellenistic Culture: Fusion and Diffusion* (New York: Norton, 1959). Georg Hanfmann and Jane C. Waldbaum, *A Survey of Sardis and the Major Monuments Outside the City Walls* (Archaeological Exploration of Sardis 1; Cambridge, Mass.: Harvard University Press, 1975). Adolf Harnack, *Marcion: Das Evangelium vom fremden Gott* (Darmstadt: Wissenschaftliche Buchgesellschaft, 1960). Harald Hegermann, "Das Griechisch sprechende Judentum" and "Philo v. Alexandrien," in Maier and Schreiner, eds., *Literatur*, 328–69; "Das hellenistische Judentum," in Leipoldt and Grundmann, eds., *Umwelt*, 1:292–345 and 2:234–314. Martin Hengel, *Judaism and Hellenism: Studies in Their Encounter in Palestine During the Early Hellenistic Period* (Philadelphia: Fortress, 1974); *Juden, Griechen, und Barbaren: Aspekte der Hellenisierung des Judentums in vorchristlicher Zeit* (SBS 76; Stuttgart: KBW, 1976); "Proseuche und Synagoge: Jüdische

Gemeinde, Gotteshaus und Gottesdienst in der Diaspora und Palästina," in Gutmann, ed., *The Synagogue*, 27–54. Sharon K. **Heyob**, *The Cult of Isis Among Women in the Greco-Roman World* (EPRO 51; Leiden: Brill, 1975). Lawrence A. **Hoffman**, "Censoring In and Censoring Out: A Function of Liturgical Language," in Gutmann, ed., *Ancient Synagogues* 19–37. Keith **Hopkins**, "Elite Mobility in the Roman Empire," in Moses I. Finley, ed., *Studies in Ancient Society* (London and Boston: Sledge & Paul, 1974) 103–20. Wilhelm **Hornbostel**, *Sarapis: Studien zur Überlieferungsgeschichte der Erscheinungsformen und Wandlungen der Gestalt eines Gottes* (Leiden: Brill, 1973). Froward **Hüttenmeister** and Gottfried **Reeg**, *Die antiken Synagogen in Israel* (Beihefte zum Tübinger Atlas des Vorderen Orients B 12/1 and 2; Wiesbaden: Reichert, 1977). Sherman E. **Johnson**, "A Sabazios Inscription from Sardis," in Neusner, ed., *Religions*, 542–50; "Asia Minor and Early Christianity," in Neusner, ed., *Christianity*, 2:77–145. Hans G. **Kippenberg**, *Religion und Klassenbildung im antiken Judäa: Eine religionssoziologische Studie zum Verhältnis von Tradition und gesellschaftlicher Entwicklung* (SUNT 14; Göttingen: Vandenhoeck & Ruprecht, 1978). Günther **Klein**, "Der Synkretismus als theologisches Problem in der ältesten christlichen Apologetik," in *Rekonstruktion und Interpretation* (BEvTh 50; Munich: Kaiser, 1969) 262–301. Helmut **Koester**, *Introduction to the New Testament* (2 vols.; Philadelphia: Fortress; Elmsford, N.Y.: De Gruyter, 1982). Helmut **Koester** and James M. **Robinson**, *Trajectories Through Early Christianity* (Philadelphia: Fortress, 1971). A. Thomas **Kraabel**, "The Diaspora Synagogue: Archaeological and Epigraphic Evidence Since Sukenik," *ANRW* 19/1: 477–510; "The Disappearance of the Godfearers," *Numen* 28/2 (1981) 113–26; "Jews in Imperial Rome," *JJS* 30 (1979) 41–58; "Paganism and Judaism: The Sardis Evidence," in A. Benoit, M. Philonenko, and C. Vogel, eds., *Paganisme, Judaisme, Christianisme: Mélanges offerts à M. Simon* (Paris: Boccard, 1978) 13–33; "The Roman Diaspora: Six Questionable Assumptions," *JJS* 33/1 and 2 (1982) 445–64; "Social Systems of Six Diaspora Synagogues," in Gutmann, ed., *Ancient Synagogues*, 79–91. Karl G. **Kuhn** and Hartmut **Stegemann**, "Proselyten," PWSup 9:1248–83. George **La Piana**, "Foreign Groups in Rome During the First Centuries," *HTR* 20 (1927) 183–403. Johannes **Leipoldt** and Walter **Grundmann**, eds., *Die Umwelt des Urchristentums* (Berlin: Evangelische Verlagsanstalt, 1965–1966). Harry J. **Leon**, *The Jews of Ancient Rome* (Philadelphia: Jewish Publication Society, 1960). Saul **Lieberman**, *Hellenism in Jewish Palestine* (New York: Jewish Theological Seminary, 1962); "How Much Greek in Palestine," in Fischel, ed., *Essays*, 325–43; "Rabbinic Interpretation of Scripture," Fischel, ed., *Essays*, 289–324. Baruch **Lifshitz**, *Donateurs et fondateurs dans les synagogues juives* (Cahiers de la Revue biblique 7; Paris: Gabalda, 1967). Ramsay **MacMullen**, *Enemies of the Roman Order: Treason, Unrest, and Alienation in the Roman Empire* (Cambridge, Mass.: Harvard University Press, 1966). Johann **Maier**, *Geschichte der jüdischen Religion von der Zeit Alexanders des Grossen bis zur Aufklärung* (New

York, N.Y.: De Gruyter, 1972). Johann **Maier** and Josef **Schreiner**, eds., *Literatur und Religion des Frühjudentums: Eine Einführung* (Würzburg and Gütersloh: Echter-Mohn, 1973). Abraham **Malherbe**, *Social Aspects of Early Christianity*, 2d ed. enl. (Philadelphia: Fortress, 1983). Ralph **Marcus**, "Antisemitism in the Hellenistic World," *Jewish Social Studies* 2 (1942) 3–25. Beele D. **Mazur**, *Studies on Jewry in Greece*, vol. 1 (Athens: Hestia, 1935). Wayne **Meeks**, *The First Urban Christians: The Social World of the Apostle Paul* (New Haven and London: Yale University Press, 1983). David G. **Mitten**, "A New Look at Ancient Sardis," *BA* 29 (1966) 26–68. Arnaldo **Momigliano**, *Alien Wisdom: The Limits of Hellenization* (Cambridge: Cambridge University Press, 1975). George F. **Moore**, *Judaism in the First Centuries of the Christian Era: The Age of the Tannaim* (3 vols.; Cambridge, Mass.: Harvard University Press, 1927–30). Reimar **Müller**, "Antike Gesellschaftstheorie, römische Weltanschauung und Philosophie," in Jürss, ed., *Geschichte* (Bibliography 5), 336–49, 453–60, 502–29, 592–600. Jacob **Neusner**, *Ancient Israel After Catastrophe: The Religious Worldview of the Mishnah* (Charlottesville: University of Virginia Press, 1983); *First Century Judaism in Crisis: Yohanan ben Zakkai and the Renaissance of Torah* (Nashville: Abingdon, 1982); *From Politics to Piety: The Emergence of Pharisaic Judaism* (Englewood Cliffs, N.J.: Prentice-Hall, 1979); *Method and Meaning in Ancient Judaism* (Brown Judaic Studies 10, 15, 16; Chico, Calif.: Scholars Press, 1979–82); *Rabbinic Traditions About the Pharisees Before 70* (Leiden: Brill, 1971); (ed.), *Christianity, Judaism, and Other Greco-Roman Cults: Studies for Morton Smith at Sixty* (Studies in Judaism in Late Antiquity; Leiden: Brill, 1975); *Religions in Antiquity: Essays in Memory of E. R. Goodenough* (Studies in the History of Religions 14; Leiden: Brill, 1968). Arthur D. **Nock**, "Hellenistic Mysteries and Christian Sacraments," in Zeph Stewart, ed., *Essays on Religion and the Ancient World* (Oxford: Clarendon, 1972) 2:791–820; "The Milieu of Gnosticism," in Zeph Stewart, ed., *Essays on Religion and the Ancient World* (Oxford: Clarendon, 1972) 1:441–51. James **Reese**, *Hellenistic Influence on the Book of Wisdom and Its Consequences* (AnBib 41; Rome: 1970). Israel **Renov**, "The Seat of Moses," in Gutmann, ed., *The Synagogue*, 233–38. Louis and J. **Robert**, "Inscriptions Grècques de side en Pamphylie," *Revue de philologie, de literature, et d'histoire* 32 (1958) 15–53; *Nouvelles inscriptions de Sardis* (Archaeological Exploration of Sardis 1; Paris: Maissoneuxs, 1964). Kurt **Rudolph**, *Gnosis: The Nature and History of Gnosticism*, trans. R. McL. Wilson (San Francisco: Harper & Row, 1977). Shmuel **Safrai** and Moses **Stern**, eds., *The Jewish People in the First Century* (Assen: van Gorkum, 1974); "Relations Between the Diaspora and the Land of Israel," in Safrai and Stern, eds., *Jewish People*, 1:84–215. E. P. **Sanders**, *Paul and Palestinian Judaism: A Comparison of Patterns of Religion* (Philadelphia: Fortress, 1977). Samuel **Sandmel**, "Philo Judaeus: An Introduction to the Man, His Writings, and His Significance," *ANRW* 2.21.1:3–46. Hans M. **Schenke**, "Die Gnosis," in Leipoldt and

Grundmann, *Umwelt*, 370–415. Carl **Schneider**, *Kulturgeschichte des Hellenismus* (Munich: Beck, 1967–69). Gershom G. **Scholem**, *Jewish Gnosticism: Merkabah Mysticism and Talmudic Tradition* (New York: Jewish Theological Seminary, 1960). Wolfgang **Schrage**, "Συναγωγή," *TDNT*, 7:798–852. Emil **Schürer**, *The History of the Jewish People in the Age of Jesus Christ, 175 B.C.–135 A.D.* (ed. Geza Vermès and F. Millar; Edinburgh: Clark, 1973). Elisabeth **Schüssler-Fiorenza**, ed., *Aspects of Religious Propaganda in Judaism and Early Christianity* (Notre Dame and London: University of Notre Dame Press, 1976); "Miracles, Mission, and Apologetics: An Introduction," in Schüssler-Fiorenza, ed., *Aspects*, 1–25. Andrew **Seager**, "Ancient Synagogue Architecture: Methodological Problems," in Gutmann, ed., *Ancient Synagogues*, 39–47; "The Architecture of the Dura and Sardis Synagogues," in Gutmann, ed., *The Synagogue*, 149–93. Jan N. **Sevenster**, *The Roots of Pagan Antisemitism in the Ancient World* (Leiden: Brill, 1975). Adriann N. **Sherwin-White**, *Racial Prejudice in Imperial Rome* (Cambridge: Cambridge University Press, 1967). Marcel **Simon**, "Remarques sur les synagogues à images de Doura et de Palestine," in *Recherches d'histoire Judéo-Chrétienne* (Paris, 1962) 188–98, 204–8. E. Mary **Smallwood**, *Jews Under Roman Rule: From Pompey to Diocletian* (Studies in Judaism in Late Antiquity 20; Leiden: Brill, 1976); *Philonis Alexandrini Legatio ad Gaium* (Leiden: Brill, 1961). Morton **Smith**, "The Image of God: Notes on the Hellenization of Judaism," *BJRL* 40 (1957–58) 473–512; "Goodenough's 'Jewish Symbols' in Retrospect," in Gutmann, ed., *The Synagogue*, 194–209; "Palestinian Judaism of the First Century," in M. Davis, ed., *Israel: Its Role in Civilization* (New York: Harper & Row, 1956) 67–81; *Palestinian Parties and Politics That Shaped the Old Testament* (New York: Columbia University Press, 1971). Victor **Tcherikover**, "Die hellenistischen Städtegründungen von Alexander dem Grossen bis auf die Römerzeit," *Philologus Sup.* 19 (1927) 182ff.; *Hellenistic Civilization and the Jews* (Philadelphia: Jewish Publication Society of America; Jerusalem: Magnes Press, 1959). Karl W. **Tröger**, "Spekulativ-esoterische Ansätze: Frühjudentum und Gnosis," in Johann Maier and Josef Schreiner, eds., *Literatur*, 310–19; (ed.), *Altes Testament—Frühjudentum—Gnosis* (Gütersloh: Mohn, 1980). Roland de **Vaux**, *Ancient Israel: Its Life and Institutions* (London: Darton, Longman & Todd, 1961). Geo **Widengren**, ed., *Der Manichäismus* (Darmstadt: Wissenschaftliche Buchgesellschaft, 1977).

EPILOGUE NOTES 28–78

28. In recent years the number of studies on biblical wisdom and its oriental counterparts has become stupendous. Jewish wisdom outside the Hebrew Bible has found much less attention. There is an abbreviated

discussion of my views on the matter, with a bibliography, in my essay "Das Wesen der Weisheit," where I present a picture of the various branches of postexilic wisdom and of the place of the Wisdom of Solomon within that.

29. Palestinian Jewry during the second century C.E. gained influence on the diaspora first and most of all because of the forced emigration of a great number of Jews from Palestine after the second Jewish War. These emigrants remained in contact with their teachers, who had stayed behind and established themselves in Galilee. Because the Pharisaic rabbinate was willing to collaborate with the Romans, the Romans rewarded them with authority over the Jewry at large (through the patriarchate which was more than the cultic centrality and moral authority Jerusalem used to have). The Romans apparently thought that measure would give them greater control over the Jews in the Roman Empire. The provision which caused the greatest change in the character of the dispersion was the Roman prohibition of Jewish proselytizing. Although not completely successful, this restriction nevertheless changed the character of the dispersion radically, closed the diaspora synagogue more or less toward the outside, and exposed it to the Palestinian rabbinate. The reduction of Jewish missionary power concurrently met Roman and Pharisaic rabbinic interest. Some other aspects are covered in J. Neusner's *From Politics* and his *First Century*, and also in M. Smallwood's *Jews*.

30. There is no justification for calling any of the Jewish writings outside the Hebrew Bible or outside the Pharisaic rabbinic tradition heterodox or less Jewish. For the historian and historian of theology, the whole range of apocrypha, pseudepigrapha, Qumran writings, and Hellenistic-Jewish writings, including Jewish Gnostic literature, has equal standing with the Mishnah, Tosephtah, and Talmud. Morton Smith, in his various studies, has given an impression of that colorful picture.

31. The comparison often made with Islam and with the role of the Qur'an within it is not correct, because in Islam the interpretation of the Qur'an clearly has a character subordinate to the Qur'an itself.

32. Whether the Palestinian rabbinate from the second century C.E. on exercised worldwide authority and control is still debated, but even if that were the case, this central authority never developed to the degree that we know from the Roman Catholic Church.

33. This is clear in Ernst Troeltsch's definition of sect operative in his *Social Teaching of the Christian Churches* (2 vols.; New York: Harper & Row, 1960). For him the sect is defined first by its antithesis to *the* church. But that church did not exist in the first three centuries. Troeltsch reads backward the *state-supported success* of one group of Jesus-believers over all the other competing ones. His description of the church's beginnings in the first volume of the work mentioned is astonishingly undifferentiated; it is amazing that he neglects the discoveries of his friends of the *Religionsgeschichtliche Schule* regarding the character and authenticity of the various groups of Jesus-believers. Recent research has confirmed and enhanced

much of the research of Troeltsch's colleagues and heavily called into question much of his own description of early Christianity and thus the consequences drawn from it in the sociology of religion and sociology at large. The same is true with respect to Max Weber, whose *Ancient Judaism* (New York: Free Press, 1967) betrays a curious unwillingness to recognize Jewish pluralism and universalism, particularly not as functioning organizational phenomena. This unwillingness, unfortunately so influential in the area of sociology, has an ideological background. In Weber's Protestant mind, Judaism is a competitor with Christianity, but it *must not be* an equal one. Thus the Jews *must be* sectarian, that is inferior, and the Pharisees are portrayed as the most authentic expression of that.

34. It has been argued that a pyramidlike organizational structure is the more successful structure, in fact, the only lasting one. In his frequently reprinted *Grammar of Politics* (London: Allen & Unwin, 1963), Harold J. Laski has said (p. 85): "A working theory of the State must, in fact, be conceived in administrative terms. Its will is the decision arrived at by a small number of men to whom is confided the legal power of making decisions." "The right to pass judgment upon the quality" of these few men is held to be necessary but is in this theory and practice of government at best a secondary effort—most often after the damage has been done already.

35. "Anarchic" here is taken in its most literal sense, i.e., "without head," which means without an elevated center of authority, power, and control, without a hierarchical structure or line of authority. In fact, "anarchy" is a frequent phenomenon today, often of considerable duration. Modern sciences, economics, trade (particularly world trade), and, not to be forgotten, Western democracies as such provide many examples.

36. On the Marcionite church, cf. A. Harnack, 143–96. On the Manicheans, cf. G. Widengren and C. Colpe, "Manichäismus," 719.

37. Prior to Marcion, neither the idea nor the practice of an *exclusive* canon of either OT or NT writings existed in the church. Even in Judaism the concept evolved only during the period of "Jamnia," but it did not completely succeed there either. Collections of writings existed already, not only of older Jewish writings (including the later "biblical" ones) but also of Paul. But none of these was understood as exclusive. Whether a four-gospel collection existed before Justin is debatable, but it certainly did not exist in any exclusive sense as the continuously ongoing production of further gospels proves, not only of Gnostic gospels. That the apocryphal gospels presuppose the four "canonical" Gospels has not been proven. Those who have argued that always confused the use of common sayings- or narrative-traditions with dependence on the gospels known to us. On canon, see further below, pp. 431–34.

38. The Manichaeans were exterminated by the Mongols in the thirteenth century. They are mentioned last in the law code of the Ming emperors, 1370–74; cf. C. Colpe, "Manichäismus," 715.

39. An interesting factor in the "Catholic" church's development of theol-

ogy and organization, especially its Western version's development, is the impact of Neoplatonic ideology. I am thinking in particular of the ideas of the one in relation to the many and of stability, much understudied features of Catholic, especially Roman Catholic, organizational ideology, and only secondarily issues of reality. Even the concept of reality itself evolving in the West is dependent on Neoplatonism as mediated through the church.

40. In the case of Jewish religion, it is known, for instance, that many towns had more than one synagogue and that the increase in the number of synagogues at a given place was not always due to an increase in the size of the local Jewish community alone but sometimes seems to have been due to differences also.

41. M. Rostovtzeff, quoted by Wayne Meeks, 11. This interplay of a vast plurality of social entities discussed above naturally entailed friction, conflict, and oppression, as well as resistance.

42. The structural resemblance and ideological similarity between the victorious branch of the church and the Diocletian-Constantinian organization, and the increase of this likeness after the merger of church and state, deserve further attention. The coalition between both powers created further success through the devastating attacks on pagans, Jews, and Christian "heretics." All this has not been studied as thoroughly as the persecutions of Christians before Constantine.

43. I call this development counterrevolutionary for two reasons: (a) because of its static counteraction against the dynamic tendency and structure of Hellenistic society and culture, which in that respect had been a permanent revolution, and (b) because it was a reaction against movements within Hellenistic culture and religion, like Gnosticism or some other oriental religions, which had radicalized the dynamic, indeed revolutionary, tendencies of their environment (as well as of their own heritage). Thus they had overtaken Hellenism and had turned against it on and from the left, as it were.

44. As covered by the Apocrypha and pseudepigrapha, the Qumran writings, Hellenistic-Jewish literature, and even some of the Nag-Hammadi tractates.

45. Unfortunately, Victor Tcherikover's unsubstantiated claims in his *Hellenistic Civilization* about the intentions of Jewish Apologetic writers have revived these prejudices. Tcherikover's book appears to be rather ideological, no match for his "Die hellenistischen Städtegründungen."

46. In many of Hadas's studies, summarized in his *Culture*.

47. The oldest extant but by no means the original version is that under the name of Pseudo-Callisthenes.

48. M. Braun (Bibliography 4) has argued convincingly that Hellenistic romances could contain elements of political and social criticism, even insubordination.

49. One highpoint in my life came in 1964, when I met Goodenough,

whom I had known only from his literary work. This encounter, occurring not long before he died, became an inspiring testament for me.

50. Morton Smith, in his review of the last volume of Goodenough's *Symbols* (Bibliography 1), has shown in a masterly fashion how much Moore's famous portrayal of rabbinic Judaism reflected Moore's own religion (and, by way of rebellion against it, also Goodenough's): "'Normative' Judaism was as he [Moore] pictured it, much like the normative, upper-class New England Protestantism of 1920: common sense, respectable, law-abiding, moral, pharasaic, in a word, square. But . . . 'normative' Judaism was not 'normative.' It was, like New England 'society,' a puritanic sect walled up in its self-made ghetto" (Smith, "Retrospect," 63).

An equally fascinating portrayal of the formative religious and political perspective of Moore's German equivalent, E. Schürer's *History* could be given, although in Schürer's case it would be a German Lutheran's apologetic need for a certain fixed image of Judaism.

51. It would be unfair to the giants mentioned in the previous footnote if I pretended that my vision of the NT environment was less influenced by my religious, cultural, and political heritage, my reaction to it and to my present world, as if my view were historical reality itself while theirs were not. But my very experience, not the least of the survival of plurality over various attempts of conformism, has made me more appreciative of variations and of the possibility that they are able to protect and further integrity and identity.

52. The person who after G. Scholem has contributed the most to our knowledge of this branch of Judaism is I. Gruenwald. In *Apocalyptic*, 134–234, he discusses the relevant texts. In the preceding chapters he discusses mystical elements in earlier Jewish, including rabbinical, literature.

53. Not only in his more recent works since his discovery of the Secret Gospel of Mark, but also in earlier studies, e.g., in "Judaism." In "Retrospect," Smith has made important remarks about the evidence pointing to a Jewish folk religion. He warns also against the ideal of a well-controlled Jewish, even rabbinic, religion after the Jewish Wars. Cf. also his "Judaism," *Parties*, and *Jesus* (the latter in Bibliography 4).

54. It is obvious from the magical papyri that Hellenistic magic was strongly influenced by Judaism. That pagan magic, including theurgic practices, influenced Jewish practice and thought has been shown by I. Gruenwald, *Apocalyptic* (see his index under "Magic—Greek papyri"). He refers also to other authors, like Urbach, who give additional information on related phenomena in rabbinic Judaism. Gruenwald, Smith, and many others, starting with the *Religionsgeschichtliche Schule*, have demonstrated convincingly that the transition from magic to mysticism in antiquity has been fluid. That mystical aspects of Jewish practice and theology, especially of Hellenistic Judaism, have been heavily influenced by non-Jewish Hellenism has been abundantly demonstrated, with Wisdom of Solomon,

Philo, and Jewish Gnosticism providing the major examples. The other direction from Judaism to Hellenism has been less researched. The history of the effect of Philo's writings would be the most prominent starting place. Wolfson's thesis (Philo; Bibliography 1) about their impact on the history of ideas needs some correction, but it deserves further scrutiny. Neopythagoreanism and Middle- and Neoplatonism might not be without Jewish traces. Jewish Gnosticism definitely had an influence on general culture, and not only through Christian Gnosticism. Here the Corpus Hermeticum, for instance, may yield more evidence than C. H. Dodd has observed already. M. Hadas, *Culture*, 108–9, speaks about possible connections of Posidonius with Jewish tradition. More on magic, pp. 403, 408, 421 n. 128.

55. At least the *Apocalypse of Adam, The Second Treatise of the Great Seth*, and *The Three Steles of Seth* are of Jewish origin: so probably *The Hypostasis of the Archons, On the Origin of the World, The Letter of Eugnostos, The Thunder, The Concept of Our Great Power, The Discourse on the Eighth and the Ninth, The Paraphrase of Shem, The Teachings of Silvanus, Zostrianos, The Thought of Norea, Marasanes, Allogenes, Hypsiphrone*, and outside the Nag Hammadi Library, the original form of *The Odes of Solomon*. The Corpus Hermeticum is under Jewish Gnostic influence too.

56. Correctly emphasized by A. T. Kraabel, "Roman Diaspora."

57. Definitely cultic considerations as to the architectural position and structure of synagogues are documented but late.

58. On Jewish residential areas, see E. M. Smallwood, *Philo*, 19–23, 214–19, 233–40; on synagogues, see ibid., 45–47, 220–24.

59. On peristyles, see Friedrich Ebert; Heinrich Sulze; and A. W. van Buren, "Peristylium," PW 19.1:860; Supp. 7:950–72.

60. On the holiness of synagogues, see M. Hengel, "Proseuche," 36–39, 50–51, 54.

61. There is no evidence that the peristyle court was associated with the Torah procession. In any case, the documentation for the existence of a Torah procession is itself very late.

62. B. Brooten, 103–38, has shown that there is next to no evidence for women's galleries in ancient Jewish synagogues, and none in the diaspora.

63. This is the result of Brooten's important study.

64. On overcoming of class distinctions in mystery religions and on their stressing of ethical responsibility, see J. Leipoldt, *Mysterien* (Bibliography 4), 10–11, 16–17, 36–37.

65. See both collections of L. and J. Robert, nos. 1 and 2; J. B. Frey; B. Lifshitz.

66. See the two cautious presentations of the problems of Jewish expansion and assimilation (presupposing more an ethnic than a missionary character) by M. Hadas, 30–44, and H. Koester, *Introduction*, 1:219–28.

Both Philo and Paul give examples for ethnic Jews bearing non-Jewish names. For Paul, Luke claims also a Hebraic name, Saul. But since Paul himself never mentions it, not even when he stresses his Jewish origin, and since Acts 13:4–12, the pericope that suggests the switch from his Hebraic name to his Roman name, has no ring of historical authenticity, the idea of the Pauline double name appears to be an expression of Luke's tendentiousness. Whether this applies to the question of Paul's Roman citizenship also is hard to say. The fact that Paul, who stems from the Eastern Mediterranean, bears a Roman name could speak for Roman citizenship, although Paul himself never mentions it. But Paul and Philo are very emphatic with respect to their Jewish ethnicity. The same would be true with Jews elsewhere who bore double names or indicated their ethnic Jewish origin otherwise (family or local connections). The total absence of any such reference puts an ethnic relationship in doubt, especially in the context of tombs but even more in the case of Italian inscriptions, where the Roman practice would suggest a preference for the retention of family ties in the name and where many Jews continue to maintain such ethnic indicators in their names. Therefore, the absence of such an indication becomes all the more telling.

67. On similarities between Pharisaic-rabbinic and Hellenistic-Jewish interpretations, see, e.g., S. Lieberman.

68. Provisions for ablutions in synagogues, for instance, in Dura, Priene, Sardis.

69. Recent research has shown that even Palestinian practice and legislation as to synagogues was much more liberal than conceded earlier.

70. Scholars to this day argue that ancient synagogues already in their majority were consciously oriented toward Jerusalem. But this is not true even for the majority of the Palestinian synagogues, as described by F. Hüttenmeister and by Chiatt, contrary to their claims. There should be at least some discussion about what degree of approximation would be necessary in order to state orientation, since the direction is so frequently very far off Jerusalem. The important question of how the layout of the synagogue related to that of the street and neighboring buildings outside the synagogue complex is rarely discussed. All this applies to the diaspora synagogues too. Here the conscious orientation direction toward Jerusalem has nowhere been proven. There is no proof that there was even a common direction of prayer of an entire Jewish congregation in the first century C.E., let alone that a worshiping community would turn collectively in a direction not identical with that of a building. We do not even possess any clear criteria as to the distinction of a front of a synagogue from its side—or its rear for that matter. The distinction between small-side and broad-side does not really help, nor do doors necessarily.

71. Extra rooms of probable guestroom function have been found in Delos (2), Aegina (2), Ostia (several), Dura (several), and Hammam Lif (several).

72. Archaeological finds relating to diaspora Judaism have given no support to the common opinion that Judaism in the Mediterranean outside

Palestine was predominantly an ethnic phenomenon and oriented toward a "homeland." The orientation of the synagogues toward Jerusalem was late. Inscriptions do not contain much, if any, geographical ideology or nostalgia, and they do not emphasize ethnicity. The inscriptions do not show anything comparable to the lists in Ezra 2 and 8 or Nehemiah 7 and 12, i.e., biblical models which—authentic or not—demonstrate connection with the homeland despite the exile. It can be imagined that there would be lists of that kind in Hellenistic times also, and for mere ideological reasons. Therefore, their absence in the context of the Jewish diaspora is significant.

The pictorial remains of the diaspora synagogues do not contribute to the concept of the Holy Land or to that of Israel's continuance as an ethnically and culturally *different* phenomenon. There is no depiction of holy geography (land, river, city, mountain, temple) as the present center of reverence. There is no hieratic stylizing of contemporary Jewish dress or customs. Hebrew and Aramaic are not treated as major, let alone holy, languages in the diaspora remains. As for material objects, there is no resemblance to peculiar Palestinian architecture.

The only holy cult object relating to Palestine is the menorah, which is a replica of a piece of temple equipment in Jerusalem. The later use of the symbol of the ark does not relate as much to the throne of God in the Jerusalem temple as to the ark of the covenant in the exodus; that is more a literary than a physical connection, based on the symbolism of interpreters like Philo who because of the Pentateuch dwell more on the desert experience than on the experience of dwelling in "eretz Israel."

The one great exception is the pilgrimage to the temple in Jerusalem, and associated with that the temple tax for the upkeep of that center of pilgrimage. But the pilgrimages literally bypassed the indigenous political and social structures of Palestine outside the temple, with the exception of those supporting the pilgrimage itself (for protection as well as convenience).

Judaism, in fact, had followed more radically a pattern which had evolved in the Hellenistic world. Together with the migration of people the Hellenistic religions had spread over larger areas. Migrants usually retained some connection with their geographical and ethnic origin. But as they took their gods and rites with them they adjusted and changed them as well, and they received "strangers" into their ranks, and even started to proselytize them. Often the geographical orientation was toward a particular polis. But as the religion evolved, city, land, and people slowly turned into mythical phenomena, partly cultural, partly nostalgic, partly eschatological. Whereas the various aspects of these religions had been related to the land and people, in Hellenistic times they became separated. And these religions started to create their own people, partly emigrants, partly converts, the latter slowly taking the initiative, most dramatically in the case of the Romans.

73. Smith, "Retrospect," 60–61.

74. On Roman elements in Dura paintings, see R. Brilliant.

75. To this day the term "syncretism" is offensive to many historians of religion, particularly those of religious persuasion, because for them the term means a hodgepodge, lacks integrity, and confuses identity. But since the first appearance of the term in Plutarch's *Moralia* (490ab), it means a determined coalition which is maintained despite and against difficulties caused by variety and difference. Thus integrity is an essential, if not central, element of the concept of syncretism. Here blending is not just accidental but intentional. Syncretism means integration, neither imperialistic absorption nor involuntary accumulation. A syncretistic phenomenon is not everything to everyone, but it possesses a hermeneutical direction which interprets the elements integrated. Whether this direction has a conservative or a revolutionary bend, or even both, depends on the particular phenomenon. Jewish Apologetic syncretism possessed a more conservative tendency, but the Jewish diaspora harbored also the more revolutionary syncretism of Gnosticism. The religio-historical school started to discuss these matters, and its efforts deserve renewed appreciation and continuation. The excellent article of C. Colpe, "Synkretismus," is a good start in that direction, and there are interesting perspectives in the article of G. Klein.

76. There was the success story of the Tobiads, then the decades of Herodian collaboration with the Romans, culminating in the liaison between Titus and Berenice, the princess. There was also the family of Philo, with the peculiar figure of Philo's nephew as the climax, a high Roman official on various assignments, then general of the Roman army which besieged Jerusalem. Poppaea, Nero's mistress, Titus Flavius Clemens, and his wife, Flavia Domitilla, sympathized with Judaism; the latter two were of the Flavian family, nephew and granddaughter of Vespasian, thus also related to Titus and to Domitian, who had designated Clemens's and Domitilla's two sons as probable successors. The parents were later tried, the husband executed, the wife banished. Like M. Smallwood, *Jews*, 378–85, I do not believe Christian hagiography which made them into Christian martyrs. Suetonius (*Domitian* 12) knows only of persecution of Jews and Jewish affiliates in Rome. The conversion of the royal house of Adiabene has already been mentioned above, p. 100. The immediate importance of Philo for non-Jewish philosophy and civilization prior to his adoption by the Christians has been postulated by H. A. Wolfson (1:158–60, see Bibliography 1), but this is still a matter for debate.

77. M. Hadas, *Culture*, stresses again and again the oriental, and particularly the Jewish, contributions to Hellenism. The particular relationship to Roman political theology is described ibid., 238–48 ("Roman Evangelists"). See also the next two chapters, "An Elect, With Sovereignty and Without" and "Authority and Law."

78. See below, pp. 394–406, 422–34.

Social Aspects of the Phenomenon
of the Divine Man

In 1964 I had moved beyond the studies of Ludwig Bieler and Hans Windisch and many since which have looked at the "divine man" as a type.[79] I became convinced that the divine man was more than a matter of ideals. Behind the image, I had discovered elements of the practice which had produced the typology, the reality of actual propaganda, and again not just of ideological concepts and propositions but of actual role models and individual propagandists.

In the meantime, through further research I have learned that propaganda in the Hellenistic age was not limited to missionary religions alone but was a general feature of the entire culture during the whole period from Alexander to Constantine, starting with the end of the Peloponnesian War.[80] I began to see also the wider role which the concept of the divine man played in this entire culture, and I noticed that many people realized this concept, and not only on the highest level. The huge number of inscriptions erected for benefactors, many trivial ones, presents evidence for that already.[81]

If I were asked to describe the main characteristic of Hellenistic culture between Alexander and Constantine, I would answer that it was committed to experiment with transcendence, literally as well as metaphorically. It represented a multifarious exploration of the limits and possibilities of humanity. It was a laboratory of the extraordinary. One probed and tested the ranges of the divine and the human and the possibilities of extension and convergence of both. Many different options were tried, not only abstractly but also concretely. Two-way traffic and reciprocity between the divine and the human were among the options, and the social and political realms were included in the experimentation as well. Later "Christian" theological alternatives of transcendence and immanence—particularly as mutually exclusive—were not a matter of course in New Testament times, not even in Judaism or the early church. Dualism undoubtedly existed in some sectors, like in Apocalypticism and Gnosticism, but was not pervasive as yet.

Talking about the extraordinary in Hellenism means talking about the θεῖος ἄνθρωπος, the divine human,[82] the foremost representative of that culture's experiment with transcendence. Celebrating the extraordinary, Hellenism presented a curious paradox, namely, that the exceptional was not limited to a few star cases. On the contrary, celebrating the extraordinary meant multiplying it. One wanted the increase of the number of phenomena meant as or understood as far beyond the common norm. Hellenism intended the integration of the extraordinary into ordinary cultural expectation and worked for the growth of possibilities and options for the exceptional. The exceptional grew in a stunning fashion—the uncommon became a common phenomenon. At least one saw it that way.

Hellenism was oriented toward the exceptional. The experience of the superhuman extended from the traditional, direct interference of the deity over the experience of sudden or unusual changes of nature, and the stupendous range of healing miracles, to the seemingly more mundane actions and experiences of poets, philosophers, and skilled and professional people of all kinds, and also of politicians, of whom Alexander the Great was but the most famous. Augustus's bringing of peace certainly had the character and impact of a sensational miracle, not only by his own decree but also by the acclamation of the sigh of relief of a whole world that had been plagued by decades of civil war from which Augustus had now liberated them. And there were many other kinds of experiences that struck Hellenistic people as manifestations of the divine in the here and now. One should not forget the physical demonstrations of the superhuman in the form of architectural and aesthetic monuments or technological feats.

Indeed, not only beauty but also the miraculous is in the eye of the beholder, and Hellenistic people *wanted* to experience the divine breaking in, mingling with the human, and the human extending to divine heights, not only metaphorically but also literally. Sensitivity for the divine increased—tremendously.

Therefore a wide range of phenomena, many more than appearances of deities alone, were considered miraculous, that is, were seen as caused by the divine, as manifestations of superhuman qualities, of superior power. But in this literally paradoxical age, the miracle, its character, and its whence and whither, was also a matter of rational reflection, of instruction, of production and reproduction. Most often no contradiction between the rational and the irrational or, better, suprarational was felt; on the contrary, there seemed to be harmony and correspondence. Mockers like Lucian were exceptions, and even they had their own private preserve for something exceptional, if it were only uncommon stylistic skill. The devotion of an age dedicated to education and to technique found curious expression in this blend of the irrational and the rational. The Hellenistic instructional features of "paradigm" and of "mimesis," of model and of imitation, were used with respect to the miraculous also.

Not that all the sometimes fantastic descriptions of individual manifestations of the miraculous were correct pictures of reality, historically authentic so to speak. They were this as little or as much as the retrospective Gospel accounts about Jesus. But there was the massive reality of people believing in miracles and drawing important conclusions about religious and cultural values from them.[83] There were also people who fed into that, by way of entertaining and narrating through reports and references. But there were, further, those who tried to correspond to these expectations as much as possible through personal manifestations of the extraordinary. And the reporting and referring was not as "indirect" either, but participated in the experience of the extraordinary as well. The miracles were not just the frosting on the cake of religious and cultural propaganda but a major element of it, and the type or, better, role model or habitus, of the "divine man" was a major prerequisite for successful propaganda.

In the discussion of the divine man problem, I have not yet been very successful convincing fellow scholars that our "enlightened" differentiations between practice and theory, abstract and concrete, practical and conceptual, literary and real, are of little use in assessing Hellenistic people, their understanding and their actions. Accounts, fictitious or not, about people considered paradigmatic by authors and/or audiences of those days yield information about the understanding authors and/or audiences then possessed of a reality worth imitating. There was no premium on originality at all, and even less on the phenomenological uniqueness of the people or events portrayed or of the persons narrating or listening. The borderline between fiction and reality was fluid everywhere. Observing a time where paradigm and imitation made past, present, and even future converge constantly, the historian cannot concentrate on the few references to certain individuals alone who were known as divine men and of whom we possess certain historical evidence.

Our own contemporary experience teaches us that the production of accounts of the extraordinary, the belief in it, and the interest in seeing and performing it form a circle. The existence of miracle stories in the Hellenistic world points not only to the people who composed them, to those who narrated them, and to audiences who believed them, but also to the people who were ready to perform them again. The question whether the extraordinary did or would occur exactly as told was of no concern. Since the range of the extraordinary was so immense, the chances that something exceptional did happen and that something out of the ordinary would occur again were better than 100 percent.

Belief and fact, as well as history, present, and future, did interact constantly in this trading of the extraordinary. This miraculous experience definitely affected the view of the world, of history and geography, often drastically. The continuous interdependence between Dionysus and Heracles myths, on the one hand, and the strategies and politics of the historical Alexander, on the other hand, is well known, resulting in the impact of that interdependence on Hellenistic knowledge of history and of geography.[84] But Alexander is only the most outstanding example for a phenomenon in which innumerable sailors, explorers, merchants, mercenaries, adventurers, job seekers, and missionaries participated as well. They felt they were under the guidance and protection of their deities. Their journeys and achievements helped to change previous perceptions of history and the world. Their ventures affected historical and geographical knowledge about peoples and countries and about the world's borders, and they changed the understanding of the divine as well. Whether the gods led humans, or vice versa, was often hard to say. And the development of the Alexander legend proves also that the two-way traffic between fact and myth could initiate legendary aggrandizement of a person's achievements during that person's lifetime already, even under the public eye and "scientific" inquiry.[85] And the person described might even have had an active interest and a hand in the whole conflation of fact and fiction.

The impact of the Alexander figure on kings and statesmen during the Hellenistic age is a familiar thing, as is the fact that the Romans could not resist the creative spell of this most successful and tragic youth either.[86] The history of the Alexander romance proves the influence of the great Macedonian on the lower classes, including the subjugated peoples too. It would be wrong to assume that this use and impact of the Alexander figure were entirely secondary and manipulative. The Mithridateses and Caesars of those days believed in their imitations of Alexander themselves, and so did their admirers and foes. And there was even more to this than imitation. Representation of Alexander, or whomever, was often considered to be *reappearance*, and not only by admirers. Metempsychosis was not a matter of Pythagorean philosophy and legend alone. People saw it occur everywhere, and they were willing to contribute to it by action, communication, and belief.

This variegated cultural context of the miraculous makes my original critique of the divine man phenomenon look premature, due to the cultural, social, and religious condescension on my part. I was as yet unaware of the importance and function of the divine and the miraculous in Hellenistic culture at large, especially about a certain democratic potential of these phenomena in those days. I identified the divine man phenomenon too quickly as aristocratic and denigrated miracle belief too hastily as crude, thus de facto working with subconscious social classifications of a Protestant intellectual of today, which caused a great lack of social logic in my description.[87]

THE IMAGE OF THE MAN OF GOD
IN SIRACH

Jews felt particularly at ease in this cultural celebration of the extraordinary because they possessed a tradition full of miraculous features.[88] It appeared to be especially advantageous that the biblical tradition presented in the Pentateuch was a close combination of legal forms and genres with narrative material, many of them miracle stories, not just about God but also about great men.

It strikes me as symptomatic, although not enough observed yet in my book, that in Sirach there is a relatively *concentrated collection of motifs and images* which, if *looked at synoptically*, present an interesting transition from the picture of the men of God of Israel's earlier scriptures to the working image of the divine man operative in Hellenistic-Jewish Apologetics. The self-understanding of the charismatic wise found in representative fashion in Sirach appears to be preformative of the self-understanding of the Jewish Apologists. There are many hints that Jewish Apologetics evolved out of the charismatic wisdom people such as Jesus ben Sirach represented.[89]

There was a good reason that the grandson of Jesus ben Sirach felt that the diaspora would be responsive to the translation of his grandfather's work. The translation speaks to Jewish Apologists, members of a new movement no doubt, but with so many connections to the old man's wisdom that he was nevertheless a kindred spirit. The synopsis now given will present a core picture of the divine man to which Jewish Apologetics and Hellenism at large would add more features. But the basic contours were already available to charismatic wisdom. It is important to note that Jesus ben Sirach knows of the confluence and similarity of that which is *valuable*, especially morally valuable, with that which is *divine, and* with that which is *miraculously present* and active, although the Hebrew version of Sirach does not have a real linguistic equivalent for the Greek term ἀρετή, which in its Hellenistic use combines all that. In the Jewish use of this term and concept, biblical and Hellenistic tendencies converge.

My synopsis is taken from Sirach 24, 38, 39, and 44–50[90] and from the latter part of the appendix in chap. 51 (vv. 18–38). The so-called hymn of the fathers (chaps. 44–50) unequivocally proves that the author wants to integrate all important (i.e., extraordinary) features of all God's agents in Israel's past into that of the wise as presented in the context, especially in the other chapters mentioned above. Thus I have included in this synopsis of extraordinary characteristics, skills, and achievements not only what is said about the wise teacher or student specifically but also what is stated about heroes of old. The book wants to draw both together, the great ones of yesteryear and the wise ones of today and tomorrow. Cumulatively Jesus Sirach's gallery of examples, ancient and contemporary, articulates a professional code for the wise, a fascinating sketch of a paradigmatic role model.

Sirach presupposes inspiration, but this inspiration is more than just infusion with a divine spirit or a demon. It means that wisdom has incorporated herself in the wise one, who turns ἔνθεος in the truest sense, just to use one Greek term out of a typology of the θεῖος ἀνήρ. Anyone reading the chapters of Sirach mentioned above, especially chap. 24, would conclude that the wise was even more ἔνθεος than Greek divine men, more even than Socrates.

Wisdom, taking possession of the wise, brings heavenly power, primeval, transcendental, eschatological. Thus she is associated—almost synonymous—with God, is more than angels, is central within the heavenly world, but also mediates creation, ruling, controlling, judging, and preserving it.

Wisdom is also the living center of Israel's cult and people, as paradisaical power possessing and mediating knowledge, life, purity, and salvation inexhaustively. She has incorporated herself in the wise since ancient times. The bearers of tradition thus have always been gifted with and have been representatives of Wisdom. Wisdom, her authority, insight, and tradition, is fully present again and again in the wise ones. But this presence, this inspiration, can be learned; it is the result of education in the wisdom school with the teacher mediating Wisdom.[91]

Through the study of law one gains the art of discovering its meaning, its secrets, the art of understanding the relationship between Wisdom, law, experience, nature, and history, of seeing divine as well as human greatness there. One is even able to uncover hidden greatness, covered by the experience of adversity, suffering, disease, death, and other catastrophes, in the heroic overcoming of them. The sage turns adversity into triumph, death into the experience of immortality.

The student of Wisdom learns the aretalogy of Wisdom and the aretalogies of her incorporations, that is, of those tested and proven as chosen by Wisdom, because they are distinguished and successful. This aretalogical knowledge, originally a privilege of prophets and poets, helps to discern miraculous presence and power and to emulate them. The wise learns how Wisdom controls and protects her covenant with the people and with the wise, and how one collaborates with her in this stabilizing activity on which history and world order hinge. Her counsel, admonition, comforting, judgment, condemnation, and forgiveness have their place, all of them extraordinary too.

In and through this continuous encounter with God's Wisdom, with her power which orders heaven and earth, the student of Wisdom learns exemplary piety, respect as well as absolute confidence, loyalty to the law, Wisdom, and God.

The wise student is called upon to test and improve this knowledge and loyalty in travels, to refine this understanding of what is truly enduring, truly great, through encounter and experience with other people. Thus the wise gains comprehensive experience and judgment. In short, the wisdom of the wise is established; the sage now can commence to communicate Wisdom, to teach, to inspire others, that is, to assist Wisdom in incorporating herself in others anew. The wise as teacher now actualizes and mediates the powers and ideas behind creation and history to others.

All this is an initiation into a communication with a continuous miraculous reality or, even better, with reality as miraculous. The basic miracle is Wisdom's mediation; thus reading and understanding the law are wonders, and so are education and becoming and being a wise person. The ability of the sage to make people participate in the miracles of Wisdom is the primary miraculous function of the teacher. This activity not only realizes the immortality of Wisdom but also contributes to it.

The wise person has absorbed the role of the prophet. The sage has visions and auditions of God and of heavenly things, of past and future, and receives oracles and has extrasensory perception. The wise has aretalogical expertise, not only vis-à-vis the past but also vis-à-vis the present, and discerns, interprets, and applies activities, Wisdom's miraculous faculties. The wise performs nature and healing miracles, miracles of punishment and of protection, and has the power to resurrect the dead. Here belongs the responsibility of the sage for society and people, the ability to establish and disestablish, the gift and faculty to take a leadership role in political council, in judicial court and in royal court. The ability to invent, to construct

and build, which is Hiskiah's faculty for instance, appears to be comparatively less impressive. But in a world geared toward civilization—and that of Jesus Sirach is part of it already—these skills are
as essential as they are extraordinary, that is, they are miraculous
too.

The primary and final miraculous tool which puts the wise into
company with Wisdom and God, above the world and even beyond
other transcendental powers, is the ability to understand and communicate wisdom as contained in scriptures. This makes the wise
vastly superior to the prophets of old, Israelite or otherwise, as interpreters of tradition.[92] Intimacy with Lady Wisdom, who is the
law of God, makes the sage intimately acquainted with the inner
workings of language, its secrets, and its possibilities. This gives all
the necessary rhetorical skills and also powerful speech. The wise
becomes familiar with the metaphorical dimensions of language,
parables, and riddles, all the mysterious and mystifying potential
that language entails.

Thus the sage demonstrates courage, counsel, comfort, judgment, independence, and superiority, in short, the freedom of a
person who excels. This is crowned by the capacity (i.e., potency) to
ascend or to be transported into heaven, at the latest upon the termination of the sage's earthly life, but actually already earlier in the
experiences of intimacy with Wisdom, especially in the various visions but also in "ordinary" exercises of interpretation which are in
reality not ordinary at all but "extraordinary." All this, certainly actual raptures in particular, means a tremendous increase in the ability to "travel" in Lady Wisdom's service. As incorporation of her,
who is the power above the angels, the wise has a seat and a voice in
the heavenly council. Thus the sage who feels heir to the ancient
prophets does not merely imitate these councilors and "secretaries
of state" of Yahweh but literally "transcends" them. It is therefore
understandable that even the dead body of God's representative,
Elisha's for instance, can—like Orpheus's head—work miracles.

Into this context of the miraculous afterlife of the wise as prophet
belong the memories of the sage's achievements in Wisdom's name.
There are physical demonstrations of the rewards of that life in the
form of financial recognition and material blessings, but there are
also even more lasting documentations of appreciation and thanks-

giving written down or inscribed. These records memorialize the extraordinary. They become efficacious records of Wisdom's continuous presence, of her immortality and the sage's immortality. These records revive themselves in subsequent generations, in the teachings and performances of future sages.

The wise stand for Wisdom's continuous success, a success that feeds on itself, a self-validating, permanent, self-fulfilling prophecy. This success story becomes its own best propaganda. If, in this process, the sages point to themselves, they do not mean self-advertisement; instead they are referring to the divine force they represent and feel obligated to propagate with all the energy available to them. What may strike us as arrogance, conceit, and aggressiveness is understood as loyalty and obedience to the divine power at work, active trust in God's Wisdom and her manifestations, past and present. The wise would take this behavior not as pompous but as modest, hiding themselves and bringing Wisdom up front, communicating God's righteousness, not self-righteousness, all of it objectively and verifiably.

The success of the wise boosts society's ability to overcome and prosper. The sages guarantee the immortality of Jewish religion, and through it the stability and well-being of the entire world. The success of civilization depends on their constant correction and their improvement of imperfections. Through their gifts, skills, and actions, most of all through their exegesis and education, the sages bring paradise unto earth and thus cosmic peace.

The world's order, its survival, rests on the wise. What Wisdom of Solomon later says through an older proverbial saying is certainly true in the eyes of Jesus ben Sirach too: "A mass of wise persons means salvation of the world" (6:24).[93] The Jewish sages guarantee God's covenants. They are more than an isolated phenomenon; they manifest what in their eyes has universal dimensions and importance and therefore demands universal recognition.[94]

THE "DIVINE MAN" IN JEWISH APOLOGETICS

It is exciting that so much is being done in Near Eastern wisdom studies,[95] an area that former generations of scholars, especially theologians, considered uninteresting. It is as if a new continent were being discovered, of which only rumors had existed before. While explorations are still going on with major discoveries still under way, historical and theological perspectives are already slowly changing all over.

But this international endeavor has done comparatively little in the vast and important section of the wisdom movement which we call Jewish Apologetics. Our ignorance starts with the lack of knowledge about exact beginnings and precise connections of this section. We do not know yet how it connected with charismatic wisdom. The number of similarities in the understanding of heavenly Wisdom and the character and role of the wise appears to be more than accidental and sets both branches of Jewish wisdom apart from Apocalypticism and Gnosticism.

It is also still a matter of debate whether or how the experiment of the "Hellenizers" in Jerusalem, which 1 and 2 Maccabees speak about, was part of that turn of Judaism toward missionary activity and thus related to the origins of Jewish Apologetics.

Whatever the unknown details of their beginnings, Jewish Apologists took the practical consequences of the universal aspects of Jewish wisdom. They were motivated for that at least as much by their Jewish heritage as they were moved and attracted by the surrounding world culture. Sirach and similar Jewish literature prove that Judaism, at least the part they represented, had made the same turn toward the dialectic between universality and particularity as the Hellenistic culture around them had. The unity of the world and of humanity was taken for granted as one concentrated on one's own particular representation of humankind as the central one, in this case not Greek but Jewish. Judaism did not turn Hellenistic because of general weakness or because of a particular person's or group's plan, conspiracy, or activity. Judaism became part of Hellenism through the force of an ecumenical *Zeitgeist*, which the Greeks had not created either but participated in as well. This *Zeitgeist* was neither conformist nor atomistic. It was liberal as well as traditionalistic, sometimes even antiquarian, but also utopian on the other side. In short, this new world culture was a creative and colorful pluralism, and Judaism was part of and contributor to it. Apologetic confidence about that is undoubtedly exaggerated, but it is not entirely wrong.

Jewish Apologists broke down the barriers of Sirach's profession-
alism and showed more trust in the Jewish congregations, those existing and those developing through their activities.[96] Not that
schooling and specialization of teaching was abandoned, but it was
now much less isolated. The ability of the community to assist in
instigating and forming the spiritual powers of an individual was
now realized more efficiently. Synagogue worship achieved an ener-
gizing potential. This presented better possibilities for proselytizing
as well as for the recruitment of missionaries. A toning down if not
disappearance of the male chauvinism expressed in Sirach helped
considerably. Women too could become sages and missionaries. Actual ability and performance became more important than biological
or professional distinction.[97]

This was made possible by a radicalizing of the connection of wisdom and scriptures, one of the first points in the synopsis given
above. I myself have shown that one saw already in Jewish scriptures, especially in the law, the basic miracle of Judaism, essential
not only for Judaism but also for culture and the world at large.
Translation and interpretation of the scriptures were seen and experienced as miracles too, essentially accompanying the basic miracle.
Thus the Jewish religion and its representatives were wondrous
phenomena also.

The aretalogical dimensions of scriptures, and of exegesis were
developed beyond practice and idea already found in Sirach. The
Apologists' evolution of the law's miraculous dimension responded
to the basic narrative and homiletical (in later Jewish terminology
haggadic) dimension of Torah and of scriptures much better than the
Pharisaic rabbinate did, when later it put this haggadic dimension
into a more secondary if not altogether marginal role.

Apologetic association of the power of the law with claims of the
law's and exegesis's contribution to the order and stability of the
world and of civilization gave glory not only to the scriptures and
tradition but also to the worship of the synagogue and to the activity
of the missionary. The Apologists saw themselves, even more than
the wise of charismatic wisdom, as social paradigms and agents, not
just of Judaism but of world society. Already that interest would
make them wonderworkers. This very society which they wanted to
contribute to experimented in transcendence, needed growth, and

this growth demanded stimulation. Extraordinary performances and achievements would provide stimulation, and thus further society and its goals.

If we compare the listing of extraordinary gifts and performances in Apologetic writings with the synopsis I have given above from Sirach, we find most of the features again, but the Apologists emphasized some more and added others. They stressed the exegetical skill too, but added the art of refined rational deliberation and explanation. Cross-cultural and intrareligious comparison led to the sophistication of the *interpretatio Graeca*, adapted to a bicultural Jewish situation. In this approach, much imagination was used to associate and explain a phenomenon of one subculture, the Jewish subculture, with that of another one, the Greek, and vice versa. Allegorical interpretation was another and even more fertile ground for the exhibition of skillful as well as imaginative learning.

That gifts of poetry, writing, and rhetoric would be drawn into this range of miraculous exegetical skills could be expected from the synopsis given above. Spiritual power and authority could not be limited to mystical exposition.[98] That the Corinthian opponents stood in this tradition is demonstrated by 2 Cor. 11:6. This is one of the many indications that, in our search for wonders, we have limited the range unjustifiably to nature and healing miracles or outright magic—which, for instance, has people or objects appear or disappear unsuspectedly—as if there were no magic in words already, spoken or written, or even more in skillfully handling them. At least for Hellenistic taste and expectation, the divine visited people in those manifestations of language. I have of course mentioned that the range of linguistic wonders in the Hellenistic synagogue included theatrical compositions too, at least tragedy as Ezekiel the Tragedian and also the tragic character of 4 Maccabees show.

For ancient people the step from language to music was small, and Jewish Apologists would know not only of the power of Orpheus's song and play but also of David's songs and lyre. A clear addition to the skills usable in the service of Wisdom and her scriptures as mentioned in Sirach would be the gifts of pictorial arts so impressively displayed in Jewish synagogues and also in works of miniature art.[99] Whereas the former demonstrate the connection between Jewish arts and exegesis, the latter show its magic dimension.

I have also discussed the fact that the use of the art of dramatic dancing, as mentioned in Philo's tractate on the Therapeutae, was clearly also in the service of the exposition of scripture.[100] And I have demonstrated the theatrical dimensions of Jewish worship.[101] Since first writing on the subject I have been struck even more by the dramatic qualities of miracle narratives and of hymnic accounts of miracles, biblical and nonbiblical, particularly on the Jewish side. Dramatic potential was often already in the object. Then came the narration. From theatrical monologue—with the ancient messenger-report being only one possibility—to actual staging, a sliding scale of options existed. These options increased as soon as sequences of episodes and narratives were collected or composed. Allegorization and allegorical interpretation could elevate the dramatization to a higher level of engagement as well.

Further study of Jewish art, particularly of the Dura paintings, lets me ask whether the conflation of mythical reality, stage and wall painting known from Pompeii and suspected elsewhere, did not occur here as well.[102] If that were so, then the stage would have served at least a structural function in the perception of those Jews. Why not presume that it reflected some ongoing reality in the synagogue as well?

I still stand by my suggestion, made to the excavators of Sardis, that the rear wall of the main room of that synagogue resembles the rear wall of the Hellenistic Roman stage well known from many wall paintings.[103] Why not assume that dramatic performances took place in front of it? The monstrous size of the room and the scarcity of seating arrangements would speak against the entire space being intended for and occupied by the audience. Dramatic arrangements that would include dance and procession as known from the Therapeutae can easily be imagined here. Those who were responsible for such performances, and those who participated in them, were involved in the meeting of the divine and the human, the bringing forth of the miraculous. The socializing which happened through that not only served the greater glory of the Jewish God and religion but was also of benefit to Hellenistic culture, or at least was so intended. That the architecture of the Sardis synagogue—at least on the inside—belonged in the area of the marvelous as far as size and probable appearance go is almost matter of course. Thus it was part of the architectural concert of a Hellenistic city, an intentionally superhuman manifestation.

Another area of convergence between the divine and the human, besides language, arts, drama, and architecture, was the world of athletics.[104] Metaphorical use enlarged its range. This happened in Hellenism already, but it became especially important in Hellenistic-Jewish Apologetics, as 4 Maccabees and Philo prove. Paul is still affected by this essential metaphor of Jewish missionary activity.[105] Not only could the display of certain skills be integrated into the demonstration of more than ordinary powers and abilities, but also the entire life of a person, group, or people, for the context of *agon* (contest) extended beyond physical faculties to include even mystical experiences. Corresponding to the Hebraic (sapiental) understanding of education as *musar* (discipline) the Hellenists and Hellenistic Jews would associate athletics and education with discipline, meaning not only the physical exercise but also other, "higher" forms of training and improvement. The ideas of "contest" and "discipline" would also be applied to the realms of conduct, morality, and knowledge.[106]

Philo is probably not the only one who would call this complex leading from the lowest to the highest "encyclopedic" or circular, that is, comprehensive (i.e., education).[107] What we now call scientific skills and disciplines would be included in this, a whole range of wondrous abilities and activities again. How much of that was exhibited during synagogue worship is difficult to say. Anything of it could have been, not least the mathematical skills, which in the form of gematria would fascinate people in the ancient world, and Philo shows how easily this could be part of exegetical exercises, certainly a divine art.

I had demonstrated the close relationship between legal and royal aspects in sapiental and Apologetic concepts of the law and the divine man. However, I had only hinted that this relationship affected the self-understanding, confidence, and actual performance of Hellenistic-Jewish missionaries. Goodenough had made me aware of these connections,[108] and I pursued them further in my study of Wisdom of Solomon.[109] This association of legal and royal motifs went beyond the merely conceptual and touched missionary practice. But this practical aspect went further.

In Philo and Josephus the association of the legal and the royal showed in political skill and prominence. Both persons were exegetical writers and political authors, and in the case of Philo we possess works of jurisprudence too. I presume that this was the case also with Josephus's lost work on Jewish laws. Philo's concrete juridical knowledge proves that he not only had had a legal education but also was of the legal profession.[110] In the case of Josephus we have no direct indication of a similar engagement. But both authors were involved in political practice. In the case of Philo it was first local involvement, some of it important already. The climax of this engagement was the embassy to Caligula, the princeps in Rome, reported in *De Legatione ad Gaium*, where Philo showed all the trademarks of a skilled, ancient diplomat. It is most often overlooked that Josephus must be compared with Philo in this respect too. Josephus tried to tackle a much more gigantic diplomatic assignment than Philo did—the reconciliation of Romans and Jews during and after the most dangerous rebellion the Romans experienced during the first century.

We are not entitled to limit this practical engagement of the Apologists to these two persons. The juridical and especially the political and diplomatic interests show heavily in Jewish Apologetics and related literature, such as 1 and 2 Maccabees. Not all the diplomatic correspondence there can be explained by the dictate of literary fashion. The number of examples and the integration of authentic documents speak against that and for more than literary preoccupation.[111] The existence of documents authored by pagan authorities granting privileges to Jewish communities demonstrate not only generosity but also the political self-interest of Gentile politicians.[112] They point to successful Jewish diplomacy as well.[113] Much of that was local, achieved by men like Philo and Josephus. They demonstrated juridical and political competence combined with diplomatic skills among the gifts and demonstrations of the Jewish θεῖος ἄνθρωπος. This deserves further scrutiny. That such an achievement could serve propagandistic purposes is obvious. A community that had such diplomatic success commended itself as a caring and protective entity, of great value in a mobile culture that created not only opportunity but also alienation and fear for the individual.

θεῖος ἄνθρωπος IN PAGAN MISSIONARY ACTIVITY AND PROPAGANDISTIC IDEOLOGY

The frequency of references to the "divine man" in recent scholarly literature shows that the importance of that concept for Hellenistic culture and society is being recognized. However, it is not yet understood that it is part of the fundamentally propagandistic character of Hellenistic (and Roman) culture, including its political side.[114] The discussion of pagan missionary activity, unfortunately not very high on the scholarly agenda, has remained limited to the religious realm, with "religious" understood in a relatively narrow sense.[115]

There was much interplay and interdependence between the spread of missionary cults and the general trends of Hellenistic culture and society. Occasional conflicts did not contradict that. The "foreignness" and hostility of some cults to their environment and the environment's occasional aversion to them, sometimes very aggressively expressed, should be taken with a grain of salt, more as conflicts within the family, heated and even bloody sometimes but not fundamental. This is true even for the relationship between "Christianity" and the Roman state. Two entities which could undergo such a thorough marriage so suddenly and so fast could not have been diametrically opposed before. These missionary cults and movements with their exotic seasonings and spices not only improved the taste of the surrounding culture but also provided a good deal of the essential stimulation, on which Hellenistic culture by its very nature depended.

I have observed for Judaism already that the propagandistic activity would not carefully distinguish between imagination and reality. Present, past, and future were not carefully separated either; on the contrary, transparency, conflation, and exchange were natural. The same was true for pagan Hellenism. A person as critical toward pompous claims and the manipulative potential of imagination as Ju-

venal, for instance, has an uncritical, idealized view of certain phenomena of the past which he understands as important and
formative, full of actualizing power, namely, all those representing
ancient Rome.[116] Lucian's attitude toward the Cynic Menippus is a
similar example.[117] In the whole area of interplay between faith,
belief, fidelity, credulity, and certainty, a *terra incognita* of sorts,
Hellenism presents for us a vast area open for exploratory ventures
by critical scholars trained in both theological and historical
criticism.[118]

There is no doubt that this transparency between imagination and
reality in Hellenism was very formative.[119] It shaped the general
cultural sense, it conditioned groups, and it formed individuals. It is
very customary to suggest that an education which took its departure from Homer as its bible was by nature different from one based
on the Pentateuch and related literature, but this is far from true.
Homer and the Pentateuch both provided, first and most of all,
imaginative models for social behavior geared toward renewed experience of the adventures described.[120] The pagan as well as the
Jewish experience and manipulation of the extraordinary, imagined
or real, included all the phenomena mentioned above with regard to
the Jewish θεῖος ἀνήρ. Actual and legendary facts and phenomena
were theologized in a similar fashion.

On the non-Jewish side, the political and societal dimensions of
the divine man concept came out even more clearly,[121] especially
as to importance and influence of the cult of the benefactor.[122] It
was not limited to great men alone, but it was all-pervasive and essential to the culture. There is a basic similarity between Augustus's
record of his extraordinary deeds in the *Res Gestae Divi Augusti* and
the inscription of the third century B.C.E. narrating the wondrous
experiences of a certain Apollonius concerning the establishment of
the Serapis cult on Delos.[123] Both relate their experiences and present themselves as pious men, active and publicly successful. They
represent divine phenomena: Augustus eternal Rome, Apollonius
the Serapis cult. Both achievements are portrayed as important for
society at large. Personal success and public benefit merge. Authors
as well as society at large believe that. The narrations become matters of public record.[124]

As for individual demonstrations, experiences, and descriptions of the extraordinary, certain features appear in pagan examples more than in Judaism, despite the basic similarity in idea and reality. Naturally, travel experiences and travelogues were common,[125] as were encounters of catastrophies and salvation in the area most directly and most dramatically associated with the powers of chaos, the sea.[126] In traveling, the chances of meeting and transcending given human limits and encountering the nonhuman were frequent. Unusual seafaring incidents, adventures abroad, and explorations of unknown regions were an essential part of a culture that did not concentrate as much on its centers as on its peripheries and on what was beyond its borders, physically and metaphorically. Levitation, ascension, and the whole range of metempsychosis belong in this Hellenistic passion for journeying.[127] The travel dimension of experiencing, staging, and narrating nature miracles should be explored much more.[128]

With regard to healing miracles, Hellenism had enlarged the medical range tremendously with inexhaustible conflation and confusion of the rational and the irrational.[129] The connection between the Asclepius cult and medicine, most prominently at the Asclepius sanctuaries and medical centers of Epidaurus and Kos, demonstrated this. On the more magical end, Hermes Trismegistos proved to be of great influence.[130] His name stands also as example for the connection of other "sciences" with the supernatural, of the rational with the irrational.[131] Outright magic and theurgics were popular.[132] Their rational dimensions were not discovered by the Neoplatonists. They could build on a long and developed tradition.

With regard to prophetic abilities and performances, pagan Hellenism is not different from Jewish Hellenism, already described. The original difference between mantics, concentrating on oracles, and prophecy, mediating communication between the divine and the human, disappeared during the Hellenistic period.[133] The prophetic dimension (of whatever particular kind) came to be most frequently identified with the θεῖος ἀνήρ. Since the function as interpreter of the divine became more and more the essential task of the prophet and thus a heavily rationalizing assignment, prophet and philosopher could converge, at the latest with Plato's Socrates, long before Philo and Plotinus.[134]

Much of the demonstration of the extraordinary in Hellenism was a matter of individual skill and interest, but nevertheless an essential element of the culture.[135] Very often these exhibitions of the superhuman were related to a mission of sorts, a cult or rite, a religion, a particular philosophy or profession. The association with certain cults, religions, or philosophies was most frequent when a prophetic ability was stressed. In all these cases the demonstration of the more than human spoke for the power of the divine and its representative, but it also entailed a persuasive element, whether directly manipulated or not. Conversion was a consideration, and certainly also interest in keeping converts.[136] This stimulated also the general interest of the culture in as many extraordinary experiences and demonstrations as possible. They provided much of the expansive and cohesive power that pluralistic civilization needed.[137]

Given the economic situation, it is a matter of course that, on the pagan side of Hellenism, the nonpersonal aspect of superhuman achievements was more prominent. I am thinking of feats of arts, architecture, and technology, sacred and secular,[138] although we have seen that Jews in Palestine and the diaspora tried their best to keep up in those fields too. It is also understandable that pagans worked at least as hard as Jews on rhetoric and other forms of mastering language(s) as a major expression of the extraordinary.[139] And philosophers and politicians competed with each other in stressing and refining the art of governing as an expression of divine capabilities.[140] Poets followed suit in lauding this, with Horace and Vergil as the most famous examples. Both, and most significantly Vergil in his *Aeneid,* brought out the propagandistic aspects and intentions of the association of the exercise of politics with the divine.[141] The ruler cult had proven this interest already, the emperor cult would perfect it. The later "Christian" association of the politics of the empire with the mission of the church was but the continuation and perfection of what had begun long before.

BIBLIOGRAPHY 4

David E. **Aune**, "Magic in Early Christianity," *ANRW* 2.23.2:1507–57. Hans Dieter **Betz**, "Gottmensch II," *RAC*, 12:234–312; (ed.), *Plutarch's Ethical Writings and Early Christian Literature* (SCHNT 4; Leiden: Brill,

1978); *Plutarch's Theological Writings and Early Christian Literature* (SCHNT 3; Leiden: Brill, 1975). H. **Beyen**, *Die pompejanische Wanddekoration vom zweiten bis zum vierten Stil* (Haag: Nijhoff, 1938, 1960). Elias **Bickerman**, *Le culte des souverains dans l'empire Romain* (Geneva: Vandoeuvres, 1973). J. D. P. **Bolton**, *Aristeas of Proconnesus* (Oxford: Clarendon, 1962). Campbell **Bonner**, "Some Changes of Religious Feeling in Later Paganism," *HTR* (1937) 119–40; *Studies in Magical Amulets* (Ann Arbor: University of Michigan Press, 1950); "The Technique of Exorcism," *HTR* 36 (1943) 39-49. Ewen L. **Bowie**, "Apollonius of Tyana: Tradition and Reality," *ANRW*, 2.16.2:1652–99. Martin **Braun**, *History and Romance in Graeco-Oriental Literature* (Oxford: Blackwell, 1938). Peter **Brown**, "The Rise and Function of the Holy Man in Late Antiquity," *JRS* 61 (1971) 80–101; "Sorcery, Demons, and the Rise of Christianity," in *Witchcraft, Confessions, and Accusations*, ed. Mary Douglas (Assoc. of Social Anthropologists Monographs 9; New York: Barnes & Noble, 1970), 17 ff. Lionel **Casson**, *Ships and Seamanship in the Ancient World* (Princeton: Princeton Univ. Press, 1971). Martin P. **Charlesworth**, *Trade-Routes and Commerce of the Roman Empire* (2d ed.; Hildesheim: Olms, 1961). Carl J. **Classen**, "Theios Aner," in *Lexikon der Alten Welt*, 3040; "Wundertäter," in *Lexikon der Alten Welt*, 3286. Gerhard **Delling**, "Zur Beurteilung des Wunders durch die Antike," in *Studien zum Neuen Testament und zum hellenistischen Judentum* (Göttingen: Vandenhoeck & Ruprecht, 1970) 53–71. Albrecht **Dieterich**, *Nekyia: Beiträge zur Erklärung der neu entdeckten Petrusapokalypse* (Stuttgart: Teubner, 1969). Eric R. **Dodds**, "Supernormal Phenomena in Classical Antiquity," *Proceedings of the Society for Psychical Research* 55 (1971) 189–237; "Telepathie und Hellsehen in der klassischen Antike," in H. Bender, ed., *Parapsychologie* WdF 4; Darmstadt: Wissenschaftliche Buchgesellschaft, 1966) 6–25. Heinrich **Dörrie**; "Neupythagoreer," *RGG*, 4:1432–33; *Platonica Minora* (Munich: Fink, 1976) herein in particular, "Kontroversen um die Seelenwanderung im kaiserzeitlichen Platonismus," 420–40; "Pythagoreer," *Der Kleine Pauly*, 4:1270–72; "Pythagoras IC: Der nachklassische Pythagoreismus," *PW* 24/1:268–77. Mary **Douglas**, "Social Preconditions of Enthusiasm and Heterodoxy," in R. F. Spencer, ed., *Forms of Symbolic Action*, Proceedings of the 1969 Annual Spring Meeting of the American Ethnological Society (Seattle: University of Washington, 1969) 69–80. Samson **Eitrem**, "La magie comme motif litteraire," *SO* 21 (1941) 39–83; *Orakel und Mysterien am Ausgang der Antike* (Albae Vigiliae NS 5; Zurich: Rhein, 1947); "La théurgie chez les neo-platoniciens et dans les papyrus magiques," *SO* 22 (1942) 49–79. Helmut **Engelmann**, ed., *Die delische Sarapisaretalogie* (Beiträge zur klass. Philologie; Meisenheim: Hain, 1964). Wolfgang **Fauth**, "Divus Epicurus: Zur Problemgeschichte philosophischer Religiosität bei Lukrez," *ANRW*, 1/4:205–25; "Katabasis," *Der kleine Pauly*, 3:152–53. Louis R. **Feldman**, "Abram, the Greek Philosopher in Josephus," *TAPA* 99 (1968)

143–56; "Josephus as an Apologist of the Greco-Roman World: His Portrait of Solomon," in Schüssler-Fiorenza, ed., *Aspects* (Bibliography 3), 68–98. Moses I. **Finley**, *The Ancient Economy* (Sather Classical Lectures 43; Berkeley and Los Angeles: University of California Press, 1973); *Slavery in Classical Antiquity: Views and Controversies* (Cambridge: Heffer, 1961). Henry A. **Fischel**, "Studies in Cynicism and the Ancient Near East: Transformation of a Chria," in Jacob Neusner, ed., *Religions* (Bibliography 3), 372–411. John G. **Gager**, *Moses in Greco-Roman Paganism* (SBLMS 16; Nashville: Abingdon, 1972). Dieter **Georgi**, "Forms of Religious Propaganda," in Hans Jürgen Schultz, ed., *Jesus in His Time* (Philadelphia: Fortress, 1967) 124–31; "The Records of Jesus in Light of Ancient Accounts of Revered Men," *SBL Proceedings* (1972) 2:527–42; "Socioeconomic Reasons for the 'Divine Man' as a Propagandistic Pattern," in Schüssler-Fiorenza, ed., *Aspects* (Bibliography 3), 27–42. Hans **Gerstinger**, "Biographie," *RAC*, 2:386–91. Judah **Golding**, "The Magic of Magic and Superstition," in Schüssler-Fiorenza, ed., *Aspects* (Bibliography 3), 115–47. Paul **Goukowsky**, *Essai sur les origines du mythe d'Alexandre* (Nancy: University of Nancy Press, 1978). Robert M. **Grant**, "Miracle and Mythology," *ZRGG* 3 (1951) 123–33. William S. **Green**, "Palestinian Holy Men: Charismatic Leadership and Rabbinic Tradition," *ANRW*, 2.19.2:619–47. J. Gwyn **Griffiths**, *Apuleius of Madauros: The Isis Book. Metamorphoses, Book XI* (EPRO; Leiden: Brill, 1975). Karl **Gross**, "Apollonius v. Tyana," *RAC*, 1:529–33. Wilhelm **Gundel**, "Astrologie," *RAC*, 1:817–31. Joseph **Gutmann**, "Programmatic Painting in the Dura Synagogue," in Gutmann, ed., *The Synagogue* (Bibliography 3), 210–32. Christian **Habicht**, *Gottmenschentum und griechische Städte* (Zetemata 14; Munich: Beck, 1970). Moses **Hadas**, "Aeneas and the Tradition of the National Hero," *American Journal of Philology* 69 (1948) 408–14; *Three Greek Romances* (Garden City, N.Y.: Doubleday, 1953). Moses **Hadas** and Morton **Smith**, *Heroes and Gods: Spiritual Biographies in Antiquity* (New York: Harper & Row, 1965). Günther **Hansen**, "Herrscherkult und Friedensidee," in Leipoldt and Grundmann, eds., *Umwelt* (Bibliography 3), 1:127–42; 2:102–13. Rudolf W. O. **Helm**, *Der antike Roman* (Göttingen: Vandenhoeck & Ruprecht, 1956). Albert **Henrichs**, "Vespasian's Visit to Alexandria," *Zeitschrift für Papyrologie und Epigraphik* 3 (1968) 51–80. Rudolf **Herzog**, "Asklepius," *RAC*, 1:795–99. Alfred **Heuss**, "Alexander der Grosse und die politische Ideologie des Altertums," *Antike und Abendland* 4 (1954) 65–104. Carl **Holladay**, *Theios Aner in Hellenistic Judaism* (SBLDS 40; Missoula, Mont.: Scholars Press, 1977). Hildebrecht **Hommel**, "Rhetorik," in *Lexikon der Alten Welt*, 2611–26. Theodor **Hopfner**, *Griechisch-ägyptischer Offenbarungszauber* (Leipzig: Haessel, 1921–24); "Mageia," *PW* 14/1:301–93; "Mantike," *PW* 14:1258–87; "Mysterien (orientalisch-hellenistisch)," *PW* 16:1315–50; "Nekromantie," *PW* 16:2218–33. John **Hull**, *Hellenistic Magic and the Synoptic Tradition* (SBT 2d ser. 28; London:

SCM Press, 1974). W. **Jayne**, *The Healing Gods of Ancient Civilization* (New Hyde Park: University Books, 1962). Howard **Kee**, *Miracle in the Early Christian World: A Study in Sociohistorical Method* (New Haven and London: Yale University Press, 1983). Otto **Kern**, "Mysterien," PW 16:1209–1304. Hans G. **Kippenberg**, "The Historical Conditions of the Emergence and Crystalization of Early Christianity," in Shmuel N. Eisenstadt, ed., *The Origins of the Axial Age and Its Diversity* (forthcoming). Leo **Koep**, "Consecration II (Kaiserapotheose)," *RAC*, 3:284–94. Helmut **Koester**, *Introduction* (Bibliography 3); "*ΝΟΜΟΣ ΦΥΣΕΩΣ*: The Concept of Natural Law in Greek Thought," in Neusner, ed., *Religions* (Bibliography 3), 521–41. "φύσις, φυσικός, φυσικώς," *TDNT*, 9:246–71. Marie C. van der **Kolf**, "Prophetes, Prophetis," PW 23/1:797–816. Jutta **Kollesch**, "Medizin," *Der Kleine Pauly*, 5:1624–28. Johannes **Leipoldt**, "Alexander von Abonuteichos," *RAC*, 1:260–61; *Von den Mysterien zur Kirche* (Hamburg: Reich, 1962). Hans P. **L'Orange**, *Apotheosis in Ancient Portraiture* (Instituttet for Sammenligende Kulturforskning, Series B, 44; Oslo: Aschehoug, 1947). Grace H. **Macurdy**, *Hellenistic Queens: A Study of Women-Power in Macedonia, Seleucid Syria, and Ptolemaic Egypt* (Johns Hopkins University Studies in Archaeology 14; Baltimore: Johns Hopkins University Press, 1932). Juliet S. M. **Maguiness**, "Heroism in Virgil," *PVS* 10 (1970–71) 45–56. Abraham J. **Malherbe**, "Ps.-Heraclitus Epistle IV: The Divinization of the Wise Man," *JAC* 21 (1978) 42–64. Henri **Marrou**, *A History of Education in Antiquity* (New York and London: Sheed & Ward, 1956). Selby **McCassland**, *By the Finger of God* (New York: Macmillan, 1951). Erwin **Mederer**, *Die Alexanderlegenden bei den ältesten Alexanderhistorikern* (Stuttgart: Kohlhammer, 1936). Wayne A. **Meeks**, "The Divine Agent and His Counterfeit in Philo and the Fourth Gospel," in Schüssler-Fiorenza, ed., *Aspects* (Bibliography 3), 43–67. Reinhold **Merkelbach**, *Die Quellen des griechischen Alexanderromans* (Zetemata 9; Munich: Beck, 1962); *Roman und Mysterium in der Antike* (Munich: Beck, 1962). Arnaldo **Momigliano**, *The Development of Greek Biography* (Cambridge, Mass.: Harvard University Press, 1971); "Seneca Between Political and Contemplative Life," *Quarto contributo alla storia degli studi classici e del mondo antico* (Rome: Ed. de Storia e letteratura, 1962) 239–56. Siegfried **Morenz**, "Vespasian, Heiland der Kranken: Persönliche Frömmigkeit im antiken Herrscherkult?" *Würzburger Jahrbücher* 4 (1949–50) 370–78. Stephen **Mott**, "The Greek Benefactor and Deliverance from Moral Distress" (Ph.D. diss., Harvard University, 1971). Herbert A. **Musurillo**, *The Acts of Pagan Martyrs: Acta Alexandrinorum* (Oxford: Clarendon Press, 1954). Allardyce **Nicoll**, *Masks, Mores, and Miracles: Studies in the Popular Theater* (New York: Cooper Square, 1963). Martin **Nilsson**, *Die Religion der griechischen Zauberpapyri* (Lund: Arsberättellse, 1947–48) 59–93. Arthur D. **Nock**, "The Cult of Heroes," in *Essays on Religion and the Ancient World* (ed. Zeph Stewart; Cambridge,

Mass.: Harvard University Press, 1972) 1:134–59; "Gnosticism," in ibid., 2:940–59; "Graeco-Egyptian Religious Propaganda," in ibid., 2:703–11; "Greek Magical Papyri," in ibid., 1:176–94; "Hellenistic Mysteries and Christian Sacraments," in ibid., 2:791–820; "Notes on Ruler Cult I–IV," in ibid., 1:134–59; "Posidonius," in ibid., 2:853–76; "Religious Symbols and Symbolism I–III," in ibid., 2:877–918; "Ruler Worship and Syncretism," in ibid., 2:551–58; "'Son of God' in Pauline and Hellenistic Thought," in ibid., 2:928–39; "Soter and Euergetes," in ibid., 2:720–35. Elpidius **Pax**, "Epiphanie," *RAC*, 5:832–909. Lionel **Pearson**, *The Lost Histories of Alexander the Great* (Philological Monographs 20; Oxford: Blackwell, 1960). Ben E. **Perry**, "The Egyptian Legend of Nectanebus," *Proceedings of American Philological Association* 97 (1966) 327–33. Gerd **Petzke**, *Die Traditionen über Apollonius von Tyana und das Neue Testament* (Studia ad Corpus Hellenisticum NT 1; Leiden: Brill, 1970). Friedrich **Pfister**, "Ekstase," *RAC*, 4:944–82; "Enthusiasmos," *RAC*, 5:455–57; "Herakles und Christus," *ARW* 34:42–60; *Kleine Schriften zum Alexanderroman* (Meisenheim: Hain, 1976); *Studien zur Mantik in der Philosophie der Antike* (Beiträge zur klassischen Philologie 64; Meisenheim: Hain, 1976). Victor **Pöschl**, ed., *Römische Geschichtsschreibung* (Wege der Forschung 90; Darmstadt: Wissenschaftliche Buchgesellschaft, 1969). Walter **Pötscher**, "Prophetes," *Der kleine Pauly*, 4:1183–84. Sarah B. **Pomeroy**, *Goddesses, Whores, Wives, and Slaves: Women in Classical Antiquity* (New York: Schocken, 1975). Anton **Priessnig**, "Die literarische Form der spätantiken Philosophenromane," *Byzantinische Zeitschrift* 30 (1929–30) 23–30. Hermann **Reich**, *Der Mimus: Ein literar-entwicklungsgeschichtlicher Versuch* (Berlin: Weidmann, 1903). Alice S. **Riginos**, *Platonica: The Anecdotes Concerning the Life and Writings of Plato* (Columbia Studies in the Classical Tradition 3; Leiden: Brill, 1976). Erwin **Rohde**, *Psyche: Seelencult und Unsterblichkeitsglaube der Criechen* (Darmstadt: Wissenschaftliche Buchgessellschaft, 1961). Dieterich **Roloff**, *Gottähnlichkeit, Vergöttlichung und Erhöhung zu seligem Leben* (Berlin: De Gruyter, 1970). Jacqueline de **Romilly**, *Magic and Rhetoric in Ancient Greece* (Cambridge, Mass.: Harvard University Press, 1975). Leopold **Sabourin**, "Hellenistic and Rabbinic Miracles," *BTB* 2 (1972) 281–397. Karl **Schefold**, *Die Antwort der griechischen Kunst auf die Siege Alexanders des Grossen* (Sitzungsberichte der bayerischen Akademie der Wissenschaften—Philosophisch-philologische und historische Klasse 4, 1979); *Pompejanische Malerei: Sinn und Ideengeschichte* (Basel: Schwabe, 1952); *Römische Kunst als religiöses Phänomen* (Hamburg: Rowohlt, 1964); *Vergessenes Pompeji: Unveröffentlichte Bilder römischer Wanddekorationen in geschichtlicher Folge* (Bremen and Munich: Francke, 1962). Willy **Schottroff**, "Gottmensch I," *RAC*, 12:155–234. Ursula **Schubert**, *Spätantikes Judentum und antike Kunst* (Vienna and Munich: Herold, 1974). Robin **Scroggs**, "The Earliest Hellenistic Christianity," in Neusner, ed., *Religions* (Bibliography

3), 176–206. Charles **Segal**, "Art and the Hero: Participation, Detachment, and Narrative Point of View in Aeneid I," *Arethusa* 1 (1981) 67–82. Erwin **Seidl**, *Ptolemäische Rechtsgeschichte* (Ägyptologische Forschungen 22; Harrisburg and New York: Glückstadt, 1962). Jonathan Z. **Smith**, "Good News Is No News: Aretalogy and Gospel," in Neusner, ed., *Christianity* (Bibliography 3), 21–38; *Map Is Not Territory* (Leiden: Brill, 1978); "Towards Interpreting Demonic Powers in Hellenistic and Roman Antiquity, "*ANRW* 2:16.1:425–39. Morton **Smith**, *Clement of Alexandria and a Secret Gospel of Mark* (Cambridge, Mass.: Harvard University Press, 1973); *Jesus the Magician* (New York: Harper & Row, 1978); "Prolegomena to a Discussion of Aretalogies, Divine Man, the Gospels, and Jesus," *JBL* 90 (1971) 174–99. Helge **Stadelmann**, *Ben Sira als Schriftgelehrter* (WUNT 26; Tübingen: Mohr, 1980). Hannes O. **Steck**, *Israel und das gewaltsame Geschick der Propheten* (WMANT 23; Neukirchen: Erziehungsverein, 1967). Walter **Stettner**, *Die Seelenwanderung bei Griechen und Römern* (Tübinger Beiträge zur Altertumswissenschaft 22; Stuttgart: Kohlhammer, 1934). Hans E. **Stier**, "Alexander der Grosse," *RAC*, 1:261–70. Georg **Strecker**, "Entrückung," *RAC*, 5:461–76. Ronald **Syme**, *The Roman Revolution* (New York and London: Oxford University Press, 1962). Fritz **Taeger**, *Charisma: Studien zur Geschichte des antiken Herrscherkultes* (Stuttgart: Kohlhammer, 1957). Gerd **Theissen**, *The Miracle Stories of the Early Christian Tradition* (Philadelphia: Fortress, 1982); *Sociology of Early Palestinian Christianity* (Philadelphia: Fortress, 1982); see also *idem.*, Bibliography 2. J. Oliver **Thomson**, *History of Ancient Geography* (Cambridge: At the University Press, 1948). Klaus **Thraede**, "Euhemerismus," *RAC*, 6:877–90; "Exorzismus," *RAC*, 7:44–117. Klaus **Thraede** and Karl **Jax**, "Erfinder," *RAC*, 5:1176–78. David L. **Tiede**, *The Charismatic Figure as Miracle Worker* (SBLDS 1; Missoula, Mont.: Scholars Press, 1972); "The Figure of Moses in the Testament of Moses," in *Studies on the Testament of Moses*, ed. George W. Nickelsburg, (Cambridge, Mass.: Harvard University Press, 1973) 86–92. "Religious Propaganda and the Gospel Literature of the Early Christian Mission," *ANRW* 2.25.2; (ed.). Karl-Wolfgang **Tröger**, *Mysterienglaube und Gnosis im Corpus Hermeticum* (TU 110; Berlin: Akademie, 1971). Ladislav **Vidman**, *Isis und Sarapis bei den Griechen und Römern: Epigraphische Studien zur Verbreitung und zu den Trägern des ägyptischen Kultes* (Berlin: De Gruyter, 1970); *Sylloge inscriptionum religionis Isiacae et Sarapicae* (Berlin: De Gruyter, 1969). Dietrich **Wachsmuth**, ΠΟΜΠΙΜΟΣ ΔΑΙΜΩΝ (diss. Univ. of Berlin, 1967); "Seewesen," *Der kleine Pauly*, 5:67–71; "Wunderglaube, -täter," *Der kleine Pauly*, 5:1395–98. Nikolaus **Walter**, "Fragmente jüdisch-hellenistischer Historiker," "Fragmente jüdisch-hellenistischer Exegeten," "Fragmente jüdisch-hellenistischer Epik, Pseudepigraphische jüdisch-hellenistische Dichtung," in Werner G. Kümmel, ed., *Jüdisches Schrifttum aus hellenistisch-römischer Zeit*, 1/2; 3/2:257–99; 4/3:135–278 (Gütersloh: Gerd Mohn,

1976, 1975, 1983). Hans **Weder**, "Wunder Jesu und Wundergeschichten," *VF* 29 (1984) 25–49. David **Winston**, "Jambulus: A Story of Greek Utopianism" (diss., Columbia University, microfilm, 1956). Antonie **Wlosok**, ed., *Römischer Kaiserkult* (Wege der Forschung 372; Darmstadt: Wissenschaftliche Buchgesellschafte, 1978). Erich **Ziebarth**, *Der griechische Kaufmann in Altertum* (Tusculum Schriften 8; Munich: Heimeran, 1934). Konrat **Ziegler**, "Paradoxographoi," PW 18/3:1137–66. L. **Ziehen**, "Mantis," PW 14/2:1345–55. Clemens **Zintzen**, "Zauberei, Zauberer," *Der kleine Pauly*, 5:1460–72.

EPILOGUE NOTES 79–141

79. The problem needs to be dealt with in terms of social history. First attempts in this direction have been made, besides by myself, also by M. Hadas, M. Smith, J. Smith, G. Theissen, and D. Tiede. The newest study in the matter, H. D. Betz's "Gottmensch II," continues the typological approach. A good deal of the criticism leveled against the revival of the interest in the "divine man" is hampered by the terminological Platonism (mentioned on p. 352 n. 1), by an apologetic preference for the biblical and Jewish tradition, by a certain hesitation to respect Hellenistic culture as a world culture with intimate ties also to the Jewish tradition, and further by an all-too-strong hesitation to go beyond the history of thought and literature. C. Holladay's dissertation reflects these deficiencies.

80. Alexander was more a symptom than a cause with respect to the Hellenistic age. The double experience of the unity of the world and of the importance of the individual had grown since the Peleponnesian War, with Socrates and Euripides as their first major expressions. The individual became dependent on the local market, which in turn became a reflection of world trade and the world economy. Monetary unification was the backbone of the sense of world unity. The worldwide activity of Greek mercenaries, among whom none less than Xenophon, demonstrated not only the limits of the *polis* but also the breakdown of Greek chauvinism. Greek mercenaries, traders, artists, and craftsmen were symptoms of the degree to which Greek skill was appreciated in the remaining world; thus they helped to spread the Greek way of life in the *ecumene*.

81. On "benefactors," cf. the unfortunately still unpublished dissertation of S. Mott.

82. Although males were predominant, it should not be overlooked that women were not completely excluded from this display of the extraordinary, from becoming divine humans. There was first the number of important Macedonian women from Alexander's mother, Olympias, down to Cleopatra VII. Then there were the women of the Julian and the Flavian dynasties, and those associated with these dynasties. Further mention should be made of wealthy Spartan, Roman, and Egyptian women. Rich

Roman women exercised great economic, political, and cultural influence. S. Pomeroy (120–89) has dealt with that. She also gives examples for women as benefactors. Then there were the priestesses of various cults, and the prophetesses of different gods. Finally, reference is made to female sorcerers and other mighty women.

83. The experience of the miraculous during the Hellenistic age has been the object of research in recent times (see C. Classen; G. Delling; E. R. Dodds; R. Grant; H. Kee; L. Sabourin; J. Smith, "Good News"; M. Smith; G. Theissen; D. Tiede; D. Wachsmuth).

The intimate relationship of this yearning for miracles to Hellenistic culture and society is not yet seen enough. It represents Hellenism's very character. Most of the studies still concentrate on religion and "superstition" alone, but these have to be seen as integral and representative parts of a culture and of a society which required secular miracles as well. Despite considerable advances in science and technology, a separate secular consciousness did not develop.

84. An historical-critical study of the life, legend, and myth of Alexander which could match the critical energy and precision of life-of-Jesus research is still missing to this day. Just as in the case of Jesus, and because of a similar nature of sources, even the best and most critical historiographer in the end will have to be satisfied with his or her own Alexander, to a high degree a construct and projection which will reflect heavily the preferences and dislikes of the modern critic. In the case of Alexander, it will be even more so than in the case of Jesus, because reliable sources on Alexander are much more removed from the person portrayed than the Gospels are from Jesus. And the Alexander evidence is not only late but also spurious.

The portrait of Alexander, literary and otherwise, reflected this interdependence of myth, history, and geography, most prominently but also symptomatically. Heracles was considered the forebear of the Macedonian dynasty. As pictorial evidence demonstrates, especially the use of the lion skin, Heracles became the paradigm for Alexander. This seemed to typify the heroic warrior, but also the restless wanderer and irresistible colonizer. The *interpretatio Graeca* of the Semitic god Melkart with Heracles seemed to have caused the conflict with Tyre. Meanwhile, the philosophical interpretation had increased the interplay of ἀγών/πόνος/ἀρετή/παιδεία in the Heracles tradition, thus turning Heracles into a model for Hellenistic culture, including its missionary civilizing zeal, transcending all previous limits and borders.

Some fifty years before Alexander was born, Euripides had written the *Bacchae* at the Macedonian court. In the first lines of this drama, Dionysus describes his invincible missionary procession to the East, literally a "triumph." These lines read like an itinerary of Alexander's campaign, although more than seventy years older. As the victorious Macedonian troops and their allies under their heroic leader progressed, the Eastern horizon of the god received clearer contours also. In the histories of the Alexander tradition and of the Dionysus tradition, it is hard to decide how much Alexander followed Dionysus and how much Dionysus followed Alexander.

85. Proof for the growth of the legend of Alexander during his lifetime is in E. Mederer. Names like Eumenes, Nearchus, Anaxarchus, Callisthenes, and Pyrrhon speak for the presence of critical intelligence around Alexander.

86. On Alexander's impact on later political figures, see A. Heuss; on the Alexander romance, see R. Merkelbach, *Quellen*, and F. Pfister, *Kleine Schriften*.

87. In the long run, an aristocratic, elitist dimension won out in the use of the divine man concept, not least because the number of divine men decreased considerably during the second century C.E. It increased again under Christian influence in the third century, as P. Brown has shown. Societal and political forces stood behind decrease and increase too.

88. There is new material in the studies of L. Feldman, J. Golding, J. Smith, M. Smith, D. Tiede, G. Theissen.

89. On charismatic wisdom in the context of the Jewish wisdom movement, see my "Wesen der Weisheit," 69–70, 78 (see Bibliography 3).

90. There is an important discussion on this in M. Hengel, *Judaism*, 157–62 (see Bibliography 3). H. Stadelmann instead renews the old Apologetic arguments about the absence of prophetic inspiration and consciousness in Jesus ben Sirach as a writer after the "biblical" prophets and before Jesus.

91. This emphasis on education is another element that corresponds to Hellenistic tendencies.

92. The confidence of the present generation that its knowledge is superior to that of the prophets of old is expressed in 1 Pet. 1:10–12. This idea, however, is nothing uniquely "Christian" but typically Jewish, a radicalization of prophetic confidence as it was furthered in wisdom circles. Heb. 11:49–50 belongs in this context too.

93. Only Jesus ben Sirach would understand this saying as this-worldly, monistically, whereas in Wisdom of Solomon it has become part of the book's dualistic message; see D. Georgi, "Weisheit Salomos," 422–23 (Bibliography 3).

94. Jesus ben Sirach therefore lodges the truly protective forces of God's creation above the level of manual labor, even above commerce and political routine (chaps. 39 and 40). The sapiential sphere of insight, word, and book is the area which counts as far as the survival of the world is concerned, not the world of everyday practice. This is an interesting analogy to if not adoption of Greek social values which had put the intellectual, especially the philosopher, above the βάναυσος, the manual laborer, particularly the craftsman. Βάναυσος therefore became synonymous with "uneducated." The interesting question is whether Paul's opponents in 2 Cor., most probably like the majority of Jewish Apologists, including Philo and Josephus, continued this social arrogance of Jesus ben Sirach in analogy

to the Greek and Hellenistic intellectual tradition. Their criticism of Paul's not accepting money and working instead manually would receive additional force that way. Paul instead followed Pharisaic tradition, that of lay people, heavily from the crafts. The Pharisaic rabbis later would drop the aversion of Jesus ben Sirach to manual labor, making it a virtue if not a requirement.

95. See my "Wesen der Weisheit," nn. 6, 10, 14 (Bibliography 3).

96. The direct connection between Apologetic literature and homiletical practice, as discussed above, pp. 84–101, proves that the basis for this Apologetic communication was in the actual worship, not only oriented to it but coming out of it.

97. The texts discussed above, pp. 101–16, demonstrate that a great variety of participants and forms of participation existed in Hellenistic-Jewish worship, also with respect to extraordinary performances.

98. As has been demonstrated above, pp. 117–22, 397–98.

99. As demonstrated by Goodenough, *Symbols* (Bibliography 1).

100. See above, p. 145.

101. See above, pp. 113–14.

102. The spirit behind this has been discussed by K. Schefold in his books on Roman paintings.

103. And from the remains of Roman theatrical buildings, like the theater of Herodes Atticus in Athens, and whatever can be reconstructed of them. On Roman theatrical architecture, see Vitruvius 5.3–6 (cf. also 7–9). On the connection between Hellenistic and Roman wallpaintings and the theater, see H. Beyen, 1:102–7, 248–53; 2.1:336–50; K. Schefold, *Pompejanische Malerei*, 59–61, 162–64. The popular theater and the mime must not be forgotten; cf., besides H. Reich, also A. Nicoll.

104. Originally the art of conducting a contest for a prize. Greek and Hellenistic culture knew many of those—sports, horse-racing, music, poetry (including the producing and performing of drama), dancing, rhetoric, and many more (all these were expressions of ἀγών, contest)—the marks of a culture which basically was agonistic, and competitive, where the prize gained gave not only civic but also divine honor and status. Over the years, *athletes* and *athletics* increasingly denoted sportsmen and sports. This did not reduce the competitive nature of the culture, but on the contrary. However, sports had been and remained the heart of that competitive culture, and thus also the basis of the metaphorical use mentioned.

105. 1 Cor. 9:24–27 and Phil. 3:14 are supported by other occurrences of ἀγών, ἀγωνίζεσθαι, δρόμος, στέφανος, etc., in Pauline and deutero-Pauline literature (including Hebrews and Luke-Acts).

106. The Cynics, Philo, Plutarch (*De Genio Socratis*); see H. D. Betz, *Plutarch's Theological Writings*, 243, etc.

107. Ἐγκυκλοπαιδεία (so Philo many a time). There is an early example in Wisd. of Sol. 7:15–21.

108. E. Goodenough, "Kingship," (Bibliography 1).

109. In "Weisheit Salomos" and "Wesen der Weisheit" (Bibliography 3).

110. E. Goodenough, *Jurisprudence* (see Bibliography 5).

111. I have spoken of the possibility of Eupolemus as diplomat, above, p. 100. Cf. also the diplomatic correspondence in 1 and 2 Maccabees.

112. The documents granting privileges to Jews prove the interest and generosity of Gentiles.

113. Sometimes these diplomats were in the service of Jerusalem, like Alexander in Josephus (*Ant.* 14.225–27) on behalf of the Jews in Ephesus. Sometimes the Jewish diaspora communities acted diplomatically for themselves, as in the case of Philo's delegation to Caligula or the case of the Jewry of Delos (Josephus, *Ant.* 14.213–16). In all these cases and in many more, Jewish diplomatic efforts had success in establishing, maintaining, or improving rights and privileges. Visits between Jewish congregations had an ambassadorial dimension too. The interest of the early church in mutual visits and the nature of her apostles, particularly in the understanding of people like Paul's opponents in 2 Cor., have to be seen in this light also, and not the least the function of letters of recommendation, all of it a diplomatic network of sorts.

114. The best discussion of the propagandistic and missionary character of Hellenistic culture, including its Roman branch, is still found in M. Hadas, *Culture* (see Bibliography 3). See also my "Socioeconomic Reasons." But these are only first steps into an almost untapped research area.

115. On the spread of pagan religions, see H. Koester, *Introduction*, 1:173–204, 356–58; and bibliography.

116. Juvenal expresses his high opinion of the ancient ways, e.g., in his first satire and in 6.286–91, 342–45.

117. Esp. in *Icaromenippus* and in the *Descent into Hades*. A good NT example is Paul's attitude toward Abraham, producing an idealized and also actualized symbol despite Paul's vitriolic opposition to the Jewish manipulation of the figure of Moses.

118. W. Wachsmuth, *Wunderglaube*, and G. Theissen, *Miracle Stories*.

119. It is interesting to note how this affected Hellenistic historiography. There is a good sketch in M. Hadas, *Culture*, 125–29 (Bibliography 3); cf. also the essays in V. Pöschl.

120. See also M. Hadas, "Livy" (Bibliography 5).

121. D. Georgi, "Socioeconomic Reasons."

122. C. Habicht and S. Mott.

123. The *Res Gestae Divi Augusti* are found in LCL (together with Velleius Paterculus). See also V. Ehrenberg (comp.), *Documents Illustrating the Reigns of Augustus and Tiberius*, 2d ed. (New York and London: Oxford University Press, 1976). On the Delos inscription, see above, p. 159.

124. In the Hellenistic world, writing things down, bringing them to general attention, and making them matters of public record (through storing in libraries or public archives or through public inscriptions) were steps and stages not only of recognition but also of legal acceptance and force; public

monuments (sculptures, altars, buildings) and coins would add to that. On aretalogies, see J. Smith, "Good News"; M. Smith, "Prolegomena"; C. Talbert (see Bibliography 6); cf. also H. Koester, *Introduction*, 1:132–40, 183–91.

125. On seafaring and commerce, see the studies by Lionel Casson and Martin Charlesworth. Many ancient Greeks were seen as wanderers, often aggrandized into heroic or divine dimensions (H. D. Betz, "Gottmensch II," 238–48). Philosophers like Pythagoras, Empedocles, Democritus, the Cynics (including Peregrinus Proteus), Apollonius, and many more were themselves migrants or were later presented as such. The traditions about Indian philosophers belong in this context too. Then there was the greatest traveler of all, Alexander the Great. Many of these journeys, real or imaginary, touched the limits of common experience or went beyond them. Thus the miraculous entered the picture easily. Many of these wanderings were therefore presented as transcending the borders of the human realm. Traveling gods and heroes, most of all Dionysus and Heracles, Isis and Hermes, epic figures like Odysseus, the Argonauts, Aeneas, and always Orpheus again, provided typological models intertwining themselves constantly with "historical" experience and interpretation. From the Greeks, Hellenism borrowed the interest in the dialectic between the exotic and the civilized, adventure and reason. Playing with the unknown, including the geographically unknown, was a major means of understanding. The borders between the description of the miraculous (the paradox), geography, and historiography, were fluid, the latter two turning often into paradoxography. Philosophy, mythology, and theology added to that.

On ancient geography and on paradoxography, see M. Hadas, *Culture*, 170–81, 212–22 (Bibliography 3); J. Thomson; and K. Ziegler.

126. Despite all the impressive nautical advancements, the sea never lost its threat for the ancients, not even for seafaring people. See D. Wachsmuth, "Daimon."

127. The idea of transmigration of souls, μετεμψύχωσις or μετενσωματώσις, had evolved into many forms, not only the original, particularly Pythagorean, form of reincarnation. It included also the ideas of the movement of certain souls beyond the limits of their bodies, of the appearance of individuals at other places or situations than their bodies would be, but particularly also of the reappearance of certain great persons of the past in figures of today. The incorporation of certain divinities in human beings is also related to this complex. Whether people experienced these extraordinary circumstances or moves beyond the common borders accidentally or voluntarily was of lesser importance. Their direction could be up or down, backward in time or forward. See J. Bolton; H. Dörrie, "Kontroversen" and "Pythagoreer"; E. Rohde, index under *Seele* (*n*) and *Seelenwanderung*; W. Stettner.

128. Both the Jewish apocalyptic literature and the Gnostic and Christian versions of it need to be mentioned here. Stories on descents into the un-

derworld as well as those of ascents into the air or into heaven belong here too. Seneca's *Apocolocyntosis* and the respective phenomena of the ruler- and the Caesar-cult are all part of this. In all this we note the transparency between dream, hope, experience, myth, and mythical enactment. And the mythological and eschatological concepts relate easily to those of journey, and vice versa. Even the idea of parousia is not too far from that. The popu- larity of all these phenomena demonstrated their importance and called for reproduction. If one could not claim any of these experiences of boundless- ness, one could participate in them through dreams, through mythical or magical reenactment, but also through pictorial, musical, and narrative means. That the latter forms of representation had magical potential or qualities for the ancient world, particularly also for the Hellenistic period, is important for our considerations. For further reference on the phenom- ena mentioned, see e.g., A. Dieterich; M. Hadas, *Culture*, 212–22 (Bibli- ography 3); H. L'Orange; D. Roloff; M. Smith, *Clement*, index under Ascent and Resurrection; and idem, *Jesus*, 100–106, 120–26, 161–62. H. Dörrie, "Pythagoreer," has shown how the biographical narration can pro- vide temporal and spatial transparency (repetition as well as identification). G. Theissen (*Miracle Stories*, 125–95, 231–302) has made important obser- vations regarding the participatory dimensions of miracle stories. They need to be expanded and critically sharpened in order to do away with his overarching apologetic interest.

129. W. Fauth, J. Kollesch.

130. A.-M. J. Festugière, *Révélation*, 1:131–36, 201–16, 283–308 (Bibli- ography 1).

131. Ibid., 187–282.

132. See D. Aune and the various studies of C. Bonner, E. R. Dodds, and S. Eitrem. See also J. Golding; J. Smith, "Towards Interpreting"; J. de Romilly; C. Zintzen; and, of course, M. Smith, *Clement* (index under Magic); idem, *Jesus*, 69–139; and W. Gundel on astrology.

133. W. Pötscher; and H. D. Betz, "Gottmensch II."

134. Empedocles needs mention here, as does Nigidius Figulus. The interplay of prophet and reason is found also in the area that traditional his- tory of religion of the Hellenistic world imprecisely has called spiritualiza- tion. Philo and the Corpus Hermeticum might be mentioned here as representatives of a much larger phenomenon.

135. This and the following is only partly recognized by Betz, "Gott- mensch II."

136. Unfortunately, A. D. Nock's famous book *Conversion* (Bibliography 1) has been seen mostly as a terminal study instead of as a seminal one.

137. See my essay "Socioeconomic Reasons."

138. Despite the elaborate art-historical research on that period, a pene- trating and comprehensive study on the phenomenon of the concept and social function of the "monumental" in Hellenism is still missing.

139. H. Koester, *Introduction*, 1:101–13; see also J. de Romilly, D.

Georgi, "Forms"; and G. Kennedy (see Bibliography 5). Even the storing and classifying of linguistic achievements reached monumental proportions; cf., e.g., the 120 books of the second director of the library in Alexandria, Callimachus, or the huge output of M. Terentius Varro (among many other writings, twenty-five books on the Latin language, forty-one books on antiquities, and further, his studies on pets, poetry, and the arts). See what is said further below, p. 432, on libraries.

140. E. Goodenough, *Politics* (Bibliography 1), on Moses; and M. Hadas, *Culture*, 249–63 (Bibliography 3). The most obvious examples for this are the ruler and the Caesar cult. But Cicero's *Somnium Scipionis* is a prominent example of the image and importance of the statesman (the princeps, in fact) as connecting heaven and earth, not as a rare exception but as a model. The Philonic model of Moses is not that outlandish. What Philo says of Augustus in *De Legatione ad Gaium*, 143–53, 309, concurs with his Moses portrait as much as with the official image of the Caesar.

141. Esp. M. Hadas, *Culture* (Bibliography 3).

CONTRIBUTIONS OF JEWISH APOLOGETICS

The success of Paul's opponents in 2 Cor. can be better understood if seen in the light of the contributions Jewish Apologetics had made to Judaism and to paganism. Paul's rivals added to the success story of Jewish Apologetics, a fact worth considering in future histories of Hellenistic Judaism. It is widely accepted that rabbinic writings of the second century C.E. and later show the influence of Hellenistic hermeneutics.[142] What is much less discussed is the mediating influence of the Jewish diaspora in that. As early as Aristobulus and as massively as in Philo and Josephus, Hellenistic Judaism demonstrated its bridging role in this transfer of knowledge.[143]

The key function of Jewish Apologetics shows especially in the legal exposition of Philo found in his treatment of biblical laws.[144] Philo here is no inventor, but he is representative of Hellenistic-Jewish missionary theology and practice, with Philo's writings still a century older than the earlier literary remains of the Pharisaic rabbinate. The similarities between Hellenistic-Jewish and rabbinical legal exposition to this day usually are considered to be caused by a dependence of the Hellenistic Jews on the Pharisaic rabbis. But historical probability speaks for the opposite.

Jews in Palestine before the year 70 had the temple and the priests for all matters of cultic law. Here Torah had been issued, expounded, and applied, even before the exile, not on internal matters of cult and priesthood alone but also in innumerable cases of public and private legal inquiry and consultation. The codification of the Pentateuch increased and eased this role of the temple priests. They, not any rabbis, were the predecessors, colleagues, and descendants of Ezra. Local courts in Palestine, the biblical tribunals "in the gate" of the individual settlements,[145] dealt with matters of civil law, but their court of reference and appeal was the temple too.[146]

From Jesus ben Sirach's elaborately demonstrated practice, therefore, one can conclude that the newly created profession of scribes[147] could concentrate on things other than legal exposition of the law. Indeed, sapiential and moral interpretation was the task of the Sirazide and his colleagues down to the times of Jesus and Paul, garnished with all the aplomb of the "divine man," as described above.

But in the diaspora the Jerusalem temple and its priests were far away. Substitutes like the temple in Leontopolis apparently did not help.[148] Thus Jews in the diaspora had to take the law into their own hands and assess and adjudicate legal issues, with the authority they had—of a Jewish community congregated around holy scriptures—and with the powers they possessed—their spirit and knowledge. The latter they shared with Gentiles.

Philo's exposition of legal texts in *De Specialibus Legibus* has been dealt with by Goodenough in his *Jurisprudence of the Jewish Courts in Egypt*.[149] Little has been done on this since 1929, which is unfortunate because the progress of research in wisdom studies, Jewish wisdom in particular, could contribute here greatly. It would correct the negative presumptions about the integrity of the efforts of Philo and his colleagues. Goodenough still shows some of the prejudice held against Jewish Apologetics when he says that Philo possessed a "probably unconscious but profound conviction that Judaism was quite inadequate in the light of Greek philosophical teaching"[150] and that the major drive in Jewish Alexandrian legal practice was toward accommodation with the Gentile situation, thus indirectly yielding the lead to the Greeks.[151] Thorough investigation of Philo's texts shows that he and his fellow Apologists were not stricken by what Goodenough calls a "crash of Judaism and Hellenism" or endeavoring to bring about a "reconciliation" between two irreconcilable entities with the biblical argument as an unrelated third, although intended as the reconciling force. The pluralistic and integrative nature of Hellenism has not yet been recognized by Goodenough, nor has the fact that Judaism was part of it, not accidentally but constitutionally, with biblical wisdom providing a major, dialogical contribution to world culture.[152]

The contribution of Hellenistic-Jewish Apologetics to Jewish and pagan hermeneutics has already been discussed above,[153] yet some points need to be stressed here. Legal application belonged in the context of the integration of diverse specifics, so essential for Hellenism. Related Jewish phenomena, Palestinian or diaspora, cannot be seen as isolated or ghettolike, nor as defensive accommodations. They are symptomatic of the Hellenistic world at large, attempts at comprehending the problems of a pluralistic world culture, its legal variety indeed. Judaism was an intimate and intrinsic part of Hellenistic culture.

The Hellenistic-Jewish hermeneutical efforts were representative of the Hellenistic search for general principles and structures, a search whose purpose was to assess, relate, and bridge differences, even those that were geographically, temporally, and culturally remote.[154] The applicability of the results of such searches was also a major concern.[155] Since the time of the first sophists, controversy existed between two different ways of comprehending the world in its entirety,[156] one through form and method ($\tau \acute{e} \chi \nu \eta$), the other through content and interpretation ($\varphi \iota \lambda o \sigma o \varphi \acute{\iota} \alpha$). The former was represented most of all by rhetoricians,[157] but they also would agree that they strove for a basic hold on things, not only for the purpose of understanding but also in order to handle and apply the knowledge gained.[158]

Goodenough has overlooked the fact that Hellenistic-Jewish Apologetics, in its attempt to overcome alienation and to synthesize discrepancies, represented a variation on a general Hellenistic theme. This was true for the discussion of legal matters too. Plato's and Aristotle's works on the state and political constitutions and Plato's work on laws present exemplary collections of a vast variety of dispersed and often contradictory data from different times and places, and also examples of attempts to reconcile them through interpretative organization.[159] These and later efforts of others were intended for education and public use.[160]

In the context of the discussion of the social role and importance of the "divine man," it is noteworthy that Hellenistic society in its various provinces considered personal competence essential for dealing with legal situations because it offered the best response to its often confusing, if not chaotic, character caused by the pluralistic nature of society. Although the controversy between form and content mentioned above often led to a mix between the two in later Hellenistic times, still, in the context of legal practice, there was a tendency to prefer the rhetorician, the representative of a certain, rhetorical τέχνη.[161]

But this must not be confused with our modern understanding of a "practical" approach. As hinted at above, the rhetorician, despite the emphasis on τέχνη, was considered not a craftsman or a specialist but a generalist.[162] In other words, the concept and reality of the division of labor developed in Greek and Hellenistic society with respect to the production of material goods, and to a degree in trade, administration, and the arts,[163] would not apply to the rhetorician (or to anybody dealing with law).[164] The rhetorician belonged in the context of what one might call the production and management of cultural goods (e.g., religion, philosophy, sciences, and law). Here the professional specialist did not count. An all-around approach and competence was required here, be it through form, content, or a blending of both.[165]

The work and person of Philo are symptomatic of the nature, and particularly of the integration, of legal practice. Philo was definitely a theologian and philosopher at heart. Within this context he created, or at least promulgated, major contributions to legal theory which continue to have some influence even in modern culture, including modern law and politics. I think of the concept of natural law, a further but characteristically Jewish development of earlier Platonic and Stoic ideas.[166] But on the other side, Philo is also involved in the practical politics and legal practice of the Jewish community at Alexandria.[167] In his exposition of the laws, particularly in the treatises on the "special laws," he proves both the concrete applicability of Torah *and* the theoretical justifiability of the practice of the Jewish courts in Alexandria in which he is heavily involved (as he bemoans in *Spec*. 3.1[168]).

Philo's heart clearly beats on the side of theory, but he follows the call of practice. This mixture calls for greater scrutiny. Taking Philo as a symptom, I want to suggest that Hellenistic-Jewish Apologists were prepared to deal with practical matters if called upon by the situation, and this would include legal matters, even court practice if necessary. These Jewish Apologists were ready to appreciate and handle local and regional problems, Jewish and others, dealing with them in a more-or-less integrative fashion. If that required legal attention and judgment, so be it; one felt enabled to give it. If it did not require such attention, one could spare the energy for something else.

An Apologist as sedentary as Philo and in a place far removed from Palestine was called on to apply his wisdom to matters of politics and law and to do so practically. He proved that he could do it. In doing so, he added to Jewish confidence and to the attractiveness of this religious offer.

An Apologist in Palestine or on a missionary tour would not as easily be under this demand. But if challenged to relate scribal wisdom and local problems he or she would be prepared to try the differentiating and synthesizing capabilities which Hellenistic-Jewish Apologists had developed in the theory and practice of hermeneutics in the diaspora.

Paul's opponents in Corinth were not needed to solve legal problems in Corinth, and thus, although they did not neglect either Torah or hermeneutics,[169] they did not need to show detailed legal interest.[170] But there were some legal questions they were concerned with. There were conflicts with Paul about authority and legitimacy, about the relationship between local and translocal, migrant authority. Judging from Paul's arguments, the dispute possessed forensic character, and the legal dimensions would be obvious and natural. The monetary question touched on several times had a legal side also. Would the opponents relate to those issues spontaneously, or was there a philosophy and practice they could follow? More work in the area of noncultic legal theory and practice in Jewish Apologetics is necessary to gain some ideas at least about options.

An area that for Jewish Apologetics was intimately related to hermeneutics has been the subject of considerable interest in recent years: the complex of tradition and its meaning and function. Studies in the various branches of biblical Jewish wisdom, of Qumran, Apocalyptic, and Gnosis in particular, have increased our knowledge considerably.[171] Similar non-Jewish phenomena have not been focused on to the same degree, for instance, the whole range of discussion and use of tradition in Roman society of the last century B.C.E. and the first century C.E.[172] Here there seem to have been direct contacts between Judaism and the Roman subculture of Hellenism.[173]

I have shown in my book that the concepts of scriptures and of canon are closely related to the issues of hermeneutics and tradition.[174] Much of our discussion of scriptures and canon still suffers from religious parochialism.[175] The concentration is generally on Jewish and "Christian" scriptures and canon, too often even separated from each other. They are more contemporary with each other than usually recognized. In fact, much of their development occurred in mutual competition and dependence.

The relatively late and then very polemical nature of the discussion of an exclusive canon has to be separated from the custom and existence of holy scriptures. Most of the New Testament writings do not yet know of a canon of biblical writings in an exclusive fashion.[176] They know of holy scriptures, but their number outside the Pentateuch remains undefined. Closely related is the observation that the Mishnah, Tosephtah, New Testament, and much of apocryphal as well as pseudepigraphical literature (Gnostic literature included) are competitive collections. They function for the communities responsible for them as authoritative interpretation of holy scriptures.

The stunning analogy in the development of the concept and reality of an *exclusive* canon of holy writ, in Jewish and "Christian" circles, has not hit home enough with scholarship. This is all the more surprising since there is also the striking "coincidence" or, I would say, competition, particularly in post-first-century Judaism and "Christianity," of collections of authoritative interpretations, combined with the simultaneous discussion of authoritative interpreters and their succession.[177] All this has remained almost completely untouched in the discussion of the development of either the Jewish or the "Christian" canon.

Albert C. Sundberg's studies on the Jewish canon have repeatedly challenged the common assumptions about a separate development in Palestine and in the diaspora. Instead he sees them interrelate—with some hints at analogies in the history of the NT canon. And yet the OT canon to this day is presented very much as a Palestinian phenomenon, the NT very much as a Gentile-Christian, non-Palestinian entity.[178]

Paul's opponents gave to their Jewish heritage an integrating role. Paul's rivals appear to have used the term "Old Testament" before Paul, and they may have used it for the first time, but they did so positively in a hermeneutically loaded interplay between inspired text and inspired interpreter, combined with the concept of inspired and inspiring tradition. All this was seen not merely as a presentation of ideas but as based on and as calling for continuous action.

Their hermeneutics and their concept of scriptures did not come out of nowhere. Scholarly discussion of the canon has not yet realized that the two oldest theoretical reflections on the Jewish canon do occur in *Hellenistic*-Jewish texts, in the grandson's preface to his translation of Jesus ben Sirach's work, and in the *Epistle of Aristeas*. It needs to be emphasized that the Hebrew work of Jesus ben Sirach does not contain any passages similar to the grandson's introductory exposition. This does not mean that the grandson turned his grandfather's opinion regarding written tradition on its head; it merely says that the discussion on holy writ had progressed considerably further since Sirach 24, and had done so most actively in the diaspora, where it had achieved a relatively advanced stage by the late second century. Now Jesus ben Sirach's grandson presents his grandfather's book as a contribution to this discussion abroad, adding his own preface as an orienting adjustment.[179]

The earlier reflections, for example, in Sirach 24, happened in wisdom circles. This remained so in the diaspora; only the kind of wisdom changed. The preface to the Greek Sirach and the *Epistle of Aristeas* relate to that. This advanced discussion belonged to the circles of Hellenistic-Jewish Apologetics. Philo and Josephus prove that Jewish Apologists stayed on the ball, although the history of rabbinic activity shows that the Pharisaic rabbis caught on to it during the latter part of the first century. In my opinion, this was influenced partly by earlier insights and achievements of Hellenistic Judaism, especially Hellenistic-Jewish Apologetics. The *Epistle of Aristeas* proves that the Apologists related the interest in the canon to general cultural trends and interests as well as to politics and that they accommodated their propaganda to that.[180] They did so not merely in theory; as LXX and LXX exegesis show, they did so also in practice.[181]

The active role of "Christian" Apologists in the development of the "Christian" canon needs to be more recognized.[182] They depended on their Jewish "colleagues." Canon discussion and canon development are not *internal* concerns alone of Jews, "Christians," or certain other Hellenistic religious groups. Closer scrutiny proves the interplay between propaganda, political power play, and missionary activity in the canonization processes. This becomes blatantly obvious if the usual artificial termination of the active canon discussion in Judaism and "Christianity" is given up. In the case of Judaism, most scholars see it terminated around 100 C.E., some around 200 C.E., that is, with the codification of the Mishnah. The "Christian" canon discussion is usually seen as finished during the early third century C.E., but a closer look demonstrates that in Judaism as well as in "Christianity" an active interest continued in subsequent generations, not only in ideas but also in the reality of the canon and its manipulation, especially also its political manipulation.[183]

The canon as a collection of holy scriptures, inclusive or exclusive, was a spiritual thing, namely a treasure house of the spirit, as the Hellenistic and Hellenistic-Jewish propagators of the canon idea understood it.[184] But the canons, Jewish, pagan, and "Christian," were worldly things too, consciously put into the competitive context of various cultural forces.

The customary idea that the Jewish as well as the "Christian" concepts of canon grew out of scriptures themselves, that is, by divine providence, the spirit's action, is nonsense. There is not only the comparability and competitiveness between two canons, one Jewish and one "Christian." There are several canonical concepts and collections in Jewish and "Christian" contexts. The fact that only two (or three, if we count the LXX separately) canons survived and established themselves is to be judged against the disappearance of competitive enterprises. Other Jewish and "Christian" concepts and collections are unfortunately to this day discredited as "heterodox," a *metabasis eis allo genos* as far as critical historical discussion is concerned.[185] It is surprising that the term "heterodoxy" was used so quickly and easily with reference to the Qumran community and their writings after their discovery. Josephus's and Philo's treatment of the Essenes should have warned against such an anachronistic and doctrinaire qualification.[186] The same has to be said against the prevailing use of the term "apocryphal" in scholarly discussion; it is used for the pragmatic distinction of what had become canonical among other revered writings, but it also commonly associates concord with the claim that the "canonical" writings indeed represented a majority phenomenon and reflected the actual theological and communal situations properly, whereas the "apocryphal" writings did not.[187]

The Jewish and the "Christian" canons which survived were relative entities, relative to each other and relative to other comparable competitive enterprises not only in their immediate religious environment but also in the larger Hellenistic culture. Jewish and "Christian" Apologists were most influential in the origin and early formation of the surviving canons. Their active interest in a definite collection of holy writings had its *Sitz im Leben* in a cultural context much wider than their own religious enterprises. This cultural context provided models and criteria for the competition the Apologists consciously joined and hoped to excel in for the greater sake of the religion they represented propagandistically.

What has been overlooked is that the rabbinic discussion about a canon and its authoritative interpretation belongs in this general context too, far beyond the Jewish subculture of Hellenism.[188] The rabbinic interest in scriptures and interpretation was certainly not a professional one alone, and not merely related to the problem of survival of a particular religious tradition either. It also had aspects of conscious concern for cultural and political survival.[189] One of the peculiar aspects of the Pharisaic contribution to the development of the Jewish canon was that they realized more than others that a religious, cultural, and political rescue of Judaism could happen only through *conformity* with certain general cultural developments and standards of their time, and only in *collaboration with* the contemporary political power which intended increasingly to control the cultural and religious aspects of world culture and its more vivid subdivisions, namely, Rome.[190]

Selective, standardized, classified, edited, and cataloged collections of written traditions had become a major objective in Hellenistic culture long before the second century C.E.[191] The development of the "canonical" and the "classical" applied not only to originals but also to works of interpretation.[192] The division between primary and secondary literature, not in name but in fact, existed already in Hellenistic culture, and just as in much of modern culture, this division was not necessarily one of rank and importance. On the contrary, both the primary and the secondary were often co-equal in actual functional importance.

Whether this Hellenistic development of idea and practice of the *canonical* and *classical* and its mediation had its origin in sophistic philosophy or in mystery religions, or both, will always remain debatable, given our fragmentary knowledge of both phenomena.[193] The formation of an authentic and authoritative core of primary sources and also of their interpretation, of the originals as well as of their competent and acceptable mediation, became clear and prominent in philosophical schools. In this environment the figure of the "divine man" proved helpful for describing the divinely gifted author and also the selected, inspired interpreter and representative.[194] The adoption of this concept of the "divine man" for this purpose could use its social-political importance gained in the culture at large.

Within and through philosophy, literary and aesthetic criticism, rhetorics, and education were infused with these concepts, worked them out further, spread them, and thus made them general cultural ideas, criteria, and even realities.[195] Libraries entered the picture and became major factors in the development.[196] The idea and practice of collections of writings through funding and supervision by kings and others brought another political dimension. Libraries turned into instruments of political power.

Whereas Plato and Aristotle led to a theoretical reflection and systematization of law and laws already, especially in and through their schools, the idea and practice of systematic codification of Hellenistic laws is of later origin.[197] Roman jurists of the first century B.C.E., masters in comprehensive systematic legal codification, with the inclusion of interpretative and, indirectly, creative jurisprudence, became a major force in this.[198] Active interference of aggressive personalities, divine men themselves, like Sulla, Cicero, Caesar, Augustus and his successors, gave this process of systematization and codification specific political direction.

These men and their circles were interested in and preoccupied with the phenomenon of "classical heritage" and its "revitalization," believed as much as manipulated.[199] Here in Rome the aggressive and powerful definition, selection, collection, and enforcement of that which is "classical" Roman was **undertaken** as a broad and multifaceted enterprise, this "classically" Roman simultaneously advertised as the authentically Hellenistic. Powerful figures, divine men, Hellenistic as well as Roman, some of them stable, some of them exchangeable, from the past to the present, became part of that core, with Augustus as one of the most important among them, as bringer of world peace and savior of world culture, a miracle worker of unusual proportions, even within those miracle-believing days.

A cultural nucleus was singled out. This was an expression of political power and became a worldwide demonstration of it. These "divine men" were put in complete correspondence with tradition. The heroes of old and the Caesars of today were presented as the central expression and authoritative representation of Roman tradition. Sculpture, monumental architecture, coinage, legislation, and jurisdiction would support and stratify that. The Caesar cult provided cohesion and motivation.[200]

It is understandable that the Pharisaic rabbis saw the application of the pattern described as a promising model for the survival of their profession, of Jewish religion, and of Jewish culture.[201] The quadruplet of basic canon, basic lore, interpretative canon, and great personalities as originators and interpreters could provide a tradition acceptable and presentable to the rabbinate at large, to the Jewish people, *and* to the Roman authorities. The first two chapters of the Mishnah tractate *Pirke Aboth* present this pattern in a nutshell, including the concept of the great men, with Hillel seen as the greatest of them.[202] This model would possess enormous power, even political clout, all the more if it would be accompanied by methodological and institutional self-discipline.

The Romans appreciated this model more than contemporary competing ones (like the Apocalyptic, Gnostic, or most Jesus-oriented ones) because the Pharisaic rabbinic model conformed most to patterns known and acceptable to the Romans, not the least because of its heavily legal dimension. In its nonsecretive, self-disciplining character the Pharisaic rabbinic model gave easy visibility and accountability for governmental supervision. It demonstrated an exemplary willingness to collaborate on the part of a previously rebellious people. Thus it presented an ideal showcase for the enactment of Roman imperial policy allowing relative autonomy to non-Roman peoples with respect to their culture and religion, and to a degree even politically.

This sketch of the history of idea and practice of the "canonical," and of its interplay with the reality of the "divine man," points to an exciting but almost unexplored area. Paul's adversaries in Corinth, people from the threshold between Palestine and the diaspora, precede the final definition and termination of the Jewish canon. Their role in the canon debate seems crucial because they relate to the Jewish development as well as to the "Christian" one. They provide precedents and links in the development toward canon and canonical interpretation and their mediation through great personalities, not only in the subsequent Jewish but also in the "Christian" Apologetic evolution of the second century. Paul's rivals can give us new clues as to the options and criteria available in this matter not only in the diaspora but also in Palestine.

I hasten to emphasize that the phenomenon usually described as the Synod of Jamnia was influenced by many more forces than Hellenistic-Jewish Apologetics. 4 Ezra, the Gospel of Matthew, and the *Assumption of Moses* present just three more options developed for the reformation, if not re-creation, of Judaism after the Jewish War.[203] All three, the *Assumption of Moses* with some fragmentary hints only, deal with the role and understanding of scriptures and their proper interpretation.[204] All these writings are understood as new, eschatologically determined formations. All three variations of eschatological holy writ mentioned attribute a key function in the proper reception of tradition to a hero figure of superhuman proportions, but in a fashion different from either Jewish Apologetics or Pharisaic rabbinate.

These models and many more were part of the discussion after the year 70. Paul's rivals in 2 Cor. had proposed another forceful alternative to the understanding and use of canon and tradition which could have worked in Palestine as well. The Pharisaic-rabbinic option finally won out at Jamnia. It was influenced by the previous discussion, in which Paul's opponents took part. We have no way of knowing how the model with which the Pharisaic rabbis entered the discussion at Jamnia looked. They may have had a variety of proposals. The winning one was that of Jokhanan ben Zaccai and his school or, better, that which evolved in his circle.[205]

Much more needs to be said and studied in the area of the theology of missionary Judaism. My attempt to present a sketch of it has remained the least discussed aspect of my book.[206] This is particularly unfortunate because of the relevance of this theology for soteriologies and eschatologies available in NT times. Historians and theologians have drawn many premature conclusions with respect to that period, and about Judaism and "Christianity," because of a limited awareness regarding contemporary possibilities.[207] The similarity between Jewish Apologetic eschatology and Roman political theology needs intensive scrutiny.[208] The eschatology of Paul's Epistle to the Romans could gain considerably from such a comparative inquiry. The several good editions and annotated translations of relevant texts which have appeared in recent years[209] provide a good basis for writing a theology of Hellenistic-Jewish Apologetics, a work long overdue.[210]

BIBLIOGRAPHY 5

Kurt **Aland**, *The Problem of the New Testament Canon* (London: Mowbray, 1962). Michael von **Albrecht**, "Arbeit," *Der kleine Pauly*, 1:490–94. Franz **Altheim**, *A History of Roman Religion* (London: Methuen, 1938). Harold W. **Attridge**, *The Interpretation of Biblical History in the Antiquities of Flavius Josephus* (HDR 7; Missoula, Mont.: Scholars Press, 1976). Ray **Barraclough**, "Philo's Politics: Roman Rule and Hellenistic Judaism," *ANRW*, 2:21.1:417–553. Edwin **Blackman**, *Marcion and His Influence* (London: SPCK, 1948). Martin **Bodmer**, ed., *Geschichte der Textüberlieferung der antiken und mittelalterlichen Literatur* (Zurich: Atlantis, 1961). Clarence E. **Boyd**, *Public Libraries and Literary Culture in Ancient Rome* (Ann Arbor, Mich.: University Microfilms, 1965). Egon **Brandenburger**, *Die Verborgenheit Gottes im Weltgeschehen: Das literarische und theologische Problem des 4. Esrabuches* (ATANT 68; Zurich: Theologischer Verlag, 1981). Karl **Büchner**, "Überlieferungsgeschichte der lateinischen Literatur des Altertums," in Bodmer, ed., *Geschichte*, 309–422. Emile **Cahen**, *Callimaque et son oeuvre poetique* (Paris: Boccard, 1929). Hans von **Campenhausen**, "Das Alte Testament als Bibel der Kirche," in *Aus der Frühzeit des Christentums* (Tübingen: Mohr, 1963) 152–96; *Die Entstehung der christlichen Bibel* (BHT 39; Tübingen: Mohr, 1968). John M. **Dillon**, *The Middle Platonists* (Ithaca, N.Y.: Cornell University Press, 1977). Ingemar **Düring**, *Aristotle in the Ancient Biographical Tradition* (Göteborgs Universitets Årsskrift 63; Göteborg: Elander, 1957); *Aristoteles* (Heidelberg: Winter, 1966). Hartmut **Erbse**, "Überlieferungsgeschichte der griechischen klassischen und hellenistischen Literatur," in Bodmer, ed., *Geschichte*, 207–307. Konrad **Gaiser**, *Platons ungeschriebene Lehre: Studien zur systematischen und geschichtlichen Begründung der Wissenschaften in der Platonischen Schule* (Stuttgart: Klett, 1963). Erwin R. **Goodenough**, *The Jurisprudence of the Jewish Courts in Egypt: Legal Administration by the Jews Under the Early Roman Empire* (Amsterdam: Philo, 1968). Frederick C. **Grant**, "The Jewish Bible in the Graeco-Roman World," in Frederick C. Grant, ed., *Roman Hellenism and the New Testament* (Edinburgh: Oliver & Boyd, 1962) 99–112. Robert M. **Grant**, *The Formation of the New Testament* (New York: Harper & Row, 1965). Felix **Grayeff**, *Aristotle and His School* (London: Duckworth, 1974). N. C. **Habel**, "Appeal to Ancient Tradition as a Literary Form," *SBLASP* 109/1 (1973) 34–54. Moses **Hadas**, "Livy as Scripture," *AJP* 6 (1940) 445–56. O. **Hampe**, *Über den sogenannten Kanon der Alexandrinen* (Jauer, 1877). Friedrich **Hauck**, "Arbeit," *RAC*, 1:586–90. Felix **Heinemann**, "Eine vorplatonische Theorie der τέχνη," in Carl J. Classen, ed., *Sophistik* (Wege der Forschung 187; Darmstadt: Wissenschaftliche Buchgesellschaft, 1976) 127–69. Herbert **Hunger**, "Antikes und mittelalterliches Buch- und Schriftwesen," in

Bodmer, ed., *Geschichte*, 25–147. Werner **Jaeger**, ed., *Das Problem des Klassischen und die Antike* (Leipzig and Berlin: Teubner, 1931). Fritz **Jürss**, ed., *Geschichte des wissenschaftlichen Denkens im Altertum* (Berlin: Akademie, 1982). Everett **Kalin**, *Argument from Inspiration in the Canonization of the New Testament* (Th.D. thesis, Harvard University, 1967). J. J. **Keaney**, "Two Notes on the Textual Tradition of Aristotle's School," *AJP* 84 (1963) 52–63. George **Kennedy**, *The Art of Persuasion in Greece* (Princeton: Princeton University Press, 1963). John **Knox**, *Marcion and the New Testament* (Chicago: University of Chicago Press, 1942). Jens **Köhn** and Elemér **Pólay**, "Römische Rechtswissenschaft," in Jürss, ed., *Geschichte*, 610–23. Wolfgang **Kunkel**, *An Introduction to Roman Legal and Constitutional History* (Oxford: Clarendon, 1966). Sid **Leiman**, *The Canonization of Hebrew Scripture: The Talmudic and Midrashic Evidence* (Hamden, Conn.: Shoe String, 1976). Johannes **Leipoldt** and Siegfried **Morenz**, *Heilige Schriften: Betrachtungen zur Religionsgeschichte der antiken Mittelmeerwelt* (Leipzig, 1953). Eduard **Lohse**, *Colossians and Philemon* (Hermeneia; Philadelphia: Fortress, 1971). Anneliese **Mannzmann**, "ἄγραφοι νόμοι," *Der Kleine Pauly*, 1:143. Rudolph **Meyer**, "Bemerkungen zum literargeschichtlichen Hintergrund der Kanontheorie des Josephus," in Otto Betz, ed., *Josephusstudien* (Göttingen: Vandenhoeck & Ruprecht, 1974) 285–99. Alain **Michel**, *Rhétoric et philosophie chez Ciceron* (Paris: Presses Université, 1980). Horst **Moehring**, "The Acta pro Judaeis in the Antiquities of Flavius Josephus: A Study in Hellenistic and Modern Apologetic Historiography," in Neusner, ed., *Christianity* (Bibliography 3), 124–58. Paul **Moraux**, *Les listes anciennes d'Aristote* (Louvain: Louvain University Press, 1951). Reimar **Müller**, "Die ersten gesellschaftstheoretischen Modelle," and "Utopie und soziale Realität in der Gesellschaftstheorie," in Jürss, ed., *Geschichte*, 336–49, 453–60. Jacob **Neusner**, *Development of a Legend: Traditions Concerning Yohanan ben Zakkai* (SPB 16; Leiden: Brill, 1970); *Early Rabbinic Judaism* (SJLA 13; Leiden: Brill, 1975); *Eliezer ben Hyrcanus: The Tradition and the Man* (SJLA 3 and 4; Leiden: Brill, 1973). Robert C. **Newman**, "The Council of Jamnia and the Old Testament Canon," *Westminster Theological Journal* 38 (1975) 319–49. Horst **Oppel**, "Kanon," *Philologus* Supp. 30/4 (1937). Harry **Orlinski**, "The Canonization of the Bible and the Exclusion of the Apocrypha," *Essays in Biblical Culture and Biblical Translation* (New York: Ktav, 1974). Rudolf **Pfeiffer**, *History of Classical Scholarship to the End of the Hellenistic Age* (Oxford: Clarendon, 1968). James D. **Purvis**, *The Samaritan Pentateuch and the Origin of the Samaritan Sect* (Cambridge, Mass.: Harvard University Press, 1968). James A. **Sanders**, *Torah and Canon* (Philadelphia: Fortress, 1972). John E. **Sandys**, *A History of Classical Scholarship* (New York: Hafner, 1967). Wolfgang O. **Schmitt**, "Antike Sprach- und Literaturwissenschaft," in Jürss, ed., *Geschichte*, 349–60, 461–70; 600–609. Hans K. **Schulte**, *Orator: Untersuchungen über das ci-*

ceronische Bildungsideal (Frankfurt: Klostermann, 1935). Fritz **Schulz,** *Geschichte der römischen Rechtswissenschaft* (Weimar: Böhlau, 1961); *Prinzipien des römischen Rechts* (Munich: Duncker & Humbolt, 1934). Erwin **Seidl,** *Römische Rechtsgeschichte und römisches Zivilprozessrecht* (Cologne: Heyman, 1962). Lou **Silberman,** "The Making of the Old Testament Canon," in *The Interpreter's One-Volume Commentary on the Bible* (Nashville: Abingdon, 1971) 1209–15. Jonathan Z. **Smith,** "Sacred Persistence: Towards a Redescription of Canon," in Greene, ed., *Approaches* (Bibliography 3), 1:11–28. Krister **Stendahl,** *The School of St. Matthew and Its Use of the Old Testament* (Philadelphia: Fortress, 1968). Albert C. **Sundberg,** "Canon Muratori: A Fourth-Century List," *HTR* 66 (1973) 1–41; "Making of the New Testament Canon," in *The Interpreter's One-Volume Commentary on the Bible* (Nashville: Abingdon, 1971) 1216–24; *The Old Testament of the Early Church* (Cambridge, Mass.: Harvard University Press, 1964); "A Revised History of the New Testament Canon," *Studia Evangelica* 4 (TU 102; 1968); "Towards a Revised History of the New Testament Canon," *Studia Evangelica* 4 (1965) 452–61. James C. **Turro** and Raymond E. **Brown,** "Canonicity," *JBC,* 515–34. Nikolaus **Walter,** *Der Thoraausleger Aristobulus* (TU 68; 1964). Klaus **Wegenast,** *Das Verständnis der Tradition bei Paulus und in den Deuteropaulinen* (WMANT 8; Neukirchen: Erziehungsverein, 1962). Fritz **Wehrli,** *Die Schule des Aristoteles: Texte und Kommentare* (Basel: Schwabe, 1969). Carl **Wendel,** "Bibliothek," *RAC,* 2:230–74. Ludwig **Wenger,** "*Canon in den römischen Rechtsquellen und in den Papyri: Eine Wortstudie* (Sitzungsberichte der Akademie der Wissenschaften, Vienna 220/2, 1942). Erik **Wolf,** *Griechisches Rechtsdenken* (4 vols.; Frankfurt: Klostermann, 1950–70). Herbert **Wright,** *The Oral Antecedents of Greek Librarianship* (Utah: Brigham Young University Press, 1977). Günther **Zuntz,** *The Text of the Epistles* (London: Oxford University Press, 1953).

EPILOGUE NOTES 142–210

142. See on this the various studies in H. Fischel, *Essays* (Bibliography 3).

143. They are our first literary evidence for detailed exegesis of biblical texts outside Qumran (and the NT).

144. On this so-called *expositio legis*, see above, p. 181 n. 59.

145. On these local courts, see, e.g., Gen. 23:10, Amos 5:10, 1 Macc. 14:9, and Matt. 10:17. Deut. 16:18 and Luke 18:2, e.g., mention professional judges (of unclear competence).

146. Higher judicial instances were the temple (e.g., Exod. 22:8–9) or the royal court (e.g., 2 Sam. 15:2–6). Various means of reconciling the highest civic and cultic authorities in one body were contemplated or

achieved (e.g., Deut. 17:8–13, 2 Chron. 19:8, 1 Macc. 12:6, 2 Macc. 1:10; cf. Josephus *BJ* 2.570–71). But the composition, procedures, and jurisdiction of these bodies are as debatable as their continuity. E. Schürer, *History* (Bibliography 1), 2.1:163–95, is too uncritical about the ideologized description of tractate Sanhedrin.

147. Different from the temple scribes, but in succession to (competition with?) the Levites, as described by H. O. Steck (Bibliography 4), 196–203 (see also 146–47).

148. Edouard Naville, *The Mound of the Jews and the City of Onias* (London: Kegan, 1890).

149. Bibliography 5.

150. Ibid., 6, 7.

151. Cf. also Goodenough's introduction to *Jurisprudence*, 1–29.

152. This dialogical skill, influenced by Apologetics, shows in Wisdom of Solomon (see D. Georgi, "Wesen der Weisheit," Bibliography 3).

153. Above, pp. 83–164.

154. The various biographies of Alexander demonstrate this, as do philosophical efforts like those of Stoicism, in particular also Posidonius, Cicero, Plutarch, and, in a further way, Pliny the Elder. At the roots of this Hellenistic trend we find Democritus, Plato, and Aristotle.

155. Plato, Aristotle, Zeno, Epicurus, Eratosthenes, Panaetius, Posidonius, and Cicero are but some of the most famous examples of the interest in the connection and interplay between theory and practice.

156. It would be wrong to presume that people like Protagoras, Gorgias, or Isocrates were not universalists. And a universal claim is made by somebody like Quintilian still, despite (perhaps better, through) the opposition to the philosophers.

157. On the connection between φιλοσοφία and τέχνη, see G. Kennedy, index under Book and under Quarrel between Rhetoric and Philosophy (see also under Delivery); E. Wolf, index under τέχνη and under φιλοσοφία. On rhetorics in general, cf. H. Hommel (Bibliography 4).

158. Aristotle and Cicero straddled both dimensions mentioned, that of τέχνη and that of φιλοσοφία. Rhetoricians as well as philosophers contributed to the first real experiment in pluralistic world culture, that of Hellenism. We are spoiled by our modern achievements in cultural exchange and understanding between different societies and subcultures, not the least also between different hermeneutical perspectives. Therefore, we look down on Hellenistic ventures in this matter, belittle their attempts to find general principles, forms, and structures from which to assess particulars and their relationships, so to estimate the applicability of the general and the theoretical to the geographically, temporally, or culturally specific, and to realize this applicability methodically. For us these Hellenistic efforts appear to be naive. Most of all, we see manipulative force. We do not appreciate the adventurous and experimental nature of the enterprise. What the Hellenists, Jews among them, tried and achieved was a first in world his-

tory, the development of a hermeneutical awareness and competence as to the existence of major cultural differences and the possibility of bridging them, thereby overcoming great distances in space, time, and character. This hermeneutical achievement was the response to a task set forth by Hellenistic culture itself, the size of which had been unheard of and unexperienced.

159. See the analysis of Plato's *Republic* and *Laws* in E. Wolf, *Griechisches Rechtsdenken* 4.1:295–410 and 4.2:197–371, and of Aristotle's concepts of law and state in I. Düring, *Aristotees*, 475–505.

160. Not only the famous seventh letter of Plato but also his *Laws* and his *Republic* prove how much politics, ethics, and education belonged together. Aristotle, author of the *Politics*, was also an ethicist and the teacher of Alexander the Great. Cicero and Philo proved that these tendencies affected not only Greeks but also other subcultures of Hellenism.

161. On the preference for rhetoricians in the area of law, cf. E. Wolf, 3.2:157–413.

162. The classical orators would stand for that as well as Cicero or the author of the work *On the Exalted* (pseudo-Longinus) prove.

163. On labor, see M. von Albrecht and F. Hauck.

164. Already the classifications of speech forms, and even more the number and variety of school topics used for the training of rhetoricians, prove a wide range of interest, competence, and involvement of Hellenistic orators. Public affairs and matters of law played a strong role in this. Rhetorical skill was employed in all areas of literature too.

165. The major force behind the importance and influence of rhetorics in Hellenism was the continuing belief that the spoken word was superior to the written word, the latter formed by the former, merely an in-between because it was to be brought to life again by new oral ventures (of which even the reading was a part, already being a reading aloud).

166. H. Koester, "*ΝΟΜΟΣ*" (Bibliography 4).

167. E. Goodenough, *Politics* (Bibliography 1), and *Jurisprudence*.

168. "There was a time when I had leisure for philosophy and for the contemplation of the universe and its contents." And then in 3.3: "But [envy sat upon me . . . plunging me into the great ocean of worries in the *πολιτεία*]."

169. Above, pp. 246–71.

170. Above, pp. 4, 248. Now these people were abroad, not sedentary anymore and therefore not called on in most matters of law either. Local authorities would usually take care of that.

171. On the discussion regarding the wisdom movement, see my "Wesen der Weisheit" (Bibliography 3).

172. Most valuable in this respect is F. Altheim.

173. M. Hadas, *Culture*, 83–104, 23–48 (Bibliography 3), has discussed this too. Further observations of his on this matter are scattered over the remainder of his book. Other material is in his "Livy."

174. A. Dewey (Bibliography 2) has furthered our understanding of the

historical context and meaning of the πνεῦμα-γράμμα antithesis. He has shown how it relates to tradition and hermeneutics and how scriptures fit into that.

175. The work of the *Religionsgeschichtliche Schule* meant a certain breakthrough here. The dividing walls between religious traditions, between "canonical" and "apocryphal," between "heretical" and "orthodox," between "classical" and "popular," "high" and "low," became transparent. But that tradition has been revived only recently, particularly in the United States. One of the most prominent recent examples of that revival is H. Koester's *Introduction* (Bibliography 3). This approach needs to be extended to the phenomenon of canonization itself.

176. The argument is often made that the idea of a division of Hebrew scriptures into "law" and "prophets," most of all, but then also the addition of "writings," presupposed an established and firm collection of individual writings (so, e.g., in the preface of Sirach). But this is not convincing at all. The assumption stated is nothing but an unproven hypothesis. It needed to be proven with respect to particular writings. This has not been done, and in my opinion it can never be done. Only the Pentateuch is commonly presupposed as a fixed exclusive collection since the third century B.C.E. at least. Evidence from Samaria and from the Diaspora (e.g., Philo) supports that. The treatment of the Pentateuch by the Samaritans and by Philo also proves its exalted state. But despite all that the term "law" in NT times has not been completely identified with a code, with the Pentateuch, as yet. New Testament authors, Pharisees, and Pharisaic rabbis, for instance, continue to attest to a wider use of the term "law."

177. On the Pharisaic rabbinic side a sequence of Jewish scriptures, oral tradition, and Mishnah (and later Tosephtah and Talmud) evolves, with the Midrash being added on the haggadic side. On the side of the church we have the same point of departure, namely, Jewish scriptures, oral tradition (not of and about Jesus alone but also prophetic, sapiential, liturgical, and general homiletical and catechetical traditions), and writings, slowly dividing themselves into primary and secondary documents. On succession, see K. Wegenast, 24–33, 121–30.

178. So, e.g., H. von Campenhausen, *Entstehung*.

179. The preface to Sirach implies knowledge of an ongoing dialogue between Jews and Gentiles in Egypt. The translator is impressed by it and intends his translation to influence that dialogue.

180. Much of the evidence presented for Philo's and Josephus's knowledge of oral tradition or oral law does not give any clues as to necessity of Palestinian rabbinic origin. In most cases it can be read the other way just as well, if not better. In fact, the whole concept of the oral not only as equal but also as superior to written (particularly also in legal matters) is explicitly Greek and Hellenistic; see R. Pfeiffer, 25–56, and A. Mannzmann.

181. The legend about the translation shows that it wants to be seen in

the context of the political as well as the cultural efforts of Ptolemy II (Philadelphus), especially his interest in universalizing the Alexandrian library. The interest not only of the legend but also of the LXX itself is to relate to a world culture. This world culture was epitomized in libraries. The LXX was a book among books which did not associate so much with the idea of being shelved and put away as with the idea of communication on a worldwide scale. The inclusion of more cosmopolitan books in the LXX collection (e.g., Wisdom of Solomon and 4 Maccabees) underlines that, so the keeping of some more "worldly" documents (e.g., Judith, 1 and 2 Maccabees, Tobit, and Esther). On the LXX, see H. Koester, *Introduction*, 1:252–55 (Bibliography 3).

182. Whereas the oldest "Christian" apologetic work, Luke's two volumes, took a monopolistic view (usurpation of Jewish scriptures—with the concept of disowning the real Jews already in mind—a replacement of earlier or contemporary gospels, repression of Paul's correspondence and a domesticated portrayal of Paul instead), the later Apologists took a more sophisticated, a library approach. They adopted this approach from Jewish and pagan apologists and from Marcion. The "Christian" Apologists intended to leave "heretics," Jews, and pagan missionary groups without their basic library(ies), essential assets in the contemporary competition over religious validity and achievement. The Apologists tried to outdo the rabbis of their time by elevating the "authoritative Christian" interpretation of scriptures, first of all the Gospels, to the level of basic/primary (exclusively canonical) literature, but the Apologists adopted this from Marcion's anti-Judaizing efforts. Whereas Marcion left the Jews with their scriptures and their piety, however, the Apologists intended to take them away from the Jews, to disown them.

183. A. Sundberg has shown in his various studies on the canons of the OT and the NT that they remained open rather long. S. Leiman has proven this for the rabbinic canon in particular. Differences about the extent of both canons continued, particularly in the branches of the church in the East.

184. It is amazing how little a role the concept of inspiration played in the later discussion (Jewish or Christian) of the canon as an exclusive phenomenon. See E. Kalin and S. Leiman.

185. Marcion's canon, the first Christian canon and the prototype for the "Catholic" canon, is the most famous of these composite collections. On its importance, see E. Blackman and H. von Campenhausen. Other examples, the writings of Basilides as the canon for the Basilidians, the works of Valentinus as scripture of the Valentinians, the books of Mani as holy writ for the Manicheans (here already intended as such by Mani, who wrote "holy scriptures" himself), and Jewish-Christian (particularly Petrine) traditions have to be discussed under this aspect too. If G. Zuntz is right, the first major collection of Pauline writings around 100 C.E. would in fact have been a col-

lection of holy writ (although not exclusive) of and for a Gnostic branch of "Christianity" with a Pauline bent.

Some Jewish examples for such collections would be the Qumran literature, the Henoch literature (not necessarily Essene), and the collection 4 Ezra presupposes at the end of his book. The literature of the Sethians and the *merkabah/hekhalot* literature could be mentioned too.

186. Philo and Josephus on the Essenes.

187. Symptomatic of this concept of canon is W. Schneemelcher's discussion "Canonical and Apocryphal" in the first volume of Edgar Hennecke and Wilhelm Schneemelcher, eds., *The New Testament Apocrypha* (Philadelphia: Westminster, 1963–65).

188. On the rabbinic canon, see S. Leiman and J. Smith.

189. But survival not in a passive sense but rather in the sense of building and construction. An impressive, indeed moving, portrayal of that effort—and its modern challenge—is found in many essays of J. Neusner's *Method*, esp. 1.41–75, 101–51; 3:61–81 (Bibliography 3). See also his *From Politics, First Century, Ancient Israel* (all Bibliography 3), and *Early Rabbinic*. Neusner stresses the integrity of that creative reconstruction.

190. E. Smallwood, *Jews* (Bibliography 3), 331–55 (88).

191. Good although by no means exhaustive introductions to the phenomenon discussed are present in the books of R. Pfeiffer and J. Sandys; see further the essays of K. Büchner, H. Erbse, and H. Hunger. Important for the concept of *the classical* is the collection of essays edited by W. Jaeger. All these studies will have to be supplemented with data that would show the intimate connection of the issues mentioned above with the larger contexts of Hellenistic society, culture, economy, politics, and the wider religious world. Not unimportant for the problems dealt with is the debate about distinctions between written and oral, and public and esoteric, in the works of Plato (and of Aristotle).

192. S. E. Bowie (Bibliography 4), E. Cahen, N. Habel, M. Hadas, W. Kunkel, R. Meyer, H. Oppel, and L. Wenger. Whereas the tendencies were similar in different schools, the success varied. It was relatively high in the case of Plato and the Academy, and also of Epicurus and the "Garden." The fortune or misfortune of the "Corpus Aristotelicum" is a matter of debate, depending greatly on the reliability of the information in Plutarch's *Sulla* 26, and Strabo 13.1.54 (see I. Düring, *Aristotle*, 393–95, esp. 337–38), which claims that the original manuscripts of Aristotle were hidden in a cellar in Skepsis (Asia Minor) and only discovered again ca. 100 B.C.E., then brought to Athens, from where Sulla had them shipped to Rome after his conquest of Athens. The reliability of this information is partly linked with the questions whether Aristotle or Theophrastus, his friend, student, and successor, were the founders of the Peripatetic school and whether Theophrastus split with the school later. There is no doubt (a) that dialogues by Aristotle were published during his lifetime (now more or

less lost), (b) that a Peripatetic school existed at least since Theophrastus, (c) that it concentrated on commenting and enlarging the works of Aristotle, and (d) that manuscripts of Aristotle were known also outside the Peripatetic school (e.g., by Epicurus and in Alexandria). However the discussion about the nature and content of the Aristotle tradition and of its actual interpretation prior to Andronicus is decided, the activity of Andronicus (in Athens and/or Rome during the first century B.C.E.) is interesting as a parallel if not a predecessor to other canonization processes in the Mediterranean. For more on the Aristotelian tradition and the survival of Aristotle's work, see F. Grayeff, J. Keaney, P. Moraux, F. Wehrli (esp. 10:117–28), and the two studies of I. Düring. Stoicism too was heavily dependent on great personalities (Zenon, Chrysippus, Panaetius, Posidonius), but this philosophical school was much less tightly organized, certainly as far as the tradition about these men and their proper transmission were concerned. Traditions about ancient commentaries, editing and publishing practices, and the methods and criteria used therein are relevant for our question too.

193. The concepts of the *canonical* and the *classical* are essentially associated with the phenomena of structured and institutionalized education for which the sophists of the fifth century B.C.E. provided the basis (R. Pfeiffer, "Sophisten"). But equally important for the growth and understanding of the concepts of the classical and the canonical were the ideas of tradition and succession practiced first of all in the mystery religions. Primary texts and secondary literature on this is conveniently collected by E. Lohse, 94–96.

194. See H. D. Betz, "Gottmensch II," esp. 238–41, 253–56, 263–70 (Bibliography 4).

195. The knowledge and traditions about great personalities served as critical paradigms for internal criticism and screening. They also provided organizing features for collection, interpretation, and representation, and they gave platforms for rhetorical demonstrations. Even greater was their strong formative importance for education through the ever-growing biographical traditions and the typological use of the concept of the divine man. The formative interplay between philosophy, religion, and interpretation can be seen best among the Neo-Pythagoreans, in Philo, and in Plutarch, but also in Hermetic Gnosticism. The tight interrelationship between biography, norm, and canon has not yet been seriously studied, either with respect to individual phenomena (Jewish and Christian ones among them) or with respect to culture at large.

196. On libraries, see C. Boyd; R. Pfeiffer, *History*, index under Libraries; H. Wright.

197. On Greek and Hellenistic legal thinking, see E. Wolf and R. Müller. This legal interest did not lead to the systematic collection of legislation and laws in Greek cities or Hellenistic states (with the exception of constitutions in the Peripatetic school).

198. On legal systematization in Cicero and others, see J. Köhn and E. Polay and the literature given there.

199. In its various forms the "classicism" of the period between Cicero and Seneca has been the object of many studies. See esp. W. Jaeger.

200. On the ruler cult, see H. Koester, *Introduction* (Bibliography 3), under Ruler Cult and the bibliographies there; also E. Goodenough, "Kingship" (Bibliography 1), C. Habicht, G. Hansen, H. L'Orange, G. Macurdy, A. Momigliano, S. Mott, and D. Roloff (all Bibliography 4).

201. Reconstruction of the recovery of Palestinian Judaism after the year 70 is difficult because the majority of the relevant texts do not show much if any historical interest. On the problems see J. Neusner, *Development*; idem, *Eliezer*, 2; and idem, *Method* (Bibliography 3), 3:61–81; see further, ibid., 2:59–75, and idem, *Early Rabbinic*, 50–70. The most puzzling problem the historian has to solve is the very moderate, almost hands-off, attitude of the Roman authorities toward the Jews in Palestine after the war, which had been clearly the most dangerous rebellion the Romans experienced in the first century C.E. The postwar moderation of the Romans drastically contrasted their sometimes cruel behavior during the latter year of the war. This apparent contrast cannot be explained by the mentalities and political philosophies of Vespasian and Titus alone. There must have been a major reason on the Palestinian Jewish side too. The Pharisaic-rabbinic maneuvers suggested above would present such a reason: an emphatic and believable trend from rebellion to collaboration, thus also a falling in line with the attitude of the Jewish communities toward the Romans in the diaspora.

202. See D. Georgi, "Records" (Bibliography 4), 529, 533, 538–39.

203. On 4 Ezra and the *Assumption of Moses*, cf. Charlesworth Apocrypha (below, n. 209). On the dating of Matthew, see W. G. Kümmel (Bibliography 2).

204. On Matthew's hermeneutics see K. Stendahl, 183–206. On 4 Ezra's hermeneutics, see E. Brandenburger, 132–38, 166–76, 186–201.

205. S. D. Georgi, "Records," 528–32.

206. Some new contributions were made by H. Attridge and N. Walter (see also Bibliography 4), pp. 119–20.

207. The most damaging but nevertheless continuing error is the claim of verifiable "Christian" uniqueness as to universalism, inclusiveness, and eschatology. Universalism and inclusiveness were present in pagan Hellenism since Alexander at least, even more in postexilic Judaism (already, e.g., in Isaiah 56 and in Jonah, even more in Wisdom traditions, and here increasingly, particularly in Apologetic and Gnostic wisdom). It is frustrating to note how Christian scholars use the term "eschatological" as a magic wand for the apologetic declaring of "Christian" uniqueness in religious comparison. Sheer invocation of that magic term "eschatological" is enough to state the basic difference—this even though the term in the history of the theology of the church, particularly also the early church, lacks clarity. It glosses over the great multifariousness of Jesus-related eschatology since

the first century. In the main text I have shown the difference between the eschatologies of Paul and of the opponents in 2 Cor. I have also shown that many miracle stories of the Synoptic tradition demonstrate an eschatology different from that of Paul, and to that the miracle stories in the Johannine sign source can be added. Then there are the well-known differences between Paul and Luke, Paul and John, Paul and James, etc. There are also the Gnostics, the Apostolic Fathers, the Apologists, and so on. On the other hand, invoking and thanking Isis or Serapis always meant addressing their ability to bring new life, personally and cosmically; and these gods had power over death. But such "eschatological" claims, if non-Christian, are denounced by Christian scholars as overstatement, fabrication, manipulation, fantasy, fantastic, etc., whereas in similar "Christian" texts the term "eschatological" would be used. Intriguing examples of this are found even in the articles of A. D. Nock cited in Bibliographies 3 and 4, e.g., "Graeco-Egyptian Religious Propaganda" or "Son of God."

208. An important step in the right direction is made by M. Hadas, *Culture* (Bibliography 3).

209. See the editions of Jewish apocryphal, pseudepigraphic, etc. writings by Werner G. Kümmel et al., *Jüdische Schriften aus hellenistisch-römischer Zeit* (Gütersloh: Mohn, 1973ff.) and James H. Charlesworth et al., *The Old Testament Pseudepigrapha*, 1 (Garden City, N.Y.: Doubleday, 1983); also the SBL series Septuagint and Cognate Studies, ed. George G. Nickelsburg et al.; the series *Studia in Veteris Testamenti Pseudepigrapha*; and the bibliography by Gerhard Delling: *Bibliographie für jüdisch-hellenistische und intertestamentarische Literatur 1900–1970*, 2d ed., TU 106, (Berlin: de Gruyter, 1975).

210. There are an increasing number of studies on the theologies of individual Hellenistic-Jewish authors and/or documents, not just of Philo or Josephus. Yet the various existing surveys still lack the penetration and differentiation we are accustomed to in NT theologies. The excuse that the literature covered is too flat for such penetration and differentiation betrays only the ahistorical and unfair attitude of the person making such an excuse. The unity and diversity of the theology of the literature in question must be judged and described vis-à-vis the challenges these theologians had to meet. The achievement of Jewish Apologetic literature can be judged more fairly if one takes into account the risks they had to face in encountering a missionary culture that was not at all—as often presumed today—decomposing and dying, but alive, demanding as well as tempting.

PAUL'S OPPONENTS IN 2 CORINTHIANS AND THE EARLY CHURCH

The importance of the θεῖος ἀνήρ concept for the christology of the early church is now almost taken for granted.[211] Its impact on the formation of the Jesus tradition is being thoroughly studied, including tendencies, differentiations, and influences which occurred in the development of the various genres summarily and somewhat incorrectly classified under the term "gospel."[212]

The connection of these phenomena with missionary interest and activities has often been recognized,[213] but little has been done with respect to the practical side of that. A thorough historical-critical investigation of the mission of the early church in the context of Jewish and Gentile propaganda is still a wish and unfortunately not yet a fact.[214] What I have contributed to that in my book and in this epilogue is only a sketch. My suggestions regarding the symptomatic character of Paul's opponents as to missionary ideology and practice have been picked up only occasionally.[215] The modular function of Jewish Apologetics and the effectiveness of the θεῖος ἀνήρ pattern for the actual organization and practice of Jesus missionaries needs to be recognized much more. This is true with respect to the nature and role of the extraordinary in the day-to-day activity of the church, and the church's propaganda, however crude the expressions of the extraordinary may appear to us.[216]

"Miracles" played a role in the weekly worship of the church. But what kind of miracles? Who performed them? What function did they have? Were miracles supposed to attract, stimulate, and motivate? Were they part of a socializing strategy not only with respect to the church alone but also with regard to Judaism and the culture at large? Did miracles contribute to the sense of identity of the Jesus-believers? How? What about the dramatic and entertaining aspects of Jesus worship? What about the dimensions of performance and achievement in celebrating Jesus? How did evaluation occur, and what were the criteria for evaluation? Was there any schooling and selecting of Jesus-missionaries? How did they relate to the local and translocal organization of Jesus-believers?

These and many more suggestive questions need to be raised and answered in future studies. What has been concluded regarding Paul's opponents in 2 Cor. seems to point to positive answers to these questions. As far as evaluation and selection were concerned, Paul's opponents entrusted the congregations with much authority, although not without their manipulative input. The meetings of the congregations for worship and celebration seem to have been the major training places also. There is no indication of any translocal organization beside the migratory activity of Paul's opponents and the other apostles.

Since I first wrote my book, the impression has grown with me that Paul's rivals were very "normal" theologians and functionaries of the early church, who anticipated much of what meanwhile has become regularly "Christian," although not of my liking. Historians as well as theologians will have to ask what this means with respect to the issue at stake in the debate. And further, did the opponents represent a majority as far as the remainder of the early church was concerned?

The practical dimensions and consequences of the debate in 2 Cor. have not yet been sufficiently recognized. They have a bearing on our understanding of the organization of the early church and of its identity. The theological trajectory from Paul's opponents to Luke proves that the common Protestant assumption is wrong, that the particular branch of the church we now call Catholic formed around fixed offices and fixed doctrine.[217] The trajectory mentioned proves that these features were secondary at best, compared with an orientation that was conscious of the larger culture, relating to it competitively as well as constructively. It becomes obvious that in this "catholic" branch of the church the issue of power was important at an early date, as was that of control, but curiously enough not firmly associated with institutionalized offices and even less with rite or doctrine.

Since my early days of study the quest of the historical Jesus had fascinated me. The reader of my book will have realized that I see the opponents of Paul as early representatives of this quest. Further intensive studies on "life of Jesus theology" have convinced me that the frequent claim that the Enlightenment brought about a decisive change in this quest is wrong. Our modern discussion about the historical Jesus since the Enlightenment is not something entirely new. It is not so different from the earlier reflections on the earthly Jesus. There is a direct connection between Moses Mendelsohn and Jewish Apologetics of NT times. There is continuity between the many modern Christian apologists who put reconstructions of the career and teaching of the earthly Jesus into the center of theology and the church, and the intentions of the opponents of Paul in 2 Cor.

The concepts of objectivity and verifiability are much older than the Enlightenment, which did not invent the idea of rationality either. The Enlightenment, by means of critical analysis and separation, has sharpened the concept of the historical, increasing the awareness of distance and the possibility of its manipulation. But it needs to be emphasized that the Enlightenment possessed paradoxical aspects: it trusted in illumination, not altogether too different from inspiration, *and* in the rational; it believed in differentiation *and* in generalizability and universality; it wanted to reconcile the rational *and* the irrational. These paradoxes resemble much of what was peculiar to Hellenistic culture, particularly the Hellenistic-Jewish subsection of it. These resemblances need further attention.[218]

BIBLIOGRAPHY 6

Paul J. **Achtemeier**, "Gospel Miracle Tradition and the Divine Man," *Int* 26/2 (1972) 174–97; "Jesus and the Disciples as Miracle Workers in the Apocryphal New Testament," in Schüssler-Fiorenza, ed., *Aspects* (Bibliography 3), 149–86; "The Origin and Formation of the Pre-Markan Miracle Catenae," *JBL* 91 (1972) 198–221. Hans Dieter **Betz**, "Jesus as Divine Man," in F. Trotter, ed., *Jesus and the Historian* (Philadelphia: Westminster, 1968) 114–33. Leonhard I. **Bredvold**, *The Brave New World of Enlightenment* (Ann Arbor: University of Michigan Press, 1961). Thomas **Budesheim**, "Jesus and the Disciples in Conflict with Judaism," *ZNW* 62 (1971) 190–209. T. Alec **Burkill**, *New Light on the Earliest Gospel: Seven Markan Studies* (Ithaca, N.Y.: Cornell University Press, 1972). Leander E. **Keck**, "Mark 3:7–12 and Mark's Christology," *JBL* 84 (1965) 341–58. Howard C. **Kee**, "Aretalogies, Hellenistic 'Lives,' and the Sources of Mark," in Wilhelm Wuellner, ed., *Colloquy 12* (Berkeley: Center for Hermeneutical Studies, 1975). Karl **Kertelge**, "Die Wunder Jesu in der neueren Exegese," *Theologische Berichte* 5 (1976) 71–105. Jack D. **Kingsbury**, "The 'Divine Man' as the Key to Mark's Christology: The End of an Era?" *Int* 35 (1981) 243–57. Helmut **Koester**, "Γνῶμαι διάφοροι: The Origin and Nature of Diversity in the History of Early Christianity," in Koester and Robinson, eds., *Trajectories* (Bibliography 3) 114–57; "Dialog und Spruchüberlieferung in den gnostischen Texten von Nag Hammadi," *EvTh* 39 (1979) 532–56; "Gnostic Writings as Witnesses for the Development of the Sayings Tradition," in Bentley Layton, ed., *Rediscovery of Gnosticism* (Leiden: Brill, 1980) 238–61; *Introduction* (Bibliography 2), index under Aretalogy, Gospel, Gospel Literature; "One Jesus and Four Primitive Gospels," in Koester and Robinson, eds., *Trajectories* (Bibliography 3) 158–204; "Romance, Biography, and Gospel: The Genre of the Gospels" (Working Papers of the SBL Task Group in the Genre of the Gospels; Missoula, Mont.: Scholars Press, 1972). Heinz Wolfgang **Kuhn**, *Ältere Sammlungen im Markusevangelium* (SUNT 8; Göttingen: Vandenhoeck & Ruprecht, 1971). Charles F. D. **Moule**, ed., *Miracles: Cambridge Studies in Their Philosophy and History* (London: Mowbray, 1965). George W. **Nickelsburg**, "The Genre and Function of the Markan Passion Narrative," *HTR* 73 (1980) 153–84. Rudolf **Pesch**, ed., *Das Markusevangelium* (Wege der Forschung 411; Darmstadt: Wissenschaftliche Buchgesellschaft, 1979). Karl **Rengstorf**, *Die Anfänge der Auseinandersetzung zwischen Christusglaube und Asklepiusfrömmigkeit* (Münster: Aschendorf, 1953). Gottfried **Schille**, *Die urchristliche Wundertradition* (Stuttgart: Calwer, 1967). Elisabeth **Schüssler-Fiorenza**, *In Memory of Her: A Feminist Theological Reconstruction of Christian Origins* (New York: Crossroad, 1983). Morton **Smith**, "The Aretalogy Used by Mark," in Wilhelm Wuellner, ed., *Colloquy 9* (Berkeley: Center for Hermeneutical Studies, 1973). Jacob **Speigel**, "Die Rolle des Wunders im vorkonstantinischen Christentum," *ZThK* 92 (1970) 287–312. Alfred **Suhl**, ed., *Der Wunderbegriff des Neuen Testaments* (Wege der Forschung 295; Darmstadt: Wissenschaftliche Buchgesellschaft, 1980). Charles **Talbert**, *What Is a Gospel? The Genre of the Canonical Gospels* (Philadelphia: Fortress, 1977). É. **Trocme**, *The Formation of the Gospel According to Mark* (Philadelphia: Westminster, 1975). Clyde Weber **Votaw**, *The Gospels and Contemporary Biographies in the Greco-Roman World* (Facet Books, Biblical Series 27; Philadelphia: Fortress, 1970). Theodore J. **Weeden**, "The Heresy That Necessitated Mark's Gospel," *ZNW* 59 (1968) 145–58; *Mark: Tradition in Conflict* (Philadelphia: Fortress, 1971).

EPILOGUE NOTES 211–219

211. H. D. Betz's "Gottmensch II" (Bibliography 4) shows, e.g., the wide range of the θεῖος ἀνήρ motif in the christologies of the early church; see also D. Tiede, "Religious Propaganda" (Bibliography 4).

212. Various articles by H. Koester redirect our understanding of gospel tradition and gospel formation. Gospel scholarship must follow this lead. It must break down further the artificial walls around the four canonical Gospels and see even more their variety and their correspondence with character and tradition of apocryphal and Gnostic gospels and with Hellenistic phenomena, pagan as well as Jewish.

213. Most recently again by D. Tiede, "Religious Propaganda" (Bibliography 4).

214. All existing Christian studies, including my own, suffer from the

Apologetic interest in justifying the success of Christianity, more or less at the expense of fairness toward the competing forces and movements.

215. I am grateful to Elisabeth Schüssler-Fiorenza for the symposium she conducted years ago at the University of Notre Dame. The volume she edited after that symposium (Bibliography 3) reflects but a start. H. Koester, J. Robinson, D. Tiede, T. Weeden have pushed the question further, as have T. Budesheim and R. Pervo in yet unpublished dissertations (Budesheim on the Gospel of Mark years ago at Heidelberg Univ., Pervo on the Acts of the Apostles at Harvard Univ. [forthcoming from Fortress Press]).

216. The selection of studies on miracles given in Bibliography 6 gives an impression of that.

217. Luke's discrepancy between his emphasis on the importance of the office of the twelve and on order in the church, on the one hand, and his failure to present actual cases which would demonstrate administrative issues, solutions, and structures, on the other hand, is curious. The whole issue of hierarchical dispersion and delegation of power remains undescribed in Acts. Occasional attempts (e.g., the election of Matthias, the selection of the seven "deacons," the mission in Samaria, the integration of the newly "converted" Paul, the organization of the mission of Antioch, the Jerusalem convention) remain vague and contradictory. There is never any attempt to describe the organization of the Pauline churches. Luke's interest in order and unity is expressed at the expense of any actual concern for organization and administration. It is also striking how abstract 1 Clement, Ignatius, Justin, and Irenaeus are concerning practical issues of governance, especially if compared with Paul. The slightly higher degree of colorfulness of the Pastoral Epistles is achieved only through the more intensive exploitation of the lists of popular philosophical and Hellenistic-Jewish propaganda, not through greater attention to actual situations of the Jesus communities. The monarchical episcopate in the second century is more wishful thinking than reality, certainly not an administrative reality, even less in the sense of a functioning hierarchical structure.

218. On the Enlightenment, see, e.g., L. I. Bredvold.

Index of Subjects

Index of Subjects

ommendation; of reconciliation, 11, 13, 22
n.35, 24 n.65, 290 n.67, 339, 343–44; of
sorrow/tears, 11, 16, 18, 22 n.36, 24 n.65.
See also Heavenly letter; Interim letter
Libertinism, 4, 5, 7, 230, 290 nn.64, 70

2 Maccabees, 206 n.320, 440 n.181
3 Maccabees, 206 n.320
4 Maccabees, 43, 49, 72 n.116, 73 n.124, 206
n.320, 217 n.441, 402, 441 n.181
Magic, 402, 408; magical texts/papyri, 70
n.81, 102, 385 n.54; magicians, 102, 103–
4, 125, 154, 191 n.147, 226 n.543
Mani/Manicheans, 362–63, 383, 441 n.185
Marcion/Marcionites, 344, 362–63, 383, 441
nn.182, 185
Martyrdom, 73 n.124
Meals, cultic/sacred, 116, 145
Merkabah/hekhalot literature, 442 n.185
Messiah, 105, 107, 150, 167
Metamorphosis. *See* Transformation
Metempsychosis, 394, 408
Middle Platonism, 386 n.54
Midrash, 247, 305 n.222, 440 n.177
Mimus. *See* Fool's speech
Miracle working/stories, 102, 112, 127, 128,
145, 166, 169, 171, 209 n.334, 222 n.485,
278, 390, 393, 394, 397, 408, 416 n.83, 421
n.128, 445 n.207, 446, 450 n.216
Mishnah, 358–59, 360, 374, 382, 427, 428,
440 n.177
Mission, of early church, 23 n.42, 84, 164–74,
225 n.523, 245, 275, 288 n.47, 315, 409,
446; pagan, 78 n.157, 150, 151–64, 218
n.451, 406–9, 441 n.182
Missionaries, 15–16, 32, 66 n.67, 77 n.153,
78 n.156, 111, 119, 248, 284 n.4, 404
Missionary consciousness/conception/the-
ology, 28, 33, 35, 38, 53, 83, 110, 118–19,
166, 175 n.1, 236, 258, 287 n.46, 358, 376,
422, 434, 446
Missionary structure, 95, 96, 361
Money. *See* Remuneration
Monism, 145
Monotheism, 41
Music, 402
Mysteries, 218 n.456, 304 n.214, 373, 386
n.64; Attis/Cybele/Great Mother, 154, 198
n.237, 219 n.459, 362; Dionysiac, 44, 153,
219 nn.459, 461; 357 n.25, 358, 361, 416–
17 n.84; esoteric communication, 115–16;
Isis and Serapis, 94, 103, 158–59, 161–62,
219 n.459, 222 n.485, 358, 362, 407, 445
n.207
Mystical experience/vision/mysticism, 36, 54,
70 n.81, 91, 110, 143, 198 n.237, 201
nn.268, 269; 203 n.289, 282, 310 n.303, 317,
369, 385 n.54
Myth, 7, 393

Nag Hammadi finds, 370, 384 n.44, 386 n.55
Names, Jewish, 125, 373–74
Nature, 70 n.81, 122, 132, 145, 149, 396;
natural theology, 52–53
Neoplatonism, 188 n.111, 384 n.39, 386 n.54,
408
Neo-Pythagoreans, 152, 157, 160–61, 205
n.311, 222 n.482, 386 n.54, 443 n.195

Oracle(s), 135, 162, 259, 408; sibylline, *see*
Index of Extra-Scriptural References
Orpheus, Testament of, 54–55, 79 n.163,
116–17, 124–25
Orthodoxy. *See* Heresy

Painting, 376, 403, 418 nn.102, 103
Palestine, 5, 12, 83, 361, 375, 382, 440 n.180,
444 n.201
Parousia. *See* Future
Past/age/archive/past-present/records, 139,
150, 163, 258–64. *See also* Canon; Future;
Time
Paul's style/thinking/strategy, 101, 287 n.44,
289 n.60, 316
Pentateuch, 86–87, 359, 388 n.72, 394, 407,
423, 440 n.176
Peripatetic school, 188 n.111
Peter party, 2
Pharisaic rabbinate, 71 n.95, 193 n.174, 347,
360, 369, 375, 382, 401, 418 n.94, 422, 429,
433, 440 nn.176, 177; 444 n.201
Pharisaism/Pharisees, 5, 87, 107, 374
Philippic. *See* Letter of sorrow
Philosophy, 19 n.5, 30, 100, 112, 125, 142,
152, 156, 160, 394, 420 n.125, 438 n.158,
442 n.192
Pictorial art. *See* Painting
Piety/pious/religious knowledge, 51, 110, 145,
148–50, 310 n.321, 374, 396
Pirke Aboth, 360, 433
Pneumatic, 5, 6, 8, 58, 66 n.67, 100, 102,
104–5, 107, 108–9, 112, 128, 141, 167–70,
235, 236, 242, 245, 258–59, 273, 280, 287
n.44, 288 n.51, 296 n.145, 308 n.283, 315.
See also Spirit. See also *πνεῦμα; θεῖος
ἀνήρ*, in Index of Greek Vocabulary
Poet/poetry, 402
Polytheism, 125, 169
Popular philosophy. *See* Cynic-Stoic
philosophy
Prayer, 113
Preachers, wandering/itinerant, 12, 20 n.16,
37, 62 n.20, 100, 104, 152, 218 n.451, 315,
318
Present. *See* Past
Priest/-ess, 91, 103, 125, 161, 226 n.543
Primordial time, 121. *See also* Past; Time
Privilege. *See* Right
Proof, 309 n.286
Prophet/prophecy, 66 n.67, 67 n.68, 74
n.133, 102–3, 106, 107, 109–11, 127, 169,
173, 213 n.379, 397
Proselyte, 92, 108, 149, 382
Public appeal/appearance/performance, 98,
152–53
Purity, cultic, 41

Qumran, 12, 347, 359, 382, 384 n.44, 427,
430, 442 n.185. *See also* Essenes

Rabbi/rabbinate, 8, 87, 359, 361, 374, 385
n.50
Reality, 277. *See also* Cosmos; Nature; Truth
Reason/rationality/rationalism, 112, 142, 209
n.335
Recommendation/letters of recommendation,
5, 8, 243–44, 246, 248, 280, 293 nn.111,

Index of
Scripture References

Index of
Extra-Scriptural References

Index of Greek Vocabulary